W9-AEW-590

BASIC ISSUES OF AMERICAN DEMOCRACY

THE CENTURY
POLITICAL SCIENCE SERIES

Edited by FREDERIC A. OGG

Frederic A. Ogg and P. Orman Ray, *Introduction to American Government,* Tenth Edition, and *Essentials of American Government,* Seventh Edition.

Hillman M. Bishop and Samuel Hendel, *Basic Issues of American Democracy,* Second Edition.

Clyde F. Snider, *American State and Local Government.*

Arthur W. Bromage, *Introduction to Municipal Government and Administration.*

Joseph P. Chamberlain, *Legislative Processes: National and State.*

Howard R. Penniman, *Sait's American Parties and Elections,* Fifth Edition.

Andrew C. McLaughlin, *A Constitutional History of the United States.*

Percy Thomas Fenn, Jr., *The Development of the Constitution.*

John M. Mathews, *American Foreign Relations: Conduct and Policies,* Revised Edition.

Graham H. Stuart, *Latin America and the United States,* Fourth Edition.

Pitman B. Potter, *An Introduction to the Study of International Organization,* Fifth Edition.

Charles G. Fenwick, *International Law,* Third Edition.

Frank M. Russell, *Theories of International Relations.*

Edward M. Sait, *Political Institutions: A Preface.*

W. F. Willoughby, *The Government of Modern States,* Revised Edition.

Francis W. Coker, *Recent Political Thought.*

Raymond G. Gettell, *History of Political Thought* and *History of American Political Thought.*

J. Mark Jacobson, *The Development of American Political Thought.*

Anna Haddow, *Political Science in American Colleges and Universities, 1636–1900.*

Everett S. Brown, *A Manual of Government Publications: United States and Foreign.*

BASIC ISSUES OF AMERICAN DEMOCRACY

A Book of Readings Selected and Edited by

HILLMAN M. BISHOP and SAMUEL HENDEL

with the collaboration of BERNARD E. BROWN

All of the Department of Government,
The College of the City of New York

New York

APPLETON-CENTURY-CROFTS, INC.

592

PRINTED IN THE UNITED STATES OF AMERICA

PREFACE

A second edition of this book was suggested by the desirability of giving greater attention, in the light of international tension and the threat of war, to the conflict both in theory and practice between communism and Western democracy, and, to major alternatives of American foreign policy. It was also deemed desirable to expand the discussion of American governmental problems to include consideration of key proposals of the President's Civil Rights Committee, the value of public opinion polls, the case for disciplined parties, the effect of pressure groups upon Congress, and the compatibility of large scale economic planning and democracy. Finally, certain topics which received attention in the first edition have been strengthened by the presentation of variant and more recent materials.

The general orientation of the first edition has not been altered. That orientation derives from the belief that descriptive phases of government should not be emphasized, in introductory American government and related courses, to the neglect of values and fundamental issues. And foremost among the values that merit study are those relating to the democratic creed itself. This view has met with increasing support and is set forth in the report of the President's Commission on Higher Education, entitled *Higher Education for American Democracy:*

> To educate our citizens only in the structure and processes of the American Government . . . is to fall far short of what is needed for the fuller realization of the democratic ideal. It is the responsibility of higher education to devise programs and methods which will make clear the ethical values and the concept of human relations upon which our political system rests. Otherwise we are likely to cling to the letter of democracy and lose its spirit, to hold fast to its procedures when they no longer serve its ends, to propose and follow undemocratic courses of action in the very name of democracy.

The process of selecting materials continued to be guided by the conviction that in dealing with vital issues it is desirable, within limits of space and without regard to our personal positions, to present the most persuasively reasoned or most authoritative statements obtainable on important sides of each controversy. We agree with John Stuart Mill that full justice can be done to arguments only if they are presented by persons "who actually believe them; who defend them in earnest, and do their very utmost for them," and that the "beliefs we have the most warrant for, have no safeguard to rest on, but a standing invitation to the whole world to prove them unfounded." And it is noteworthy that this principle of selection has meant the inclusion of materials representing some of the truly great names in political science.

With regard to the extent to which these guiding desiderata have been realized in this volume, some explanation is necessary. It has obviously not been possible, within the compass of this brief book, to deal with all of the salient issues of our democracy. It should also be noted that, while on major issues direct and sharp conflict will usually be found, cleavage may not always appear with respect to each of the supporting arguments, since the material on one side of a controversy was not ordinarily written in reply to that on another. Nothwithstanding these reservations, we believe that there is no other book of readings that gives as much emphasis to, and with as great consistency presents, diverse positions on the fundamental values and problems of American government and democracy.

What purposes are served by this emphasis? We believe that it contributes to a realization of the following: (*a*) It compels the student to reëxamine the foundations of his beliefs and brings "clearer perception and livelier impression" to those to which he adheres; particularly, we think, it heightens his understanding of the meaning and value of democracy. (*b*) It requires the student to analyze conflicting viewpoints and to make value judgments; habits and skills thus developed in the classroom may assist him in making choices among alternative policies which confront him as a citizen. (*c*) It increases interest in political discussion and may lead to more active interest and participation in political life outside the classroom. Comments received from many teachers who have used the first edition encourage the belief that these objectives were furthered by this approach.

This volume, we suggest, may be adapted to the primary political science course, or to one semester of an integrated social science course, in a number of ways. At some colleges, for purposes of day-to-day classroom discussion, assignments consist of selections from these readings; in addition, students are required to read particular chapters in a standard textbook. While the textbook chapters are not discussed in the classroom, knowledge of this largely descriptive, factual material is tested in periodic examinations. At other colleges, instructors prefer to rely upon a standard textbook, supplemented at appropriate points with required reading from this volume.

We are indebted to the publishers, editors, and authors who graciously granted permission to reproduce the material in this book. Our obligation to Professor Walter R. Sharp, former chairman, and to other members of the Department of Government at the College of the City of New York is considerable. In particular, we are indebted to Dr. Bernard E. Brown for his valued collaboration in the preparation of this edition. Our wives, too, Clara Hendel and Georgiana Bishop, merit our very great thanks for their assistance with many final tasks.

S.H.
H.M.B.

CONTENTS

Part II

THE LIVING CONSTITUTION

Part III

PROBLEMS OF POLITICAL CONTROL

SOURCES OF READINGS

(Bracketed numbers refer to pages in this volume)

Books, Articles, and Addresses

Agar, Herbert (b. 1897)	"Why Have A Labor Party?" [284]
Beard, Charles A. (1874–1948)	"Method in Political Science" [21]
Becker, Carl (1873–1945)	*Freedom and Responsibility In the American Way of Life* [53]
	"Some Generalities That Still Glitter" [48]
Bellows, Henry A. (1885–1939)	"In Defense of Lobbying" [310]
Benson, George C. S. (b. 1908)	*The New Centralization* [215]
Bryce, James (1838–1922)	*The American Commonwealth* [291]
	Modern Democracies [24]
Burnham, James (b. 1905)	*The Struggle for the World* [359]
Burns, James M. (b. 1918)	*Congress on Trial* [262, 301]
Butler, Nicholas M. (1862–1947)	*The World Today* [277]
Cardozo, Benjamin N. (1870–1938)	*The Nature of the Judicial Process* [212]
Cohen, Morris R. (1880–1942)	"Is Judicial Review Necessary?" [202]
	"Why I Am Not a Communist" [65]
Commager, Henry Steele (b. 1902)	*Majority Rule and Minority Rights* [118]
	"Who Is Loyal to America?" [159]
Cousins, Norman (b. 1913)	*Modern Man Is Obsolete* [436]
Cushman, Robert E. (b. 1889)	"The Rôle of the Supreme Court in a Democratic Nation" [192]
Dewey, John (b. 1859)	*Essays in Experimental Logic* [15]
	"Social Science and Social Control" [11]
Fairbank, John K. (b. 1907)	"Competition with Communism, Not Containment" [423]
Finer, Herman (b. 1898)	*Road to Reaction* [348]
	The Theory and Practice of Modern Government [319]
Gallup, George (b. 1901)	"The Case for the Public Opinion Poll" [250]
Great Britain	"Note to the Soviet Union (February, 1951)" [385]
Hayek, Friedrich (b. 1899)	*The Road to Serfdom* [337]
Hazlitt, Henry (b. 1894)	*A New Constitution Now* [324]
Herring, Pendleton (b. 1903)	*The Politics of Democracy* [269, 297]

CASES

He who knows only his own side of the case, knows little of that. His reasons may be good, and no one may have been able to refute them. But if he is equally unable to refute the reasons on the opposite side; if he does not so much as know what they are, he has no ground for preferring either opinion. The rational position for him would be suspension of judgment, and unless he contents himself with that, he is either led by authority, or adopts, like the generality of the world, the side to which he feels most inclination. Nor is it enough that he should hear the arguments of adversaries from his own teachers, presented as they state them, and accompanied by what they offer as refutations. That is not the way to do justice to the arguments, or bring them into real contact with his own mind. He must be able to hear them from persons who actually believe them; who defend them in earnest, and do their very utmost for them. He must know them in their most plausible and persuasive form; he must feel the whole force of the difficulty which the true view of the subject has to encounter and dispose of; else he will never really possess himself of the portion of truth which meets and removes that difficulty.

John Stuart Mill—*On Liberty*

Part I

POLITICS AND DEMOCRACY

SECTION I

The Study of Politics

Preliminary to the study of complex political issues, there must be some understanding of the extent to which it is possible to draw verifiable conclusions from such study. Philosophers and students of politics are by no means agreed. Machiavelli, for example, believed that his *Prince* was a "scientific" guide to action for rulers. Engels, too, stated: "Just as Darwin discovered the law of evolution in organic nature, so Marx discovered the law of evolution in human history." In differing degrees, scholars like John Dewey and Barbara Wootton, while laying claim to no such over-all synthesis, insist upon the fruitfulness of applying scientific method to the study of politics. On the other hand, Professor MacIver, also represented by a selection, rejects the view that a body of knowledge can be developed "that can serve as a definite guide to the statesman, a science of how to govern, an applied science that does or can do in its field what medicine, say, or engineering does in its field." Others, like Charles A. Beard, point out that it is possible to have wrong data and yet "mirror with a high degree of accuracy the political movements of an age, its underlying and hidden currents, no less than its outward pomp and circumstance."

The issue is worth considering, we believe, if for no other reasons than that (1), a realization of the difficulties involved in drawing "scientific" conclusions from the study of politics may induce a salutary humility; and (2), an appreciation for something at least resembling scientific method may result in a degree of open-mindedness and objectivity.

Topic 1

POLITICS—SCIENCE OR ART?

THE VALUE OF SCIENTIFIC METHOD

Barbara Wootton *

The contrast between man's amazing ability to manipulate his material environment and his pitiful incompetence in managing his own affairs is now

* Professor of Social Studies at the University of London. Author of *Lament for*

as commonplace as it is tragic. The world of atomic energy and nylon is for millions still the world of poverty, hunger, misgovernment, crime, domestic unhappiness or personal frustration. And mastery over earth and air and sea and atom has brought us only to daily fear of sudden death of our own making.

No one has any doubt how that mastery has been won. It is by rigorous devotion to scientific method that we have made our conquests over the material environment. Nor are we troubled by doubts as to the validity of the results which scientific research has thus achieved in the understanding of, and the consequent power to manipulate, inanimate things. The Christian and the Muslim, the Fascist and the Liberal, the idealist and the logical positivist may dispute endlessly about their views on human life and the nature of things; but they all accept the facts that steam engines will pull trains and amplifiers make their speeches more widely heard. Even the most primitive peoples quickly learn to put their trust in firearms.

It is no less obvious that this method, which has been so brilliantly successful in the natural sciences, is not normally applied to the field of our most disastrous failures. The personal relations of human beings, individual and collective, are conducted in a quite different way: these are for the most part governed by a medley of primitive impulses, kindly or harsh, sometimes even noble, modified by rules of thumb, and set in the framework of a traditional morality which varies from place to place and from age to age. In these matters science plays little part and commands but meagre respect. It may be true that of recent years the findings of the psychologists—often in seriously distorted versions—have begun to seep into this area of experience, affecting the personal relationships of individuals and the upbringing of children quite considerably, penal codes and practice somewhat less noticeably, national politics still less, and international politics hardly at all. In these developments, as also in the growing prestige of empirical economic science, and in the gradual influence of anthropology upon the dealings of one cultural group with another, we may perhaps discern the beginnings of a very different future. But these are marginal occurrences: they have still not seriously modified the division of experience into two sharply divided sections—that in which science speaks with authority, and that in which she whispers furtively, or is dumb.

This contrast surely seems to point a simple moral—that we ought seriously to ask whether the tool that has worked such wonders in the one job could not be used for the other. More than a century has passed since Auguste Comte said that the rational reform of society must be brought about by the application of scientific method to social problems. If not very much has happened since to prove him right, certainly even less has hap-

---

Economics, Freedom Under Planning, and other works. The selection is from Barbara Wootton, *Testament for Social Science* (New York, W. W. Norton & Co., Inc., 1951), *passim.* By permission of W. W. Norton & Co., Inc.

pened to prove him wrong. In the intervening century scientific method has marched from victory to victory in the field of natural phenomena, while those human problems which have not enjoyed its attentions remain as intractable as ever.

It is, therefore, the first purpose of this essay to ask how far these problems also might be tackled by the methods of science. This is not, indeed, a simple matter; for scientific method is no magic formula whose incantation will perform any trick that may be desired. Certainly there are, at least in the present state of knowledge, real differences between the material to be handled by the social and the natural sciences respectively. Human bodies may be bundles of atoms, but men and women are not atoms; and their behaviour may, as we shall see, prove in some respects even more disorderly than that of the particles of which they are composed.

Nevertheless, as I hope to show, the potential contribution of science in this field is far greater than anything we have yet seen: the differences between the material of the social and the natural sciences are differences of degree, rather than of kind; and even these are easily exaggerated. And the rewards of success are inestimable. Every fresh advance in the natural sciences—at least in physics, chemistry and bacteriology—now widens the gap between our material success and our social failure, and endangers still further the hope of happiness and civilised living, if not of actual survival, for the majority of mankind. That gap could be closed if, in the perspective of history, the age that lies before us could be as memorable in the social, as the nineteenth and twentieth centuries are already in the natural, sciences.

There are secondary rewards also. Our lives are darkened not only by the familiar threats, if not the actualities, of poverty, unemployment, famine, war, and all their attendant miseries and cruelties. Most of us also live under the clouds of one or other form of superstition; and the dignity of our species is diminished by the gods and idols that we have created in our own image. The scientific method, which has enabled us to master our material environment, might dissipate those clouds also: for, while there may be questions which science cannot answer, yet a scientific approach to life enables us to face the universe both with greater realism and with a new sense of dignity and independence. And, finally, science may have far more to contribute than we yet realise towards the enrichment of the emotional and aesthetic experiences which are among the greatest delights of that peculiar organ of our species—the mind.

The consistency of the scientific approach to all the problems that concern us is, indeed, the underlying theme of this [essay]. Science has already reshaped our material environment from top to bottom, and now stands ready, I suggest, to take up with equal zest, and we may fairly hope with hardly less effectiveness, the task of unravelling the tangled complexities of our own relationships. . . .

As soon as we set out to frame hypotheses in the hope of establishing parallel laws of association in the social sciences, we are met by the formidable allegation that human affairs are wholly intractable by this process or at least insufficiently tractable to make the effort worth while. Hence before we can discuss any special features of the search for hypotheses in this field, we have to take up this challenge to the very existence of the laws which every hypothesis seeks to anticipate. Clearly, if there are no laws, no hypothesis can anticipate them, and the attempt to frame such hypotheses is a waste of everybody's time.

The main grounds of this challenge appear to be as follows. First, it is argued that there is an indeterminacy inherent in human behaviour which precludes the formulation of any valid laws of association. Men and women, it is said, act incalculably, just as from time to time it may seem good to them to act. . . .

The laws of natural science are only statements of association of varying degrees of probability. If associations of comparable probability (or of any degree of probability higher than pure chance) can be demonstrated by observation to hold good of human affairs (as I hope to show that they can), then the meaning of law in both natural and social science is fundamentally the same. Moreover, we should do well to remind ourselves that the effects upon our generalisations of our own ignorance on the one hand, or of inherent disorderliness in our data on the other hand, would, as in the natural sciences, be identical. Both pull us down in the scale of probability; and no one can say whether lack of certainty means that no reliable associations exist, or that associations are present but still undiscovered. And we should still further remind ourselves that the natural sciences, just as much as social science, would come to a dead stop, if we now decided to make the assumption that everything beyond the present frontiers of knowledge is devoid of regularities and therefore inaccessible to scientific method. Such an assumption would, of course, have been equally well warranted, if it had been made before the earliest beginnings of scientific investigations. To have acted upon it then would obviously have effectively prevented the accumulation of all our present scientific knowledge. It would be a disaster if a comparable defeatism were allowed to stultify the potentialities of scientific method in the relatively unexplored field of human affairs.

A second challenge to the possibility of formulating valid laws of association in human affairs stems from the complexity of the situations with which the social scientist has to deal, and the rarity of the cases in which effectively controlled experiment is possible. This is a real problem, but it is easily exaggerated. There are several reasons for facing it with optimism.

The first is the conspicuous fact that, even without any refined scientific technique, many valid generalisations about human behaviour are in fact constantly made. Civilised life, or indeed any social life at all, even at a quite primitive level, would be impossible without them. The baker can *generally* be relied on to bake, the postman to deliver the letter, and the addressee to be willing and able to read it. It would be safe to bet long odds that Aunt Mary will remember your birthday, and that Uncle Tom will bring any conversation round to himself. If none of these associations reaches the certainty of the statement that water will bubble and steam at a given temperature, all of them are much more often right than they would be if the matter were one of pure chance. And many of them have a higher degree of probability than have some of the more tentative associations established by recognized natural sciences. All of us can probably forecast in a limited number of specific situations the behaviour of a few people whom we know intimately with a degree of probability which, while it falls short of that with which astronomers foretell eclipses, yet easily surpasses the success with which the meteorologists prophesy tomorrow's weather in England. Certainly we do not lack hypotheses to explain our own or our neighbor's behaviour, even if the selection of data is differently weighted, and the relevant hypothesis differently framed, in the two cases. And if our generalisations about social behavior do fail from time to time, it is arguable that our guesses make quite as good a showing in relation to the data as did our opinions about natural phenomena before these had been satisfactorily explained. We are probably making big mistakes about, say, the causes of war and the forms of government best adapted to our needs and natures. But it was also a big mistake to think that the sun went round the earth.

Secondly, the fact that possible associations can be established by crude observation should encourage the view that in the social, as in the natural, sciences, better observation would yield generalisations of a higher degree of probability. Here again, a sensible person conducts his ordinary life on this assumption. He does not argue that to make a small chance of being right into a larger one is not worth while in cases where one cannot hope to attain complete certainty. If you are particular about food and drink, and you propose to take a holiday in a place that you have not previously visited, you do not choose your hotel at random from the directory. You make such enquiries as you can from the hotels themselves; and, since in these matters experience has shown that independent evidence is of superior value, you will also, if you can, get advice from other people who know the place.

In this context, devotees of racing and of football pools should be a lesson to us. The data on which they have to work are generally such as only permit forecasts of very low probability. Nevertheless, thousands of enthusiasts study form with meticulous care in the hope of raising a small chance into one slightly larger. And where there is little to be gleaned from the actual data, they are eager to get all the help that they can from mathematical theory in choosing their permutations.

In any case, the complexity of the conditions to be unravelled in human problems varies greatly in different cases. We should do well to get ahead with those that are comparatively simple, the more so as these often turn out to be directly related to the other more complicated tasks. Psychology is the one human science that can to some extent avail itself of laboratory experiments, and can, therefore, study, under controlled conditions, certain carefully isolated aspects of human behaviour. In this way a body of knowledge is in process of being built up showing what human beings really are like. If the social scientists are not yet ready to make pronouncements on larger issues such as the psychological causes of war, let us remember that the physicists had to engage in most elaborate studies of minutiae before they could produce results that would blow up the world. Laboratory experiments, and near-laboratory work such as the close observations of individuals made by psychiatrists, are beginning to enable us to classify temperaments, to measure intelligence, to distinguish between hereditary traits and those that are environmentally produced, and to map the conditions with which guilt and aggression are associated. Knowledge on these topics is the basis of understanding of the larger problems of, say, government and economic relationships, just as the work of the cultural anthropologists is the beginning of wisdom in international affairs.

Psychology is, indeed, so demonstrably the foundation of the social sciences that it is from many points of view to be regretted that these are not all regarded as branches of it. This is not just a matter of convenience of academic classification; for there is a real risk that other studies will go wrong because their psychology is false. In the absence of scientific knowledge based on accurate empirical observations, historians, economists and political theorists have worked on a few crude assumptions about human nature. They have, in consequence, only too often produced sweeping interpretations or intricate intellectual systems far removed from actuality. Man is neither wholly brutish and nasty, nor completely dominated by the economic calculus; and he will not learn how to govern himself satisfactorily or to satisfy his bodily needs until he has a much clearer idea about the proportions in which these and other ingredients are compounded in his make-up, and the measure in which the mixture can be modified to taste.

The answer, then, to the challenge that social affairs are too complex to be susceptible of scientific treatment is threefold. In the first place, nothing more is involved by that challenge than an admission that we must for the present be content with fairly low degrees of probability; though it would be unwise to prejudge the rate at which progress may be made to higher levels. Secondly, since we are all making generalisations anyhow, it is only common sense to get these as nearly accurate as possible; and, thirdly, the complexity of conditions and the impossibility of simplifying them by experiment is a much more formidable obstacle in some fields than in others; and it is fortunate that the departments in which these obstacles are least terrifying are also those in which advance is most clearly a precondition of progress everywhere else. Meanwhile, whatever the measure of probability which the generalisations of social science have so far achieved, the generalisations themselves can only be reached by the same process as the laws of the natural sciences. . . .

The final stage of the scientific process is reached when the hypothesis passes the test of empirical verification and is promoted to the rank of law. It is at this stage that the technique of controlled experiment has proved so valuable. Since nature does not often oblige us with the identical situations necessary for exact comparisons, we proceed to construct these artificially in the laboratory whenever we can. Even so, however, we need by no means despair of making any advances in knowledge at all in circumstances in which controlled experiment is precluded. We have, for instance, acquired a creditable knowledge of astronomy without being able as yet to make the stars dance to our tune. In this case it is no doubt a help that the relevant conditions are comparatively simple. But at the other end of the scale even the meteorologists are not deterred by the complexity of their data and the impossibility of controlled experiment from research into the vagaries of the weather. The difference between controlled experiment and uncontrolled observation is, in fact, one of degree.

Observation that "depends upon a definite interest and involves selection from the whole that is presented in experience is always of the nature of experiment, assuming that by an experiment is meant a controlled observation such that the number of variables is finite and known. The ideal of experiment is never attained. It would mean that the whole universe proceeded uniformly while we varied one ingredient." In practice we must recognise a scale from the almost wholly uncontrolled to the almost wholly controlled; but naturally, the degree of probability attaching to the results is likely to correspond to the position on this scale of the observations upon which these results are based. . . .

In the social sciences this final stage of the scientific process—empirical testing of the hypothesis—in its turn follows, in principle, the same course as in the natural sciences. Just as in the natural sciences this is the point at which controlled experiment is generally conclusive, so in the social sciences it is here that experimental methods are most seriously missed. But as has just been said, no hard and fast line separates controlled experiment from controlled observation. Hypothesis must be tested by the nearest approximation to controlled experiment that is available. And if this is conscientiously done, even in the social sciences hypotheses need no longer waste their fruitful potentialities in rank proliferation into the field of pure imagination.

In the absence of experiment, we must, however, normally be content with probabilities that fall in varying degrees short of certainty. . . . The proof of the social science pudding must be in the eating; and that, of course, lies mostly in the future, for the greater part of the pudding is not yet cooked, and, as we have seen, the public are reluctant to taste the few morsels that are ready. Further, the ingredients are expensive; and the social sciences have hitherto been much less liberally endowed with the public or private benefactions for research which provide those ingredients, than have at least the more advanced, the more conspicuously useful, or the more potentially destructive branches of natural science.

Money, however, begins to be forthcoming on a much more generous scale; and, all in all, the established results of research in every branch of the human sciences now fill a substantial specialised literature of their own. Some of these researches already have been, and some look as if they soon would be, of real help in the solution of our immediate practical problems. The psychologists in particular have made large contributions, larger perhaps than has, as yet, any other branch of social science. Their work in vocational selection has, for instance, made possible the elimination of thousands of square pegs from round holes: recent advances in psychiatry have enlarged our understanding of the nature of the conditions for mental health, and of the treatment of mental illness: and much light has been thrown on the causes of crime and on the probable success of various methods of treatment. In the long run perhaps one of the most significant of all the pieces of psychological enquiry of our day will prove to be the close investigation of the personality of Rudolph Hess, which the happy accident of his flight to England made possible; for in this for the first time the psychiatrists, first of England, then later also of the United States, France and Russia were able intimately to observe the character-structure of a (till then) successful paranoiac tyrant, and its relation to the social environment of contemporary Germany; and, no less significantly, all these experts, including those from Russia, reached final agreement about the case. That, indeed, may have been the first step to full understanding of what makes the Hitlers and the Hess's of this world.

The ethnologists in their turn have wholly exposed the illusion that existing racial groups correspond at all closely to distinct biological stocks; and all the evidence that they and the psychologists together have so far collected supports a sceptical attitude as to the presence of significant innate mental differences between different races. The ground is thus cut from under the feet of the many cocksure myths about racial superiority; and the excuse for all the indignities and injustices which are inflicted in their name is destroyed. Meanwhile, the social anthropologists, by their exploration of the interactions of personality and culture, have illuminated the varying presuppositions of different moral codes—explaining incidentally how Japanese prisoners of war could give information to their captors without any sense of treachery, and how genuinely puzzled they were that English and American soldiers would not do the same in similar circumstances; whilst nearer home the surveys of the sociologists make it possible to relate the structure and planning of new urban communities to the known needs of their inhabitants; and the economists are hot on the trail of the scourge of unemployment and the trade cycle.

Of the fields still to be cultivated, one in which development is perhaps needed with particular urgency is that which lies in the borderland of politics (national and international) and psychology. The psychology of political life is still extremely crude: international politics too often reflect the psychological relationships of infancy, whilst on the national scale the reciprocal relations of politician and elector seem to be largely based on mental stereotypes. Little, too, is known of the psychology of the elector; of the forces which make him politically indifferent or active, or a supporter of this or that party; or of the measure in which his interest is directed towards shaping policy at the centre or taking part in its execution at the circumference. Even the distribution of power between the several organs of government changes under the involuntary pressure of circumstances, rather than in response to any informed conception of the requirements of sensitive and efficient government—and this in a generation when constitution after constitution in Europe and in Asia has been remade.

Certainly, the social sciences have their hands full; but their achievements give ground for hope, and experience is on their side. The "sordid and savage story of history has been written by man's irrationality, and the thin precarious crust of civilization which has from time to time been built over the bloody mess has always been built by reason."

Social Science and Social Control

John Dewey *

"SOCIAL SCIENCE" †

It would require a technical survey, which would be out of place here, to prove that the existing limitations of "social science" are due mainly to unreasoning devotion to physical science as a model, and to a misconception of physical science at that. Without making any such survey, attention may be directly called to one outstanding difference between physical and social facts. The ideal of the knowledge dealing with the former is the elimination of all factors dependent upon distinctively human response. "Fact," physically speaking, is the ultimate residue after human purposes, desires, emotions, ideas and ideals have been systematically excluded. A

* Professor of Philosophy at Columbia University, 1905–1931; now Emeritus Professor. Author of *Human Nature and Conduct, The Public and Its Problems, Liberalism and Social Action,* and numerous other books and articles on philosophy, politics, and education.

† Reprinted from an article in *New Republic,* July 29, 1931, by permission.

social "fact," on the other hand, is a concretion in external form of precisely these human factors.

An occurrence is a physical fact only when its constituents and their relations remain the same, irrespective of the human attitude toward them. A species of mosquitoes is the carrier of the germs of malaria, whether we like or dislike malaria. Drainage and oil-spraying to destroy mosquitoes are a social fact because their use depends upon human purpose and desire. A steam locomotive or a dynamo is a physical fact in its structure; it is a social fact when its existence depends upon the desire for rapid and cheap transportation and communication. The machine itself may be understood physically without reference to human aim and motive. But the railway or public-utility system cannot be understood without reference to human purposes and human consequences.

I may illustrate the present practice of slavishly following the technique of physical science and the uselessness of its results by the present zeal for "fact finding." Of course, one cannot think, understand and plan without a basis of fact, and since facts do not lie around in plain view, they have to be discovered. But for the most part, the data which now are so carefully sought and so elaborately scheduled are not social facts at all. For their connection with any system of human purposes and consequences, their bearing as means and as results upon human action, are left out of the picture. At best they are mere physical and external facts. They are unlike the facts of physical science, because the latter are found by methods which make their interrelations and their laws apparent, while the facts of social "fact finding" remain a miscellaneous pile of meaningless items. Since their connections with human wants and their effect on human values are neglected, there is nothing which binds them together into an intelligible whole.

It may be retorted that to connect facts with human desires and their effect upon human values is subjective and moral, and to an extent that makes it impossible to establish any conclusions upon an objective basis: that to attempt inference on this point would land us in a morass of speculative opinion. Suppose, for example, all the facts about the working of the prohibition law and its enforcement were much more completely known than they are; even so, to establish a connection between these facts and the human attitudes lying back of them would be a matter of guesswork. As things stand, there is much force in the objection. But if made universal, it would overlook the possibility of another kind of situation.

Wherever purposes are employed deliberately and systematically for the sake of certain desired social results, there it is possible, within limits, to determine the connection between the human factor and the actual occurrence, and thus to get a complete social fact, namely, the actual external occurence in its human relationships. Prohibition, whether noble or not, is not an experiment in any intelligent scientific sense of the term. For it was undertaken without the effort to obtain the conditions of control which are essential to any experimental determination of fact. The Five Year Plan of Russia, on the other hand, whether noble or the reverse, has many of the traits of a social experiment, for it is an attempt to obtain certain specified social results by the use of specified definite measures, exercised under conditions of considerable, if not complete, control.

The point I am making may be summed up by saying that it is a complete error to suppose that efforts at social control depend upon the prior existence of a social science. The reverse is the case. The building up of social science, that is, of a body of knowledge in which facts are ascertained in their significant relations, is dependent upon putting social planning into effect. It is at this point that the misconception about physical science, when it is taken as a model for social knowledge, is important. Physical science did not develop because inquirers piled up a mass of facts about observed phenomena. It came into being when men intentionally experimented, on the basis of ideas and hypotheses, with observed phenomena to modify them and disclose new observations. This process is self-corrective and self-developing. Imperfect and even wrong hypotheses, when *acted upon,* brought to light significant phenomena which made improved ideas and improved experimentations possible. The change from a passive and accumulative attitude into an active and productive one is the secret revealed by the progress of physical inquiry. Men obtained knowledge of natural energies by trying deliberately to control the conditions of their operation. The result was knowledge, and then control on a larger scale by the application of what was learned.

It is a commonplace of logical theory that laws are of the "if-then" type. *If* something occurs, *then* something else happens; if certain conditions exist, they are accompanied by certain other conditions. Such knowledge alone is knowledge of a fact in any intelligible sense of the word. Although we have to act in order to discover the conditions underlying the "if" in physical matters, yet the material constituting the "if" is there apart from our action; like the movements of sun and earth in an eclipse. But in social phenomena the relation is: "If we *do* something, something else will happen." The objective material constituting the "if" belongs to us, not to something wholly independent of us. We are concerned, not with a bare relation of cause and effect, but with one of means and consequences, that is, of causes deliberately used for the sake of producing certain effects. As far as we intentionally do and make, we shall know; as far as we "know" without making, our so-called knowledge is a miscellany, or at most antiquarian, and hence without relevance to future planning. Only the knowledge which is itself the fruit of a technology can breed further technology.

I want to make the same point with reference to social prediction. Here, too, the assumption is generally made that we must be able to predict before we can plan and control. Here again the reverse is the case. We can predict the occurrence of an eclipse precisely because we cannot control it. If we could control it, we could not predict, except contingently; just as we can predict a collision when we see two trains approaching on the same track—provided that a human being does not foresee the possibility and take measures to avert its happening. The other day I ran across a remark of Alexander Hamilton's to the effect that instead of awaiting an event to know what measures to take, we should take measures to bring the event to pass. And I would add that only then can we genuinely forecast the future in the world of social matters.

Empirical, rule-of-thumb practices were the mothers of the arts. But the practices of the arts were in turn the source of science, when once the empirical methods were freed in imagination and used with some degree of freedom of experimentation. There cannot be a science of an art until the art has itself made some advance, and the significant development occurs when men intentionally try to use such art as they have already achieved in order to obtain results which they conceive to be desirable. If we have no social technique at all, it is impossible to bring planning and control into being. If we do have at hand a reasonable amount of technique, then it is by deliberately using what we have that we shall in the end develop a dependable body of social knowledge. If we want foresight, we shall not obtain it by any amount of fact finding so long as we disregard the human aims and desires producing the facts which we find. But if we decide upon what we want socially, what sort of social consequences we wish to occur, and then use whatever means we possess to effect these intended consequences, we shall find the road that leads to foresight. Forethought and planning must come before foresight.

I am not arguing here for the desirability of social planning and control. That is another question. Those who are satisfied with present conditions and who are hopeful of turning them to account for personal profit and power will answer it in the negative. What I am saying is that if we want something to which the name "social science" may be given, there is only one way to go about it, namely, by entering upon the path of social planning and control. Observing, collecting, recording and filing tomes of social phenomena without deliberately trying to do something to bring a desired state of society into existence only encourages a conflict of opinion and dogma in their interpretation. If the social situation out of which these facts emerge is itself confused and chaotic because it expresses socially unregulated purpose and haphazard private intent, the facts themselves will be confused, and we shall add only intellectual confusion to practical disorder. When we deliberately employ whatever skill we possess in order to serve the ends which we desire, we shall begin to attain a measure of at least intellectual order and understanding. And if past history teaches anything, it is that with intellectual order we have the surest possible promise of advancement to practical order.

EXPERIMENTAL VERIFICATION AND TRUTH *

If we exclude acting upon the idea, no conceivable amount or kind of intellectualistic procedure can confirm or refute an idea, or throw any light upon its validity. How does the non-pragmatic view consider that verification takes place? Does it suppose that we first look a long while at the facts and then a long time at the idea, until by some magical process the degree and kind of their agreement become visible? Unless there is some such conception as this, what conception of agreement is possible except the experimental or practical one? And if it be admitted that verification involves action, how can that action be relevant to the truth of an idea, unless the idea is itself already relevant to action? If by acting in accordance with the experimental definition of facts (viz., as obstacles and conditions), and the experimental definition of the end or intent (viz., as plan and method of action) a harmonized situation effectually presents itself, we have the adequate and the only conceivable verification of the intellectual factors. If the action indicated be carried out and the disordered or disturbed situation persists, then we have not merely confuted the tentative positions of intelligence, but we have in the very process of acting introduced new data and eliminated some of the old ones, and thus afforded an opportunity for the resurvey of the facts and the revision of the plan of action. By acting faithfully upon an inadequate reflective presentation, we have at least secured the elements for its improvement. This, of course, gives no absolute guaranty that the reflection will at any time be so performed as to prove its validity in fact. But the self-rectification of intellectual content through acting upon it in good faith is the "absolute" of knowledge, loyalty to which is the religion of intellect.

The Limits of Scientific Proof

R. M. MacIver †

THE "SCIENCE" OF GOVERNMENT ‡

When we speak of a science of government we are not raising doubts concerning the feasibility of political science, as that expression is commonly used. There is an important body of systematic knowledge about the state, about the conditions under which different types of government emerge, about the characteristics of the different types, about the relation of gov-

* From John Dewey, *Essays in Experimental Logic* (Chicago, University of Chicago Press, 1917), pp. 231–241. By permission.

† Professor of Political Philosophy and Sociology at Columbia University. Author of *The Modern State, Leviathan and the People, Toward an Abiding Peace, The More Perfect Union,* and others.

‡ From R. M. MacIver, *The Web of Government* (New York, The Macmillan Co., 1947), pp. 8–11. By permission.

ernment to the governed in different historical situations, about the modes in which governments carry on their functions according to their kind, and so forth. This body of knowledge may properly be named a science. We do not take sides with the purists who deny the title of "science" to any knowledge that does not present us with eternal laws or that cannot be expressed in quantitative terms. There is really no intelligent issue here. If in their zeal for immutable exactitude these purists are offended when other kinds of knowledge are referred to as sciences, we can call them by some other name—and the knowledge will be just as good and as useful as before. What, however, we are rejecting is the claim that there is a systematic body of knowledge, already in existence or awaiting development, that can serve as a definite guide to the statesman, a science of how to govern, an applied science that does or can do in its field what medicine, say, or engineering does in its field.

Men have often dreamed of a science of government in this sense, and some have even claimed to inaugurate it. From Plato to George Bernard Shaw there have been champions of the view that in the development of this science lies the salvation of mankind. Plato was dominated by one myth-complex,* and George Bernard Shaw by another. So it will always be. What then would a full-fledged science of government be? A science of how men *are* governed? We have much on that score, but it is historical description and not systematic knowledge. A science of how men *should* be governed? But the *should* is always expressive of the thinker's own myth-complex, is always subject to his presuppositions, and so lies outside the ambit of science—a fact that in no wise lessens its social importance, since the *it should be* of the mythical is as necessary as the *it is so* of the evidential. A science of how men *can* be governed? Perhaps this seems more hopeful. Machiavelli set the example to the modern world of presenting to the ruler pragmatic principles for his guidance. Men who have had much experience in public affairs, statesmen, diplomats, policy-makers, party bosses, the counselors of presidents and of kings have written memoirs in which they have exposed the secrets of political success. Psychologists, publicists, propaganda analysts, have studied the modes of mass response and the devices by which they can be manipulated or evoked. Enlightening as these records are they do not, however, meet the requirements of a science. They are reflections and observations on the art of government rather than the serviceable data for a science of government.

What is the difference? Let us examine, for example, the famous precepts of Machiavelli. Best known of these is his advice to the ruler that he combine cunning and ruthlessness, that he disregard whenever necessary

* The author elsewhere states that "by *myths* we mean the value-impregnated beliefs and notions that men hold, that they live by or live for. Every society is held together by a myth-system, a complex of dominating thought-forms that determines and sustains all its activities. All social relations, the very texture of human society, are myth-born and myth-sustained."

the accepted code of morals but always make a show of observing it. Machiavelli's experience in politics led him to believe that by following this advice a prince could best safeguard his throne. He wrote at a time marked by turbulence and instability. For such times, and for such rulers, the advice might be good, within discretionary limits—but who can assign the limits? Many who have followed Machiavelli's precepts have ended in disaster. Where is the clean-cut nexus that science desiderates? Discretionary precepts for the attainment of particular goals—that is all we are given. That is all we find in the whole series, down to the latest behind-the-scenes writer who informs us that a successful President of the United States must be all things to all men.

Moreover, most of these precepts are concerned not with the larger issues of government but with the much narrower question of how a ruler or a ruling group can gain or retain power; and we cannot reduce the vast business of government to a few precarious techniques for holding on to office. The tasks of government are manifold and comprehensive, emerging from complicated and ever changing conditions. What science prescribes these tasks? The people over whom government is exercised are moved by various conflicting sentiments and impulses, have different needs and different demands from time to time. What science envisages the endless conjunctures to which government must address itself?

Policy-making depends on the assessing of alternatives with a view to translating one of them into action. A bill or an executive action is up for consideration. There is then the primary question: will the proposed measure advance the purposes of the government? It must be not only such that the government itself regards it with approval, it must furthermore not entail any untoward consequences such as in the judgment of the government would outweigh the direct advantages. To what reactions will it give rise? There are numerous pros and cons. How weigh the one against the other? At the close of the war, to take an example, there rose the question whether the United States, Great Britain, and Canada should either immediately communicate to their allies in the struggle the secret of the construction of the atomic bomb or should reserve the secret until at least the negotiations for the peace settlement were concluded or until arrangements for a satisfactory system of control over that terrifying agency were completed. This is, for short, a rough and inadequate statement of the alternatives. It was an issue that no government had ever faced before, but in this respect it differed only in degree from every other question that comes before a government, since every situation is for the policy-maker a new one. There were many aspects to the situation; many interests would be affected by the decision. There was the major question whether a world system more satisfactory to the holders of the secret would be attainable if the other allies, and one of them in particular, were—or were not—entrusted with the secret. We need not enter into detail. A plausible case could be made for withholding, another for giving. It is so with every issue of policy. Always the situation is many-sided. Always there is a complex set of reactions to be foreseen and assessed. What science can lay down exact rules for that task? What science can postulate explicit and clearly relevant principles to guide the legislator or the minister in the exploration of the alternatives, in the forevision of the consequences, in the practical evaluation of the various considerations that are relevant to his decision?

Let us take again the situation where a particular policy has already been adopted. The New York State legislature has, for example, decided in favor of an anti-discrimination measure. But the framing of the measure, on which its success and efficacy depend, still raises many questions. Should it apply to all forms of employment, including professional employment on all levels? Should it apply not only to employment but also to admission to trade unions, colleges, and so forth? Should it apply to employment units that involve only three or four workers as well as to those that involve hundreds or thousands? What is the test of discrimination? How far can it be made to work in practice? How can evasion be controlled? How can the measure be guarded against the danger that it will create resistance and resentment such as will stimulate in some quarters a stronger spirit of discrimination? How should the board controlling the operation of the act be constituted? What minority groups should be represented in it? What system of inspection and of enforcement should be set up? There are various groups each with its own myth-complex, and their respective susceptibilities and responses must be taken into account. There are no formulas, no clear-cut rules to which we can refer. At every point decisions have to be made that call for experience, knowledge of the intricacies of the situation, the good judgment as well as the good will of the legislator. . . .

PHYSICAL AND SOCIAL SCIENCE *

Social science has hitherto suffered greatly from the attempt to make it conform to methods derived from the older and more abstract sciences. It has led us, for one thing, to look for impossible results, and to be disappointed at not getting them. We inquire, for example, after the manner of physical sciences, which of two related social phenomena is cause and which effect. It usually turns out, in the social sphere, that both are cause and both are effect. Does the kind of education account for the standard of intelligence in a community? True, but does not the standard of intelligence account for the standard of education? Was slavery in the ancient world due in part to the lack of technical development? Doubtless, but

* From R. M. MacIver, *The Elements of Social Science* (London, Methuen & Co., Ltd., 1949), pp. 12–18. By permission.

was not the lack of technical development due in part to the institution of slavery? Was the severity of the criminal code a hundred years ago due to the amount of crime? May it not be replied that the amount of crime was also due to the severity of the criminal code? Are low wages a cause of poverty? Yes, but is not poverty a cause of low wages? Intemperance is a source of destitution, but destitution is also a source of intemperance. Such examples could be multiplied indefinitely. One can reverse, with some degree of truth, almost any statement of social causation. Social causation is nearly always reciprocal. Unless we realize this fact we will be asking wrong questions and finding wrong answers—though questions of a type that might be legitimately asked in other scientific spheres where another kind of causation prevails.

It is a common view that science begins and ends with measurement. Whether or not this is true of physical science, it is certainly not true of social science. Even in the physical sphere the mind that discovers measure is really seeking something more. It seeks to understand, not merely to compute. Light and colour mean more to the mind than vibrations and wave-lengths, and that more always eludes measurement. Heat is not to be understood as the dance of atoms. It is something we feel. Music is more than combinations of sound waves, nor will all the computation in the world bring the knowledge of harmony. Or take our knowledge of time itself. The real time we live through refuses to be broken up into a succession of mathematical points. We are apt to think we know what time is because we can measure it, but no sooner do we reflect upon it than that illusion goes.

So it appears that the range of the measurable is not the range of the knowable. There are things we can measure, like time, but yet our minds do not grasp their meaning. There are things we cannot measure, like happiness or pain, and yet their meaning is perfectly clear to us. Perhaps, after all, we can measure only the external, the unknown, and can know only the internal, the conscious state, the incommensurate. In which case science, if it is limited to the measurable, is limited to the unknown, perhaps even to the unknowable. It is then a means to power, not to understanding. It is our weapon to conquer and control nature, not to comprehend her. It is only quantity we can measure, but it is only quality we can experience. Science then counts the throbs of nature, but does not feel them. They are to her as the beats of a vast mechanism, fulfilling eternally eternal laws. But the question, Why?—the only question that matters, the first question of childhood, the last of age—that she cannot answer.

All this follows if science is confined to measurement. But it would be too paradoxical to conclude that science, the express term for all that is clear and illuminate, is concerned only with the unknown. But here our object is only to vindicate the claim of social science. In the study of society we have to do with the relationships of conscious beings, with the motives and purposes that determine these, with the ways of living and acting which depend upon them. None of these things can be measured. There is a very common confusion of the commensurate and the incommensurate in social science. We can add the wealth of a group or a nation and get some kind of total. We can add its man-power and get a total. But we cannot make a sum of its health or its habits or its culture. A thousand weak purposes cannot be rolled into one strong purpose as a thousand weak units of force are joined into one strong force. We cannot add wisdom as we can add wealth. A thousand mediocrities do not sum up into one genius. Likewise of joy and sorrow. The suffering of a thousand is not more intense than that of a single heart, for it is a thousand who suffer it. The woe of a stricken people is a myriad circles of woe which its members feel only as individuals—save in so far as their sympathy for their kind adds to each a further suffering. In times of general misfortune this is a legitimate consolation, for it can come only to those who abjure the mass-idea of mankind, who know that one heart can suffer whatever there is of suffering and enjoy whatever there is of joy.

The root distinction here is that between means and ends. Social science is concerned with the relation of means to ends, as it is actually worked out in the structure of society. Power and wealth are means, not ends; they are the means to some kind of satisfaction or fulfillment, and have no significance apart from that. Only means are cumulative, nor can we measure the degree of fulfillment in terms of the amassing of the means through which it is sought. The divorce of means from ends, the engrossment in projects of power or wealth, as if these were significant in themselves, the assumption that the measure of the means is also the measure of the ends, this has been a most dangerous delusion in many an age, our own not least. . . .

In the scale of the sciences, from our present viewpoint, mathematics stands at one end and social science at the other. The former deals with the most abstract, the latter with the most concrete, of subjects; the one with the ultimate forms of mere existence, the other with the ultimate of realities. Quantitative relations hold of social as of all other facts, but they are quite inadequate to reveal the nature of the former. The social scientist needs, for example, statistics, not for their own sake, but because they serve as indices to facts of another order altogether. Thus what are called vital statistics give us most necessary and valuable indications of changes taking place within society, changes not merely in health conditions, but changes in mode of life and thought, changes in the character of the family, in the whole system of ideals and traditions that animate society. To get the figures is, or should be, easy; to interpret them is the much more arduous task of the social scientist. . . .

THE ART OF GOVERNMENT *

We should then be content to think of government rather as an art than as a science. Like every other art it makes use of the appropriate sciences. Among these sciences is social psychology. Analysts of public opinion are learning to measure more accurately the various responses of different groups both to appeals and to situations. From this science, and from others—including economics which though still very inadequate has at least shown the potentiality of becoming systematic knowledge—the practitioners of government can draw much valuable information. But no science can tell men how to govern, as the science of engineering can tell men how to throw a bridge across a river. And for this difference we return to our first argument. The techniques of engineering are relatively independent of the myths of the bridge-maker, or of the bridge-user, and they are not contingent on the purposes of the company that undertakes to build the bridge or of the public authority that sanctions the building of it. But the business of governing is inextricably bound up with the elaborate and ever varying myth-complex that links the governors and the governed.

The Uses of Political Philosophy

Charles A. Beard †

What constitutes significant work in [political science], work that stands out above the flood of time? Rousseau's *Social Contract* is significant in this sense. Why? His data are generally wrong, but it so happened that he reflected in his conclusions a vast social movement then under way in France and the rest of the Western World. Rousseau was a part of that movement; he mirrored its desires and its becoming. The *Federalist* is significant. Its data are most realistic, but not all embracing. Why its significance? It too mirrored a huge realistic movement in American politics, the practical consequences of which are still powerful with us. Marx's *Capital* is a significant work, for similar reasons. Hence we seem constrained to say that great works in political science mirror with a high degree of accuracy the political movements of an age, its underlying and hidden currents, no less than its outward pomp and circumstance. They constitute in no mystical way a part of the world's process of becoming conscious of itself, indicating its proximate direction, and giving the force of rationality

* From R. M. MacIver, *The Web of Government* (New York, The Macmillan Co., 1947), pp. 11–12. By permission.

† Professor of Politics at Columbia University, 1904–1917. Author of *An Economic Interpretation of the Constitution, The Republic*. Co-author of *Rise of American Civilization*. The selection is from Charles A. Beard, "Method in Political Science," *Essays on Research in the Social Sciences* (Washington, D.C., The Brookings Institution, 1931), pp. 58–63. By permission of the Brookings Institution.

to its own realization. Such, as Hegel would say, seems to be the decision which the present state of our knowledge requires.

It must not be assumed that this is academic. The directing statesman, no less than the student, also represents immense movements of human and material forces. The data with which he works are more real than those of the laboratory, the data of political experience. He too selects, arranges, interprets, and decides. If his mental picture corresponds realistically with the long movement of actuality about him, he holds a place as a statesman; if not, he becomes a politician in the American sense of that word. A study of the memoirs of great statesmen shows most of them working under a sense of destiny not of their own making, choosing and applying expedients under its limitations, and thus divining the future which they are helping to make. The accuracy of the divination seems to determine the degree of immortality attained by the statesman, as of the writer on political science. Lincoln's place is higher than that of Calhoun, not because he was a greater logician but because he more accurately reflected the titanic movement of forces which was to dominate the close of the nineteenth century. More people read Marx than Gladstone because the former more effectively conceived the inevitabilities inherent in the Victorian age.

If so, what then is the immediate upshot? It is that while we must work more zealously and carefully than ever with the immediate substance of political science, we can only illuminate it and give enduring form to conclusions respecting it by constant and laborious effort to relate it to the widest possible periphery of knowledge, understanding, and actuality. Even the smallest effort to do this contributes to the fruition of great efforts. When an age is characterized by similar efforts among many thinkers, a concentration and enrichment of thought takes place, and at the proper moment some Newton, making use of all fragments around him, kindles a light that illuminates the heavens. Even the smallest of us can help to prepare the way for the higher generalization; indeed it is certain that unless we work wisely and laboriously at our tasks the intellectual heritage for truly penetrative judgments cannot be supplied. Unless the least of us dares to dare, the greatest cannot conquer a single segment of the barrier between ignorance and understanding.

SECTION II

What Is Democracy?

Few concepts in political theory are so enmeshed in controversy over scope and definition as is the concept of democracy. So great is its appeal that radically differing régimes have, at one time or another, claimed the name and sanction of democracy.

Most Americans identify democracy with the political systems of the United States and Western Europe. But to Adolph Hitler nazism was "Germanic" democracy and a leading philosopher called fascist Italy "the democratic state—par excellence." Soviet leaders distinguish between the "true" democracy of the U.S.S.R. and the "sham" democracy of the West. Russia and America differ, too, over whether democracy exists in certain Eastern European countries.

One result of this apparent confusion might be to brush aside the whole question as a mere matter of semantics. This would be unfortunate, for disagreement over definition may derive from deep-lying differences over values and may manifest itself in the institutional devices designed to realize these values.

What has been said is not intended to suggest that there is some *one* correct definition of democracy. It is rather to point to the urgency of thinking through the problem of definition, for obviously while other considerations are involved, an evaluation of the institutions and techniques of the American constitutional system, such as federalism, the party process, Congress, the presidency, and judicial review, will be profoundly affected by the answer to the question: "What is democracy?"

(For Lenin's views on "democracy" see Topic 5.)

Topic 2

A SYMPOSIUM ON DEMOCRACY

George C. Marshall *

I realize that the word "democracy" is given many interpretations. To the American Government and citizens it has a basic meaning. We believe

* Secretary of Defense. Formerly Chief of Staff, U.S. Army, Ambassador to China,

that human beings have certain inalienable rights—that is, rights which may not be given or taken away.

They include the right of every individual to develop his mind and his soul in the ways of his own choice, free of fear and coercion—provided only that he does not interfere with the rights of others. To us a society is not democratic if men who respect the rights of their fellow men are not free to express their own beliefs and convictions without fear that they may be snatched away from their home or family. To us a society is not free if law-abiding citizens live in fear of being denied the right to work or deprived of life, liberty and the pursuit of happiness.

James Bryce *

The word Democracy has been used ever since the time of Herodotus to denote that form of government in which the ruling power of a State is legally vested, not in any particular class or classes, but in the members of the community as a whole. This means, in communities which act by voting, that rule belongs to the majority, as no other method has been found for determining peaceably and legally what is to be deemed the will of a community which is not unanimous. . . . Where the will of the whole people prevails in all important matters, even if it has some retarding influences to overcome, or is legally required to act for some purposes in some specially provided manner, that may be called a Democracy. . . . I use the word in its old and strict sense, as denoting a government in which the will of the majority of qualified citizens rules, taking the qualified citizens to constitute the great bulk of the inhabitants, say, roughly, at least three-fourths, so that the physical force of the citizens coincides (broadly speaking) with their voting power.

Walter Lippmann †

A false ideal of democracy can lead only to disillusionment and to meddlesome tyranny. If democracy cannot direct affairs, then a philosophy

U.S. Secretary of State. The selection is from Secretary of State Marshall's statement to the Moscow Conference of the Council of Foreign Ministers, *New York Times,* March 15, 1947. By permission of *The New York Times* and the Associated Press.

* British Ambassador to the United States, 1907–1913. Former President of the American Political Science Association. Author of *The Holy Roman Empire, Modern Democracies, The American Commonwealth,* etc. The selection is from James Bryce, *Modern Democracies* (New York, The Macmillan Co., 1929), Vol. I, pp. 20–22. By permission.

† Newspaper columnist. Formerly newspaper editor. Author of *Public Opinion, A Preface to Politics, A Preface to Morals, The Good Society, U.S. Foreign Policy,* and numerous other books. The selection is from Walter Lippmann, *The Phantom Public* (New York, The Macmillan Co., 1927), pp. 41, 42, 55–62, 126–128, 155. By permission.

which expects it to direct them will encourage the people to attempt the impossible. . . . The actual governing is made up of a multitude of arrangements on specific questions by particular individuals. These rarely become visible to the private citizen. Government, in the long intervals between elections, is carried on by politicians, officeholders and influential men who make settlements with other politicians, officeholders, and influential men. The mass of people see these settlements, judge them, and affect them only now and then. They are altogether too numerous, too complicated, too obscure in their effects to become the subject of any continuing exercise of public opinion.

Nor in any exact and literal sense are those who conduct the daily business of government accountable after the fact to the great mass of the voters. They are accountable only, except in spectacular cases, to the other politicians, officeholders and influential men directly interested in the particular act. Modern society is not visible to anybody, nor intelligible continuously and as a whole. One section is visible to another section, one series of acts is intelligible to this group and another to that. Even this degree of responsible understanding is attainable only by the development of fact-finding agencies of great scope and complexity. . . .

The more clearly it is understood what the public can do and what it cannot, the more effectively it will do what lies within its power to do well and the less it will interfere with the liberties of men. The role of public opinion is determined by the fact that its relation to a problem is external. The opinion affects an opinion, but does not itself control the executive act. A public opinion is expressed by a vote, a demonstration of praise or blame, a following or a boycotting. But these manifestations are in themselves nothing. They count only if they influence the course of affairs. They influence it, however, only if they influence an actor in the affair. And it is, I believe, precisely in this secondary, indirect relationship between public opinion and public affairs that we have the clue to the limits and the possibilities of public opinion.

It may be objected at once that an election which turns one set of men out of office and installs another is an expression of public opinion which is neither secondary nor indirect. But what in fact is an election? We call it an expression of the popular will. But is it? We go into a polling booth and mark a cross on a piece of paper for one of two, or perhaps three or four names. Have we expressed our thoughts on the public policy of the United States? Presumably we have a number of thoughts on this and that with many buts and ifs and ors. Surely the cross on a piece of paper does not express them. It would take us hours to express our thoughts, and calling a vote the expression of our mind is an empty fiction.

A vote is a promise of support. It is a way of saying: I am lined up with these men, on this side. I enlist with them. I will follow. . . . The public does not select the candidate, write the platform, outline the policy any more than it builds the automobile or acts the play. It aligns itself for or against somebody who has offered himself, has made a promise, has produced a play, is selling an automobile. The action of a group as a group is the mobilization of the force it possesses.

The attempt has been made to ascribe some intrinsic moral and intellectual virtue to majority rule. It was said often in the nineteenth century that there was a deep wisdom in majorities which was the voice of God. Sometimes this flattery was a sincere mysticism, sometimes it was the self-deception which always accompanies the idealization of power. In substance it was nothing but a transfer to the new sovereign of the divine attributes of kings. Yet the inherent absurdity of making virtue and wisdom dependent on 51 per cent of any collection of men has always been apparent. The practical realization that the claim was absurd has resulted in a whole code of civil rights to protect minorities and in all sorts of elaborate methods of subsidizing the arts and sciences and other human interests so they might be independent of the operation of majority rule.

The justification of majority rule in politics is not to be found in its ethical superiority. It is to be found in the sheer necessity of finding a place in civilized society for the force which resides in the weight of numbers. I have called voting an act of enlistment, an alignment for or against, a mobilization. These are military metaphors, and rightly so, I think, for an election based on the principle of majority rule is historically and practically a sublimated and denatured civil war, a paper mobilization without physical violence. . . . Hans Delbruck puts the matter simply when he says that the principle of majority rule is "a purely practical principle. If one wants to avoid a civil war, one lets those rule who in any case would obtain the upper hand if there should be a struggle; and they are the superior numbers."

I do not wish to labor the argument any further than may be necessary to establish the theory that what the public does is not to express its opinions but to align itself for or against a proposal. If that theory is accepted, we must abandon the notion that democratic government can be the direct expression of the will of the people. We must abandon the notion that the people govern. Instead we must adopt the theory that, by their occasional mobilizations as a majority, people support or oppose the individuals who actually govern. We must say that the popular will does not direct continuously but that it intervenes occasionally. . . . To support the Ins when things are going well; to support the Outs when they seem to be going badly, this, in spite of all that has been said about tweedledum and tweedledee, is the essence of popular government. . . . A community where there is no choice does not have popular government. It is subject to some form of dictatorship or it is ruled by the intrigues of the politicians in the lobbies. . . .

In the United States, Great Britain, Canada, Australia and in certain of the Continental countries an election rarely means even a fraction of what the campaigners said it would mean. It means some new faces and perhaps a slightly different general tendency in the management of affairs. The Ins may have a bias toward collectivism; the Outs will lean toward individualism. The Ins may have been suspicious and noncooperative in foreign affairs; the Outs will perhaps be more trusting or entertain another set of suspicions. The Ins may have favored certain manufacturing interests; the Outs may favor agricultural interests. But even these differing tendencies are very small as compared with the immense area of agreement, established habit and unavoidable necessity.

Harold J. Laski *

No definition of democracy can adequately comprise the vast history which the concept connotes. To some it is a form of government, to others a way of social life. Men have found its essence in the character of the electorate, the relation between government and the people, the absence of wide economic differences between citizens, the refusal to recognize privileges built on birth or wealth, race or creed. Inevitably it has changed its substance in terms of time and place. What has seemed democracy to a member of some ruling class has seemed to his poorer fellow citizen a narrow and indefensible oligarchy. Democracy has a context in every sphere of life; and in each of those spheres it raises its special problems which do not admit of satisfactory or universal generalization. . . .

[The] notion of equality points the way to the essence of the democratic idea—the effort of men to affirm their own essence and to remove all barriers to that affirmation. All differentials by which other men exercise authority or influence they do not themselves possess hinder their own self-realization. To give these differentials the protection of the legal order is to prevent the realization of the wishes and interests of the mass of men. The basis of democratic development is therefore the demand for equality, the demand that the system of power be erected upon the similarities and not the differences between men. Of the permanence of this demand there can be no doubt; at the very dawn of political science Aristotle insisted that its denial was the main cause of revolutions. Just as the history of the state can perhaps be most effectively written in terms of the expanding claims of the common man upon the results of its effort, so the development of the realization of equality is the clue to the problem of democracy. . . .

* Late Professor of Political Science at London School of Economics. Formerly Chairman of the British Labor Party Executive Committee. Author of numerous books on political subjects, including *Grammar of Politics, Democracy in Crisis, State in Theory and Practice, The American Democracy*. The selection is from Harold J. Laski, "Democracy," *Encyclopaedia of Social Sciences* (New York, The Macmillan Co., 1942). By permission.

It is because political equality, however profound, does not permit the full affirmation of the common man's essence that the idea of democracy has spread to other spheres. The discovery that men may be politically equal without attaining a genuine realization of their personalities was seen by not a few during the Puritan revolution, and the demand for economic equality was loudly and ably voiced there by Winstanley and his followers. It was only, however, with the French Revolution that economic equality may be said to have become a permanent part of the democratic creed. From that time, particularly in the context of socialist principles, it has been increasingly insisted that in the absence of economic equality no political mechanisms will of themselves enable the common man to realize his wishes and interests. Economic power is regarded as the parent of political power. To make the diffusion of the latter effective, the former also must be widely diffused. To divide a people into rich and poor is to make impossible the attainment of a common interest by state action. Economic equality is then urged as the clue upon which the reality of democracy depends. . . .

Democratic government during the nineteenth century may be said to have been successful so long as it confined its activities to the purely political field. While it occupied itself with matters of religious freedom, formal political equality, the abrogation of aristocratic privilege, its conquests were swift and triumphant. But the attainment of these ends did not solve any of the major social and economic issues. The masses still remained poor; a small number of rich men still exercised a predominant influence in the state. With the grant of the franchise to the workers therefore a movement toward collectivism was inevitable. Political parties had to attract their support; the obvious method was to offer the prospect of social and economic legislation which should alleviate the workers' condition. And from the early days of the French Revolution there had appeared the portent of socialism with its insistence that only in the rigorous democratization of economic power could a solution to the social problem be found. Incoherent at first, the development of trade unions and the growth of doctrines like that of Marx made what seemed visionary utopianism into a movement. By the eighties of the nineteenth century socialism could represent itself as the natural and logical outcome of democratic theory. It could outbid the older parties on ground which universal suffrage had made the inevitable territory of conflict. In the opening years of the twentieth century the central theme of debate had become the power of the state to satisfy the economic wants of the working class. . . .

If the hypothesis of self-government is valid in the political sphere it must be valid in the economic sphere also; whence is born the insistence upon constitutional government in industry. Not only must the state interfere to this end in the general details of economic life, but it cannot realize its end if the operation of the profit making motive is admitted in any industry of basic importance to the community. The new ideals of democracy therefore foreshadow a functional society in which the older conception of liberty of contract has no place. Any state in which the economic sphere is left largely uncontrolled is necessarily a class society tilted to the advantage of the rich; it lacks that necessary basis of unity which enables men to compose their differences in peace. The claim for the sovereignty of the state no longer rests upon the strong basis provided by the old liberal hypothesis of a society equal in fact because formally equal in political power. Largely the new democratic theory accepts a quasi-Marxian interpretation of the state while refusing to draw therefrom the inference that revolution is its only satisfactory corrective. . . .

[The new democratic theory] regards the right of men to share in the results of social life as broadly equal; and it regards differences of treatment as justifiable only in so far as they can be shown to be directly relevant to the common good. It takes its stand firmly on the need for a close economic equality on the ground that the benefits a man can obtain from the social process are, at least approximately and in general, a function of his power of effective demand, which in turn depends upon the property he owns. It is thus hostile to all economic privilege as being in its nature fatal to the end at which a democratic society must aim. For the new democratic theory liberty is necessarily a function of equality. . . .

The new trend of democracy is not less hostile to dictatorship in any form than the old. Whatever the original purpose of dictatorship, history indicates that it cannot avoid degeneration; and when that occurs the benefits of the dictatorship are bound to be confined to those who share in its operation. Further, modern democratic theory is built upon the notion that the only way of responding to the wants of total experience in modern communities is to give that experience the full opportunity of expression; and the only way to give it that freedom is to offer it in its various aspects the responsibility of sharing in power.

One final remark may be made. It is not the view of modern democratic theory that a political man can be constructed whose interest in the public business of the community is assured. It does believe that increased educational opportunity will increase that interest; a belief which further emphasizes the need for equality. It does argue further that the main result of inequality is so to depress the moral character of those at the basis of the social pyramid as to minimize their power to get attention for their experience. Again therefore it sees in equality the path to the end democracy seeks to serve. It has far less assurance than in the past that the end may be attained, but it is not less convinced than its predecessors of the nobility of the ideal.

R. M. MacIver *

DEMOCRACY AND THE WILL OF THE PEOPLE †

Democracy cannot mean the rule of the majority or the rule of the masses. This was the manner in which democracy was interpreted by the Greek philosophers, at a time before there was any representative system or any party system—and this fact may help to explain why they on the whole disapproved of it. The meaning of democracy was then obscure. Even today, with all our experience of democracy, it is often misunderstood. Democracy is not a way of governing, whether by majority or otherwise, but primarily a way of determining who shall govern and, broadly, to what ends. The only way in which the people, *all the people,* can determine who shall govern is by referring the question to public opinion and accepting on each occasion the verdict of the polls. Apart from this activity of the people there is no way of distinguishing democracy from other forms of government. Any kind of government can claim to rest on "the will of the people," whether it be oligarchy or dictatorship or monarchy. One kind of government alone rests on the constitutional exercise of the will of the people. Every other kind prevents the minority—or the majority—from freely expressing opinion concerning the policies of government, or at the least from making that opinion the free determinant of government. Quite possibly in Russia, at the time of writing, a larger proportion of the people approves and supports its government than may be found in democratic countries to support their governments. But that fact is quite irrelevant to the question of democracy. In the Soviet Union, under these conditions, there is no free exercise of opinion on matters of policy, nor any constitutional means by which the changing currents of opinion can find political expression. It would therefore be the sheerest confusion to classify the Soviet system as democratic.

The growth of democracy has always been associated with the free discussion of political issues, with the right to differ concerning them, and with the settlement of the difference, not by *force majeure* but by resort to the counting of votes. It has always been associated with the growing authority of some assembly of the people or of the people's representatives, such as the Greek *ecclesia,* the Roman *comitia,* the English parliament. The right to differ did not end with the victory of the majority but was inherent in the system. It was a necessary condition of democracy everywhere that opposing doctrines remained free to express themselves, to seek converts, to form organizations, and to compete for success before the tribunal of public opinion. Any major trend of opinion could thus register itself in the character and in the policies of government. . . .

* Professor Emeritus of Political Philosophy and Sociology at Columbia University.
† R. M. MacIver, *The Web of Government* (New York, The Macmillan Co., 1947), pp. 198–199. By permission.

THE RÔLE OF FREE OPINION *

Democracy constitutionally guarantees certain fundamental rights to all citizens. Apart from these rights—the right to think and believe after one's own mind and heart, the right to express one's opinions and to organize for their furtherance, the right to vote according to one's opinions, and so forth—democracy cannot exist. But the rights in question are not the same thing as a form of government. They may properly be made a *test* of its existence but they do not constitute it. Secretary of State George C. Marshall applied this test when the Western Powers were in dispute with Soviet Russia regarding the implementation of a pledge made under the Yalta agreement of 1945. The allied plenipotentiaries pledged themselves to use "democratic means" for the solution of the problems of the occupied countries of Europe, and again at the Berlin Conference they gave directions "for the eventual reconstruction of German political life on a democratic basis." But when it came to performance the Soviet Union and the Western powers were completely opposed, the former claiming that its own restrictive and high-handed methods were in accordance with the democratic pledge. General Marshall insisted that the essence of democracy was the recognition that "human beings have certain inalienable rights—that is, rights that may not be given or taken away," and that until these rights were granted and guaranteed the pledge was not fulfilled. These rights included "the right of every individual to develop his mind and his soul in the ways of his own choice, free of fear and coercion—provided only that he does not interfere with the rights of others." "To us," he said, "a society is not free if law-abiding citizens live in fear of being denied the right to work or being deprived of life, liberty and the pursuit of happiness."

The argument was just, in the light of the whole history of what the world has known as democracy. For our purpose of definition, however, we must look beyond the possession of such rights to the constitutional order that gives and guards the assurance. This constitutional order, in any of its varieties, *is* democracy. Now then we must ask: what kind of order is it that can *constitutionally* assure these rights? We find that both historically and logically it is an order that, to establish the right of opinion, gives free opinion itself a politically creative rôle. In other words, the government must be dependent on, and responsive to, the changes of public opinion. More closely, each successive administration is voted into office by an election or series of elections at which the people freely express their effective preference for one group of candidates over another group or other groups. In order that this process may be constitutionally possible the law must bind the relations of men in the areas to which it applies but must not bind their opinions in any areas. (We shall not pause here to examine the apparent

* From R. M. MacIver: *The Ramparts We Guard,* copyright 1950 by Robert MacIver, and used with the permission of The Macmillan Co. Pp. 49–51.

but not genuine exceptions to this principle that fall under laws relating to libel, slander, incitement to violence, and so forth.) In a democracy those who oppose the policies of the government lose no civil rights and those who support its policies acquire thereby no civil rights. In a democracy minority opinion remains as untrammeled as majority opinion.

The importance of the creative rôle assigned to public opinion under democracy lies primarily in the fact that if opinion is free then the whole cultural life of man is free. If opinion is free, then belief is free and science is free and art and philosophy and all the variant styles and modes in which men manifest and develop their values and tastes and ways of living—always up to the limit where they endeavor by oppression or violence to deprive their fellowmen of these same prerogatives. Democracy alone assures the citadel of human personality against the deadly invasions of power. If only we could comprehend what this means we would never let our disappointments with the defects and weaknesses that the workings of democracy may reveal blind us to the intrinsic superiority of democracy over all other systems of government. . . .

"POLITICAL" AND "ECONOMIC" DEMOCRACY *

Some recent writers draw a distinction between "political democracy" and "economic democracy." They regard "economic democracy" as either the complement or the fulfillment of "political democracy." Sometimes they treat "political democracy" as less important than "economic democracy." Not infrequently they refer to the Soviet system as embodying this superior form of democracy. Mr. Harold Laski, who follows this line, writes: "If the hypothesis of self-government is valid in the political sphere it must be valid in the economic sphere also." Now when Mr. Laski speaks of "economic democracy" he is not speaking of *democracy* in any sense. He does not mean that the workers should elect by ballot the managers and the executive boards of industrial corporations or banks and decide what policies they should pursue in the conduct of their business. He certainly can offer no evidence that these democratic procedures are applied in Soviet Russia. Moreover, the economic program he is concerned about is one he wants the state to implement. His program is a *political* one. He wants democratic countries to adopt a collectivist system. But he should not identify a collectivist system with democracy, whether "economic" or "political." A democracy may approve a collectivist program or may reject it. It is still a democracy, and either way it is taking action "in the economic sphere." "The economic sphere" can never be separated from "the political sphere." What policy a democracy follows in this sphere depends on the conditions, and immediately on public opinion. Mr. Laski, like many others, is apt to

* R. M. MacIver, *The Web of Government* (New York, The Macmillan Co., 1947), pp. 206–208. By permission.

identify democracy with the things he would like democracy to do. In some of his writings he suggests that if a democracy should adopt a "revolutionary" socialist program it might meet such resistance from the propertied classes that democracy itself would come to an end and dictatorship take its place. It is indeed possible, but where the democratic spirit prevails, as in England, the United States, the self-governing British Dominions, and the Scandinavian countries, it seeks to avoid such drastic alternatives; it prefers to move to its goals by steps, not by one convulsive act. The point, however, is that should such a convulsion take place Mr. Laski's socialist program would be achieved at the price of democracy. Nor could it reasonably be argued that "economic democracy" had taken the place of "political democracy." There might be greater economic equality, but we have no ground, either in logic or in history, for assuming that collectivist equality, arrived at on such terms, would become the boon companion of democracy. . . .

THE FUNCTION OF THE PUBLIC *

There are those who condemn democracy because, they say, the people are unfit to rule. And there are those who, in a more friendly spirit, deplore the plight of democracy because the people simply cannot undertake the task it imposes on them, the task of coping with all the complex issues of modern government. In one of his earlier books, *The Phantom Public,* Walter Lippmann put forward the plaint that the democratic man was baffled and disenchanted. He could not make his sovereign voice heard concerning a thousand tangled affairs, and how could he? How could he have an effective opinion about the situation in China today and about the sewers of Brooklyn tomorrow, and the next day about the effects of subsidies to agriculture, and the next day about some deal with Yugoslavia, and so on without end? He gave it up. He was disillusioned about democracy. He could not live up to its demands.

If any "man in the street" holds these views about his democratic obligations it is quite proper he should be disillusionized. But not, we hope, about democracy. Only about his illusions about democracy. Representative democracy, the only kind that has any meaning under modern conditions, does not put any such impossible strain on the citizen. The people, let us repeat, do not and cannot govern; they control the government. In every live democracy they decide the broad march of politics. They decide whether there is to be more social legislation or less, more collectivization or somewhat more play for private enterprise, more dependence on an international system of security or more self-sufficiency and relative isolation, and so forth. They decide these issues, not one at a time but by voting

* From R. M. MacIver: *The Ramparts We Guard,* copyright 1950 by Robert MacIver, and used with the permission of The Macmillan Co. Pp. 27–30.

for an administration favorable to one or another "platform." They decide them partly—and in the last resort—at the polls, and partly by the continuously manifested indications of public sentiment. To make decisions easier there is in every community a sense of alternative directions, marked respectively left and right, and a sway of opinion in one or the other direction. The signposts marking "left" and "right" may not always be clear, but they are always understood. The greater trends in either direction reveal the deep hidden workings of group and folk consciousness, down on a level that the recorders of opinion-changes and the political forecasters never fathom and sometimes entirely ignore.

This incessant activity of popular opinion is the dynamic of democracy. It decides between the larger alternatives of policy-making and in that way has an impact on a thousand issues. Mr. Lippmann, in the book referred to, was clearly off the beam when he suggested that it is not the business of the public to decide the substantive policies of government but merely to see that the government abides by the rules, like a referee who watches the players but takes no part in the game. The greater changes in the socio-economic policies of Western European countries in the nineteenth and twentieth centuries—the whole trend towards social legislation and the control of economic power—were due to the swelling currents of public opinion, responsive to changing conditions. Or we may cite the more recent experience of the United States, where a new manifestation of public opinion, opposed by most of the prestige-bearers and of the well-to-do, carried to power and maintained in power the party of the "New Deal."

That is how the citizens of a democracy make their citizenship effective. Not as individuals deciding for themselves the successive problems of politics, each in speculative detachment registering his opinion on every issue. Not merely as units casting their separate votes every few years as election time comes round—the citizens of a democracy are *continuously* engaged in a massive give-and-take of creative opinion-making. Certainly not as experts who must willy-nilly do the job of the administration, that is, by finding the answers to the very specific questions that the administration must face from day to day. No business is run that way, and no government can be. Executive jobs are for executives, whether in business or in government. The public—or the workers or the shareholders—may very well entertain an opinion on whether the management is doing well or badly, but that is a different matter altogether.

We observe in passing that in a democracy there are two stages of decision-making before the *proper* job of the expert begins. First, there is the primary function of policy-making, the choice between directions, the function of the people. Second, there is the delineation of policy by the legislators and the heads of the government—in accordance with the "mandate" thus entrusted to them. Third, there is the implementation of policy. At this third stage the expert finds his place. It is here, and here alone, that he belongs. He is the technician or the craftsman in the art of government.

It is an eminently logical system. The representatives of the people have the authority. They are presumably—they always become at least—more conversant with the ways of governing than are the lay citizens, but they are not experts. They mark out the lines of advance and the experts build the roads. The logic is admirable, but as in all human affairs it is subject to distortion. These three functions are not clear-cut and separable in practice. The limits of each in relation to the others must be discretionary and flexible. Which means also that there may be conflict, confusion, and encroachment between the participants. The legislator may not let the expert do his proper job or, more commonly, he permits the expert to follow his own devices into the area of policy-making. The cabinet officers may ignore the spirit of their mandate, particularly in the screened-off sector of foreign policy. The expert may become a worshipper of routine, a jealous guardian of the secrets of office, a bureaucrat in the less honorable sense of the word.

Such things happen everywhere, and perhaps there is no safeguard except the vigilance of the public, as it becomes better educated in the ways of democracy and armed with fuller knowledge of its practical operation. What indeed appears throughout, as we study democracy at work, is that the defects and shortcomings it exhibits are due not to any inherent weakness in its principle but to the greater responsibilities it imposes on those who carry it out. These responsibilities are in themselves reasonable and never excessive, but interest and pride and office are always at hand, to deflect, to distort, and to betray. The ever-active democratic process checks these tendencies. How effectively it does so is in the keeping of the public, who have the authority and the means to control those whom they entrust with the business of governing.

SECTION III

Democracy in a Changing World

That governments derive "their just powers from the consent of the governed" appears to many Americans so self-evident as to require no demonstration. Many introductory textbooks in American government, in any event, proceed on this major, if inarticulate, premise and are concerned almost exclusively with the implementation to the neglect of evaluation of democracy. To examine this major premise would seem a prerequisite to any systematic study of politics, but in view of the present world crisis this task is particularly imperative.

Democracy exists in a world which offers alternatives, and it must be tested, ultimately, in the light of these alternatives. Extracts from Frederick L. Schuman and Arthur Koestler, which present quite different interpretations of life under the Soviet state, have been included in this section because of a belief that comparisons between democracy and dictatorship in terms of principles and theory alone are not enough. Defenders of democracy, in fact, frequently maintain that the strongest arguments for democracy are based on what happens to individuals living under other forms of government.

It may be asked why a book on American government should include excerpts from Lenin's *State and Revolution* and Stalin's speech "On the New Soviet Constitution." An excellent answer can be found in John Stuart Mill's famous essay "On Liberty" (Topic 15): "They [who] have never thrown themselves into the mental position of those who think differently from them and considered what such persons may have to say . . . do not, in any proper sense of the word, know the doctrine which they themselves profess," or, at best their conclusion is held "in a manner of a prejudice, with little comprehension or feeling of its rational grounds." (It should be noted, however, that while Lenin claims that his interpretation of Marx is the only correct one, this view has been challenged by other Marxist scholars.)

This section begins with selections from Edward Sait and Alexis de Tocqueville who maintain that there are serious weaknesses in traditional democratic theory and practice. While the particular selection from de Tocqueville is highly critical of American democracy, it must be said that de Tocqueville himself believed that much could be said for democracy as well as aristocracy. In evaluating these arguments, consideration should be given to the validity of these criticisms and to what extent the weaknesses, if found to exist, are inherent in the very nature of democracy or might be remedied by changes in our institutions and attitudes. In the concluding topic of this section Carl Becker emphasizes the fundamental values which democracy promotes.

In later topics (15 and 16), consideration is given to the value and limits of free discussion in a functioning democracy. The case for free speech is obviously an integral part of the case for democracy and arguments which support one will ordinarily support the other.

Topic 3
ATTACK ON DEMOCRACY

The Decline of Democracy
Edward McChesney Sait *

The triumphs of democracy in the nineteenth century bred a strange mystical faith that did not allow itself to be disturbed by facts. The mystical democrat—he still survives among us—has passed through a religious experience. . . . The fundamentalist holds fast to the original creed by lifting it above the plane of reason and argument. It is revealed truth. No matter what strange anomalies confront him in its practical application, he must keep this precious inheritance whole and undefiled. The cure for the shortcomings of democracy, he always maintains, is more democracy. If he is confronted with facts, with the contradiction between those facts and his theory, he replies that "democracy must not be judged by its yesterday, or by its to-day, but by its to-morrow"—its always receding to-morrow; and that, as Chesterton says of Christianity, it has not been tried and found wanting, but found hard and not tried.

The fundamentalist takes a sanguine view of human nature and of average human capacity. He believes that, notwithstanding the evil propensities of individuals, men taken in the mass spontaneously generate the truth, or at least, by some mysterious power of divination, recognize the truth and resolutely follow it. The voice of the people is the voice of God. . . .

Now, since the voice of the people is the voice of God, a peculiar spiritual quality attaches to the ballot, through which the people speak. The ballot has magical properties. A century ago, the English fundamentalists embodied their aspirations—universal suffrage, annual elections, vote by ballot, etc.—in the People's Charter and took Feargus O'Connor as their prophet. Deploring the misery of the masses, O'Connor said: "Laws made

* Late Professor of Government, Pomona College. Author of *American Parties and Elections, Democracy*. The selection is from Edward McChesney Sait, *Political Institutions: A Preface* (New York, Appleton-Century-Crofts, Inc., 1938), Ch. XIX. By permission.

by all would be respected by all. . . . Universal Suffrage would, at once, change the whole character of society from a state of watchfulness, doubt, and suspicion, to that of brotherly love, reciprocal interest, and universal confidence. . . . Away, then, with the whole system at once: The wound is too deep to be healed by partial remedies; the nation's heart's blood is flowing too rapidly to be stopped by ordinary stypticks. . . . Give us, then, the only remedy for all our social ills and political maladies; make every man in his artificial state as he might be in his natural state, his own doctor, by placing the restorative in his hand, which is UNIVERSAL SUFFRAGE!!! . . . Six months after the Charter is passed every man, woman, and child in the country will be well fed, well housed, and well clothed." . . .

According to the Greek view—the view of Plato and Aristotle and Polybius—forms of government perpetually change and succeed each other in some definite cycle; but, according to the fundamentalist, democracy is the perfect and permanent flower of a completed evolution. It is an everlasting flower which, without the help of the watering-can, will keep its bloom through the ages. No matter if it is neglected utterly: never will a petal fall.

This belief in the permanence of democracy does not harmonize well with an age that has the facts of history at its command and which prates about a scientific attitude. Yet quite a few educated persons entertain it. A Socialist, like Franz Oppenheimer, may be forgiven; he must not look outside his Marxian bible, being intellectually free, as the medieval schoolmen were, only within rigidly-set limits. Perhaps Woodrow Wilson may be forgiven; he wrote at the end of the nineteenth century, before the symptoms of democratic decay had become manifest. Less lenience can be shown to college professors of the present day. Harold J. Laski says: "Democratic government is doubtless a final form of political organisation in the sense that men who have once tasted power will not, without conflict, surrender it." This opinion is all the more curious in view of the fact that it was expressed several years after the Italian people had cheerfully surrendered their power to Mussolini. Robert M. MacIver says: "If we are right in our interpretation of the state as an organ of community, we must regard all states in which the general will is not active as imperfect forms. This view seems to be confirmed by a study of the historical process, for it appears to be true that, in spite of reversions, the main trend of the state, *after it has finally emerged as a state,* is toward democracy. . . . No institutions are secure, but those which rest on the sustaining power of the community are the strongest. A people can overthrow every form of government but its own—then it finds no alternative. A republic may be destroyed from without, but it is as nearly invincible from within as anything human." On this statement it is enough to say for the moment that the people are not like an individual; they divide in opinion; and, if they divide on fundamental issues, chaos supervenes and opens the way for monarchy.

SYMPTOMS OF DECLINE

Is democracy the final flower of political evolution? Perhaps, to scientific minds, it appears rather as a system which, in a world of ceaseless change, has shown itself best adapted to a certain set of temporary conditions. Yesterday the rule of One was all but universal; to-day the rule of the Many has supplanted it. There is no reason to suppose that to-morrow will be as to-day. Institutions are set up and modified and abandoned, sometimes by the caprice of man or what seems like it, sometimes by the stern pressure of circumstances. Will democracy still fit our circumstances twenty-five, fifty, or one hundred years from now? There are obscure, underlying forces that act quite independently of the human will and shape the social structure. These forces may be exerting an influence that will ultimately undermine the foundations of democracy. . . .

Hilaire Belloc, analyzing a different set of social forces and proceeding along a different route, arrives at a position incompatible with democracy. His argument appears in *The Servile State.* That brilliant and ingenious essay, which was published in 1912, seeks to prove that the capitalist régime—unstable in equilibrium, incapable of guaranteeing sufficiency and security to the mass of the wage-earners—is moving toward something quite different from the socialist solution and quite at variance with the democratic ideal. The future society will be a servile society. "We are," says Belloc, "rapidly coming nearer to the establishment of compulsory labour among an unfree majority of non-owners for the benefit of a free minority of owners." The very legislation that is designed to improve the lot of the masses—employers' liability, insurance against sickness and unemployment, old-age pensions, the minimum wage—carries with it the implication of servitude. The State guarantees to the proletarian, as the master did to his slave, sufficiency and security; and the next step, the fatal corollary of the first—already foreshadowed in the attitude of the State toward its employees—will lead it to impose the obligation to work. Belloc believes that, except for the active and adventurous few, men like slavery when they experience it; they get the things most valued in life: sufficiency, security, and relief from responsibility. The people of the U.S.S.R. have had experience of something akin to it latterly; and, whether they really like it or not, they seem quiescent.

LOSS OF FAITH

No human institution can stand still; the process of transformation goes steadily forward. . . . The late Lord Bryce was unrivaled in his acquaintance with political affairs and unsurpassed in sobriety and penetration of judgment. His sympathies were strongly democratic. Yet at the close of his life his optimism faltered. The time had come for men to face the facts and be done with fantasies. "Few are the free countries," he wrote, "in which freedom seems safe for a century or two ahead. . . . When the spiritual oxygen which has kept alive the attachment to liberty and self-government in the minds of the people becomes exhausted, will not the flame burn low and perhaps flicker out?" No one thought of trying to revive popular government when it disappeared in Greece and Rome. "The thing did happen: and whatever has happened may happen again. People that had known and prized political freedom resigned it, did not much regret it, and forgot it." These lines were written before the March on Rome by Mussolini's Black Shirts.

Unquestionably the growing skepticism about democracy must be attributed in part to the excesses committed in its name. The franchise has been given to all adults, women as well as men; special privileges or immunities have been granted to organized labor and other interests; the rich have been taxed for the benefit of the poor. Let us remember the warning of Montesquieu: Governments decline and fall as often by carrying their principles to excess as by neglecting them altogether. . . . Evidence of popular disillusionment, of declining faith in democracy, can be found in many different places. Within the last twenty years, for example, the critical literature has assumed formidable proportions. . . .

The most obvious of all the disquieting phenomena is the fallen prestige of representative assemblies. Cynicism is not, of course, peculiar to our own time. Carlyle, after taking Emerson to "the national talk-shop," the House of Commons, asked him if he did not now believe in a personal devil; Lavelaye observed that Italy was fortunate in the situation of her capital, since the Roman malaria effectively abridged the sessions of parliament. . . . Ridicule and contempt [of Congress] are the familiar language of the Press and of men prominent in the business world. The country feels safest, according to the New York *Times,* when Congress is not in session. The worst thing we have, according to E. H. Gary, is our American Congress. "There has never been a time," says Representative Robert Luce, whose scholarly books and long service in the House give his words some authority, "when the legislative branch of the government, both national and state, has been held in such low esteem." Even the British House of Commons—doubtless regarded more highly, both at home and abroad, than any other representative body—suffers from a perpetual bombardment of derisory missiles. . . .

That representative assemblies have sunk low in prestige will probably be admitted without the submission of more evidence. However, our state constitutions offer cogent proof. In pre-democratic days these constitutions went no farther than to lay down a few principles and describe the framework of government. They were brief documents, running to no more than ten or twelve pages in Thorpe's collection. What influence was at work, then, to produce monstrosities like the Oklahoma constitution of 1907, which—though not now the longest—spreads itself over seventy-odd pages? If one glances through those dreary pages, the answer becomes apparent: the legislature had to be put under restraint. . . . Our state legislatures, with half a dozen exceptions, are permitted to meet only once every two years, and, even so, are limited in more than half the states to a session of sixty days or less. According to the *New Republic,* business associations wish "to reduce the sessions of the state legislatures, which are supposed to safeguard American social welfare, to once every four years." May we not expect in the future some still more drastic curtailment of power? The popular attitude suggests it. When the legislature completes its little span of active life, a sigh of relief shakes the atmosphere. The newspapers busily set to work estimating the damage that the "people-chosen" have done.

The typical product of popular rule is the politician. Since it is his function to make the laws and guide the destinies of the community, he must be chosen, one would suppose, because of his outstanding qualifications. Yet the politician, far from commanding respect, is the perpetual butt of sarcasms. H. G. Wells describes him as "an acutely humiliating caricature of the struggling soul of our race." He is, says Émile Faguet, "a man who, in respect of his personal opinions, is a nullity, in respect of education, a mediocrity; he shares the general sentiments and passions of the crowd. . . . He is precisely the thing of which democracy has need. He will never be led away by his education to develop ideas of his own; and having no ideas of his own, he will not allow them to enter into conflict with his prejudices. His prejudices will be, at first, a feeble sort of conviction, afterwards, by reason of his own interest, identical with those of the crowd. . . ."

It is absurd to blame the politician because he is not a superman. In order to become a politician, he had first of all to be a mediocrity.

The masses resent superiority as reflecting upon their own condition, and fear it as subversive of the democratic régime. . . . Democracy loves a crowd, but, fearing the individuals who compose it, tries to blot out human prestige and minimize the influence of personality. "Democracy has achieved its perfect work," says Ralph Adams Cram, "and has now reduced all mankind to a dead level of incapacity, where great leaders are no longer wanted or brought into existence, while society itself is unable, of its own power as a whole, to lift itself from the nadir of its own uniformity. . . . For exactly a hundred years democracy has suffered from progressive deterioration until it is now not a blessing, but a menace." Mr. Cram's esthetic feelings are outraged as he watches the mountains being levelled and the valleys filled in. Professor Irving Babbitt has horrid presentiments of the future American society as "a huge mass of standardized mediocrity . . . , one of the most trifling brands of the human species that the world has ever seen." Is that the direction in which democracy is taking us? There go the millions, ballot in hand, on their way to the polls: the same ballot for each individual, irrespective of his mental and moral endowments; the same ballot for high and low, intelligent and stupid, energetic and inert; and, since each voter among the millions makes the same infinitesimal contribution, must we not suppose that the élite will be submerged, crushed by weight of numbers?

POLITICS AND ECONOMICS

To-day everybody is impressed with the complexity of our economic, and consequently of our social, life. In place of the simple conditions of the frontier, which gave President Jackson the idea that, without preliminary training or special aptitudes, any one was competent to hold public office, we are confronted now with the most baffling and intricate problems. How striking the change has been may be gathered by comparing the national party platforms of the present era with the platforms of the forties or even the seventies. The problems have grown highly technical, transcending the capacities of ordinary citizens and requiring the attention of experts. Can democracy, with its belief in the average man and its distrust of the specialist, endure this new strain? Bismarck said quite truly that institutions must be judged by what is accomplished through them. Democracy will be judged—and is being judged—by its success or failure in supervising a highly specialized economic mechanism. According to Bryce: "Neither the conviction that power is better entrusted to the people than to a ruling One or Few, nor the desire of the average man to share in the government of his own community, has in fact been a strong force inducing political change. Popular government has been usually sought and won and valued, not as a good thing in itself, but as a means of getting rid of tangible grievances or securing tangible benefits, and when these objects had been attained, the interest in it has gradually tended to decline. If it be improbable, yet it is not unthinkable that, as in many countries impatience with tangible evils substituted democracy for monarchy or oligarchy, a like impatience might some day reverse the process."

The task of government has become vastly more difficult during the past generation. Have the people acquired a corresponding increase in competence? We are sometimes told, if public affairs have grown terribly complicated, terribly hard to penetrate, the capacity of the masses to control them has, like the efficiency of the naval gun, increased at a higher ratio. The masses are educated, enlightened. How could it be otherwise when we spend more than two billion dollars yearly on our public schools in the United States and at the same time diffuse the highest forms of culture through the moving pictures, the radio, and the Sunday supplement?

What the average citizen has obtained is the rudiments of knowledge.

He can write a letter; he can read a book. But, unfortunately, his smattering of education has made him arrogant and bold in situations that call for modesty and caution in expressing a judgment. The more remote things are from his experience and the less he knows about them, the more definite his opinions seem to be. It is doubtful that bigger doses of education would do him any good. Education can train, but not create, intelligence. When Dr. Joseph Collins tells about the prevalence of adult-infantilism and when the testers fix the average mental age of the electorate at fourteen, there may be some excuse for regarding the electorate as incurably stupid.

Wyndham Lewis, master of devastating satire and picturesque phrase, . . . says: ". . . Although we have called this prodigious mass of people 'infantile,' they are of course outwardly grown up. They do not call themselves infantile as a community. They claim to be treated as responsible, accomplished, intelligent beings. They want to have official bulletins every morning of all accidents, fires, murders, rapes that have occurred throughout the night and part of the preceding day. They wish a detailed account of how their agents and ministers of state have 'fulfilled their trust,' as they call it, in the conduct of that great and sacred affair, the commonwealth. And they wish to be informed punctually of the results of all racing, ball-games, paper-chases, bull-fights, and other similar events."

The potentialities of education have been exaggerated grotesquely. Education can only "lead forth" inborn talents, not create them; and many biologists believe that the germ-plasm of Western peoples is deteriorating. Not only is warfare dysgenic,—it "but straws the wheat and saves the chaff with a most evil fan,"—but the best stock, rising to the top in the social scale, resorts to birth-control or becomes sterile. It is the Infant Class . . . that is setting the future tone of the human species. This tendency has been confirmed by the growth of a somewhat indiscriminate humanitarian spirit in the West. Help is extended prodigally to those who cannot or will not help themselves. The doctrine of equality, which justifies the raising of the low and the leveling of the high, becomes a doctrine of inequality in practice, when the energetic and thrifty Few are called upon to provide housing, food, medical care, education, amusements, and much besides for the slothful and improvident Many, the very dregs of society. The worst specimens are coddled, and encouraged to breed, as if they were the best. They are even maintained at public expense without the necessity of working. From the standpoint of heritable qualities, the political competence of the people as a whole declines, while the complexity of the problems of government increases.

Political interest is declining. Apathy is attested not only by the bewildered complaints of democratic fundamentalists, but by the statistics of elections. . . . By way of generalization, it is enough to say of the

American situation that half the potential voters ignore the election and that three-quarters ignore the primary. The diagnostician, as he observes the pallid countenance of democracy, the wasting-away of a once robust physique, recognizes the symptoms of a fatal malady: there is no hope for the patient; this is persistent anemia. What has become of the devotion and enthusiasm that marked the democratic crusade in the nineteenth century or the suffragette movement of the early twentieth? The crusading spirit is gone now. . . .

The ordinary voter is ill-informed, apathetic, and indolent. Political issues do not touch him closely. He is preoccupied, first of all, with the task of making a living and, then, with his home and family. If he is a religious man, the church attracts him more than the polling booth. And can we be surprised that, after the exhausting labors of the day, he wants to keep his few hours of leisure for recreation and amusement? Now that political issues have grown so complicated as to be unintelligible to the average voter, civic duty does not attract his jaded mind. He will not listen to the pious doctrine that, in addition to being wise about his own personal affairs, he must now be wise about everybody else's as well. "When the private man has lived through the romantic age," says Walter Lippmann, "and is no longer moved by the stale echoes of its hot cries, when he is sober and unimpressed, his own part in public affairs appears to him a pretentious thing, a second-rate, an inconsequential. You cannot move him with a good straight talk about service and civic duty, nor by waving a flag in his face, nor by sending a boy scout after him to make him vote. He is a man back home from a crusade to make the world something or other it did not become. . . ."

Many of the issues that are presented to the voters are utterly remote from his experience, utterly beyond his comprehension, and at the same time dreary. . . . "To-day the interest in politics is on the wane," says Sir Charles Petrie, "and save on exceptional occasions they are rarely discussed by younger people outside the ranks of the professional politicians. Various reasons, mostly the reverse of flattering to those concerned, have been advanced to account for this, but the real cause is undoubtedly the fact that *the problems which face the rulers of mankind are such that no ordinary layman can understand them. . . . The interest in politics has declined because they have become unintelligible.*"

EXPERTS AS A MENACE

There is no use blinking the fact: democracy everywhere is on trial. On all sides the gospel of efficiency is being preached. . . . Here lies the dilemma: democracy without experts—and it has a justifiable fear of them—faces the danger of collapse; with experts—they being a lean and hungry crowd—it faces the danger of being devoured by its own offspring. It is on the latter horn of the dilemma that democracy is being impaled.

More than twenty-five years ago Ramsay Muir came to the pessimistic conclusion that Englishmen, gradually ceasing to feel a sense of personal responsibility for public affairs, were losing, in consequence, the habit of self-government. He attributed this tragic condition to the steady, persistent, and powerful influence of the great permanent officials, whose actions are never submitted to the judgment of the electorate and whose names are never—or very seldom—mentioned by newspapers. . . . Parliament has delegated a vast range of legislative power to the departments. Delegation has gone so far that, in one statute at least, the minister (in practice, his technical advisers) was empowered to do anything "which appears to him necessary or expedient" for the purpose named, even to the point of modifying the provisions of the Act. Most of the departmental rules and orders do not require any affirmative action by Parliament. What we encounter, therefore, is parliamentary abdication in the interest of efficiency. In the second place, there has been an equally marked tendency to confer upon the administrative experts judicial or quasi-judicial power, without allowing appeal to the ordinary courts. The expert makes the law, applies it, and penalizes offenders. Yet he lives somewhere in the shadows, beyond the range of the light that beats upon Parliament, the police, and the courts. . . .

All thoughtful Englishmen must now be aware that a "new despotism" is taking shape. Americans should recognize a similar phenomenon in their own country. Long before the danger was made obvious by the New Deal, the note of alarm had been sounded.

THE COLLAPSE OF CONSENSUS

Democracy implies in one sense the rule of all, and in another sense the rule of the majority. We speak of all as ruling when all respect the right of the majority to rule. Since unanimous decisions are rare, whether in the popular choice of representatives or in the passing of laws, it has been the practice of democracies from time immemorial to accept the voice of the majority as the voice of all. Without such a compromise, little business could be transacted. But such a compromise is possible only when the disagreements between majority and minority touch upon matters of secondary importance and when there is a coincidence of interest in matters of primary concern, unless the latter have been removed from the arena of normal party conflict by some artificial contrivance such as a constitutional bill of rights. The accord between majority and minority goes by the name of consensus.

Democracy cannot exist without consensus, or a near approach to it.

. . . The twentieth century witnesses a sudden growth of social cleavages and violent class hatreds, such as kept Spain in turmoil for years and at last plunged her into a savage civil war. Russia, Italy, and Germany have found a way out through the suppression of irreconcilable minorities and the creation of an artificial uniformity. . . . At any rate, the collapse of consensus will always and everywhere entail the collapse of democracy. On that point there can be no doubt whatever. . . .

In Great Britain, notwithstanding the rise of a Socialist party and the deleterious effect of urban life upon the masses, the native inclination to compromise still runs strong, as does also the respect for law. Yet Professor Laski says:

> The success of the British Parliamentary system has been built upon the fact that the major parties in the state could agree to accept each other's legislation, since neither altered the essential outlines of that social-economic system in which the interests of both were involved. With the emergence of the Labor party as the alternative government, a different position has come into view. The Labor party aims at the transformation of a capitalist into a socialist society. It seeks, therefore, directly to attack, by means of Parliament, the ownership of the means of production by those classes which constitute the foundation of Tory and Liberal strength. Its principles are a direct contradiction of those of its rivals. It denies the validity of the whole social order which the nineteenth century maintained. Is it likely that it can obtain its objectives in the peaceful and constitutional fashion which was characteristic of the Victorian epoch? . . . A change in the essential methods of production, such as the Labor party envisages, involves changes in the legal and political institutions which are literally fundamental. However generous be the compensation to established expectations, the interference with vested interests which the policy predicates is momentous in amount. Are the owners of property likely to accept the peaceful destruction of their position in the state?

Such are the views of a prominent British socialist.

In the United States the situation is, in some respects, more reassuring. It is true that the urban population now exceeds the rural and that class-consciousness has spread among the ranks of the proletariat, especially with the growth of industrial unionism since 1936. These factors will make themselves felt in the partisan realignment that seems to be impending. The proletariat is far from being a class-conscious unit, however; the skilled trades—constituting a sort of aristocracy of labor—incline to something like a middle-class mentality; and, with the middle-classes, they stand in the way of a clear-cut social division in party politics. Far more effective as an obstacle to such a division are the agricultural interests, which cannot be harmonized with those of the wage-earners. As long as agriculture retains anything like its present character and importance, there is no good prospect for the formation of a major party that openly advocates a Marxian solution. There still seems to be a vast reservoir of moderate opinion that makes itself heard in time of crisis. But that alone does not guarantee the survival of consensus.

The Tyranny of the Majority

Alexis de Tocqueville *

I hold it to be an impious and an execrable maxim that, politically speaking, a people has a right to do whatsoever it pleases, and yet I have asserted that all authority originates in the will of the majority. Am I, then, in contradiction with myself? . . .

A majority taken collectively may be regarded as a being whose opinions, and most frequently whose interests, are opposed to those of another being, which is styled a minority. If it be admitted that a man, possessing absolute power, may misuse that power by wronging his adversaries, why should a majority not be liable to the same reproach? Men are not apt to change their characters by agglomeration; nor does their patience in the presence of obstacles increase with the consciousness of their strength. And for these reasons I can never willingly invest any number of my fellow creatures with that unlimited authority which I should refuse to any one of them. . . .

I am of opinion that some one social power must always be made to predominate over the others; but I think that liberty is endangered when this power is checked by no obstacles which may retard its course, and force it to moderate its own vehemence.

Unlimited power is in itself a bad and dangerous thing; human beings are not competent to exercise it with discretion, and God alone can be omnipotent, because his wisdom and his justice are always equal to his power. But no power upon earth is so worthy of honor for itself, or of reverential obedience to the rights which it represents, that I would consent to admit its uncontrolled and all-predominant authority. When I see that the right and the means of absolute command are conferred on a people or upon a king, upon an aristocracy or a democracy, a monarchy or a republic, I recognize the germ of tyranny, and I journey onward to a land of more hopeful institutions.

In my opinion the main evil of the present democratic institutions of the United States does not arise, as is often asserted in Europe, from their weakness, but from their overpowering strength; and I am not so much alarmed at the excessive liberty which reigns in that country as at the very inadequate securities which exist against tyranny.

When an individual or a party is wronged in the United States, to whom can he apply for redress? If to public opinion, public opinion constitutes the majority; if to the legislature, it represents the majority, and implicitly obeys its injunctions; if to the executive power, it is appointed by the majority, and remains a passive tool in its hands; the public troops consist of the

* Noted French statesman and critic. Author of *The Old Government and the Revolution* and other works on political and social subjects. The selection is from Alexis de Tocqueville, *Democracy in America* (Henry Reeve translation, 1835), Vol. I, Chs. XIII–XV.

majority under arms; the jury is the majority invested with the right of hearing judicial cases; and in certain States even the judges are elected by the majority. However iniquitous or absurd the evil of which you complain may be, you must submit to it as well as you can. . . .

I do not say that tyrannical abuses frequently occur in America at the present day, but I maintain that no sure barrier is established against them, and that the causes which mitigate the government are to be found in the circumstances and the manners of the country more than in its laws. . . .

In America, the majority raises very formidable barriers to the liberty of opinion: within these barriers an author may write whatever he pleases, but he will repent it if he ever step beyond them. Not that he is exposed to the terrors of an *auto-da-fé,* but he is tormented by the slights and persecutions of daily obloquy. His political career is closed forever, since he has offended the only authority which is able to promote his success. . . .

Monarchical institutions have thrown an odium upon despotism; let us beware lest democratic republics should restore oppression, and should render it less odious and less degrading in the eyes of the many, by making it still more onerous to the few. . . .

Topic 4

DEFENSE OF DEMOCRACY

Some Generalities That Still Glitter

Carl Becker *

We do accept democracy somewhat perfunctorily—less so now that Hitler has brought into strong relief its essential virtues, but still rather from habit than from profound conviction. Long familiarity with democracy as a going concern, by disclosing its glaring defects and discords, has bred in many quarters a half-cynical skepticism which is alternately directed against the democratic reality as something scarcely worth preserving, and against the ideal as something impossible to achieve. The result is that if we go all out for the reality we are in danger of being thought hypocritical, while if we go all out for the ideal we are sure to be thought naïve. We can therefore only accept democracy with reservations, and it is difficult indeed to go all out for reservations.

This is the normal price paid by all religious and social systems for

* Late Professor of History at Cornell University. Author of *The Declaration of Independence, Our Great Experiment in Democracy, Modern Democracy, How New Will the Better World Be?, Freedom and Responsibility in the American Way of Life,* etc. The selection is from Carl Becker, "Some Generalities That Still Glitter," *The Yale Review* (Summer, 1940), XXIX, No. 4, pp. 650, 651, 663–667. Copyright Yale University Press. By permission.

success and long life. Having conquered the world, they are subdued to it. The ideological faiths that originally gave them intellectual coherence and moral support, being gradually assimilated to the worldly conventions, come to be accepted as a matter of course, without serious reservations perhaps, but at least without the disturbing zeal engendered by deep conviction. If then, under the stress of profound discords in the system, the ideology is subjected to skeptical criticism and analysis, it is likely to fade away into the realm of myth, leaving nothing but inertia or naked force to preserve the system from decay or destruction.

Since primitive times most religious and social systems have attempted to avoid this fate by forbidding free criticism and analysis, either of the established institutions or of the doctrines that sustain them. Democracy is the one system that cannot employ this method of self-preservation, since the cardinal principle of its ideology is that free criticism and analysis by all and sundry is the highest virtue. Democracy, if it be consistent, must welcome the critical examination, not only of its current institutions and policies but even of the fundamental assumptions on which it rests. Democracy is thus a stupendous gamble for the highest stakes. It offers long odds on the capacity of the human mind. It wagers all it has that the freest exercise of the human reason will never disprove the proposition that only by the freest exercise of the human reason can a tolerably just and rational society ever be established.

The play is still going on, the outcome of the wager is still uncertain, but the gamble seems now a more desperate one than it did a century ago. During the last hundred years, the assumptions of the democratic faith have been subjected to the freest possible and the most penetrating critical examination; and the result is to leave us somewhat doubtful, not perhaps of the capacity of the human mind at its best, but certainly of the capacity of the average human mind to perceive that which is true and to cleave to that which is good. Our doubt in this respect arises in part from the fact that our conception of human reason, of its capacity to devise a rational system of law and government, and of the part it plays in shaping the conduct of men, is in certain important respects different from that which inspired the early prophets and protagonists of democracy. . . .

The trend of thought variously known as anti-intellectualism, relativism, activism, assumes its crudest and least defensible form in the dictum of Thrasymachus that "might makes right, justice is the interest of the stronger." For more than half a century this doctrine, in more or less diluted form, has slowly, insidiously, not altogether unashamed, warped itself into the fabric of democratic thought and practice; and now, under pressure of economic collapse and social frustration, it has been exalted to the level of a complete philosophy of life in certain countries which have frankly abandoned democratic institutions. In their theoretical exposition of ultimate aims, both communism and fascism pay tribute to certain ideal values—the welfare and happiness of the community, the progress of mankind—which are assumed to be in some mystical fashion identified with an abstract entity, called in the one case the dialectic of history, in the other, the totalitarian state. Yet both assume that the abstract entity is realized in the activities of an inspired leader to whom the truth has been revealed and the direction of affairs committed; and as they exhibit themselves in action under the leader both represent a direct attack upon intelligence, an unqualified denial of any obligation to be guided by rational thinking or humane dealing. Both assume that the individual man has no importance except as an instrument to be used, with whatever degree of brutality may be necessary, for the common good as the leader understands it. Both subordinate reason to will, identify law and morality with naked force as an instrument of will, and accord value to the disinterested search for truth only in so far as the leader judges it to be momentarily useful for the attainment of immediate political ends. Herein the anti-intellectual, relativist trend of thought reaches a final, fantastic form: truth and morality turn out to be relative to the purposes of any egocentric somnambulist who can succeed, by a ruthless projection of his personality, in creating the power to impose his unrestrained will upon the world.

Hitler and Stalin represent an exorbitant price for a little wisdom. But they have at least done something to strengthen the cause of democracy. More than anything else in recent years, their incredible sophistries and ruthless brutalities have revealed to us the advantages of democratic institutions and the reality of the rational and humane values that are traditionally associated with them. The Declaration of Independence may now be referred to without apology, and even policemen on the beat are becoming dimly aware that there is such a thing as the Bill of Rights. What associations for the defense of civil liberties could not accomplish, Hitler and Stalin have in some measure accomplished; and they have accomplished it by frankly accepting, ruthlessly applying, and thereby reducing to an absurdity the principle that law and morality are nothing more than the right of the stronger.

The absurdity is that this principle, accepted with the moral obtuseness and applied with the cynical brutality of the Hitlers and the Stalins, eliminates from the world those rational and humane values which for more than two thousand years men have commonly accepted as the test of civilized living, however little their actual conduct may have conformed to them. The exertion of brute force is a fact which we cannot ignore; but to justify the brute fact by its existence and pressure is to end with no means of distinguishing fact from illusion, since illusion is a fact the existence of which is undeniable and the pressure of which may be immense. Might and right are discordant and incommensurable terms, and while it is necessary to submit to that which is stronger, there is nothing which men have more persistently or universally denied than that it is right to approve of it for that reason. To say that justice is the right of the stronger is to dispense with right and justice altogether. There is then nothing but the fact, or rather nothing but what is, which is neither good nor bad, fact nor illusion, but merely that which is "existential," as the philosophers say. There is then no place for law or morality. There is then no place for reason, even as an instrument functionally developed to serve the interest of a biological organism. For if reason is a functional instrument, then it must have a function, and what function can it have if it be not to discriminate the relatively true from the relatively false, the dependable fact from the deceptive illusion, in order that the organism may pursue the better rather than the less good interest? Granted that reason is an instrument developed to serve the interest of the organism, the chief service it can perform is to determine which of many interests it is best for the organism to pursue. The choice in any particular instance may be a good one, but whether it is so or not cannot be determined by the fact that the organism has chosen to respond to a purely egoistic impulse and has exhibited the power required to gratify it.

It does not matter that we cannot share the belief of an earlier generation in the easy triumph of the right-thinking man. We may still believe in his triumph. We may admit that mind is an integral part of the animal organism, and that the pronouncements of reason are subtly shaped by subconscious desire and emotion. We may admit it, and we should admit it gladly, since to know the limitations of reason is to increase its power in the long run. If we know (and we knew it long before Freud) that the wish is father to the thought, that the heart has reasons that reason knows not of, it was, after all, reason that revealed this secret to us, and the secret, once revealed, enables reason to avoid illusions that would otherwise vitiate its conclusions. The fallacy is to suppose that because truth is in some sense relative it cannot be distinguished from error, or that the margin of error cannot be progressively reduced. The fallacy is to suppose that reason cannot transcend its lowly animal origin, to suppose that because it is a function of the organism's total activity and can be and is employed in the service of purely egoistic and brutal impulses, it cannot serve purposes of a more humane and impersonal import. On the contrary, whatever success men have had since the Stone Age in lifting themselves above the level of brute existence, has been the result of the slowly developing capacity of reason to distinguish fact from illusion, and to prefer the values that exalt the humane and rational qualities of the human personality to the values that deny and degrade them.

To have faith in the dignity and worth of the individual man as an end in himself, to believe that it is better to be governed by persuasion than by coercion, to believe that fraternal good will is more worthy than a selfish and contentious spirit, to believe that in the long run all values are inseparable from the love of truth and the disinterested search for it, to believe that knowledge and the power it confers should be used to promote the welfare and happiness of all men rather than to serve the interests of those individuals and classes whom fortune and intelligence endow with temporary advantage—these are the values which are affirmed by the traditional democratic ideology. But they are older and more universal than democracy and do not depend upon it. They have a life of their own apart from any particular social system or type of civilization. They are the values which, since the time of Buddha and Confucius, Solomon and Zoroaster, Plato and Aristotle, Socrates and Jesus, men have commonly employed to measure the advance or the decline of civilization, the values they have celebrated in the saints and sages whom they have agreed to canonize. They are the values that readily lend themselves to rational justification, yet need no justification. No one ever yet found it necessary to justify a humane and friendly act by saying that it was really a form of brutality and oppression; but the resort to coercion in civil government, in war and revolution, in the exploitation of the poor or the liquidation of the rich, has always to be justified by saying that the apparent evil is an indirect means of achieving the greater or the ultimate good. Even the Hitlers and the Stalins, in order to win the support of their own people, find it necessary to do lip service to the humane values, thus paying the customary tribute of hypocrisy which virtue exacts from vice.

Whatever the limitations of reason may be, it is folly to renounce it, since it is the only guide we have—the only available means of enlarging the realm of scientific knowledge, the only means of discriminating the social value of the various uses to which such knowledge may be put. Whatever the limitations of reason may be, they are not so great that the civilized man cannot recognize the existence and the necessity of naked force and coercion in an imperfect social world, without attributing to them the creation of those humane and rational values which by their very nature affirm that naked force and coercion are at best necessary evils.

The case for democracy is that it accepts the rational and humane values as ends, and proposes as the means of realizing them the minimum of coercion and the maximum of voluntary assent. We may well abandon the cosmological temple in which the democratic ideology originally enshrined these values without renouncing the faith it was designed to celebrate. The essence of that faith is belief in the capacity of man, as a rational and humane creature, to achieve the good life by rational and humane means. Apart from this faith, there is no alternative for the modern man except cynicism or despair—or the resort to naked force, which is itself but masked despair or cynicism disguised. For even more obvious now than in the seventeenth century is the truth of Pascal's famous dictum: "Thought makes the whole dignity of man; therefore, endeavor to think well, that is the only morality." The chief virtue of democracy, and the sole reason for cherishing it, is that with all its faults it still provides the most favorable conditions for the maintenance of that dignity and the practice of that morality.

We may, I think, find some measure of assurance in the fact that democracy accepts in theory, and realizes in practice better than other forms of government, the humane and rational values of life, and that it is to that extent in harmony with the age-long human impulse to know that which is true and to follow that which is good—the impulse that throughout the ages, although often frustrated and sometimes defeated, has been the determining factor in lifting mankind above the life that, as Hobbes said, is "nasty, brutish and short." In all times past this inherent and indefeasible impulse has proved to be, with whatever reverses, the wave of the future; in the time that is before us, I think it will likewise prove to be, with whatever reverses, the wave of the future.*

For the moment we are living in one of the periods of reverses, in a time when, as the poet Jeffers says, we seem to feel "a gathering in the air of something that hates humanity." Something that hates humanity and, for that reason, the truth too. The best case for democracy, and our best reason for having faith in the freedom of learning and teaching which it fosters, is that in the long history of civilization humanity has proved stronger than hate, and falsehood less enduring than truth.

Topic 5

COMMUNISM AND DEMOCRACY

STATE AND REVOLUTION

V. I. Lenin †

THE STATE AS THE PRODUCT OF THE IRRECONCILABILITY OF CLASS ANTAGONISMS

Marx's doctrines are now undergoing the same fate, which, more than once in the course of history, has befallen the doctrines of other revolutionary thinkers and leaders of oppressed classes struggling for emancipation. During the lifetime of great revolutionaries, the oppressing classes have invariably meted out to them relentless persecution, and received their teach-

* This and the following paragraph are from Carl Becker, "Freedom of Learning and Teaching," *Freedom and Responsibility In the American Way of Life* (New York: Alfred A. Knopf, Inc., 1945), p. 64. Reprinted by permission of Alfred A. Knopf, Inc.

† Outstanding leader of the Russian Bolshevik Revolution. First President of the Council of Peoples' Commissars, U.S.S.R. Author of *Imperialism: The Highest Stage of Capitalism* and numerous other books and articles. *State and Revolution,* written in 1917, is presented here in abridged and rearranged form.

ing with the most savage hostility, most furious hatred, and a ruthless campaign of lies and slanders. After their death, however, attempts are usually made to turn them into harmless saints, canonizing them, as it were, and investing their name with a certain halo by way of "consolation" to the oppressed classes, and with the object of duping them; while at the same time emasculating and vulgarizing the real essence of their revolutionary theories and blunting their revolutionary edge. At the present time the bourgeoisie and the opportunists within the Labor Movement are co-operating in this work of adulterating Marxism. They omit, obliterate, and distort the revolutionary side of its teaching, its revolutionary soul, and push to the foreground and extol what is, or seems, acceptable to the bourgeoisie. . . .

Let us begin with the most popular of Engels' works, *The Origin of the Family, Private Property, and the State*. Summarizing his historical analysis Engels says:

> The State in no way constitutes a force imposed on Society from outside. Nor is the State "the reality of the Moral Idea," "the image and reality of Reason" as Hegel asserted. The State is the product of Society at a certain stage of its development. The State is tantamount to an acknowledgment that the given society has become entangled in an insoluble contradiction with itself, that it has broken up into irreconcilable antagonisms, of which it is powerless to rid itself. And in order that these antagonisms, these classes with their opposing economic interests may not devour one another and Society itself in their sterile struggle, some force standing, seemingly, above Society, becomes necessary so as to moderate the force of their collisions and to keep them within the bounds of "order." And this force arising from Society, but placing itself above it, which gradually separates itself from it—this force is the State.

Here, we have, expressed in all its clearness, the basic idea of Marxism on the question of the historical role and meaning of the State. The State is the product and the manifestation of the irreconcilability of class antagonisms. When, where and to what extent the State arises, depends directly on when, where and to what extent the class antagonisms of a given society cannot be objectively reconciled. And, conversely, the existence of the State proves that the class antagonisms *are* irreconcilable.

It is precisely on this most important and fundamental point that distortions of Marxism arise along two main lines.

On the one hand, the bourgeois and particularly the petty-bourgeois ideologists, compelled by the pressure of indisputable historical facts to recognize that the State only exists where there are class antagonisms and class struggles, "correct" Marx in such a way as to make it appear that the State is an organ for the *reconciliation* of classes. According to Marx, the State can neither arise nor maintain itself if a reconciliation of classes is possible. But with the petty-bourgeois and philistine professors and publicists, the State (and this frequently on the strength of benevolent references to Marx) becomes a mediator and conciliator of classes. According to

Marx, the State is the organ of class *domination,* the organ of oppression of one class by another. Its aim is the creation of order which legalizes and perpetuates this oppression by moderating the collisions between the classes. But in the opinion of the petty-bourgeois politicians, the establishment of order is equivalent to the reconciliation of classes, and not to the oppression of one class by another. To moderate their collisions does not mean, according to them, to deprive the oppressed class of certain definite means and methods in its struggle for throwing off the yoke of the oppressors, but to conciliate it. . . .

But what is forgotten or overlooked is this:—If the State is the product of the irreconcilable character of class antagonisms, if it is a force standing above society and "separating itself gradually from it," then it is clear that the liberation of the oppressed class is impossible without a violent revolution, and without the destruction of the machinery of State power, which has been created by the governing class and in which this "separation" is embodied. . . .

What does this force consist of, in the main? It consists of special bodies of armed men who have at their command prisons, etc. We are justified in speaking of special bodies of armed men, because the public power peculiar to every State "is not identical" with the armed population, with its "self-acting armed organization." . . .

For the maintenance of a special public force standing above society, taxes and State loans are indispensable.

> Wielding public power and the right to exact taxes, the officials [Engels writes] are raised as organs of society, *above* society. The free voluntary respect enjoyed by the organs of the tribal (clan) society is no longer sufficient for them, even could they win it. . . .

BOURGEOIS DEMOCRACY

In capitalist society, under the conditions most favorable to its development, we have a more or less complete democracy in the form of a democratic republic. But this democracy is always bound by the narrow framework of capitalist exploitation, and consequently always remains, in reality, a democracy only for the minority, only for the possessing classes, only for the rich. Freedom in capitalist society always remains more or less the same as it was in the ancient Greek republics, that is, freedom for the slave owners. The modern wage-slaves, in virtue of the conditions of capitalist exploitation, remain to such an extent crushed by want and poverty that they "cannot be bothered with democracy," have "no time for politics"; that, in the ordinary peaceful course of events, the majority of the population is debarred from participating in public political life. . . .

Democracy for an insignificant minority, democracy for the rich—that is the democracy of capitalist society. If we look more closely into the mechanism of capitalist democracy, everywhere—in the so-called "petty" details of the suffrage (the residential qualification, the exclusion of women, etc.), in the technique of the representative institutions, in the actual obstacles to the right of meeting (public buildings are not for the "poor"), in the purely capitalist organization of the daily press, etc., etc.—on all sides we shall see restrictions upon restrictions of democracy. These restrictions, exceptions, exclusions, obstacles for the poor, seem slight—especially in the eyes of one who has himself never known want, and has never lived in close contact with the oppressed classes in their hard life, and nine-tenths, if not ninety-nine hundredths, of the bourgeois publicists and politicians are of this class! But in their sum these restrictions exclude and thrust out the poor from politics and from an active share in democracy. Marx splendidly grasped the *essence* of capitalist democracy, when, in his analysis of the experience of the Commune, he said that the oppressed are allowed, once every few years to decide which particular representatives of the oppressing class are to represent and repress them in Parliament! . . .

In a democratic Republic, Engels continues "wealth wields its power indirectly, but all the more effectively," first, by means of "direct corruption of the officials" (America); second, by means of "the alliance of the government with the stock exchange" (France and America). At the present time, imperialism and the domination of the banks have reduced to a fine art both these methods of defending and practically asserting the omnipotence of wealth in democratic Republics of all descriptions. . . .

We must also note that Engels quite definitely regards universal suffrage as a means of capitalist domination. Universal suffrage, he says (summing up obviously the long experience of German Social-Democracy), is "an index of the maturity of the working class; it cannot and never will, give anything more in the present state." The petty-bourgeois democrats such as our Socialist-Revolutionaries and Mensheviks and also their twin brothers, the Social-Chauvinists and opportunists of Western Europe, all expect a "great deal" from this universal suffrage. They themselves think and instil into the minds of the people the wrong idea that universal suffrage in the "present state" is really capable of expressing the will of the majority of the laboring masses and of securing its realization. . . .

Take any parliamentary country, from America to Switzerland, from France to England, Norway and so forth; the actual work of the State is done behind the scenes and is carried out by the departments, the chancelleries and the staffs. Parliament itself is given up to talk for the special purpose of fooling the "common people." . . .

Two more points. First: when Engels says that in a democratic republic, "not a whit less" than in a monarchy, the State remains an "apparatus for the oppression of one class by another," this by no means signifies that the *form* of oppression is a matter of indifference to the proletariat, as some anarchists "teach." A wider, more free and open form of the class struggle and class oppression enormously assists the proletariat in its struggle for the annihilation of all classes.

Second: only a new generation will be able completely to scrap the ancient lumber of the State—this question is bound up with the question of overcoming democracy, to which we now turn.

DICTATORSHIP OF THE PROLETARIAT

The forms of bourgeois States are exceedingly various, but their substance is the same and in the last analysis inevitably the *Dictatorship of the Bourgeoisie.* The transition from capitalism to Communism will certainly bring a great variety and abundance of political forms, but the substance will inevitably be: the *Dictatorship of the Proletariat.* . . .

The State is a particular form of organization of force; it is the organization of violence for the purpose of holding down some class. What is the class which the proletariat must hold down? It can only be, naturally, the exploiting class, i.e., the bourgeoisie. The toilers need the State only to overcome the resistance of the exploiters, and only the proletariat can guide this suppression and bring it to fulfillment, for the proletariat is the only class that is thoroughly revolutionary, the only class that can unite all the toilers and the exploited in the struggle against the bourgeoisie, for its complete displacement from power. . . .

But the dictatorship of the proletariat—that is, the organization of the advance-guard of the oppressed as the ruling class, for the purpose of crushing the oppressors—cannot produce merely an expansion of democracy. *Together* with an immense expansion of democracy—for the first time becoming democracy for the poor, democracy for the people, and not democracy for the rich folk—the dictatorship of the proletariat will produce a series of restrictions of liberty in the case of the oppressors, exploiters and capitalists. We must crush them in order to free humanity from wage-slavery; their resistance must be broken by force. It is clear that where there is suppression there must also be violence, and there cannot be liberty or democracy. . . .

The replacement of the bourgeois by the proletarian State is impossible without a violent revolution. . . . There is [in *Anti-Dühring*] a disquisition on the nature of a violent revolution; and the historical appreciation of its role becomes, with Engels, a veritable panegyric on violent revolution. . . . Here is Engels' argument:

That force also plays another part in history (other than that of a perpetuation of evil), namely a *revolutionary* part; that, as Marx says, it is the midwife of every old society when it is pregnant with a new one; that force is the instrument and the means by which social movements hack their way through and break up the dead and fossilized political forms—of all this not a word by Herr Dühring. Duly, with sighs and groans, does he admit the possibility that for the overthrow of the system of exploitation force may, perhaps, be necessary, but most unfortunate if you please, because all use of force, forsooth, demoralizes its user! And this is said in face of the great moral and intellectual advance which has been the result of every victorious revolution! And this is said in Germany where a violent collision—which might perhaps be forced on the people—should have, at the very least, this advantage that it would destroy the spirit of subservience which has been permeating the national mind ever since the degradation and humiliation of the Thirty Years' War. And this turbid, flabby, impotent, parson's mode of thinking dares offer itself for acceptance to the most revolutionary party which history has known!

In the *Communist Manifesto* are summed up the general lessons of history, which force us to see in the State the organ of class domination, and lead us to the inevitable conclusion that the proletariat cannot overthrow the bourgeoisie without first conquering political power, without obtaining political rule, without transforming the State into the "proletariat organized as the ruling class"; and that this proletarian State must begin to wither away immediately after its victory, because in a community without class antagonisms, the State is unnecessary and impossible.

WHAT IS TO REPLACE THE SHATTERED STATE MACHINERY?

In 1847, in the *Communist Manifesto,* Marx was as yet only able to answer this question entirely in an abstract manner, stating the problem rather than its solution. To replace this machinery by "the proletariat organized as the ruling class," "by the conquest of democracy"—such was the answer of the *Communist Manifesto*. . . .

Refusing to plunge into Utopia, Marx waited for the experience of a mass movement to produce the answer to the problem as to the exact forms which this organization of the proletariat as the dominant class will assume and exactly in what manner this organization will embody the most complete, most consistent "conquest of democracy." Marx subjected the experiment of the [Paris] Commune, although it was so meagre, to a most minute analysis in his *Civil War in France*. Let us bring before the reader the most important passages of this work. . . .

The Commune was the direct antithesis of the Empire. It was a definite form . . . of a Republic which was to abolish, not only the monarchical form of class rule, but also class rule itself.

What was this "definite" form of the proletarian Socialist Republic? What was the State it was beginning to create?

"The first decree of the [Paris] Commune was the suppression of the standing army, and the substitution for it of the armed people," says Marx. . . . But let us see how, twenty years after the Commune, Engels summed up its lessons for the fighting proletariat. . . .

Against this inevitable feature of all systems of government that have existed hitherto, viz., the transformation of the State and its organs from servants into the lords of society, the Commune used two unfailing remedies. First, it appointed to all posts, administrative, legal, educational, persons elected by universal suffrage; introducing at the same time the right of recalling those elected at any time by the decision of their electors. Secondly, it paid all officials, both high and low, only such pay as was received by any other worker. The highest salary paid by the Commune was 6,000 francs (about £240).

Thus was created an effective barrier to place-hunting and career-making, even apart from the imperative mandates of the deputies in representative institutions introduced by the Commune over and above this.

Engels touches here on the interesting boundary where a consistent democracy is, on the one hand, *transformed* into Socialism, and on the other, *demands* the introduction of Socialism. For, in order to destroy the State, it is necessary to convert the functions of the public service into such simple operations of control and bookkeeping as are within the reach of the vast majority of the population, and, ultimately, of every single individual. And, in order to do away completely with the political adventurer, it must be made impossible for an "honorable," though unsalaried, sinecure in the public service to be used as a jumping-off ground for a highly profitable post in a bank or a joint stock company, as happens *constantly* in the freest capitalist countries. . . .

In this connection the special measures adopted by the Commune and emphasized by Marx, are particularly noteworthy: the abolition of all representative allowances, and of all special salaries in the case of officials; and the lowering of the remuneration of *all* servants of the State to the level of the *"workingmen's wages."* Here is shown, more clearly than anywhere else, the *break*—from a bourgeois democracy to a proletarian democracy; from the democracy of the oppressors to the democracy of the oppressed; from the domination of a "special force" for the suppression of a given class to the suppression of the oppressors by the whole force of the majority of the nation—the proletariat and the peasants. And it is precisely on this most obvious point, perhaps, the most important so far as the problem of the State is concerned, that the teachings of Marx have been forgotten. It is entirely neglected in all the innumerable popular commentaries. It is not "proper" to speak about it as if it were a piece of old-fashioned "naiveté"; just as the Christians, having attained the position of a State religion "forget" the "naiveté" of primitive Christianity, with its revolutionary democratic spirit.

The lowering of the pay of the highest State officials seems simply a naive, primitive demand of democracy. One of the "founders" of the newest opportunism, the former Social-Democrat, E. Bernstein, has more than once exercised his talents in the repetition of the vulgar capitalist jeers at "primitive" democracy. Like all opportunists, like the present followers of Kautsky, he quite failed to understand that, first of all, the transition from capitalism to Socialism is impossible without "return," in a measure, to "primitive" democracy. How can we otherwise pass on to the discharge of all the functions of government by the majority of the population and by every individual of the population. And, secondly, he forgot that "primitive democracy" on the basis of capitalism and capitalist culture is not the same primitive democracy as in pre-historic or pre-capitalist times. Capitalist culture has created industry on a large scale in the shape of factories, railways, posts, telephones, and so forth: and *on this basis* the great majority of functions of "the old State" have become enormously simplified and reduced, in practice, to very simple operations such as registration, filing and checking. Hence they will be quite within the reach of every literate person, and it will be possible to perform them for the usual "working man's wage." This circumstance ought to and will strip them of all their former glamour as "government," and, therefore, privileged service.

The control of all officials, without exception, by the unreserved application of the principle of election and, *at any time,* re-call; and the approximation of their salaries to the "ordinary pay of the workers"—these are simple and "self-evident" democratic measures, which harmonize completely the interests of the workers and the majority of peasants; and, at the same time, serve as a bridge leading from capitalism to Socialism. . . .

The dictatorship of the proletariat, the period of transition to Communism, will, for the first time, produce a democracy for the people, for the majority, side by side with the necessary suppression of the minority constituted by the exploiters. Communism alone is capable of giving a really complete democracy, and the fuller it is the more quickly will it become unnecessary and wither away of itself. In other words, under capitalism we have a State in the proper sense of the word: that is, a special instrument for the suppression of one class by another, and of the majority by the minority at that. Naturally, for the successful discharge of such a task as the systematic suppression by the minority of exploiters of the majority of exploited, the greatest ferocity and savagery of suppression is required, and seas of blood are needed, through which humanity has to direct its path, in a condition of slavery, serfdom and wage labor.

Again, during the *transition* from capitalism to Communism, suppression is *still* necessary; but in this case it is suppression of the minority of exploiters by the majority of exploited. A special instrument, a special machine for suppression—that is, the "State"—is necessary, but this is now a transitional State, no longer a State in the ordinary sense of the term. For the suppression of the minority of exploiters, by the majority of those who were *but yesterday* wage slaves, is a matter comparatively so easy, simple and natural that it will cost far less bloodshed than the suppression of the risings of the slaves, serfs or wage laborers, and will cost the human race far less. And it is compatible with the diffusion of democracy over such an overwhelming majority of the nation that the need for any *special machinery* for *suppression* will gradually cease to exist. The exploiters are unable, of course, to suppress the people without a most complex machine for performing this duty; but *the people* can suppress the exploiters even with a very simple "machine"—almost without any "machine" at all, without any special apparatus—by the simple *organization of the armed masses* (such as the Councils of Workers' and Soldiers' Deputies, we may remark, anticipating a little).

Finally, only under Communism will the State become quite unnecessary, for there will be *no one* to suppress—"no one" in the sense of a *class,* in the sense of a systematic struggle with a definite section of the population. We are not utopians, and we do not in the least deny the possibility and inevitability of excesses by *individual persons,* and equally the need to suppress such excesses. But, in the first place, for this no special machine, no special instrument of repression is needed. This will be done by the armed nation itself, as simply and as readily as any crowd of civilized people, even in modern society, parts a pair of combatants or does not allow a woman to be outraged. And, secondly, we know that the fundamental social cause of excesses which violate the rules of social life is the exploitation of the masses, their want and their poverty. With the removal of this chief cause, excesses will inevitably begin to "wither away." We do not know how quickly and in what stages, but we know that they will be withering away. With their withering away, the State will also wither away.

THE "WITHERING AWAY" OF THE STATE

Engels' words regarding the "withering away" of the State enjoy such a popularity, are so often quoted, and reveal so clearly the essence of the common adulteration of Marxism in an opportunist sense that we must examine them in detail. Let us give the passage from which they are taken.

> The proletariat takes control of the State authority and, first of all, converts the means of production into State property. But by this very act it destroys itself, as a proletariat, destroying at the same time all class differences and class antagonisms, and with this, also, the State.

Engels speaks here of the *destruction* of the capitalist State by the proletarian revolution, while the words about its withering away refer to the remains of a *proletarian* State *after* the Socialist revolution. The capitalist State does not wither away, according to Engels, but is *destroyed* by the proletariat in the course of the revolution. Only the proletarian State or semi-State withers away after the revolution. . . .

A general summary of his views is given by Engels in the following words:—

> Thus, the State has not always existed. There were societies which did without it, which had no idea of the State or of State power. At a given stage of economic development which was necessarily bound up with the break up of society into

classes, the State became a necessity, as a result of this division. We are now rapidly approaching a stage in the development of production, in which the existence of these classes is not only no longer necessary, but is becoming a direct impediment to production. Classes will vanish as inevitably as they inevitably arose in the past. With the disappearance of classes the State, too, will inevitably disappear. When organizing production anew on the basis of a free and equal association of the producers, Society will banish the whole State machine to a place which will then be the most proper one for it—to the museum of antiquities side by side with the spinning-wheel and the bronze axe.

FIRST PHASE OF COMMUNIST SOCIETY: SOCIALISM

It is this Communist society—a society which has just come into the world out of the womb of capitalism, and which, in all respects, bears the stamp of the old society—that Marx terms the first, or lower, phase of Communist society.

The means of production are now no longer the private property of individuals. The means of production belong to the whole of society. Every member of society, performing a certain part of socially-necessary labor, receives a certificate from society that he has done such and such a quantity of work. According to this certificate, he receives from the public stores of articles of consumption, a corresponding quantity of products. After the deduction of that proportion of labor which goes to the public fund, every worker, therefore, receives from society as much as he has given it.

"Equality" seems to reign supreme. . . . But different people are not equal to one another. One is strong, another is weak; one is married, the other is not. One has more children, another has less, and so on.

With equal labor [Marx concludes] and, therefore, with an equal share in the public stock of articles of consumption, one will, in reality, receive more than another, will find himself richer, and so on. To avoid all this, "rights," instead of being equal, should be unequal.

The first phase of Communism, therefore, still cannot produce justice and equality; differences and unjust differences in wealth will still exist, but the *exploitation* of one man by many, will have become impossible, because it will be impossible to seize as private property the *means of production,* the factories, machines, land, and so on. While tearing to tatters Lassalle's small bourgeois, confused phrase about "equality" and "justice" in *general,* Marx at the same time shows the *line of development* of Communist society, which is forced at first to destroy *only* the "injustice" that the means of production are in the hands of private individuals. *It is not capable* of destroying at once the further injustice which is constituted by the distribution of the articles of consumption according to "work performed" (and not according to need). . . .

"He who does not work neither shall he eat"—this Socialist principle is *already* realized. "For an equal quantity of labor an equal quantity of products"—this Socialist principle is also already realized. Nevertheless, this is not yet Communism, and this does not abolish "bourgeois law," which gives to unequal individuals, in return for an unequal (in reality) amount of work, an equal quantity of products.

This is a "defect," says Marx, but it is unavoidable during the first phase of Communism; for, if we are not to land in Utopia, we cannot imagine that, having overthrown capitalism, people will at once learn to work for society *without any regulations by law;* indeed, the abolition of capitalism does not *immediately* lay the economic foundations for such a change. . . .

The State is withering away in so far as there are no longer any capitalists, any classes, and, consequently, any *class* whatever to suppress. But the State is not yet dead altogether, since there still remains the protection of "bourgeois law," which sanctifies actual inequality. For the complete extinction of the State complete Communism is necessary.

THE HIGHER PHASE OF COMMUNIST SOCIETY: COMMUNISM

Marx continues:

> In the higher phase of Communist society, after the disappearance of the enslavement of man caused by his subjection to the principle of division of labor; when, together with this, the opposition between brain and manual work will have disappeared; when labor will have ceased to be a mere means of supporting life and will itself have become one of the first necessities of life; when with the all-round development of the individual, the productive forces, too, will have grown to maturity, and all the forces of social wealth will be pouring an uninterrupted torrent—only then will it be possible wholly to pass beyond the narrow horizon of bourgeois laws, and only then will society be able to inscribe on its banner: "From each according to his ability; to each according to his needs."

Only now can we appreciate the full justice of Engels' observations when he mercilessly ridiculed all the absurdity of combining the words "freedom" and "State." While the State exists there can be no freedom. When there is freedom there will be no State.

The economic basis for the complete withering away of the State is that high stage of development of Communism when the distinction between brain and manual work disappears; consequently, when one of the principal sources of modern *social* inequalities will have vanished—a source, moreover, which it is impossible to remove immediately by the mere conversion of the means of production into public property, by the mere expropriation of the capitalists.

This expropriation will make it possible gigantically to develop the forces of production. And seeing how incredibly, even now, capitalism *retards* this development, how much progress could be made even on the basis of modern technique at the level it has reached, we have a right to say, with the fullest confidence, that the expropriation of the capitalists will result inevitably in a gigantic development of the productive forces of human society. But how rapidly this development will go forward, how soon it will reach the point of breaking away from the division of labor, of the destruction of the antagonism between brain and manual work, of the transformation of work into a "first necessity of life"—this we do not and *cannot* know.

Consequently, we are right in speaking solely of the inevitable withering away of the State, emphasizing the protracted nature of this process, and its dependence upon the rapidity of development of the *higher phase* of Communism; leaving quite open the question of lengths of time, or the concrete forms of this withering away, since material for the solution of such questions is not available.

The State will be able to wither away completely when society has realized the formula: "From each according to his ability; to each according to his needs"; that is when people have become accustomed to observe the fundamental principles of social life, and their labor is so productive, that they will voluntarily work *according to their abilities.* "The narrow horizon of bourgeois law," which compels one to calculate, with the pitilessness of a Shylock, whether one has not worked half-an-hour more than another, whether one is not getting less pay than another—this narrow horizon will then be left behind. There will then be no need for any exact calculation by society of the quantity of products to be distributed to each of its members; each will take freely "according to his needs." . . .

But the scientific difference between Socialism and Communism is clear. That which is generally called Socialism is termed by Marx the first or lower phase of Communist society. In so far as the means of production become public property, the word Communism is also applicable here, providing that we do not forget that it is not full Communism. . . .

Democracy implies equality. The immense significance of the struggle of the proletariat for equality and the power of attraction of such a battle-cry are obvious, if we but rightly interpret it as meaning the *annihilation of classes.* But the equality of democracy is *formal* equality—no more; and immediately after the attainment of the equality of all members of society in respect of the ownership of the means of production, that is, of equality of labor and equality of wages, there will inevitably arise before humanity the question of going further from equality which is formal to equality which is real, and of realizing in life the formula, "From each according to his ability; to each according to his needs." By what stages, by means of what practical measures humanity will proceed to this higher aim—this we do not and cannot know. But it is important that one should realize how infinitely mendacious is the usual capitalist representation of Socialism as something lifeless, petrified, fixed once for all. In reality, it is only with Socialism that there will commence a rapid, genuine, real mass advance, in which first the majority and then the *whole* of the population will take part—an advance in all domains of social and individual life.

WHY I AM NOT A COMMUNIST

Morris Raphael Cohen *

What distinguishes present-day Communists is not . . . their professed ultimate goal or their analysis of our economic ills, but their political remedy or program—to wit, the seizure of power by armed rebellion [1] and the setting up of a dictatorship by the leaders of the Communist Party. To be sure, this dictatorship is to be in the name of the *proletariat,* just as the fascist dictatorship is in the name of *the whole nation.* But such verbal tricks cannot hide the brute facts of tyrannical suppression necessarily involved in all dictatorship. For the wielders of dictatorial power are few, they are seldom if ever themselves toilers, and they can maintain their power only by ruthlessly suppressing all expression of popular dissatisfaction with their rule. And where there is no freedom of discussion, there is no freedom of thought.

This program of civil war, dictatorship, and the illiberal or fanatically intolerant spirit which war psychology always engenders may bring more miseries than those that the Communists seek to remove; and the arguments to prove that such war is desirable or inevitable seem to me patently inadequate.

Communists ignore the historic truth that civil wars are much more destructive of all that men hold dearest than are wars between nations; and all the arguments that they use against the latter, including the late "war to end war," are much more cogent against civil wars. Wars between nations are necessarily restricted in scope and do not prevent—to a limited extent they even stimulate—co-operation within a community. But civil wars necessarily dislocate all existing social organs and leave us with little social capital or machinery to rebuild a better society. The hatreds which fratricidal wars develop are more persistent and destructive than those developed by wars that terminate in treaties or agreements.

Having lived under the tyranny of the Czar, I cannot and do not condemn all revolutions. But the success and benefits of any revolution depend on the extent to which—like the American Revolution of 1776, the French Revolution of 1789, and the anti-Czarist Revolution of March 1917—it approximates national unanimity in the co-operation of diverse classes.

* Late Professor of Philosophy, College of the City of New York. President of the American Philosophical Association, 1929. Author of *Reason and Nature, Law and the Social Order, Faith of a Liberal,* and other works. The selection is from Morris Raphael Cohen, "Why I Am Not a Communist," *Modern Monthly* (April, 1934), Vol. 8, No. 3. Reprinted in *The Meaning of Marx: A Symposium,* by Bertrand Russell, John Dewey, Morris Cohen, Sidney Hook, and Sherwood Eddy (New York, Rinehart & Co., Inc., 1934). Reprinted with permission of the administrators of the estate of Morris Raphael Cohen.

[1] (Author's footnote.) Since this article was written armed intervention seems to have largely replaced armed rebellion as a technique for the seizure of power.

When armed uprisings have been undertaken by single oppressed classes, as in the revolt of the gladiators in Rome, the various peasant revolts in England, Germany, and Russia, the French Commune of 1871, or the Moscow uprising of 1905, they have left a deplorably monotonous record of bloody massacres and oppressive reaction. The idea that armed rebellion is the only or the always effective cure for social ills seems to me no better than the old superstition of medieval medicine that blood-letting is the only and the sovereign remedy for all bodily ills.

Communists may feel that the benefits of their Revolution of 1917 outweigh all the terrific hardships which the Russian people have suffered since then. But reasonable people in America will do well to demand better evidence than has yet been offered that they can improve their lot by blindly imitating Russia. Russian breadlines, and famine without breadlines, are certainly not *prima facie* improvements over American conditions. At best a revolution is a regrettable means to bring about greater human welfare. It always unleashes the forces that thrive in disorder, the brutal executions, imprisonments, and, what is even worse, the sordid spying that undermines all feeling of personal security. These forces, once let loose, are difficult to control and they tend to perpetuate themselves. If, therefore, human well-being, rather than mere destruction, is our aim, we must be as critically-minded in considering the consequences of armed revolution as in considering the evils of the existing regime.

One of the reasons that lead Communists to ignore the terrific destruction which armed rebellion must bring about is the conviction that "the revolution" is inevitable. In this they follow Marx, who, dominated by the Hegelian dialectic, regarded the victory of the proletariat over the bourgeoisie as inevitable, so that all that human effort can hope to achieve is "to shorten and lessen the birth pangs" of the new order. There is, however, very little scientific value in this dialectic argument, and many Communists are quite ready to soft-pedal it and admit that some human mistake or misstep might lead to the triumph of fascism. The truth is that the dialectic method which Marx inherited from Hegel and Schelling is an outgrowth of speculations carried on in theologic seminaries. The "system" of production takes the place of the councils or the mills of the gods. Such Oriental fatalism has little support in the spirit and method of modern science. Let us therefore leave the pretended dialectic proof and examine the contention on an historical basis.

Historically, the argument is put thus: When did any class give up its power without a bloody struggle? As in most rhetorical questions, the questioner does not stop for an answer, assuming that his ignorance is conclusive as to the facts. Now, it is not difficult to give instances of ruling classes giving up their sovereignty without armed resistance. The English landed aristocracy did it in the Reform Bill of 1832; and the Russian nobility did it in 1863 when they freed their serfs, though history showed clearly that in this way not only their political power but their very existence was doomed (for money income has never been so secure as direct revenue from the land, and life in cities reduced the absolute number of noble families). In our own country, the old seaboard aristocracy, which put over the United States Constitution and controlled the government up to the Jacksonian era, offered no armed resistance when the backwoods farmers outvoted them and removed church and property qualifications for office and for the franchise.

But it is not necessary to multiply such instances. It is more important to observe that history does not show that any *class* ever gained its enfranchisement through a bloody rebellion carried out by its own unaided efforts. When ruling classes are otherthrown it is generally by a combination of groups that have risen to power only after a long process. For the parties to a rebellion cannot succeed unless they have more resources than the established regime. Thus the ascendancy of the French bourgeoisie was aided by the royal power which Richelieu and Colbert used in the seventeenth century to transform the landed barons into dependent courtiers. Even so, the French Revolution of 1789 would have been impossible without the co-operation of the peasantry, whose opposition to their ancient seigneurs was strengthened as the latter ceased to be independent rulers of the land. This is in a measure also true of the supposedly purely Communist Revolution in Russia. For in that revolution, too, the peasantry had a much greater share than is ordinarily assumed. After all, the amount of landed communal property (that of the crown, the church, etc.) which was changed by the peasants into individual ownership may have been greater than the amount of private property made communal by the Soviet regime. Even the system of collective farms is, after all, a return to the old *mir* system, using modern machinery. The success of the Russian Revolution was largely due to the landlords' agents who, in their endeavor to restore the rule of the landlords, threw the peasantry into the arms of the Bolshevists. Indeed, the strictly Marxian economics, with its ideology of surplus-value due to the ownership of the means of production, is inherently inapplicable to the case of the peasant who cultivates his own piece of ground.

Even more important, however, is it to note that no amount of repetition can make a truth of the dogma that the capitalist class alone rules this country and like the Almighty can do what it pleases. It would be folly to deny that, as individuals or as a class, capitalists have more than their proportionate share of influence in the government, and that they have exercised it unintelligently and with dire results. But it is equally absurd to maintain that they have governed or can govern without the co-operation of the farmers and the influential middle classes. None of our recent constitutional amendments—not the income-tax amendment, not the popular election of the United States Senators, not woman suffrage, neither prohibition nor its repeal—nor any other major bit of legislation can be said to have been imposed on our country in the interests of the capitalist class. The farmers, who despite mortgages still cling to the private ownership of their land, are actually the dominant political group even in industrial states like New York, Pennsylvania, and Illinois.

The Communist division of mankind into workingmen and capitalists suffers from the fallacy of simplism. Our social structure and effective class divisions are much more complicated. As the productivity of machinery increases, the middle classes increase rather than decrease. Hence a program based entirely on the supposed exclusive interests of the proletariat has no reasonable prospect. Any real threat of an armed uprising will only strengthen the reactionaries, who are not less intelligent than the Communist leaders, understand just as well how to reach and influence our people, and have more ample means for organization. If our working classes find it difficult to learn what their true interests are and do not know how to control their representatives in the government and in the trade unions, there is little prospect that they will be able to control things better during a rebellion or during the ensuing dictatorship.

If the history of the past is any guide at all, it indicates that real improvements in the future will come like the improvements of the past—namely, through co-operation among different groups, each of which is wise enough to see the necessity of compromising with those with whom we have to live together and whom we cannot or do not wish to exterminate.

I know that this notion of compromise or of taking counsel as the least wasteful way of adjusting differences is regarded as hopelessly antiquated and bourgeois, but I do not believe that the ideas of so-called Utopian socialists have really been refuted by those who arrogate the epithet "scientific" to themselves. The Communists seem to me to be much more Utopian and quite unscientific in their claims that the working class alone can by its own efforts completely transform our social order.

I do not have very high expectations from the efforts of sentimental benevolence. Yet I cannot help noticing that the leaders of the Communists and of other revolutionary labor movements—Engels, Marx, Lassalle, Luxemburg, Liebknecht, Lenin, and Trotsky—have not been drawn to it by economic solidarity. They were not workingmen nor even all of workingmen's families. They were driven to their role by human sympathy. Sympathy with the sufferings of our fellow men is a human motive that cannot be read out of history. It has exerted tremendous social pressure. Without it you cannot explain the course of nineteenth-century factory legislation, the freeing of serfs and slaves, or the elimination of the grosser forms of human exploitation. Though some who regard themselves as followers of Karl Marx are constantly denouncing reformers who believe in piecemeal improvement and hope rather that things will get worse so as to drive people into a revolution, Marx himself did not always take that view. Very wisely he attached great importance to English factory legislation which restricted the number of hours per working day, for he realized that every little bit that strengthens the workers strengthens their resistance to exploitation. Those who are most oppressed and depressed, the inhabitants of the slums, do not revolt—they have not energy enough to think of it. When, therefore, Mr. Strachey and others criticize the socialists for not bringing about the millennium when they get into power, I am not at all impressed. I do not believe that the socialists or the Labor Party in England have been free from shameful error. But neither have the Communists, nor any other human group, been free from it. Trite though it sounds, it is nevertheless true that no human arrangement can bring about perfection on earth. And while the illusion of omniscience may offer great consolation, it brings endless inhumanity when it leads us to shut the gates of mercy. Real as are our human conflicts, our fundamental identity of interest in the face of hostile nature seems to me worthy of more serious attention than the Communists have been willing to accord it.

If liberalism were dead, I should still maintain that it deserved to live, that it had not been condemned in the court of human reason, but lynched outside of it by the passionate and uncompromisingly ruthless war spirit, common to Communists and Fascists. But I do not believe that liberalism is dead, even though it is under eclipse. There still seems to me enough reason left to which to appeal against reckless fanaticism.

It is pure fanaticism to belittle the gains that have come to mankind from the spirit of free inquiry, free discussion, and accommodation. No human individual or group of individuals can claim omniscience. Hence society can only suffer serious loss when one group suppresses the opinions and criticisms of all others. In purely abstract questions compromise may often be a sign of confusion. One cannot really believe inconsistent principles at the same time. But in the absence of perfect or even adequate knowledge in regard to human affairs and their future, we must adopt an experimental attitude and treat principles not as eternal dogmas, but as hypotheses, to be tried to the extent that they indicate the general direction of solution to specific issues. But as the scientist must be ever ready to modify his own hypothesis or to recognize wherein a contrary hypothesis has merits or deserves preference, so in practical affairs we must be prepared to learn from those who differ with us, and to recognize that however contradictory diverse views may appear in discourse they may not be so in their practical applications.

Thus, the principles of Communism and individualism may be held like theologic dogmas, eternally true and on no occasion ever to be contaminated one by the other. But in fact, when Communists get into power they do not differ so much from others. No one ever wished to make everything communal property. Nor does anyone in his senses believe that any individual will ever with impunity be permitted to use his "property" in an antisocial way when the rest of the community is aroused thereby. In actual life, the question how far Communism shall be pushed depends more upon specific analyses of actual situations—that is, upon factual knowledge. There can be no doubt that individualism à la Herbert Hoover has led millions to destruction. Nevertheless, we must not forget that a Communist regime will, after all, be run by individuals who will exercise a tremendous amount of power, no less than do our captains of industry or finance today. There is no real advantage in assuming that under Communism the laboring classes will be omniscient. We know perfectly well how labor leaders like John Lewis keep their power by bureaucratic rather than democratic methods. May it not be that the Stalins also keep their power by bureaucratic rather than democratic methods?

Indeed the ruthless suppression of dissent within the Communist Party in Russia and the systematic glorification of the national heroes and military objectives of Czarist days suggest that the Bolshevik Revolution was not so complete a break with the Russian past as most of its friends and enemies assumed in earlier days. In any event we have witnessed in the history of the Communist movement since 1917 a dramatic demonstration of the way in which the glorification of power—first as a means of destroying a ruling class, then as a means of defending a beleaguered state from surrounding enemies, and finally as a means of extending Communism to neighboring lands—comes imperceptibly to displace the ends or objectives which once formed the core of Communist thought. Thus, one by one, the worst features of capitalist society and imperialism, against which Communism cut its eye teeth in protest—extreme inequality in wages, speed-up of workers, secret diplomacy, and armed intervention as a technique of international intercourse—have been taken over by the Soviet Union, with only a set of thin verbal distinctions to distinguish the "good" techniques of Communism from the corresponding "bad" techniques used by capitalism. As is always the case, the glorification of power dulls the sense of righteousness to which any movement for bettering the basic conditions of human living must appeal.

The Communist criticism of liberalism seems to me altogether baseless and worthless. One would suppose from it that liberalism is a peculiar excrescence of capitalism. This is, however, not true. The essence of liberalism—freedom of thought and inquiry, freedom of discussion and criticism—is not the invention of the capitalist system. It is rather the mother of Greek and modern science, without which our present industrial order and the labor movement would be impossible. The plea that the denial of freedom is a temporary necessity is advanced by all militarists. It ignores the fact that, when suppression becomes a habit, it is not readily abandoned. Thus, when the Christian Church after its alliance with the Roman Empire began the policy of "compelling them to enter," it kept up the habit of intolerant persecution for many centuries. Those who believe that many of the finer fruits of civilization were thereby choked should be careful about strengthening the forces of intolerance.

When the Communists tell me that I must choose between their dictatorship and Fascism, I feel that I am offered the choice between being shot and being hanged. It would be suicide for liberal civilization to accept this as exhausting the field of human possibility. I prefer to hope that the present wave of irrationalism and of fanatical intolerance will recede and that the great human energy which manifests itself in free thought will not perish. Often before, it has emerged after being swamped by passionate superstitions. There is no reason to feel that it may not do so again.

Topic 6

CHALLENGE OF THE SOVIET SYSTEM

On the Soviet Constitution

Joseph Stalin *

The complete victory of the socialist system in all spheres of the national economy is now a fact. This means that exploitation of man by man is abolished—liquidated—while the socialist ownership of the implements and means of production is established as the unshakable basis of our Soviet society.

As a result of all these changes in the national economy of the U.S.S.R., we have now a new socialist economy, knowing neither crises nor unemployment, neither poverty nor ruin, and giving to the citizen every possibility to live prosperous and cultured lives.

Such, in the main, are the changes which took place in our economy during the period from 1924 to 1936. Corresponding to these changes in the sphere of the economy of the U.S.S.R., the class structure of our society has also changed. As is known, the landlord class had already been liquidated as a result of the victorious conclusion of the Civil War.

As for the other exploiting classes, they share the fate of the landlord class. The capitalist class has ceased to exist in the sphere of industry. The kulak class has ceased to exist in the sphere of agriculture. The merchants and speculators have ceased to exist in the sphere of distribution. In this way, all exploiting classes are proved to have been liquidated. . . .

How are these changes in the life of the U.S.S.R. reflected in the draft

* General Secretary of the Communist Party of the Soviet Union and Chairman of the Council of Ministers, U.S.S.R. Author of *Foundations of Leninism, Problems of Leninism* and numerous articles on Communism. The selection is from the report of Joseph Stalin to the Special Eighth All-Union Congress of Soviets, delivered November 25, 1936.

of the new Constitution? In other words, what are the main specific features of the draft Constitution submitted for consideration at the present congress? . . .

Our Soviet society succeeded in achieving socialism, in the main, and has created a socialist order, *i.e.*, has achieved what is otherwise called among Marxists the first or lower phase of communism, that is, socialism.

It is known that the fundamental principle of this phase of communism is the formula: "From each according to his abilities; to each according to his deeds." . . . But Soviet society has not yet succeeded in bringing about the highest phase of communism where the ruling principle will be the formula: "From each according to his abilities; to each according to his needs," although it sets itself the aim of achieving the materialization of this higher phase, full communism, in the future.

Unlike the bourgeois constitutions, the draft of the new Constitution of the U.S.S.R. proceeds from the fact that antagonistic classes no longer exist in our society, that our society consists of two friendly classes: the workers and peasants, that precisely these toiling classes are in power, that the state guidance of society (dictatorship) belongs to the working class as the advanced class of society, that the Constitution is needed to consolidate the social order desired by and of advantage to the toilers. . . .

The draft of the new Constitution of the U.S.S.R. is . . . profoundly international. It proceeds from the premise that all nations and races have equal rights. It proceeds from the premise that color or language differences, differences in cultural level or the level of state development as well as any other difference among nations and races, cannot serve as grounds for justifying national inequality of rights.

It proceeds from the premise that all nations and races irrespective of their past or present position, irrespective of their strength or weakness, must enjoy equal rights in all spheres, economic, social, state and the cultural life of society. Such is a feature of the draft of the new Constitution. [Another] specific feature of the draft of the new Constitution is its consistent and fully sustained democracy. For it all citizens are equal in their rights. Neither property status nor national origin, nor sex, nor official standing, but only the personal capabilities and personal labor of every citizen determine his position in society.

A specific feature of the draft of the new Constitution is that it does not limit itself to recording formal rights of citizens, but transfers the center of gravity to questions of the guarantee of these rights, to the question of the means of exercising them.

It does not merely proclaim the equality of the rights of citizens but ensures them by legislative enactment of the fact of liquidation of the regime of exploitation, by the fact of liberation of citizens from any exploitation.

It not only proclaims the right to work, but ensures it by legislative enactment of the fact of non-existence of crises in Soviet society, and the fact of abolition of unemployment. It not merely proclaims democratic liberties but guarantees them in legislative enactments by providing definite material facilities.

It is clear, therefore, that the democracy of the new Constitution is not the "usual" and "generally recognized" democracy in general, but socialist democracy. . . .

BOURGEOIS CRITICS OF THE CONSTITUTION

A few words about bourgeois criticism of the draft Constitution. . . . Whereas [one] group charges that the draft Constitution renounced the dictatorship of the working class, [another] group, on the contrary, charges that the draft makes no change in the existing position of the U.S.S.R.; that it leaves the dictatorship of the working class intact, does not provide for freedom of political parties, and preserves the present leading position of the Communist Party of the U.S.S.R. And, at the same time, this group of critics believes that the absence of freedom for parties in the U.S.S.R. is an indication of the violation of the fundamental principles of democracy.

I must admit the draft of the new Constitution really does leave in force the regime of the dictatorship of the working class, and also leaves unchanged the present leading position of the Communist Party of the U.S.S.R.

If our venerable critics regard this as a shortcoming of the draft Constitution, this can only be regretted. We Bolsheviks, however, consider this as a merit of the draft Constitution. As for freedom for various political parties, we here adhere to somewhat different views.

The party is part of the class, its vanguard section. Several parties and consequently freedom of parties can only exist in a society where antagonistic classes exist whose interests are hostile and irreconcilable, where there are capitalists and workers, landlords and peasants, kulaks and poor peasants.

But in the U.S.S.R. there are no longer such classes as capitalists, landlords, kulaks, etc. In the U.S.S.R. there are only two classes, workers and peasants, whose interests not only are not antagonistic but, on the contrary, amicable. Consequently there are no grounds for the existence of several parties, and therefore for the existence of freedom of such parties in the U.S.S.R. There are grounds for only one party, the Communist Party, in the U.S.S.R. Only one party can exist, the Communist Party, which boldly defends the interests of the workers and peasants to the very end. And there can hardly be any doubt about the fact that it defends the interests of these classes.

They talk about democracy. But what is democracy? Democracy in capitalist countries where there are antagonistic classes is in the last analysis the democracy for the strong, democracy for the propertied minority. Democracy in the U.S.S.R., on the contrary, is democracy for all. But from this it follows that the principles of democracy are violated not by the draft of the new Constitution of the U.S.S.R. but by the bourgeois constitutions.

That is why I think that the Constitution of the U.S.S.R. is the only thoroughly democratic constitution in the world.

Achievements of the Soviet System

Frederick L. Schuman *

The whole structure and spirit of the Soviet State were imposed upon its rulers, as the price of survival, by the armed struggle which its foes commenced against it. In the absence of attack from without, supported by counter-revolution from within, the Marxist gospel, superimposed by its Russian apostles on the wreckage of the Muscovite autocracy, might have found concrete expression in any one of a number of possible shapes so long as State power could be said to rest on the Soviets and could be somehow described as a dictatorship of the proletariat and poorest peasants, dedicated to socialism. It did, in fact, assume at the outset a political form having little in common with its ultimate configuration. In the sequel the Soviet State would doubtless have become something wholly different from what it actually became, both in its program at home and its policies abroad, had it not been made the target of those resolved upon its destruction. . . .

The war of the revolution against intervention and counter-revolution converted a quasi-coalition regime into a one-party despotism. It transformed cooperation and compromise into force and terrorism. It changed tolerance into intolerance, democracy into dictatorship, socialist gradualism into "war communism." It produced the first of the "totalitarian" States of the 20th Century, whose unique devices of persecution, persuasion and perquisites were later copied, for wholly different purposes, by the demagogue-despots of Fascism. These devices are everywhere abhorred by democrats. They constitute the chief counts in the indictment of Soviet "totalitarianism" by the democracies. What is commonly forgotten in the West is that Soviet "totalitarianism" was not inevitable nor necessarily implicit in the Bolshevism of 1917–18 but was forced upon it, with death as the alternative, by the decisions of Russian democrats and of the Western Democracies. . . .

An ancient aphorism holds that "war is the father of all things." The war of the Russian Revolution begot many of the enduring features of the young Soviet State. . . . The foundation posts of the Soviet Constitu-

* Professor of Political Science at Williams College. Author of *International Politics —An Introduction to the Western State System, The Nazi Dictatorship, Europe on the Eve,* and other books and articles. The selection is from Frederick L. Schuman, *Soviet Politics at Home and Abroad* (New York, Alfred A. Knopf, Inc., 1946), *passim.* By permission of the author and publisher.

tion, of the one-party totalitarian State, of the Comintern, of the Red Army, the political police and the higher propaganda, of economic planning in socialized industry, of rural collectivization and "class war in the villages" were all forged in the flames of war which swirled around Red Muscovy in the ghastly and heroic years of civil strife and foreign intervention. . . .

Viewed in the long perspective of man's devices for the management of men, the cause of liberty has sometimes been served by dictatorship—but only when dictators resist the temptation to become despots and unselfishly serve democratic purposes in times of trouble or of dynamic new departures in social engineering. . . .

The decisive internal factor which has promoted the perpetuation of the dictatorship has been the resolve of the Soviet elite to remake man and society in a new image in order that a new freedom might ultimately be attained. The reforging of the land and people, in the heat of fierce propaganda and under the hammer of ruthless compulsion, has been shown by events to have been a necessity for national survival. It has been no less necessary as a means of liquidating evil legacies of ignorance, prejudice and technical backwardness. . . .

Soviet experience, and indeed much experience elsewhere, particularly in war-time, suggests that in the current stage of interpersonal relations and the industrial arts, some equivalent of "dictatorship" is indispensable for the effective performance of those functions of centralized planning and distribution without which there can be no total utilization of land, labor and capital for community purposes. The abrupt transplantation into Soviet society of the premises and practices of Western parliamentary democracy (assuming that such a cultural miracle were conceivable) would almost inevitably generate political groups or factions representing the differing demands and expectations of collective farmers, urban workers, and Soviet technocrats and managers. . . .

In the present phase of Soviet economy, it may be doubted whether such decisions could be made and executed wisely or well in a bourgeois-democratic context of competing politicians, parties, factions, lobbies, pressure groups, and rival propagandists appealing against one another for public favor. That these devices are satisfactory in the Western democracies or even conducive to the commonweal under current conditions is questioned by many reflective observers who are free of all taint of Marxism. Such procedures would be wholly unworkable in the USSR. The Party has the function of reflecting in its own composition and activity the various interests and expectations which must be reconciled, and translating the resulting consensus into programs for action which, once adopted, are for the most part beyond the possibility of further challenge or discussion. "Dictatorship" in Soviet society is not a means (save in isolated instances, flowing from abuses of power) whereby a privileged and parasitic oligarchy exploits the community to its own advantage. Neither is it a formula for "tyranny," nor an institutionalization of the corruption which often goes with absolute power. It is rather the means of integrating elite and mass, preserving the true faith, promoting high morale and group purpose, maintaining discipline and *élan,* and evolving and administering the broad All-Union directives for serving the general welfare and the common defense. Soviet planning involves cooperation and collaboration by millions at all levels and stages of the process. But the necessary continuity, crusading fervor, and coordination from a common center are supplied, and at present can only be supplied, by maintaining the Party's monopoly of legality and leadership. . . .

The industrialization of a great community is by itself obviously not unique. It has been experienced by England, Germany and the United States and may in days to come be experienced by China and India. What is unique in the USSR is that a single decade saw developments which required half a century or more elsewhere. Industrialization was achieved, moreover, without private capital, without foreign investments (save in the form of engineering skills and technical advice), without private profit as a spur to individual initiative, without private ownership of any of the means of production, and with no unearned increment or private fortunes accruing to entrepreneurs or lucky investors. Resources were developed, labor was recruited, trained and allocated, capital was saved and invested not through the price mechanism of a competitive market but through a consciously devised and deliberately executed national economic plan, drawn up by quinquennia, by years, and by quarters for every segment of the economy, for every region, city, town and village, for every factory, farm, mine and mill, for every store, bank and school, and even for every hospital, theater and sports club. Politburo, Sovnarkom and Gosplan supplied direction and coordination to the effort. But almost all Soviet citizens participated in planning, contributed to fulfillment in proportion to their abilities, and shared in the results in accordance with their contribution. Nothing remotely comparable to this endeavor had ever been before attempted. Most outside observers were therefore certain that the effort would fail. Long after it was launched, many were equally certain that it had failed or was failing. But in all that was decisive for the future, Party and people carried through their self-imposed tasks to success. . . .

Between the poverty-stricken year of 1924, when Lenin died, and the relatively abundant year of 1940, the cultivated area of the USSR expanded by 74%; grain crops increased 11%; coal production was multiplied by 10; steel output by 18; engineering and metal industries by 150; total national income by 10; industrial output by 24; annual capital investment (*c.* 40 billion rubles in 1940) by 57. . . . Factory and office workers grew from 7,300,000 to 30,800,000, and school and college students from 7,900,000 to 36,600,000. Between 1913 (roughly comparable in most fields of production to the levels of 1927) and 1940, oil production increased from 9 to 35 million tons; coal from 29 to 164; pig-iron from 4 to 15; steel from 4 to 18; machine tools from 1,000 to 48,000 units, tractors from 0 to over 500,000; harvester combines from 0 to 153,500; electrical power output from 2 billion kilowatt hours to 50 billion; and value of industrial output from 11 billion rubles to more than 100 billions by 1938. If the estimated volume of total industrial production in 1913 be taken as 100, the corresponding indices for 1938 are 93.2 for France; 113.3 for England; 120 for the United States; 131.6 for Germany and 908.8 for the Soviet Union. . . .

These and a thousand other transformations, viewed in terms of personal living, meant for scores of millions hope, heroism, opportunity, the realization of the promise of 1917, the collective inspiration of dynamic purposes shared in cooperative endeavor, and the triumph of new techniques of planning and management in guiding all to a more meaningful and abundant life than any of them had known before. They also meant bureaucracy, red-tape and costly fumblings; overcrowding, wretched housing and meager food and clothing for the sake of heavy industry; and incredible quantum of backbreaking labor and heartbreaking tragedy; and appalling sacrifices, ruthless cruelty toward laggards, and the relentless driving of the entire population to the edge of physical and nervous exhaustion. In the perspective of recent years the question of whether the results were worth the price has found its answer in events. The ultimate alternatives were victory or death. The road to victory was watered with sweat, tears and blood long before the Nazi invaders burst into the Soviet land. . . .

Living standards, measured in consumers' goods and housing, although not in social services and educational opportunities, declined during the first Plan. The result was a ceaseless migration of workers from district to district in search of more favorable conditions, with a labor turnover of amazing proportions. Under the second Plan, 1933–38, life became easier, if not less hectic, and the labor supply became more stable. . . .

The passion for unity finds renewed expression in the legislative procedure of all Soviets. All votes are unanimous. Deputies make, and listen to, speeches and reports on many controversial issues. But no question is brought to a vote unless unanimity is assured. This practice leads many Western observers to conclude anew that the deputies are merely puppets whose every motion is a result of strings pulled behind the scenes by Party bosses. Closer observation would suggest that in Soviet legislatures, as in elections, means other than yes-and-no votes are employed to reconcile divergencies and arrive at an effective consensus. In the USSR the law-making process, like the electoral process, is not a method of making decisions on national policy as it is in the West. But neither is it a simple business of "rubber-stamping" decisions made elsewhere. It is rather to be thought of as one of the important means whereby the Party leaders maintain close contact with the non-Party masses and adjust the line to popular complaints, aspirations and demands within limits determined by the leaders' judgment of what is possible and what is necessary. . . .

What may justly be said is that the dictatorship of the Party, operating through pseudo-democratic structures and procedures, has thus far been a necessity for the building of socialism, the defense of the State, and the salvation and victory of the Soviet peoples in a hostile and formidably menacing world. Survival is the first law of life, in politics as elsewhere. Had the USSR been a political democracy of the Western type during the past 20 years, had its people been permitted to choose what was soft, easy and pleasant rather than what was hard, painful and necessary, the Soviet Union would not exist today. Its destroyers would also, in all likelihood, have destroyed the independence of Britain and the freedom of America as well, for the military collapse of Russia would have rendered the victors invulnerable and invincible. Dictatorship has been the price of survival for the USSR and for the United Nations. Herein lies its justification—save in the eyes of those who are concerned only with the propriety of means and never with the primacy of ends, or with the eternal verities to the exclusion of the tough tasks of the day, or with the virtues of national suicide under unrestricted freedom as against the vices of national survival by way of coercion.

Despite the lamentations or sadistic rejoicings of irreconcilable haters and embittered ex-lovers, there are no solid reasons for assuming that the dictatorial means thus far used have forever destroyed the possibility of attaining democratic ends in the USSR. The Marxist dream stems from democratic values. Its Soviet apostles have returned to them in form. They will yet return to them in substance if the non-Soviet world will permit them to. The Soviet citizenry has meanwhile found in its own system the elements of creative discipline and unity necessary for collective survival and for all the hopes of the future.

"Real liberty," declared Stalin to Roy Howard in 1936, "can be had only where exploitation is destroyed, where there is no oppression of one people by another, where there is no unemployment and pauperism, where a person does not shiver in fear of losing tomorrow his job, home, bread. Only in such a society is it possible to have real, and not paper, liberty, personal and otherwise." . . .

Freedom from unemployment, exploitation and overwork, and from neglect and penury in sickness, disability and old age, are among the major objectives of the Soviet State. These social rights (cf. §§118–120) represent the great gains of the Revolution and are among the best protected of all rights of the Soviet citizen. Within the inevitable limits of ideological conformity, and of available facilities amid the growing pains of rapid industrialization, all have a right to work, to payment proportionate to contribution, to leisure and vacations with full pay, to insurance against illness and old age and to free medical and dental service at all times. The nationwide system of socialized medicine is one of the brightest stars in the Soviet crown. Its progress is indicated by comparative figures for 1913, 1928 and 1941: physicians, 19,785, 63,162 and 130,348—almost half of them women; urban and rural medical centers, 5,597, 13,204 and 26,973; sanatoria and health resorts, 2,000, 36,100 and 132,000; maternity hospitals, 6,824, 27,338 and 141,873; and hospital beds, 142,310, 217,744 and 661,431—as compared with 1,324,381 in the United States. Soviet citizens as yet are less well protected against the hazards of disease, accident and senescence than members of the upper and middle income groups in the West. But they may fairly be said to be far better protected than scores of millions of the underprivileged in the Atlantic communities.

Freedom from ignorance through free public education for all (§121) has ever been a central purpose of the Soviet regime. The liquidation of illiteracy, along with the abolition of racial and national discrimination, must be regarded by all just observers, without respect to their views of property and profits, as a gigantic contribution of the USSR to the emancipation of man. Russian elementary and secondary schools in 1914–15 numbered 105,524 with 7,896,249 pupils. In the USSR of 1930–31 there were 152,813 schools with 17,614,537 pupils; and in 1938–39, 171,579 with 31,517,375 pupils. . . . A decree of October 2, 1940, introduced small tuition fees in upper secondary schools and universities, with a system of scholarships for talented but indigent pupils and a program of free vocational training for the rest.

These departures from the principles of free and "progressive" education have been widely interpreted abroad as evidence of "reaction" and of the restoration of "class privileges" in the USSR. They are more simply and accurately explained in terms of the desire of the Party leadership to foster a larger measure of individual and family responsibility for education; to raise standards of higher education to the level of those best fitted for intellectual work; and, in the light of the appalling human losses of war, to interest Soviet womanhood in home-making and child-rearing as well as in careers in the trades and professions. All three objectives appear to be well on their way toward realization. . . .

Freedom from lawlessness and from arbitrary acts of officialdom are as much the goals of jurisprudence in the USSR as they are in the Western democracies. But in the Soviet Union the commands of the State are fully equated with the welfare of society. Law is envisaged not as a set of norms anterior and superior to government, but as a tool of politics and a weapon of class rule—pending the complete attainment of the "classless society" and the "withering away of the State." Wrote Marx: "Personal freedom is possible only in the collectivity." This principle, coupled with fear of foreign aggression, has meant that in Soviet law public order invariably takes precedence over private liberty. . . . At all points the protection of the State against treason and crime is deemed more important than the protection of the individual against abuse of authority.

Yet the widespread impression in the United States that Soviet citizens "have no rights" and that Soviet officials are vested with arbitrary power, unrestrained by law, is contrary to fact. . . . In considering the work of these various bodies in the light of the Russian past and the contemporary exigencies of revolution, reconstruction, socialization and war, it would be manifestly absurd for foreign observers to expect as high standards of legal logic, procedural safeguards and abstract justice as are to be found in the English-speaking lands with their relative freedom from invasion or internal strife and their centuries-old tradition of "a government of laws and not of men." Even more absurd are the efforts of many to deny the achievements of Soviet law and justice and to depict all Soviet jurisprudence as a farce, played by terrorists at the expense of a population of slaves.

These efforts in recent years have reached a *reductio ad absurdum* in connection with Soviet penal colonies. Soviet treatment of criminals has always displayed a combination of the most severe measures of punishment for political offenders with the most enlightened practices of psychiatric and occupational rehabilitation for non-political culprits. Since 1929 extensive use has been made of Correctional Labor Camps, whose inmates have engaged in road construction, canal-building, and other public works, often under highly adverse conditions of climate, housing, nutrition, and sanitation. Many such convicts have received amnesties, prizes, and honors for work well done. For reasons which seem to them sufficient, the Soviet authorities have not seen fit to publish statistics regarding these penal institutions. In so vast a land no private observer, inside or outside of such camps, can possibly estimate the total number of inmates. If arrests for crimes of violence and theft were to number 2,000,000 annually in the USSR, with prisoners serving long-term sentences totalling 200,000, the result would be proportionate to the situation in the United States. There may well be a comparable number of political prisoners in penal camps. All such estimates, however, are guesswork. Official Soviet secrecy has combined with ignorance and malice abroad to encourage anti-Soviet journalists to engage in a truly amazing competition in this field. . . .

Thus Koestler on a single page . . . "reveals" that 15,000,000 people turned up "missing" in the Soviet census of 1937 and says seven lines later that "eye-witnesses put the mortality among prisoners at 30% per annum." The "guesswork" here is particularly interesting, since such a mortality among the 20,000,000 or more persons continuously domiciled (by Koestler, et al.) in labor camps during the past decade would mean that at least 6,000,000 died annually, with total deaths of 60,000,000. . . . More clever calculators, however, have been skeptical of the possibility of persuading even the most credulous that more than a third of the Soviet population has died in imprisonment, with a tenth of the survivors still in confinement.

Confusion can be reduced at the outset by recognizing that the Soviet disciples of the true faith according to Marx, Engels, and Lenin have not achieved, and have never hoped or intended to achieve during the present historical epoch, a society in which all wealth would be shared equally or pecuniary incentives would be abolished, or all incomes would be identical. The principle of "socialism" has ever been: "From each according to his ability, to each according to his work." . . . Lenin . . . toyed for a time, to be sure, with the notion of a moderate levelling of incomes. Under "War Communism," and to a lesser extent under the NEP, wage and salary scales were influenced by this idea. Once the building of socialism was embarked upon in earnest, however, the gap between the best paid and the worst paid grew ever greater. . . .

And thus Stalin . . . [said]

> The consequence of wage equalization is that the unskilled worker lacks the incentive to become a skilled worker and is thus deprived of the prospect of advancement; as a result he feels himself a "sojourner" in the factory, working only temporarily so as to earn a little and then go off to "seek his fortune" elsewhere. . . . Hence the heavy turnover of labor power. In order to put an end to this evil we must abolish wage equalization. . . . We cannot tolerate a situation where a rolling-mill hand in a steel mill earns no more than a sweeper. . . .

Yet the oft-repeated statements in the Western press (sometimes intended as an indictment, and sometimes as a eulogy) that the gap between the best-paid and the worst-paid is greater under socialism than capitalism admits of no verification and would almost certainly prove to be untrue if the necessary data were available for a fair comparison.[1] Satisfactory statistics on the distribution of incomes are difficult to come by. In normal years in the United States, corporation salaries of over a quarter of a million dollars go to a few dozen movies stars, cinema magnates, and executives in the fields of luxury goods having a mass distribution. Recipients of incomes of a million dollars and more (from all sources) have ranged in number from 513 in 1929 to 20 in 1932, with much larger figures probable for the recent years of war prosperity. In 1929 the 36,000 wealthiest American families received as much of the national income as the 11,000,000 poorest families, of whom over half (21% of all families) had incomes of less than $1,000 a year. . . .

[1] (Author's footnote.) Thus Manya Gordon in *Workers Before and After Lenin* (New York, E. P. Dutton & Company, 1941) seeks to show, by omitting or minimizing the imponderables and completely ignoring the danger of the war which came to Russia four months after her book appeared, that Russian workers enjoyed a better living standard under the Tsars than under the Soviets. Hubbard (p. 164 of *Soviet Labor and Industry*) devises an index of "real wages" according to which the figure of average real wages in 1929 was 154 (with 1913 as 100) and only 68 in 1937. F. Forest in *The New International* (Jan.–Feb., 1943), quoted by Koestler in *The Yogi and the Commissar* (p. 158), arrived at "real wage" indices of 100 for 1913, 125 for 1928 and 62 for 1940. All such attempts, even when honestly intentioned, are all but meaningless since the various components of living standards, apart from money wages and commodity price levels, are not adequately weighted and render incomparable the situations sought to be compared.

These patterns have no counterpart in the USSR. The Soviet fiscal system, to be sure, does not embrace the current Anglo-American practice of penalizing high incomes through virtually confiscatory taxes. Well-paid executives, moreover, are furnished with comfortable homes, cars and sometimes even yachts at no cost to themselves. In the Soviet wage structure the disparity of compensation between skilled and unskilled, and between efficient and inefficient, is far greater than in Britain or the United States. But there is no group of well-to-do employers, owners, investors and speculators who regularly receive 1,000 times the money income of the poorest paid worker.

This fact, however, is neither praiseworthy nor blameworthy, save in the eyes of the naive who regard private wealth as an end in itself or as an evil *per se*. Nor does it disclose the significant differences between the two systems. Comparisons of money wages are misleading because the mass of Soviet workers receive a variety of social services and special benefits (including free medical and dental care, comprehensive insurance, vacations with pay, low rentals, low-price factory restaurants, etc.) which are still in process of inauguration in the Atlantic democracies. At the same time Soviet producers in the mass are much poorer than Western workers, since their productivity is still inferior. . . .

Who rules with the old rulers gone? The best answer is not "The Proletariat," or "Workers and Peasants," or even "The Communist Party," but "The Soviet Intelligentsia." In Stalin's formulation: "No ruling class has managed without its own intelligentsia. There are no grounds for believing that the working class of the USSR can manage without its own industrial and technical intelligentsia." . . .

But what is impossible for the Soviet Intelligentsia is to become a propertied class or a leisured class living on unearned income. These are the earmarks of every landed aristocracy. To live without labor is the dream of every Western businessman, and indeed the secret hope of almost all men and women everywhere, since the species is allergic to work, craves luxuries, preferably on a silver platter, and prefers a horizontal to a vertical position whenever possible. The pecuniary elites of the West consist in part of hard-working and hard-driving executives and managers, and in part of idle rich. The latter indulge in conspicuous consumption and live without work by virtue of astute selection of ancestors, schools, colleges, fraternity brothers, wives and/or business associates, affording access to (or skill in acquiring) adequate quantities of unearned increments. . . .

Not only is the Soviet Intelligentsia a functional elite of diligent and desperately busy experts, but it is lacking in both the virtues and the vices inculcated by an acquisitive culture which places premiums on private possessions and pride of ancestry. Its privileges are strictly contingent upon performance. Advancement is extraordinarily rapid and rewarding for the capable. Demotion is equally speedy for the failures. Circulation up and down the social scale is swift and easy. Most intellectuals are children of peasants and workers. If more in the future are children of intellectuals, a tendency already manifesting itself, this will be less a result of any self-perpetuation of a new caste than of the circumstance that manual laborers and farmers constitute a diminishing proportion of the total population with further advances of technology and productivity. "Striking it rich" is impossible. . . .

"Dictatorship" in Soviet society is not a means (save in isolated instances, flowing from abuses of power) whereby a privileged and parasitic oligarchy exploits the community to its own advantage. Neither is it a formula for "tyranny," nor an institutionalization of the corruption which often goes with absolute power. It is rather the means of integrating elite and mass, preserving the true faith, promoting high morale and group purpose, maintaining discipline and *élan,* and evolving and administering the broad All-Union directives for serving the general welfare and the common defense. Soviet planning involves cooperation and collaboration by millions at all levels and stages of the process. But the necessary continuity, crusading fervor, and coordination from a common center are supplied, and at present can only be supplied, by maintaining the Party's monopoly of legality and leadership.

Only those observers who are invincibly ignorant, or blinded by irrational fear and hatred, will deny that the Soviet system of business and power has, for all its abuses and crudities, promoted the liberation of men from impoverishment, exploitation, illiteracy, and prejudice and served the cause of human dignity and self-respect on an immense scale. These purposes are of the essence of the democratic dream. In this sense the USSR is a democratic polity—in its ends and in its achievements, if not always in its means.

Topic 7

REPLY TO THE SOVIET CHALLENGE

Soviet Myth and Reality

Arthur Koestler *

Denial of facts about Soviet reality may be conscious or unconscious. If it is conscious, it falls under the next heading. But mostly it is unconscious, based on ignorance.

Ignorance of Soviet reality among the addicts of the Soviet myth is

* Foreign correspondent in the Middle East, 1926–1931. Traveled in Russia, 1932–1933. Covered the Spanish Civil War for the London *News Chronicle* and was im-

stupendous. Nine out of ten are shocked and incredulous when told, for instance, that the workers' right to strike is abolished in Russia, and that striking, or the incitement to it, is punishable by capital punishment; or that the Soviet electorate's only function is to vote "yes" or "no" to a single list of officially appointed candidates. This ignorance is partly due to the difficulty of obtaining factual information, partly to an unconscious fear of disappointment. One could almost say that the more importance people attach to Russia the more reluctant they seem to find out the facts. . . .

SUPPRESSION OF FACTS

Foreign newspapers were and are forbidden in Russia. The Soviet press is controlled to a degree which Nazism could never achieve. Each town in the Union, Moscow included, has two morning papers: a government organ and a party organ. All government papers throughout the country appear every morning with one uniform leader, distributed by radio and telegraph: the leader of the Moscow *Izvestia*. Party papers all over the country appear with the leader from the Moscow *Pravda*. Both foreign and home news are similarly distributed by the official TASS agency. Local news consists of official hand-outs.

The effect of this total centralisation of news in a country with vast distances is that the great mass of people are kept in ignorance not only of events abroad, but also of events outside their immediate neighborhood. Here is one example of how the system works:

I spent the winter of 1932–33 mainly in Kharkov, then capital of Ukraine. It was the catastrophic winter after the first wave of collectivisation of the land; the peasants had killed their cattle, burned or hidden their crops and were dying of starvation and typhoid; the number of deaths in Ukraine alone is estimated at about two millions. Travelling through the countryside was like running the gantlet: the stations were lined with begging peasants with swollen hands and feet, the women holding up to the carriage windows horrible infants with enormous wobbling heads, sticklike limbs, swollen, pointed bellies. You could swap a loaf of bread for Ukrainian embroidered kerchiefs, national costumes and bedcovers; foreigners could sleep with practically any girl except party members for a pair of shoes or stockings. Under my hotel room window in Kharkov funeral processions marched past all day. The electricity supply in Kharkov had broken down; there was no light in the town, and the trams functioned only for an hour or so a day to take workers to the factories and back. There was also no fuel or petrol in the town and the winter was hard even for Ukraine, with

prisoned by General Franco, later by the Vichy French. Author of *The Gladiators, Darkness at Noon, Arrival and Departure, Thieves in the Night, The Age of Longing*. The selection is from Arthur Koestler, "Soviet Myth and Reality," *The Yogi and the Commissar and Other Essays* (New York, The Macmillan Co., 1946). By permission.

temperatures of 30 degrees below zero. Life seemed to have come to a standstill, the whole machinery on the verge of collapse. . . .

Today, the catastrophe of 1932–33 is more or less frankly admitted in Soviet circles; but at the time not the slightest allusion to real conditions was allowed to appear in the Soviet press, including the newspapers of Ukraine itself. Each morning when I read the Kharkov *Kommunist* I learned about plan-figures reached and over-reached, about competitions between factory shock brigades, awards of the Red Banner, new giant combines in the Urals, and so on; the photographs were either of young people, always laughing and always carrying a banner in their hands, or of some picturesque elder in Uzbekistan, always smiling and always learning the alphabet. Not one word about the local famine, epidemics, the dying out of whole villages; even the fact that there was no electricity in Kharkov was not once mentioned in the Kharkov newspaper. It gave one a feeling of dreamlike unreality; the paper seemed to talk about some quite different country which had no point of contact with the daily life we led; and the same applies to the radio.

The consequence of all this was that the vast majority of people in Moscow had no idea of what went on in Kharkov, and even less of what went on in Tashkent, or Archangel or Vladivostok. . . . The enormous land was covered by a blanket of silence and nobody outside the small circle of initiated could form a comprehensive picture of the situation.

A second belt of silence isolated the country from contacts with the outside world. . . . The cumulative effect of all this was a picture distorted by half-truths and systematic omissions. This was the foundation on which direct Soviet propaganda could build. . . .

THE INHERITANCE OF PRIVILEGE

One of the first tenets of socialism is that each child born into this world should have equal opportunities of education and career. Accordingly inheritance through relationship, last will, or life insurance was abolished shortly after the revolution. . . .

The new Constitution of 1936 re-established inequality from birth. Inheritance was made legal again and the right of unrestricted disposal of property by last will guaranteed to each individual citizen. Death insurance was also reinstated. . . . Not even the most purist critic could expect a sudden jump to total equalitarianism. But one was entitled to expect from a regime moving however slowly towards a socialist goal that it should make efforts to minimize the effects on the child of the unavoidable inequality among the parents, i.e., to prevent the emergence of privilege from the cradle. Soviet policy took exactly the opposite course. Inheritance was revived, death insurance encouraged; moreover, the children of prominent people are endowed with special money grants from the state upon their coming of age. . . .

Thus inequality is not restricted to grown-up wage-earners, but carried straight into the nursery by a deliberate policy of the regime. Children in Soviet Russia grow up rich and poor as in capitalist countries. The first bulwark against inherited privilege fell when the new Constitution sanctioned the inheritance of property; the second and more important bulwark fell when free education was abolished by the introduction of fees for higher education.

The decree of October 2, 1940, fixed the tuition fee for secondary schools (technical, normal, agricultural, medical, etc.) at 150 to 200 roubles per year, for universities at 300 to 500 roubles. The fees for the first term had to be paid within one month from the promulgation of the new law; 600,000 students of poor parents who couldn't pay the fee, had to leave school. Thus higher education (from the fifteenth year onward) became a privilege of the children of parents who could afford it; i.e., bureaucracy, technocracy and the new intelligentsia. . . .

The introduction of school fees in 1940 was the crowning piece of this development. But it did not halt there. Special schools reserved for the children of the bureaucracy, and cadet schools ("Suvorov Military Academies") with special entrance facilities for officers' sons (decree of August 23, 1943) followed. At the same time children whose parents cannot afford the fees for secondary education are conscripted on leaving school to four years' compulsory labour service. (Decree of October 2, 1940.) They are given "vocational training" lasting from six months to two years, and are obliged for a further four years to work wherever directed. The upshot of the whole development is that on the average the children of manual workers and peasants remain manual workers and peasants, whereas the children of the upper strata are automatically put on the road to jobs in the upper strata.

There are, of course, scholarships for the poor, but their conditions are harsher than in most capitalist countries: two-thirds "excellent" marks and the remainder "good" on the examination paper. The very fact that the child of poor parents has to show special gifts to be granted the benefits of education which the son of rich parents obtains as a matter of course indicates the presence of a class barrier, a filter through which only the exception can pass.

The whole development can be summarized in two stages. First, the population became stratified according to income-classes which was unavoidable; secondly, this economic division is transferred to the following generation from the cradle, by deliberate government policy. A hereditary bureaucracy, technocracy and military caste emerges in the framework of a new type of class-society, based no longer on the ownership of the means of production, but on control of the levers of the state, and following the same trend towards self-perpetuation which characterises all stable class rule in history.

It is hard to see how the series of decrees which conditioned this development could be explained as "temporary expedients" or "emergency measures." The restoration of inheritance is embodied in the Constitution which was certainly not meant as a temporary expedient. The abolition of the Workers' Nucleus policy in 1932 can hardly be explained as a gesture of appeasement towards Roosevelt or Churchill, nor could the introduction of school fees be expected to speed up the opening of the Second Front. . . .

PAUPERS AND PROLETARIAN MILLIONAIRES

I have emphasised that inequality in earnings is inevitable during a considerable transition period and as such cannot be the object of criticism of the present Soviet regime. But criticism becomes legitimate when we inquire into the degree of this inequality and into its tendency to increase or decrease.

The starting point of the whole development is Lenin's principle, laid down in *State and Revolution,* of the "Maximum Income"—viz., that no member of the State-Bureaucracy up to the President of the Republic should receive a higher salary than a qualified worker. It was one of the three fundamental principles to protect the dictatorship of the proletariat against bureaucratic degeneration (the other two being the unification of executive and legislative power, and the electorate's right to recall any state official at any time from his post). . . .

The maximum income (of about 400 roubles per month) remained in force for party members, and those who earned more—NEP men, Russian and foreign "non-party specialists" were regarded with contempt as a necessary evil. During the first five-year plan contrasts in earnings became more prominent, but the basic and radical change came with Stalin's famous six-point speech in June, 1931. It was a declaration of war against "Uravnilovka," or equality of pay.

Equalitarianism in wages was to cease once and for all, since it was "alien and detrimental to socialist production." Equalitarianism became a "petty bourgeois deviation," a crime against the State, a bogey word like "Counter-revolution" and "Trotskyism." Stalin's speech was followed by the usual nationwide propaganda campaign, a holy crusade against "Uravnilovka," with the effect that the majority among the people became honestly convinced that inequality of pay was a fundamental principle of socialism. . . .

A new incentive had to be found at all costs to increase production and the quality of output; it was found in the temporary expedient of differentiating salaries and wages to an extent which soon "reached and surpassed" the inequality of income under capitalism, as we shall presently see. It should be noted that the new policy was not presented as a transitory measure or necessary evil, but as a triumph of socialist ethics. . . . To take an example: according to the Moscow paper *Trud* (20/1/36) sixty employees of a Donetz mine earned monthly wages of 1,000–2,500 roubles per head;

seventy-five employees earned 800–1,000 roubles per head; four hundred earned 500–800 roubles per head and the remaining thousand *averaged* 125 roubles. The top wages in this average mine were about thirty times higher than the minimum wages. But the director of a mine of 1,500 employees belongs only to the medium stratum of the technocracy; the salaries of directors, chief engineers and administrators in the top stratum are up to 100 times higher than the average wage and up to 300 times higher than the minimum wage. In 1943 the appearance of the first "proletarian millionaires," enthusiastically welcomed by the Soviet press, completed the development.

The apologist may argue that, regrettably unequal as Soviet incomes may be, they still represent *salaries* and not *profits* as in capitalist countries. The theoretical implications of this argument form part of the doctrine of the "unshaken foundations" with which we shall deal later. But from a practical point of view it makes little difference whether Comrade Berdyebekov, the Director of a State Farm in Kazakstan who became the first officially proclaimed Soviet Millionaire, owns the farm or merely directs it. His powers over the employees under the present labour legislation are actually greater than the powers of ownership in capitalist countries; his children will be privileged by wealth, educational and social opportunities. Their income will be just as "unearned" as that of any capitalist millionaire's offspring. The only difference is that Berdyebekov cannot buy land or a factory of his own; but who wants to *buy* a factory if he can enjoy all the benefits of ownership without the financial risks?

The true significance of the proletarian millionaires can be appreciated only when set against the background of the living conditions of the proletarian paupers. The Soviet Union is the only great country in the world which publishes no standard of living index, no statistics about the distribution of income groups and spending. Russian statistics make a deafening noise with their figures of industrial production; about the consumer they are silent. Individual reports about the dismal living conditions of the masses by people who lived among them and had both the chance to get abroad and the courage to speak up, e.g., Ciliga, Sedov, Yvon, Serge, are dismissed as Trotskyite slander. There are nevertheless methods to establish the truth by careful analysis of official Soviet sources which are *ex hypothesi* beyond doubt. Thus for example *Planovoie Khoziaistvo* ("Planned Economy"), an official Soviet periodical, published in 1938 some figures about the food consumption of an average family of St. Petersburg textile workers under Tsarism. Using this as a basis, Hubbard (*Soviet Labour and Industry,* p. 164) arrives at the following figures:

		1913	1929	1937
Cost of 1 week's food	Roubles	3.40	5.90	49.60
Index of food prices	Per cent	100	172	1449
Average (monthly) money wages ...	Roubles	25	66	245
Index of real wages	Per cent	100	154	68

Thus the average standard of living had risen from the Revolution to 1929 by 54 per cent and had by 1937 dropped to a level 32 per cent lower than the pre-revolutionary standard.

[Here the author cites similar studies by F. Forest and Colin Clark.]

To the best of my knowledge no Soviet or communist authority has so far attempted either to refute these figures or to publish different standard-of-living estimates. This would in any case be a difficult undertaking as the results were obtained by calculation based on official Soviet figures for food production, average money wages, population census, etc. . . .

Workers, peasants and soldiers being the three pillars of the Soviet state, the army could not lag behind industry and agriculture in the socialist struggle against "petit-bourgeois equalitarianism" (Stalin). The private soldier in the Red army is paid today 10 roubles per month; a lieutenant 1,000 roubles, a colonel 2,400 roubles. The ratio of a private's to a subaltern's pay in the British army is approximately 1:4, in the American army 1:3, in the Soviet army 1:100. It may be of some interest to hear what the Soviet apologist has to say about this phenomenon. In *Soviet Millionaires,* a pamphlet issued in 1943 in the communist "Russia Today" series, written by Reg Bishop, we read:

> Another item on which there has been a great deal of misunderstanding concerns army remuneration, the fact that whereas a private soldier gets a mere pittance, Red army officers receive relatively high pay—a lieutenant gets approximately 1,000 roubles a month, a colonel something over 2,000 roubles, and so on for the higher grades.
>
> Obviously, Soviet millionaires are not going to develop on the pay of a ranker, but equally obviously this is no question of class differentiation, but one of sound socialist policy, in line with the general wages policy of the U.S.S.R. . . .

ASPECTS OF SOVIET LEGISLATION

[A] law, equally unprecedented in the legislation of any country, decrees the deportation for five years "to the remote regions of Siberia" of all the dependents of a man who escapes military service by deserting abroad, *if they did not know about his crime.* If they did know about it, the penalty is five to ten years of imprisonment and confiscation of property. Paragraph 3 of the decree of June 8, 1934 (published in *Izvestia,* June 9, 1934), runs:

> 3. In the event of flight or escape abroad of a military person, the adult members of his family, if they have in any way assisted the preparations or the commitment of the act of treason, or even if they have known about it without bringing it to the knowledge of the authorities, will be punished with 5 to 10 years of imprisonment with confiscation of their property.
>
> The other adult members of the traitor's family, living with him or being his dependents at the time of treason, are deprived of their electoral rights and deported for 5 years to the remote regions of Siberia.

The decree revives the primitive conception of the collective responsibility of the family or clan for crimes. Since 1935 the routine of deporting relatives of arrested people has been extended to all forms of high treason and counter-revolutionary activity—terms which cover practically any offence: political dissent, "wrecking," absenteeism. What it amounts to in practice is that every individual has to regard his whole family as potential hostages for his conduct. . . .

THE NEW RULING CLASS

The nucleus of power in the Soviet Union is the Party. The radical changes both in leadership and membership which the Bolshevik Party underwent during the last decade are of fundamental importance for the understanding of the new regime; they give in a nutshell the significance of Stalinism.

[Here the author cites the official Report of the 17th Party Congress in 1934 before the purge and the 18th Party Congress in 1939 to show changes in the social composition of the Communist Party and to claim that nine-tenths of party members and delegates to the 17th Party Congress did not survive the purge.]

Who then is the Party, the all-powerful body of a million and a half people who occupy all responsible positions and administer the country? Who are the 90.7 per cent among the delegates who were already in 1934 *not* "workers from production"? The Soviet State knows only one great class of people besides them: the administrators of economy and state-apparatus—bureaucracy and technocracy. About one-third of the Soviet government consists of engineers; the rest of administrators. We have seen in previous sections how this new "managerial" ruling class became more and more segregated from the masses, how it succeeded in creating a new framework for the inheritance of privilege, so as to approach the criteria of a hereditary caste (similar to the old Russian administrative aristocracy) and how it gradually closed its ranks against newcomers from below by legislation, differentiation of income, educational restrictions, and the abandonment of the "workers' nucleus" principle in the higher schools. The purging and "taking over" of the Party by the bureaucracy was the decisive step from the dictatorship of the proletariat to the stabilisation of the new ruling class.

FORCED LABOUR—A PARENTHESIS

There is one question connected with the political changes during the past two decades which cannot be satisfactorily answered: the number of Soviet citizens who in connection with these changes lost life or liberty. The wall of silence around Russia which so effectively prevents information even regarding relatively trivial matters from leaking through, is at its densest where this question is concerned. It has been officially admitted by the Soviet Government that the White Sea Canal was built entirely, and the Turksib-Railway partly, by Forced Labour Brigades; gigantic enterprises which involved the labour of a million men. But here official information ends; no figures were published and no outsider was ever permitted to visit those camps. . . . [Many] may have perished in the Forced Labour Brigades where eye-witnesses put the mortality among the prisoners at 30 per cent per annum. But all this is guesswork. . . .

[Here the author makes extensive reference to and quotes from the testimony of Lucien Blit, a leading member of the Bund (the Jewish Socialist Party of Poland) who "shared the average fate of Polish refugees to Russia."]

Blit was released, together with other Poles, after the German attack on Russia in 1941 and the subsequent signing of the Stalin-Sikorsky treaty. He joined the Polish army then under formation in Alma-Ata. For the Soviet citizen no such happy event is possible. Once sent to one of the Arctic labour camps he never returns, doomed to perish in the cold inferno of the polar night.

How many of them? There is no means of ascertaining it; but the estimates by people who have glimpsed behind the Soviet scene suggest about 10 per cent of the total population. This is not so fantastic as it seems, since the five million Kulaks officially deported in the years of Collectivisation already represent a solid core of 3½ per cent. Then came the crushing of the various oppositions of Left and Right—Trotskyites, Bukharinites, etc., culminating in the purges. . . .

"I have lived with a number of Russian families," B. says at the end of his narrative, "and there was not a single case in which at least one member among the relatives or friends of the family was not 'absent.' When I spoke to a well-known Soviet journalist in Kuibishev he emphasized, with some pride in his voice, that there were not more than 18 million of them; everything else was exaggeration. Officials of the regime grew very angry at estimates over 20 million; up to that figure their attitude was one of tacit admission."

This is one first-hand report among many, whose authors are personally known to me as reliable and responsible persons. I am fully aware, however, that to the Soviet addict, and also to many uninformed sympathisers, this report will sound like a tale from the moon. One is generally prepared to accept a correction of one's ideas by, say, 10 per cent; a correction by 1,000 per cent is beyond one's capacity of immediate adaptation. . . .

[This] is the only part of this survey whose contents are based on private, not on official data. The indignant reader is at liberty to disbelieve them, to call me a Trotskyite agent, a menshevik counter-revolutionary, a Japanese spy, a howling hyena or any other name applied to critics of Russia.

But he won't be able to take the same attitude towards the official Soviet sources, Soviet laws, decrees, statistics, etc., quoted in the rest of this work. I have selected Blit's testimony as an illustration. The reader may discard the illustration without affecting the text. . . .

Economically the Soviet Union represents State Capitalism. The State owns the means of production and controls the production and distribution of goods. The distinction between State Capitalism and State Socialism is from the economist's point of view meaningless. The difference between the two lies in the political and social structure of the country, in the question "The State controls everything, but who controls the State?" We have seen that the Soviet masses have no means to control either through elections or through trade unions, through political or economic pressure, the decisions of the State. The workers of the coal mines in the Urals have less influence on their wages, their working hours, their living conditions than the miners in Britain or the U.S.A. They cannot strike, they cannot elect their Union delegates, they cannot start a row in Parliament, in the press or in the streets. The Soviet workers "are not owners of their factories any more than the British citizen is owner of the British Navy" (Polanyi). . . .

The Russian Revolution has failed in its aim to create a new type of human society in a new moral climate. The ultimate reason for its failure was the arid nineteenth-century materialism of its doctrine. It had to fall back on the old opiates because it did not recognise man's need for spiritual nourishment.

Reflections on the Russian Revolution

Sidney Hook *

DEMOCRACY AND THE DICTATORSHIP OF THE PARTY

The key to the Russian economy, to the evolution of Russian culture since the early years of the revolution, to its ghastly purges and juridical frame-ups, is to be found in the character of the Russian state power. The Russian state is marked by the concentration of all political and economic power in the hands of the Communist Party. Other political parties of the working class are forbidden, even in the "democratic" Stalin Constitution. The organization of factions within the Communist Party is punishable by exile to concentration camps or by death. The Soviets and Parliament have

* Professor of Philosophy at New York University. Author of *Towards the Understanding of Karl Marx, From Hegel to Marx, The Hero in History,* and numerous articles on political and philosophical subjects. The selection is from Sidney Hook, "Reflections on the Russian Revolution," *Southern Review,* Vol. IV (Winter, 1939), No. 3, pp. 429–462. Reprinted in *Reason, Social Myths, and Democracy* (New York, John Day Co., Inc., 1940). Reprinted by permission of author and *Southern Review.*

the same function in Russia as [had] the Reichstag in Germany—emphatic rubber stamps for policies decided by the Political Committee of the Party. Begun as a dictatorship of a class, the Russian Revolution developed through the dictatorship of the Communist Party into the dictatorship of the Secretariat. . . .

It does not require much perspicacity to realize that the dictatorship of a political party cannot for long be effective without its own internal organization becoming dictatorial. The necessity of *controlling* the mass of the population over whom the party wields a dictatorship, of effectively combating enemies, real and alleged, of imposing a uniform ideology, compels the party to assume a military, sometimes called monolithic, structure. The interests of the nonparty masses which cannot be openly expressed because of the absence of free political institutions naturally tend to express themselves in differences within the party itself, in factional groupings of various sorts. But the dictatorship of the party cannot be effectively wielded unless the facts and appearance of division in its own ranks are concealed from the nonparty masses. To conceal this division and to parade the maximum amount of unity, the ruling group in the party must regulate and control the expression of opinion among the rank and file. It must exercise an even stricter supervision of the party press than it does of the nonparty press. Now in order to exercise the proper supervision the leading group must itself be unified. Dissidents are isolated, gagged into silence, exiled, deported, and shot. The rule of the leading group must be fortified by a mythology which glorifies "the leader," "the beloved disciple," "the man of iron" who tops the pyramidal structure and whose word on any subject is law. Opposition of any kind is equated with treason. Decisions are "unanimously" approved; failure, no matter for what reason, becomes sabotage; silence today a sign of betrayal tomorrow; the instruments of one purge become the victims of another. Historical variations may appear in some points in this evolution from the dictatorship *of* a political party to the dictatorship *over* the party. The general pattern of Russian development, however, fits the facts: from the outlawing of other working-class political parties, to the prohibition of factions in the Communist Party (in March, 1920), to ruthless police terror against *all* dissidents under Stalin.

THE SOURCES OF STALINISM

Although he denies that the explanation of the present political regime in Russia is to be found in its natural evolution from party dictatorship to dictatorship of the secretariat, Trotsky [in *The Revolution Betrayed*] gives himself great pains to show that the dictatorship of the party is no part of the theory of Bolshevism, and that its rise in Russia, and the concomitant absence of workers' democracy, "was a measure of defence of the dictatorship [of the proletariat as a class] in a backward and devastated country, surrounded by enemies on all sides." In this way, he seeks to refute those Marxist critics who lay the totalitarian form of the Stalin regime and its bloody excesses at the door of Bolshevism as well as those non-Marxist critics who see in what has transpired in Russia a final judgment upon the whole tradition of Marxism. . . .

I shall begin by showing that it is false, in fact, to say that the prohibition of other working-class parties in Russia was a temporary exigency adopted because of peculiar Russian circumstances, but that it followed from the Bolshevik theory of leadership and conquest of power. . . .

That the Bolsheviks considered the dictatorship of the proletariat to be the dictatorship of the Communist Party is evidenced by (1) the existence of a polemic literature, long before the October Revolution, and to which Trotsky himself contributed, charging them with that view. (2) The critique of groups like that of Rosa Luxemburg, which shared the international social program of the October Revolution but protested against the abrogation of Soviet democracy. (3) Their oppressive treatment of other working-class organizations, press, and leaders even before the country was rent by civil war. (4) The substantial identification of the dictatorship of the party and the dictatorship of the class in the theoretical writings, after 1917, of Lenin, Trotsky, Bukharin, Zinoviev, and Stalin. And (5) most important of all, as far as this specific point is concerned, the program of the Communist International, which left no room for doubt that the Communist Parties of respective countries would liquidate at the first opportunity other working-class parties.[1] Despite Trotsky's claim that the one-party dictatorship was the result of the Russian backward economy and other local conditions, the Theses and Resolutions of the Fourth Congress of the Communist International which were mandatory upon *all* Communist Parties *everywhere,* specifically state that the dictatorship of the proletariat can only be achieved by a purely Communist government. At most other forms of working-class government must be regarded as a starting point of the struggle for party dictatorship. . . . [For development of the first four of the foregoing points see original article.]

By their curiously mystical, but highly convenient, doctrine that the Communist Party knew better than the working class itself what was good for it, the Bolshevik leaders could pretend that any workers who disagreed with them were agents of the enemy. But among themselves they spoke quite frankly about imposing their will upon the working class when it was in a reactionary mood. They, of course, were the *sole* judges as to when that mood was reactionary. . . .

This is not to maintain that in the early years of the Revolution no demo-

[1] (Author's footnote.) The openness with which this was proclaimed varied with the strategical exigencies of the moment, but see for the U.S. William Z. Foster's *Towards Soviet America* (1932), p. 275. "Under the dictatorship, all the capitalistic parties—Republican, Democratic, Progressive, Socialist (*sic!*)—will be liquidated, the Communist Party functioning alone as the Party of the toiling masses."

cratic processes whatsoever existed within the Soviets. Compared to their complete absence from 1924 down to the present, they loom large. Nor can the existence of genuine democracy within the highly centralized Communist Party during the early years be disputed. But the tendency towards complete domination of the Soviets by the minority Communist Party, reënforced by a thousand and one sanctions that the possession of state power bestows, was there. Nothing demonstrates this more clearly than the attitude of the Bolshevik leaders to the slogans of "freely elected Soviets" which were raised by their working-class opponents after the October Revolution. This was really nothing more than another form of the slogan "All Power to the Soviets" under which the Bolsheviks had marched to the conquest of power. But because here and there, some Cadets took up the slogan in hope that under its cover they could carry on anti-Soviet propaganda, *all* who made the demand for democratically elected Soviets, including the heroic Kronstadt sailors, were regarded as counterrevolutionists. It was in Lenin's own time that *Pravda* proclaimed that "All power to the Soviets" had been replaced by "All power to the Cheka." . . .

That the identification of the dictatorship of the party and the class is an integral part of the Bolshevik theory, and not a removable appendage, must be the inescapable conclusion of any critical inquiry into its party documents and historical practice. Article 126, the prize joker of the Stalin Constitution, which lays down as the law of the land that the Communist Party is "to constitute the guiding nucleus of all organizations, both social and governmental" states candidly what was already true in the time of Lenin. . . .

The history of the Russian Revolution has demonstrated that a minority one-party dictatorship has led to an increase of the power of man over man, to a power exercised more brutally and accompanied by greater servility than anywhere else in the world with the possible exception of Germany. There is every reason to believe on economic, psychological, and historic grounds that a one-party dictatorship would lead to similar results everywhere in the world today. The presence of a superior productive technique would confer no immunity; it would merely make the engines of repression more efficient. . . .

The socialist movement originally appeared in Western Europe as the heir of the great traditions of political democracy which were imperiled by the absence of corresponding democracy in social and economic life. Its program, its axioms, its faith—called for better and more democracy, not less. The fate of the Russian Revolution is impressive testimony of a negative sort that no set of economic arrangements from which democratic control is absent, can ever achieve the moral and material promise of the socialist ideal.

Part II

THE LIVING CONSTITUTION

Some Fundamental Constitutional Principles

The Constitution: "Road or Gate"?

What Limits on Free Speech?

Judicial Review

Federalism

SECTION I

Some Fundamental Constitutional Principles

Although the American Constitution has been changed by amendments and modified by more than a century and a half of political practice, it still embodies, to a considerable extent, the philosophy of the Founding Fathers. This philosophy is most authoritatively expressed in *The Federalist,* written by James Madison, Alexander Hamilton, and John Jay. The eighty-five articles which comprise *The Federalist* originally appeared in several New York journals from October, 1787, to August, 1788. Although written specifically to help secure ratification of the Constitution in New York, the various articles received immediate recognition as political exposition of the highest order, and they were widely reprinted throughout the states. Most political scientists would agree that they are America's greatest contribution to political thought.

Number 10, written by James Madison, is the most famous and widely quoted *Federalist* paper. In it Madison expressed the fear that a majority, unless checked, would often decide measures not according to "justice" but through force of numbers. One of the chief merits of the Constitution, he maintained, was that it would, through the advantages accruing from the "republican" principle help to secure impartial justice.

Recent research has established that Madison, and not Hamilton, wrote Number 51 as well as Number 47 of *The Federalist.* In these papers the author explains how, through a system of separation of powers and checks and balances, the Constitution is designed to protect the minority and the individual citizen from the depredations of a majority.

Professor Hofstadter, in his essay, interprets the motives and work of the Founding Fathers. The basic fear of majority factions set forth in *The Federalist* is underscored by the selection from Walter Lippmann. That fear is in marked contrast, however, to Thomas Jefferson's belief, as Henry Steele Commager explains, in the capacity of the common man to govern himself. Jefferson looked to the self-restraint of the majority to safeguard minority rights.

(This section, and particularly Professor Commager's article, is closely related to the discussion of judicial review in Topics 17 and 18.)

Topic 8
THE CONTROL OF MAJORITY "FACTIONS"

THE FOUNDING FATHERS
Richard Hofstadter *

Democratic ideas are most likely to take root among discontented and oppressed classes, rising middle classes, or perhaps some sections of an old, alienated, and partially disinherited aristocracy, but they do not appeal to a privileged class that is still amplifying its privileges. With a half-dozen exceptions at the most, the men of the Philadelphia Convention were sons of men who had considerable position and wealth, and as a group they had advanced well beyond their fathers. Only one of them, William Few of Georgia, could be said in any sense to represent the yeoman farmer class which constituted the overwhelming majority of the free population. In the late eighteenth century "the better kind of people" found themselves set off from the mass by a hundred visible, tangible, and audible distinctions of dress, speech, manners, and education. There was a continuous lineage of upper-class contempt, from pre-Revolutionary Tories like Peggy Hutchinson, the Governor's daughter, who wrote one day: "The dirty mob was all about me as I drove into town," to a Federalist like Hamilton, who candidly disdained the people. Mass unrest was often received in the spirit of young Gouverneur Morris: "The mob begin to think and reason. Poor reptiles! . . . They bask in the sun, and ere noon they will bite, depend upon it. The gentry begin to fear this." Nowhere in America or Europe—not even among the great liberated thinkers of the Enlightenment—did democratic ideas appear respectable to the cultivated classes. Whether the Fathers looked to the cynically illuminated intellectuals of contemporary Europe or to their own Christian heritage of the idea of original sin, they found quick confirmation of the notion that man is an unregenerate rebel who has to be controlled.

And yet there was another side to the picture. The Fathers were intellectual heirs of seventeenth-century English republicanism with its opposition to arbitrary rule and faith in popular sovereignty. If they feared the advance of democracy, they also had misgivings about turning to the extreme right. Having recently experienced a bitter revolutionary struggle with an external power beyond their control, they were in no mood to

* Associate Professor of History at Columbia University. Author of *Social Darwinism in American Thought*. The selection is reprinted from *The American Political Tradition* by Richard Hofstadter, pp. 3-17, by permission of Alfred A. Knopf, Inc.

follow Hobbes to his conclusion that any kind of government must be accepted in order to avert the anarchy and terror of a state of nature. They were uneasily aware that both military dictatorship and a return to monarchy were being seriously discussed in some quarters—the former chiefly among unpaid and discontented army officers, the latter in rich and fashionable Northern circles. . . .

Unwilling to turn their backs upon republicanism, the Fathers also wished to avoid violating the prejudices of the people. "Notwithstanding the oppression and injustice experienced among us from democracy," said George Mason, "the genius of the people is in favor of it, and the genius of the people must be consulted." Mason admitted "that we had been too democratic," but feared that "we should incautiously run into the opposite extreme." James Madison, who has quite rightfully been called the philosopher of the Constitution, told the delegates: "It seems indispensable that the mass of citizens should not be without a voice in making the laws which they are to obey, and in choosing the magistrates who are to administer them." James Wilson, the outstanding jurist of the age, later appointed to the Supreme Court by Washington, said again and again that the ultimate power of government must of necessity reside in the people. This the Fathers commonly accepted, for if government did not proceed from the people, from what other source could it legitimately come? . . .

What the Fathers wanted was known as "balanced government," an idea at least as old as Aristotle and Polybius. This ancient conception had won new sanction in the eighteenth century, which was dominated intellectually by the scientific work of Newton, and in which mechanical metaphors sprang as naturally to men's minds as did biological metaphors in the Darwinian atmosphere of the late nineteenth century. Men had found a rational order in the universe and they hoped that it could be transferred to politics, or, as John Adams put it, that governments could be "erected on the simple principles of nature." Madison spoke in the most precise Newtonian language when he said that such a "natural" government must be so constructed "that its several constituent parts may, by their mutual relations, be the means of keeping each other in their proper places." A properly designed state, the Fathers believed, would check interest with interest, class with class, faction with faction, and one branch of government with another in a harmonious system of mutual frustration. . . .

It is ironical that the Constitution, which Americans venerate so deeply, is based upon a political theory that at one crucial point stands in direct antithesis to the main stream of American democratic faith. Modern American folklore assumes that democracy and liberty are all but identical, and when democratic writers take the trouble to make the distinction, they usually assume that democracy is necessary to liberty. But the Founding Fathers thought that the liberty with which they were most concerned was menaced by democracy. In their minds liberty was linked not to democracy but to property.

What did the Fathers mean by liberty? What did Jay mean when he spoke of "the charms of liberty"? Or Madison when he declared that to destroy liberty in order to destroy factions would be a remedy worse than the disease? Certainly the men who met at Philadelphia were not interested in extending liberty to those classes in America, the Negro slaves and the indentured servants, who were most in need of it, for slavery was recognized in the organic structure of the Constitution and indentured servitude was no concern of the Convention. Nor was the regard of the delegates for civil liberties any too tender. It was the opponents of the Constitution who were most active in demanding such vital liberties as freedom of religion, freedom of speech and press, jury trial, due process, and protection from "unreasonable searches and seizures." These guarantees had to be incorporated in the first ten amendments because the Convention neglected to put them in the original document. Turning to economic issues, it was not freedom of trade in the modern sense that the Fathers were striving for. Although they did not believe in impeding trade unnecessarily, they felt that failure to regulate it was one of the central weaknesses of the Articles of Confederation, and they stood closer to the mercantilists than to Adam Smith. Again, liberty to them did not mean free access to the nation's unappropriated wealth. At least fourteen of them were land speculators. They did not believe in the right of the squatter to occupy unused land, but rather in the right of the absentee owner or speculator to pre-empt it.

The liberties that the constitutionalists hoped to gain were chiefly negative. They wanted freedom from fiscal uncertainty and irregularities in the currency, from trade wars among the states, from economic discrimination by more powerful foreign governments, from attacks on the creditor class or on property, from popular insurrection. They aimed to create a government that would act as an honest broker among a variety of propertied interests, giving them all protection from their common enemies and preventing any one of them from becoming too powerful. The Convention was a fraternity of types of absentee ownership. All property should be permitted to have its proportionate voice in government. Individual property interests might have to be sacrificed at times, but only for the community of propertied interests. Freedom for property would result in liberty for men—perhaps not for all men, but at least for all worthy men. Because men have different faculties and abilities, the Fathers believed, they acquire different amounts of property. To protect property is only to protect men in the exercise of their natural faculties. Among the many liberties, therefore, freedom to hold and dispose property is paramount. Democracy, unchecked rule by the masses, is sure to bring arbitrary redistribution of property, destroying the very essence of liberty.

The Fathers' conception of democracy, shaped by their practical experience with the aggressive dirt farmers in the American states and the urban mobs of the Revolutionary period, was supplemented by their reading in history and political science. Fear of what Madison called "the superior force of an interested and overbearing majority" was the dominant emotion aroused by their study of historical examples. The chief examples of republics were among the city-states of antiquity, medieval Europe, and early modern times. Now, the history of these republics—a history, as Hamilton said, "of perpetual vibration between the extremes of tyranny and anarchy"—was alarming. Further, most of the men who had overthrown the liberties of republics had "begun their career by paying an obsequious court to the people; commencing demagogues and ending tyrants."

All the constitutional devices that the Fathers praised in their writings were attempts to guarantee the future of the United States against the "turbulent" political cycles of previous republics. By "democracy," they meant a system of government which directly expressed the will of the majority of the people, usually through such an assemblage of the people as was possible in the small area of the city-state. . . .

Government, thought the Fathers, is based on property. Men who have no property lack the necessary stake in an orderly society to make stable or reliable citizens. Dread of the propertyless masses of the towns was all but universal. George Washington, Gouverneur Morris, John Dickinson, and James Madison spoke of their anxieties about the urban working class that might arise some time in the future—"men without property and principle," as Dickinson described them—and even the democratic Jefferson shared this prejudice. Madison, stating the problem, came close to anticipating the modern threats to conservative republicanism from both communism and fascism:

> In future times, a great majority of the people will not only be without landed but any other sort of property. These will either combine, under the influence of their common situation—in which case the rights of property and the public liberty will not be secure in their hands—or, what is more probable, they will become the tools of opulence and ambition, in which case there will be equal danger on another side.

What encouraged the Fathers about their own era, however, was the broad dispersion of landed property. The small land-owning farmers had been troublesome in recent years, but there was a general conviction that under a properly made Constitution a *modus vivendi* could be worked out with them. The possession of moderate plots of property presumably gave them a sufficient stake in society to be safe and responsible citizens under the restraints of balanced government. Influence in government would be proportionate to property: merchants and great landholders would be dominant, but small property-owners would have an independent and far from negligible voice. It was "politic as well as just," said Madison, "that the interests and rights of every class should be duly represented and understood in the public councils," and John Adams declared that there could be "no free government without a democratical branch in the constitution." . . .

After the Constitution was adopted, conflict between the ruling classes broke out anew, especially after powerful planters were offended by the favoritism of Hamilton's policies to Northern commercial interests. The planters turned to the farmers to form an agrarian alliance, and for more than half a century this powerful coalition embraced the bulk of the articulate interests of the country. As time went on, therefore, the main stream of American political conviction deviated more and more from the anti-democratic position of the Constitution-makers. Yet, curiously, their general satisfaction with the Constitution together with their growing nationalism made Americans deeply reverent of the founding generation, with the result that as it grew stronger, this deviation was increasingly overlooked.

There is common agreement among modern critics that the debates over the Constitution were carried on at an intellectual level that is rare in politics, and that the Constitution itself is one of the world's masterpieces of practical statecraft. On other grounds there has been controversy. At the very beginning contemporary opponents of the Constitution foresaw an apocalyptic destruction of local government and popular institutions, while conservative Europeans of the old regime thought the young American Republic was a dangerous leftist experiment. Modern critical scholarship, which reached a high point in Charles A. Beard's *An Economic Interpretation of the Constitution of the United States,* started a new turn in the debate. The antagonism, long latent, between the philosophy of the Constitution and the philosophy of American democracy again came into the open. Professor Beard's work appeared in 1913 at the peak of the Progressive era, when the muckraking fever was still high; some readers tended to conclude from his findings that the Fathers were selfish reactionaries who do not deserve their high place in American esteem. Still more recently, other writers, inverting this logic, have used Beard's facts to praise the Fathers for their opposition to "democracy" and as an argument for returning again to the idea of a "republic."

In fact, the Fathers' image of themselves as moderate republicans standing between political extremes was quite accurate. They were impelled by class motives more than pietistic writers like to admit, but they were also controlled, as Professor Beard himself has recently emphasized, by a statesmanlike sense of moderation and a scrupulously republican philosophy. Any attempt, however, to tear their ideas out of the eighteenth-century context is sure to make them seem starkly reactionary. Consider, for example, the favorite maxim of John Jay: "The people who own the country ought to govern it." To the Fathers this was simply a swift axiomatic statement of the stake-in-society theory of political rights, a moderate conservative position under eighteenth-century conditions of property distribution in America. Under modern property relations this maxim demands a drastic restriction of the base of political power. A large portion of the modern middle class—and it is the strength of this class upon which balanced government depends—is propertyless; and the urban proletariat, which the Fathers so greatly feared, is almost one half the population. Further, the separation of ownership from control that has come with the corporation deprives Jay's maxim of twentieth-century meaning even for many propertied people. The six hundred thousand stockholders of the American Telephone & Telegraph Company not only do not acquire political power by virtue of their stock-ownership, but they do not even acquire economic power: they cannot control their own company.

From a humanistic standpoint there is a serious dilemma in the philosophy of the Fathers, which derives from their conception of man. They thought man was a creature of rapacious self-interest, and yet they wanted him to be free—free, in essence, to contend, to engage in an umpired strife, to use property to get property. They accepted the mercantile image of life as an eternal battleground, and assumed the Hobbesian war of each against all; they did not propose to put an end to this war, but merely to stabilize it and make it less murderous. They had no hope and they offered none for any ultimate organic change in the way men conduct themselves. The result was that while they thought self-interest the most dangerous and unbrookable quality of man, they necessarily underwrote it in trying to control it. They succeeded in both respects: under the competitive capitalism of the nineteenth century America continued to be an arena for various grasping and contending interests, and the federal government continued to provide a stable and acceptable medium within which they could contend; further, it usually showed the wholesome bias on behalf of property which the Fathers expected. But no man who is as well abreast of modern science as the Fathers were of eighteenth-century science believes any longer in unchanging human nature. Modern humanistic thinkers who seek for a means by which society may transcend eternal conflict and rigid adherence to property rights as its integrating principles can expect no answer in the philosophy of balanced government as it was set down by the Constitution-makers of 1787.

The Union as a Safeguard Against Domestic Faction

The Federalist, No. 10

James Madison

Among the numerous advantages promised by a well-constructed Union, none deserves to be more accurately developed than its tendency to break and control the violence of faction. The friend of popular governments never finds himself so much alarmed for their character and fate, as when he contemplates their propensity to this dangerous vice. He will not fail, therefore, to set a due value on any plan which, without violating the principles to which he is attached, provides a proper cure for it. The instability, injustice, and confusion introduced into the public councils have, in truth, been the mortal diseases under which popular governments have everywhere perished; as they continue to be the favorite and fruitful topics from which the adversaries to liberty derive their most specious declamations. The valuable improvements made by the American constitutions on the popular models, both ancient and modern, cannot certainly be too much admired; but it would be an unwarrantable partiality, to contend that they have as effectually obviated the danger on this side, as was wished and expected. Complaints are everywhere heard from our most considerate and virtuous citizens, equally the friends of public and private faith, and of public and personal liberty, that our governments are too unstable; that the public good is disregarded in the conflicts of rival parties; and that measures are too often decided, not according to the rules of justice, and the rights of the minor party, but by the superior force of an interested and overbearing majority. However anxiously we may wish that these complaints had no foundation, the evidence of known facts will not permit us to deny that they are in some degree true. It will be found, indeed, on a candid review of our situation, that some of the distresses under which we labor have been erroneously charged on the operation of our governments; but it will be found, at the same time, that other causes will not alone account for many of our heaviest misfortunes; and, particularly, for that prevailing and increasing distrust of public engagements, and alarm for private rights, which are echoed from one end of the continent to the other. These must be chiefly, if not wholly, effects of the unsteadiness and injustice with which a factious spirit has tainted our public administrations.

By a faction, I understand a number of citizens, whether amounting to a majority or a minority of the whole, who are united and actuated by some common impulse of passion, or of interest, adverse to the rights of other citizens, or to the permanent and aggregate interests of the community.

There are two methods of curing the mischiefs of faction: the one, by removing its causes; the other, by controlling its effects.

There are again two methods of removing the causes of faction: the one, by destroying the liberty which is essential to its existence; the other, by giving to every citizen the same opinions, the same passions, and the same interests.

It could never be more truly said than of the first remedy, that it was worse than the disease. Liberty is to faction what air is to fire, an aliment without which it instantly expires. But it could not be less folly to abolish liberty, which is essential to political life, because it nourishes faction, than it would be to wish the annihilation of air, which is essential to animal life, because it imparts to fire its destructive agency.

The second expedient is as impracticable as the first would be unwise. As long as the reason of man continues fallible, and he is at liberty to exercise it, different opinions will be formed. As long as the connection subsists between his reason and his self-love, his opinions and his passions will have a reciprocal influence on each other; and the former will be objects to which the latter will attach themselves. The diversity in the faculties of men, from which the rights of property originate, is not less an insuperable obstacle to a uniformity of interests. The protection of these faculties is the first object of government. From the protection of different and unequal faculties of acquiring property, the possession of different degrees and kinds of property immediately results; and from the influence of these on the sentiments and views of the respective proprietors, ensues a division of the society into different interests and parties.

The latent causes of faction are thus sown in the nature of man; and we see them everywhere brought into different degrees of activity, according to the different circumstances of civil society. A zeal for different opinions concerning religion, concerning government, and many other points, as well of speculation as of practice; an attachment to different leaders ambitiously contending for pre-eminence and power; or to persons of other descriptions whose fortunes have been interesting to the human passions, have, in turn, divided mankind into parties, inflamed them with mutual animosity, and rendered them much more disposed to vex and oppress each other, than to co-operate for their common good. So strong is this propensity of mankind to fall into mutual animosities, that where no substantial occasion presents itself, the most frivolous and fanciful distinctions have been sufficient to kindle their unfriendly passions and excite their most violent conflicts. But the most common and durable source of factions has been the various and unequal distribution of property. Those who hold and those who are without property have ever formed distinct interests in society. Those who are creditors, and those who are debtors, fall under a like discrimination. A landed interest, a manufacturing interest, a mercantile interest, a moneyed interest, with many lesser interests, grow up of necessity in civilized nations, and divide them into different classes, actuated by different sentiments and views. The regulation of these various and interfering interests forms the principal task of modern legislation, and involves the spirit of party and faction in the necessary and ordinary operations of the government.

No man is allowed to be a judge in his own cause, because his interest would certainly bias his judgment and, not improbably, corrupt his integrity. With equal, nay, with greater reason, a body of men are unfit to be both judges and parties at the same time; yet what are many of the most important acts of legislation, but so many judicial determinations, not indeed concerning the rights of single persons, but concerning the rights of large bodies of citizens? And what are the different classes of legislators, but advocates and parties to the causes which they determine? Is a law proposed concerning private debts? It is a question to which the creditors are parties on one side and the debtors on the other. Justice ought to hold the balance between them. Yet the parties are, and must be, themselves the judges; and the most numerous party, or, in other words, the most powerful faction, must be expected to prevail. Shall domestic manufacturers be encouraged, and in what degree, by restrictions on foreign manufactures? are questions which would be differently decided by the landed and the manufacturing classes, and probably by neither with a sole regard to justice and the public good. The apportionment of taxes on the various descriptions of property is an act which seems to require the most exact impartiality; yet there is, perhaps, no legislative act in which greater opportunity and temptation are given to a predominant party, to trample on the rules of justice. Every shilling with which they overburden the inferior number, is a shilling saved to their own pockets.

It is in vain to say that enlightened statesmen will be able to adjust these clashing interests, and render them all subservient to the public good. Enlightened statesmen will not always be at the helm. Nor, in many cases, can such an adjustment be made at all, without taking into view indirect and remote considerations, which will rarely prevail over the immediate interest which one party may find in disregarding the rights of another or the good of the whole.

The inference to which we are brought is, that the *causes* of faction cannot be removed, and that relief is only to be sought in the means of controlling its *effects*.

If a faction consists of less than a majority, relief is supplied by the republican principle, which enables the majority to defeat its sinister views by regular vote. It may clog the administration, it may convulse the society; but it will be unable to execute and mask its violence under the forms of the Constitution. When a majority is included in a faction, the form of popular government, on the other hand, enables it to sacrifice to its ruling passion or interest both the public good and the rights of other citizens. To secure the public good and private rights against the danger of such a faction, and at the same time to preserve the spirit and the form of popular government, is then the great object to which our inquiries are directed. Let me add that it is the great desideratum, by which alone this form of government can be rescued from the opprobrium under which it has so long labored, and be recommended to the esteem and adoption of mankind.

By what means is this object attainable? Evidently by one of two only. Either the existence of the same passion or interest in a majority at the same time must be prevented; or the majority, having such coexisting passion or interest, must be rendered, by their number and local situation, unable to concert and carry into effect schemes of oppression. If the impulse and the opportunity be suffered to coincide, we well know that neither moral nor religious motives can be relied on as an adequate control. They are not found to be such on the injustice and violence of individuals, and lose their efficacy in proportion to the number combined together; that is, in proportion as their efficacy becomes needful.

From this view of the subject it may be concluded that a pure democracy, by which I mean a society consisting of a small number of citizens, who assemble and administer the government in person, can admit of no cure for the mischiefs of faction. A common passion or interest will, in almost every case, be felt by a majority of the whole; a communication and concert result from the form of government itself; and there is nothing to check the inducements to sacrifice the weaker party or an obnoxious individual. Hence it is that such democracies have ever been spectacles of turbulence and contention; have ever been found incompatible with personal security, or the rights of property; and have in general been as short in their lives as they have been violent in their deaths. Theoretic politicians, who have patronized this species of government, have erroneously supposed that by reducing mankind to a perfect equality in their political rights, they would at the same time be perfectly equalized and assimilated in their possessions, their opinions, and their passions.

A republic, by which I mean a government in which the scheme of representation takes place, opens a different prospect, and promises the cure for which we are seeking. Let us examine the points in which it varies from pure democracy, and we shall comprehend both the nature of the cure and the efficacy which it must derive from the Union.

The two great points of difference between a democracy and a republic are: first, the delegation of the government, in the latter, to a small number of citizens elected by the rest; secondly, the greater number of citizens, and greater sphere of country, over which the latter may be extended.

The effect of the first difference is, on the one hand, to refine and enlarge the public views, by passing them through the medium of a chosen body of citizens, whose wisdom may best discern the true interests of their country, and whose patriotism and love of justice will be least likely to sacrifice it to temporary or partial considerations. Under such a regulation, it may well happen that the public voice, pronounced by the representatives of the people, will be more consonant to the public good than if pronounced by the people themselves, convened for the purpose. On the other hand, the effect may be inverted. Men of factious tempers, of local prejudices, or of sinister designs, may, by intrigue, by corruption, or by other means, first obtain the suffrages, and then betray the interests of the people. The question resulting is, whether small or extensive republics are more favorable to the election of proper guardians of the public weal; and it is clearly decided in favor of the latter by two obvious considerations.

In the first place, it is to be remarked that, however small the republic may be, the representatives must be raised to a certain number, in order to guard against the cabals of a few; and that, however large it may be, they must be limited to a certain number, in order to guard against the confusion of a multitude. Hence, the number of representatives in the two cases not being in proportion to that of the two constituents, and being proportionally greater in the small republic, it follows that if the proportion of fit characters be not less in the large than in the small republic, the former will present a greater option, and consequently a greater probability of a fit choice.

In the next place, as each representative will be chosen by a greater number of citizens in the large than in the small republic, it will be more difficult for unworthy candidates to practice with success the vicious arts, by which elections are too often carried; and the suffrages of the people, being more free, will be more likely to centre in men who possess the most attractive merit and the most diffusive and established characters.

It must be confessed that in this as in most other cases, there is a mean, on both sides of which inconveniences will be found to lie. By enlarging too much the number of electors, you render the representative too little acquainted with all their local circumstances and lesser interests; as by reducing it too much, you render him unduly attached to these, and too little fit to comprehend and pursue great and national objects. The federal Constitution forms a happy combination in this respect; the great and aggregate interests being referred to the national, the local and particular to the State legislatures.

The other point of difference is, the greater number of citizens and extent of territory which may be brought within the compass of republican than of democratic government; and it is this circumstance principally which renders factious combinations less to be dreaded in the former than in the latter. The smaller the society, the fewer probably will be the distinct parties and interests composing it; the fewer the distinct parties and interests, the more frequently will a majority be found of the same party; and the smaller the number of individuals composing a majority, and the smaller the compass within which they are placed, the more easily will they concert and execute their plans of oppression. Extend the sphere, and you take in a greater variety of parties and interests; you make it less probable that a majority of the whole will have a common motive to invade the rights of other citizens; or if such a common motive exists, it will be more difficult for all who feel it to discover their own strength, and to act in unison with each other. Besides other impediments, it may be remarked that where there is a consciousness of unjust or dishonorable purposes, communication is always checked by distrust in proportion to the number whose concurrence is necessary.

Hence it clearly appears that the same advantage which a republic has over a democracy, in controlling the effects of faction, is enjoyed by a large over a small republic—is enjoyed by the Union over the States composing it. Does the advantage consist in the substitution of representatives, whose enlightened views and virtuous sentiments render them superior to local prejudices, and to schemes of injustice? It will not be denied that the representation of the Union will be most likely to possess these requisite endowments. Does it consist in the greater security afforded by a greater variety of parties, against the event of any one party being able to outnumber and oppress the rest? In an equal degree does the increased variety of parties, comprised within the Union, increase this security? Does it, in fine, consist in the greater obstacles opposed to the concert and accomplishment of the secret wishes of an unjust and interested majority? Here, again, the extent of the Union gives it the most palpable advantage.

The influence of factious leaders may kindle a flame within their particular States, but will be unable to spread a general conflagration through the other States. A religious sect may degenerate into a political faction in a part of the confederacy; but the variety of sects dispersed over the entire face of it must secure the national councils against any danger from that source. A rage for paper money, for an abolition of debts, for an equal division of property, or for any other improper or wicked project will be less apt to pervade the whole body of the Union than a particular member of it; in the same proportion as such a malady is more likely to taint a particular county or district, than an entire State.

In the extent and proper structure of the Union, therefore, we behold a republican remedy for the diseases most incident to republican government. And according to the degree of pleasure and pride we feel in being republicans, ought to be our zeal in cherishing the spirit and supporting the character of federalists.

PUBLIUS.

Topic 9

"SINCE ANGELS DO NOT GOVERN MEN"

SEPARATION OF POWERS

The Federalist, No. 47

James Madison

One of the principal objections inculcated by the more respectable adversaries to the Constitution, is its supposed violation of the political maxim that the legislative, executive, and judiciary departments ought to be separate and distinct. In the structure of the federal government, no regard, it is said, seems to have been paid to this essential precaution in favor of liberty. The several departments of power are distributed and blended in such a manner as at once to destroy all symmetry and beauty of form, and to expose some of the essential parts of the edifice to the danger of being crushed by the disproportionate weight of other parts.

No political truth is certainly of greater intrinsic value, or is stamped with the authority of more enlightened patrons of liberty, than that on which the objection is founded. The accumulation of all powers, legislative, executive, and judiciary, in the same hands, whether of one, a few, or many, and whether hereditary, self-appointed, or elective, may justly be pronounced the very definition of tyranny. Were the federal Constitution, therefore, really chargeable with the accumulation of power, or with a mixture of powers, having a dangerous tendency to such an accumulation, no further arguments would be necessary to inspire a universal reprobation of the system. I persuade myself, however, that it will be made apparent to everyone that the charge cannot be supported, and that the maxim on which it relies has been totally misconceived and misapplied. In order to form correct ideas on this important subject, it will be proper to investigate the sense in which the preservation of liberty requires that the three great departments of power should be separate and distinct.

The oracle who is always consulted and cited on this subject is the celebrated Montesquieu. If he be not the author of this invaluable precept in the science of politics, he has the merit at least of displaying and recommending it most effectually to the attention of mankind. Let us endeavor, in the first place, to ascertain his meaning on this point.

The British Constitution was to Montesquieu what Homer has been to the didactic writers on epic poetry. As the latter have considered the work of the immortal bard as the perfect model from which the principles and rules of the epic art were to be drawn, and by which all similar works were to be judged, so this great political critic appears to have viewed the Constitution of England as the standard, or to use his own expression, as the mirror of political liberty, and to have delivered, in the form of elementary truths, the several characteristic principles of that particular system. That we may be sure, then, not to mistake his meaning in this case, let us recur to the source from which the maxim was drawn.

On the slightest view of the British Constitution we must perceive that the legislative, executive, and judiciary departments are by no means totally separate and distinct from each other. The executive magistrate forms an integral part of the legislative authority. He alone has the prerogative of making treaties with foreign sovereigns, which, when made, have, under certain limitations, the force of legislative acts. All the members of the judiciary department are appointed by him, can be removed by him on the address of the two Houses of Parliament, and form, when he pleases to consult them, one of his constitutional councils. One branch of the legislative department forms also a great constitutional council to the executive chief; as, on another hand, it is the sole depositary of judicial power in cases of impeachment, and is invested with the supreme appellate jurisdiction in all other cases. The judges, again, are so far connected with the legislative department as often to attend and participate in its deliberations, though not admitted to a legislative vote.

From these facts, by which Montesquieu was guided, it may clearly be inferred that in saying "There can be no liberty where the legislative and executive powers are united in the same person or body of magistrates," or, "if the power of judging be not separated from the legislative and executive powers," he did not mean that these departments ought to have no *partial agency* in, or no *control* over, the acts of each other. His meaning, as his own words import, and still more conclusively as illustrated by the example in his eye, can amount to no more than this, that where the *whole* power of one department is exercised by the same hands which possess the *whole* power of another department, the fundamental principles of a free constitution are subverted. This would have been the case in the Constitution examined by him if the King, who is the sole executive magistrate, had possessed also the complete legislative power, or the supreme administration of justice; or if the entire legislative body had possessed the supreme judiciary or the supreme executive authority. This, however, is not among the vices of that Constitution. The magistrate in whom the whole executive power resides cannot of himself make a law, though he can put a negative on every law; nor administer justice in person, though he has the appointment of those who do administer it. The judges can exercise no executive prerogative, though they are shoots from the executive stock; nor any legislative function, though they may be advised with by the legislative councils. The entire legislature can perform no judiciary act; though by the joint act of two of its branches the judges may be removed from their offices, and though one of its branches is possessed of the judicial power in the last resort. The entire legislature, again, can exercise no executive prerogative, though one of its branches constitutes the supreme executive magistracy, and another, on the impeachment of a third, can try and condemn all the subordinate officers in the executive department.

The reasons on which Montesquieu grounds his maxim are a further demonstration of his meaning. "When the legislative and executive powers are united in the same person or body," says he, "there can be no liberty, because apprehensions may arise lest *the same* monarch or Senate should *enact* tyrannical laws to *execute* them in a tyrannical manner." Again: "Were the power of judging joined with the legislative, the life and liberty of the subject would be exposed to arbitrary control, for the *judge* would then be the *legislator*. Were it joined to the executive power, the *judge* might behave with all the violence of *an oppressor*." Some of these reasons are more fully explained in other passages; but briefly stated as they are here, they sufficiently establish the meaning which we have put on this celebrated maxim of this celebrated author.

If we look into the constitutions of the several States, we find that, notwithstanding the emphatical and in some instances the unqualified terms in which this axiom has been laid down, there is not a single instance in which the several departments of power have been kept absolutely separate and distinct. . . .

[Here the author examines the constitutions of the original thirteen states, excepting those of Rhode Island and Connecticut which were formed prior to the American Revolution.]

What I have wished to evince is, that the charge brought against the proposed Constitution, of violating a sacred maxim of free government, is warranted neither by the real meaning annexed to that maxim by its author nor by the sense in which it has hitherto been understood in America.

PUBLIUS

Checks and Balances

The Federalist, No. 51

James Madison

To what expedient, then, shall we finally resort, for maintaining in practice the necessary partition of power among the several departments, as laid down in the Constitution? The only answer that can be given is, that as all these exterior provisions are found to be inadequate, the defect must be supplied, by so contriving the interior structure of the government as that its several constituent parts may, by their mutual relations, be the means of keeping each other in their proper places. Without presuming to undertake a full development of this important idea, I will hazard a few general observations, which may perhaps place it in a clearer light, and enable us to form a more correct judgment of the principles and structure of the government planned by the Convention.

In order to lay a due foundation for that separate and distinct exercise of the different powers of government, which to a certain extent is admitted on all hands to be essential to the preservation of liberty, it is evident that each department should have a will of its own; and consequently should be so constituted that the members of each should have as little agency as possible in the appointment of the members of the others. Were this principle rigorously adhered to, it would require that all the appointments for the supreme executive, legislative, and judiciary magistracies should be drawn from the same fountain of authority, the people, through channels having no communication whatever with one another. Perhaps such a plan of constructing the several departments would be less difficult in practice than it may in contemplation appear. Some difficulties, however, and some additional expense would attend the execution of it. Some deviations, therefore, from the principle must be admitted. In the constitution of the judiciary department in particular, it might be inexpedient to insist rigorously on the principle: first, because peculiar qualifications being essential in the members, the primary consideration ought to be to select that mode of choice which best secures these qualifications; secondly, because the permanent tenure by which the appointments are held in that department must soon destroy all sense of dependence on the authority conferring them.

It is equally evident that the members of each department should be as little dependent as possible on those of the others, for the emoluments annexed to their offices. Were the executive magistrate, or the judges, not independent of the Legislature in this particular, their independence in every other would be merely nominal.

But the great security against a gradual concentration of the several powers in the same department, consists in giving to those who administer each department the necessary constitutional means and personal motives to resist encroachments of the others. The provision for defence must in this, as in all other cases, be made commensurate to the danger of attack. Ambition must be made to counteract ambition. The interest of the man must be connected with the constitutional rights of the place. It may be a reflection on human nature, that such devices should be necessary to control the abuses of government. But what is government itself, but the greatest of all reflections on human nature? If men were angels, no government would be necessary. If angels were to govern men, neither external nor internal controls on government would be necessary. In framing a government which is to be administered by men over men, the great difficulty lies in this: you must first enable the government to control the governed; and in the next place oblige it to control itself. A dependence on the people is, no doubt, the primary control on the government; but experience has taught mankind the necessity of auxiliary precautions.

This policy of supplying, by opposite and rival interests, the defect of better motives, might be traced through the whole system of human affairs, private as well as public. We see it particularly displayed in all the subordinate distributions of power, where the constant aim is to divide and arrange the several offices in such a manner as that each may be a check on the other—that the private interest of every individual may be a sentinel over the public rights. These inventions of prudence cannot be less requisite in the distribution of the supreme powers of the State.

But it is not possible to give to each department an equal power of self-defence. In republican government, the legislative authority necessarily predominates. The remedy for this inconveniency is to divide the legislature into different branches; and to render them, by different modes of election and different principles of action, as little connected with each other as the nature of their common functions and their common dependence on the society will admit. It may even be necessary to guard against dangerous encroachments by still further precautions. As the weight of the legislative authority requires that it should be thus divided, the weakness of the executive may require, on the other hand, that it should be fortified. An absolute negative on the legislature appears at first view to be the natural defence with which the executive magistrate should be armed. But perhaps it would be neither altogether safe nor alone sufficient. On ordinary occasions it might not be exerted with the requisite firmness, and on extraordinary occasions it might be perfidiously abused. May not this defect of an absolute negative be supplied by some qualified connection between this weaker department and the weaker branch of the stronger department, by which the latter may be led to support the constitutional rights of the former, without being too much detached from the rights of its own department?

If the principles on which these observations are founded be just, as I persuade myself they are, and they be applied as a criterion to the several State constitutions, and to the federal Constitution, it will be found that if the latter does not perfectly correspond with them, the former are infinitely less able to bear such a test.

There are, moreover, two considerations particularly applicable to the federal system of America, which place that system in a very interesting point of view.

First. In a single republic all the power surrendered by the people is submitted to the administration of a single government, and the usurpations are guarded against by a division of the government into distinct and separate departments. In the compound republic of America, the power surrendered by the people is first divided between two distinct governments, and then the portion allotted to each subdivided among distinct and separate departments. Hence a double security arises to the rights of the people. The different governments will control each other, at the same time that each will be controlled by itself.

Second. It is of great importance in a republic not only to guard the society against the oppression of its rulers, but to guard one part of the society against the injustice of the other part. Different interests necessarily exist in different classes of citizens. If a majority be united by a common interest, the rights of the minority will be insecure. There are but two methods of providing against this evil: the one by creating a will in the community independent of the majority, that is, of the society itself; the other by comprehending in the society so many separate descriptions of citizens as will render an unjust combination of a majority of the whole very improbable, if not impracticable. The first method prevails in all governments possessing an hereditary or self-appointed authority. This, at best, is but a precarious security; because a power independent of the society may as well espouse the unjust views of the major as the rightful interests of the minor party, and may possibly be turned against both parties. The second method will be exemplified in the federal republic of the United States. Whilst all authority in it will be derived from and dependent on the society, the society itself will be broken into so many parts, interests and classes of citizens, that the rights of individuals, or of the minority will be in little danger from interested combinations of the majority. In a free government the security for civil rights must be the same as that for religious rights. It consists in the one case in the multiplicity of interests, and in the other in the multiplicity of sects. The degree of security in both cases will depend on the number of interests and sects; and this may be presumed to depend on the extent of country and number of people comprehended under the same government. This view of the subject must particularly recommend a proper federal system to all the sincere and considerate friends of republican government, since it shows that in exact proportion as the territory of the Union may be formed into more circumscribed confederacies, or States, oppressive combinations of a majority will be facilitated; the best security under republican forms, for the rights of every class of citizens, will be diminished; and, consequently, the stability and independence of some member of the government, the only other security, must be proportionally increased. Justice is the end of government. It is the end of civil society. It ever has been and ever will be pursued until it be obtained, or until liberty be lost in the pursuit. In a society under the forms of which the stronger faction can readily unite and oppress the weaker, anarchy may as truly be said to reign as in a state of nature, where the weaker individual is not secured against the violence of the stronger; and as in the latter state even the stronger individuals are prompted by the uncertainty of their condition to submit to a government which may protect the weak as well as themselves; so, in the former state, will the more powerful factions or parties be gradually induced, by a like motive, to wish for a government which will protect all parties, the weaker as well as the more powerful. It can be little doubted that if the State of Rhode Island was separated from the confederacy, and left to itself, the insecurity of rights under the popular form of government within such narrow limits would be displayed by such reiterated oppressions of factious majorities that some power altogether independent of the people would soon be called for by the voice of the very factions whose misrule had proved the necessity of it. In the extended republic of the United States, and among the great variety of interests, parties, and sects which it embraces, a coalition of a majority of the whole society could seldom take place on any other principles than those of justice and the general good; whilst there being thus less danger to a minor from the will of a major party, there must be less pretext, also, to provide for the security of the former, by introducing into the government a will not dependent on the latter; or, in other words, a will independent of the society itself. It is no less certain than it is important, notwithstanding the contrary opinions which have been entertained, that the larger the society, provided it lie within a practical sphere, the more duly capable it will be of self-government. And happily for the *republican cause*, the practicable sphere may be carried to a very great extent, by a judicious modification and mixture of the *federal principle*.

PUBLIUS

Topic 10
MAJORITY RULE AND MINORITY RIGHTS

IN DEFENSE OF MAJORITY RULE

Henry Steele Commager *

It was in America that the doctrine of majority rule was first successfully asserted and effectuated; it was in America that the principle of limited government was first institutionalized and that machinery for maintaining it was first fashioned.

These statements may require some elaboration. What we have here are two fundamental—perhaps the two most fundamental—principles of American politics: the principle that men make government, and the principle that there are limits to the authority of government. The philosophical origins of the first principle may be found in the natural-rights philosophy of the seventeenth century—in the notion that all rights inhered originally in men and that men, living in a state of nature, came together for mutual self-protection and set up government, and that the governments thus instituted derive all their just powers from the consent of the governed. . . .

The second great basic principle—that governments are limited, that there are things no government may do, rights no government may impair, powers no government may exercise—traces its philosophical origins deep into the past but again derives authority from American experience with Parliamentary and royal pretensions. It held, simply enough, that as government was instituted to secure certain rights, its jurisdiction was strictly limited to the fields assigned to it, and that if it over-stepped the bounds of its jurisdiction its acts were not law. In the great words of Samuel Adams, addressed to Shelburne and Rockingham and Camden, "in all free states the constitution is fixed; it is from thence that the legislative derives its authority; therefore it cannot change the constitution without destroying its own foundations." . . .

* Professor of History at Columbia University. Author of *The American Mind*. Co-author of *The Growth of the American Republic, The Heritage of America* and other works. Contributor to many journals and periodicals. The selection is from Henry Steele Commager, *Majority Rule and Minority Rights* (New York, Oxford University Press, 1943), Chs. I and III. By permission of author and publisher.

[The] generation [of the American Revolution], more conscious of the dangers than of the potentialities of government, more concerned with protection against governmental tyranny than with the promotion of majority welfare, devised cunning mechanisms for putting limitations upon government. When we contemplate the ingenuity of the Fathers in setting up their system of checks and balances we are deeply impressed, almost dismayed. That the limits of governmental authority might not be misunderstood, that authority was described—for the first time—in written constitutions, and to these constitutions were added bills of rights. But this was merely elementary. There were, in addition, the checks and balances of the federal system, of the tripartite division of powers, of the bicameral legislatures, of frequent elections, and of impeachment. And atop all this there developed—I would not say there was established—the practice of judicial review.

But in their laudable zeal to give reality to John Dickinson's description of a free people—"Not those over whom government is reasonably and equitably exercised, but those who live under a government so constitutionally checked and controlled, that proper provision is made against its being otherwise exercised"—the framers of our constitutions confused, it would seem, jurisdiction with power, and the confusion has persisted down to our own day. They failed properly to distinguish between the authority government should have, and the manner in which government might exercise that authority which it did have. They set up limits on the jurisdiction of government, enumerating things no government could do; and this was eminently proper and in harmony with the philosophy of the Revolutionary era. But they went farther. So fearful were they of governmental tyranny that even where they granted to government certain necessary powers they put obstacles in the way of the effective exercise of those powers. They set up not only boundaries to government but impediments in government. Thus they not only made it difficult for government to invade fields denied to it, but they made it difficult for government to operate at all. They created a system where deadlock would be the normal character of the American government—a situation from which political parties rescued us.

So here we have two institutions which are—or would appear to be—fundamentally contradictory. We have first the institutionalization of the principle that men can alter, abolish, and institute governments, can, in short, make government conform to their will. But over against this we have the institutionalization of the principle that governments are limited—that there are things not even a majority may require government to do because they are outside the jurisdiction of any government. If the majority may use government to do its will, is that not an attack upon the inalienable rights of men over against government? if there are limits upon what governments may do, is that not a challenge to or even a denial of the principle of majority rule? Here is a paradox not yet resolved in our political philosophy or our constitutional system.

This paradox is presented in most familiar form in Jefferson's First Inaugural Address: "All, too, will bear in mind this sacred principle, that though the will of the majority is in all cases to prevail, that will to be rightful must be reasonable; that the minority possess their equal rights which equal law must protect, and to violate would be oppression." And throughout our history runs this theme of majority will and minority rights. Jefferson, as we shall see, emphasized majority will, and so did Jefferson's successors, Jackson and Lincoln—Jackson, who brushed aside judicial interposition, Lincoln, who reminded us that

> A majority . . . is the only true sovereign of a free people. Whoever rejects it does, of necessity, fly into anarchy or to despotism. Unanimity is impossible; the rule of a minority, as a permanent arrangement, is wholly inadmissible; so that, rejecting the majority principle, anarchy or despotism in some form is all that is left.

But the emphasis since the Civil War has been increasingly on minority rights—an emphasis so marked, between Reconstruction and the New Deal, that it is no great exaggeration to say that tenderness for the minority became the distinguishing characteristic of the American constitutional system.

Underlying this distinction are, of course, the assumptions that majority will and minority rights are antithetical, that majority rule constantly threatens minority rights, and that the principal function of our constitutional system is to protect minority rights against infringement.

So plausible are these assumptions that there has developed, in course of time, the theory of the "tyranny of the majority"—a theory which derived much support abroad as well as here from the misleading observations of Tocqueville. Tocqueville, who leaned heavily for material and authority on that pillar of conservatism, Joseph Story, confessed that "the very essence of democratic government consists in the absolute sovereignty of the majority," and concluded from this that the prospects for American democracy were bleak indeed. His analysis of the consequences that flow from the tyranny of the majority has given comfort, ever since, to those who fear democracy. So persuasive is this theory of the tyranny of the majority that many Americans have come to believe that our constitutional system is not, in fact, based upon the principle of majority rule. And they have found support and consolation in the curious notion that ours is a "republican" form of government, and that a republic is the very opposite of a democracy.

The fear of the tyranny of the majority has haunted many of the most distinguished and respectable American statesmen and jurists since the days of the founding of the Republic; it persists today, after a century and a half of experience. It was first formulated, in elaborate and coherent fashion, by John Adams in his famous *Defense of the Constitutions of Government of the United States of America* (1786). The people, Adams urges, are not to be trusted, nor are their representatives, without an adequate system of checks and balances:

> If it is meant by the people . . . a representative assembly, . . . they are not the best keepers of the people's liberties or their own, if you give them all the power, legislative, executive and judicial. They would invade the liberties of the people, at least the majority of them would invade the liberties of the minority, sooner and oftener than any absolute monarch. . . .

[And in No. 51 of *The Federalist,* the warning was given that]

> It is of great importance in a republic not only to guard the society against the oppression of its rulers, but to guard one part of the society against the injustice of the other part. Different interests necessarily exist in different classes of citizens. If a majority be united by a common interest, the rights of the minority will be insecure. . . . Justice is the end of government. It is the end of civil society. . . . In a society under the forms of which the stronger faction can readily unite and oppress the weaker, anarchy may as truly be said to reign as in a state of nature where the weaker individual is not secured against the violence of the stronger. . . .

Confronted by these different interpretations of the American constitutional system, of democracy and of republicanism, we may turn with some confidence to Thomas Jefferson. On these questions he is, indubitably, our leading authority. He helped to create and to establish the new political systems in America, and he furnished them with a good part of their political philosophy. He never wrote a formal treatise on the subject (as did his old friend John Adams), but in his public papers and his private letters we can find the most comprehensive and consistent statement of the nature of American democracy that has come down to us from the generation of the founders.

And it must be observed, first, that Jefferson was by no means unaware of the dangers inherent in majority rule. . . . [To him] majority rule is neither anarchy nor absolutism, but government within self-imposed restraints. And we search in vain through the voluminous writings of Jefferson for any expression of distrust of the virtue or the wisdom of the people. What we do find, on the contrary, from the beginning to the end of Jefferson's career, is an unterrified and unflinching faith in majority rule.

"I am not among those who fear the people," he wrote to Kercheval in 1816; "they and not the rich, are our dependence for continued freedom." . . . Writing to Madison [he said], . . . "After all, it is my principle that the will of the majority should prevail." And to another Virginia friend, Colonel Carrington, went the same reassurance:

> I am persuaded myself that the good sense of the people will always be found to be the best army. They may be led astray for a moment, but will soon correct themselves. The people are the only censors of their governors; and even their errors will tend to keep these to the true principles of their institution.

That the people, if led astray, would "soon correct themselves" was a fixed conviction and one which, *mirabile dictu,* found confirmation in their tenacious support of his own administration. Thus to John Tyler in 1804:

> No experiment can be more interesting than that we are now trying, and which we trust will end in establishing the fact that man may be governed by reason and truth. . . . The firmness with which the people have withstood the late abuses of the press, the discernment that they have manifested between truth and falsehood, show that they may safely be trusted to hear everything true and false, and to form correct judgment between them. . . .

This was the consistent note—that the people may—and must—be trusted. "No government can continue good," he assured John Adams, "but under the control of the people"; and again, to that doughty opponent of judicial pretensions, Spencer Roane, "Independence can be trusted nowhere but with the people in the mass. They are inherently independent of all but the moral law." "I know of no safe depository of the ultimate powers of the society," he told William Jarvis, "but the people themselves; and if we think them not enlightened enough to exercise their control with a wholesome discretion, the remedy is not to take it from them, but to inform their discretion by education." And recalling Hume's argument that "all history and experience" confounded the notion that "the people are the origin of all just power," Jefferson burst out with uncharacteristic violence: "And where else will this degenerate son of science, this traitor to his fellow men, find the origin of just powers, if not in the majority of the society? Will it be in the minority? Or in an individual of that minority?" And we hear an echo of that question which the First Inaugural submits to the contemporary world: "Sometimes it is said that man can not be trusted with the government of himself. Can he, then, be trusted with the government of others? Or have we found angels in the forms of kings to govern him? Let history answer this question." For himself, Jefferson knew the answer. His devotion to the people was not that of the benevolent despot, the party boss, or the dictator, but of the good citizen, and his whole career is a monument to the sincerity of his confession to Du Pont de Nemours. "We both love the people," he said, "but you love them as infants, whom you are afraid to trust without nurses; and I as adults whom I freely leave to self-government."

To all of this many of Jefferson's contemporaries could have subscribed without reservation: he, assuredly, had no monopoly on faith in popular government. "We of the United States," as he explained simply, "are constitutionally and conscientiously democrats." But in one respect Jefferson went farther than most of his contemporaries, went so far, indeed, that his argument sounds bizarre and almost alien to our ears. That was his advocacy of what we may call the doctrine of the continuing majority. It was easy enough for most Americans to subscribe to the compact theory of government—the compact made, of course, by the original majority—just as it is easy for us to subscribe, now, to the doctrine that we are, all of us, bound by the compact made at Philadelphia in 1787 and ratified by the majority of that time. And just as we have invested that Constitution with sacrosanctity, so—in England, in France, in America of the eighteenth century—there was a tendency to regard the original compact, the product of the Golden Age of the past, with reverence and to invest it with a peculiar sanctity. Such an attitude was foreign to Jefferson. His conviction, however, that each new majority must write its own fundamental law has sometimes been regarded as merely an amusing exaggeration, a whimsey to be indulged along with the whimsey that a little rebellion, now and then, is an excellent thing. But there can be no doubt of Jefferson's sincerity in the matter, nor of his persuasion that the issue was one of fundamental importance.

This problem is more fundamental, and more complex, than might appear at first glance—this problem of the original *versus* the continuing majority. All of us seem to agree that we are bound by the original majority—by the majority of 1787, or that which decreed our state constitutions. But what if the will of the present majority conflicts with that of the original majority? Is majority will valid only for some past generation? The easy answer is that the present majority can, if it chooses, change the original compact by constitutional amendment or by substituting an entirely new constitution. But it takes more than a majority to amend a constitution or to write a new one, and under our present system a determined minority can, if it will, effectively veto any change in the federal document and in most state documents. Not only this, but the courts have pretty consistently held that the current majority may not even interpret the original constitution to accommodate it to felt needs. . . .

Jefferson, as we know, entertained no reverence for the constitutional dogmas of the past. His attitude, set forth in the famous letter to Samuel Kercheval, of July 1816, is too familiar to justify quotation in full:

> Let us [not] weakly believe that one generation is not as capable as another of taking care of itself, and of ordering its own affairs. Let us . . . avail ourselves of our reason and experience, to correct the crude essays of our first and unexperienced, although wise, virtuous and well-meaning counsels. And lastly, let us provide in our Constitution for its revision at stated periods. What these periods should be, nature herself indicates. . . . Each generation is as independent of the one preceding, as that was of all which had gone before. It has, then, like them, a right to choose for itself the form of government it believes most promotive of its own happiness . . . and it is for the peace and good of mankind that a solemn opportunity of doing this every nineteen or twenty years should be provided by the Constitution. . . .

"The People," a distinguished contemporary statesman has said in a phrase already classic, "have no right to do wrong." It is at least suggestive that Eamon de Valera, who has fought pretty consistently for his people and who regards himself as a democrat, should have found it necessary to invoke the techniques of totalitarianism to prevent the people from "doing wrong." And it is a characteristic of almost every anti-democratic philosophy that it purports to serve the welfare of the people but refuses to trust the judgment of the people on questions affecting their welfare. . . .

Our constitutional system, as has already been observed, is one of checks and balances: these have already been noted. It is sometimes forgotten that our political system is one of checks and balances too. Anyone who has followed the slow and tortuous course of a major public issue—the poll tax, for example, or neutrality, through the arena of public opinion, into the party conventions and caucuses, into the halls of Congress and the rooms of appropriate committees, knows how much of delay, of balance, of compromise, is implicit in our political machinery. A good part of our politics, indeed, seems to be concerned with reconciling majority and minority will, class hostilities, sectional differences, the divergent interests of producer and consumer, of agriculture and labor, of creditor and debtor, of city and country, of tax-payer and tax-beneficiary, of the military and the civilian. In small issues as in great, the result is generally a compromise. Democracy, in short, whether from instinct or from necessity, furnishes its own checks and balances—quite aside from such as may be provided in written constitutions.

Indeed it might plausibly be argued that it is one of the major advantages of democracy over other forms of government that it alone can indulge in the luxury of tolerating minority and dissenting groups because it alone has developed the technique for dealing with them. It is sometimes charged as a criticism of democracy that it cannot act speedily and effectively in an emergency—as can totalitarian or despotic governments. The charge is not sound—as witness the efficiency of our own democracy in the spring of 1933 or the winter of 1941–2—but it is true that in a democracy it requires a real emergency to produce prompt and effective action.

But there is this to be said of the checks and balances of democratic politics—that they are natural, not artificial; that they are flexible rather than rigid; that they can yield to public opinion and to necessity. They do, sometimes, enable the majority to ride down the minority; they do, far more frequently, enable the minority to delay and defeat the majority. But the responsibility in all this is with the people themselves—where it belongs. Where they indulge their apathy, their carelessness, their blindness, they pay the price, and it is right that they should pay the price. As the fault is theirs, so, too, the remedy. Where issues appear sufficiently important the majority can have its way even against the recalcitrance of minorities who take refuge in the labyrinths of our party and our legislative systems. But against minorities entrenched in the judiciary there is no effective appeal except through the complicated and slow process of constitutional amendment. Here it is true today as it was in 1801 that the minority can "retire into the judiciary as a stronghold," and "from that battery" beat down the works of republicanism. . . .

This is the crucial objection to judicial nullification of majority will in any field: that "education in the abandonment of foolish legislation is itself a training in liberty." If our democracy is less educated in this respect than we might wish, if our legislatures are less alert to constitutional principles than might seem desirable, a heavy responsibility rests upon the courts. For these, by taking over to themselves the peculiar guardianship of the Constitution and of civil liberties, have discouraged the people's active and intelligent interest in these matters. Judges—and liberals—have ignored what Professor Chafee finely says, that "the victories of liberty of speech must be won in the mind before they are won in the courts." For in the long run only an educated and enlightened democracy can hope to endure. . . .

Our own experience, I believe, justifies Jefferson's faith that men need no masters—not even judges. It justifies us, too, in believing that majority will does not imperil minority rights, either in theory or in operation. It gives us firm basis for a belief that the people themselves can be trusted to realize that the majority has a vital interest in the preservation of an alert and critical minority and that, conversely, the minority can have no rights fundamentally inimical to the commonwealth. It justifies us in the belief that only in a democracy where there is free play of ideas, where issues are freely fought out in the public forum,—where, in short, the safety valves of public discussion and experimentation and reconsideration are always open—can there be assurance that both majority and minority rights will be served. It is the glory of democracy that it—and it alone—can tolerate dissent. It is the strength of democracy that dissent, where tolerated, is helpful rather than harmful.

Minorities Should Not Be Coerced

Walter Lippmann *

Although the question before the Senate is whether to amend the rules, the issue is not one of parliamentary procedure. It is whether there shall be a profound and far-reaching constitutional change in the character of the American government. The proposed amendment to Rule XXII would enable two-thirds of the Senate to close the debate and force any measure, motion, or other matter to a vote. If the amendment is carried, the existing power of a minority of the states to stop legislation will have been abolished.

"Stripped of all mumbo-jumbo and flag waving," says "The New York

* Newspaper columnist. Formerly newspaper editor. Author of *Public Opinion, A Preface to Politics, A Preface to Morals, The Good Society, U.S. Foreign Policy,* and numerous other books. The selection is from a column by Walter Lippmann in the *New York Herald Tribune,* March 3, 1949. Copyright, 1949, New York Herald Tribune, Inc. By permission.

Times," the issue "is whether the country's highest legislative body will permit important measures to be kept from a vote through the activities of a few leather-throated, iron-legged members who don't want democratic decision." This is an unduly scornful and superficial way to dispose of a great constitutional problem. For the real issue is whether any majority, even a two-thirds majority, shall now assume the power to override the opposition of a large minority of the states.

In the American system of government, the right of "democratic decision" has never been identified with majority rule as such. The genius of the American system, unique I believe among the democracies of the world, is that it limits all power—including the power of the majority. Absolute power, whether in a king, a president, a legislative majority, a popular majority, is alien to the American idea of "democratic decision."

The American idea of a democratic decision has always been that important minorities must not be coerced. When there is strong opposition, it is neither wise nor practical to force a decision. It is necessary and it is better to postpone the decision—to respect the opposition and then to accept the burden of trying to persuade it.

For a decision which has to be enforced against the determined opposition of large communities and regions of the country will, as Americans have long realized, almost never produce the results it is supposed to produce. The opposition and the resistance, having been overridden, will not disappear. They will merely find some other way of avoiding, evading, obstructing or nullifying the decision.

For that reason it is a cardinal principle of the American democracy that great decisions on issues that men regard as vital shall not be taken by the vote of the majority until the consent of the minority has been obtained. Where the consent of the minority has been lacking, as for example in the case of the prohibition amendment, the "democratic decision" has produced hypocrisy and lawlessness.

This is the issue in the Senate. It is not whether there shall be unlimited debates. The right of unlimited debates is merely a device, rather an awkward and tiresome device, to prevent large and determined communities from being coerced.

The issue is whether the fundamental principle of American democratic decision—that strong minorities must be persuaded and not coerced—shall be altered radically, not by constitutional amendment but by a subtle change in the rules of the Senate.

The issue has been raised in connection with the civil rights legislation. The question is whether the vindication of these civil rights requires the sacrifice of the American limitation on majority rule. The question is a painful one. But I believe the answer has to be that the rights of Negroes will in the end be made more secure, even if they are vindicated more slowly, if the cardinal principle—that minorities shall not be coerced by majorities—is conserved.

For if that principle is abandoned, then the great limitations on the absolutism and tyranny of transient majorities will be gone, and the path will be much more open than it now is to the demagogic dictator who, having aroused a mob, destroys the liberties of the people.

SECTION II

The Constitution: "Road or Gate"?

Marbury v. *Madison* established the power of the Supreme Court to declare Acts of Congress unconstitutional and unenforceable. The Constitution provided for the exercise of similar power by the Court with respect to state legislation. The scope of both federal and state power to deal with the exigencies of governing has depended, in the last analysis, therefore, upon the decisions of the Supreme Court. That the Court has enjoyed considerable discretion in defining that scope is manifest from the cases dealt with in this section.

McCulloch v. *Maryland,* in which Chief Justice Marshall gave elastic scope to Congressional power generally under the Constitution, is not merely of historic interest but proved of great importance in helping to sustain much of the New Deal legislation and continues as the foundation of broad federal authority.

On the other hand, the *Schechter* case, in which the Supreme Court unanimously invalidated the National Industrial Recovery Act, reflects a restricted view of delegated Congressional power. This was one of several blows to New Deal legislation which led President Roosevelt in 1937 to seek to reorganize the Supreme Court. (See Dorothy Thompson in Topic 18.) *Wickard* v. *Filburn,* decided in the decade of the 40's, is representative of sweeping extensions of federal power over the economy upheld by the Court in its greatly expanded view of Congressional prerogative under the Constitution.

The due process clauses of the Constitution have been the most fecund source of Supreme Court decisions invalidating social legislation. Due process in the Fifth Amendment has limited the exercise of federal delegated power and a similar clause in the Fourteenth Amendment has proven, to an even greater extent, a restraint upon the state police power to govern in the general interest. No clearer illustration of judicial discretion on issues of constitutionality exists than in the vicissitudes of minimum wage for women legislation under due process challenge. In 1917 such legislation was sustained as constitutional by an evenly divided Court. Only six years later, after some changes in the Court, in *Adkins* v. *Children's Hospital,* a similar law was invalidated by a vote of five to three. In 1925 and again in 1927, without opinion, and on the authority of the *Adkins* decision, the Court found similar Arizona and Arkansas statutes unconstitutional. In 1936, by vote of five to four, a New York minimum wage for women law was struck down by the Court. Finally, in *West Coast Hotel* v. *Parrish,* decided the next year, such legislation was upheld when one justice altered his position. This latter decision, giving expanded scope to the police power of the state, is representative of the more recent decisions of the Supreme Court.

(For a general evaluation of judicial review, see Topics 17 and 18.)

Topic 11
THE JUDICIAL POWER

MARBURY V. MADISON *

[On March 2, 1801, two days before the close of his term, President John Adams appointed William Marbury, among others, as a justice of the peace in the District of Columbia. The appointment was confirmed by the Senate, the commission was signed by the President, countersigned by the Secretary of State and the seal of the United States was affixed. Through some inadvertence the commission was left on the desk of the Secretary of State when President Adams' term expired at midnight, March 3rd. Upon Thomas Jefferson's accession to the presidency, he directed his Secretary of State, James Madison, to refuse delivery of the commission. Marbury appealed to the Supreme Court sitting as a court of original jurisdiction for a writ of mandamus to compel delivery of the commission. This specific writ was sought under a section of the Judiciary Act of 1789 which provided that, "The Supreme Court . . . shall have power to issue . . . writs of mandamus in cases warranted by the principles and usages of law, to any persons holding office, under the authority of the United States." Chief Justice John Marshall, speaking for the entire court, held this provision unconstitutional as an attempt to enlarge the original jurisdiction of the Supreme Court beyond that provided by Article III, Section 2 of the Constitution of the United States which reads in part as follows: "In all cases affecting ambassadors, other public ministers and consuls, and those in which a State shall be Party, the Supreme Court shall have *original jurisdiction.*"]

The following opinion of the court was delivered by the CHIEF JUSTICE [Marshall]. . . .

The question, whether an act, repugnant to the constitution, can become the law of the land, is a question deeply interesting to the United States; but, happily, not of an intricacy proportioned to its interest. It seems only necessary to recognize certain principles, supposed to have been long and well established, to decide it. That the people have an original right to

* 1 Cranch 137 (1803).

establish, for their future government, such principles as, in their opinion shall most conduce to their own happiness, is the basis on which the whole American fabric has been erected. The exercise of this original right is a very great exertion; nor can it, nor ought it, to be frequently repeated. The principles, therefore, so established, are deemed fundamental; and as the authority from which they proceed is supreme, and can seldom act, they are designed to be permanent.

This original and supreme will organizes the government, and assigns to different departments their respective powers. It may either stop here, or establish certain limits not to be transcended by those departments. The government of the United States is of the latter description. The powers of the legislature are defined and limited; and that those limits may not be mistaken, or forgotten, the constitution is written. To what purpose are powers limited, and to what purpose is that limitation committed to writing, if these limits may, at any time, be passed by those intended to be restrained? The distinction between a government with limited and unlimited powers is abolished, if those limits do not confine the persons on whom they are imposed, and if acts prohibited and acts allowed, are of equal obligation. It is a proposition too plain to be contested, that the constitution controls any legislative act repugnant to it; or that the legislature may alter the constitution by an ordinary act.

Between these alternatives, there is no middle ground. The constitution is either a superior paramount law, unchangeable by ordinary means, or it is on a level with ordinary legislative acts, and, like other acts, is alterable when the legislature shall please to alter it. If the former part of the alternative be true, then a legislative act, contrary to the constitution, is not law; if the latter part be true, then written constitutions are absurd attempts, on the part of the people, to limit a power, in its own nature, illimitable.

Certainly, all those who have framed written constitutions contemplate them as forming the fundamental and paramount law of the nation, and consequently, the theory of every such government must be, that an act of the legislature, repugnant to the constitution, is void. This theory is essentially attached to a written constitution, and is, consequently, to be considered, by this court, as one of the fundamental principles of our society. It is not, therefore, to be lost sight of, in the further consideration of this subject.

If an act of the legislature, repugnant to the constitution, is void, does it, notwithstanding its invalidity, bind the courts, and oblige them to give it effect? Or, in other words, though it be not law, does it constitute a rule as operative as if it was a law? This would be to overthrow, in fact, what was established in theory; and would seem, at first view, an absurdity too gross to be insisted on. It shall, however, receive a more attentive consideration.

It is, emphatically, the province and duty of the judicial department, to say what the law is. Those who apply the rule to particular cases, must of necessity expound and interpret that rule. If two laws conflict with each other, the courts must decide on the operation of each. So, if a law be in opposition to the constitution; if both the law and the constitution apply to a particular case, so that the court must either decide that case, conformably to the law, disregarding the constitution; or conformably to the constitution, disregarding the law; the court must determine which of these conflicting rules governs the case; this is of the very essence of judicial duty. If then, the courts are to regard the constitution, and the constitution is superior to any ordinary act of the legislature, the constitution, and not such ordinary act, must govern the case to which they both apply.

Those, then, who controvert the principle, that the constitution is to be considered, in court, as a paramount law, are reduced to the necessity of maintaining that courts must close their eyes on the constitution, and see only the law. This doctrine would subvert the very foundation of all written constitutions. It would declare that an act which, according to the principles and theory of our government, is entirely void, is yet, in practice, completely obligatory. It would declare, that if the legislature shall do what is expressly forbidden, such act, notwithstanding the express prohibition, is in reality effectual. It would be giving to the legislature a practical and real omnipotence, with the same breath which professes to restrict their powers within narrow limits. It is prescribing limits, and declaring that those limits may be passed at pleasure. That it thus reduces to nothing, what we have deemed the greatest improvement on political institutions, a written constitution, would, of itself, be sufficient, in America, where written constitutions have been viewed with so much reverence, for rejecting the construction. But the peculiar expressions of the constitution of the United States furnish additional arguments in favor of its rejection. The judicial power of the United States is extended to all cases arising under the constitution. Could it be the intention of those who gave this power, to say, that in using it, the constitution should not be looked into? That a case arising under the constitution should be decided, without examining the instrument under which it arises? This is too extravagant to be maintained. In some cases, then, the constitution must be looked into by the judges. And if they can open it at all, what part of it are they forbidden to read or to obey?

There are many other parts of the constitution which serve to illustrate this subject. It is declared, that "no tax or duty shall be laid on articles exported from any state." Suppose, a duty on the export of cotton, of tobacco, or of flour; and a suit instituted to recover it. Ought judgment to be rendered in such a case? ought the judges to close their eyes on the constitution, and only see the law?

The constitution declares "that no bill of attainder or *ex post facto* law shall be passed." If, however, such a bill should be passed, and a person should be prosecuted under it; must the court condemn to death those victims whom the constitution endeavors to preserve?

"No person," says the constitution, "shall be convicted of treason, unless on the testimony of two witnesses to the same overt act, or on confession in open court." Here, the language of the constitution is addressed especially to the courts. It prescribes, directly for them, a rule of evidence not to be departed from. If the legislature should change that rule, and declare one witness, or a confession out of court, sufficient for conviction, must the constitutional principle yield to the legislative act?

From these, and many other selections which might be made, it is apparent, that the framers of the constitution contemplated that instrument as a rule for the government of courts, as well as of the legislature. Why otherwise does it direct the judges to take an oath to support it? This oath certainly applies in an especial manner, to their conduct in their official character. How immoral to impose it on them, if they were to be used as the instruments, and the knowing instruments, for violating what they swear to support!

The oath of office, too, imposed by the legislature, is completely demonstrative of the legislative opinion on this subject. It is in these words: "I do solemnly swear, that I will administer justice, without respect to persons, and do equal right to the poor and to the rich; and that I will faithfully and impartially discharge all the duties incumbent on me as ——, according to the best of my abilities and understanding, agreeably to the constitution and laws of the United States." Why does a judge swear to discharge his duties agreeably to the constitution of the United States, if that constitution forms no rule for his government? if it is closed upon him, and cannot be inspected by him? If such be the real state of things, this is worse than solemn mockery. To prescribe, or to take this oath, becomes equally a crime.

It is also not entirely unworthy of observation, that in declaring what shall be the supreme law of the land, the constitution itself is first mentioned; and not the laws of the United States, generally, but those only which shall be made in pursuance of the constitution, have that rank.

Thus, the particular phraseology of the constitution of the United States confirms and strengthens the principle, supposed to be essential to all written constitutions, that a law repugnant to the constitution is void; and that courts, as well as other departments, are bound by that instrument.

The rule must be discharged.

Topic 12

"IT IS A CONSTITUTION WE ARE EXPOUNDING"

McCulloch v. Maryland *

Error to the Court of Appeals of the State of Maryland.

[Congress in 1816 passed an act to incorporate the Bank of the United States, and in the following year the bank established a branch in Baltimore. In 1818 the state of Maryland required all banks not chartered by the state to pay an annual tax of $15,000 or to pay a stamp tax on each bank note issued. McCulloch, the cashier of the Baltimore branch of the Bank of the United States, issued bank notes in violation of the state law whereupon the state of Maryland brought suit against him. The state courts decided in favour of Maryland. McCulloch appealed the case to the U.S. Supreme Court on a writ of error.]

Marshall, Chief Justice, delivered the opinion of the court. . . .

The first question made in the cause is, has congress power to incorporate a bank? . . . The power now contested was exercised by the first congress elected under the present constitution. The bill for incorporating the Bank of the United States did not steal upon an unsuspecting legislature, and pass unobserved. Its principle was completely understood, and was opposed with equal zeal and ability. After being resisted, first in the fair and open field of debate, and afterwards in the executive cabinet, with as much persevering talent as any measure has ever experienced, and being supported by arguments which convinced minds as pure and as intelligent as this country can boast, it became a law. The original act was permitted to expire; but a short experience of the embarrassments to which the refusal to revive it exposed the government, convinced those who were most prejudiced against the measure of its necessity, and induced the passage of the present law. It would require no ordinary share of intrepidity to assert, that a measure adopted under these circumstances, was a bold and plain usurpation, to which the constitution gave no countenance. These observations belong to the cause: but they are not made under the impression that, were the question entirely new, the law would be found irreconcilable with the constitution.

In discussing this question, the counsel for the state of Maryland have deemed it of some importance, in the construction of the constitution, to consider that instrument not as emanating from the people, but as the act of sovereign and independent states. The powers of the general govern-

* 4 Wheaton 316 (1819).

ment, it has been said, are delegated by the states, who alone are truly sovereign; and must be exercised in subordination to the states, who alone possess supreme dominion. It would be difficult to sustain this proposition. The convention which framed the constitution was, indeed, elected by the state legislatures. But the instrument, when it came from their hands, was a mere proposal, without obligation, or pretensions to it. It was reported to the then existing congress of the United States, with a request that it might "be submitted to a convention of delegates, chosen in each state by the people thereof, under the recommendation of its legislature, for their assent and ratification." This mode of proceeding was adopted; and by the convention, by congress, and by the state legislatures, the instrument was submitted to the *people*. They acted upon it, in the only manner in which they can act safely, effectively, and wisely, on such a subject, by assembling in convention. . . . From these conventions, the constitution derives its whole authority. The government proceeds directly from the people; is "ordained and established" in the name of the people; and is declared to be ordained, "in order to form a more perfect union, establish justice, insure domestic tranquility, and secure the blessings of liberty to themselves and to their posterity." . . . The government of the Union, then, is emphatically and truly, a government of the people. In form, and in substance, it emanates from them. Its powers are granted by them, and are to be exercised directly on them, and for their benefit.

This government is acknowledged by all, to be one of enumerated powers. The principle, that it can exercise only the powers granted to it, would seem too apparent, to have required to be enforced by all those arguments, which its enlightened friends, while it was depending before the people, found it necessary to urge; that principle is now universally admitted. But the question respecting the extent of the powers actually granted, is perpetually arising, and will probably continue to arise, as long as our system shall exist. In discussing these questions, the conflicting powers of the general and state governments must be brought into view, and the supremacy of their respective laws, when they are in opposition, must be settled.

If any one proposition could command the universal assent of mankind, we might expect that it would be this—that the government of the Union, though limited in its powers, is supreme within its sphere of action. This would seem to result, necessarily, from its nature. It is the government of all; its powers are delegated by all; it represents all, and acts for all. Though any one state may be willing to control its operations, no state is willing to allow others to control them. The nation, on those subjects on which it can act, must necessarily bind its component parts. But this question is not left to mere reason: the people have, in express terms, decided it, by saying, "this constitution, and the laws of the United States, which shall be made in pursuance thereof," "shall be the supreme law of the land," and by requiring that the members of the state legislatures, and the officers of the executive and judicial departments of the state, shall take the oath of fidelity to it. The government of the United States, then, though limited in its powers, is supreme; and its laws, when made in pursuance of the constitution, form the supreme law of the land, "anything in the constitution or laws of any state, to the contrary notwithstanding."

Among the enumerated powers, we do not find that of establishing a bank or creating a corporation. But there is no phrase in the instrument which, like the articles of confederation, excludes incidental or implied powers; and which requires that everything granted shall be expressly and minutely described. Even the 10th amendment, which was framed for the purpose of quieting the excessive jealousies which had been excited, omits the word "expressly," and declares only that the powers "not delegated to the United States, nor prohibited to the states, are reserved to the states or to the people"; thus leaving the question, whether the particular power which may become the subject of contest, has been delegated to the one government, or prohibited to the other, to depend on a fair construction of the whole instrument. The men who drew and adopted this amendment had experienced the embarrassments resulting from the insertion of this word in the articles of confederation, and probably omitted it, to avoid those embarrassments. A constitution, to contain an accurate detail of all the subdivisions of which its great powers will admit, and of all the means by which they may be carried into execution, would partake of the prolixity of a legal code, and could scarcely be embraced by the human mind. It would, probably, never be understood by the public. Its nature, therefore, requires, that only its great outlines should be marked, its important objects designated, and the minor ingredients which compose those objects, be deduced from the nature of the objects themselves. That this idea was entertained by the framers of the American constitution, is not only to be inferred from the nature of the instrument, but from the language. Why else were some of the limitations, found in the 9th section of the 1st article, introduced? It is also, in some degree, warranted, by their having omitted to use any restrictive term which might prevent its receiving a fair and just interpretation. In considering this question, then, we must never forget, that it is a *constitution* we are expounding.

Although, among the enumerated powers of government, we do not find the word "bank," or "incorporation," we find the great powers, to lay and collect taxes; to borrow money; to regulate commerce; to declare and conduct war; and to raise and support armies and navies. . . . A government, intrusted with such ample powers, on the due execution of which the happiness and prosperity of the nation so vitally depends, must also be intrusted with ample means for their execution. The power being given, it is the interest of the nation to facilitate its execution. It can never be their interest, and cannot be presumed to have been their intention, to clog and embarrass its execution, by withholding the most appropriate means.

Throughout this vast republic, from the St. Croix to the Gulf of Mexico, from the Atlantic to the Pacific, revenue is to be collected and expended, armies are to be marched and supported. The exigencies of the nation may require, that the treasure raised in the north should be transported to the south, that raised in the east, conveyed to the west, or that this order should be reversed. Is that construction of the constitution to be preferred, which would render these operations difficult, hazardous, and expensive? Can we adopt that construction (unless the words imperiously require it), which would impute to the framers of that instrument, when granting these powers for the public good, the intention of impeding their exercise by withholding a choice of means? If, indeed, such be the mandate of the constitution, we have only to obey; but that instrument does not profess to enumerate the means by which the powers it confers may be executed; nor does it prohibit the creation of a corporation, if the existence of such a being be essential, to the beneficial exercise of those powers. It is, then, the subject of fair inquiry, how far such means may be employed.

It is not denied, that the powers given to the government imply the ordinary means of execution. That, for example, of raising revenue, and applying it to national purposes, is admitted to imply the power of conveying money from place to place, as the exigencies of the nation may require, and of employing the usual means of conveyance. But it is denied, that the government has its choice of means, or, that it may employ the most convenient means, if, to employ them, it be necessary to erect a corporation. . . . The government which has a right to do an act, and has imposed on it the duty of performing that act, must, according to the dictates of reason, be allowed to select the means; and those who contend that it may not select any appropriate means, that one particular mode of effecting the object is excepted, take upon themselves the burden of establishing that exception. . . .

But the constitution of the United States has not left the right of congress to employ the necessary means, for the execution of the powers conferred on the government, to general reasoning. To its enumeration of powers is added, that of making "all laws which shall be necessary and proper, for carrying into execution the foregoing powers, and all other powers vested by this constitution, in the government of the United States, or in any department thereof." . . .

The argument on which most reliance is placed, is drawn from the peculiar language of this clause. Congress is not empowered by it to make all laws, which may have relation to the powers conferred on the government, but only such as may be "necessary and proper" for carrying them into execution. The word "necessary" is considered as controlling the whole sentence, and as limiting the right to pass laws for the execution of the granted powers, to such as are indispensable, and without which the power would be nugatory. That it excludes the choice of means, and leaves to congress, in each case, that only which is most direct and simple.

Is it true, that this is the sense in which the word "necessary" is always used? Does it always import an absolute physical necessity, so strong, that one thing, to which another may be termed necessary, cannot exist without that other? We think it does not. If reference be had to its use, in the common affairs of the world, or in approved authors, we find that it frequently imports no more than that one thing is convenient, or useful, or essential to another. . . . A thing may be necessary, very necessary, absolutely or indispensably necessary. To no mind would the same idea be conveyed by these several phrases. This comment on the word is well illustrated by the passage cited at the bar, from the 10th section of the 1st article of the constitution. It is, we think, impossible to compare the sentence which prohibits a State from laying "imposts, or duties on imports or exports, except what may be absolutely necessary for executing its inspection laws," with that which authorizes congress "to make all laws which shall be necessary and proper for carrying into execution" the powers of the general government, without feeling a conviction, that the convention understood itself to change materially the meaning of the word "necessary" by prefixing the word "absolutely." This word, then, like others, is used in various senses; and, in its construction, the subject, the context, the intention of the person using them, are all to be taken into view.

Let this be done in the case under consideration. The subject is the execution of those great powers on which the welfare of a nation essentially depends. It must have been the intention of those who gave these powers, to insure, as far as human prudence could insure, their beneficial execution. This could not be done, by confining the choice of means to such narrow limits as not to leave it in the power of congress to adopt any which might be appropriate, and which were conducive to the end. This provision is made in a constitution, intended to endure for ages to come, and consequently, to be adapted to the various crises of human affairs. To have prescribed the means by which government should, in all future time, execute its powers, would have been to change, entirely, the character of the instrument, and give it the properties of a legal code. It would have been an unwise attempt to provide, by immutable rules, for exigencies which, if foreseen at all, must have been seen dimly, and which can be best provided for as they occur. To have declared, that the best means shall not be used, but those alone, without which the power given would be nugatory, would have been to deprive the legislature of the capacity to avail itself of experience, to exercise its reason, and to accommodate its legislation to circumstances. If we apply this principle of construction to any of the powers of the government, we shall find it so pernicious in its operation that we shall be compelled to discard it. [The Court here cites the law requiring an oath of office in addition to the oath prescribed by the Constitution.]

So, with respect to the whole penal code of the United States whence arises the power to punish, in cases not prescribed by the constitution? All admit, that the government may, legitimately, punish any violation of its laws; and yet, this is not among the enumerated powers of congress. . . .

The baneful influence of this narrow construction on all the operations of the government, and the absolute impracticability of maintaining it, without rendering the government incompetent to its great objects, might be illustrated by numerous examples drawn from the constitution, and from our laws. The good sense of the public has pronounced, without hesitation, that the power of punishment appertains to sovereignty, and may be exercised, whenever the sovereign has a right to act, as incidental to his constitutional powers. It is a means for carrying into execution all sovereign powers, and may be used, although not indispensably necessary. It is a right incidental to the power, and conducive to its beneficial exercise.

If this limited construction of the word "necessary" must be abandoned, in order to punish, whence is derived the rule which would reinstate it, when the government would carry its powers into execution, by means not vindictive in their nature? If the word "necessary" means "needful," "requisite," "essential," "conducive to," in order to let in the power of punishment for the infraction of law; why is it not equally comprehensive, when required to authorize the use of means which facilitate the execution of the powers of government, without the infliction of punishment? . . .

We admit, as all must admit, that the powers of the government are limited, and that its limits are not to be transcended. But we think the sound construction of the constitution must allow to the national legislature that discretion, with respect to the means by which the powers it confers are to be carried into execution, which will enable that body to perform the high duties assigned to it, in the manner most beneficial to the people. Let the end be legitimate, let it be within the scope of the constitution, and all means which are appropriate, which are plainly adapted to that end, which are not prohibited, but consist with the letter and spirit of the constitution, are constitutional.

That a corporation must be considered as a means not less usual, not of higher dignity, not more requiring a particular specification than other means, has been sufficiently proved. . . . If a corporation may be employed, indiscriminately with other means, to carry into execution the powers of the government, no particular reason can be assigned for excluding the use of a bank, if required for its fiscal operations. To use one, must be within the discretion of congress, if it be an appropriate mode of executing the powers of government. That it is a convenient, a useful, and essential instrument in the prosecution of its fiscal operations, is not now a subject of controversy. . . .

But were its necessity less apparent, none can deny its being an appropriate measure; and if it is, the degree of its necessity, as has been very justly observed, is to be discussed in another place. Should congress, in the execution of its powers, adopt measures which are prohibited by the constitution; or should congress, under the pretext of executing its powers, pass laws for the accomplishment of objects not intrusted to the government; it would become the painful duty of this tribunal, should a case requiring such a decision come before it, to say, that such an act was not the law of the land. But where the law is not prohibited, and is really calculated to effect any of the objects intrusted to the government, to undertake here to inquire into the degree of its necessity, would be to pass the line which circumscribes the judicial department, and to tread on legislative ground. This court disclaims all pretensions to such a power.

After this declaration, it can scarcely be necessary to say, that the existence of state banks can have no possible influence on the question. No trace is to be found in the constitution of an intention to create a dependence of the government of the Union on those of the states, for the execution of the great powers assigned to it. Its means are adequate to its ends; and on those means alone was it expected to rely for the accomplishment of its ends. To impose on it the necessity of resorting to means which it cannot control, which another government may furnish or withhold, would render its course precarious, the result of its measures uncertain, and create a dependence on other governments, which might disappoint its most important designs, and is incompatible with the language of the constitution. But were it otherwise, the choice of means implies a right to choose a national bank in preference to state banks, and congress alone can make the election.

After the most deliberate consideration, it is the unanimous and decided opinion of this court, that the act to incorporate the Bank of the United States is a law made in pursuance of the constitution, and is a part of the supreme law of the land.

The branches, proceeding from the same stock, and being conducive to the complete accomplishment of the object, are equally constitutional.

[The remainder of the case deals with the power of the state of Maryland to tax the bank.]

Topic 13

THE COMMERCE POWER

A RESTRICTED VIEW

[In 1933 Congress passed the National Industrial Recovery Act. In signing the bill President Roosevelt said, "History probably will record the National Industrial Recovery Act as the most important and far-reaching legislation ever enacted by the American Congress." The purpose of the law according to the President was to promote re-employment, to shorten hours and increase wages, and to prevent unfair competition.

The first section of the act attempted to provide a constitutional basis for the legislation, stating:

"Section 1. A national emergency productive of widespread unemployment and disorganization of industry, which burdens interstate and foreign commerce, affects the public welfare, and undermines the standards of living of the American people, is hereby declared to exist. It is hereby declared to be the policy of Congress to remove obstructions to the free flow of interstate and foreign commerce which tend to diminish the amount thereof; and to provide for the general welfare by promoting the organization of industry for the purpose of cooperative action among trade groups, to induce and maintain united action of labor and management under adequate competitive practices, to promote the fullest possible utilization of the present productive capacity of industries, to avoid restriction of production (except as may be temporarily required), to increase the consumption of industrial and agricultural products by increasing purchasing power, to reduce and relieve unemployment, to improve standards of labor, and otherwise to rehabilitate industry and to conserve natural resources."

On May 27, 1935 the Supreme Court in a unanimous opinion declared the National Industrial Recovery Act unconstitutional on the grounds that (1), it "attempted delegation of legislative power" and (2), it "attempted regulation of intrastate transactions which affect interstate commerce only indirectly."]

SCHECHTER POULTRY CORP. V. UNITED STATES *

[The Schechter Poultry Corporation conducted a wholesale poultry slaughterhouse market in Brooklyn. It ordinarily purchased live poultry from commission men in New York City or at the railroad terminals and after slaughtering the poultry sold it to retail dealers and butchers. The Court stated that "New York City is the largest live-poultry market in the United States. Ninety-six per cent of the live poultry there marketed comes from other States." However, "Defendants do not sell poultry in interstate commerce."]

MR. CHIEF JUSTICE HUGHES delivered the opinion of the court.

(1) Were these transactions *"in"* interstate commerce? Much is made of the fact that almost all the poultry coming to New York is sent there from other States. . . . Neither the slaughtering nor the sales by defendants were transactions in interstate commerce. . . . So far as the poultry here in question is concerned, the flow in interstate commerce had

* 295 U.S. 495 (1935).

ceased. The poultry had come to a permanent rest within the State. . . .

(2) Did the defendants' transaction directly *"affect"* interstate commerce so as to be subject to federal regulation? . . . In determining how far the federal government may go in controlling intrastate transactions upon the ground that they "affect" interstate commerce, there is a necessary and well-established distinction between direct and indirect effects. The precise line can be drawn only as individual cases arise, but the distinction is clear in principle. . . . [And] where the effect of intrastate transactions upon interstate commerce is merely indirect, such transactions remain within the domain of state power. . . .

The question of chief importance relates to the provision of the Code as to the hours and wages of those employed in defendants' slaughterhouse markets. It is plain that these requirements are imposed in order to govern the details of defendants' management of their local business. The persons employed in slaughtering and selling in local trade are not employed in interstate commerce. Their hours and wages have no direct relation to interstate commerce. . . . If the federal government may determine the wages and hours of employees in the internal commerce of a State, because of their relation to cost and prices and their indirect effect upon interstate commerce, it would seem that a similar control might be exerted over other elements of cost, also affecting prices, such as the number of employees, rents, advertising, methods of doing business, etc. All the processes of production and distribution that enter into cost could likewise be controlled. If the cost of doing an intrastate business is in itself the permitted object of federal control, the extent of the regulation of cost would be a question of discretion and not of power.

The government also makes the point that efforts to enact state legislation establishing high labor standards have been impeded by the belief that, unless similar action is taken generally, commerce will be diverted from the states adopting such standards, and that this fear of diversion has led to demands for federal legislation on the subject of wages and hours. The apparent implication is that the federal authority under the commerce clause should be deemed to extend to the establishment of rules to govern wages and hours in intrastate trade and industry generally throughout the country, thus overriding the authority of the states to deal with domestic problems arising from labor conditions in their internal commerce.

It is not the province of the Court to consider the economic advantages or disadvantages of such a centralized system. It is sufficient to say that the Federal Constitution does not provide for it. Our growth and development have called for wide use of the commerce power of the federal government in its control over the expanded activities of interstate commerce and in protecting that commerce from burdens, interferences, and conspiracies to restrain and monopolize it. But the authority of the federal government may not be pushed to such an extreme as to destroy the distinction, which the commerce clause itself establishes, between commerce "among the several States" and the internal concerns of a State. The same answer must be made to the contention that is based upon the serious economic situation which led to the passage of the Recovery Act,—the fall in prices, the decline in wages and employment, and the curtailment of the market for commodities. Stress is laid upon the great importance of maintaining wage distributions which would provide the necessary stimulus in starting "the cumulative forces making for expanding commercial activity." Without in any way disparaging this motive, it is enough to say that the recuperative efforts of the federal government must be made in a manner consistent with the authority granted by the Constitution.

[The portion of the opinion dealing with the "attempted delegation of legislative power" is omitted. The concurring opinion of Mr. Justice Cardozo is also omitted.]

An Expanded View

WICKARD, SECRETARY OF AGRICULTURE, V. FILBURN *

[The Agricultural Adjustment Act of 1938, as related to wheat, sought to control the volume moving in interstate and foreign commerce in order to avoid surpluses and shortages and consequent abnormalities of price and obstructions to commerce. The Act, as amended, provided procedures which resulted in the fixing of a market quota applicable to each farm and laid a penalty upon any excess brought to market by the farmer. The basic provision of this law was sustained in *Mulford* v. *Smith,* 307 U.S. 38 (1939).

The question in the instant case is whether Congress may constitutionally regulate *production* of wheat, not intended in any part for commerce, but wholly for *consumption* on the farm.]

MR. JUSTICE JACKSON delivered the opinion of the Court. . . .

[Filburn] says that this is a regulation of production and consumption of wheat. Such activities are, he urges, beyond the reach of congressional power under the commerce clause, since they are local in character, and their effects upon interstate commerce are at most "indirect." In answer the government argues that the statute regulates neither production nor consumption, but only marketing; and, in the alternative, that if the Act does go beyond the regulation of marketing it is sustainable as a "necessary and proper" implementation of the power of Congress over interstate commerce.

* 317 U.S. 111 (1942).

The government's concern lest the Act be held to be a regulation of production or consumption rather than of marketing is attributable to a few dicta and decisions of this Court which might be understood to lay it down that activities such as "production," "manufacturing," and "mining" are strictly "local" and, except in special circumstances which are not present here, cannot be regulated under the commerce power because their effects upon interstate commerce are, as matter of law, only "indirect." Even today, when this power has been held to have great latitude, there is no decision of this Court that such activities may be regulated where no part of the product is intended for interstate commerce or intermingled with the subjects thereof. We believe that a review of the course of decision under the commerce clause will make plain, however, that questions of the power of Congress are not to be decided by reference to any formula which would give controlling force to nomenclature such as "production" and "indirect" and foreclose consideration of the actual effects of the activity in question upon interstate commerce.

At the beginning Chief Justice Marshall described the federal commerce power with a breadth never yet exceeded. Gibbons *v.* Ogden, 9 Wheat. 1, 194, 195. He made emphatic the embracing and penetrating nature of this power by warning that effective restraints on its exercise must proceed from political rather than from judicial processes. 9 Wheat. at page 197.

For nearly a century, however, decisions of this Court under the commerce clause dealt rarely with questions of what Congress might do in the exercise of its granted power under the clause and almost entirely with the permissibility of state activity which it was claimed discriminated against or burdened interstate commerce. During this period there was perhaps little occasion for the affirmative exercise of the commerce power, and the influence of the clause on American life and law was a negative one, resulting almost wholly from its operation as a restraint upon the powers of the states. In discussion and decision the point of reference instead of being what was "necessary and proper" to the exercise by Congress of its granted power, was often some concept of sovereignty thought to be implicit in the status of statehood. Certain activities such as "production," "manufacturing," and "mining" were occasionally said to be within the province of state governments and beyond the power of Congress under the commerce clause.

It was not until 1887 with the enactment of the Interstate Commerce Act that the interstate commerce power began to exert positive influence in American law and life. This first important federal resort to the commerce power was followed in 1890 by the Sherman Anti-Trust Act and, thereafter, mainly after 1903, by many others. These statutes ushered in new phases of adjudication, which required the Court to approach the interpretation of the commerce clause in the light of an actual exercise by Congress of its power thereunder.

When it first dealt with this new legislation, the Court adhered to its earlier pronouncements, and allowed but little scope to the power of Congress. United States *v.* E. C. Knight Co., 156 U.S. 1. These earlier pronouncements also played an important part in several of the five cases in which this Court later held that acts of Congress under the commerce clause were in excess of its power.

Even while important opinions in this line of restrictive authority were being written, however, other cases called forth broader interpretations of the commerce clause destined to supersede the earlier ones, and to bring about a return to the principles first enunciated by Chief Justice Marshall in Gibbons *v.* Ogden, *supra.*

Not long after the decision of United States *v.* E. C. Knight Co., *supra,* Mr. Justice Holmes, in sustaining the exercise of national power over intrastate activity, stated for the Court that "commerce among the states is not a technical legal conception, but a practical one, drawn from the course of business." Swift & Co. *v.* United States, 196 U.S. 375, 398. It was soon demonstrated that the effects of many kinds of intrastate activity upon interstate commerce were such as to make them a proper subject of federal regulation. In some cases sustaining the exercise of federal power over intrastate matters the term "direct" was used for the purpose of stating, rather than of reaching, a result; in others it was treated as synonymous with "substantial" or "material"; and in others it was not used at all. Of late its use has been abandoned in cases dealing with questions of federal power under the commerce clause.

In the Shreveport Rate Cases (Houston, E. & W. T. R. Co. *v.* United States), 234 U.S. 342, the Court held that railroad rates of an admittedly intrastate character and fixed by authority of the state might, nevertheless, be revised by the federal government because of the economic effects which they had upon interstate commerce. The opinion of Mr. Justice Hughes found federal intervention constitutionally authorized because of "matters having such a close and substantial relation to interstate traffic that the control is essential or appropriate to the security of that traffic, to the efficiency of the interstate service, and to the maintenance of the conditions under which interstate commerce may be conducted upon fair terms and without molestation or hindrance." 234 U.S. at page 351.

The Court's recognition of the relevance of the economic effects in the application of the commerce clause exemplified by this statement has made the mechanical application of legal formulas no longer feasible. Once an economic measure of the reach of the power granted to Congress in the commerce clause is accepted, questions of federal power cannot be decided simply by finding the activity in question to be "production" nor can consideration of its economic effects be foreclosed by calling them "indirect." The present Chief Justice has said in summary of the present state of the law: "The commerce power is not confined in its exercise to the regulation of commerce among the states. It extends to those activities intrastate which so affect interstate commerce or the exertion of the power of Congress over it, as to make regulation of them appropriate means to the attainment of a legitimate end, the effective execution of the granted power to regulate interstate commerce. . . . The power of Congress over interstate commerce is plenary and complete in itself, may be exercised to its utmost extent, and acknowledges no limitations other than are prescribed in the Constitution. . . . It follows that no form of state activity can constitutionally thwart the regulatory power granted by the commerce clause to Congress. Hence the reach of that power extends to those intrastate activities which in a substantial way interfere with or obstruct the exercise of the granted power." United States *v.* Wrightwood Dairy Co., 315 U.S. 110, 119.

Whether the subject of the regulation in question was "production," "consumption," or "marketing" is, therefore, not material for purposes of deciding the question of federal power before us. That an activity is of local character may help in a doubtful case to determine whether Congress intended to reach it. The same consideration might help in determining whether in the absence of congressional action it would be permissible for the state to exert its power on the subject matter, even though in so doing it to some degree affected interstate commerce. But even if appellant's activity be local and though it may not be regarded as commerce, it may still, whatever its nature, be reached by Congress if it exerts a substantial economic effect on interstate commerce and this irrespective of whether such effect is what might at some earlier time have been defined as "direct" or "indirect."

The parties have stipulated a summary of the economics of the wheat industry. Commerce among the states in wheat is large and important. Although wheat is raised in every state but one, production in most states is not equal to consumption. Sixteen states on average have had a surplus of wheat above their own requirements for feed, seed, and food. Thirty-two states and the District of Columbia, where production has been below consumption, have looked to these surplus-producing states for their supply as well as for wheat for export and carryover.

The wheat industry has been a problem industry for some years. Largely as a result of increased foreign production and import restrictions, annual exports of wheat and flour from the United States during the ten-year period ending in 1940 averaged less than 10 percent of total production, while during the 1920's they averaged more than 25 percent. The decline in the export trade has left a large surplus in production which in connection with an abnormally large supply of wheat and other grains in recent years caused congestion in a number of markets; tied up railroad cars; and caused elevators in some instances to turn away grains, and railroads to institute embargoes to prevent further congestion. . . .

In the absence of regulation the price of wheat in the United States would be much affected by world conditions. During 1941 producers who cooperated with the Agricultural Adjustment program received an average price on the farm of about $1.16 a bushel as compared with the world market price of 40 cents a bushel. . . .

The effect of consumption of home-grown wheat on interstate commerce is due to the fact that it constitutes the most variable factor in the disappearance of the wheat crop. Consumption on the farm where grown appears to vary in an amount greater than 20 percent of average production. The total amount of wheat consumed as food varies but relatively little, and use as seed is relatively constant.

The maintenance by government regulation of a price for wheat undoubtedly can be accomplished as effectively by sustaining or increasing the demand as by limiting the supply. The effect of the statute before us is to restrict the amount which may be produced for market and the extent as well to which one may forestall resort to the market by producing to meet his own needs. That [Filburn's] own contribution to the demand for wheat may be trivial by itself is not enough to remove him from the scope of federal regulation where, as here, his contribution, taken together with that of many others similarly situated, is far from trivial. National Labor Relations Board *v.* Fainblatt, 306 U.S. 601, 606, *et seq.*, 307 U.S. 609; United States *v.* Darby, *supra,* 312 U.S. at page 123.

It is well established by decisions of this Court that the power to regulate commerce includes the power to regulate the prices at which commodities in that commerce are dealt in and practices affecting such prices. One of the primary purposes of the Act in question was to increase the market price of wheat and to that end to limit the volume thereof that could affect the market. It can hardly be denied that a factor of such volume and variability as home consumed wheat would have a substantial influence on price and market conditions. This may arise because being in marketable condition such wheat overhangs the market and, if induced by rising prices, tends to flow into the market and check price increases. But if we assume that it is never marketed, it supplies a need of the man who grew it which would otherwise be reflected by purchases in the open market. Home-grown wheat in this sense competes with wheat in commerce. The stimulation of commerce is a use of the regulatory function quite as definitely as prohibitions or restrictions thereon. This record leaves us in no doubt that Congress may properly have considered that wheat consumed on the farm where grown if wholly outside the scheme of regulation would have a substantial effect in defeating and obstructing its purpose to stimulate trade therein at increased prices. . . .

Reversed.

Topic 14

THE POLICE POWER

A Restricted View

ADKINS V. CHILDREN'S HOSPITAL *

[The question raised by appeal to the Supreme Court was the constitutionality of the Act of Congress of September 19, 1918, providing for the creation *in the District of Columbia* of a Minimum Wage Board to investigate, among others, the wages paid women in varying occupations and to declare "standards of minimum wages for women in any occupation in the District of Columbia, and what wages are inadequate to supply the necessary cost of living to any such women workers to maintain them in good health and to protect their morals." Employers were forbidden under penalty of law to employ women at wages lower than those fixed by the Board.]

MR. JUSTICE SUTHERLAND delivered the opinion of the court.

This court, by an unbroken line of decisions from Chief Justice Marshall to the present day, has steadily adhered to the rule that every possible presumption is in favor of the validity of an act of Congress until overcome beyond rational doubt. But, if by clear and indubitable demonstration a statute be opposed to the Constitution, we have no choice but to say so. . . .

The statute now under consideration is attacked upon the ground that it authorizes an unconstitutional interference with the freedom of contract included within the guaranties of the due process clause of the Fifth Amendment. That the right to contract about one's affairs is a part of the liberty of the individual protected by this clause is settled by the decisions of this Court and is no longer open to question. [Authorities.] Within this liberty are contracts of employment of labor. In making such contracts, generally speaking, the parties have an equal right to obtain from each other the best terms they can as the result of private bargaining. . . .

There is, of course, no such thing as absolute freedom of contract. It is subject to a great variety of restraints. But freedom of contract is, nevertheless, the general rule and restraint the exception; and the exercise of legislative authority to abridge it can be justified only by the existence of exceptional circumstances. Whether these circumstances exist in the present case constitutes the question to be answered. It will be helpful to this end to review some of the decisions where the interference has been upheld and consider the grounds upon which they rest. [Here follows an elaborate review of the decisions.]

* 261 U.S. 525 (1923).

If now, in the light furnished by the foregoing exceptions to the general rule forbidding legislative interference with freedom of contract, we examine and analyze the statute in question, we shall see that it differs from them in every material respect. It is not a law dealing with any business charged with a public interest, or with public work, or to meet and tide over a temporary emergency. It has nothing to do with the character, methods or periods of wage payments. It does not prescribe hours of labor or conditions under which labor is to be done. It is not for the protection of persons under legal disability or for the prevention of fraud. It is simply and exclusively a price-fixing law, confined to adult women (for we are not now considering the provisions relating to minors), who are legally as capable of contracting for themselves as men. It forbids two parties having lawful capacity—under penalties as to the employer—to freely contract with one another in respect of the price for which one shall render service to the other in a purely private employment where both are willing, perhaps anxious, to agree, even though the consequence may be to oblige one to surrender a desirable engagement and the other to dispense with the services of a desirable employee. . . .

The standard furnished by the statute for the guidance of the board is so vague as to be impossible of practical application with any reasonable degree of accuracy. What is sufficient to supply the necessary cost of living for a woman worker and maintain her in good health and protect her morals is obviously not a precise or unvarying sum—not even approximately so. The amount will depend upon a variety of circumstances: the individual temperament, habits of thrift, care, ability to buy necessaries intelligently, and whether the woman live alone or with her family. . . . The relation between earnings and morals is not capable of standardization. It cannot be shown that well paid women safeguard their morals more carefully than those who are poorly paid. Morality rests upon other considerations than wages; and there is, certainly, no such prevalent connection between the two as to justify a broad attempt to adjust the latter with reference to the former. As a means of safeguarding morals the attempted classification, in our opinion, is without reasonable basis. No distinction can be made between women who work for others and those who do not; nor is there ground for distinction between women and men, for, certainly, if women require a minimum wage to preserve their morals men require it to preserve their honesty. For these reasons, and others which might be stated, the inquiry in respect of the necessary cost of living and of the income necessary to preserve health and morals, presents an individual and not a composite question, and must be answered for each individual considered by herself and not by a general formula prescribed by a statutory bureau. . . .

The law takes account of the necessities of only one party to the contract. It ignores the necessities of the employer by compelling him to pay not less than a certain sum, not only whether the employee is capable of earning it, but irrespective of the ability of his business to sustain the burden, generously leaving him, of course, the privilege of abandoning his business as an alternative for going on at a loss. Within the limits of the minimum sum, he is precluded, under penalty of fine and imprisonment, from adjusting compensation to the differing merits of his employees. It compels him to pay at least the sum fixed in any event, because the employee needs it, but requires no service of equivalent value from the employee. It therefore undertakes to solve but one-half of the problem. The other half is the establishment of a corresponding standard of efficiency, and this forms no part of the policy of the legislation, although in practice the former half without the latter must lead to ultimate failure, in accordance with the inexorable law that no one can continue indefinitely to take out more than he puts in without ultimately exhausting the supply. The law is not confined to the great and powerful employers but embraces those whose bargaining power may be as weak as that of the employee. It takes no account of periods of stress and business depression, of crippling losses, which may leave the employer himself without adequate means of livelihood. To the extent that the sum fixed exceeds the fair value of the services rendered, it amounts to a compulsory exaction from the employer for the support of a partially indigent person, for whose condition there rests upon him no peculiar responsibility, and therefore, in effect, arbitrarily shifts to his shoulders a burden which, if it belongs to anybody, belongs to society as a whole.

The feature of this statute which perhaps more than any other, puts upon it the stamp of invalidity is that it exacts from the employer an arbitrary payment for a purpose and upon a basis having no causal connection with his business, or the contract or the work the employee engages to do. The declared basis, as already pointed out, is not the value of the service rendered but the extraneous circumstances that the employee needs to get a prescribed sum of money to insure her subsistence, health and morals. . . . In principle, there can be no difference between the case of selling labor and the case of selling goods. If one goes to the butcher, the baker or grocer to buy food, he is morally entitled to obtain the worth of his money but he is not entitled to more. If what he gets is worth what he pays he is not justified in demanding more simply because he needs more; and the shopkeeper, having dealt fairly and honestly in that transaction, is not concerned in any peculiar sense with the question of his customer's necessities. Should a statute undertake to vest in a commission power to determine the quantity of food necessary for individual support and require the shopkeeper, if he sell to the individual at all, to furnish that quantity at not more than a fixed maximum, it would undoubtedly fall before the constitutional test. The fallacy of any argument in support of the validity of such a statute would be quickly exposed. The argument in support of that now being considered is equally fallacious, though the weakness of it may not be so plain. A statute requiring an employer to pay in money, to pay at prescribed and regular intervals, to pay the value of the services rendered, even to pay with fair relation to the extent of the benefit obtained from the service, would be understandable. But a statute which prescribes payment without regard to any of these things and solely with relation to circumstances apart from the contract of employment, the business affected by it and the work done under it, is so clearly the product of a naked, arbitrary exercise of power that it cannot be allowed to stand under the Constitution of the United States.

We are asked, upon the one hand, to consider the fact that several States have adopted similar statutes, and we are invited, upon the other hand, to give weight to the fact that three times as many States, presumably as well informed and as anxious to promote the health and morals of their people, have refrained from enacting such legislation. We have also been furnished with a large number of printed opinions approving the policy of the minimum wage, and our own reading has disclosed a large number of the contrary. These are all proper enough for the consideration of the lawmaking bodies, since their tendency is to establish the desirability or undesirability of the legislation; but they reflect no legitimate light upon the question of its validity, and that is what we are called upon to decide. The elucidation of that question cannot be aided by counting heads. . . .

Finally, it may be said that if, in the interest of the public welfare, the police power may be invoked to justify the fixing of a minimum wage, it may, when the public welfare is thought to require it, be invoked to justify a maximum wage. The power to fix high wages connotes, by like reasoning, the power to fix low wages. If, in the face of the guaranties of the Fifth Amendment, this form of legislation shall be legally justified, the field for the operation of the police power will have been widened to a great and dangerous degree. If, for example, in the opinion of future lawmakers, wages in the building trades shall become so high as to preclude people of ordinary means from building and owning homes, an authority which sustains the minimum wage will be invoked to support a maximum wage for building laborers and artisans, and the same argument which has been here urged to strip the employer of his constitutional liberty of contract in one direction will be utilized to strip the employee of his constitutional liberty of contract in the opposite direction. A wrong decision does not end with itself; it is a precedent, and, with the swing of sentiment, its bad influence may run from one extremity of the arc to the other.

It has been said that legislation of the kind now under review is required in the interest of social justice, for whose ends freedom of contract may lawfully be subjected to restraint. The liberty of the individual to do as he pleases, even in innocent matters, is not absolute. It must frequently yield to the common good, and the line beyond which the power of interference may not be pressed is neither definite nor unalterable but may be made to move, within limits not well defined, with changing need and circumstance. Any attempt to fix a rigid boundary would be unwise and futile. But, nevertheless, there are limits to the power, and when these have been passed, it becomes the plain duty of the courts in the proper exercise of their authority to so declare. To sustain the individual freedom of action contemplated by the Constitution, is not to strike down the common good but to exalt it; for surely the good of society as a whole cannot be better served than by the preservation against abritrary restraint of the liberties of its constituent members.

It follows from what has been said that the act in question passes the limit prescribed by the Constitution, and, accordingly, the decrees of the court below are affirmed.

[Mr. Justice Brandeis took no part in the consideration or decision of this case.]

[The dissenting opinion of Chief Justice Taft, with which Mr. Justice Sanford concurred, is omitted.]

MR. JUSTICE HOLMES, dissenting.

I confess that I do not understand the principle on which the power to fix a minimum for the wages of women can be denied by those who admit the power to fix a maximum for their hours of work. I fully assent to the proposition that here as elsewhere the distinctions of the law are distinctions of degree, but I perceive no difference in the kind or degree of interference with liberty, the only matter with which we have any concern, between the one case and the other. The bargain is equally affected whichever half you regulate. Muller v. Oregon, I take it, is as good law today as it was in 1908. It will need more than the Nineteenth Amendment to convince me that there are no differences between men and women, or that legislation cannot take those differences into account. I should not hesitate to take them into account if I thought it necessary to sustain this act. . . .

This statute does not compel anybody to pay anything. It simply forbids employment at rates below those fixed as the minimum requirement of health and right living. It is safe to assume that women will not be employed at even the lowest wages allowed unless they earn them, or unless the employer's business can sustain the burden. . . .

The criterion of constitutionality is not whether we believe the law to be for the public good. We certainly cannot be prepared to deny that a reasonable man reasonably might have that belief in view of the legislation of Great Britain, Victoria and a number of the States of this Union. The belief is fortified by a very remarkable collection of documents submitted on behalf of the appellants, material here, I conceive, only as showing that the belief reasonably may be held. In Australia the power to fix a minimum for wages in the case of industrial disputes extending beyond the limits of any one State was given to a Court, and its President wrote a most interesting account of its operation. 29 Harv. Law Rev. 13. If a legislature should adopt what he thinks the doctrine of modern economists of all schools, that "freedom of contract is a misnomer as applied to a contract between an employer and an ordinary individual employee," ibid. 25, I could not pronounce an opinion with which I agree impossible to be entertained by reasonable men. If the same legislature should accept his further opinion that industrial peace was best attained by the device of a Court having the above powers, I should not feel myself able to contradict it, or to deny that the end justified restrictive legislation quite as adequately as beliefs concerning Sunday or exploded theories about usury. I should have my doubts, as I have them about this statute—but they would be whether the bill that has to be paid for every gain, although hidden as interstitial detriments, was not greater than the gain was worth: a matter that it is not for me to decide.

I am of opinion that the statute is valid and that the decree should be reversed.

AN EXPANDED VIEW

WEST COAST HOTEL COMPANY V. PARRISH *

MR. CHIEF JUSTICE HUGHES delivered the opinion of the court.

This case presents the question of the constitutional validity of the minimum wage law of the State of Washington.

The Act, entitled "Minimum Wages for Women," authorizes the fixing of minimum wages for women and minors. Laws of 1913 (Washington) chap. 174; Remington's Rev. Stat. (1932), §§7623 *et seq.* It provides:

"Section 1. The welfare of the State of Washington demands that women and minors be protected from conditions of labor which have a pernicious effect on their health and morals. The State of Washington, therefore, exercising herein its police and sovereign power declares that inadequate wages and unsanitary conditions of labor exert such pernicious effect.

"Sec. 2. It shall be unlawful to employ women or minors in any industry or occupation within the State of Washington under conditions of labor detrimental to their health or morals; and it shall be unlawful to employ women workers in any industry within the State of Washington at wages which are not adequate for their maintenance.

"Sec. 3. There is hereby created a commission to be known as the 'Industrial Welfare Commission' for the State of Washington, to establish such standards of wages and conditions of labor for women and minors employed within the State of Washington, as shall be held hereunder to be reasonable

* 300 U.S. 379 (1937).

and not detrimental to health and morals, and which shall be sufficient for the decent maintenance of women." . . .

The appellant conducts a hotel. The appellee Elsie Parrish was employed as a chambermaid and (with her husband) brought this suit to recover the difference between the wages paid her and the minimum wage fixed pursuant to the state law. The minimum wage was $14.50 per week of 48 hours. The appellant challenged the act as repugnant to the due process clause of the Fourteenth Amendment of the Constitution of the United States.

[Here follows comment on *Morehead* v. *New York* ex rel. *Tipaldo,* 298 U.S. 587, and other minimum wage decisions.]

The principle which must control our decision is not in doubt. The constitutional provision invoked is the due process clause of the Fourteenth Amendment governing the States, as the due process clause invoked in the Adkins Case governed Congress. In each case the violation alleged by those attacking minimum wage regulation for women is deprivation of freedom of contract. What is this freedom? The Constitution does not speak of freedom of contract. It speaks of liberty and prohibits the deprivation of liberty without due process of law. In prohibiting that deprivation the Constitution does not recognize an absolute and uncontrollable liberty. Liberty in each of its phases has its history and connotation. But the liberty safeguarded is liberty in a social organization which requires the protection of law against the evils which menace the health, safety, morals and welfare of the people. Liberty under the Constitution is thus necessarily subject to the restraints of due process, and regulation which is reasonable in relation to its subject and is adopted in the interests of the community is due process.

This essential limitation of liberty in general governs freedom of contract in particular. More than twenty-five years ago we set forth the applicable principle in these words, after referring to the cases where the liberty guaranteed by the Fourteenth Amendment had been broadly described:

"But it was recognized in the cases cited, as in many others, that freedom of contract is a qualified and not an absolute right. There is no absolute freedom to do as one wills or to contract as one chooses. The guaranty of liberty does not withdraw from legislative supervision that wide department of activity which consists of the making of contracts, or deny to government the power to provide restrictive safeguards. Liberty implies the absence of arbitrary restraint, not immunity from reasonable regulations and prohibitions imposed in the interests of the community." *Chicago, B. & Q. R. Co.* v. *McGuire,* 219 U.S. 549, 567.

This power under the Constitution to restrict freedom of contract has had many illustrations. That it may be exercised in the public interest with respect to contracts between employer and employee is undeniable. . . .

The point that has been strongly stressed that adult employees should be deemed competent to make their own contracts was decisively met nearly forty years ago in *Holden* v. *Hardy,* 169 U.S. 366, where we pointed out the inequality in the footing of the parties. We said (*Id.,* 397): "The legislature has also recognized the fact, which the experience of legislators in many States has corroborated, that the proprietors of these establishments and their operatives do not stand upon an equality, and that their interests are, to a certain extent, conflicting. The former naturally desire to obtain as much labor as possible from their employees, while the latter are often induced by the fear of discharge to conform to regulations which their judgment, fairly exercised, would pronounce to be detrimental to their health or strength. In other words, the proprietors lay down the rules and the laborers are practically constrained to obey them. In such cases self-interest is often an unsafe guide, and the legislature may properly interpose its authority." . . .

It is manifest that this established principle is peculiarly applicable in relation to the employment of women in whose protection the State has a special interest. That phase of the subject received elaborate consideration in *Muller* v. *Oregon* (1908), 208 U.S. 412, where the constitutional authority of the State to limit the working hours of women was sustained. We emphasized the consideration that "woman's physical structure and the performance of maternal functions place her at a disadvantage in the struggle for subsistence" and that her physical well-being "becomes an object of public interest and care in order to preserve the strength and vigor of the race." . . .

This array of precedents and the principles they applied were thought by the dissenting Justices in the *Adkins* case to demand that the minimum wage statute be sustained. The validity of the distinction made by the Court between a minimum wage and a maximum of hours in limiting liberty of contract was especially challenged. 261 U.S., p. 564. That challenge persists and is without any satisfactory answer. . . .

[The court here quotes from the dissenting opinions of Justice Holmes and of Chief Justice Taft in the *Adkins* case.]

We think that the views thus expressed are sound and that the decision in the *Adkins* case was a departure from the true application of the principles governing the regulation by the State of the relation of employer and employed. Those principles have been reenforced by our subsequent decisions. [Case references are omitted.]

With full recognition of the earnestness and vigor which characterize the prevailing opinion in the *Adkins* case, we find it impossible to reconcile that ruling with these well-considered declarations. What can be closer to the public interest than the health of women and their protection from unscrupulous and overreaching employers? And if the protection of women is a legitimate end of the exercise of state power, how can it be said that the requirement of the payment of a minimum wage fairly fixed in order to meet the very necessities of existence is not an admissible means to that end? The legislature of the State was clearly entitled to consider the situation of women in employment, the fact that they are in the class receiving the least pay, that their bargaining power is relatively weak, and that they are the ready victims of those who would take advantage of their necessitous circumstances. The legislature was entitled to adopt measures to reduce the evils of the "sweating system," the exploiting of workers at wages so low as to be insufficient to meet the bare cost of living, thus making their very helplessness the occasion of a most injurious competition. The legislature had the right to consider that its minimum wage requirements would be an important aid in carrying out its policy of protection. The adoption of similar requirements by many States evidences a deep-seated conviction both as to the presence of the evil and as to the means adapted to check it. Legislative response to that conviction cannot be regarded as arbitrary or capricious, and that is all we have to decide. Even if the wisdom of the policy be regarded as debatable and its effects uncertain, still the legislature is entitled to its judgment.

There is an additional and compelling consideration which recent economic experience has brought into a strong light. The exploitation of a class of workers who are in an unequal position with respect to bargaining power and are thus relatively defenceless against the denial of a living wage is not only detrimental to their health and well-being but casts a direct burden for their support upon the community. What these workers lose in wages the taxpayers are called upon to pay. The bare cost of living must be met. We may take judicial notice of the unparalleled demands for relief which arose during the recent period of depression and still continue to an alarming extent despite the degree of economic recovery which has been achieved. It is unnecessary to cite official statistics to establish what is of common knowledge through the length and breadth of the land. While in the instant case no factual brief has been presented, there is no reason to doubt that the State of Washington has encountered the same social problem that is present elsewhere. The community is not bound to provide what is in effect a subsidy for unconscionable employers. The community may direct its law-making power to correct the abuse which springs from their selfish disregard of the public interest. The argument that the legislation in question constitutes an arbitrary discrimination, because it does not extend to men, is unavailing. This Court has frequently held that the legislative authority, acting within its proper field, is not bound to extend its regulation to all cases which it might possibly reach. The legislature "is free to recognize degrees of harm and it may confine its restrictions to those classes of cases where the need is deemed to be clearest." If "the law presumably hits the evil where it is most felt, it is not to be overthrown because there are other instances to which it might have been applied." There is no "doctrinaire requirement" that the legislation should be couched in all embracing terms. [Case references are omitted.] This familiar principle has repeatedly been applied to legislation which singles out women, and particular classes of women, in the exercise of the State's protective power. [Case references are omitted.] The relative need in the presence of the evil, no less than the existence of the evil itself, is a matter for the legislative judgment.

Our conclusion is that the case of *Adkins* v. *Children's Hospital,* 261 U.S. 525, should be, and it is, overruled. The judgment of the Supreme Court of the State of Washington is affirmed.

MR. JUSTICE SUTHERLAND, dissenting:

MR. JUSTICE VAN DEVANTER, MR. JUSTICE MCREYNOLDS, MR. JUSTICE BUTLER and I think the judgment of the court below should be reversed.

The principles and authorities relied upon to sustain the judgment, were considered in *Adkins* v. *Children's Hospital,* 261 U.S. 525, and *Morehead* v. *New York* ex rel. *Tipaldo,* 298 U.S. 587; and their lack of application to cases like the one in hand was pointed out. A sufficient answer to all that is now said will be found in the opinions of the court in those cases. Nevertheless, in the circumstances, it seems well to restate our reasons and conclusions. [The restatement is omitted.]

SECTION III

What Limits on Free Speech?

The age which acclaimed the Declaration of Independence and added a Bill of Rights to the Federal Constitution considered freedom of opinion one of the great natural rights which governments were instituted to protect. It believed that this sacred and inalienable right could not be justly impaired by any state, even with the consent of the majority. (See the definition of democracy by former Secretary of State Marshall, pp. 23–24). Today "the Laws of Nature and of Nature's God" seem to have less influence on "the opinions of mankind," and the case for freedom of opinion must find a more rational and pragmatic basis.

Most Americans would readily agree with the writers who maintain that freedom of speech is fundamental to the democratic process. Too few, however, adequately comprehend *why* freedom of speech is indispensable to our way of life. Why should the majority tolerate the propagation of minority doctrines which the majority regards as false, and even loathsome?

The words of the First Amendment are absolute and unqualified: "Congress shall make *no* law . . . abridging the freedom of speech, or of the press. . . ." If taken literally this would seem to prohibit *all* legislation by Congress which in any degree interferes with freedom of expression. However, no serious thinker has ever contended that freedom of speech is, or should be, entirely unlimited.

Should freedom of speech include the right to advocate revolution and dictatorship? Should those who seek to destroy freedom of speech and democracy be allowed to take advantage of the very democratic liberties which they would deny to others? This is one of the great dilemmas which democracy faces, and it has been the subject of a number of important Supreme Court decisions.

Schenck v. *United States* was the first important judicial decision on freedom of speech in war time. The so-called "clear and present danger" test, first enunciated in this case—although not always followed by the Supreme Court, especially in the years immediately following this decision—is today the cornerstone of most contemporary judicial discussion of freedom of speech.

In the case of *Gitlow* v. *New York,* decided in 1925, the majority of the Supreme Court in sustaining the Criminal Anarchy law of New York said:

"A single revolutionary spark may kindle a fire that, smouldering for a time, may burst into a sweeping and destructive conflagration. It cannot be said that the State is acting arbitrarily or unreasonably when in the exercise of its judgment as to the measures necessary to protect the public peace and safety, it seeks to extinguish the spark without waiting until it has enkindled the flame or blazed into the conflagration."

The dissent of Justice Holmes regarded this decision as a departure from the clear and present danger test enunciated in the *Schenck* case. He said:

"If what I think the correct test is applied it is manifest that there was no present danger of an attempt to overthrow the government by force on the part of the admittedly small minority who shared the defendant's view. . . . Whatever may be thought of the redundant discourse before us, it had no chance of starting a present conflagration."

Dennis v. *United States,* which arose out of the trial of eleven Communist Party leaders, involves a reconsideration of freedom of speech in the light of the present international situation.

Topic 15

THE DILEMMA OF FREEDOM

"Free Trade in Ideas"

*Justice Oliver Wendell Holmes, Jr.**

Persecution for the expression of opinions seems to me perfectly logical. If you have no doubt of your premises or your power and want a certain result with all your heart you naturally express your wishes in law and sweep away all opposition. To allow opposition by speech seems to indicate that you think the speech impotent, as when a man says that he has squared the circle, or that you do not care wholeheartedly for the result, or that you doubt either your power or your premises. But when men have realized that time has upset many fighting faiths, they may come to believe even more than they believe the very foundations of their own conduct that the ultimate good desired is better reached by free trade in ideas—that the best test of truth is the power of the thought to get itself accepted in the competition of the market, and that truth is the only ground upon which their wishes safely can be carried out. That, at any rate, is the theory of our Constitution. It is an experiment, as all life is an experiment. Every year if not every day we have to wager our salvation upon some prophecy based upon imperfect knowledge. While that experiment is part of our system I think that we should be eternally vigilant against attempts to check

* The selection is from his dissenting opinion in *Abrams* v. *United States,* 250 U.S. 616, 624 (1919).

the expression of opinions that we loathe and believe to be fraught with death, unless they so imminently threaten immediate interference with the lawful and pressing purposes of the law that an immediate check is required to save the country. I wholly disagree with the argument of the Government that the First Amendment left the common law as to seditious libel in force. History seems to me against the notion. I had conceived that the United States through many years had shown its repentance for the Sedition Act of 1798 by repaying fines that it imposed. Only the emergency that makes it immediately dangerous to leave the correction of evil counsels to time warrants making any exception to the sweeping command, "Congress shall make no law . . . abridging the freedom of speech." Of course I am speaking only of expressions of opinion and exhortations, which were all that were uttered here, but I regret that I cannot put into more impressive words my belief that in their conviction upon this indictment the defendants were deprived of their rights under the Constitution of the United States.

Who Is Loyal to America?

Henry Steele Commager *

On May 6 a Russian-born girl, Mrs. Shura Lewis, gave a talk to the students of the Western High School of Washington, D.C. She talked about Russia—its school system, its public health program, the position of women, of the aged, of the workers, the farmers, and the professional classes—and compared, superficially and uncritically, some American and Russian social institutions. The most careful examination of the speech—happily reprinted for us in the *Congressional Record*—does not disclose a single disparagement of anything American unless it is a quasi-humorous reference to the cost of having a baby and of dental treatment in this country. Mrs. Lewis said nothing that had not been said a thousand times, in speeches, in newspapers, magazines, and books. She said nothing that any normal person could find objectionable.

Her speech, however, created a sensation. A few students walked out on it. Others improvised placards proclaiming their devotion to Americanism. Indignant mothers telephoned their protests. Newspapers took a strong stand against the outrage. Congress, rarely concerned for the political or economic welfare of the citizens of the capital city, reacted sharply when its intellectual welfare was at stake. . . . Mr. Danowsky,

* Professor of History at Columbia University. Author of *The American Mind*. Co-author of *The Growth of the American Republic, The Heritage of America* and other works. Contributor to many journals and periodicals. The selection is from Henry Steele Commager, "Who Is Loyal to America?" *Harper's Magazine,* Vol. 195 (September, 1947), pp. 193 ff.

the hapless principal of the Western High school, was "the most shocked and regretful of all." The District of Columbia Committee would be happy to know that though he was innocent in the matter, he had been properly reprimanded!

It is the reaction of the educators that makes this episode more than a tempest in a teapot. . . . We expect hysteria from Mr. Rankin and some newspapers; we are shocked when we see educators, timid before criticism and confused about first principles, betray their trust. And we wonder what can be that "philosophy of education" which believes that young people can be trained to the duties of citizenship by wrapping their minds in cotton-wool.

Merely by talking about Russia Mrs. Lewis was thought to be attacking Americanism. It is indicative of the seriousness of the situation that during this same week the House found it necessary to take time out from the discussion of the labor bill, the tax bill, the International Trade Organization, and the world famine, to meet assaults upon Americanism from a new quarter. This time it was the artists who were undermining the American system, and members of the House spent some hours passing around reproductions of the paintings which the State Department had sent abroad as part of its program for advertising American culture. We need not pause over the exquisite humor which congressmen displayed in their comments on modern art: weary statesmen must have their fun. But we may profitably remark the major criticism which was directed against this unfortunate collection of paintings. What was wrong with these paintings, it shortly appeared, was that they were un-American. "No American drew those crazy pictures," said Mr. Rankin. Perhaps he was right. The copious files of the Committee on Un-American Activities were levied upon to prove that of the forty-five artists represented "no less than twenty were definitely New Deal in various shades of Communism." The damning facts are specified for each of the pernicious twenty; we can content ourselves with the first of them, Ben-Zion. What is the evidence here? "Ben-Zion was one of the signers of a letter sent to President Roosevelt by the United American Artists which urged help to the USSR and Britain after Hitler attacked Russia." He was, in short, a fellow-traveler of Churchill and Roosevelt.

The same day that Mr. Dirksen was denouncing the Washington school authorities for allowing students to hear about Russia ("In Russia equal right is granted to each nationality. There is no discrimination. Nobody says, you are a Negro, you are a Jew") Representative Williams of Mississippi rose to denounce the *Survey-Graphic* magazine and to add further to our understanding of Americanism. The *Survey-Graphic,* he said, "contained 129 pages of outrageously vile and nauseating anti-Southern, anti-Christian, un-American, and pro-Communist tripe, ostensibly directed toward the elimination of the custom of racial segregation in the South." It was written by "meddling un-American purveyors of hate and indecency."

All in all, a busy week for the House. Yet those who make a practice of reading their *Record* will agree that it was a typical week. For increasingly Congress is concerned with the eradication of disloyalty and the defense of Americanism, and scarcely a day passes that some congressman does not treat us to exhortations and admonitions, impassioned appeals and eloquent declamations, similar to those inspired by Mrs. Lewis, Mr. Ben-Zion, and the editors of the *Survey-Graphic*. And scarcely a day passes that the outlines of the new loyalty and the new Americanism are not etched more sharply in public policy.

And this is what is significant—the emergence of new patterns of Americanism and of loyalty, patterns radically different from those which have long been traditional. It is not only the Congress that is busy designing the new patterns. They are outlined in President Truman's recent disloyalty order; in similar orders formulated by the New York City Council and by state and local authorities throughout the country; in the programs of the D.A.R., the American Legion, and similar patriotic organizations; in the editorials of the Hearst and the McCormick-Patterson papers; and in an elaborate series of advertisements sponsored by large corporations and business organizations. In the making is a revival of the red hysteria of the early 1920's, one of the shabbiest chapters in the history of American democracy; and more than a revival, for the new crusade is designed not merely to frustrate Communism but to formulate a positive definition of Americanism, and a positive concept of loyalty.

What is the new loyalty? It is, above all, conformity. It is the uncritical and unquestioning acceptance of America as it is—the political institutions, the social relationships, the economic practices. It rejects inquiry into the race question or socialized medicine, or public housing, or into the wisdom or validity of our foreign policy. It regards as particularly heinous any challenge to what is called "the system of private enterprise," identifying that system with Americanism. It abandons evolution, repudiates the once popular concept of progress, and regards America as a finished product, perfect and complete.

It is, it must be added, easily satisfied. For it wants not intellectual conviction nor spiritual conquest, but mere outward conformity. In matters of loyalty it takes the word for the deed, the gesture for the principle. It is content with the flag salute, and does not pause to consider the warning of our Supreme Court that "a person gets from a symbol the meaning he puts into it, and what is one man's comfort and inspiration is another's jest and scorn." It is satisfied with membership in respectable organizations and, as it assumes that every member of a liberal organization is a Communist, concludes that every member of a conservative one is a true American. It has not yet learned that not everyone who saith Lord, Lord, shall enter into the kingdom of Heaven. It is designed neither to discover real disloyalty nor to foster true loyalty.

II

What is wrong with this new concept of loyalty? What, fundamentally, is wrong with the pusillanimous retreat of the Washington educators, the barbarous antics of Washington legislators, the hysterical outbursts of the D.A.R., the gross and vulgar appeals of business corporations? It is not merely that these things are offensive. It is rather that they are wrong—morally, socially, and politically.

The concept of loyalty as conformity is a false one. It is narrow and restrictive, denies freedom of thought and of conscience, and is irremediably stained by private and selfish considerations. "Enlightened loyalty," wrote Josiah Royce, who made loyalty the very core of his philosophy,

> means harm to no man's loyalty. It is at war only with disloyalty, and its warfare, unless necessity constrains, is only a spiritual warfare. It does not foster class hatreds; it knows of nothing reasonable about race prejudices; and it regards all races of men as one in their need of loyalty. It ignores mutual misunderstandings. It loves its own wherever upon earth its own, namely loyalty itself, is to be found.

Justice, charity, wisdom, spirituality, he added, were all definable in terms of loyalty, and we may properly ask which of these qualities our contemporary champions of loyalty display.

Above all, loyalty must be to something larger than oneself, untainted by private purposes or selfish ends. But what are we to say of the attempts by the NAM and by individual corporations to identify loyalty with the system of private enterprise? Is it not as if officeholders should attempt to identify loyalty with their own party, their own political careers? Do not those corporations which pay for full-page advertisements associating Americanism with the competitive system expect, ultimately, to profit from that association? Do not those organizations that deplore, in the name of patriotism, the extension of government operation of hydro-electric power expect to profit from their campaign?

Certainly it is a gross perversion not only of the concept of loyalty but of the concept of Americanism to identify it with a particular economic system. This precise question, interestingly enough, came before the Supreme Court in the Schneiderman case not so long ago—and it was Wendell Willkie who was counsel for Schneiderman. Said the Court:

> Throughout our history many sincere people whose attachment to the general Constitutional scheme cannot be doubted have, for various and even divergent reasons, urged differing degrees of governmental ownership and control of natural resources, basic means of production, and banks and the media of exchange,

either with or without compensation. And something once regarded as a species of private property was abolished without compensating the owners when the institution of slavery was forbidden. Can it be said that the author of the Emancipation Proclamation and the supporters of the Thirteenth Amendment were not attached to the Constitution?

There is, it should be added, a further danger in the willful identification of Americanism with a particular body of economic practices. Many learned economists predict for the near future an economic crash similar to that of 1929. If Americanism is equated with competitive capitalism, what happens to it if competitive capitalism comes a cropper? If loyalty and private enterprise are inextricably associated, what is to preserve loyalty if private enterprise fails? Those who associate Americanism with a particular program of economic practices have a grave responsibility, for if their program should fail, they expose Americanism itself to disrepute.

The effort to equate loyalty with conformity is misguided because it assumes that there is a fixed content to loyalty and that this can be determined and defined. But loyalty is a principle, and eludes definition except in its own terms. It is devotion to the best interests of the commonwealth, and may require hostility to the particular policies which the government pursues, the particular practices which the economy undertakes, the particular institutions which society maintains. "If there is any fixed star in our Constitutional constellation," said the Supreme Court in the Barnette case, "it is that no official, high or petty, can perscribe what shall be orthodox in politics, nationalism, religion, or other matters of opinion, or force citizens to confess by word or act their faith therein. If there are any circumstances which permit an exception they do not now occur to us."

True loyalty may require, in fact, what appears to the naïve to be disloyalty. It may require hostility to certain provisions of the Constitution itself, and historians have not concluded that those who subscribed to the "Higher Law" were lacking in patriotism. We should not forget that our tradition is one of protest and revolt, and it is stultifying to celebrate the rebels of the past—Jefferson and Paine, Emerson and Thoreau—while we silence the rebels of the present. "We are a rebellious nation," said Theodore Parker, known in his day as the Great American Preacher, and went on:

> Our whole history is treason; our blood was attainted before we were born; our creeds are infidelity to the mother church; our constitution, treason to our fatherland. What of that? Though all the governors in the world bid us commit treason against man, and set the example, let us never submit.

Those who would impose upon us a new concept of loyalty not only assume that this is possible, but have the presumption to believe that they are competent to write the definition. We are reminded of Whitman's defiance of the "never-ending audacity of elected persons." Who are those who would set the standards of loyalty? They are Rankins and Bilbos, officials of the D.A.R. and the Legion and the NAM, Hearsts and McCormicks. May we not say of Rankin's harangues on loyalty what Emerson said of Webster at the time of the Seventh of March speech: "The word honor in the mouth of Mr. Webster is like the word love in the mouth of a whore."

What do men know of loyalty who make a mockery of the Declaration of Independence and the Bill of Rights, whose energies are dedicated to stirring up race and class hatreds, who would straitjacket the American spirit? What indeed do they know of America—the America of Sam Adams and Tom Paine, of Jackson's defiance of the Court and Lincoln's celebration of labor, of Thoreau's essay on Civil Disobedience and Emerson's championship of John Brown, of the America of the Fourierists and the Come-Outers, of cranks and fanatics, of socialists and anarchists? Who among American heroes could meet their tests, who would be cleared by their committees? Not Washington, who was a rebel. Not Jefferson, who wrote that all men are created equal and whose motto was "rebellion to tyrants is obedience to God." Not Garrison, who publicly burned the Constitution; or Wendell Phillips, who spoke for the underprivileged everywhere and counted himself a philosophical anarchist; not Seward of the Higher Law or Sumner of racial equality. Not Lincoln, who admonished us to have malice toward none, charity for all; or Wilson, who warned that our flag was "a flag of liberty of opinion as well as of political liberty"; or Justice Holmes, who said that our Constitution is an experiment and that while that experiment is being made "we should be eternally vigilant against attempts to check the expression of opinions that we loathe and believe to be fraught with death."

III

There are further and more practical objections against the imposition of fixed concepts of loyalty or tests of disloyalty. The effort is itself a confession of fear, a declaration of insolvency. Those who are sure of themselves do not need reassurance, and those who have confidence in the strength and the virtue of America do not need to fear either criticism or competition. The effort is bound to miscarry. It will not apprehend those who are really disloyal, it will not even frighten them; it will affect only those who can be labeled "radical." It is sobering to recall that though the Japanese relocation program, carried through at such incalculable cost in misery and tragedy, was justified to us on the ground that the Japanese were potentially disloyal, the record does not disclose a single case of Japanese disloyalty or sabotage during the whole war. The warning sounded by the Supreme Court in the Barnette flag-salute case is a timely one:

> Ultimate futility of such attempts to compel obedience is the lesson of every such effort from the Roman drive to stamp out Christianity as a disturber of pagan unity, the Inquisition as a means to religious and dynastic unity, the Siberian exiles as a means to Russian unity, down to the fast-failing efforts of our

present totalitarian enemies. Those who begin coercive elimination of dissent soon find themselves exterminating dissenters. Compulsory unification of opinion achieves only the unanimity of the graveyard.

Nor are we left to idle conjecture in this matter; we have had experience enough. Let us limit ourselves to a single example, one that is wonderfully relevant. Back in 1943 the House Un-American Activities Committee, deeply disturbed by alleged disloyalty among government employees, wrote a definition of subversive activities and proceeded to apply it. The definition was admirable, and no one could challenge its logic or its symmetry:

> Subversive activity derives from conduct intentionally destructive of or inimical to the Government of the United States—that which seeks to undermine its institutions, or to disort its functions, or to impede its projects, or to lessen its efforts, the ultimate end being to overturn it all.

Surely anyone guilty of activities so defined deserved not only dismissal but punishment. But how was the test applied? It was applied to two distinguished scholars, Robert Morss Lovett and Goodwin Watson, and to one able young historian, William E. Dodd, Jr., son of our former Ambassador to Germany. Of almost three million persons employed by the government, these were the three whose subversive activities were deemed the most pernicious, and the House cut them off the payroll. The sequel is familiar. The Senate concurred only to save a wartime appropriation; the President signed the bill under protest for the same reason. The Supreme Court declared the whole business a "bill of attainder" and therefore unconstitutional. Who was it, in the end, who engaged in "subversive activities"—Lovett, Dodd, and Watson, or the Congress which flagrantly violated Article One of the Constitution?

Finally, disloyalty tests are not only futile in application, they are pernicious in their consequences. They distract attention from activities that are really disloyal, and silence criticism inspired by true loyalty. That there are disloyal elements in America will not be denied, but there is no reason to suppose that any of the tests now formulated will ever be applied to them. It is relevant to remember that when Rankin was asked why his Committee did not investigate the Ku Klux Klan he replied that the Klan was not un-American, it was American!

Who are those who are really disloyal? Those who inflame racial hatreds, who sow religious and class dissensions. Those who subvert the Constitution by violating the freedom of the ballot box. Those who make a mockery of majority rule by the use of the filibuster. Those who impair democracy by denying equal educational facilities. Those who frustrate justice by lynch law or by making a farce of jury trials. Those who deny freedom of speech and of the press and of assembly. Those who press for special favors against the interest of the commonwealth. Those who regard public office as a source of private gain. Those who would exalt the military over the civil. Those who for selfish and private purposes stir up national antagonisms and expose the world to the ruin of war.

Will the House Committee on Un-American Activities interfere with the activities of these? Will Mr. Truman's disloyalty proclamation reach these? Will the current campaigns for Americanism convert these? If past experience is any guide, they will not. What they will do, if they are successful, is to silence criticism, stamp out dissent—or drive it underground. But if our democracy is to flourish it must have criticism, if our government is to function it must have dissent. Only totalitarian governments insist upon conformity and they—as we know—do so at their peril. Without criticism abuses will go unrebuked; without dissent our dynamic system will become static. The American people have a stake in the maintenance of the most thorough-going inquisition into American institutions. They have a stake in nonconformity, for they know that the American genius is nonconformist. They have a stake in experimentation of the most radical character, for they know that only those who prove all things can hold fast that which is good.

IV

It is easier to say what loyalty is not than to say what it is. It is not conformity. It is not passive acquiescence in the status quo. It is not preference for everything American over everything foreign. It is not an ostrich-like ignorance of other countries and other institutions. It is not the indulgence in ceremony—a flag salute, an oath of allegiance, a fervid verbal declaration. It is not a particular creed, a particular version of history, a particular body of economic practices, a particular philosophy.

It is a tradition, an ideal, and a principle. It is a willingness to subordinate every private advantage for the larger good. It is an appreciation of the rich and diverse contributions that can come from the most varied sources. It is allegiance to the traditions that have guided our greatest statesmen and inspired our most eloquent poets—the traditions of freedom, equality, democracy, tolerance, the tradition of the higher law, of experimentation, co-operation, and pluralism. It is a realization that America was born of revolt, flourished on dissent, became great through experimentation.

Independence was an act of revolution; republicanism was something new under the sun; the federal system was a vast experimental laboratory. Physically Americans were pioneers; in the realm of social and economic institutions, too, their tradition has been one of pioneering. From the beginning, intellectual and spiritual diversity have been as characteristic of America as racial and linguistic. The most distinctively American philosophies have been transcendentalism—which is the philosophy of the Higher Law—and pragmatism—which is the philosophy of experimentation and pluralism. These two principles are the very core of Americanism: the principle of the Higher Law, or of obedience to the dictates of conscience rather than of statutes, and the principle of pragmatism, or the rejection of a single good and of the notion of a finished universe. From the beginning Americans have known that there were new worlds to conquer, new truths to be discovered. Every effort to confine Americanism to a single pattern, to constrain it to a single formula, is disloyalty to everything that is valid in Americanism.

Heresy and Conspiracy

Sidney Hook *

The "hot war" in Korea makes it even more urgent that we clarify our thinking on the "cold war" of ideologies. At the heart of the matter are basic philosophical issues which in more settled times would have been dismissed as of no practical concern. One of them is the meaning of "liberalism," which becomes important because communism invokes the freedom of a liberal society in order to destroy that society. Many proposals have been made to cope with this problem. All of them must face the question whether in advocating such measures the principles of liberalism are themselves being consistently applied or compromised.

It is easier to say what liberalism is not than what it is. It is not belief in laissez-faire or free enterprise in economics—the temper of Great Britain has remained liberal despite the shifting economic programs and institutions of the last century. Neither is liberalism the philosophy of invariable compromise or the comforting notion that it is always possible to find a middle ground—if a man demands my purse, to grant him half of it is not a liberal solution. Nor can liberalism be identified with the traditional belief in absolute or inalienable rights—every right is, in fact, evaluated in terms of its consequences for society, and is, therefore, subject to modification if it endangers other rights of equal or greater validity.

When one right limits another, the final adjudication of their conflict, in a liberal society, is made in the reflective light of the total situation and of that set of rationally preferred freedoms whose preservation may require the temporary abridgment of some specific freedom. To say that we cannot preserve our freedoms by sacrificing them is, therefore, an empty piece of rhetoric. Our common experience brings home to us the necessity of sacrificing some particular freedom to preserve other freedoms just as we must sometimes surrender a genuine good for the sake of other and better goods. Here the readiness to reflect is all.

* Professor of Philosophy at New York University. Author of *Towards the Understanding of Karl Marx, From Hegel to Marx, The Hero in History,* and numerous articles on political and philosophical subjects. The selection is from Sidney Hook, "Heresy, Yes—But Conspiracy, No," *New York Times Magazine,* July 9, 1950. By permission of the author and *The New York Times.*

This provides a key to the abiding meaning of the liberal tradition from Socrates to John Dewey and Justice Holmes.

Liberalism is, in the memorable words of Justice Holmes, the belief "in the free trade of ideas—that the test of truth is the power of thought to get itself accepted in the competition of the market."

There are at least two presuppositions of this belief in the free market of ideas. One of them, explicitly drawn by Justice Holmes, is that the free expression and circulation of ideas may be checked wherever their likely effects constitute a clear and present danger to public peace or the security of the country. The second presupposition is that in the free market of ideas the competition will be honestly and openly conducted. What the liberal fears is the systematic corruption of the free market of ideas by activities which make intelligent choice impossible. In short, what he fears is not heresy but conspiracy.

The failure to recognize the distinction between heresy and conspiracy is fatal to a liberal civilization, for the inescapable consequence of their identification is either self-destruction, when heresies are punished as conspiracies, or destruction at the hands of their enemies, when conspiracies are tolerated as heresies.

A heresy is a set of unpopular ideas or opinions on matters of grave concern to the community. The right to profess and advocate heresy of any character, including communism, is an essential element of a liberal society. The liberal stands ready to defend the honest heretic no matter what his views against any attempt to curb him. It is enough that the heretic pays the price of unpopularity which he cannot avoid and from which he cannot reasonably plead exemption, or use as a pretext for conspiracy. In some respects each of us is a heretic, but a liberal society can impose no official orthodoxies of belief, disagreement with which entails legal sanctions of any kind.

A conspiracy, as distinct from a heresy, is a secret or underground movement which seeks to attain its ends not by normal political or educational process but by playing outside the rules of the game. Because it undermines the conditions which are required in order that doctrines may freely compete for acceptance, because where successful it ruthlessly destroys all heretics and dissenters, conspiracies cannot be tolerated without self-stultification in a liberal society.

A heresy does not shrink from publicity. It welcomes it. Not so a conspiracy. The signs of a conspiracy are secrecy, anonymity, the use of false labels, and the calculated lie. It does not offer its wares openly but by systematic infiltration into all organizations of cultural life, it seeks to capture strategic posts to carry out a policy alien to the purposes of the organizations. There is political conspiracy which is the concern of the state. But there may also be a conspiracy against a labor union, a cultural or professional association, or an educational institution which is not primarily the concern of the state but of its own members. In general, whoever subverts the rules of a democratic organization and seeks to win by chicanery what cannot be fairly won in the processes of free discussion is a conspirator.

This suggests what the guiding principle of liberalism should be toward communism. Communist ideas are heresies, and liberals need have no fear of them where they are freely and openly expressed. The Communist movement, however, is something much more than a heresy, for wherever it exists it operates along the lines laid down by Lenin as guides to Communists of all countries, and perfected in all details since then.

"It is necessary," so Lenin instructs all Communists, "to agree to any and every sacrifice and even—if need be—resort to all sorts of stratagems, maneuvers, and illegal methods, to evasions and subterfuges . . . in order to carry on Communist work." Further: "In all organizations without exception . . . (political, industrial, military, co-operative, educational, sports), groups or nuclei of Communists should be formed . . . mainly open groups but also secret groups."

There are no exceptions: "In all countries, even the freest, 'legal' and 'peaceful' in the sense that the class struggle is least acute in them, the time has fully matured when it is absolutely necessary for every Communist party systematically to combine legal with illegal work, legal and illegal organizations. . . . Illegal work is particularly necessary in the Army, the Navy, and police."

Under present conditions of political and military warfare it is not hard to see what immense dangers to the security of liberal institutions is implicit in this strategy of infiltration and deceit. Even a few men in sensitive posts can do incalculable harm. These instructions, combined with explicit directives to Communists to transform any war in which their country is involved, except one approved by the Soviet Union, into a civil war against their own Government, indicate that members of the Communist party are not so much heretics as conspirators, and regard themselves as such.

There may be some justification for conspiratorial activity in undemocratic countries where heresies are proscribed, but Lenin, as we have seen, makes no exceptions.

How faithfully the Communist movement pursues the pattern laid down by its authoritative leaders in the political sphere is a matter of historical record. But unfortunately for the peace of mind of liberals the same tactics are followed in other areas of social and cultural life. The history of American labor is replete with illustrations.

Every large labor organization in the United States has been compelled to take disciplinary action against Communist party elements, not because of their beliefs—their heresies—but because their pattern of conduct made the Communist party, and ultimately the Kremlin, the decisive power in the life of the union, and not the needs and wishes of the membership.

President Philip Murray of the C.I.O., in the recent expulsion of the

Mine, Mill and Smelter Workers Union, exposed the technique in detail. In all these situations it is not fear of Communist ideas which has led to disciplinary action. The charge against the Communists is that it is they who fear the open and honest confrontation of ideas. They operate through "fronts," the charge continues, because they fear that if the membership is given a free choice of honestly labeled alternatives they will be rejected; and once they slip into power they consolidate their position by terrorizing any opposition.

By now it should be apparent that liberals in the twentieth century are confronted by a situation quite unfamiliar to their forebears. For they must contend, not with fearless heretics—indigenous elements of the community—who like the Abolitionists and revolutionists of old scorn concealment, and who make no bones about their hostility to the principles of liberalism. They find themselves in a unique historical predicament of dealing with native elements who by secrecy and stratagem serve the interests of a foreign power which believes itself entitled to speak for all mankind, and whose victory spells the end of all liberal civilization and with it the right to heresy.

The problems this creates for a liberal society are of tremendous magnitude. They cannot be dismissed by a quotation from Jefferson. Nor can they be solved by placing the Communist movement and its entire periphery outside the law by special legislation. They require constructive intelligence, the discovery and application of techniques in each field which will meet the conspiratorial threats to the proper functioning of liberal institutions without creating still greater ones.

Failure to take this approach is characteristic of some current wholesale responses to the problem. The first is that of frightened reactionaries who cannot distinguish between heresy and conspiracy, and in addition, identify communism with any decent thing they wish to destroy. By making reckless charges of conspiracy where there is only honest heresy, they prevent intelligent choice. And by labeling all progressive ideas as communistic they help the Communist strategy. If this reactionary movement gains momentum it will petrify the status quo and destroy the possibilities of peaceful social change.

Then there is a small but influential group of men who believe that they can check Communist conspiracy merely by passing laws against it, and that they can protect institutions from subversives by requiring all individuals, particularly teachers, to take loyalty oaths. As if any member of the Communist party regarded any oath except one to the Communist party and the Soviet Union as binding!

A third group consists of those whom we may call ritualistic, as distinct from realistic, liberals. They ignore or blithely dismiss the mass of evidence concerning the conspiratorial character of the Communist movement in all institutions in which it is active. They regard communism merely as an unpleasant heresy, just a little worse than a crotchety theory of disease or finance. They sometimes characterize a prosecution of a conspirator for espionage or perjury as a persecution of heresy. This gives a new lease of life to the reactionaries who now tend to regard the ritualistic liberals as the dupes or accomplices of the Communists, thus confirming in turn the illusions of these liberals that there really is no problem of Communist conspiracy.

Ritualistic liberals legitimately criticize the dangerous nonsense of those who proscribe heresy. But they carry their criticism to a point where they give the impression that the country is in the grip of a reign of terror or hysteria much more dangerous than Communist expansion from without and infiltration from within.

Because some security regulations in government are questionable and because some blunders have been made, the ritualistic liberals intimate that no security regulations are necessary and that the existing laws against treason and criminal conspiracy are sufficient for all purposes. By artfully collecting instances of foolishness from the press and blowing up their significance, and by disregarding counter-instances of equal or greater significance, they paint a very misleading picture of the actual state of American civil liberties comparable to an account of American business composed only of bankruptcies, or an account of public order that featured only crime stories.

David Lilienthal, a realistic not a ritualistic liberal, has warned us against the "Scare-the-dopes!" method of discussing nuclear energy. There is also a "Scare-the-dopes" method of discussion of the problem of Communist conspiracy. It is used by those who with scandalous looseness employ the term Communist for any economic or political heresy, and who shout conspiracy where there is only heresy. It is also used by those who do not tell us how to meet the real dangers of Communist conspiracy but shout, "Hysteria" and "Fascism" or "Police State" when the first faltering efforts are made to cope with dangers hitherto unprecedented.

The position of realistic liberalism in three troubled centers of American life in which overt conspiratorial activity of a criminal nature is not involved may be briefly indicated.

Where government service is concerned, the operating maxim for every sensitive and policy-making post should be a principle enunciated by Roger Baldwin, former head of the American Civil Liberties Union: "A superior loyalty to a foreign Government disqualifies a citizen for service to our own." The difficulty is to determine what constitutes sufficient evidence to warrant the inference that a particular individual is unsafe. No hard and fast rules can be laid down in advance, for in some cases even past membership in subversive organizations is not conclusive. The criterion for establishing unreliability obviously must be less stringent than those which lead us to deprive an individual of freedom. The main problem is not punitive but preventive.

In labor organizations the existence of Communist party leaderships is extremely dangerous because of the Communists' unfailing use of the strike as a political instrument at the behest of the Kremlin.

The history of Communist-led trade unions here and abroad is instructive enough. The most effective way of meeting this situation, however, is not by requiring non-Communist oaths on the part of union officers, for this can be circumvented by delegating office to individuals who are faithful non-card holding Communists. The most intelligent procedure here is to let labor clean its own house. Free and independent trade unions which are essential to a democracy cannot be liberated from the organizational stranglehold of the Communist party by government intervention. Only an aroused membership can do it.

The question of freedom and control in the schools is not political. It does not involve civil rights but the ethics of professional conduct. Heresy in the schools, whether in science, economics, or politics, must be protected against any agency which seeks to impose orthodoxy. For the scholar there are no subversive doctrines but only those that are valid or invalid or not proved in the light of evidence. The primary commitment of the teacher is to the ethics and logic of inquiry. It is not his beliefs, right or wrong; it is not his heresies, which disqualify the Communist party teacher but his declaration of intention, as evidenced by official statements of his party, to practice educational fraud.

The common sense of the matter is clear and independent of the issue of communism. An individual joins an organization which explicitly instructs him that his duty is to sabotage the purposes of the institution in which he works and which provides him with his livelihood. Is it necessary to apprehend him in the act of carrying out these instructions in order to forestall the sabotage? Does not his voluntary and continuous act of membership in such an organization constitute prima facie evidence of unfitness?

This is a matter of ethical hygiene, not of politics or of persecution. And because it is, the enforcement of the proper professional standards should rest with the teachers themselves and not with the state or Regents or even boards of trustees. The actual techniques of handling such issues must be worked out but the problem should not be confused with the issue of heresy.

Liberalism in the twentieth century must toughen its fiber, for it is engaged in a fight on many different fronts. Liberalism must defend the free market in ideas against the racists, the professional patrioteer, and those spokesmen of the status quo who would freeze the existing inequalities of opportunity and economic power by choking off criticism.

Liberalism must also defend freedom of ideas against those agents and apologists of Communist totalitarianism who, instead of honestly defending their heresies, resort to conspiratorial methods of anonymity and other techniques of fifth columnists. It will not be taken in by labels like "left" and "right." These terms came into use after the French Revolution but the legacy of the men who then called themselves "left"—the strategic freedoms of the Bill of Rights—is everywhere repudiated by those who today are sometimes euphemistically referred to as "leftists" but who are actually Communists more reactionary than many parties conventionally called "right."

Realistic liberalism recognizes that to survive we must solve many hard problems, and that they can be solved only by intelligence and not by pious rhetoric. It recognizes that our greatest danger today is not fear of ideas but absence of ideas—specific ideas, addressed to concrete problems here and now, problems of such complexity that only the ignorant can be cocksure or dogmatic about the answers to them.

Finally, liberalism conceives of life not in terms of bare survival or peace at any price but in the light of ideals upon which it is prepared to stake everything. Among these ideals are the strategic freedoms of the liberal American tradition which make the continuous use of intelligence possible.

Topic 16

FREE SPEECH UNDER THE CONSTITUTION

Freedom of Speech in War Time

SCHENCK V. UNITED STATES *

Error to the District Court of the United States for the Eastern District of Pennsylvania.

Mr. Justice Holmes delivered the opinion of the court.

This is an indictment in three counts. The first charges a conspiracy to violate the Espionage Act of June 15, 1917, c. 30, §3, 40 Stat. 217, 219, by causing and attempting to cause insubordination, &c., in the military and naval forces of the United States, and to obstruct the recruiting and enlistment service of the United States, when the United States was at war with the German Empire, to-wit, that the defendants wilfully conspired to have printed and circulated to men who had been called and accepted for military service under the Act of May 18, 1917, a document set forth and alleged to be calculated to cause such insubordination and obstruction. The count alleges overt acts in pursuance of the conspiracy, ending in the distribution of the document set forth. The second count alleges a conspiracy to commit an offense against the United States, to-wit, to use the mails for the transmission of matter declared to be non-mailable by Title XII, §2 of the Act of June 15, 1917, to-wit, the above mentioned

* 249 U.S. 47 (1919).

document, with an averment of the same overt acts. The third count charges an unlawful use of the mails for the transmission of the same matter and otherwise as above. The defendants were found guilty on all the counts. They set up the First Amendment to the Constitution forbidding Congress to make any law abridging the freedom of speech, or of the press, and bringing the case here on that ground have argued some other points also of which we must dispose. . . .

The document in question upon its first printed side recited the first section of the Thirteenth Amendment, said that the idea embodied in it was violated by the Conscription Act and that a conscript is little better than a convict. In impassioned language it intimated that conscription was despotism in its worst form and a monstrous wrong against humanity in the interest of Wall Street's chosen few. It said, "Do not submit to intimidation," but in form at least confined itself to peaceful measures such as a petition for the repeal of the act. The other and later printed side of the sheet was headed "Assert Your Rights." It stated reasons for alleging that any one violated the Constitution when he refused to recognize "your right to assert your opposition to the draft," and went on, "If you do not assert and support your rights, you are helping to deny or disparage rights which it is the solemn duty of all citizens and residents of the United States to retain." It described the arguments on the other side as coming from cunning politicians and a mercenary capitalist press, and even silent consent to the conscription law as helping to support an infamous conspiracy. It denied the power to send our citizens away to foreign shores to shoot up the people of other lands, and added that words could not express the condemnation such coldblooded ruthlessness deserves, &c., winding up, "You must do your share to maintain, support and uphold the rights of the people of this country." Of course the document would not have been sent unless it had been intended to have some effect, and we do not see what effect it could be expected to have upon persons subject to the draft except to influence them to obstruct the carrying of it out. The defendants do not deny that the jury might find against them on this point.

But it is said, suppose that that was the tendency of this circular, it is protected by the First Amendment to the Constitution. Two of the strongest expressions are said to be quoted respectively from well-known public men. It well may be that the prohibition of laws abridging the freedom of speech is not confined to previous restraints, although to prevent them may have been the main purpose, as intimated in *Patterson* v. *Colorado,* 205 U.S. 454, 462. We admit that in many places and in ordinary times the defendants in saying all that was said in the circular would have been within their constitutional rights. But the character of every act depends upon the circumstances in which it is done. *Aikens* v. *Wisconsin,* 195 U.S. 194, 205, 206. The most stringent protection of free speech would not protect a man in falsely shouting fire in a theatre and causing a panic. It does not even protect a man from an injunction against uttering words that may have all the effect of force. *Gompers* v. *Buck Stove & Range Co.,* 221 U.S. 418, 439. The question in every case is whether the words used are used in such circumstances and are of such a nature as to create a clear and present danger that they will bring about the substantive evils that Congress has a right to prevent. It is a question of proximity and degree. When a nation is at war many things that might be said in time of peace are such a hindrance to its effort that their utterance will not be endured so long as men fight and that no Court could regard them as protected by any constitutional right. It seems to be admitted that if an actual obstruction of the recruiting service were proved, liability for words that produced that effect might be enforced. The statute of 1917 in §4 punishes conspiracies to obstruct as well as actual obstruction. If the act (speaking, or circulating a paper), its tendency and the intent with which it is done are the same, we perceive no ground for saying that success alone warrants making the act a crime. *Goldman* v. *United States,* 245 U.S. 474, 477. Indeed that case might be said to dispose of the present contention if the precedent covers all *media concludendi.* But as the right to free speech was not referred to specially, we have thought fit to add a few words. . . .

Judgments affirmed.

Democracy May Defend Itself

DENNIS ET AL. V. UNITED STATES *

Mr. Chief Justice Vinson announced the judgment of the court and an opinion in which Mr. Justice Reed, Mr. Justice Burton and Mr. Justice Minton join.

Petitioners were indicted in July, 1948, for violation of the conspiracy provisions of the Smith Act, 54 Stat. 671, 18 U.S.C. (1946 Ed.) Section 11, during the period of April, 1945, to July, 1948. . . .

The indictment charged the petitioners with willfully and knowingly conspiring (1) to organize as the Communist Party of the United States of America a society, group and assembly of persons who teach and advocate the overthrow and destruction of the Government of the United States by force and violence, and (2) knowingly and willfully to advocate and teach the duty and necessity of overthrowing and destroying the Government of the United States by force and violence.

The indictment further alleged that Section 2 of the Smith Act proscribes these acts and that any conspiracy to take such action is a violation of Section 3 of the act.

The trial of the case extended over nine months, six of which were devoted to the taking of evidence, resulting in a record of 16,000 pages. . . .

Petitioners dispute the meaning to be drawn from the evidence, con-

* No. 336, October Term, 1950, dec. June 4, 1951.

tending that the Marxist-Leninist doctrine they advocated taught that force and violence to achieve a Communist form of government in an existing democratic state would be necessary only because the ruling classes of that state would never permit the transformation to be accomplished peacefully, but would use force and violence to defeat any peaceful political and economic gain the Communists could achieve.

But the Court of Appeals held that the record supports the following broad conclusions:

By virtue of their control over the political apparatus of the Communist Political Association, petitioners were able to transform that organization into the Communist party; that the policies of the Association were changed from peaceful cooperation with the United States and its economic and political structure to a policy which had existed before the United States and the Soviet Union were fighting a common enemy—namely, a policy which worked for the overthrow of the Government by force and violence; that the Communist party is a highly disciplined organization, adept at infiltration into strategic positions, use of aliases and double-meaning language; that the party is rigidly controlled; that Communists, unlike other political parties, tolerate no dissension from the policy laid down by the guiding forces, but that the approved program is slavishly followed by the members of the party; that the literature of the party and the statements and activities of its leaders, petitioners here, advocate, and the general goal of the party was, during the period in question, to achieve a successful overthrow of the existing order by force and violence.

It will be helpful in clarifying the issues to treat next the contention that the trial judge improperly interpreted the statute by charging that the statute required an unlawful intent before the jury could convict. More specifically, he charged that the jury could not find the petitioners guilty under the indictment unless they found that petitioners had the intent "to overthrow the Government by force and violence as speedily as circumstances permit."

Section 2 (A) (1) makes it unlawful "to knowingly or willfully advocate, . . . or teach the duty, necessity, desirability or propriety of overthrowing or destroying any government in the United States by force or violence. . . ."

Section 2 (A) (3), "To organize or help to organize any society, group or assembly of persons who teach, advocate or encourage the overthrow."

Because of the fact that Section 2 (A) (2) expressly requires a specific intent to overthrow the Government, and because of the absence of precise language in the foregoing subsections, it is claimed that Congress deliberately omitted any such requirement. We do not agree. . . . We hold that the statute requires, as an essential element of the crime, proof of the intent of those who are charged with its violation to overthrow the Government by force and violence. . . .

The obvious purpose of the statute is to protect existing government, not from change by peaceable, lawful and constitutional means, but from change by violence, revolution and terrorism.

That it is within the *power* of the Congress to protect the Government of the United States from armed rebellion is a proposition which requires little discussion. Whatever theoretical merit there may be to the argument that there is a "right" to rebellion against dictatorial governments, is without force where the existing structure of the government provides for peaceful and orderly change.

We reject any principle of governmental helplessness in the face of preparation for revolution, which principle, carried to its logical conclusion, must lead to anarchy. No one could conceive that it is not within the power of Congress to prohibit acts intended to overthrow the Government by force and violence. The question with which we are concerned here is not whether Congress has such *power,* but whether the *means* which it has employed conflict with the First and Fifth Amendments to the Constitution.

One of the bases for the contention that the means which Congress has employed are invalid takes the form of an attack on the face of the statute on the grounds that, by its terms, it prohibits academic discussion of the merits of Marxism-Leninism, that it stifles ideas and is contrary to all concepts of a free speech and a free press. . . .

The very language of the Smith Act negates the interpretation which petitioners would have us impose on that act. It is directed at advocacy, not discussion. Thus, the trial judge properly charged the jury that they could not convict if they found that petitioners did "no more than pursue peaceful studies and discussions or teaching and advocacy in the realm of ideas." He further charged that it was not unlawful "to conduct in an American college and university a course explaining the philosophical theories set forth in the books which have been placed in evidence."

Such a charge is in strict accord with the statutory language, and illustrates the meaning to be placed on those words. Congress did not intend to eradicate the free discussion of political theories, to destroy the traditional rights of Americans to discuss and evaluate ideas without fear of governmental sanction. Rather, Congress was concerned with the very kind of activity in which the evidence showed these petitioners engaged. . . .

We pointed out in [*American Communications Ass'n.* v. *Douds,* 339 U.S. 382 (1950)] that the basis of the First Amendment is the hypothesis that speech can rebut speech, propaganda will answer propaganda, free debate of ideas will result in the wisest governmental policies. It is for this reason that this Court has recognized the inherent value of free discourse.

An analysis of the leading cases in this Court which have involved direct limitations on speech, however, will demonstrate that both the majority of the Court and the dissenters in particular cases have recognized that this is not an unlimited, unqualified right, but that the societal value of speech must, on occasion, be subordinated to other values and considerations.

No important case involving free speech was decided by this court prior to *Schenck* v. *United States,* 249 U.S. 47 (1919). Indeed, the summary treatment accorded an argument based upon an individual's claim that the First Amendment protected certain utterances indicates that the Court at earlier dates placed no unique emphasis upon that right.

It was not until the classic dictum of Justice Holmes in the Schenck case, that speech *per se* received that emphasis in a majority opinion. That case involved a conviction upon the Criminal Espionage Act, 40 Stat. 217. The question the Court faced was whether the evidence was sufficient to sustain the conviction.

Writing for a unanimous court, Justice Holmes stated that the "question in every case is whether the words used are used in such circumstances and are of such a nature as to create a clear and present danger that they will bring about the substantive evils that Congress has a right to prevent." 249 U.S. at 52.

But the force of even this expression is considerably weakened by the reference at the end of the opinion to *Goldman* v. *United States,* 245 U.S. 474 (1918), a prosecution under the same statute. Said Justice Holmes, "Indeed (Goldman) might be said to dispose of the present contention if the precedent covers all *media concludendi,* but as the right to free speech was not referred to specially, we have thought fit to add a few words." 249 U.S. at 52.

The fact is inescapable, too, that the phrase bore no connotation that the danger was to be any threat to the safety of the Republic. The charge was causing and attempting to cause insubordination in the military forces and obstruct recruiting. The objectionable document denounced conscription and its most inciting sentence was, "You must do your share to maintain, support and uphold the rights of the people of this country." 249 U.S. at 51.

Fifteen thousand copies were printed and some circulated. This insubstantial gesture toward insubordination in 1917 during war was held to be a clear and present danger of bringing about the evil of military insubordination. . . .

The rule we deduce . . . is that where an offense is specified by a statute in nonspeech or nonpress terms, a conviction relying upon speech or press as evidence of violation may be sustained only when the speech or publication created a "clear and present danger" of attempting or accomplishing the prohibited crime, e. g., interference with enlistment. . . .

[It was never] envisioned that a shorthand phrase should be crystallized into a rigid rule to be applied inflexibly without regard to the circumstances of each case. Speech is not an absolute, above and beyond control by the Legislature when its judgment, subject to review here, is that certain kinds of speech are so undesirable as to warrant criminal sanction.

Nothing is more certain in modern society than the principle that there are no absolutes, that a name, a phrase, a standard has meaning only when associated with the considerations which gave birth to the nomenclature. See *Douds,* 339 U.S. at 397. To those who would paralyze our Government in the face of impending threat by encasing it in a semantic straitjacket we must reply that all concepts are relative.

In this case we are squarely presented with the application of the "clear and present danger" test, and must decide what that phrase imports.

We first note that many of the cases in which this Court has reversed convictions by use of this or similar tests, have been based on the fact that the interest which the state was attempting to protect was itself too insubstantial to warrant restriction of speech. [Citations omitted.]

Overthrow of the Government by force and violence is certainly a substantial enough interest for the Government to limit speech. Indeed, this is the ultimate value of any society, for if a society cannot protect its very structure from armed internal attack, it must follow that no subordinate value can be protected. If, then, this interest may be protected, the literal problem which is presented is what has been meant by the use of the phrase "clear and present danger" of the utterances bringing about the evil within the power of Congress to punish.

Obviously, the words cannot mean that before the Government may act, it must wait until the *putsch* is about to be executed, the plans have been laid and the signal is awaited. If Government is aware that a group aiming at its overthrow is attempting to indoctrinate its members and to commit them to a course whereby they will strike when the leaders feel the circumstances permit, action by the Government is required.

The argument that there is no need for Government to concern itself, for Government is strong, it possesses ample powers to put down a rebellion, it may defeat the revolution with ease, needs no answer. For that is not the question.

Certainly an attempt to overthrow the Government by force, even though doomed from the outset because of inadequate numbers or power of the revolutionists, is a sufficient evil for Congress to prevent. The damage which such attempts create both physically and politically to a nation, makes it impossible to measure the validity in terms of the probability of success, or the immediacy of a successful attempt.

In the instant case, the trial judge charged the jury that they could not convict unless they found that petitioners intended to overthrow the Government "as speedily as circumstances would permit." This does not mean, and could not properly mean, that they would not strike until there was certainty of success. What was meant was that the revolutionists would strike when they thought the time was ripe. We must therefore reject the contention that success or probability of success is the criterion.

The situation with which Justice Holmes and Brandeis were concerned in *Gitlow* was a comparatively isolated event, bearing little relation in their minds to any substantial threat to the safety of the community. Such also is true of cases like *Fiske* v. *Kansas,* 274 U.S. 380 (1927), and *Dejone* v. *Oregon,* 299 U.S. 353 (1937); but cf. *Lazar* v. *Pennsylvania,* 286 U.S. 532 (1932).

They were not confronted with any situation comparable to the instant one—the development of an apparatus designed and dedicated to the overthrow of the Government, in the context of world crisis after crisis.

Chief Judge Learned Hand, writing for the majority below, interpreted the phrase as follows: "In each case (courts) must ask whether the gravity of the 'evil,' discounted by its improbability, justifies such invasion of free speech as is necessary to avoid the danger." 183 F. 2D at 212.

We adopt this statement of the rule. As articulated by Chief Judge Hand, it is as succinct and inclusive as any other we might devise at this time. It takes into consideration those factors which we deem relevant, and relates their significances. More we cannot expect from words.

Likewise, we are in accord with the court below, which affirmed the trial court's finding that the requisite danger existed. The mere fact that, from the period 1945 to 1948, petitioners' activities did not result in an attempt to overthrow the Government by force and violence is, of course, no answer to the fact that there was a group that was ready to make the attempt.

The formation by petitioners of such a highly organized conspiracy, with rigidly disciplined members subject to call when the leaders, these petitioners, felt that the time had come for action, coupled with the inflammable nature of world conditions, similar uprisings in other countries, and the touch-and-go nature of our relations with countries with whom petitioners were in the very least ideologically attuned, convince us that their convictions were justified on this score.

And this analysis disposes of the contention that a conspiracy to advocate, as distinguished from the advocacy itself, cannot be constitutionally restrained, because it comprises only the preparation. It is the existence of the conspiracy which creates the danger. Cf. *Pinkerton* v. *United States,* 328 U.S. 640 (1946); *Goldman* v. *United States,* 245 U.S. 474 (1918); *United States* v. *Rabinowich,* 238 U.S. 78 (1915).

If the ingredients of the reaction are present, we cannot bind the Government to wait until the catalyst is added. . . .

The argument that the action of the trial court is erroneous, in declaring as a matter of law that such violation shows sufficient danger to justify the punishment, despite the First Amendment, rests on the theory that a jury must decide a question of the application of the First Amendment. We do not agree.

When facts are found that establish the violation of a statute, the protection against conviction afforded by the First Amendment is a matter of law. The doctrine that there must be a clear and present danger of a substantive evil that Congress has a right to prevent is a judicial rule to be applied as a matter of law by the courts.

The guilt is established by proof of facts.

Whether the First Amendment protects the activity which constitutes the violation of the statute must depend upon a judicial determination of the scope of the First Amendment applied to the circumstances of the case. . . .

The question in this case is whether the statute which the Legislature has enacted may be constitutionally applied. In other words, the Court must examine judicially the application of the statute to the particular situation, to ascertain if the Constitution prohibits the conviction. We hold that the statute may be applied where there is a "clear and present danger" of the substantive evil which the Legislature had the right to prevent. Bearing as it does, the marks of a "question of law," the issue is properly one for the judge to decide.

There remains to be discussed the question of vagueness—whether the statute, as we have interpreted it, is too vague, not sufficiently advising those who would speak of the limitations upon their activity. It is urged that such vagueness contravenes the First and Fifth Amendments. . . .

We agree that the standard as defined is not a neat, mathematical formulary. Like all verbalizations, it is subject to criticism on the score of indefiniteness. But petitioners themselves contend that the verbalization, "clear and present danger," is the proper standard. We see no difference from the standpoint of vagueness, whether the standard of "clear and present danger" is one contained in *haec verba* within the statute, or whether it is the judicial measure of constitutional applicability. . . .

We think it well serves to indicate to those who would advocate constitutionally prohibited conduct, that there is a line beyond which they may not go—a line, which they, in full knowledge of what they intend and the circumstances in which their activity takes place, will well appreciate and understand. . . .

Where there is doubt as to the intent of the defendants, the nature of their activities, or their power to bring about the evil, this Court will review the convictions with the scrupulous care demanded by our Constitution. But we are not convinced that because there may be borderline cases at some time in the future, these convictions should be reversed because of the argument that these petitioners could not know that their activities were constitutionally proscribed by the statute. . . . Petitioners intended to overthrow the Government of the United States as speedily as the circumstances would permit. Their conspiracy to organize the Communist Party and to teach and advocate the overthrow of the Government of the United States by force and violence created a "clear and present danger" of an attempt to overthrow the Government by force and violence. They were properly and constitutionally convicted for violation of the Smith Act. The judgments of conviction are *Affirmed.*

MR. JUSTICE CLARK took no part in the consideration or decision of this case.

MR. JUSTICE JACKSON, concurring.

This prosecution is the latest of never-ending, because never successful, quests for some legal formula that will secure an existing order against revolutionary radicalism. It requires us to reappraise, in the light of our own times and conditions, constitutional doctrines devised under other circumstances to strike a balance between authority and liberty.

Activity here charged to be criminal is conspiracy—that defendants conspired to teach and advocate, and to organize the Communist Party to teach and advocate, overthrow and destruction of the Government by force and violence. There is no charge of actual violence or attempt at overthrow.

The principal reliance of the defense in this Court is that the conviction cannot stand under the Constitution because the conspiracy of these defendants presents no "clear and present danger" of imminent or foreseeable overthrow.

The statute before us repeats a pattern, originally devised to combat the wave of anarchistic terrorism that plagued this country about the turn of the century, which lags at least two generations behind Communist Party techniques. . . .

Communism, the antithesis of anarchism, appears today as a closed system of thought representing Stalin's version of Lenin's version of Marxism. As an ideology, it is not one of spontaneous protest arising from American working-class experience. It is a complicated system of assumptions, based on European history and conditions, shrouded in an obscure and ambiguous vocabulary, which allures our ultrasophisticated intelligentsia more than our hard-headed working people. From time to time it champions all manner of causes and grievances and makes alliances that may add to its foothold in government or embarrass the authorities.

The Communist Party, nevertheless, does not seek its strength primarily in numbers. Its aim is a relatively small party whose strength is in selected, dedicated, indoctrinated, and rigidly disciplined members. From established policy it tolerates no deviation and no debate. It seeks members that are, or may be, secreted in strategic posts in transportation, communications, industry, government, and especially in labor unions where it can compel employers to accept and retain its members. It also seeks to infiltrate and control organizations of professional and other groups. Through these placements in positions of power it seeks a leverage over society that will make up in power of coercion what it lacks in power of persuasion.

The Communists have no scruples against sabotage, terrorism, assassination, or mob disorder; but violence is not with them, as with the anarchists, an end in itself. The Communist Party advocates force only when prudent and profitable. Their strategy of stealth precludes premature or uncoordinated outbursts of violence, except, of course, when the blame will be placed on shoulders other than their own. They resort to violence as to truth, not as a principle but as an expedient. Force or violence, as they would resort to it, may never be necessary, because infiltration and deception may be enough.

Force would be utilized by the Communist Party not to destroy government but for its capture. The Communist recognizes that an established government in control of modern technology cannot be overthrown by force until it is about ready to fall of its own weight. Concerted uprising, therefore, is to await that contingency and revolution is seen, not as a sudden episode, but as the consummation of a long process.

The United States, fortunately, has experienced Communism only in its preparatory stages and for its pattern of final action must look abroad. Russia, of course, was the pilot Communist revolution, which to the Marxist confirms the Party's assumptions and points its destiny. But Communist technique in the overturn of a free government was disclosed by the *coup d'etat* in which they seized power in Czechoslovakia. There the Communist Party during its preparatory stage claimed and received protection for its freedoms of speech, press, and assembly. Pretending to be but another political party, it eventually was conceded participation in government, where it entrenched reliable members chiefly in control of police and information services. When the government faced a foreign and domestic crisis, the Communist Party had established a leverage strong enough to threaten civil war. In a period of confusion the Communist plan unfolded and the underground organization came to the surface throughout the country in the form chiefly of labor "action committees." Communist officers of the unions took over transportation and allowed only persons with party permits to travel. Communist printers took over the newspapers and radio and put out only party-approved versions of events. Possession was taken of telegraph and telephone systems and communications were cut off wherever directed by party heads. Communist unions took over the factories, and in the cities a partisan distribution of food was managed by the Communist organization. A virtually bloodless abdication by the elected government admitted the Communists to power, whereupon they instituted a reign of oppression and terror, and ruthlessly denied to all others the freedoms which had sheltered their conspiracy.

The foregoing is enough to indicate that, either by accident or design, the Communist strategem outwits the anti-anarchist pattern of statute aimed against "overthrow by force and violence" if qualified by the doctrine that only "clear and present danger" of accomplishing that result will sustain the prosecution.

The "clear and present danger" test was an innovation by Mr. Justice Holmes in the Schenck case, reiterated and refined by him and Mr. Justice

Brandeis in later cases, all arising before the era of World War II revealed the subtlety and efficacy of modernized revolutionary techniques used by totalitarian parties. In those cases, they were faced with convictions under so-called criminal syndicalism statutes aimed at anarchists but which, loosely construed, had been applied to punish socialism, pacifism, and left-wing ideologies, the charges often resting on far-fetched inferences which, if true, would establish only technical or trivial violations. They proposed "clear and present danger" as a test for the sufficiency of evidence in particular cases.

I would save it, unmodified, for application as a "rule of reason" in the kind of case for which it was devised. When the issue is criminality of a hot-headed speech on a street corner, or circulation of a few incendiary pamphlets, or parading by some zealots behind a red flag, or refusal of a handful of school children to salute our flag, it is not beyond the capacity of the judicial process to gather, comprehend, and weigh the necessary materials for decision whether it is a clear and present danger of substantive evil or a harmless letting off of steam. It is not a prophecy, for the danger in such cases has matured by the time of trial or it was never present. The test applies and has meaning where a conviction is sought to be based on a speech or writing which does not directly or explicitly advocate a crime but to which such tendency is sought to be attributed by construction or by implication from external circumstances. The formula in such cases favors freedoms that are vital to our society, and, even if sometimes applied too generously, the consequences cannot be grave. But its recent expansion has extended, in particular to Communists, unprecedented immunities. Unless we are to hold our Government captive in a judge-made verbal trap, we must approach the problem of a well-organized, nation-wide conspiracy, such as I have described, as realistically as our predecessors faced the trivialities that were being prosecuted until they were checked with a rule of reason.

I think reason is lacking for applying that test to this case.

If we must decide that this Act and its application are constitutional only if we are convinced that petitioner's conduct creates a "clear and present danger" of violent overthrow, we must appraise imponderables, including international and national phenomena which baffle the best informed foreign offices and our most experienced politicians. We would have to foresee and predict the effectiveness of Communist propaganda, opportunities for infiltration, whether, and when, a time will come that they consider propitious for action, and whether and how fast our existing government will deteriorate. And we would have to speculate as to whether an approaching Communist *coup* would not be anticipated by a nationalistic fascist movement. No doctrine can be sound whose application requires us to make a prophecy of that sort in the guise of a legal decision. The judicial process simply is not adequate to a trial of such far-flung issues. The answers given would reflect our own political predilections and nothing more.

The authors of the clear and present danger test never applied it to a case like this, nor would I. If applied as it is proposed here, it means that the Communist plotting is protected during its period of incubation; its preliminary stages of organization and preparation are immune from the law; the Government can move only after imminent action is manifest, when it would, of course, be too late.

The highest degree of constitutional protection is due to the individual acting without conspiracy. But even an individual cannot claim that the Constitution protects him in advocating or teaching overthrow of government by force or violence. I should suppose no one would doubt that Congress has power to make such attempted overthrow a crime. But the contention is that one has the constitutional right to work up a public desire and will to do what it is a crime to attempt. I think direct incitement by speech or writing can be made a crime. . . .

As aptly stated by Judge Learned Hand in *Masses Publishing Co.* v. *Patten,* 244 F. 535, 540: "One may not counsel or advise others to violate the law as it stands. Words are not only the keys of persuasion, but the triggers of action, and those which have no purport but to counsel the violation of law cannot by any latitude of interpretation be a part of that public opinion which is the final source of government in a democratic state."

Of course, it is not always easy to distinguish teaching or advocacy in the sense of incitement from teaching or advocacy in the sense of exposition or explanation. It is a question of fact in each case.

What really is under review here is a conviction of conspiracy, after a trial for conspiracy, on an indictment charging conspiracy, brought under a statute outlawing conspiracy. With due respect to my colleagues, they seem to discuss anything under the sun except the law of conspiracy. One of the dissenting opinions even appears to chide me for "invoking the law of conspiracy." As that is the case before us, it may be more amazing that its reversal can be proposed without even considering the law of conspiracy.

The Constitution does not make conspiracy a civil right. The Court has never before done so and I think it should not do so now. Conspiracies of labor unions, trade associations, and news agencies have been condemned, although accomplished, evidenced and carried out, like the conspiracy here, chiefly by letter-writing, meetings, speeches and organization. Indeed, this Court seems, particularly in cases where the conspiracy has economic ends, to be applying its doctrines with increasing severity. While I consider criminal conspiracy a dragnet device capable of perversion into an instrument of injustice in the hands of a partisan or complacent judiciary, it has an established place in our system of law, and no reason appears for applying it only to concerted action claimed to disturb interstate commerce and withholding it from those claimed to undermine our whole Government. . . .

There is lamentation in the dissents about the injustice of conviction in the absence of some overt act. Of course, there has been no general uprising against the Government, but the record is replete with acts to carry out the conspiracy alleged, acts such as always are held sufficient to consummate the crime where the statute requires an overt act.

But the shorter answer is that no overt act is or need be required. The Court, in antitrust cases, early upheld the power of Congress to adopt the ancient common law that makes conspiracy itself a crime. Through Mr. Justice Holmes, it said: "Coming next to the objection that no overt act is laid, the answer is that the Sherman Act punished the conspiracies at which it is aimed on the common law footing—that is to say, it does not make the doing of any act other than the act of conspiring a condition of liability." *Nash* v. *United States,* 229 U.S. 373, 378. Reiterated, *United States* v. *Socony-Vacuum Oil Co.,* 310 U.S. 150, 252. It is not to be supposed that the power of Congress to protect the Nation's existence is more limited than its power to protect interstate commerce. . . .

The defense of freedom of speech or press has often been raised in conspiracy cases, because, whether committed by Communists, by businessmen, or by common criminals, it usually consists of words written or spoken, evidenced by letters, conversations, speeches or documents. Communication is the essence of every conspiracy, for only by it can common purpose and concert of action be brought about or be proved. However, when labor unions raised the defense of free speech against a conspiracy charge, we unanimously said:

"It rarely has been suggested that the constitutional freedom for speech and press extends its immunity to speech or writing used as an integral part of conduct in violation of a valid criminal statute. We reject the contention now. . . .

"Such an expansive interpretation of the constitutional guaranties of speech and press would make it practically impossible ever to enforce laws against agreements in restraint of trade as well as many other agreements and conspiracies deemed injurious to society." *Giboney* v. *Empire Storage & Ice Co.,* 336 U.S. 490, 498, 502. . . .

While I think there was power in Congress to enact this statute and that, as applied in this case, it cannot be held unconstitutional, I add that I have little faith in the long-range effectiveness of this conviction to stop the rise of the Communist movement. Communism will not go to jail with these Communists. No decision by this Court can forestall revolution whenever the existing government fails to command the respect and loyalty of the people and sufficient distress and discontent is allowed to grow up among the masses. Many failures by fallen governments attest that no government can long prevent revolution by outlawry. Corruption, ineptitude, inflation, oppressive taxation, militarization, injustice, and loss of leadership capable of intellectual initiative in domestic or foreign affairs are allies on which the Communists count to bring opportunity knocking to their door. Sometimes I think they may be mistaken. But the Communists are not building just for today—the rest of us might profit by their example.

MR. JUSTICE DOUGLAS, dissenting.

If this were a case where those who claimed protection under the First Amendment were teaching the techniques of sabotage, the assassination of the President, the filching of documents from public files, the planting of bombs, the art of street warfare, and the like, I would have no doubts. The freedom to speak is not absolute; the teaching of methods of terror and other seditious conduct should be beyond the pale along with obscenity and immorality. This case was argued as if those were the facts. The argument imported much seditious conduct into the record. That is easy and it has popular appeal, for the activities of Communists in plotting and scheming against the free world are common knowledge. But the fact is that no such evidence was introduced at the trial. There is a statute which makes a seditious conspiracy unlawful.[1] Petitioners, however, were not charged with a "conspiracy to overthrow" the Government. They were charged with a conspiracy to form a party and groups and assemblies of people who teach and advocate the overthrow of our Government by force or violence and with a conspiracy to advocate and teach its overthrow by force and violence. It may well be that indoctrination in the techniques of terror to destroy the Government would be indictable under either statute. But the teaching which is condemned here is of a different character.

So far as the present record is concerned, what petitioners did was to organize people to teach and themselves teach the Marxist-Leninist doctrine contained chiefly in four books: [2] *Foundations of Leninism* by Stalin (1924), *The Communist Manifesto* by Marx and Engels (1848), *State and Revolution* by Lenin (1917), *History of the Communist Party of the Soviet Union* (B) (1939).

Those books are to Soviet Communism what Mein Kampf was to Nazism. If they are understood, the ugliness of Communism is revealed, its deceit and cunning are exposed, the nature of its activities becomes apparent, and the chances of its success less likely. That is not, of course, the reason why petitioners chose these books for their classrooms. They are fervent Communists to whom these volumes are gospel. They preached the creed with the hope that some day it would be acted upon.

The opinion of the Court does not outlaw these texts nor condemn them to the fire, as the Communists do literature offensive to their creed. But if

[1] 18 U.S.C. §2384 provides: "If two or more persons in any State or Territory, or in any place subject to the jurisdiction of the United States, conspire to overthrow, put down, or to destroy by force the Government of the United States, or to levy war against them, or to oppose by force the authority thereof, or by force to prevent, hinder, or delay the execution of any law of the United States, or by force to seize, take, or possess any property of the United States contrary to the authority thereof, they shall each be fined not more than $5,000 or imprisoned not more than six years, or both."

[2] Other books taught were *Problems of Leninism* by Stalin, *Strategy and Tactics of World Communism* (H. Doc. No. 619, 80th Cong., 2d Sess.), and *Program of the Communist International.*

the books themselves are not outlawed, if they can lawfully remain on library shelves, by what reasoning does their use in a classroom become a crime? It would not be a crime under the Act to introduce these books to a class, though that would be teaching what the creed of violent overthrow of the government is. The Act, as construed, requires the element of intent—that those who teach the creed believe in it. The crime then depends not on what is taught but on who the teacher is. That is to make freedom of speech turn not on *what is said,* but on the *intent* with which it is said. Once we start down that road we enter territory dangerous to the liberties of every citizen. . . .

Free speech has occupied an exalted position because of the high service it has given our society. Its protection is essential to the very existence of a democracy. The airing of ideas releases pressures which otherwise might become destructive. When ideas compete in the market for acceptance, full and free discussion exposes the false and they gain few adherents. Full and free discussion even of ideas we hate encourages the testing of our own prejudices and preconceptions. Full and free discussion keeps a society from becoming stagnant and unprepared for the stresses and strains that work to tear all civilizations apart.

Full and free discussion has indeed been the first article of our faith. We have founded our political system on it. It has been the safeguard of every religious, political, philosophical, economic, and racial group amongst us. We have counted on it to keep us from embracing what is cheap and false; we have trusted the common sense of our people to choose the doctrine true to our genius and to reject the rest. This has been the one single outstanding tenet that has made our institutions the symbol of freedom and equality. We have deemed it more costly to liberty to suppress a despised minority than to let them vent their spleen. We have above all else feared the political censor. We have wanted a land where our people can be exposed to all the diverse creeds and cultures of the world.

There comes a time when even speech loses its constitutional immunity. Speech innocuous one year may at another time fan such destructive flames that it must be halted in the interests of the safety of the Republic. That is the meaning of the clear and present danger test. When conditions are so critical that there will be no time to avoid the evil that the speech threatens, it is time to call a halt. Otherwise, free speech which is the strength of the Nation will be the cause of its destruction.

Yet free speech is the rule, not the exception. The restraint to be constitutional must be based on more than fear, on more than passionate opposition against the speech, on more than a revolted dislike for its contents. There must be some immediate injury to society that is likely if speech is allowed. The classic statement of these conditions was made by Mr. Justice Brandeis in his concurring opinion in *Whitney* v. *California,* 274 U.S. 357, 376–377,

"Fear of serious injury cannot alone justify suppression of free speech and assembly. Men feared witches and burnt women. It is the function of speech to free men from the bondage of irrational fears. To justify suppression of free speech there must be reasonable ground to fear that serious evil will result if free speech is practiced. There must be reasonable ground to believe that the danger apprehended is imminent. There must be reasonable ground to believe that the evil to be prevented is a serious one. Every denunciation of existing law tends in some measure to increase the probability that there will be violation of it. Condonation of a breach enhances the probability. Expressions of approval add to the probability. Propagation of the criminal state of mind by teaching syndicalism increases it. Advocacy of law-breaking heightens it still further. But even advocacy of violation, however reprehensible morally, is not a justification for denying free speech where the advocacy falls short of incitement and there is nothing to indicate that the advocacy would be immediately acted on. The wide difference between advocacy and incitement, between preparation and attempt, between assembling and conspiracy, must be borne in mind. In order to support a finding of a clear and present danger it must be shown either that immediate serious violence was to be expected or was advocated, or that the past conduct furnished reason to believe that such advocacy was then contemplated.

"Those who won our independence by revolution were not cowards. They did not fear political change. They did not exalt order at the cost of liberty. To courageous, self-reliant men, with confidence in the power of free and fearless reasoning applied through the processes of popular government, no danger flowing from speech can be deemed clear and present, unless the incidence of the evil apprehended is so imminent that it may befall before there is opportunity for full discussion. *If there be time to expose through discussion the falsehood and fallacies to avert the evil by the processes of education, the remedy to be applied is more speech, not enforced silence.*" (Italics added.)

I had assumed that the question of the clear and present danger, being so critical an issue in the case, would be a matter for submission to the jury. . . .

Yet, whether the question is one for the Court or the jury, there should be evidence of record on the issue. This record, however, contains no evidence whatsoever showing that the acts charged, *viz.*, the teaching of the Soviet theory of revolution with the hope that it will be realized, have created any clear and present danger to the Nation. The Court, however, rules to the contrary. It says, "The formation by petitioners of such a highly organized conspiracy, with rigidly disciplined members subject to call when the leaders, these petitioners, felt that the time had come for action, coupled with the inflammable nature of world conditions, similar uprisings in other countries, and the touch-and-go nature of our relations with countries with whom petitioners were in the very least ideologically attuned, convince us that their convictions were justified on this score."

That ruling is in my view not responsive to the issue in the case. We might as well say that the speech of petitioners is outlawed because Soviet Russia and her Red Army are a threat to world peace.

The nature of Communism as a force on the world scene would, of course, be relevant to the issue of clear and present danger of petitioners' advocacy within the United States. But the primary consideration is the strength and tactical position of petitioners and their converts in this country. On that there is no evidence in the record. If we are to take judicial notice of the threat of Communists within the nation, it should not be difficult to conclude that *as a political party* they are of little consequence. Communists in this country have never made a respectable or serious showing in any election. I would doubt that there is a village, let alone a city or county or state which the Communists could carry. Communism in the world scene is no bogey-man; but Communists as a political faction or party in this country plainly is. Communism has been so thoroughly exposed in this country that it has been crippled as a political force. Free speech has destroyed it as an effective political party. It is inconceivable that those who went up and down this country preaching the doctrine of revolution which petitioners espouse would have any success. In days of trouble and confusion when bread lines were long, when the unemployed walked the streets, when people were starving, the advocates of a short-cut by revolution might have a chance to gain adherents. But today there are no such conditions. The country is not in despair; the people know Soviet Communism; the doctrine of Soviet revolution is exposed in all of its ugliness and the American people want none of it.

How it can be said that there is a clear and present danger that this advocacy will succeed is, therefore, a mystery. Some nations less resilient than the United States, where illiteracy is high and where democratic traditions are only budding, might have to take drastic steps and jail these men for merely speaking their creed. But in America they are miserable merchants of unwanted ideas; their wares remain unsold. The fact that their ideas are abhorrent does not make them powerful. . . .

The First Amendment provides that "Congress shall make no law . . . abridging the freedom of speech." The Constitution provides no exception. This does not mean, however, that the Nation need hold its hand until it is in such weakened condition that there is no time to protect itself from incitement to revolution. Seditious conduct can always be punished. But the command of the First Amendment is so clear that we should not allow Congress to call a halt to free speech except in the extreme case of peril from the speech itself. The First Amendment makes confidence in the common sense of our people and in their maturity of judgment the great postulate of our democracy. Its philosophy is that violence is rarely, if ever, stopped by denying civil liberties to those advocating resort to force. The First Amendment reflects the philosophy of Jefferson "that it is time enough for the rightful purposes of civil government for its officers to interfere when principles break out into overt acts against peace and good order." The political censor has no place in our public debates. Unless and until extreme and necessitous circumstances are shown our aim should be to keep speech unfettered and to allow the processes of law to be invoked only when the provocateurs among us move from speech to action.

Vishinsky wrote in 1948 in *The Law of the Soviet State,* "In our state, naturally there can be no place for freedom of speech, press, and so on for the foes of socialism."

Our concern should be that we accept no such standard for the United States. Our faith should be that our people will never give support to these advocates of revolution, so long as we remain loyal to the purposes for which our Nation was founded.

MR. JUSTICE BLACK, dissenting.

At the outset I want to emphasize what the crime involved in this case is, and what it is not. These petitioners were not charged with an attempt to overthrow the government. They were not charged with nonverbal acts of any kind designed to overthrow the government. They were not even charged with saying anything or writing anything designed to overthrow the government. The charge was that they agreed to assemble and to talk and publish certain ideas at a later date: the indictment is that they conspired to organize the Communist party and to use speech or newspapers and other publications in the future to teach and advocate the forcible overthrow of the government. No matter how it is worded, this is a virulent form of prior censorship of speech and press, which I believe the first amendment forbids. I would hold (section) 3 of the Smith Act authorizing this prior restraint unconstitutional on its face and as applied. . . .

I have always believed that the first amendment is the keystone of our government, that the freedoms it guarantees provide the best insurance against destruction of all freedom. . . .

So long as this court exercises the power of judicial review of legislation, I cannot agree that the first amendment permits us to sustain laws suppressing freedom of speech and press on the basis of Congress' or our own notions of mere "reasonableness." . . .

Public opinion being what it now is, few will protest the conviction of these Communist petitioners. There is hope, however, that in calmer times, when present pressures, passions and fears subside, this or some later court will restore the first amendment liberties to the high preferred place where they belong in a free society.

MR. JUSTICE FRANKFURTER also wrote a concurring opinion.

SECTION IV

Judicial Review

Judicial review, by which is meant the power of American courts and finally of the Supreme Court to set aside national and state legislation as unconstitutional, has served as, and remains, at least potentially, one of the most important restraints upon majority rule provided by our Constitution. (The power of judicial review with respect to federal legislation, as has been seen, was established in the case of *Marbury* v. *Madison.*) The question of the compatibility of judicial review with democracy has been sharply and persistently raised. And the answer, in turn, in no small part will depend on how democracy is defined. Apart from its democratic or undemocratic nature, however, the issue remains whether its values to the American people have been greater than its vices.

The material we have included on this issue sets forth some leading arguments for and against judicial review. The included extract from Justice Cardozo has been characterized by D. W. Brogan, the eminent British political scientist, as "the best defense of judicial review, at any rate in the field of constitutional guarantees where its activities have been most often and most vigorously condemned." The statement of Dorothy Thompson in support of judicial review was made in 1937 in a Hearing of the Senate Committee on the Judiciary which was considering President Roosevelt's proposal to reorganize the Court.

Topic 17

ATTACK ON JUDICIAL REVIEW

THE RÔLE OF THE SUPREME COURT IN A DEMOCRATIC NATION

Robert E. Cushman *

Back in 1801 Jefferson wrote to a friend: "The Federalists have retired into the judiciary as a stronghold—and from that battery all the works of republicanism are to be beaten down and erased." Some people to-day be-

* Professor and Head of Government Department at Cornell University. Author of *The Independent Regulatory Commissions*. Editor of *Leading Constitutional Decisions*. Contributor to legal and other periodicals. The selection is from Robert E. Cushman,

lieve that in a democracy no court should have power to invalidate laws passed by the representatives of the people. Many others believe that we need a Supreme Court with power to declare laws unconstitutional; but they also feel that in the use of that authority the Court has dangerously assumed powers which belong to the legislature, powers which in a democratic government ought not to be exercised by a court of law. This is the problem which I wish to explore. What is the rôle of the Supreme Court in our constitutional democracy? . . .

I should like *first* to show the nature and growth of the Supreme Court's power to invalidate laws. *Second,* I wish to show that the Court in reviewing legislation determines not merely the constitutionality of law but the wisdom and desirability of legislative policy. . . .

I. *The nature and growth of the Supreme Court's power over legislation.* Let us turn to the first of these [two] topics,—the nature and growth of the Supreme Court's power over legislation. I do not enter here upon any analysis of the theory of judicial review. I do not wish to make any comment upon the old, old dispute as to whether the framers of the Constitution intended to have the Supreme Court invalidate acts of Congress. We may accept judicial review as a going concern without worrying about its lineage. I should like, however, to trace the stages in the development of the power of the Supreme Court to declare laws unconstitutional, from the rather modest beginning in John Marshall's famous decision in the case of *Marbury* v. *Madison,* to the broad and drastic power which the Court now enjoys. This will make more clear the actual working relations between the Supreme Court and the Congress. There are at least four stages in this evolution of the Court's power, and these I wish to discuss.

First, let us examine briefly the case in which the Supreme Court first declared an act of Congress unconstitutional. This was the case of *Marbury* v. *Madison*. . . . [See Topic 11.] Now there are two facts about *Marbury* v. *Madison* which should be carefully noted. In the first place, the act of Congress held void was an act in which Congress had, in the Court's opinion, unconstitutionally tampered with the Court's own jurisdiction. It had tried to give to the Court powers which could not validly be given and the Court had protected itself against this legislative assault on its own integrity. Jefferson himself could not logically quarrel with the basic theory of the Court's action. He believed that each of the three departments of the Government must interpret the Constitution in so far as it bears upon its own powers and status, and may properly follow its own interpretation. No department is bound by the constitutional interpretation of any other department. In *Marbury* v. *Madison* the Court is simply saying to the Congress, "You must keep your hands off from us. You cannot enlarge our jurisdiction beyond

"The Rôle of the Supreme Court in a Democratic Nation," Edmund Janes James Lecture at the University of Illinois, March 9, 1938. Reprinted by permission of the author and the University of Illinois Press.

constitutional limits." While some of Marshall's language is more generous, the case of *Marbury* v. *Madison,* viewed on its facts, does not establish the power of the Court to reach over its own fence and pass upon the validity of Congressional or Presidential acts which in no way affect the prerogatives or jurisdiction of the Court itself. Marshall nowhere asserts the superiority of the Court over Congress or the Executive, nor does he lay claim on the Court's behalf to any general power of supervision over the other two departments. In the second place, no other act of Congress was invalidated until the Dred Scott case in 1857. If the Supreme Court, under the doctrine of *Marbury* v. *Madison,* was supposed to enjoy the broad power to supervise the constitutional correctness with which Congress and the President exercised their own powers, it is rather surprising that during the fifty years following no attempt was made to seek the Court's decision as to the constitutionality of the Bank of the United States, a protective tariff, the acquisition of Louisiana, the annexation of Texas, and numerous other legislative or executive acts which aroused bitter constitutional dispute.

The second stage in the development of the power of judicial review was reached in the Dred Scott case decided in 1857. We cannot go into the fascinating story of this great case. It is enough for our purposes to know that the Court held that a Negro slave could not become a citizen of the United States, and that the Missouri Compromise Act of 1820, which forbade slavery in the federal territories north of 36° 30″, was unconstitutional. In thus forbidding slavery in the territories Congress had exercised a power not granted to it in the Constitution, a power which could not validly be implied from the delegated power to govern the territories. This represents an important enlargement of the scope of judicial review over the doctrine of *Marbury* v. *Madison.* Marshall's early decision had held that the Court could refuse to enforce laws purporting to change its own jurisdiction when the Court believed those laws to be invalid. In the Dred Scott case Taney and his colleagues go much further. They hold that the judgment of Congress as to the scope of one of its own legislative powers, this time a power in no way concerning the Court, is wrong and that the act so passed is unconstitutional. The Court, in other words, takes on the task of determining whether Congress has exercised powers which the Constitution has not delegated to it. Congress must stay in its own constitutional backyard and the Supreme Court, not Congress, is to determine whether it has done so.

The third stage in the growth of judicial guardianship over legislation came in the late eighties with the emergence of the Court's modern doctrine of due process of law. Here the Court added to its power of deciding whether Congress exercised undelegated power the much more far-reaching power of deciding whether Congress has exercised delegated power in an improper manner. Due process of law is a test, not of the existence of legislative power, but of the method of its exercise. The story back of this can be sketched only in the briefest way. The guarantee of due process of law traces its ancestry back to Magna Charta. After many permutations we find it set forth in the Fifth Amendment of the Federal Bill of Rights. There we read, "no person shall be deprived of life, liberty, or property without due process of law." Similar clauses are found in most state constitutions, and in 1868 the Fourteenth Amendment included an identical due process clause which applies to the states. The early history of due process of law was not spectacular. For a hundred years due process was held to be a limitation upon governmental procedure and not upon the substance or content of legislative policy. It required notice and hearing and a fair trial, but it did not forbid the legislature to regulate a social or economic problem.

After the Fourteenth Amendment was adopted the Supreme Court, in its first case construing it, held that the due process clause had no relevance to, and could not, therefore, forbid an arbitrary state police regulation setting up a slaughterhouse monopoly in New Orleans. Due process seemed destined to remain the "forgotten clause" of the Constitution. But vast economic changes were taking place. The states began to deal with social and economic problems through more drastic exercises of their police powers, while the regulatory powers of Congress, especially under the commerce clause, were pushed far beyond previous limits. All this legislative activity was a sharp challenge to our American pioneer philosophy of *laissez faire*. Vested interests felt keenly the need of a constitutional weapon with which to combat the onward march of the new social control, and after a period of some wavering and uncertainty the Supreme Court, abandoning the precedents of a hundred years, converted the due process clauses of the Fifth and Fourteenth Amendments into judicial yardsticks by which to measure the validity of the substance and content of social legislation. Under the new rule a state or federal law was void as a denial of due process of law if in the opinion of the Court it impinged in an "arbitrary" manner upon the liberty or property rights of the individual. This step, taken without ostentation, constituted the greatest expansion of the Court's power to review legislation which has thus far occurred. Let me give a single illustration of the way in which the new doctrine enlarged judicial power. In 1898 Congress passed the Erdman Act regulating interstate railroads. One section of that act, aimed at the promotion of collective bargaining, forbade any interstate railroad to discharge one of its men because he belonged to a labor union. The Supreme Court held the act void on two grounds. It held first that this provision was not a regulation of interstate commerce because the relations between the railroad and its men had nothing to do with interstate commerce and did not, therefore, fall within the delegated power of Congress to regulate that commerce. It held, secondly, that, even if Congress had exercised its commerce power in passing the act, it had exercised it in so arbitrary and unreasonable a manner as to deprive the railroads of their liberty and property without due process of law. Congress had tried to exercise a power it did not have; but even if it had had the power, it had exercised it in an unconstitutional manner.

There is a fourth step in the development I am tracing. By it the Court has added to its scrutiny of the constitutional propriety of the *method* by which a granted power has been exercised by Congress, the further job of judging the constitutional propriety of the *purpose* for which the power has been used. This new technique was first employed in invalidating the first federal child labor act in 1918 in the case of *Hammer* v. *Dagenhart*. This act had forbidden the shipment in interstate commerce of the products of mines and factories in which children were employed in violation of standards set up in the act. In a five-to-four decision this was held void on two grounds. First, child labor is not closely enough connected with interstate commerce to make the statute a bona fide exercise of the delegated power to regulate commerce. Secondly, even if the statute were a bona fide exercise of the commerce power, it was an exercise of the commerce power for an unconstitutional *purpose,* namely, the regulation of child labor, a matter lying within the powers reserved to the states by the Tenth Amendment. Three New Deal measures of importance were invalidated on this same ground, that they constituted exercises of valid federal powers for invalid purposes. These acts were the Agricultural Adjustment Act, the Municipal Bankruptcy Act, and the Guffey Coal Act. In invalidating the AAA in the Butler case Mr. Justice Roberts did not hold the processing taxes and the paying of crop reduction benefits void on the ground that Congress was not exercising its delegated power to spend money. He held it void because the tax was levied in order to raise money to be spent for financing a scheme for the regulation of agriculture, an object which lies outside the delegated powers of Congress. The power was there, the method was regular, but the purpose was wrong. The Court has thus extended its supervision to the *motives* which have led Congress to exercise its delegated powers. "Thus," as Mr. Justice Cardozo put it, "the process of psychoanalysis has spread to unaccustomed fields."

To summarize this whole growth of judicial power, we find the Court at the outset protecting itself and its jurisdiction from unconstitutional interference by Congress. It next assumed the power to keep Congress from exercising powers not delegated to it by the Constitution. By a third step, the Court took over the authority to see that Congress and the States do not exercise their admitted powers by methods which seem to the Court to be arbitrary. Finally, the Court has undertaken to scrutinize legislative motives and to invalidate exercises of valid powers, by valid methods, but for wrongful purposes. Thus the judicial camel has got himself pretty completely into the legislative tent.

II. *The legislative and policy-determining character of the Supreme Court's power to declare laws void.* This brings me to the second major part of my discussion—the substitution, through the Court's power of judicial review, of judicial for legislative judgments on major questions of legislative policy. Has this come about in any large measure? If so, how has it come about, and with what practical results? My own view is that the Supreme Court now exercises wide power over the actual content of legislative policy. A very large proportion of the social and economic legislation invalidated in recent years has been held void not because it conflicted clearly and unmistakably with the clauses of the Constitution, but because a majority of the members of the Supreme Court believed the legislation to be economically unsound and objectionable. The Court exercises what I believe to be essentially a legislative veto. It is doing the legislature's job over again.

I am well aware that this charge would be sternly denied by the Supreme Court. As Professor Thomas Reed Powell has neatly put it, the Court has a very keen appreciation of "the role of rigmarole" in the judicial process. Proceeding on the theory "let not thy left hand know what thy right hand doeth," the Court continues to insist that the invalidating of a statute is an almost mechanical judicial process in which there is no room for personal opinion as to the social or economic merits of the legislation involved. In the very process of holding the Agricultural Adjustment Act void on grounds so strained and loosely reasoned as to reach almost a new low in judicial technique, Mr. Justice Roberts takes time out to restate the old orthodox incantation:

> When an act of Congress is appropriately challenged in the Courts as not conforming to the constitutional mandate, the judicial branch of the Government has only one duty—to lay the article of the Constitution which is invoked beside the statute which is challenged—and to decide whether the latter squares with the former. All the Court does, or can do, is to announce its considered judgment upon the question.

All of which sounds as though the justices, with the aid of compasses and slide rules, should reach a perfectly accurate result with which there can be no disagreement.

Now, certain clauses of the Constitution can be interpreted by the Supreme Court in this coldly mechanical manner. If Congress should fix federal income tax rates at a higher level in Illinois than in New York there could not be the slightest doubt that such an act violates the requirement of geographical uniformity in accordance with which the Constitution states that such taxes must be levied. It would be impossible for Congress to regulate criminal procedure in the federal courts in such a way as to violate the provisions of the federal Bill of Rights guaranteeing trial by jury, or protection against compulsory self-incrimination. It may be readily agreed that in such cases the Court could put the statute and the constitutional provision side by side and see at a glance that they do not jibe. Cases of this kind are exceedingly rare. They are rare because legislatures are not likely to indulge in self-advertised violations of the Constitution.

But these are not the cases in which the validity of social and economic legislation is involved or in which broad questions of legislative policy are at issue. If we examine the cases in which important legislative measures have been held by the Supreme Court to be valid or to be invalid over the last twenty years, we shall see that the constitutional provisions which these laws are supposed to violate do not have any clear, certain, and established meaning. What, for instance, are the major constitutional issues on which the validity of the principal New Deal measures turned? They are three in number. *First,* has Congress exercised some power not delegated to it? Or, concretely, can you reasonably hang the National Industrial Recovery Act on the constitutional "peg" of the commerce power, which Congress thought it was exercising when it passed the statute? *Second,* has Congress, or have the states, exercised some power in a manner so arbitrary or unreasonable as to amount to a deprivation of liberty or property without due process of law? *Third,* has Congress exercised some delegated power, such as the commerce power, or the taxing power, for a purpose believed by the Court to be unconstitutional? There are no sharp, clear lines here between the constitutional and the unconstitutional, no categories of black and white, and in settling these issues the Court has come to exercise a type of judgment and discretion which is essentially legislative in character. Let us examine more closely just how the judicial process actually works in dealing with problems of this sort.

Let us turn first to the Minimum Wage Cases. In 1923 the Supreme Court by a five-to-three decision held that the due process clauses of the Constitution guarantee the right to pay women and children starvation wages. The Court clung to this shocking doctrine until last year when it held by a five-to-four vote that its previous decision was wrong and that minimum wage laws for women and minors do not deny due process of law. Now what actually happened here? A minimum wage law is an exercise of what we call the police power. The police power is that vital power of the American states to legislate for the public welfare. More specifically it is the power of the state to restrict individual freedom of action, or the free use of private property, in order to protect the health, morals, good order, convenience, or general welfare. A parking regulation, a quarantine of contagious disease, or an act forbidding gambling is each an exercise of the police power. Each exercise of the police power contains two elements. It restricts individual liberty and it protects or promotes some public social interest. The Court's task when it applies the test of due process of law to a legislative exercise of the police power is to weigh these two conflicting interests one against the other. If, in the opinion of the Court, the restriction upon individual liberty outweighs the social advantage claimed for the act, then it denies due process of law. Thus a majority of the Court prior to March, 1937, believed that minimum wage laws imposed upon employers and employees a burdensome restriction of their right to make free contracts with each other about wages, and that this restriction was not offset or compensated for by any equivalent social gain. The valued right of women and minors to work for next to nothing was at stake, and there was no substantial advantage to the community in having them paid a living wage. Then suddenly light came to one of the members of the Court and this balance between social advantage and restricted bargaining power was reversed. There were now five justices who believed that starvation wages for women and children were a sufficient social menace to warrant a legislative restriction on the free bargaining power of employers and employees, and as a result minimum wage laws suddenly became constitutional.

Now in reaching these important decisions the words of the Constitution have played no real part. The Constitution does not mention minimum wages and it does not explain what it means by due process of law. The Court therefore must decide whether or not a minimum wage law is valid without any direct help from the Constitution itself. The question is in essence not a legal question at all. It is a question of individual judgment and opinion and the answer which the individual judge makes to it will depend upon his social and economic philosophy, which, in turn, will depend upon his early environment and education and his business or professional associations. This is what Mr. Justice Stone was driving at when he said, "It is difficult to imagine any grounds, other than our own personal economic predilections," for holding a minimum wage law void. And when the Supreme Court invalidates important legislation on the basis of its "own economic predilections" it is doing the work of a legislature and not of a court; it is determining questions of legislative policy and not questions of law. Minimum wage laws were unconstitutional for fourteen years not because the Constitution forbids them but because a majority of the Court believed them unsound and objectionable.

Let us examine next the Schechter case in which the Supreme Court held void the National Industrial Recovery Act. We may pass by that part of the Court's decision holding that the NIRA invalidly delegated legislative power to the President, because the statute could easily have been amended to avoid that constitutional defect. The crucial issue in the case was whether Congress in the exercise of its delegated power to regulate interstate commerce could validly authorize the application of a code of fair competition to a Brooklyn wholesale poultry market and punish violations of that code. The Court, in a unanimous decision, held that it could not. The Government urged that the transactions in the Schechters' poultry market, and other similar establishments covered by the code, vitally affected the stream of interstate commerce in poultry in the metropolitan area. Congress therefore could properly take measures to protect that interstate commerce against the harmful effects of bad labor conditions and unfair competitive practices prevailing in the local markets. In a substantial number of cases the Court had permitted federal power to penetrate into local affairs in order to protect interstate commerce from the effects of local evils or local discrimination. The Supreme Court did not repudiate these earlier decisions. It did not even deny that conditions prevailing in the Schechters' poultry market had an influence upon the interstate commerce which Congress might lawfully regulate. It merely held that that influence was "indirect" and not "direct" and therefore the code could not be sustained under the commerce power. Here is an important act of Congress stricken down by the Court because it falls on the wrong side of the line by which the Court separates those transactions and interests which are "directly" connected with interstate commerce from those which are only "indirectly" connected with it. It is perfectly clear that in making such a decision and in drawing such a line the Court translates into a rule of constitutional law its own opinions as to how far the policy of federal centralization under the commerce power should be permitted to go, again a question of policy, a question of expediency, thinly disguised as a question of law.

There is a third type of decision in which the Court even more clearly assumes the role of the lawmaker. These are the cases in which the Court invalidates acts of Congress because delegated powers have been used for what the Court regards as wrongful purposes. Some of the best illustrations have arisen under the federal taxing power. In 1902, Congress, under pressure from the powerful lobby representing the dairy interests of the country, drove colored oleomargarine out of the market by levying on it a prohibitive tax of ten cents per pound. Two years later in the McCray case the Supreme Court upheld the statute against the charge that it was an abuse of the federal taxing power since its purpose was not revenue but destruction. The Court refused to inquire into or worry about the motives which had led Congress to pass the act. Such motives cannot properly be made the subject of judicial scrutiny. The oleomargarine tax is "on its face" a revenue measure. It is, in short, "objectively" constitutional, and whether it is "subjectively" unconstitutional, whether Congress had an ulterior and unconstitutional purpose in levying it, is none of the Court's business. A year ago this doctrine was reaffirmed in a case in which Congress had imposed a special license tax of $200 per year upon those engaged in selling machine-guns, sawed-off shotguns or rifles, and silencers. "On its face," says Mr. Justice Stone, "it is a taxing measure" and "inquiry into the hidden motives which may move Congress to exercise a power constitutionally conferred upon it is beyond the competency of the Court." The good faith of Congress is evidenced by the fact that twenty-seven people paid the tax in 1934 and twenty-two in 1935, so it must have been a revenue measure. In 1919, however, Congress imposed a tax of ten percent upon the net income of those employing children in violation of the standards set up in the act. It had also passed the Future Trading Act by which a tax of twenty cents a bushel was laid upon all grain sold on future contracts upon grain exchanges which were not registered with the Secretary of Agriculture and subject to his regulations. The Supreme Court held both of these statutes unconstitutional. The taxes levied were not really taxes at all. They were penalties imposed on those who indulge in practices which Congress objects to but may not directly forbid. Speaking of the child labor tax Chief Justice Taft declared, "Its prohibitory and regulatory effect and purpose are palpable. All others can see and understand this. How can we properly shut our minds to it?" How indeed, except by just following the sound and wholesome doctrine of the oleomargarine tax case that the motives leading Congress to exercise a delegated power are not a proper subject for judicial examination. But this the Court was not willing to do. Last year the Court applied the rule of the Child Labor Tax Case to a federal statute imposing an annual license tax of $1000 upon anyone engaging in the business of selling liquor in violation of the laws of a state. This, again, is a fiscal penalty and not a tax and encroaches, therefore, upon state power.

Now the Court in these tax cases has very deftly managed to eat its cake and keep it too. It invalidated the child labor tax without overruling its decision in the oleomargarine tax case. It has, therefore, both rules to play with and can select with a good deal of freedom which prohibitory or regulatory federal taxes it is going to hold valid and which it is going to hold void. Looking at them realistically there is no essential difference in the nature of these taxes or the privileges or interests upon which they fall. Congress taxes the privilege of making colored oleomargarine, the privilege of employing children, the privilege of selling the kinds of weapons with which gangster crimes are usually committed, or the privilege of operating as a bootlegger within a state. Congress could not directly forbid anyone to exercise any of these privileges on which it has laid its tax. In every case the tax is for a non-fiscal purpose and everybody knows it. When the Court approves of the regulatory policy involved in the tax it turns a blind eye to the obvious effect of the tax and applies the test of "objective constitutionality." But with equal ease it can invalidate a similar regulatory tax, by taking into account "what everybody knows" and applying the test of "subjective constitutionality." In deciding which formula to use the Court is able to give effect to its own views as to the expediency of the legislative policy involved, it is able to exercise a policy-determining power.

I have no patience with the pious verbal expressions and legal epigrams by which certain judges and lawyers seek to camouflage or to conceal the essentially legislative power which the Court exercises in the handling of these three groups of cases and many others. In applying these vague and general clauses of the Constitution to concrete cases the Court has the opportunity, and it embraces the opportunity, of giving effect to its hunches, its predilections, and its prejudices. In interpreting due process of law it may read into the Constitution either a progressive social philosophy or a Mid-Victorian theory of "rugged individualism." In setting the limits to the commerce power it may swing the balance toward an aggressive federal centralization or toward an equally vigorous protection of state rights. In my judgment the legislative power which the Supreme Court now wields in the exercise of its power of judicial review of legislation is far greater than can be soundly adjusted to the principles of democratic government. Our constitutional system rests on the principle that the legislative power of the United States is vested in the Congress. It is not vested in the Supreme Court. It seems to me one of the vicious paradoxes of our national democracy that so many vital questions of national policy are determined in the last analysis by the "personal economic predilections" of Supreme Court justices. . . .

Is Judicial Review Necessary?

Morris Raphael Cohen *

The power of the Supreme Court to declare acts of Congress unconstitutional does not, as a practice, exist in any other civilized country. One or two cases in Australia and Canada, under unusual conditions, are the exceptions which prove the general rule. Those who argue for its *necessity* rely on old fictions and ignore the facts. Thus, they claim that it is a necessary part of our Anglo-Saxon liberties, but Anglo-Saxon England has never allowed this power to its courts. Marshall's argument that it follows from the nature of written constitutions, is obviously refuted by the constitutions of France and of other countries where life, liberty and property are as safe, if not safer than they are here; and the argument that Federal Government is impossible without it, ignores the Swiss and other Federal states.

But the main fallacy is the argument that since the Constitution declares itself to be the supreme law of the land, therefore Congress and the Executive must accept the Court's interpretation of it, though they are supposed to be coordinate and not subordinate powers. This is the fallacy of *non sequitur*. A Constitution is adopted by the people, who ought to know what they vote for, and this cannot exclude the people's representatives in the Congress and in the Executive, mostly lawyers in any case. What the Constitution in fact does say, is that *it and the laws and treaties of the United States made in pursuance* of it, should be the supreme law of the land. Now, the members of Congress and the Executive swear to obey the Constitution,

* Late Professor of Philosophy at the College of the City of New York. President of the American Philosophical Association, 1929. Author of *Reason and Nature, Law and the Social Order, Preface to Logic, Faith of a Liberal*, and other works. The selection is from Morris Raphael Cohen, "Is Judicial Review Necessary?", an address given at the New School Forum, April 24, 1936. Also printed in slightly modified form in the *New Leader* (May 30, 1936), Vol. 19, p. 5.

and how can they make laws and treaties under it without interpreting its meaning? And why must they disregard their own conscientious reading of the Constitution because a different opinion is held by a majority of the Supreme Court, which may not be a majority even of all the judges that pass on the act? The notion that the court must necessarily have the *exclusive* and final power to declare what the Constitution means is neither historically nor logically tenable. Indeed, the Supreme Court itself abandons it when it admits that the meaning of the term "republican form of government" in the Constitution must be left to Congress and to the Executive.

Let us get behind legalistic hair-splitting and look at the question in the light of common sense and the logic that is no respecter of traditional dogmas. No one really believes that the human beings who adopted the Constitution in the 18th century foresaw all our modern conditions and made unmistakable provision as to what Congress may or may not enact into law. And the notion that they laid down certain principles from which every decision of the Supreme Court is deduced with absolute rigor and without regard to the personal opinion of the judges, must be pronounced ridiculous by the logic of modern science. History shows unmistakably that decisions on constitutional issues depend upon the political, social and economic opinions of the judges. Taney differed from Marshall, Field from Waite, and McReynolds from Holmes. And who honestly doubts that if the personnel of the court were to change tomorrow, its decisions would be different? It is certainly not through the will of the people and the express words of the Constitution that the power to regulate interstate commerce includes the power to prohibit lotteries but not to regulate insurance, to prohibit the passage of liquor from some States to others or to compel railroads to install certain safety appliances, but not to prohibit them from posting notices that they will discharge their men who join trade unions. Only recently this power to regulate interstate commerce was held to include the power to order a system of workmen's compensation but not a pension system. These and a thousand other subtle distinctions are points on which well-informed men and even judges honestly differ, and how the court will rule on any actual act of Congress, is largely a matter of guess work even for lawyers. It is unbelievable that the framers of the Constitution in 1787 had settled these matters beyond a reasonable doubt. When, therefore, a mere majority of the court insists that no rational being can doubt that Congress has misread or violated the plain provisions of the Constitution, their sense of humor as well as of courtesy to their fellow judges and to the coordinate powers of the government is rather esoteric.

Consider now the practical arguments for judicial review.

It has been defended as a necessary appeal from the passion and haste of Congress to the calm and deliberate judgment of the Courts; but this rests on a number of untenable assumptions. It is psychologically weird to suppose that judges are not human or free from human passions. One has only to recall Justice McReynolds' dissent in the Gold Case or the passionate outburst of Chief Justice Chase and the minority in connection with the second Legal Tender Case. Even more important is the fact that our courts are so constituted that their deliberation cannot possibly be based on adequate knowledge. For the court cannot institute investigation. It cannot hold prolonged hearings. The life of the judge does not permit him to be fully cognizant of all that is going on in our modern complicated civilization. And the fiction that judges only pass on the law and not on the actual facts makes them satisfied to decide fateful questions of public policy by listening to two lawyers argue for a few hours on submitted briefs, which is hardly an intelligent way of determining any great issue or the affairs of a nation.

Moreover, the assumption that all restraints on Congressional action are good is utterly thoughtless. One might well say that it is a good thing to tie us to stones so as to prevent us from running and possibly breaking our necks. Safety often depends upon quick action, as when our house is on fire or someone is to be rescued from danger. Indeed, this argument for the necessity of restraints on the people's representatives is precisely the one that used to be advanced in England for the House of Lords. When, however, the English people discovered that such restraints were in fact exercised in the interests of a given class, and against the popular will, they curbed that power to delay legislation. So we may likewise curb the power of our courts to suspend Congressional legislation until the people go through the elaborate process of a Constitutional Amendment. The trouble with Congress is not only its haste but more often its cumbrous slowness. In any case, it is safer to be subject to accidental majorities of a Congress that is in touch with and responsive to popular needs than to be at the mercy of an accidental and very small majority of the Supreme Court. For the mistakes of Congress can be corrected more quickly, while to overcome the mistakes of the Supreme Court, as in the Income Tax Case of 1895, took eighteen years. Actually there have been very few acts of Congress that have been felt to be unjust or unconstitutional by a majority of our people, and from which the courts have saved us. The liberties which the courts have enforced have more often been the liberty of powerful vested interests to exploit the poor who work for a living—witness the minimum wage cases, the child labor case, the enforcement of yellow dog contracts and iniquitous injunctions, and the like. In the two cases where Congress did admittedly violate the plain command of the Constitution, to wit, in refusing from 1922 to 1932 to reapportion representation according to the latest census or to reduce representation in accordance with the plain provision of the 14th Amendment, the courts have done nothing or have been helpless. The rights and liberties of the people are safe only in the hands of a vigilant and intelligent electorate.

The power of the courts to declare legislation unconstitutional has in fact made our law uncertain and has degraded our political life. For when a law is planned no one knows with reliable certainty how the courts will rule on a Congressional enactment, and the result is that instead of discussing issues on their merits, we discuss them in terms of what a few elderly gentlemen on the Supreme Court bench will think of their constitutionality. *The worst of all possible systems of government is that which divorces power from responsibility, and that is what we do when we give the last word to judges who are not answerable to any earthly authority.*

It is vain to say the people can amend the Constitution. Not only is that process very cumbrous, requiring three-quarters of the States rather than a majority of the people, but no one knows what the courts will make of the Amendment when it is passed. Thus, when the people adopted the 11th Amendment prohibiting a foreign citizen from suing a State, it was practically nullified by Marshall permitting such suits against the officers of the State. When the people, after the Civil War, adopted the 14th Amendment to safeguard the rights of the Negroes, the latter got very little real protection from it, but it became instead an instrument to prevent the former free States from protecting their white laborers by regulating hours, wages and the like. The people recalled the court's decision of 1895 when they empowered Congress to tax incomes *from whatever source derived.* Nevertheless, the courts do not allow the taxing of incomes from child labor and other sources, thus creating a privileged class free from taxation. The words *"from whatever source derived"* are as plain as human words can be, but the courts pay more attention to obsolete political theories and Marshall's dictum that the power to tax is the power to destroy—a dictum, however, which they disregard when they allow Congress, through heavy taxation, to drive out oleomargarine and State notes.

The arbitrary assumption that federal government cannot exist without the judicial review, ignores the fact that the harmonious adjustment between the constituent States of a federal union depends upon changing social, economic and political conditions and cannot be absolutely fixed in advance in purely legal terms. It is, therefore, properly a matter for a federal council, as Jefferson, indeed, suggested for the United States. If the distinctive virtue of a federal law is that it allows the different States to try diverse provisions for a common good, that virtue has been nearly killed by the way our Supreme Court has stretched the 14th Amendment—intended by the people to protect the Negroes—to prohibit all legislation that does not appeal to elderly and conservative gentlemen who refuse to think in terms of the actual conditions of today.

It has frequently been urged that since the judicial review has been our accepted tradition since the beginning of our national life, and since we have prospered under it, it is unpatriotic to try to change it. Even if the historic facts here assumed were true, the conclusion would not follow in logic or ethics. But the history thus assumed is not quite accurate. In the early days of the Republic the matter was by no means settled, as can be seen by Chief Justice Gibson's refutation of the arguments advanced by Marshall in *Marbury* v. *Madison.* The first case in which the Supreme Court undertook to set aside a Congressional enactment of general interest was really the Dred Scott case, and it was certainly not tacitly accepted. It is only since the Civil War that this power has become an active and important factor in the affairs of our country.

As a student of philosophy, I must decline the challenge to name the exact alternative to the mode prevailing today. There are many possible alternatives and we shall probably not anticipate the actual historic consequences of proposed changes any more accurately than those who adopted the 14th Amendment. But there can be no doubt that the strength of judicial review rests on the popular misconception that the Constitution is some esoteric document which in some mysterious way contains a solution to every problem, revealed only to a majority of the judges on the Supreme Court Bench. When the people at large begin to discount sanctimonious fictions and to look at the naked facts—as our advanced legal scholars and progressive jurists are already doing—they will see what all honest thinkers have seen all along, namely, that constitutional law is just what the judges make it, that our Supreme Court is, in fact, a continuous Constitutional Convention, and that the people or their elected representatives ought to have an effective way of ratifying or rejecting the results. Otherwise the will of the majority will continue to be frustrated and representative government exist in name only.

Topic 18

DEFENSE OF JUDICIAL REVIEW

The Supreme Court and Constitutional Morality

Dorothy Thompson *

I am not an expert on constitutional law, and my only justification for taking your time is that I have been for some years, as a foreign correspondent, an observer at the collapse of constitutional democracies. You might say I have been a researcher into the mortality of republics. The outstanding fact of our times is the decline and fall of constitutional democracy. A great need of our time is for more accurate analysis of the pathology of

* Newspaper columnist, lecturer, radio commentator, and foreign correspondent. Contributor to many periodicals. The selection is from a statement by Miss Dorothy Thompson at a hearing before the Senate Committee on the Judiciary. Reorganization of the Federal Judiciary, Hearings before the Committee on the Judiciary, United States Senate, 75th Congress, 1st Session on S. 1392, A Bill to Reorganize the Judicial Branch of the Government. (Washington, D.C., U.S. Government Printing Office, 1937), pp. 859–867.

constitutional government, of why constitutional government perishes. A great deal of such analysis has been made, but the more thoughtful students have not made much impress on public opinion. And there are a great many people in the United States, for instance, who think that fascism is completely described as a plot of big business to seize government and run it in their own interests, through a dictator who is their stooge. Or they think that fascism has come about through some evil man, perhaps an evil genius of overwhelming ambition, bent on personal power, who suppressed free institutions by violence. Or they think that fascism is a peculiar institution of certain peoples, arising from special and limited conditions. For instance, that Germany became national socialist because of the Treaty of Versailles; or that Italy became fascist because she did not get what she expected to get out of the war. Or they think that constitutional democracies have fallen because they "failed to meet human needs" and pass adequate social legislation. I refer to that because that, apparently, is the President's view. That is what he said, in his first speech in support of his proposals for reforming the judiciary. He said:

> In some countries a royalist form of government failed to meet human needs and fell. In other countries a parliamentary form of government failed to meet human needs and fell. In still other countries, governments have managed to hold on, but civil strife has flared, or threats of upheaval exist.

That is what the President said, and apparently the moral of that is that unless Congress is made perfectly free to make any sort of legislation it may hit upon and then pass it on to a Supreme Court representative of the ideas of the majority, we shall see the end of democracy. Also, Mr. Harry Hopkins, in a radio address recently said, "The cure for the evils of democracy is more democracy." That is just another expression of the thought that democracies perish if they are curbed, or if they fail to respond immediately to all the economic and social demands of powerful groups of the community. . . .

The dangers that threaten democracies are two: One is that the legal pattern should be too rigid; that the dynamics in society should shatter themselves against a Chinese wall which can be broken only by revolution. That argument is constantly advanced these days by the advocates of rapid and drastic change. That argument is implicit in the President's speech at the Democratic Party rally. It is the threat of revolution. I am not impressed by that argument. I am not impressed by it, because in the past 17 years I have attended the funerals of many democracies and I have not seen one in which the cause of death could be so diagnosed. This danger confronts absolutist systems, where popular opinion is not allowed to function, where there is no representative government, where insurrection is the only outlet. Mr. Hitler faced such a danger in the summer of 1934; in Moscow, recently, we have had trials indicating that Mr. Stalin has been facing such a danger, or the danger can arise in a sudden and acute crisis such as occurred here, in 1932, when thousands of people were threatened by actual starvation, by bankruptcy, and by the complete break-down of economic life. Such emergencies from time to time hit all republics, and often, during them the constitution is tacitly suspended, by almost universal consent. Such an emergency occurred in France in 1926–27 when the franc fell catastrophically. For 2 years, Poincaré was virtually a dictator. It happened here and elsewhere during the war. But wise democracies do not attempt during such emergencies to fundamentally alter the continuing structure of the State or set precedents for new procedures, and they return as rapidly as possible to the traditional pattern of procedure.

I think the second danger to democracies is far greater: It is that reforms, often very good and much needed reforms, should be rushed through at a rate in which they cannot be digested in society. It is the danger that eager and unchecked majorities should set up new instruments of power, before they are equipped properly to administer such instruments. It is that the will of powerful pressure groups, even when such groups embrace a majority of voters, should find expression in total disregard of the feelings, apprehensions, and interests of large and important minorities. All of those things, for instance, would hold true if you analyzed the pathology of the Austrian Republic. There is the danger that radical changes, affecting the social structure, should take place without the guidance or the check of any clear unequivocal principles. I think the greater the demand for popular franchises and rights, the greater is the need for constitutional control. Otherwise, this struggle for democratic rights—or, if you want to call it that, for new economic freedoms—can very rapidly degenerate into a chaotic redistribution of privileges. That again is what happened in Austria. There are always hundred percenters for democracy, those who want pure democracy. They want to do away with every impediment and march at high speed toward what they call a real or modern democracy, or the democracy in harmony with the times. But precisely in such revolutionary times—and we live in one—it is most necessary to have a point of reference, a warrant, an instrument which confidently assures the legitimacy of what is being done. For without such a point of reference, there ceases to be a spontaneous social cohesion and what you then get as sure as fate is social cohesion by coercion. . . .

I think the disciplines of law are particularly needed in democracies and are especially needed at any moment when a powerful majority is in temporary control of the current political situation almost to the exclusion of minority representation. We have such a situation in this country now. The men who designed the structure of this Republic realized this. They did not believe that the cure for the evils of democracy was more democracy. They believed that the prevention against a democracy running away with itself, the prevention against a powerful majority riding roughshod over the temporary minority and selling short the whole future of the country, the prevention against today's majority mortgaging tomorrow's majority, lay in a written constitution and an independent Supreme Court to interpret that constitution.

There is a reason why Supreme Court judges are appointed for life, and removable only by impeachment. That reason is obvious. It was certain that successive executives and successive Senates would seek to put upon the Supreme Court Bench men responsive to their own ideas. Everybody is human, but it was arranged that the Supreme Court, only by the merest chance, by a very remote mathematical chance, would ever coincide with the majority of the moment. It was so arranged that the Court should represent, not the momentary dominant majority, but the continuity and tradition in American life.

The difference between a regime of pure democracy, which moves from majority to majority, one often overthrowing the other and seeking to destroy all or much of what its predecessor has done—the difference between that kind of government, which I do not think has ever worked on this globe—and our own constitutional democracy is the difference between legislation which is haphazard, which is directed by powerful forces at large in society, and legislation which is somewhat checked by the will to continuity. It is true that the Supreme Court is conservative. I think it is conservative by its very nature. And that, gentlemen, is its function—to conserve. It represents, the opponents say, the past. Yes; perhaps it does. It represents continuity; it demands that today's laws shall be checked against the whole body of law and the principles governing the state, and thus it insures that new laws shall be designed in some conformity with certain long-established customs and ways of life. And just because it represents continuity, because it exerts a constant reminder on the people that they have a past, a past to which they have a duty; just because it reminds them that when they act, however radically, however drastically, they must keep an eye on long-established patterns of law and behavior—just for that reason I think it safeguards the future. For certainly those political democracies, gentlemen, have been proved safest which have the longest and most unbroken traditions. You might say that just because we have a past, we can be most confident that we have a future.

This question is essentially a political, and not a juridical, one, and I do not know how to discuss it except on the basis of a philosophy of politics. I know that the President's proposal is legally constitutional. But I am convinced that it is not politically constitutional. It strikes the Supreme Court and the Constitution in the most radical and drastic fashion imaginable. Because it proposes to switch the Supreme Bench into line with the current political majority. That was frankly admitted by the President in his metaphor about the three-horse team. It proposes to create a court whose eyes are fixed, not upon the Constitution, and upon the whole body of existing law, but upon the White House and the ruling majority in Congress. It proposes to make the Supreme Court the instrument of that majority. The proposal suggests that its framers were in a confusion about the functions of society, the State, and the Government.

The Supreme Court is essentially an instrument of the State, not of government, which is a temporary majority running the state machinery. That is to say, it is a part of the entire legal apparatus. It is not there to guarantee that the will of the majority shall be expressed but to see that the will of the majority does not infringe the basic guaranteed rights of any individual citizen who wants to appeal against that will to a higher institution of reference. In fact, the very existence of the Supreme Court is an affirmation not only that every individual citizen has equality before the law, but that any individual citizen may, at some point, assert his equality with the whole political set-up. The conception that the individual may appeal to a court of reference which is above the majority; that he can stand there, all alone, and demand a right which perhaps 99 percent of the people do not want or cherish, is the most grandiose concept of political freedom. It was recognized as such by foreign critics and students of our system of government, such as Lord Brougham, Bryce, and Gladstone. Incidentally, 40 years ago Bryce pointed out that the power of the President to expand the Supreme Court was the weakest point in the whole system. And it has reality only if the Court is independent of the Government, and that independence has been arranged for by a way of appointment and removal which gives every mathematical chance of success. If it becomes the instrument of the majority today, what possible guaranty have you that it will not become the instrument of another majority tomorrow? If, in our desire—a desire which I share with many members of this administration—to see a greater national consolidation, to extend the economic control of government over chaotic economic forces—an objective with which in the large sense I am in sympathy—if in order to do that, we pack the Court, what possible guaranty have we that tomorrow a government which believes that a national emergency demands the curbing of free speech, the dissolution of certain political parties, the control over the radio will not pack it again?

We have had times in our history when honest men tried to suppress all civil liberties—we have been told a lot about Supreme Court decisions that have balked social legislation and we are asked to turn back history and remember the *Dred Scott case,* which, they say, brought on the Civil War. But some of you gentlemen in this committee are from the South, and I wonder if you are lawyers. Do you remember the role that the Supreme Court played in the reconstruction era, in the days of the carpetbaggers, when men like Thaddeus Stevens—who were the radicals of their day—were trying to fasten a hideous tyranny forever on the South? In those days the Supreme Court alone stood between the people of the South and a black terror organized by white northerners. In those days the

South was in the minority; in those days the North, in its own mind, represented all the forces of national union and solidarity, progressiveness, and enlightenment. And like lots of enlightened, progressive, world-savers in history they were ready to resort to any means whatever to make the forces of what they called justice prevail. . . .

I have never suggested that President Roosevelt is trying to establish a dictatorship. I would not be so foolish. But I have said that if any President wanted to establish a dictatorship and do so with all the appearance of legality, this is the way he would take. The modern coup d'état, by which so many democratic systems have fallen, does not destroy the legal apparatus of the State. The modern revolution is not made by violence. It keeps it, for the coup d'état wishes to appear legal. It only alters its spirit and its aim. Mr. Hitler took an oath to the Constitution of Weimar, and he has never offered another constitution. He has just obliterated it by a series of decrees backed by a supine parliament. . . .

One must not push analogies too far. Analogies as well as metaphors are always dangerous. But neither can one divorce events in this country from ideas and tendencies which are manifest throughout the world. The problems which we face are not unique. Everywhere constitutional democracies have had to face the question of how to make new integrations between economic and political power. We want power. That is the whole problem, the basic problem, of the New Deal. Everywhere constitutional democracies have had to meet increased demands from the masses for a greater share of the national wealth and for more security. Everywhere there is a demand for more efficient instruments of political power. And accompanying these demands is a growing tendency toward personal leadership and personal government, and for a very simple reason: Personal leadership and personal government are the quickest and easiest way to get the things that people want. It is always easier to change the men than to change the law.

People grow restive under the checks imposed by a regime of law. And yet all history proves that what Aristotle said is correct—that regimes tend to turn into their opposites, if the political principle which they represent is allowed to develop to the bitter end. If democracy becomes so pure and so immediate that the popular will is subjected to no standards, it rapidly moves into tyranny.

The whole world today has a new vision of freedom; economic freedom. That actually means a redistribution of wealth which will diminish the privileges of the few for the sake of the under-privileged many. From both a moral and an economic viewpoint that demand is justified and made inevitable, by our era of mass production. But that economic freedom—I do not think this can be said too often—will prove a complete mirage unless it is accomplished with the maintenance of political freedom. Political freedom is the condition of all freedom, as the people of Russia have learned, as the people of Italy have learned, and as the people of Germany have learned. They gave up political freedom to get something else which they thought at the moment was very much more important, and then they found out that there is not anything more important. And the first condition of political freedom is that we should stick to a regime of law, and not move off the path toward a regime of men.

It is precisely because we live in a revolutionary age that it is most necessary for us to guard with the greatest caution the traditional procedures of government. I believe there is a constitutional crisis in this country. I said so in print last June. I feel very strongly that the way to meet it is to meet it in law and not in personnel. I do not like the constant reiteration that something—anything—must be done now, at this moment, in this instant, otherwise the whole country is going to bust. What social forces are threatening to overthrow everything if they are not immediately conciliated? Who is encouraging them? I do not like the talk about an outworn Constitution, or the pillorying of judges as "defeatist" lawyers—judges, incidentally, who are hampered by their very office from defending themselves. Precisely because we live in a revolutionary period, it is no time to break down public confidence in the basic institutions. And I am very sure that this proposal of the President would break down confidence. On the contrary, this is the moment to make clear to the people of the United States that social advances can only be won in conformity with established procedures, which require political effort on the part of the people themselves.

The Utility of a Restraining Power

Justice Benjamin N. Cardozo *

Some critics of our public law insist that the power of the courts to fix the limits of permissible encroachment by statute upon the liberty of the individual is one that ought to be withdrawn. It means, they say, either too much or too little. If it is freely exercised, if it is made an excuse for imposing the individual beliefs and philosophies of the judges upon other branches of the government, if it stereotypes legislation within the forms and limits that were expedient in the nineteenth or perhaps the eighteenth century, it shackles progress, and breeds distrust and suspicion of the courts. If, on the other hand, it is interpreted in the broad and variable sense which I believe to be the true one, if statutes are to be sustained unless they are so plainly arbitrary and oppressive that right-minded men and women could not reasonably regard them otherwise, the right of supervision, it is said,

* Distinguished American jurist. Appointed to the New York Court of Appeals in 1914, and to the United States Supreme Court in 1932. Author of *The Growth of Law, Law and Literature and Other Essays,* etc. The selection is from Benjamin N. Cardozo, *The Nature of the Judicial Process* (New Haven, Yale University Press, 1921), pp. 91–94. By permission of the publisher.

is not worth the danger of abuse. "There no doubt comes a time when a statute is so obviously oppressive and absurd that it can have no justification in any sane polity." Such times may indeed come, yet only seldom. The occasions must be few when legislatures will enact a statute that will merit condemnation upon the application of a test so liberal; and if carelessness or haste or momentary passion may at rare intervals bring such statutes into being with hardship to individuals or classes, we may trust to succeeding legislatures for the undoing of the wrong. That is the argument of the critics of the existing system.

My own belief is that it lays too little stress on the value of the "imponderables." The utility of an external power restraining the legislative judgment is not to be measured by counting the occasions of its exercise. The great ideals of liberty and equality are preserved against the assaults of opportunism, the expediency of the passing hour, the erosion of small encroachments, the scorn and derision of those who have no patience with general principles, by enshrining them in constitutions, and consecrating to the task of their protection a body of defenders. By conscious or subconscious influence, the presence of this restraining power, aloof in the background, but none the less always in reserve, tends to stabilize and rationalize the legislative judgment, to infuse it with the glow of principle, to hold the standard aloft and visible for those who must run the race and keep the faith. I do not mean to deny that there have been times when the possibility of judicial review has worked the other way. Legislatures have sometimes disregarded their own responsibility and passed it on to the courts. Such dangers must be balanced against those of independence from all restraint, independence on the part of public officers elected for brief terms, without the guiding force of a continuous tradition. On the whole, I believe the latter dangers to be the more formidable of the two. Great maxims, if they may be violated with impunity, are honored often with lip-service, which passes easily into irreverence. The restraining power of the judiciary does not manifest its chief worth in the few cases in which the legislature has gone beyond the lines that mark the limits of discretion. Rather shall we find its chief worth in making vocal and audible the ideals that might otherwise be silenced, in giving them continuity of life and of expression, in guiding and directing choice within the limits where choice ranges. This function should preserve to the courts the power that now belongs to them, if only the power is exercised with insight into social values, and with suppleness of adaptation to changing social needs.

SECTION V

Federalism

The United States is the first great experiment in federalism. Prior to the framing of the Constitution in 1787, history had witnessed the rise and fall of a number of confederacies, and the world had experienced numberless centralized or unitary states.

Our Constitution establishes a system under which, generally speaking, the federal government, subject to specific prohibitions, enjoys supremacy in the exercise of delegated sovereign powers, while the states, also subject to specific prohibitions and those inferred from grants to the federal government, exercise reserved sovereign powers. Theoretically this distribution of powers can be changed only by constitutional amendment. In actual practice, however, the elastic scope recently accorded by the Supreme Court to federal power, in spheres previously regarded as reserved to state action, demonstrates that the balance is a changing one.

Notwithstanding this increase in federal authority, it is argued that the present pattern of our federal system is not compatible with the urgent continuing needs of the twentieth century. On the other hand, a position taken is that the virtues of decentralization outweigh its weaknesses. A third view affirms that it is possible and desirable to increase political centralization but maintain administrative decentralization to realize the advantages of both and minimize the disadvantages of either. Apart from these general issues, the specific crucial question raised is: Should the poll tax, segregation, and discriminatory employment practices, affecting particularly but not exclusively Negroes in the South, be dealt with by federal action or be left to the states?

Topic 19

CENTRALIZATION VS. DECENTRALIZATION

THE BRIEF FOR DECENTRALIZATION

George C. S. Benson *

It must be remembered that the "decentralization" which this essay attempts to evaluate is a somewhat protean word. It can mean political decentralization or it can mean administrative decentralization. The latter is pre-eminently a question of management policy. It may exist—and often has done so—in countries highly centralized politically. When Madison said during the constitutional controversy in 1787–88, "It would not be difficult to show that if [the states] were abolished, the general government would be compelled, by the principle of self-preservation, to reinstate them in their proper jurisdiction," he was by no means pacifying his opponents. Every ardent Antifederalist realized too clearly the difference between political and administrative decentralization to accept, as a substitute for the former, a system based on the expediency of breaking down a large area into more workable units of control.

This difference must be constantly in mind in any consideration of the pros and cons of decentralization. When in the course of this study the word "decentralization" is used alone, the political meaning is implied. Administrative decentralization is meant only when fully expressed. Most—but not all—of the advantages and disadvantages outlined in this and the following chapter apply to political decentralization. The most exclusively political of the arguments are more properly applicable in the federal-state sphere, but much of the material is also helpful in illuminating state-local relations.

BULWARK AGAINST USURPATION

In this era of fascist dictatorships it is often felt that one of the greatest advantages of the decentralized system is its latent capacity for resisting dictatorial regimentation. If—to be fanciful—a president wished to become dictator, he would be forced to negotiate forty-nine coups rather than one. Certainly a respectable number of governors—all of the opposition party

* President of Claremont Men's College. Formerly Professor of Public Administration, Northwestern University, and Chief Resident Consultant, Council of State Governments. The selection is from George C. S. Benson, *The New Centralization* (New York, Rinehart & Co., Inc., 1941), Ch. II. By permission of the publisher.

and undoubtedly many others—would rise up with rugged individualism to resist coercion from Washington on matters of internal concern, and in the event of military pressure would undoubtedly call out the National Guard before turning over their state houses to *staathalters* (men placed in charge of the German states by the Hitler regime). Moreover, it is undoubtedly true that the average American citizen is probably less "national minded" as a result of a century and a half of federalism than are the inhabitants of many other countries. That is not, of course, to say that it is impossible to influence the American population on a national scale. But there does exist sufficient confusion of loyalties between state and national governments that one or more governors raising the banner against "fascism" could achieve a considerable amount of counterpropaganda.

INSULATION

Justice Holmes coined the happy phrase "the insulated chambers" of the several states. He was referring to their utility for purposes of governmental experimentation, but the phrase is equally descriptive of their capacity for localizing some of the more undesirable manifestations of public intolerance and wrongheadedness. The sovereignty of the states, which undoubtedly does give rise to many vexing problems of interlevel adjustment, works in both directions to check "oppression of minorities." For instance, it seems unlikely that any widespread and organized anti-Semitism, even if it infected other states, could prevail in New York, the population of whose chief city is one third Jewish; moreover, it seems likely that the protection of the largest and wealthiest state in the Union might go far to alleviate the situation elsewhere. Conversely, although the federal government has been unable to enforce nondiscriminatory treatment of the Negro by Southern state governments, it is notable that legalized prejudicial treatment has not spread northward. There is much shameful social and economic discrimination against our colored fellow citizens, but it has not extended to the legal sphere. For example, in a large Midwest metropolitan area a Negro has long held one of the highest and most important administrative positions. Bryce stated this value of federalism: "If social discord or an economic crisis has produced disorders or foolish legislation in one member of the federal body, the mischief may stop at the state frontier instead of spreading through and tainting the nation at large." And to return to the second point hinted above, the fact that the disease is isolated may in itself tend to promote the cure. Montesquieu, praising the values of federalism, pointed out: "Should abuses creep into one part, they are reformed by those that remain sound." It is striking how quickly Louisiana has returned to the main current of American governmental ideology after the Long regime. It may well be that the localization of the prejudice against the Negroes has been an important factor in the considerable improvement in Southern attitude and in the decrease in annual lynchings during the past fifty years from 231 to 3. No state desires for too long to play the role of solitary or even minority villain.

SEPARATION OF ISSUES

Potentially, at least, the federal system makes possible the very salutary separation of state and local from national issues. One of the great difficulties even now for the thoughtful voter is the number of judgments registered by a single × on the November ballot. The choice between presidential candidate A whose foreign policy we approve and whose domestic policy we abhor and candidate B whose domestic policy we should like to support but whose foreign policy we consider disastrous, is sufficiently painful, but if—as under a unitary system—that same × covered decisions on state sales taxes, county relief administration, and municipal sewage disposal plans, we should in effect be abrogating our right to decide on nine tenths of the issues involved. It is true that the full value of this aspect of federalism is far from being achieved. The form of ballot which encourages block party voting and the human tendency, especially in presidential election years, to subordinate our judgments on state and local candidates to those on national affairs both tend to counteract the advantage. But the fact remains that these mechanical or psychological factors are not fundamental. The nature of the federal system permits us to register our conviction that the program of one party is nationally advantageous, that the state program of another party is superior within the state and that perhaps a "non-partisan" local administration may promise the best results.

ADMINISTRATIVE EFFICIENCY

Even while granting that most of the states are inferior to Washington in administrative efficiency, many students of government are convinced that a government adequate to a large country necessarily becomes unwieldy when its administration is too highly centralized. Economists tell us that it is possible for corporations to reach a size at which the economies of large-scale operation are more than counter-balanced by the inefficiency of a top-heavy overhead management. It is, of course, difficult to say just where this point of diminishing returns occurs. Some people feel that it has already been reached in the federal government—that a million civil employees is an unmanageable staff; that scores of relatively independent federal agencies must inevitably fail to co-ordinate their activities; that the machinery is so bewilderingly complex that not even the well-intentioned and persevering can find and root out waste and duplication and inefficiency and that the inertia of large-scale organization is difficult to overcome. . . .

Some of the federal administrative problems stem directly from the huge area of the United States. For instance, all would admit that the maintenance of efficiency in hundreds of thousands of post offices from Maine to California is, under any system, a difficult task and under a completely centralized system, a stupendous one. It would occur to few of us to lay the discourtesy of our mail carrier at the postmaster general's door; yet, under the existing order, it is the postmaster general who is responsible. The same geographical difficulties of remote control occur in other fields—law enforcement, regulation, service programs. It is, of course, true that the difficulties are not insuperable. Examples of excellent federal administration exist, as do a few examples of excellent retail business enterprise on a nation-wide scale. But the fact that a problem can be overcome does not prove that it might not be wiser to obviate it. . . .

POLITICAL LABORATORIES

Mr. Justice Holmes was not the only one who believed in the "experimental" value of the federal system. Bryce said: "Federalism enables a people to try experiments in legislation and administration which could not be safely tried in a large centralized country. A comparatively small commonwealth like an American state easily makes and unmakes its laws; mistakes are not serious, for they are soon corrected; other states profit by the experience of a law or a method which has worked well or ill in the state that has tried it." And another English writer remarked that "the western states have been the Scandinavia and Switzerland of the New World—laboratories for innumerable experiments in direct democracy." While the objection that the scientific aspects of this experimentation have too often been negligible is not without foundation and will be discussed elsewhere, it is true that many policies and techniques later adopted by other states or by the federal government have been tried out on state testing grounds. Workmen's compensation, for example, has spread from state to state until today almost everywhere in the Union laborers have some security against injury. For fifty years states have been "experimenting" with declaratory judgment acts, whereby courts are permitted in certain circumstances to pronounce judgments even when there is no clash of interest—of the conventional "case" type—over a law. Five years ago the federal government decided to adopt such an act. Nation-wide prohibition may have been a "great experiment" but it was a clumsy and wasteful one. Since its repeal, far more significant experimentation is taking place in the field of liquor control, for the various states are trying out diversified methods. For instance, more than a dozen states have established governmental monopolies of liquor sales. It will take time and study to secure the maximum benefit from this experimentation, but there is reason to hope that practice will sift out the unsatisfactory and confirm the better systems.

However inadequate many of the earlier pieces of state social legislation may have been, they were precedents and harbingers of the federal Social Security Act, and their educational value was considerable. Wisconsin, of course, preceded the federal government in the field of unemployment compensation, and it is by no means generally agreed that her system of employer reserves is inferior to the more widely used plan of pooled reserves. Whether or not for other reasons unemployment compensation is properly a matter of state administration, the present organization does facilitate the accumulation of comparative data.

There has been an unusual amount of state experimentation in so-called "direct democracy." Popular referenda on certain issues, popular recall of public officials, direct primary elections to nominate party candidates, popular initiative of laws or constitutional amendments—all have been tried out by the states. Although some of these devices have worked badly and students of government are not agreed definitely on which ones can be fitted harmoniously into the total system, it is nevertheless encouraging that the states are eager and able to carry out these experiments. . . .

EDUCATION OF THE CITIZENRY

The educational advantages of the federal system are twofold. In the first place the fact that it has become a cliché does not alter the truth of the statement that the existence of democratic government depends upon a population trained to democracy. The persistently undemocratic nature of eastern European and Asiatic governmental systems has long been explained by this principle, and recent events indicate that its operation is not confined to the so-called backward areas.

Just how is a population "trained to democracy"? Ideally the schools should be competent to the task, but that ideal is only partially realized at present. To some extent the inadequate school training can be supplemented later by participation in the activities of vigorous and independent local governments. Thus a realization of the problems, responsibilities, and privileges of popular government can be widely diffused by virtue of the possibility of "lay" membership on school boards, city councils, boards of supervisors, and similar small governmental bodies.

In the second place, for the individual interested in more continuous government service—either legislative or administrative—this local training is important. Congressmen are often "graduates" of these same city councils and boards of supervisors and of the state legislatures. For example, 35 of the senators and 149 of the representatives in the Seventy-third Congress (34 per cent and 36 per cent of the respective totals) had served "apprenticeships" of an average length of four and a half years in state legislatures. With the extension of civil service, local governmental elective positions become an increasingly important training ground for politicians. . . .

ADAPTATION TO LOCAL NEEDS

The impossibility of adjusting blanket policies and techniques to all the diversified local problems and conditions in so extensive a country as this has long been a chief argument for decentralization. Social legislation adapted to Northern states, it was claimed, was neither feasible nor desirable in certain Southern areas. Laws suitable in a thickly populated, largely urbanized, and highly industrial state would ill fit the situation in Nebraska or Nevada.

Certainly it is possible to cite instances both of uniform legislation and of uniform administrative policies which have failed simply because they did not respect these essential differences. For example, prior to 1919, several states had adopted state-wide prohibition laws. Many of these laws had been in effect for years and apparently were proving relatively satisfactory. Prohibition was consonant to the wishes of a substantial majority of the local citizens in each case and enforcement proved more or less possible, though somewhat handicapped by interstate evasion. But the total failure of the attempt to impose a national prohibition law is notorious. Popular reaction was prompt and vigorous. The example of those fifteen years when respect for law and for government officials sank to a shameful ebb, when state and local officers—backed by public opinion—co-operated feebly or not at all with federal agents, points clearly the potential dangers of ill-advised efforts to disregard local differences. . . .

CONCLUSIONS

It is apparent that the traditional American decentralization possesses many advantages—advantages not to be lightly discarded in a sudden "reform movement" toward centralization. A system of relatively autonomous units is valuable as a safeguard against possible *coups d'état,* as a quarantine against sociological diseases, as a device for separating political issues which need separation. It permits administration on a more workable scale, adaptation to local needs, and training in self-government. However, the very fact that there exists a definite trend toward centralization proves that decentralization has either failed to achieve its inherent advantages or that other advantages not inherent to it seem increasingly significant. This other side of the problem will be considered in the following chapter.

The Brief for Centralization

George C. S. Benson *

Commentators who regard federalism as the key which has opened a Pandora's box of governmental ills are probably as remote from the truth as those who regard it as the key to a governmental celestial city; nevertheless it must be realized that many evils have resulted because of—or in spite of—decentralization. In some cases the machinery is not geared to the theory. For instance, the military weakness of the states limits their powers against would-be dictators. The fact that national, state, and local elections are held simultaneously plays into the hands of politicians who desire to confuse the issues. In other cases every advantage is partially offset by some disadvantage. While citizens in office are being trained in self-government, their communities may be suffering from the effects of their well-meaning but inexperienced legislative and administrative efforts. The following are the chief charges leveled at our decentralized system.

OBSTRUCTION OF SOCIAL LEGISLATION

It will be recalled that under the Tenth Amendment to the Constitution all powers not expressly granted to the federal government are reserved to the states. The powers so granted do not include the general "police power"—the authority to legislate for the public health, safety, and welfare. It is true that the courts have declared certain aspects of the police power to be implied in the powers of taxation and of regulation of interstate commerce, but the great bulk of social legislation remains within the jurisdiction of the state. At first glance it seems not unreasonable that this should be so. Social legislation is closely bound up with local economic conditions with which the state governments are in close contact. However, it will also be recalled that freedom of commerce between the states is constitutionally guaranteed. In actual practice this very seriously affects a state's theoretical independence in the matter of social legislation. . . . [While] the lack of state activity in this field is only partly due to state hesitancy and partly to judicial checks, on the whole there has developed a situation in which the states would not, and the national government could not, pass certain socially desirable legislation affecting internal conditions. . . .

Many a state honestly felt that its hesitation was due not to lack of desire but to fear of economic consequences. Prohibited by the federal Constitution from "protecting" their own industries by tariffs or other legislation restricting imports, the states argued that laws requiring shorter hours or higher wages for women and children or otherwise improving working conditions would handicap their manufacturers, who would be competing

* The selection is from Benson, *ibid.*, Ch. III.

against manufacturers in states which permitted long hours and low wages. Influenced by such an argument, the legislator who hesitated to vote for progressive legislation did not necessarily "sell out" to "ruthless business." He may sincerely have felt that the possible decline of industry in his state as a consequence of social legislation and the resulting unemployment and distress were themselves genuine social evils.

But a still more specific fear withheld him from voting for improved working conditions or imposing taxes on industry with which to finance social welfare activities—the fear that large industries would move out of his state and into the jurisdiction of some more lenient legislature. It is probable that this view was not entirely groundless. . . .

But—groundless or not—the fears were a potent factor in impeding social legislation. If legislators *believed* their industries likely to migrate, they would hesitate to test the reality of the threats by passing laws unpalatable to the business interests. As Harold Groves, a former tax commissioner of Wisconsin, comments: "Whether or not taxation is a vital factor in the relocation of industry is open to question. But there can be little question that the threat of relocation is a vital factor in shaping state and local tax systems. The author knows of one liberal state legislature which actually modified its inheritance tax because one old person of considerable wealth threatened to leave the state and establish residence in California. Quite characteristically, the state legislature took no pains at all to determine whether or not the California inheritance tax law was less favorable than that of the state which made the change. There never has been a debate concerning the adoption of a state income tax in any state, so far as the speaker knows, where the threat of industrial migration did not play a large part in the deliberation."

A detailed study of Massachusetts manufacturing during the last decade prepared by the Massachusetts Commission on Interstate Cooperation and presented to the General Court of the state in June, 1939, did not substantiate the theory that high taxation or high labor standards were important causes of the severe decline of the state's textile and boot and shoe industries, and the commission definitely did not recommend the widely circulated proposals to restrict wage and hour standards to the federal levels or to repeal certain other labor legislation. However, it is interesting to note that even this commission in its basically progressive recommendations as to taxation and legislation did suggest that "in adopting additional labor and industrial legislation, due regard be given to the status of such legislation in competing states." The impact of free competition on internal social policies cannot be overlooked. . . .

Because the major stress in this section has been laid on problems dealing with industrial evils, it should not be imagined that this is the only field where obstruction is encountered. Many desirable conservation programs have been checked by this same conflict of interstate commerce and internal policy. Although European countries, for instance, legislate against the excessive cutting of privately owned forests, the failure of the American states to do so can be traced in large part to the contention that such restrictions increase the cost of production and handicap the local industry in its competition with lumber companies in other states. Oil-conservation measures were long postponed for a similar reason.

INTERSTATE EVASION

The industrial migration mentioned in the preceding section is, of course, one method of evading the laws of one state by taking "sanctuary" under the laws of another. But decentralization gives rise to many other types of interstate evasion. Just as in federated India citizens temporarily "move" from states prohibiting child marriages to states permitting it and return as soon as their children have been married, so in America people "move" to Nevada for six weeks to acquire a divorce either because they are unwilling to wait the statutory period required in their home states or because the grounds for divorce are less extensive in the latter. . . .

Law enforcement is seriously handicapped by the facility with which criminals can elude the jurisdiction of local police and state troopers by the simple process of crossing an unpatrolled geographical line. In an era when criminals in a high-powered car can race through a dozen counties and four or five states in a single afternoon, the weakness of decentralized police jurisdiction is obvious. Some of our law-enforcement officers have made earnest and at least partly successful efforts to overcome this boundary difficulty by arranging to co-operate with law-enforcement officers in neighboring jurisdictions. Despite their attempts, however, it is still frequently true that a police officer of one city or state has no legal power in another city or state. When he is out of his jurisdiction he loses the legal right of making arrests necessary for effective action by any peace officer. Under prevailing conditions it is difficult to secure the prompt arrest of a fugitive who has escaped to another state, and matters are further complicated by the legal formalities which must be observed before such a fugitive can be returned to the state where the crime was committed.

Under the so-called "Golden Rule" employed by some municipal police forces the city agrees not to bother criminals who do not operate within its limits. Although such an agreement eliminates many problems for a few police commissioners or mayors, it has been very damaging for the country as a whole. Granted comparative security in some cities, gangs of criminals, in these days of rapid transportation, can prey more readily on others.

These same factors also promote tax evasion. There can be little doubt that the service stations which line the highway at each point where it passes from a low gas-tax state to a high gas-tax state do not make all their profits from tourists. Many of the permanent residents of the high gas-tax state undoubtedly seize this opportunity for evasion. . . .

Delaware and other states are notorious for the laxness of their corporation charter laws. W. Z. Ripley gives a number of examples of advertisements for incorporation:

"Charters—Delaware Best, Quickest, Cheapest, Most Liberal. Nothing need be paid in. Do business and hold meetings anywhere. Free forms. Colonial Charter Company, Wilmington, Delaware."

"This beats New Jersey—Charters procured under South Dakota laws for a few dollars. Write for corporation laws, blanks, by-laws, and forms to Philip Lawrence, late Assistant Secretary of State, Huron, Beadle Co., South Dakota."

In the large industrial state of Michigan, to take a more or less typical example, many of the biggest concerns—the bulk of whose productive activities are centered in Michigan—have Delaware or other out-of-state charters. In a very real sense this practice involves an encroachment on state sovereignty since for a small charter fee one state can sell to a company relative freedom from the regulatory program of the other state or states in which the company is to operate. Yet the federal Constitution demands that one state accept another's charter and thus abrogate its right to regulate the powers, privileges, and financial structure of its major industries. Provisions regarding the fiscal and other responsibilities of the directors of the corporation, the power of the corporation to conduct a wide variety of unrelated activities, the type of accounting to the shareholders and the public, the nature of the securities outstanding—all these are subject to the laws of the state in which the charter is granted. Unquestionably it is wise to permit corporations to operate in various states, but it is unfortunate that certain states grant corporate charters so freely.

DECENTRALIZATION AND THE FINANCING OF SERVICES

There is certainly disagreement as to the desirable extent of governmental services, but within reasonable limits these services are approved by all. No one today challenges the inclusion of education, road construction and maintenance, fire and police protection, certain health and welfare activities within the governmental sphere. Traditionally most of these have been deemed of "local" or at most "state" concern, and the danger of "centralization" has been a constant cry of those interested in maintaining unchanged our federal system. But it has become increasingly apparent that the problem is not one of political theory alone—it is one of economic fact as well. It is as true now as when Hamilton said it that "money is the vital principle of the body politic" and the successful retention of the decentralized pattern depends upon our ability to reconcile it with two facts.

First, in the gigantic economic system of the United States the wealth of different areas varies widely. The citizens of Massachusetts, New York, and California possess a proportion of wealth far above the national average. On the other hand, the profits from the major economic activities of such states as West Virginia and Arkansas are in part drained off to security holders in other state. Within a state the disparity of tax resources between areas may be even greater. Complete decentralization—complete local responsibility for governmental services—may then result in a "spread" between the standards of different districts which would shock even the uncritical believer in a national "American" standard. Of course, the situation was dramatically evident in the early years of the depression. The relief burden went far beyond the tax resources of countless localities and even states, and President Hoover's initial contention that "relief" was a local problem simply indicated a failure to see that economic disaster nullified political theory. Actually, the dream of local responsibility at such a time was particularly fanciful since the areas and communities which in normal times had the lowest tax resources were in many cases those in which the tax resources were hardest hit and the relief load was the heaviest.

But the same weakness is evident even in normal times. It has been estimated that a reasonable effort to tax available resources and to administer the revenue efficiently would mean—in the field of education—that the sum of money annually available for the education of each child would vary among the states from a high of $125 in New York to a low of $12 in Mississippi. Admittedly these figures are estimates, but the actual expenditures per pupil in the various states for 1935–36 seem to indicate that the spread is approximately correct. In New York the sum was $134—in Mississippi $27. There is undoubtedly a difference in living costs, but it is not great enough to equalize these differences in tax resources. Obviously, state and local government in Mississippi simply will not be able to finance the quality of education available in New York. One shocking situation—the existence of a considerable amount of illiteracy in this great and wealthy country—is in large part a result of these financial inequities. The 1940 census reports almost three million illiterate Americans. Another interesting fact is evident from the figures published by the Advisory Committee on Education which show that on the whole the poorer states, the ones with substandard schools, are making more strenuous efforts than the wealthy states to achieve good educational systems. They not only have higher general tax rates, they also devote a higher percentage of their total tax resources to the support of public schools. Although, absolutely speaking, Mississippi's $27 per child falls far below the national average, it far exceeds the national average of percentage of revenue devoted to education. Actually, on the other hand, New York's $134 is *below* the national average percentage allocated to that purpose. Here is one case where there can be no question of equalization running counter to a state *policy*. . . .

INTER-AREAL BARRIERS

Many recent writers have focused their attention on "interstate barriers" and in so doing have probably created an exaggerated impression of the dangerous tendencies of such governmental action. The mass of literature on the subject in all probability is merely one expression of a "depression psychology," but the theory of "protecting" intrastate business constitutes a serious challenge to the federal system. Whatever potential value true "protection" may possess is not achieved by these state devices. For instance, discriminatory tax legislation increases the cost of specific commodities within the state without materially increasing wages. As we have already noted, the fear of losing industry prevents the logical "bargaining" of protection for higher wage levels. Moreover, the actual gains to the industry are slight because retaliatory legislation by other states inevitably follows.

There are six major fields in which these barriers have been used.

(1) The Twenty-first Amendment, when repealing prohibition, also removed, in connection with the liquor traffic, the constitutional interdiction against state interference with interstate commerce. . . . Many states availed themselves of this right, retaliatory legislation in other states promptly followed, and interstate "beer wars" and "wine wars" have been the rule since 1933.

(2) Interstate trucking has been seriously handicapped by the diversity of state standards for size, lighting, or equipment of trucks. . . .

(3) Sometimes, in its proprietary or business capacity, the state raises interstate barriers by forbidding governmental employment of nonresidents or purchase of goods from out-of-state merchants. . . .

(4) The so-called "Green River" ordinances which forbid uninvited calls on private residences by peddlers, itinerant merchants, and transient vendors are municipal devices primarily intended to protect local merchants against outside competition. . . .

(5) Regulatory activities, legitimate in themselves, have been twisted so as to achieve the effect of impeding interstate trade. For instance, in 1932, New York imposed a quarantine against the importation of any dairy cattle into the state—even if free from Bang's disease—from herds which had not on three occasions during the previous year been certified as completely free from Bang's disease. It is questionable whether a single herd within New York State met the requirement—but the quarantine effectively secured the local market for the local dairies. . . .

(6) Use and excise taxes can also be potent protective weapons. Use taxes are generally a substitute for a state sales tax on articles purchased out of the state. . . .

COMPETITIVE BIDDING

Closely related to the problem of interstate evasion discussed in an earlier section is that of inter-area bidding by wealthy individuals or corporations. More than a dozen years ago the writer, driving through one of the Southern states, noted numerous large billboards "advertising" the fact that the state had neither income nor inheritance taxes. Every reader is familiar with the extensive advertising of recreational facilities by both state and local governments. Most of these attempts to secure either the tourist trade or the residence of individuals are not of great governmental significance. Neither, indeed, is the bulk of the public advertising done by governmental units even when designed to attract industries as well as individuals. . . .

Far more serious is the tendency, chiefly displayed by cities and towns but also by some states, to offer as inducements to industrial migration entire freedom from—or greatly reduced—taxes, as well as free factory sites, free power, guarantees against labor trouble and similar extraordinary privileges. . . .

THE FAILURE AS EXPERIMENTAL LABORATORIES

[It appears that] in spite of the examples we have noted in the previous chapter, state and local units do not seem generally to have functioned as satisfactory experimental laboratories. It is true that new devices and programs are often tried out in restricted areas, but the utility of such "experiments" is questionable if no scientific recording or evaluation of results occurs and if there is no consistent effort to transmit to other units the conclusions drawn from the experiment. Sometimes the blame is to be laid on the experimenting unit when it fails to make available in practical form the results of its experience. More frequently indifference, venality, or incapacity on the part of officials in other communities is responsible for the relatively small degree to which intelligent use of the existing data is made. . . .

ADMINISTRATIVE WEAKNESS OF STATES

We have noted in the preceding chapter that proponents of decentralization insist that it increases administrative efficiency. Experience, especially on the state level, does not seem to substantiate this conclusion. With [some exceptions] state governments are inferior administratively to the federal government. Two thirds of the states lack genuine merit systems for selection of personnel, and only three or four have salary levels sufficiently high to attract competent administrative or professional staffs. Progressive governmental units have long recognized that the general electorate is ill qualified to judge legal, financial, or technical administrative performance; yet in most states the chief counsel (the attorney general), the chief clerk (the secretary of state), the treasurer and other financial officers are still elective. Moreover, those departments which in every state show uniformly high administrative efficiency are generally those in which the federal government, through grants-in-aid, is exerting some pressure for the maintenance of standards.

LEGISLATIVE WEAKNESS OF STATES AND LOCAL UNITS

While theoretically local legislatures should be most sensitive to local needs, best acquainted with local circumstances, and best able to solve local problems, that ideal presupposes certain conditions lacking in many of the states. In an age of increasingly complex economic factors and of generally increasing governmental activity, a body of men who are satisfactorily to meet the varying problems of society must possess more than good intentions. They must possess knowledge as well. They should receive salaries commensurate with the importance of their position. Yet the state legislatures—constitutionally entrusted with the most important and extensive of legislative responsibility and power—are on the whole ill equipped for intelligent consideration of the vital concerns of their area. There are so many members that individuals in the busy, short session are unable to attract public attention to themselves. Individual legislators rarely have either the time or the fiscal resources for adequate research on even a few bills, and only a handful of states have set up fully satisfactory research bureaus to which the legislators can turn for assistance. . . .

NEED OF LARGE-SCALE OPERATIONS AND PLANNING

The fact that certain governmental problems require large-scale administrative operations or large-scale administrative planning difficult or impossible for governments limited to the area of a particular city, county, or state constitutes another argument against decentralization. A small city cannot regulate the rates of a large electric power company when it must determine what constitutes a reasonable return on that company's entire operations in 50 cities in order to allocate overhead costs justly. A state like New Hampshire cannot be expected to conduct flood control operations on the Upper Connecticut River for the benefit of the states lower down the river. . . .

CONCLUSION

It is, of course, obvious that the various weaknesses noted in this chapter differ widely in type, and that solutions must similarly differ. For instance, it is hard to escape the feeling that federal action is necessary in some cases.

Desirable nation-wide social legislation must almost inevitably depend upon Congress. Fiscal equalization between states is another national problem. Some of the state trade barriers are definitely unconstitutional violations of unrestricted interstate commerce, and it is generally agreed that it is the province of Congress to legislate against them. Certainly the quarantines mentioned in this chapter could easily be superseded by federal regulation.

Some of the other problems, particularly those mentioned under "interstate evasion," could best be met through interstate co-operation. In fact, steps have already been taken in the form of reciprocal agreements between states on marriage requirements and co-ordinated police activities. Many of the interstate barriers which are not within federal jurisdiction could also be eliminated by mutual agreement. Probably most elusive are the difficulties arising from tax programs and certain regulatory activities which are not only legitimate but to a limited extent locally desirable. The control of interstate competitive bidding seems confined to gentlemen's agreements between the states.

The state could very well undertake equalization between the communities in its borders and it could also control intrastate competitive bidding and intermunicipal barriers.

Unless they are willing to confess their political bankruptcy and welcome the extension of federal activities, the states must themselves attempt to correct the last three weaknesses. Constitutional changes which would make certain offices appointive rather than elective, longer and more frequent legislative sessions, higher legislative salaries, the establishment of adequate research bureaus, some effective mechanism for the exchange of experiences—all seem reasonable hopes for the future.

At present, however, these problems remain unsolved and a glance at the shifting points of emphasis in our governmental structure indicates the rise of new problems.

Political Centralization and Administrative Decentralization

David E. Lilienthal *

I am not one who is attracted by that appealing combination of big business and little government. I believe that the federal government must have large grants of power progressively to deal with problems that are national in their consequences and remedy, problems too broad to be handled by local political units. I am convinced, as surely most realistic men

* Formerly Chairman, U.S. Atomic Energy Commission, and Chairman, Tennessee Valley Authority. Author of several articles on politics. The selection is from David E. Lilienthal, *TVA, Democracy on the March* (New York, Harper & Bros., 1944), pp. 155–164. Copyright, 1944, by David E. Lilienthal. By permission of Harper & Bros.

must be, that in the future further responsibilities will have to be assumed by the central government to deal with national issues which centralized business inevitably creates. The war has advanced this trend.

The people have a right to demand that their federal government provide them an opportunity to share in the benefits of advances in science and research, the right to demand protection from economic abuses beyond the power of their local political units to control. But they have the further right to insist that the methods of administration used to carry out the very laws enacted for their individual welfare will not atrophy the human resources of their democracy.

It is folly to forget that the same dangers and the same temptations exist whether the centralization is in government or in mammoth business enterprises. In both cases the problem is to capture the advantages that come with such centralized authority as we find we must have, and at the same time to avoid the hazards of overcentralized *administration* of those central powers. It can be done. It can be done in many business operations as well as in government activities. . . .

Congress established the TVA as a national agency, but one confined to a particular region. This provided an opportunity for decentralization. A limited region, its outlines drawn by its natural resources and the cohesion of its human interests, was the unit of federal activity rather than the whole nation.

TVA's methods are, of course, not the only ones that must be tried. There will be different types and other methods of administration suitable to other problems and different areas. Diversity will always be the mark of decentralized administration, just as surely as uniformity (often for its own sake) is the mark of central and remote control.

Decentralization in action has been anything but an easy task. Its course will never be a smooth one, without setbacks and disappointments. Everywhere, nevertheless, the problem must be faced if we are to conserve and develop the energies and zeal of our citizens, to keep open the channels through which our democracy is constantly invigorated.

"Centralization" is no mere technical matter of "management," of "bigness versus smallness." We are dealing here with those deep urgencies of the human spirit which are embodied in the faith we call "democracy." It is precisely here that modern life puts America to one of its most severe tests; it is here that the experience in this valley laboratory in democratic methods takes on unusual meaning.

The chief purpose . . . of decentralization is to provide greater opportunity for a richer, more interesting, and more responsible life for the individual, and to increase his genuine freedom, his sense of his own importance. Centralization in administration promotes remote and absentee control, and thereby increasingly denies to the individual the opportunity to make decisions and to carry those responsibilities by which human personality is nourished and developed.

I find it impossible to comprehend how democracy can be a living reality if people are remote from their government and in their daily lives are not made a part of it, or if the control and direction of making a living—industry, farming, the distribution of goods—is far removed from the stream of life and from the local community. . . .

In the Tennessee Valley's power system . . . we have centralized only the activities in connection with electric supply which are common to a large integrated area and can best be carried on by a single agency, that is, producing the power and then transmitting it from the dams and steam-electric plants to the gates of communities. . . . The ownership and management of the distribution systems are decentralized. Here, I believe, is one example, among many, of an effective combination of the advantages of the *decentralized administration of centralized authority.*

ADMINISTRATION IN THE FIELD

The distinction between authority and its administration is a vital one. For a long time all of us—administrators, citizens, and politicians—have been confused on this point. We have acted on the assumption that because there was an increasing need for centralized authority, the centralized execution of that authority was likewise inevitable. We have assumed that, as new powers were granted to the government with its seat at Washington, these powers therefore must also be administered from Washington. Out of lethargy and confusion we have taken it for granted that the price of federal action was a top-heavy, cumbersome administration. Clearly this is nonsense. *The problem is to divorce the two ideas of authority and administration of authority.*

Our task is to invent devices of management through which many of the powers of the central government will be administered not by remote control from Washington but in the field.

A national capital almost anywhere is bound to suffer from lack of knowledge of local conditions, of parochial customs. And in a country as vast as the United States, in which local and regional differences are so vital and so precious, many citizens and administrators are coming to see more and more that powers centrally administered from Washington cannot take into account the physical and economic variations within our boundaries. The national strength and culture that flows from that very diversity cannot be nourished by centralized administration. . . .

Centralization at the national capital or within a business undertaking always glorifies the importance of pieces of paper. This dims the sense of reality. As men and organizations acquire a preoccupation with papers they become less understanding, less perceptive of the reality of those matters with which they should be dealing: particular human problems, particular human beings, actual things in a real America—highways, wheat, barges, drought, floods, backyards, blast furnaces. The reason why there is and always has been so much bureaucratic spirit, such organizational intrigue, so much pathologic personal ambition, so many burning jealousies and vendettas in a capital city (any capital city, not only Washington), is no mystery. The facts with which a highly centralized institution deals tend to be the men and women of that institution itself, and their ideas and ambitions. To maintain perspective and human understanding in the atmosphere of centralization is a task that many able and conscientious people have found well-nigh impossible.

THE HUMAN ELEMENT

Making decisions from papers has a dehumanizing effect. Much of man's inhumanity to man is explained by it. Almost all great observers of mankind have noted it. In *War and Peace* Tolstoy makes it particularly clear. Pierre Bezukhov is standing a captive before one of Napoleon's generals, Marshal Davout.

> At the first glance, when Davout had only raised his head from *the papers where human affairs and lives were indicated by numbers,* Pierre was merely a circumstance, and Davout could have shot him without burdening his conscience with an evil deed, but now he saw in him a human being . . .

To see each citizen thus as a "human being" is easy at the grass roots. That is where more of the functions of our federal government should be exercised.

The permanence of democracy indeed demands this. For the cumulative effect of overcentralization of administration in a national capital is greatly to reduce the effectiveness of government. It is serious enough in itself when, because of remoteness and ignorance of local conditions or the slowness of their operation, laws and programs fail of their purposes. We are threatened, however, with an even more disastrous sequence, the loss of the people's confidence, the very foundation of democratic government. Confidence does not flourish in a "government continually at a distance and out of sight," to use the language of Alexander Hamilton, himself a constant advocate of strong central authority. . . .

We who believe devoutly in the democratic process should be the first to urge the use of methods that will keep the administration of national functions from becoming so concentrated at the national capital, so distant from the everyday life of ordinary people, as to wither and deaden the average citizen's sense of participation and partnership in government affairs. *For in this citizen participation lies the vitality of a democracy.*

Federal functions can be decentralized in their administration. But it requires a completely changed point of view on the part of citizens and their representatives. For this business of centralization is not wholly the fault of government administrators. Statutes are rarely designed to provide an opportunity for ingenuity in the development of new techniques in administration. Only infrequently do you find a new law which in its terms recognizes the hazards of overcentralization. . . .

This country is too big for such a pyramiding of responsibilities. In the general atmosphere of bigness, men continue to come about the same size. There is a limit to the energy and wisdom of the best; the ancient lust for power for its own sake burns in the worst.

In the case of TVA, Congress did enact a statute which permitted a decentralized administration. Had not Congress created that opportunity, the TVA could not have developed its administration at the grass roots. An area of manageable proportions—the watershed of a river as its base—was the unit of administration. Decisions could be made and responsibility taken at a point that was close to the problems themselves. That is the test of decentralization.

It is not decentralization to open regional offices or branches in each state, if decisions have to be made in Washington and the officers in the field prove to be merely errand boys. Genuine decentralization means an entirely different point of view in the selecting and training of personnel. It means an emigration of talent to the grass roots. But if the important tasks, the real responsibilities, are kept at the center, men of stature will not go to the "field."

TOUCHSTONES OF DECENTRALIZATION

Neither is it decentralization when bureaus or departments are moved out of crowded Washington. It may be necessary and entirely wise—but it is not decentralization. You do not get decentralization as we know it in the TVA unless you meet two tests:

First, do the men in the field have the power of decision?

Second, are the people, their private and their local public institutions, actively participating in the enterprise? . . .

There is generous lip service to decentralization on every hand. But little will be done about it unless there is real understanding of what it means, and an urgent and never ceasing demand from citizens. . . .

The practices of decentralized administration have made considerable headway; the tendency, however, continues the other way. Lip service is paid to decentralization by legislators and administrators; they then proceed to draw to Washington the very elements of discretion and the power to decide which impose centralization in its worst forms. Members of Congress will inveigh against the evils of "concentrating power in Washington," and then almost in the same breath (unwittingly, without a doubt) will speed up that very process by passing legislation that sets up additional managerial controls in a central Washington bureau. An able Member of Congress, sincerely interested in the necessity of federal decentralization, recently introduced a comprehensive resolution proposing a broad study of the means of achieving decentralization in the government; but only a few months later the same Member introduced another measure to combine all federally owned power operations in a central "power administration" in Washington! . . .

The often flabby muscles of community and individual responsibility will never be invigorated unless the muscles are given work to do. They grow strong by use; there is no other way. Although it is true that decentralization at times is ineffective because of the quality of local officials or field officers, the virtues, by comparison, of what can be done in central headquarters are somewhat illusory. For, without the co-operation of citizens (an admittedly difficult goal) and of institutions familiar to them, no detailed and far-reaching economic or social policy and no democratic planning can be made effective. Surely there can be little doubt about the truth of this statement. . . . The daily experience of the average citizen confirms it unanswerably. . . .

I would be rendering a disservice if I left the impression that the TVA's methods offer a ready-made pattern to be copied literally, in all manner of situations, or that genuine decentralization in the administration of every and any kind of national function is feasible. Many functions of the federal government present entirely different problems from the development and improvement of land, water, forests, minerals. Resources have a fixed *situs* and can only be dealt with adequately at that *situs*. TVA's methods can be readily adapted to such problems. But whether regional decentralization in the genuine sense is feasible for many other functions is not a subject for generalization. While different devices must be invented, TVA's methods and experience may be of considerable aid in that process.

Topic 20

HOW TO SECURE THESE RIGHTS?

THE NATIONAL GOVERNMENT MUST LEAD

President's Committee on Civil Rights *

There are several reasons why we believe the federal government must play a leading role in our efforts as a nation to improve our civil rights record.

First, many of the most serious wrongs against individual rights are

* The selection is from *The Report of the President's Committee on Civil Rights* (Washington, D.C., U.S. Government Printing Office, 1947), *passim*.

committed by private persons or by local public officers. In the most flagrant of all such wrongs—lynching—private individuals, aided upon occasion by state or local officials, are the ones who take the law into their own hands and deprive the victim of his life. The very fact that these outrages continue to occur, coupled with the fact that the states have been unable to eliminate them, points clearly to a strong need for federal safeguards.

Second, it is a sound policy to use the idealism and prestige of our whole people to check the wayward tendencies of a part of them. It is true that the conscience of a nation is colored by the moral sense of its local communities. Still, the American people have traditionally shown high national regard for civil rights, even though the record in many a community has been far from good. We should not fail to make use of this in combating civil rights violations. The local community must be encouraged to set its own house in order. But the need for leadership is pressing. That leadership is available in the national government and it should be used. We cannot afford to delay action until the most backward community has learned to prize civil liberty and has taken adequate steps to safeguard the rights of every one of its citizens.

Third, our civil rights record has growing international implications. These cannot safely be disregarded by the government at the national level which is responsible for our relations with the world, and left entirely to government at the local level for proper recognition and action. Many of man's problems, we have been learning, are capable of ultimate solution only through international co-operation and action. The subject of human rights, itself, has been made a major concern of the United Nations. It would indeed be ironical if in our own country the argument should prevail that safeguarding the rights of the individual is the exclusive, or even the primary concern of local government. . . .

Interference with the right of a qualified citizen to vote locally cannot today remain a local problem. An American diplomat cannot forcefully argue for free elections in foreign lands without meeting the challenge that in many sections of America qualified voters do not have free access to the polls. Can it be doubted that this is a right which the national government must make secure?

Fourth, the steadily growing tendency of the American people to look to the national government for the protection of their civil rights is highly significant. . . . The American people are loyal to the institutions of local self-government, and distrust highly centralized power. But we have never hesitated to entrust power and responsibility to the national government when need for such a course of action has been demonstrated and the people themselves are convinced of that need.

Finally, the national government should assume leadership in our American civil rights program because there is much in the field of civil rights that it is squarely responsible for in its own direct dealings with millions of persons. It is the largest single employer of labor in the country. . . . By scrupulously following fair employment practices, it not only sets a model for other employers to follow, but also directly protects the rights of more than two million workers to fair employment.

THE RIGHT TO VOTE

The denial of the suffrage on account of race is the most serious present interference with the right to vote. Until very recently, American Negro citizens in most southern states found it difficult to vote. Some Negroes have voted in parts of the upper South for the last twenty years. In recent years the situation in the deep South has changed to the point where it can be said that Negroes are beginning to exercise the political rights of free Americans. In the light of history, this represents progress, limited and precarious, but nevertheless progress. . . .

The poll tax—an important legal obstacle to full suffrage in some southern states—limits white as well as Negro suffrage. The poll tax has frequently had an unequal racial effect, since . . . it has been administered in a discriminatory manner. It has been very effective as an anti-Negro device. A poll tax simply places the payment of a fee between the voter and the ballot box. In some states it is cumulative; taxes not paid in years when the voter does not go to the polls pile up and he must pay more than one year's tax before he can vote.

The poll tax has curtailed the size of the entire electorate, white and Negro. Seven states—Alabama, Arkansas, Mississippi, South Carolina, Tennessee, Texas, and Virginia—still maintain this tax as a prerequisite to voting. Since 1921 four other states have abandoned the poll tax. These are North Carolina, Louisiana, Florida, and Georgia. [The poll tax has recently been abolished in South Carolina and Tennessee.]

It was estimated on the floor of the House of Representatives on July 21, 1947, that:

> In the Presidential elections of 1944, 10 per cent of the potential voters voted in the seven poll-tax states, as against 49 per cent in the free-vote states. In the congressional elections of 1946, the figures are 5 per cent for the poll-tax states as compared with 33 per cent for the free-voting states.

It has frequently been pointed out that the congressional representation of poll tax states is based on proportionately fewer voters than the representation of other jurisdictions. It has also been urged that the poll tax is in reality a tax levied by the state upon the citizen's federal right to vote for members of Congress. In recent years there has been a strong drive for federal legislation forbidding the requirement of a poll tax as a prerequisite to voting in federal elections. The House of Representatives passed an anti-poll tax bill for the fourth time in July of 1947. The three previous bills passed by the House were killed in the Senate. . . .

THE RIGHT OF EMPLOYMENT

A man's right to an equal chance to utilize fully his skills and knowledge is essential. The meaning of a job goes far beyond the paycheck. Good workers have a pride in the organization for which they work and feel satisfaction in the jobs they are doing. A witness before a congressional committee has recently said:

> Discrimination in employment damages lives, both the bodies and the minds, of those discriminated against and those who discriminate. It blights and perverts that healthy ambition to improve one's standard of living which we like to say is peculiarly American. It generates insecurity, fear, resentment, division and tension in our society. . . .

Discriminatory hiring practices.—Discrimination is most acutely felt by minority group members in their inability to get a job suited to their qualifications. Exclusions of Negroes, Jews, or Mexicans in the process of hiring is effected in various ways—by newspaper advertisements requesting only whites or gentiles to apply, by registration or application blanks on which a space is reserved for "race" or "religion," by discriminatory job orders placed with employment agencies, or by the arbitrary policy of a company official in charge of hiring.

A survey conducted by the United States Employment Service and contained in the Final Report of the Fair Employment Practice Committee reveals that of the total job orders received by USES offices in 11 selected areas during the period of February 1–15, 1946, 24 percent of the orders were discriminatory. Of 38,195 orders received, 9,171 included specifications with regard to race, citizenship, religion, or some combination of these factors. . . .

The Fair Employment Practice Committee was established by President Roosevelt in an Executive Order dated June 25, 1941. Its mandate was to eliminate discriminatory employment practices within the federal government and in companies and unions which had contracts with the government or which were engaged in the production of materials necessary to the war effort. The FEPC, as a practical matter, served as a clearing house for complaints alleging various types of employment discrimination. It had no enforcement powers of its own; and no recourse to the courts.

The effectiveness of the FEPC was due almost entirely to its success as a mediation body in persuading a union or employer to revise the particular policy or practice complained of. During its most active two years, FEPC closed an average of 250 cases a month, about 100 of which were satisfactorily adjusted. The Committee's work ended in June, 1946, when Congress failed to appropriate funds for the ensuing fiscal year. In a letter of

June 28, 1946, to the Committee accepting the resignation of its members, President Truman said:

> The degree of effectiveness which the Fair Employment Practice Committee was able to attain has shown once and for all that it is possible to equalize job opportunity by governmental action, and thus eventually to eliminate the influence of prejudice in the field of employment. . . .

THE TIME IS NOW

The pervasive gap between our aims and what we actually do is creating a kind of moral dry rot which eats away at the emotional and rational bases of democratic beliefs. There are times when the difference between what we preach about civil rights and what we practice is shockingly illustrated by individual outrages. There are times when the whole structure of our ideology is made ridiculous by individual instances. And there are certain continuing, quiet, omnipresent practices which do irreparable damage to our beliefs.

As examples of "moral erosion" there are the consequences of suffrage limitations in the South. The fact that Negroes and many whites have not been allowed to vote in some states has actually sapped the morality underlying universal suffrage. Many men in public and private life do not believe that those who have been kept from voting are capable of self rule. They finally convince themselves that disfranchised people do not really have the right to vote. . . .

Finally, the cost of prejudice cannot be computed in terms of markets, production, and expenditures. Perhaps the most expensive results are the least tangible ones. No nation can afford to have its component groups hostile toward one another without feeling the stress. People who live in a state of tension and suspicion cannot use their energy constructively. The frustrations of their restricted existence are translated into aggression against the dominant group. Myrdal says:

> Not only occasional acts of violence, but most laziness, carelessness, unreliability, petty stealing and lying are undoubtedly to be explained as concealed aggression. . . . The truth is that *Negroes generally do not feel they have unqualified moral obligations to white people.* . . . The voluntary withdrawal which has intensified the isolation between the two castes is also an expression of Negro protest under cover.

It is not at all surprising that a people relegated to second-class citizenship should behave as second-class citizens. This is true, in varying degrees, of all of our minorities. What we have lost in money, production, invention, citizenship, and leadership as the price for damaged, thwarted personalities—these are beyond estimate.

The United States can no longer afford this heavy drain upon its human wealth, its national competence.

Our position in the postwar world is so vital to the future that our smallest actions have far-reaching effects. We have come to know that our own security in a highly interdependent world is inextricably tied to the security and well-being of all people and all countries. Our foreign policy is designed to make the United States an enormous, positive influence for peace and progress throughout the world. We have tried to let nothing, not even extreme political differences between ourselves and foreign nations, stand in the way of this goal. But our domestic civil rights shortcomings are a serious obstacle.

In a letter to the Fair Employment Practice Committee on May 8, 1946, the Honorable Dean Acheson, then Acting Secretary of State, stated that:

> . . . the existence of discrimination against minority groups in this country has an adverse effect upon our relations with other countries. We are reminded over and over by some foreign newspapers and spokesmen, that our treatment of various minorities leaves much to be desired. While sometimes these pronouncements are exaggerated and unjustified, they all too frequently point with accuracy to some form of discrimination because of race, creed, color, or national origin. Frequently we find it next to impossible to formulate a satisfactory answer to our critics in other countries; the gap between the things we stand for in principle and the facts of a particular situation may be too wide to be bridged. . . .

THE COMMITTEE'S RECOMMENDATIONS

To strengthen the right to citizenship and its privileges, the President's Committee recommends:

Action by the states or Congress to end poll taxes as a voting prerequisite.

Considerable debate has arisen as to the constitutionality of a Federal statute abolishing the poll tax. In four times passing an anti-poll tax bill, the House of Representatives has indicated its view that there is a reasonable chance that it will survive a court attack on constitutional grounds. We are convinced that the elimination of this obstacle to the right of suffrage must not be further delayed. It would be appropriate and encouraging for the remaining poll-tax states voluntarily to take this step. Failing such prompt state action, we believe that the Nation, either by act of Congress, or by constitutional amendment should remove this final barrier to universal suffrage. . . .

To strengthen the right to equality of opportunity, the President's Committee recommends:

In general:

The elimination of segregation, based on race, color, creed, or national origin, from American life. . . .

The conditioning by Congress of all federal grant-in-aid and other forms of federal assistance to public or private agencies for any pur-

pose on the absence of discrimination and segregation based on race, color, creed, or national origin.

We believe that Federal funds supplied by taxpayers all over the Nation, must not be used to support or perpetuate the pattern of segregation in education, public housing, public health services, or other public services and facilities generally. . . .

A minority of the Committee favors the elimination of segregation as an ultimate goal but opposes the imposition of a Federal sanction. It believes that Federal aid to the states for education, health, research and other public benefits should be granted provided that the states do not discriminate in the distribution of the funds. It dissents, however, from the majority's recommendation that the abolition of segregation be made a requirement, until the people of the states involved have themselves abolished the provisions in their state constitutions and laws which now require segregation. Some members are against the non-segregation requirement in educational grants on the ground that it represents Federal control over education. They feel, moreover, that the best way ultimately to end segregation is to raise the educational level of the people in the states affected; and to inculcate both the teachings of religion regarding human brotherhood and the ideals of our democracy regarding freedom and equality as a more solid basis for genuine and lasting acceptance by the peoples of the states.

[*With respect to*] *employment:*

The enactment of a federal Fair Employment Practice Act prohibiting all forms of discrimination in private employment, based on race, color, creed, or national origin. . . .

The enactment by the states of similar laws.

A Federal fair employment practice statute will not reach activities which do not affect interstate commerce. To make fair employment a uniform national policy, state action will be needed. The successful experiences of some states warrant similar action by all of the others.

The enactment of a Federal mandate against discrimination in government employment and the creation of adequate machinery to enforce this mandate.

Federal Action Is Unnecessary

Clyde R. Hoey *

What is involved in the civil-rights program? I do not want to discuss the subject as a southerner, although I am an intense southerner, but I wish to discuss it as an American citizen, because I am more intense as an American.

* U.S. Senator from North Carolina since 1945. Former Governor of North Carolina. The selection is from his speech of March 2, 1949, in the U.S. Senate.

I know something about the proposals recommended by the President's Civil Rights Committee, and recommended by the President. The . . . proposals are known to the American people in general, but their implications are not well known, and their dangers have not been fully presented; the viciousness of the measures has not been sufficiently discussed, so that the people can understand fully just what is involved.

Let us consider . . . the poll tax, which has caused considerable comment and discussion. It is a very insignificant matter when it is analyzed. The Constitution of the United States provides that the States shall have the right to prescribe the qualifications of electors. That was one of the rights reserved by the States when the Constitution was formed. There has never been any challenge of that authority. Each State has the right to regulate and prescribe the qualifications of its electors. That is subject to one single exception, and that is that we cannot deny the voting privilege to anyone because of race, color, or previous condition of servitude. The poll tax does neither of those things. It applies to every voter. Therefore, there is nothing offensive in the payment of a poll tax as a requirement for voting, so far as race, color, and previous condition of servitude are concerned.

Presently, there are only seven States which have poll taxes as a requirement for voting. Practically all States have poll taxes levied on the citizens, but ordinarily they go to support the public-school funds. In my State a poll tax is levied from the time a man becomes 21 years of age until he is 50 years of age. The tax is levied on male citizens. For 29 years it has not been required in North Carolina that a tax be paid in order to vote, but the tax is still collected. It is from $1 to $2 a year. Yet, from the hue and cry heard regarding the discussion of the matter, it would be thought that it is a great and exorbitant tax which is being levied upon persons to deny them their right of franchise.

We hear a great deal said about the fact that in the Southern States only a small vote is cast in general elections, and that is attributed to the fact that the voters have to pay a poll tax, and therefore it is said many are disqualified from voting. That is not the cause at all. Why are only a small number of votes cast in many Southern States? It is because one political party is dominant in those States, and because every voter knows that every candidate for whom he would vote will be elected without regard to whether the voter goes to the polls or not. Therefore there is no incentive for a man to go to the polls. If he belongs to the minority party it is hopeless for him to go to the polls, and he does not do so.

On the question of the poll tax, three of the seven States which now have it are preparing to do away with it. In the course of another year or so that question will therefore be settled. Should Congress and the Senate undertake to invade the rights of the States, and say, "You are not getting rid of this thing as quickly as we would like to have you, therefore we are going to exercise the sovereign power of the Federal Government to determine what sort of law you should have in prescribing the qualifications of your electors."

Our opposition to that is on the ground that it is unconstitutional. Moreover, we take the position that if the Federal Government has a right to enter a sovereign State and to say what qualifications it should prescribe with reference to the payment of a poll tax to entitle one to vote, then the same government has the right to go into a State and undertake to prescribe other qualifications for its voters and electors, and that very soon we would reach the point where the Federal Government would undertake to dictate the qualifications of the electors of all the sovereign States, and the reservation of that power which was made to the sovereign States when the Constitution was adopted would be trampled underfoot. . . .

I pass . . . to another measure, namely, the antisegregation measure. What is the necessity for passing such a measure? To begin with, the Congress has nothing in the world to do with segregation within the limits of a State. The Federal Government has no power or authority to override the law of a State and say what shall happen with reference to segregation within the confines of a State, with the sole exception of transportation that may involve interstate commerce. The Supreme Court of the United States has already decided that question. The Court said that the States have no power and no authority to legislate about interstate commerce, and therefore, State segregation laws applying to interstate commerce were null and void. Now what more can be done? Why pass any more segregation laws?

Do we want the Federal Government to say what shall happen with reference to the internal affairs of a State? The Constitution of the United States does not say that segregation is discrimination. That is where many persons make a mistake. We hear many talk about segregation as if it were discrimination. The fact is that it is not discrimination. The Supreme Court of the United States has gone far afield in deciding a great many of these questions, but it has never yet held that segregation is discrimination. In reality it is just the reverse. Why, then, undertake to have Congress pass a law in the teeth of the Supreme Court, in the teeth of the Constitution. . . .

Donald R. Richberg *

People are pleased to be told that they have a "right" to do what they want to do. They applaud the politician who assures them that they have a "right" to enjoy the things they desire.

It is much more comforting to be assured that you have a right to obtain a good job from some one, than to be informed that you have a duty to do

* Noted Washington lawyer, long active in politics and administration. Author of *Government and Business Tomorrow* and several other books on politics and law. The selection is from an article which appeared originally in the Washington *Evening Star* and was reprinted in *Congressional Digest,* February, 1950. By permission of the Washington *Evening Star*.

a good job for some one. But, let's not forget, that no right can be enforced for one person without compelling another to fulfill a duty. In the language of the courts: "When a right is invaded a duty is violated." "There is no right where there is no remedy."

Even the basic right of my individual liberty cannot be enforced except by imposing restraints on your individual liberty. The claim of a right is worthless against more and more domestic conflicts, less and less internal peace. . . . The surest way to destroy the fundamental freedoms of American life would be to build up a vast legal structure of social, economic and political rights, all of them creating corresponding duties, and all of them enforced by governmental restraints upon individual freedom. . . .

In the name of "liberty," [the recent report of the President's Committee on Civil Rights] proposes to compel American men, women and children to live and work in a social and economic system created and regulated by Government, a system in which their most profound emotions and ambitions are to be suppressed at the will of political monitors. Here are the two most fundamental recommendations of the committee, in its own language:

"The elimination of segregation, based on race, color, creed or national origin, from American life."

"The enactment of a Federal Fair Employment Practice Act, prohibiting all forms of discrimination in private employment, based on race, color, creed or national origin."

Please note that segregation is to be eliminated—not only from Government operations, but everywhere "from American life." That is precisely the aim of the committee, which announces, with the voice of omnipotent omniscience: "We can tolerate no restrictions upon the individual which depend upon irrelevant factors such as his race, his color, his religion or the social position to which he was born."

Hundreds of millions of Protestants, Catholics, Jews, Mohammedans, Buddhists and Hindus have believed and taught for centuries the One Way of Living, or the One Road to Salvation, was divinely ordained and revealed in the articles of their particular faith. Any one's religion is necessarily a restriction on him and, if he is to be free in the exercise of his religion (a freedom expressly guaranteed in our Constitution), then he must be free to restrict his associations with others in accordance with his feelings and his convictions as to what is necessary and desirable. Yet the committee would have a man forced by law into associations which may be repulsive to him—not because of any narrow prejudice but because of his profound religious convictions.

Race and color may seem "irrelevant" to the committee. Yet differences of race and color have divided mankind for centuries. They may fade in the coming centuries. But they cannot be wiped out by a state or federal law; and every such foolish effort only intensifies prejudice and intolerance, creates disrespect for law, and is itself an intolerant violation of individual liberty.

Curiously enough the committee observed that an essential part of our freedom is that we "are free to be different." Evidently the committee is willing to have us differ in our taste for cigarettes, but not in our taste for companions. But, in another breath, the committee says: "In a democracy, each individual must have freedom to choose his friends and to control the pattern of his personal and family life." Nevertheless in order to eliminate "segregation" and to prevent "discrimination," the committee insists that this "free" American shall be compelled to spend his working life with undesirable associates, and to send his children to schools, to eat in restaurants, to live in hotels and enjoy all public amusements, in the company of those whose company he would not voluntarily choose.

The logic of the report is very difficult to follow. But, as the King said in Alice in Wonderland, "If there's no meaning in it that saves a world of trouble, you know, as we needn't try to find any."

Let us assume, however, that every like or dislike based or race, color or religion is unreasonable and unfair, and that such prejudices ought to be eliminated from human thinking. Nevertheless, is it proper or even possible for the Government of a free people to attempt to prevent men and women in business or social life from acting in accord with their prejudices? Now this is an entirely different question from asking whether the Government itself should deny equality of opportunity to some of its citizens.

Political equality, in the right to vote, in the administration of justice and in the rendering of public services, is due to all citizens. But unless Government is to destroy an economic system of competitive freedom and a social system of free association, it cannot undertake to level down the inequalities that result from differing abilities and opportunities, or to interfere with the voluntary selection of one's associates in work or play.

No one would dare to propose that an employer be given the right by law to compel a man to work for him. That would be "involuntary servitude"—slavery. Yet it is solemnly proposed that an employer shall be forbidden to refuse to employ a "qualified" man because of his race or religion. This means, in practical effect, that if a Government regulator says that a man is "qualified" and rules that he has been denied employment because of race, color or religion, then he must be employed.

We know from experience under the Wagner Act that the employer would be presumed to be wrong. "Sentence first, verdict afterwards" is the conventional procedure. It seems to be forgotten that an employer works for his employes, just as they do for him. He is obligated by law to do a great many things for his employe. So the proposed law would force an employer into involuntary servitude to men who are under no obligation to work for him.

Superficially, it may seem to be a noble project for government to insure to all citizens an equality of opportunity to earn a livelihood and "to enjoy the benefits of society." But, no government can insure equality of opportunity to human beings who differ so widely in natural capacity and who, because of parental variances in ability and fortune, are so differently nurtured. It should also be pointed out that the benefits of a democratic, free society are not gathered by an omnipotent government into one treasure house for distribution to a dependent population. On the contrary, individuals in a host of big and little enterprises, work and produce things and seek to gain out of their cooperation with others the benefits and satisfactions which they desire and for which they are willing to work and sacrifice. . . .

It is most significant that the shrill slogan of all those fomenting the civil rights hysteria is "equality," although the great declared purpose of the Constitution was, not to achieve an impossible equality among unequal human beings, but to "secure the blessings of liberty" so that men could be free to be different and to realize their differing ambitions with their differing abilities. Every law which seeks to give a man a right to something which as a free man he cannot gain for himself, must impose burdens and restraints on the freedom of other men.

We may, reasonably, tax the fortunate to give aid to the less fortunate. We may reasonably, prevent the abuse of freedom by those who heedlessly or ruthlessly injure others in the pursuit of selfish gain. We may, reasonably, enact laws to protect the right of every citizen to an equal participation in government and to equal treatment in all government operations. But, let us be watchful against every effort to create by law a "right" in one man to compel others to associate with him or to accept obligations to him in the domain of private enterprise or private life. Let us realize, not only that it is a part of our heritage that "a man's house is his castle," but also that freedom of association in work or play is the most precious of all our liberties.

It is well at this time to recall the words of the late Justice Brandeis—whom no one would ever accuse of religious intolerance or racial prejudice. He wrote:

> The makers of our Constitution undertook to secure conditions favorable to the pursuit of happiness. They recognized the significance of man's spiritual nature, of his feelings, and of his intellect. They knew that only a part of the pain, pleasure and satisfactions of life are to be found in material things. They sought to protect Americans in their beliefs, their thoughts, their emotions and their sensations. They conferred, as against the Government, the right to be let alone—the most comprehensive of rights and the right most valued by civilized men.

Part III

PROBLEMS OF POLITICAL CONTROL

The Politics of a Democracy
President and Congress
Government and the Economy

SECTION I

The Politics of a Democracy

The Constitution which established the basic framework of our government did not mention public opinion or political parties. The Framers, to be sure, took cognizance of the potential power of organized public opinion and political parties and attempted to curb their influence through the electoral college, the indirect election of senators, and other devices. Yet, today, the force of both public opinion and political parties is recognized as a vital concomitant of our democratic and constitutional system.

Public opinion expresses itself periodically through the ballot and more frequently, if sporadically, through direct correspondence with legislative and executive officers. Increasingly, however, opinion polls are being utilized to ascertain public views on crucial issues of the day with the explicit or implicit inference that these views should carry great or even controlling influence. But is it possible to measure public opinion accurately or meaningfully? And how much weight, if any, should our representatives accord to the wishes of their constituents as against their own considered judgments?

Political parties have made so many contributions to our functioning democracy that without them democracy would now be hardly conceivable. Apart from participating in the process of framing issues, organizing the electorate and electing officials, the parties have helped to democratize the machinery of government. Notwithstanding these contributions, some critics like James M. Burns maintain that the lack of centralized responsibility of our major parties makes them poor instrumentalities in serving the national interest as against local and special interests. Others, like Harold J. Laski, go further and argue that, in addition to centralization of control, our parties must be economically realigned or they will continue to serve similar interests and deny to the electorate any real choices. Nicholas Murray Butler favors realignment for other reasons. On the other hand, writers like Pendleton Herring and Herbert Agar insist that the very amorphousness of our parties is vital to the preservation of our federal system and our democracy.

Topic 21

PUBLIC OPINION IN A DEMOCRACY

THE VALUE OF PUBLIC OPINION POLLS

George Gallup *

The critics of polls have had their innings since Nov. 2 [1948]. Now I think the public should hear the other side. Naturally, I am a prejudiced witness.

I feel that the public opinion poll has an important place in democracy—so important that all thinking persons ought to be in a position to arrive at a fair and unbiased appraisal of polling. The volume of criticism leveled at the polls is in itself a testimony to their importance.

Critics of polls have raised questions as to whether polls can measure opinion on complex issues, whether questions can be phrased fairly, whether the samples taken are accurate guides, whether polls are detrimental to the democratic process, whether they can indicate future action, and whether they can really measure private opinions.

I believe that anyone who examines the full record of poll results over the past thirteen years will see that they have been able to do all those things. No claim that polls have reached a stage of absolute perfection has ever been made. We poll-takers are thoroughly aware of how much there is still to be learned. But it seems significant to me that no responsible critic has ever attempted to prove that any other system of appraising public opinion can do a better or more reliable job than the public-opinion poll.

It is interesting to speculate on what might have happened in the last ten years if there had been no polls—if public opinion had been left to manifest itself through the traditional channels. Let's take a few examples to see what might have happened. During the summer of 1940 one of the big issues facing the country was the question of a peacetime military draft. The pressure put on Congressmen by letter writers was overwhelmingly against the draft. An analysis published in the Public Opinion Quarterly of more than 30,000 letters received by fourteen Senators during the summer concerning the Burke-Wadsworth Selective Service Bill showed: For the bill, 10 per cent; against the bill, 90 per cent.

During that same time a survey by the American Institute of Public Opinion found a cross-section of the nation's voters overwhelmingly in

* Director of the American Institute of Public Opinion, Princeton University. Author of *The Pulse of Democracy, Guide to Public Opinion Polls,* and numerous articles on public opinion. The selection is from George Gallup, "The Case for the Public Opinion Polls," *New York Times Magazine,* February 27, 1949. By permission of the author and *The New York Times.*

favor of the draft. If the fourteen Senators had based their vote solely on the huge outpouring of mail they received they would have gone counter to the wishes of a majority of the people, and in the light of subsequent events would have done incalculable harm to our military establishment.

Other examples could be cited. The pay-as-you-go income tax, the Lend-Lease act, the Marshall Plan and many other vital steps taken by the Government might have been long delayed if there had been no accurate way of knowing whether the public would resist such steps, or support them, and how willingly.

The difficulty of trying to judge public opinion without some such systematic gauge was well described by James Bryce in "The American Commonwealth" more than sixty years ago. "Such is the din of voices," wrote Bryce, "that it is hard to say which cry prevails, which is swelled by many, which only by a few throats. The organs of opinion seem almost as numerous as the people themselves, and they are all engaged in representing their own views as that of the people."

But how can polls possibly measure opinions on so complex a subject as the Marshall Plan? Can we measure a person's competence to judge such an issue? Anyone asking such questions is clearly not very familiar with what the polls have been doing to meet just such situations.

The whole point of the Institute's five published surveys on the Marshall Plan between July, 1947, and March, 1948, was to accomplish precisely the thing referred to in the foregoing paragraph, i. e., to find out how many voters were competent to judge it. The polling consisted of a series of questions designed to find out the degree of knowledge among voters on the Marshall Plan. It put respondents "on the spot" by requiring them to say exactly what they understood the Plan to be. From the answers it was possible to classify each voter according to whether he was well informed, moderately informed, only vaguely informed or misinformed. The opinions of each of these groups were then sounded regarding the Plan itself. Thus attitudes on the subject could be studied as if in a spectrum, ranging from opinions of the best informed down to those of the most ignorant. The published reports of these studies showed that over-all sentiment among voters who had heard of the Plan was favorable and that those who were most informed about it were the most in favor of it.

The above is not just an isolated example. For nearly three years we have been using what is known as the "quintamensional plan of question design" for sounding attitudes on the more complex public issues. By this technique the issues are covered from five aspects with a series of questions. The voter is made to prove what he knows about the subject before his opinion is asked. Thus, any such poll as one allegedly taken on the "Metallic Metals Act," a nonexistent bill, by a polling prankster would be utterly impossible.

One of the most unfounded criticisms of polls is that a 3,000-ballot sample is not large enough to measure opinion on issues because, if you were to divide that total by the 435 Congressional districts, you would get only 6.9 ballots per district. Obviously, opinion cannot be satisfactorily measured with six cases and it would be absurd even to try it. But polltakers do not attempt, or claim, to predict opinion in a Congressional district. If they did they would have to get as many cases or ballots in a district as they do in the whole nation. To measure national opinion the polltakers gather the views of a small number of persons in a large number of places and their aggregate gives a picture of national sentiment. Sample sizes for polling are based on well-known statistical tables.

Let me make another thing clear. No polltaker that I know of has ever said that political leaders should suspend their own judgment and follow polls blindly. That would be absurd. What we do say is this: To the extent that a political leader does take public opinion into account in making his decisions, he should have an accurate and objective measure of that opinion rather than mere guesswork. What polls endeavor to supply is a more systematic and more objective measure of opinions. The need for this was pointed out many years ago by Lincoln, who said, "What I want to get done is what the people desire to have done, and the question for me is how to find that out exactly."

The question has been raised whether polls might not harm democracy by shutting off the process of debate and discussion which informs voters and brings out the implications of proposals being considered. The charge that polls put a closure on debate seems to me baseless. For example, the discussion over whether the nation should have a postwar military draft continued in intense fashion for two full years (1945–47), when our polls were showing majority sentiment in favor of the draft.

The national polls were wrong in selecting the winner of the 1948 election. But a general impression has been created that they were much "wronger" than was actually the case. The Institute's error nationally on the Truman vote was 5.3 percentage points, the difference between the forecast of 44.5 per cent and the actual Truman vote of 49.8 per cent. (This way of computing error is a standard procedure among opinion researchers.) On Dewey the difference was 4.1 points, on Wallace 1.6, on Thurmond 0.4. The average was 2.9. Figured on the basis of the two leading parties, it was 4.7. We had repeatedly in the years prior to 1948 pointed out that election polling was subject to a 4-percentage-point error.

With those who say that this is not good enough, particularly in close elections, I quite agree. The problem of election forecasting is the problem of reducing the present average error of 4 percentage points down to 3 or possibly to 2. I believe that this can be done during the next few years if we get the full cooperation of social scientists, and if we ourselves carry forward the intensive experimental programs now being outlined.

The reasons for the 1948 error are worth examining. Some critics have assumed that the failure of the polls was a failure of the sampling technique or procedure—that the tool itself is faulty. While some of the error was due to the selection of the sample, let me correct the impression that it was the major cause.

The error resulted primarily from mistakes in the management or use of the sampling tool. One mistake was in ending the polling too soon before election day. The bulk of the interviewing for our final forecast was completed ten to twelve days prior to Nov. 2. We assumed, as other poll directors did, that few voters change their minds in the closing days of a campaign. This assumption proved wrong.

Another mistake in management was the assumption that, because of general apathy, so few of the persons undecided at the time of our last poll would vote that this group could be excluded. Actually, many did vote, and we now know that a large majority of these voted for Truman.

What makes election forecasting much more difficult than other kinds of predicting is the line drawn between winner and loser. This same difficulty does not apply to polls on issues. In an issue poll it is not a matter of drawing a line between a winner and loser which makes you right if you are on the right side and wrong if you are on the other. A margin of error of 4 or 5 percentage points does not invalidate the results of a poll on an issue.

The need for accurate and systematic knowledge of public opinion on issues has been expressed many times by many people, but never more eloquently than by Bryce in "Modern Democracies." He wrote:

"In saying that public opinion is the real ruler of America, I mean that there exists a judgment and sentiment of the whole nation which is imperfectly expressed through its representative legislatures, is not to be measured by an analysis of votes cast at elections, is not easily gathered from the most diligent study of the press, but is nevertheless a real force, impalpable as the wind, yet a force which all are trying to discover and nearly all to obey."

It seems to me that public opinion polls not only fill this need better than any other method, but have also shown their value in many demonstrable ways, as follows:

Public opinion polls constitute almost the only check on the growing power of pressure groups. The influence of lobbies on Congress has been a matter of increasing concern to many. The claims of pressure groups presuming to speak for millions can be tested by polls. This has been done many times in the past, and it has been shown that some of the leaders of pressure groups represent only a minority within their own groups and that their threats of political reprisal on legislators who refused to bow to their wishes were baseless.

Polls have uncovered many areas of ignorance. It is a mistake to assume that the public opinion polls confine themselves simply to measuring opinion.

A major service which they perform is that of finding out what the public knows about the issues that confront government.

Polls have helped administrative departments of Government make better decisions. Federal, state and local officials are confronted with the problem of dealing intelligently with the public. Government is learning what American business learned years ago—that any program designed to influence the public must be based upon accurate knowledge of public attitudes.

Polls speed up the process of democracy by accurate and swift reporting on public opinion. A miniature national referendum can be conducted in a matter of hours by this method. Examples of the peacetime draft, lend-lease, the Marshall Plan and others have been cited.

Polls help define the mandate of the people in national elections. History is full of baffling questions as to what an election outcome really meant. Was Hoover's victory over Al Smith in 1928 a mandate to keep liquor prohibition? Was Harding's victory in 1920 a mandate to stay out of the League of Nations? Did Franklin D. Roosevelt's 1936 victory give him a mandate to curb the Supreme Court? By sounding opinion on specific issues, as divorced from sentiment on candidates, polls are able to tell what was in the minds of voters who went to the polls on election day.

And so I say that the sampling poll is too valuable to be abandoned or curtailed because of the failure to name the winner in one election. We are continually experimenting and continually learning. This process will never stop. New methods which we are now developing will be tested in the field. The nation may look to substantial improvement in one of the most useful instruments of democracy ever devised.

THE POLLSTERS' FALSE PREMISES

Lindsay Rogers *

Public-opinion polling, if not a major, is a large and important American industry whose tycoons and their academic acolytes have been far from reticent in boasting of achievements. "The speed with which sampling referenda can be completed for the entire nation," writes Dr. George Gallup, "is such that public opinion on any given issue can be reported within forty-eight hours if the occasion warrants. Thus the goal has nearly been reached when public opinion can be 'ascertainable at all times.' " . . .

I concede that polls on a wide variety of questions have become a significant feature of journalism in the United States and in other countries, and that they are a new kind of reporting which gives the reading public data that it did not previously possess and that are sometimes worthy of

* Professor of Public Law at Columbia University. Author of *The American Senate, Crisis Government,* and other works. The selection is reprinted from *The Pollsters* by Lindsay Rogers, by permission of Alfred A. Knopf, Inc. Copyright 1949 by Alfred A. Knopf, Inc.

analysis. But the data conceal more than they reveal and will have different meanings for different analysts. And for the pollsters to maintain that percentages of "yeses," "noes," "no opinion," "never heard of it," disclose public opinion on the policy that they have inquired about, and to which many respondents may not have given a moment's thought before they were interrogated, is to advertise a mouthwash as a cure for anemia. If the pollsters sold their product in bottles instead of as news, the Federal Trade Commission would long since have been after them.

Why the misbranding? It results, I think, from two great sins of omission of which the pollsters are guilty. They have never attempted to define what it is they are measuring. . . . And this is the second great omission—that in the now enormous literature on polling methods and the data that have been secured, one never—well almost never—finds any reasoned statement of premises concerning the nature of the political society in which public opinion should be the ruler. When, as if by accident, premises are articulated, they prove to be false. They have to be, because, if they were not, the pollsters would not be able to make the exaggerated claims that they do about the meaning of the data they present for consideration. They would see that they are talking nonsense when they speak of "implementing democracy," "making it more articulate," and "speeding up its processes." Moreover, they do not bother to say how they define "democracy," which may be anything from a non-snobbish sentimental interest in the underdog to the system that Stalin and the Politburo impose on Russia. . . .

Most men and women do not study public questions and endeavor to form rational opinions. They have neither time nor interest. What they learn from newspapers or the radio gives them incomplete, ofttimes unintentionally, and sometimes intentionally, distorted information. People follow the "pictures" in their heads, which Lippmann called "stereotypes." There is in fact and need be no public opinion on an issue until it has already been shaped and has its advocates and opponents. Even then people will really concern themselves only if they are directly interested. The Reciprocal Trade Agreements policy, for example, may affect importers and exporters. In the long run it may be of vital importance to the economy of the nation as a whole. Apart from those who feel an immediate self-interest, there are few people—mostly persistent students of public affairs—who know of or care one way or the other about the Reciprocal Trade Agreements. As Doob wisely remarks, "What is discouraging about democracy in the modern world and what elsewhere has helped give rise to alternate forms of government is the increasing complexity of the affairs with which government must deal. If the forces of democracy have enabled information to be spread at an arithmetically increasing rate, it can be said without much exaggeration that technology and social changes have increased at a geometrical rate the amount of information which needs to be known for the electorate to be intelligent and reasonably expert." The Athenians could choose members of administrative bodies by lot because then any intelligent citizen had sufficient knowledge of the matters that must be dealt with. This is no longer true. . . .

"The task of government, and hence of democracy as a form of government, is not to express an imaginary popular will, but to effect adjustments among the various special wills and purposes which at any given time are pressing for realization." * And to do this, I might add, after full discussion in the country and mature deliberation in the representative assembly. . . . The pollsters overlook the really vital role of representative assemblies in focusing attention on political issues. If there were no Congress, with its clash of personalities, parties, and sections, could questions be asked, for example, about the Taft-Hartley Act or the Marshall Plan? If they were, "no opinion" would be by far the most frequent reply. . . .

There are few questions suitable for mass answers by yes or no. This the pollsters must ignore when they talk about sample referenda implementing democracy and making it articulate. A man may say that he is in favor of a protective tariff, but would it be worth while to ask him? No one in his senses would propose that a series of tariff schedules should be submitted for rejection or acceptance at the polls, yet the schedules determine whether there is to be any tariff protection and if so, how much. A man can be for or against the Taft-Hartley Act, but what would this mean? Few who know anything about the statute would say that all its provisions are good or that all are bad.

How, in the postwar period, could any issue of foreign policy have been put to the electorate for decision? The Marshall Plan? Its essence lay in the amounts of money, the strings attached to its use, and the concern of our government in respect of the ancillary measures to be taken by receiving states. Policy toward Russia? What questions could be put to an electorate? In an age when 531 representatives and senators who are paid so well for their time that they do not have to have other means of livelihood, and who are staffed for the investigation of the merits of proposed legislation, have to throw up their hands and say there are many details on which they cannot pass and which they must leave to administrative determination, it is absurd to suggest that counting the public pulse can give any light or leading save on the simplest kind of a proposition. And on such simple propositions the wishes of the public can usually be known without the assistance of a poll.

Harold J. Laski writes:

> If it [a referendum] is confined to obtaining answers to questions of principle, then, in the absence of concrete details, the questions are devoid of real meaning. If it is enlarged to consider the full amplitude of a complicated statute, then it

* John Dickinson, "Democratic Realities and Democratic Dogma," *American Political Science Review,* Vol. XXIV (1930), p. 283.

is useless to pretend that a mass judgment upon its clauses is in any way a valid one. . . .

The public's lack of information on certain important issues suggests that in many cases even the pollsters should have viewed their percentages with suspicion and should have boldly declared that there was no opinion for them to try to measure. . . . After the Atlantic Charter had been discussed for some little while, 60 per cent of the population had "never heard of it" and 95 per cent could not name a single one of its provisions. A later poll disclosed eight in ten admitting that they had not read or heard about the Charter. Only one citizen in ten could name the Four Freedoms. Slightly more than one half of the people thought that Lend-Lease operated in reverse, but a majority of these believed that the return was "good will and co-operation" rather than substantial amounts of goods. At the time, polling organizations were telling us what "public opinion" was on the kind of peace settlement that was desirable (1944); and when there was a good deal of discussion of schemes for a new world organization, more than one half of the population thought we had joined the old League of Nations. The same year, seven out of ten did not know that the Senate must approve treaties by a two-thirds vote. . . . In 1946, 31 per cent of a sample had never heard of the Bill of Rights; 36 per cent had heard of it but could not identify it; and 12 per cent gave confused or contradictory answers. . . . And what of opinion on the Taft-Hartley Act? One poll disclosed 61 per cent claiming to have heard of the law, but of this "informed group" 75 per cent could not mention any specific provision that they considered particularly good, and 85 per cent could not pick out a provision that they thought particularly bad. . . .

A premise the pollsters do not make articulate is that if there is a majority public opinion, it should prevail, and presumably at once. They have never bothered to examine what majority rule means in the government the founding fathers proposed, which was accepted, and which, in its main outlines, no section of opinion save the Communists has since challenged. That system is not majority rule pure and simple, which is what the pollsters seem to assume it is. Our arrangements are fashioned as much to protect minorities as they are to enable majority opinion to prevail. Moreover . . . we endeavor to make the arrangements work in a federal system of government. . . . Under the American system of government we take many fateful decisions by less than a majority and sometimes prevent the larger part from having its way against the smaller part. . . .

From the grimness of the contemporary world it is sometimes useful to turn back to a piece of political literature that is still pertinent and suggestive and that deserves rereading. . . . [In 1774, Edmund] Burke made a speech that has been frequently quoted by those who have concerned themselves with the relations between representatives and their constituencies. Burke referred to the fact that his successful colleague at the election (Bristol returned two members to the House of Commons) had declared that "the topic of instructions has occasioned much altercation and uneasiness in this city," and had expressed himself "in favour of the coercive authority of such instructions." That view Burke vehemently repudiated.

> Certainly, gentlemen, [he declared], it ought to be the happiness and glory of a representative to live in the strictest union, the closest correspondence, and the most unreserved communication with his constituents. Their wishes ought to have great weight with him; their opinion high respect; their business unremitted attention. It is his duty to sacrifice his repose, his pleasures, his satisfactions, to theirs; and above all, ever, and in all cases, to prefer their interest to his own. But his unbiassed opinion, his mature judgment, his enlightened conscience, he ought not to sacrifice to you; to any man, or to any set of men living. These he does not derive from your pleasure; no, nor from the law and the constitution. They are a trust from Providence, for the abuse of which he is deeply answerable. Your representative owes you, not his industry only, but his judgment; and he betrays, instead of serving you, if he sacrifices it to your opinion.

Burke said that his colleague had declared that "his will ought to be subservient to yours." If that were all, there would be no objection.

> If government were a matter of will upon any side, yours, without question, ought to be superior. But government and legislation are matters of reason and judgment, and not of inclination; and what sort of reason is that, in which the determination precedes the discussion; in which one set of men deliberate, and another decide; and where those who form the conclusion are perhaps three hundred miles distant from those who hear the arguments?

Of course it was the right of all men to deliver opinions, and those expressed by constituents would be "weighty and respectable." A representative ought always to be glad to hear them and he ought always most seriously to consider them. "But *authoritative* instructions, *mandates* issued, which the member is bound blindly and implicitly to obey, to vote, and to argue for, although contrary to the clearest conviction of his judgment and conscience—these are things utterly unknown to the laws of this land, and which arise from a fundamental mistake of the whole order and tenor of our constitution."

Then follows the passage that has been quoted most frequently:

> Parliament is not a *congress* of ambassadors from different and hostile interests; which interests each must maintain, as an agent and advocate, against other agents and advocates; but parliament is a *deliberative* assembly of *one* nation, with *one* interest, that of the whole; where, not local purposes, not local prejudices ought to guide, but the general good, resulting from the general reason of the whole. You choose a member indeed; but when you have chosen him, he is not a member of Bristol, but he is a member of *parliament*. If the local constituent should have an interest, or should form an hasty opinion, evidently opposite to the real good of the rest of the community, the member for that place ought to be as far, as any other, from any endeavour to give it effect. . . .

The principles on which Burke insisted are more frequently ignored than honored. He himself stated them in too extreme a form. He was indifferent to the value of discussion, which is indispensable in any community that seeks to govern itself rather than to permit itself to be ruled. As Sir Ernest Barker has suggested, "Burke regarded himself and his fellow members in the light of 'publick-Counsellors,' or as we may say in the language of that book of Ecclesiastes which he knew and quoted, 'leaders of the people by their counsels and by their knowledge of learning meet for the people wise and eloquent instruction.' He remained something of a scholar of Trinity House, 'damned absolute'; something of a professor who even in the House of Commons was apt to speak *ex cathedra.*"

On the other hand, too many men have thought too exclusively of staying in a legislature or holding onto their seals of office. They have hesitated to express their convictions and have been content to follow rather than to lead public opinion. In Burke, wrote Lord Morley, "there was none of that too familiar casuistry, by which public men argue themselves out of their consciences in a strange syllogism, that they can best serve the country in Parliament; that to keep their seats they must follow their electors; and that, therefore, in the long run they serve the country best by acquiescing in ignorance and prejudice." In other public men who do not thus deceive themselves, hesitation and softness may result from the fact that they are tired; that swimming with the tide requires much less exertion than going against the tide; that plaudits are usually more pleasant than criticism. I could select innumerable illustrations of what I mean, but one will suffice. . . .

In November 1936 Stanley Baldwin told the House of Commons "that not once but on many occasions, in speeches and in various places, when I have been speaking and advocating as far as I am able the democratic principle, I have stated that a democracy is always two years behind the dictator. I believe that to be true." So far as British rearmament was concerned, Mr. Baldwin had made it true as he proceeded to explain to the House with what he himself described as "an appalling frankness." In order to win an election he had deceived Great Britain on Germany's rearmament program.

"Supposing I had gone to the country and said that Germany was rearming and that we must rearm, does anybody think that this pacific democracy would have rallied to that cry at that moment? I cannot think of anything that would have made the loss of the election from my point of view more certain." But the consequences of the policy were far more appalling than the frankness of the statement. To be sure, Mr. Baldwin's successor as Prime Minister had time in which he could have retrieved the error at least partially. But until the war came in September 1939, and Churchill, Eden, and others entered the Cabinet, there had been in the British executive little of that "energy" which in *The Federalist* papers Alexander Hamilton described as "a leading character in the definition of good government."

Energy is not to be found in those who do no more than follow—in those who look upon a legislative assembly as a congress of ambassadors. In Burke's day the sentiment of a constituency had to be ascertained from its leading members. Now legislators quail under a deluge of telegrams or letters, and not only keep their ears to the ground, but wonder whether they would not be wise to use the acousticon of public-opinion polls. . . .

Party first, mandated representatives, sectional and special interests—this is the setting in which free peoples, in Burke's phrase, now expect their governments to be contrivances of human wisdom to provide for human wants. It would be comforting to accept the sales patter of the pollsters and agree that what they call "public-opinion polls" really do "implement democracy." For reasons already given, I think that even to talk in such a fashion discloses reasoning that is fantastically muddled. To do more than talk—to permit the pollsters' pronouncements to influence policy would be disastrous politically. . . .

The great problem, Lord Acton once said, is not to discover "what governments prescribe but what they ought to prescribe." We cannot wait to obtain the prescription from the perfectionists who, as someone remarked, are people who have no solution for any difficulty but are, nevertheless, able to find a difficulty in any proposed solution. The great question so far as public opinion is concerned is not what it wants, but what it ought to want. . . .

During pre-Munich days, for example, the "essential wisdom" of the British people was latent because the nation had no leadership. Every people, it is cynically and untruthfully said, have as good a government as they deserve. But a government may have no better an electorate than it deserves because it fails to give leadership. In the days of Baldwin and Chamberlain, British politicians congratulated themselves on being able to catch buses they were supposed to be driving. Later, as Bertrand Russell said, the British people were magnificent.

"In a multitude of counsellors there is wisdom," wrote Huxley, "but only in a few of them." *Vox populi* cannot help democratic governments to decide what they ought to do. Political and intellectual leaders must propose alternative policies. They must educate the electorate, and if the leadership and education are effective, then the people will demonstrate their "essential wisdom." "It is the few," said Guicciardini, "which commonly give the turn to affairs" and to which "any general temper in a nation" may be traced.

True it is that in a free state public opinion rules, but this is no reason for more than interest in the yeses and noes that may be disclosed by sampling. A baker can ask a sample of consumers whether it wants the loaf of bread sliced or unsliced, and, if the answer is two to one for sliced, can decide to distribute loaves in that proportion. A housing authority *should* ask a sample whether it prefers flats or single dwellings. The British Broadcasting Corporation can ask its listeners whether they prefer jazz or classical music, but the directors of the BBC have a duty that goes beyond satisfying what the public says is its taste. They should endeavor to change that taste for the better.

"Shall income taxes be reduced?" can be asked of a sample, but the Secretary of the Treasury and congressional committees on appropriations should take note of the answers only for the purpose of endeavoring to change those answers if they do not agree with them.

> It is the business of a statesman to lead [wrote the London *Times*], and with his ear perpetually to the ground he is in no posture of leadership. The honest leader determines his course by the light of his own conscience and the special knowledge available to him, not by ascertaining the views of his necessarily less well-informed followers, in order that he may meekly conform. Having decided for himself what is right, he has then to convince the rank and file, knowing that if he fails to win or hold their support they will dismiss him and transfer their trust to another. That, and that only, is the sanction for the ultimate control of public opinion over policy. By no other means can the general will be formulated and elicited. A leader, in war or peace, who hesitates to take his political life in his hands will not be followed; neither social surveys nor any other mechanical device can be manipulated as an insurance by a politician playing for safety. Democracy implies and demands leadership in the true sense, and founders without it.

The United States has been fortunate in that it had leadership at critical times. The chief incidents are well known. Jefferson made the Louisiana Purchase without consulting Congress. "A John Randolph," he wrote, "would find means to protract the proceeding on it by Congress until the ensuing spring, by which time new circumstances would change the mind of the other party." Public opinion approved Jefferson's acquisition. President Monroe announced what for a century was the basis of American foreign policy in a message to Congress—the Monroe Doctrine. Abraham Lincoln took courageous action that he admitted was beyond his legal power as President but that he thought was not beyond the constitutional competence of Congress, which would be called upon to approve it. . . .

Franklin Roosevelt made his "New Deal" and took his decisions on the transfer of destroyers in return for the use of British bases and of convoying before he was sure of congressional or public approval. Even if a sample poll had shown majority criticism, and its findings had had support from other quarters, the decisions should have stood and the President could have waited for the "essential wisdom" of the people to manifest itself. The polls did show support for the President, and this was better than if they had shown lack of support, which might have caused a little but only temporary embarrassment.

What of leadership now? What foreign policies should we have? What, domestically, should be our program? Answers to these questions are not my present subject. The pollsters will not be able to discover what our policies should be from samples in which each respondent says "yes" or "no" or "don't know." That method may be suitable for predicting election results, and should work *if the sample is properly chosen*. But the method is not suitable for measuring public opinion on the foreign or domestic proposals that statesmen may make. Each member of the electorate casts a ballot that is the equal of every other ballot. But who are the people who favor certain policies? How influential are they? Whom do they represent. How well are they organized? How much do they care? . . . In politics it is not the accumulation of facts but insight that will find the highroad if and when it is found.

The facts that the pollsters accumulate and endeavor to explain they create themselves. Bernard Shaw once declared that he was unable to see a great deal of difference between the controversies of the schoolmen over how many angels could stand on the point of a needle and the discussions of the physicists over the number of electrons in an atom. There is a difference: the physicist proposes to do something with his answer when he gets it, and he knows that it will be accepted by all other physicists. The pollsters get answers—yeses and noes—that are frequently suspect on their faces, that are not the same answers as other pollsters get, and that sometimes cancel each other out.

Since they must maintain that their work is important, the pollsters use a false premise: that our political system must accept and act on their answers. . . . So far as the pollers of public opinion are concerned, the light they have been following is a will-o'-the-wisp. They have been taking in each other's washing, and have been using statistics in terms of the Frenchman's definition: a means of being precise about matters of which you will remain ignorant.

Topic 22

IS CENTRALIZATION OF OUR PARTIES DESIRABLE?

The Need for Disciplined Parties

James M. Burns *

OUR MULTI-PARTY SYSTEM

If the thousands of organized interests in a democracy reflect group antagonisms, it is the two-party system which, under ideal conditions, exploits the underlying solidarity among people. It is that system which,

* Assistant Professor of Political Science at Williams College. Formerly Legislative Assistant, United States Congress. The selection is from James M. Burns, *Congress on Trial* (New York, Harper & Bros., 1949), pp. 33–34. Copyright, 1949, by Harper & Bros.

functioning properly, manages to express the concurrence of a majority.

How does the two-party system accomplish this vital task? The answer is not hard to find. In any democracy a major party seeks control of the government. To achieve that goal it bids for support throughout the community. To gain that support the party must broaden its platform through a series of compromises with organized groups and with unorganized voters. No narrow program will do the job. Constantly searching for the beliefs that bind diverse groups, the party's policy-makers define the issues that transcend the claims of special interests and find response among great masses of the people. Since the politicians attempt to attract as many "customers" as possible, the party system becomes, in the words of Lord Bryce, "the best instrument for the suppression of dissident minorities democracy has yet devised." For in a democracy the parties can hold a minority in check without stifling its creative function in the polity.

In the United States especially, a major party must find the common denominator among a large and varied group of voters, for it hopes to pluck the biggest plum of all at the next election—the Presidency. To elect a Chief Executive it must produce an electoral majority, and in doing so it forces adjustments among minority groups. As Carl Becker has said, "the fundamental compromises are, in the first instance, made not between the major parties but within them." Once having gone through this process of compromise in each of their camps, the two parties can offer the voters a relatively simple "either-or" choice rather than a confused array of alternatives. The two parties take up new ideas and attract new voters in order to survive in rigorous competition, and in doing so they display the inclusiveness that is central to democracy.

Such, ideally, are the benefits of a two-party system. But in the United States we do not enjoy these benefits because our two-party system breaks down in the legislative branch. What we have in Congress might better be called a multi-party system. Instead of a grand encounter between the rallied forces of the two great parties in House and Senate, the legislative battle often degenerates into scuffles and skirmishes among minority groups. On matters of vital public policy the major parties fail to hold their lines. They leave the field in possession of the pressure politicians and other members of Congress who are faithful to a locality or to a special interest but not to the national platform of their party.

A glance at virtually any House or Senate roll call will demonstrate the inability of the party to enforce discipline even if it should try. In recent years the Democratic party has been especially vulnerable to the disruptive effects of bloc voting, but the Republicans too are rarely able to prevent at least a few of their adherents from crossing party lines. Party irresponsibility also affects the shaping of bills in committee and on the floor before the final roll call is reached. Indeed, it is hardly proper even to use the term "party responsibility" in discussing Congress, for the most rudimentary underpinnings of such responsibility do not exist. The party members in Congress have no common political program; as Pendleton Herring has said, "On the majority of issues the party takes no stand." And if there were such a program, little machinery exists in House or Senate to enforce it.

As a result of this situation we have in Congress, as far as public policy is concerned, a group of splinter parties. They are the Southern Democratic party, the Farmers' party, the Labor party, the New Deal party, the Liberal Republican party, the Veterans' party, the Silver party, and many others, along with the faithful adherents of the Republican and Democratic parties. A President of the United States is a Democrat or Republican, but key Senators and Representatives are more than likely to vote as members of a multi-party system.

This congressional patchwork is neither new nor accidental. It is rooted in American political organization. As national institutions, our parties are decrepit. They are coalitions of state and local party organizations, pulling together in awkward harmony every four years in an attempt to elect a President, going their own way the rest of the time.

The bosses who run the party machines are concerned more with private spoils than with public policy. The pressure groups that work through and around the parties are interested in their own designs, which may or may not coincide with the general welfare.

Lacking central control and discipline, the major party cannot hold its congressmen responsible to the broad majority of the voters in the nation who put the party into power. The national committee and chairman of the party have little control over national policy. They can do nothing for the congressman—he feels no responsibility to them.

Senators and Representatives can blithely disregard the national political platform; if they bother to pay it lip service, they usually do so because the program is so broad as to permit the widest leeway. In their states and districts the congressmen are responsible to fragments of the party—fragments that assume a variety of shapes under the impact of economic, sectional, ideological, and other forces.

BRITAIN: PARTY GOVERNMENT IN ACTION

We have much to learn from the English on this matter of political organization in a democracy. For over the course of many years they have forged a system of party government in the full sense of the term. That system serves three cardinal purposes. It unites the various branches of the government in order to carry out the will of a popular majority. It staves off the thrusts for power of minority groups. And as recent events have made clear, it offers the voters a genuine choice between two fairly distinct programs, rather than the Tweedledum-Tweedledee alternatives that often characterize political encounters in the United States. . . .

The difference between the British system and ours is not, of course, one of personality, but one of basic political organization. There the party is supreme. Its role in national life is so meaningful and decisive that most Englishmen vote in terms of the party program and record, rather than on the basis of the personality, salesmanship, and promises of the individual candidate.

On first look such a scheme might seem to bear an authoritarian stamp. But in fact the British party system is an almost ideal form of representative government. By forcing candidates for Parliament to run on the national platforms, it gives the voter a real choice between two opposing programs. And the voter expects the successful candidate to support that program once he takes his seat in the Commons, for faithfulness to that cause is part of the bargain between voter, candidate, and party. The parties make no pretense of responding to every ripple of public opinion, or to every pressure of some organized minority. They have the more vital function of expressing the broad political aspirations of a majority of the people. While in this country Congress often seems to represent every group except the majority, in Britain the major parties, operating at the highest level of political organization, give the national welfare right of way over minority interests.

Despite the omnipotence of party in Britain, the legislature is not a dead letter. On the contrary, Parliament enjoys enormous prestige in that country and throughout much of the world. "It has occupied the centre of the political stage for centuries," Jennings has written. "So much of the history of freedom is part of the history of Parliament that freedom and parliamentary government are often considered to be the same thing." . . .

How to explain the contrast between party domination of the legislative in Britain and the constant disruption of party lines in Congress? The answer, in part, lies in the greater homogeneity of the British people that permits a more cohesive political structure. But that is not the whole answer, for Britain too has her sectional rivalries that cut across parties, her special interests that would use either party in their quest for influence. The main reason for that contrast is the organization of political power in Britain as compared with America.

The Conservative Party, and to an even greater extent the Labour party, are centralized agencies. Ample control over funds, program, and the choice of candidates is lodged in the national office of each party. Because each is responsible for judgment and action on a national scale it requires its parliamentary members to vote in national terms. In contrast to the loose decentralized party structure of the United States, continually disintegrating in Congress under the impact of organized minorities, the British parties have the means of holding their M.P.'s in line.

It is not a matter simply of enforcement machinery. Discipline in the British party rests also on the fact that, except perhaps in times of fast-moving political developments, its program is a genuine compromise among the various groups making up the party. That program is carefully devised not only to consolidate the support of the rank and file but to attract independent voters as well. On the theory that an M.P. is more easily led than driven, it may even make concessions to local and sectional interests. But those concessions are never so fundamental as to endanger seriously the party's loyalty to its national program. It is precisely in this respect—at least as far as discipline in the legislative body is concerned—that the American parties differ so drastically from their British counterparts.

MAKE-BELIEVE MAJORITIES

Lacking the party rule that invigorates the British parliamentary system, Congress is often unable to furnish majorities for even the most urgent measures. While Parliament automatically musters enough votes to enact the program of the party in power, or else must face dissolution, the majority party in Congress cannot control its own rank and file. Hence bills in Congress get stymied in committee; they survive in one chamber only to stall in the other; a few fail in conference between Senate and House. When measures become marooned somewhere in the winding legislative channels, the villain of the piece may well be a minority group holding a strong position in committee or chamber, and the majority may be powerless to come to the rescue.

How, then, do bills get passed? Partly as a result of the appeals and threats of a President acting as chief legislator as well as chief executive. The President's control of patronage, his means of mobilizing public opinion, the authority of his office often enable him to drive measures through the legislature. In many cases, too, legislation is enacted largely as a result of bi-party coalitions responding to group pressures of some sort. Such important measures as the McNary-Haugen proposals for farm surplus control in the 1920's, the Smoot-Hawley tariff of 1930, the Economy Act of 1933, the National Industrial Recovery Act of the same year, the Employment Act of 1946, the Greek-Turkish aid bill of 1947, to name only a few, were passed by Congress as a result of bi-party support.

Least significant of all in the enactment of legislation seems to be the party as such. Half a century ago A. Lawrence Lowell set out to discover how often more than nine-tenths of the party members in Congress voted on the same side of a question. He found such party cohesion in less than eight per cent of the important bills considered by the Thirty-Eighth Congress, elected in 1862; and party influence on legislation was even less in other samples he studied.

Party cohesion is still slight today. And as for straight party voting—where every Republican lines up on one side of an issue and every Democrat on the opposite side—it would be difficult indeed to find an example of such voting on an important issue (aside from "organizing" the House or Senate) in the last quarter century.

In the absence of party voting Congress at times falls back on curious methods of producing majorities. One of these might be termed the "majority by threat." It is the most primitive of all means of securing a working combination. Rather than agreeing on a common program, blocs threaten to withhold their votes from bills backed by other blocs unless support is forthcoming for their own.

It is a sort of log-rolling in reverse, with the advocates of a measure saying in effect: "If you dare to vote against our bill, we will vote against yours." Thus in 1937 the labor bloc in Congress threatened to oppose agricultural legislation unless farm representatives supported a wages and hours bill. In considering the price control bill of 1942 the majority leader issued a similar warning to the farm group. There is a vast difference between such attempts to win votes through fugitive alliances in reverse, and the effecting of agreement by intra-party action based on awareness of a broad but genuine identity of interest.

Another crude method of achieving joint action on bills is "evasion by delegation"—the consignment of broad powers of decision to the President when congressional blocs cannot agree on a closely defined policy. Not because of the need for administrative discretion but because of its own failure to find a basis for agreement, Congress passes important policy-making powers on to the Chief Executive.

An example of such delegation is found in the consideration of the National Industrial Recovery Act in 1933; protectionist and anti-protectionist Senators were at odds over an embargo provision, and as a "compromise" they left the matter to the discretion of Mr. Roosevelt. This type of delegation is a form of legislative abdication.

Such behavior by congressional majorities should not be confused with genuine majority rule. It is one thing for a party to present its platform and candidates to the voters and, when vested with power, to make specific policies in terms of the approved program. It is quite another matter when bi-party majorities, operating without the endorsement of a majority of the voters, capture the machinery of law-making. Such majorities in Congress raise hob with the representative process. They have little responsibility to the people. They may gain their ends and disappear overnight. Their actions may be good or bad, but in either case the bi-party coalitions can ignore with impunity the national party platforms which, however vague and irresolute, at least must pass some kind of public inspection. Bi-party blocs cannot long provide real majority rule. The fleeting majorities that they muster are often not truly representative of the majority of the voters.

If these coalitions do not provide real majority rule, what does? In a democracy majority rule is assumed to be the best means of discovering and satisfying the "public interest." But what kind of majority? There are many types—the majority required to pass an amendment to the Constitution, that needed to push a bill through Congress, that involved in electing a President, and others.

The most democratic, stable, and effective type of majority, however, is a popular majority—namely, one half of all the pooled votes throughout the nation, plus one (or more). This is a different sort of majority than that represented by a coalition in Congress responding to minorities organized in the various states and districts. "No public policy could ever be the mere sum of the demands of the organized special interests," says Schattschneider; ". . . the sum of the special interests, especially the organized special interests, is not equal to the total of all interests of the community, for there are vital common interests that cannot be organized by pressure groups."

Not only do pressure groups often fail to represent fairly the interests of many of their own members. Also in the interstices of the pressure groups one finds voting fragments that see their main stake in the well-being of the community at large. The marginal members of pressure groups, those who are not members of pressure groups, and the voters who are torn between allegiance to competing pressure groups—all these have significant weight in a nation-wide popular election, but far less weight in the sum total of local elections. In short, they are far more influential in choosing Presidents (even with the electoral college) than in choosing members of Congress.

Consequently, a popular majority tends to be more representative and democratic than a "segmented" majority. It is more stable too, because it cannot be manipulated by a few pressure politicians who are able to mobilize organized interests in various states and districts. A simple, mass, nation-wide, popular majority is often feared as leading to the "tyranny of the majority." Actually it is the safest kind of majority. Building a nation-wide coalition of twenty or more millions of voters is no mean feat. It requires the presidential candidate to find a basis of harmony among diverse groups and to widen his platform to attract those groups and the millions of independent voters. A popular majority, like democratic politics in general, furnishes its own checks and balances.

The nation-wide political party is the natural vehicle for a popular majority. But it is also a rickety one. "Coalition fever" in Congress reflects the weakness of the American parties—their inertia, their slackness, their fear of assuming leadership. Organized interest groups display precisely the traits that the parties should display but do not—discipline over their representatives in office, alertness, the capacity to submerge internal differences in a united drive toward the more decisive group objectives. The special interests operate through either or both major parties with a cynical disregard for the party platform. "In a Republican district I was Republican; in a Democratic district I was a Democrat; and in a doubtful district I was doubtful," said Jay Gould, "but I was always Erie."

Similarly with the organized interests of today. It would be inconceivable for a dairy Senator from Wisconsin, a silver Congressman from Colorado, a cotton Senator from Alabama to desert their respective groups to uphold the party platform or the general welfare. In a Congress lacking sturdy party organization, many of the nation's pressure groups seem to enjoy greater representation than the majority of the voters.

THE CASE FOR DECENTRALIZED PARTIES

Pendleton Herring *

In this country the whole ideology of party is still closely bound to Edmund Burke's definition of it—the view which regards a political party as a body of men united for promoting by their joint endeavor the national interest upon some particular principle in which they are all agreed. If this be our definition of political parties, something is very wrong with our system. The only bodies answering this description are the short-lived and ineffective third parties, fatally dedicated to forwarding limited interests or specific panaceas. Perhaps the chief reason for the prevalence of Burke's notion lies in the fact that the interpretation of American political institutions has been deeply affected by assumptions derived from a study of the British government. An interesting study in the transmigration of symbols and ideas might be attempted in noting the vast influence of James Bryce, A. Lawrence Lowell, and Woodrow Wilson, the three great figures largely responsible for the birth of political science and all deeply imbued with the English tradition. It is fair to say that the standards for judging party government in the United States have been based most persistently upon norms derived from studying the Mother of Parliaments.

Our party system is better tested not by traditional theoretical assumptions but rather in terms of its political environment in the United States. How does it meet the demands made by this environment?

Party government has operated within a society basically unified by a confidence in a system of free enterprise. We have proceeded on a gospel of trust in God and the devil take the hindmost. Planning and forethought, while necessary for private pursuits, have not been regarded as essential for public affairs.

The significance of our system lies not in the alignment of voters pro and con in purely intellectualistic terms but rather in the maintenance of

* Executive Associate of the Carnegie Corporation, a research institution. Formerly Professor of Government, Harvard University, and Professor, Harvard Graduate School of Public Administration. Author of *Group Representation Before Congress, Public Administration and the Public Interest, Presidential Leadership,* and other works. The selection is from Pendleton Herring, *The Politics of Democracy: American Parties in Action* (New York, Rinehart & Co., Inc., 1940), *passim.* By permission of the publisher.

institutions which keep political power contingent and provide alternative sets of rulers. It is well to repeat that in practice our major political parties are primarily concerned not with framing issues and drawing up distinctive programs but in trying to discover some way of bringing together into a reasonably harmonious relationship as large a proportion of the voters as possible. The methods employed to this end are dictated by the times, the circumstances, and the kind of men in control of the organization. Principles and issues must remain relative to these conditions. . . .

Faced with the necessity of holding together in one organization the many varied elements that go to make it up, the party leaders find it inexpedient and unwise to commit themselves in advance to a definite program. In the first place they might not get general support for the program, nor could they secure agreement upon its contents. This causes much head-wagging as to the meaninglessness and futility of our parties. Yet the very lack of agreement results in such a degree of personal freedom for the individual congressman as would be impossible were the party to sponsor a set of specific issues. The legislator may stand forth as the spokesman of the most powerful and aggressive elements within his constituency, or under the pressure from divergent interests he may take a conciliatory attitude. Whatever his reaction may be, he is seldom bound by the stand of the party.

This situation has prompted some to decry the influence of special minorities which are thus left free to make their power felt. It is protested that "Congress has become the tool of selfish interests." Yet in what more appropriate place than in Congress, pray, could such forces come forward with their demands? The conflict and confusion there are indicative of the vital character of this assembly. Our congressmen may at times appear as quarrelsome politicians, but this very independence protects them from becoming automatons. They retain a greater degree of personal political responsibility than do most lawmakers in other countries. It is their manifest duty as public representatives to weigh the forces of various interests according to their conception of the general welfare. That they are often unable to meet this responsibility is no reflection on the political party itself.

Little would be gained by shifting the struggle to a party conclave and compromising differences in private caucuses in order that the party might offer the appearance of solidarity. In a parliamentary government the ministers do this bargaining and commit their followers to a particular course of policy in the light of such arrangements. To say that a party has a program is to say that it has agreed upon a *modus operandi* with the social and economic interests that constitute the underlying power in political affairs. . . .

Congress itself is handicapped in acting as an agency entrusted with the formulation of national policy. First, the organization of its chambers makes control and responsibility exceedingly difficult. Authoritative leadership lacks a focal point. The only discipline which can be achieved comes through presidential control. Second, the operation of the seniority rule places in position of less influence representatives with the newest popular mandate, namely, the last election returns. . . .

Parties cannot be pictured realistically as coming forward with a program, winning office, and then putting their platform into effect. This view is based on a mandate theory of government. The essence of democracy does not lie in the plebescite or even in the initiative and referendum. A recording of ayes and noes by uninformed persons cannot be justified by any scheme of government that values individual integrity and judgment. It is better for the voter to act upon limited empiric evidence than to base his judgment upon vague promises and to act upon fuzzy notions about broad public problems far beyond his experience and capacity for evaluation. In presidential elections the voter has usually been able to cast his ballot upon an estimate of the candidate's personality. A president may point to a great popular mandate, but this gesture is necessarily a political argument rather than authority for action on any specific issues.

Defenders of the popular mandate theory of democracy point to the British system as providing the means for a clear expression of opinion. "Elections in Great Britain," they say, "mean so much more. You know what you are voting for." This is not the view taken by Ivor Jennings, one of the most careful students of British institutions. He shows how time and again arguments have arisen as to "whether a mandate has been given and of what a mandate consists." Of the many issues put before the voters upon which must the government respond? . . .

If it is difficult under a responsible ministry in Great Britain to establish just what has been decided by an election, it is impossible to identify a clear line of policy with the voice of the people in this country. To commit a party to a long-term program is to discount the unpredictable. Politicians must face issues as they arise and in concrete terms. To do more is to invite debate on abstractions. The New Deal has carried forward a process of basic readjustments with a minimum of debate on final ends. Once such questions are posed sharply by opposing political camps the probability of peaceful change is reduced. Then men focus their eyes not on the task demanding attention but on more distant horizons. There is no point in fighting today to settle a question which you now assume will be pressing in the unpredictable future.

To have two distinctive parties, each determined to carry out its program, would necessitate a change in our form of government. Obviously such a system is not compatible with staggered elections for House and Senate and with an independent executive. Nor could we then tolerate having a majority of Congress and the president of different parties. Even more important would be the abolition of fixed terms of office. Under such a system the electorate must be able to throw out of office a party whose program no longer holds popular confidence. If all those wanting change were able to gang up and force through a sweeping party program, while all those of the party against change were expected to stand by until an election occurred two or four years hence, the pent-up feeling and the resulting clash would probably blow the dome off the Capitol.

An acceptable theory of party must take into full account the context within which our parties function. The development of new criteria rather than the repetition of old criticisms would make for a better understanding of political problems. This might serve to show the voter where and how to direct his attention to politics. The apathy of the citizen is due not to a lack of interest in public affairs but rather to a feeling of helplessness at the booming, buzzing confusion. Accordingly, any standards of judgment, if they are to prove usable, must be simple and understandable.

The achievement of harmony within the party suggests itself as an appropriate criterion. Has the party demonstrated its power to compromise the differences of its members coming from the various localities? During the course of one administration the unity or disunity within the party is sure to appear. Has the party developed among its followers a consciousness of party responsibility that stimulates a willingness to co-operate in the solution of public questions?

To what extent has rule by the party in the majority resulted in efficient administration? Accomplishments certainly provide a basis for judgment superior to promises. Viewed as an organization with a continuing life and a definite leadership and membership, the political party stands forth as a body that can be called to task for the standards of public conduct of the politicians enrolled; it can be demanded of the party that the candidates put forward in its name be honest and able public servants.

The party can be judged according to the quality of its personnel. What kind of men does the party offer? The public is quick to decide as to the personalities associated with the party. If stuffed shirts are placed in positions of authority and bosses left to connive in the background, the situation soon stirs common gossip. Is authority within the party exercised directly and openly or deviously and darkly? Politicians cannot depend upon the force of party discipline to guarantee control of the legislature. Has the party sponsored an executive official who has succeeded in winning wide support? Has the party picked a leader?

Having asked these questions of the party, one may question the candidate directly as to his stand on particular measures of concern to groups and individuals. To require the party to stand flatly on an issue is simply another way of demanding that a particular position be urged upon the elected representatives through the party leaders of the national organization. The contact had better be direct, since party discipline is far from dependable. For the proposal of policies and the responsibility of promises, individual statesmen alone can be held accountable. Commitments on specific issues demand clear and direct answerability.

Limitations upon the party as an expounder of principles and supporter of issues make the need of leadership in the presidential office all the more urgent at times when positive action is required. The chief executive is in a strategic position to initiate policy and gain national support for legislative measures. His is the only nation-wide constituency. Not only chief executive but often also national representative-at-large, he is capable of holding the strongest mandate from the electorate. With party lines providing little guidance to public policy, with control in the legislative body disparate and uncertain, the presidential will must be positive and clear if Congress is to carry through a consistent program.

For a statesman to secure a following in support of his measures it is not necessary or even always desirable to identify the party itself with these policies. Under our system, government has often been conducted on a personal rather than a partisan plane. The problem has been one of individual and not party leadership. The American political party has not adhered to a fixed set of doctrines for deciding specific policies. It has done little more than launch leaders selected for their availability and their capacity to attract political support.

The voter can judge the political party more clearly in terms of its leaders than by its promises. If the validity of appraising our party system in accordance with these standards were recognized, much artificial dissatisfaction with political parties might disappear. The political system could then be evaluated not by criteria removed from reality but by standards that are human, direct, and comprehensible to all. . . .

To survive in our dynamic society, parties must try to anticipate the broadest interest alignments of the nation. Their highest function is to readjust existing forces into more effective patterns for action. Parties do not contest with each other on basic questions of policy. Their real gamble is with the future. The fate of the party is determined by the skill with which it adjusts and coalesces these emergent economic and social forces. Hence our party system as a whole tends to go toward the left or toward the right. This is the characteristic pedestrian pace of democratic government. It distresses those who desire a system offering clear objectives. . . .

A basic difference between the British and the American situations is found in the almost unlimited powers centralized in the House of Commons. Parliament determines economic policies. Hence, political policies are worked out by national parties in national terms. Public policy in the United States is divided between at least forty-nine different governments. Hence, each of the major parties may have forty-nine different platforms.

More striking is the fact that our national party organization is a mechanism ill designed to support national policy. Today we face such problems with a political machinery based on local politics. Out of the narrow desires of city machine and state and county leaders we expect a national support to arise.

Our national party committees are removed from the present basis of strength in the United States today. They stand isolated except to the extent that the jollying and conniving of the national chairmen can establish ties with the communities. Localism is the inevitable result. The leader looks downward for what support he can muster. Opportunism becomes his creed. "My first job is to stay in Congress. I must watch my district." Thus frankly spoke one of the most sincere members of the Progressive bloc. Congressmen must not think of national policy without considering the local interests that may be involved.

Our party structure is one product of our system of geographical representation. At best it is broadly sectional, at worst narrowly parochial. National economic policies are before us—their appropriate institutional support today comes through organizing the individuals along functional lines affected. More significant than the party as sources of policy are the trade association, the trade union, and the farmers' organizations. Policy can be worked out by experts trying to take a broad view and then passed along to the followers for criticism and support. Policy formulation in these terms is to be seen operating in federal agencies such as the Department of Agriculture and in nonofficial organizations as well. Unless we are ready to develop these avenues we are thrown back upon the necessity of building unified, disciplined national parties.

Disciplined national parties cannot be democratically reconciled with unity and leadership unless a national harmony exists. The diversity of the nation has been so great that nationally it has seldom been possible even for a *sub rosa* organization to assume control. Today, however, with the increase of national responsibilities the demand for national political control emerges, and we see—and condemn—the subterfuge created to meet the situation.

The demands made upon government may force political parties to attempt a more authoritative line. Carefully devising a program would be pointless unless the party leaders were determined to carry it through. This would entail central control, which in turn would entail sanctions to make such power effective. The easygoing, rough-and-tumble politics and compromise and barter would then give way to disciplined parties. The British have frankly recognized the necessity of demanding compliance from the rank and file if the party is to stand for a line of policy. They are willing to pay the price for more orderly politics. This entails such a concentration of power in the Central Office of the party as would be unthinkable in this country at present.

Professor James K. Pollock in a recent investigation finds that "today the Central Office is the keystone of the whole party organization. It is the focal point of party control, and its activities extend to every phase of party life. More and more does the whole party turn to the Central Office for guidance." . . . Once the nominees are selected, the Central Office imposes its control over the policies and promises of the candidates. . . .

Under this system the member of Parliament becomes the creature of the party organization rather than being dependent entirely upon his constituents. The Central Office not only exercises crucial influence in the selection of candidates and the disbursement of campaign funds but also plays an important role in recommending persons for the honors list. It is very significant to note that "the larger part of the list is prepared by the Chairman of the Party Organization, who also collects most of the money for the running expenses of the organization."

Pollock noted "the lessening influence of the local constituencies in the control not only of the party but of their own affairs." The member of Parliament is "much more the agent of his party than of his constituency." . . .

The traditional American attitude toward party control is one of grave distrust. Political corruption and machine domination are closely associated ideas. The abuses that arise under control by such political rings are best illustrated in our cities and states. The rigidity has become so great at times that men can best think of these political relationships as a machine. A classic example of such a system was the organization perfected by Boss Tom Platt in New York State.

William Barnes, in telling Theodore Roosevelt of Platt's methods, said:

> Your know yourself, Mr. Roosevelt, the Senator does not bully. He does not have to. That the man who went into politics and wanted to go ahead found out for himself that he could not get ahead if he didn't do what the organization, what the leader, what the boss wished. That it was not necessary to give orders; it was quite sufficient to have it understood by example that the man that stood by the organization benefited because the organization stood by him and that if he did not stand by the organization he got punished and that the ordinary man found this out for himself. If he declined to learn, then he got dropped; he failed to make a record, he could not satisfy his constituents, that his bills were not passed or his work failed in other ways, and that he did not get a renomination and he was eliminated.

It is not always necessary to give orders and to insist upon personal obedience. There is the tacit understanding that the men who stand by the organization will receive their reward. Obvious coercion is not necessary here. Moral suasion is a weapon of great power in the armory of the boss. . . .

We cannot forget our experiences with strong and disciplined party organization in the United States. The strength of our local party organization is in marked contrast to the protean character of the party viewed nationally.

We have escaped in this wider realm the rigidities that have made democracy a mockery in our cities. To call the roll of state and city bosses is to remind ourselves of the consequences that have followed from a concentration of power in the hands of unscrupulous men.

Is it enough to say that we must get better men? As we have already argued, the leaders who come to the top politically are one expression of the underlying pattern of interests. Our system can work successfully only when there is effective political support for leaders who follow the conventions imposed by belief in rule by law. Where bossism prevails, constitutional morality lags. An inner ring may so completely control the avenues for the expression of opinion that those out of power despair of gaining a chance to influence government through legal means. Assassination stopped Huey Long. His regime and that of Hitler might be called similar in kind if not in degree. In each case, party leaders place their will and purpose above the limits imposed by constitutional morality.

While this has happened here in the United States, our dictators have been local bosses tolerated by a citizenry too little disturbed to reassert the standards of justice and morality latent in the community. The diversity of the country has protected the preoccupied voter from the consequences of his own inattention to national politics. The common national interests of bankers and large industrialists offer a possible basis for dictatorship. It is conceivable that a highly class-conscious labor movement might provide a context favorable to national political control by a small clique.

A higher degree of party control from the top down to the precincts may be the price that we shall have to pay for more coherence and direction in national policy. It may be that the future of our national politics calls for a higher degree of centralized control from party headquarters. This cannot be made effective, however, without great changes in our laws and customs, in our attitude toward politics, and in the distribution of powers between the states and the federal government, between the legislative and the executive branches. . . .

Our system will work so long as men with widely differing views can content themselves with a middle ground for action. Our two parties must face change together, though one may use caution and the other zest. It is not my object to argue that compromise is a good in itself or that it is necessary to seek compromise in all things. My aim is to explain rather than to advocate. My point is that, no matter what men's visions may be, where their goals differ and where a peaceful adjustment is sought, compromise is the product. In a world already bitterly divided in many areas and easily capable of further cleavages, a system that gives us half a loaf is a system to be cherished. While munching this crust, we can then take thought concerning the next move.

Topic 23

IS REALIGNMENT OF OUR PARTIES DESIRABLE?

THERE SHOULD BE TWO NEW PARTIES

Nicholas Murray Butler *

An entirely new group of doctrines and policies—economic, social and political—has come upon the scene and wholly displaced those which a generation ago were the basis of our political discussion and political action. These new principles and policies have little to do with the existing Democrat and Republican party traditions, but in reality separate those two parties, as they have heretofore existed, into wholly new groups. It cannot be long before the present party organizations are entirely reconstructed, in order to be adjusted to the consideration of these new principles and policies, and to taking practical action in accordance with such of those principles and policies as may gain the preference in public opinion. The one-time powerful Whig party, led by Henry Clay and Daniel Webster, had just this experience when the conditions which resulted in the Civil War came to the forefront in the field of public interest.

It is not difficult to see what the new party alignment must be. It will, on the one hand, bring together those liberal Republicans and those liberal Democrats whose fundamental political philosophy is that of the Federal Constitution and its Bill of Rights, and who will resist to the end the overthrow of progressive American liberalism by any one of the many reactionary forms of totalitarianism, whether these be given the name of State socialism, of communism or of any other of the new and widely heralded isms of the moment.

The party which is to defend fundamental American liberalism cannot bear the name Republican. The reason is that that party will be composed in very considerable part of the present-day Democrats in the Southern and Southwestern States. The traditions of the Civil War and the echoes of names of an already distant past would make it quite impossible for this great body of American citizens to call themselves Republicans or to vote a ticket bearing the name Republican.

It is for reasons such as these that the party to come into existence under the new alignment might well be called Constitutional Liberal. This would mean that its members were prepared to move forward, meeting new prob-

* Late President of Columbia University. Author of *Across the Busy Years* and many other books on philosophy and politics. The selection is reprinted from *The World Today* by Nicholas Murray Butler; copyright 1946 by Nicholas Murray Butler; used by permission of the publishers, Charles Scribners' Sons.

lems as they arise, but always on the basis and in terms of the Federal Constitution and its Bill of Rights.

The opposing group would consist of those who, while calling themselves progressive and liberal, are really in highest degree reactionary. Their aim is the institution of some form or kind of totalitarianism, particularly in the field of the nation's economic life. . . . It is useless to attempt to continue the once-honored party names, which have now wholly lost their one-time significance. The sooner this change is made, the better for the American people, for their happiness and prosperity and for their new world leadership. . . .

TIME FOR REALIGNMENT

Harold J. Laski *

No small part of the future of federal institutions in the United States depends upon the development, above all on the plane of ideas, of its political parties. . . . A distinction between the Republicans and the Democrats is far from easy to draw. In part it is geographical. No one, for instance, expects Maine or Vermont to go Democratic, as no one expects Georgia or Mississippi to go Republican. There is a slight tendency in the Democratic party to be more agrarian than industrial, though it has great influence in the big cities, more inclined to a low than a high tariff, more interested, for historical reasons, in the problems of the debtor class than of the creditor class, than its rival. But the tendency is no more than slight. . . . Leading industrialists have admitted without embarrassment that, at the time of a presidental election, they subscribed to both major parties in order to exercise a proportionate influence on either should it win at the polls. No one seriously supposes that either the Republicans or the Democrats have a clear and coherent political philosophy. Their platforms, as formulated at the presidential conventions, are little more than a *cri de cœur* of quite temporary significance, in which the attack upon their opponents is far more genuine than their promises of measures which will accompany their victory. It is, indeed, hardly an exaggeration to say that what gives the major parties their character is, above everything, the character of the candidate they adopt for president. For, at least until the election is decided, it is what their nominee has to say that makes the unattached voter decide the direction in which he will cast his ballot.

* Late Professor of Political Science at London School of Economics. Formerly Chairman of the British Labor Party Executive Committee. Author of numerous books on political subjects, including *Grammar of Politics, Democracy in Crisis, State in Theory and Practice, The American Democracy*. The selection is from Harold J. Laski, *The American Democracy*, pp. 129–137. Copyright 1948 by the Viking Press, Inc. Reprinted by permission of the Viking Press, Inc., New York.

This appears quite unmistakably if one compares the outlook of Democrats and Republicans in the period of the New Deal. There have been men of an ardent progressive outlook in each; and each has contained reactionaries not less ardent. . . . The real truth is that, since the Civil War at any rate, no candidate of any party would have found any intellectual difficulty in being the nominee of the opposing party. . . . If one follows, for example, the speeches of the candidates in the election of 1944, it is not an unfair description of Governor Dewey's campaign to describe it as a promise to maintain the New Deal of President Roosevelt but to administer its principles more efficiently than his rival. And that has been broadly true of the conflict between American parties with a real prospect of power ever since General Grant entered the White House. . . .

I am assuming that one digs beneath the promises to the performance. On that assumption, it is difficult to argue that a presidential election in America is, with all its excitement, very different from a choice by the voters between the two wings of a single Conservative party. The emphasis may differ at different times; but that is the reality of the choice. No doubt there are variations in the pattern of the choice; the Democratic party when led by Grover Cleveland is different from the Democratic party when led by Franklin Roosevelt, just as the Republican Party was not the same under Calvin Coolidge as it was in the brief months when Wendell Willkie was its standard bearer. But the vital fact is that the two major American parties do not seriously differ from each other in outlook and philosophy. They are more easily distinguished by the men who lead them than by the doctrines they profess.

Nor must one omit the significance of the fact that the parties on the Left have very little hold on the electoral mind. The American Socialist party consists of a few hundred thousand people among sixty million voters; and they speak to one another without being heard, or, at least, without being taken seriously, by the public at large. . . . It is true to say that, since the Civil War, no third party has been able to establish itself as at once a permanent and profound influence in the politics of America. Even the Progressive party of Theodore Roosevelt in 1912, though it aroused deep passions among its members, was no more, in essence, than a temporary split in the Republican party. . . .

From the angle of a European, and especially of a British observer, it is difficult to understand the political attitude of the American working classes. Under both Mr. Gompers and Mr. William Green, the American Federation of Labor has consistently refrained from adopting a coherent political philosophy. It has, so to say, traded the votes of its members, now to one party, and now to another, in the effort to secure particular measures in which it was interested. The party outlook of the Railroad Brotherhoods has not differed very markedly from the party outlook of Main Street.

The Congress of Industrial Organizations has, indeed, since its foundation worked hard, above all in 1940 and 1944, for the return of President Roosevelt; though it is notable that Mr. John L. Lewis, the leader of the United Mine Workers, when he left the C.I.O., sought to throw all the influence of his organization against Mr. Roosevelt's re-elections. . . . Whereas, in fact, the tendency in Europe has been for the trade-unions to give birth, not always directly, but fairly definitely, to a socialist party, as in Britain, or as in France and Germany and Belgium, to provide the main support for such a party, the American experience has been wholly different.

Anyone who analyses the party position in the United States must be careful to realize that the absence of effective parties on the Left does not for one moment mean the absence of Left policies. Certainly Jefferson and, to a limited degree, Andrew Jackson were the sponsors of Left policies in the period before the Civil War; there was a definitely liberal tinge in the conservatism of Theodore Roosevelt and Woodrow Wilson; and the first term, at least, of Franklin Roosevelt saw policies put into operation to which the quality of radicalism may be fairly applied. Yet it is broadly an accurate generalization to say that, historically, a conservative party, by whatever name it called itself, has always been in power in the United States, and that, on the federal plane, no radical party has ever been able seriously to challenge its authority. By what reasons can this curious phenomenon be explained? . . . What really emerges from a comparison of the American party position with that of all Europe, save Russia since the October Revolution, is the central fact that conservatives in the United States pursued a policy which differed in degree, rather than in kind, from the policy of a radical or even a socialist government in any important European state until 1945. . . .

There is, indeed, a probability, if the evidence of the Gallup polls is valid, that there are two important aspects in which the Democratic party is different from the Republican. It seems to emerge that, on the whole, the supporters of the Democrats are younger than the supporters of the Republicans; and, what perhaps follows from this conclusion, the prosperous voter is to be found among the Republicans, and the voter of modest means among the Democrats. It is certainly, I think, significant that the main sources of hostility to Franklin Roosevelt were among the wealthy classes; and that this has a relation of some permanence is suggested by the fact that the main supporters of "appeasement" at the time of the Civil War were the wealthy manufacturers and merchants of New York and Boston and Philadelphia. It is clear, too, that if one makes a correlation between the census returns and the election results, the drift in the cities is towards a Democratic emphasis among the poorer sections and a Republican emphasis among the more well-to-do. But against this must be set the fact that the large owners of cotton and tobacco are mostly Democrats by tradition, while the farmers of New England and the Northwest are mainly Republican. From this it follows that each party is historically a coalition in which the antagonism of each part to the other emerges as soon as one examines the direction of its economic interests.

One is tempted to conclude from all this that the time is rapidly approaching for a realignment of political parties in the United States. It is significant that the wealthy in both parties combined, after the first few months of Mr. Roosevelt's first administration, to limit his power to secure the passage of radical legislation. It is, I think, still more significant that, with the development of the Congress of Industrial Organizations, the tendency becomes more marked for the unions which compose it to take an increasing part in politics. And this tendency is likely to grow for the simple but inevitable reason that the growth of federal intervention in economic affairs is certain to continue. The coming of social security, the implications of the Labor Relations Act, the federal control of hours and wages, these, to take instances only, involve the need to establish criteria of action in the shaping of which labour is bound to take an increasing interest in order to take an increasing share; the Taft-Hartley Act is likely to strengthen this need. The point at which this development is likely to emerge is set by the experience of Europe. Where the period of economic expansion reaches its limit there emerges always a disparity of opportunity which results, sooner or later, in an antagonism of interest. And where that antagonism begins to take a conscious form the result is always that a party is formed to safeguard interests, on both sides, which feel themselves to be in jeopardy.

No one can examine the main political parties in the United States today without seeing quite clearly that they are in essence great coalitions of interests which range from the Left to the Right, though each, no doubt, excludes, if it can, the extreme Left. . . . Both parties have always offered, so far, enough concessions to the forces of Labour to be able to divide the votes of the workers; and it is only in recent years that the trade-unionist in the cities has begun to suspect a special affiliation between the Republican party and business interests which would be harmful to him if a Republican were to reach the White House.

It was easy to maintain this agreement upon fundamentals, as well as this continuity in techniques, until at least some such period as the Great Depression of 1929. . . . Until 1929, the rise of third parties always served to correct any large departure from public expectation among Democrats or Republicans. And, until 1929, there was always sufficient economic elbowroom in the United States to make a third party little more than an incentive to adjustment. Until the nineties there was the frontier; after the possibilities of the land began to be exhausted, there was the immense internal growth upon the industrial plane; while during that growth, and beyond it, there was the continued creation of purchasing power for the little man by the different bonus schemes for veterans of the wars in which America participated. . . .

But the problem since 1929 has begun to assume a shape quite different from that in the earlier years of the republic. With both the major parties committed to an individualist social policy (which does not, of course, prevent each from accusing the other of betraying traditional American ideas at each election), it becomes ever more dubious whether full employment is available in terms of individualism. The trend of modern economic theory rejects the concepts of free enterprise upon which the main American parties rely; it is, indeed, no exaggeration to say that in the last generation full employment has been attained only in periods of war as a result of the immense orders placed by government with manufacturers. With the cessation of those orders, the pursuit of the historic American policy of free enterprise is likely to result either in mass unemployment or in a grave reduction in the standard of living. To avoid being impaled upon the horns of this dilemma it becomes necessary both for Republicans and Democrats to accept a distribution of purchasing power quite different from anything that America has previously known. But to accept that difference means, quite simply, the recognition that the age of free enterprise has gone. That recognition, in its turn, means a wide extension of federal ownership and control in industry and agriculture and, therewith, a fundamental alteration in the kind of economic privileges which the leaders of American industry have enjoyed. The situation then emerges in which either the political parties are at odds with the leadership of industry, or that leadership refuses to accept the new principles of organization to which political parties seeking an electoral majority are bound to move. At this point, as I think, the organized workers of the United States are faced with the necessity of acting upon postulates which business leaders quite obviously reject. And I do not see how they can accept the necessity of such action within the framework of the existing party structure. American labour, in short, will be driven into independent political action in the post-war period much as circumstances forced the British trade-unions into a similar path. They have been able to play both sides so far much as the British workingmen were either liberal or conservative until 1906. It is even possible that some of the American labour leaders will resist the tendency to independence, as Mr. Ramsay MacDonald did so long as he hoped for a Liberal seat in the House of Commons, or as Labour men like Mr. G. N. Barnes and Mr. G. H. Roberts did at the close of the war of 1914 when they clung to Mr. Lloyd George. But they will increasingly find that the more adamant the demands of labour, the more unified will be the activity of the Republican and Democratic parties; and the more unified that activity, the wider will be the gap which separates capital from labour in the United States. It is difficult, indeed, not to infer from the Political Action Committee which Mr. Sidney Hillman formed in 1944 the first effective emergence of political independence among the trade-unions. Too, while it may be true that the influence of that Committee was overwhelmingly thrown on Mr. Roosevelt's side, it is reasonably clear that the reason for the Committee's decision lay less in the character of the Democratic party than in the policy on labour matters it imputed to Mr. Roosevelt, and, still more, to his opponent Mr. Dewey. It is no more likely to retain what may be termed the habit of coalition than the Labour party in Great Britain was likely to retain the habit of coalition with Mr. Churchill. On this assumption, it is at least probable that American trade-unionism will pass through two phases on the political plane. As soon as a conservative Democrat fights for the presidency against a conservative Republican . . . the American workers, like the British workers in 1906, will move swiftly towards independent political action. In the first phase of that independence, no doubt, they will be a relatively minor party on the federal stage, insisting that they inherit the traditions of Jefferson and Lincoln. But, in that first phase also, they will make clear the fact that Republicans and Democrats alike speak for an America from which, in any profound way, the interest of the workingman is excluded on all fundamental matters. They will then be driven to the Left, like the British Labour party; and they will find not only that this movement, whatever name it be given, makes them in fact a socialist party; they will find, also, that their opponents, both Republican and Democratic, will discover that there is little essential difference between them. When this emerges, the American party situation is not likely to differ in fundamentals from that upon the Continent in Europe. It is even possible, moreover, that the arrival of this situation may be quickened by the influence of the Soviet Union upon the industrial and political habits of Western and even Asiatic civilization.

I add that I do not think this view is falsified by the traditional habits of the "Solid South." For it is important to remember that the South is being industrialized at a great speed; that great numbers of its Negro population are migrating to the North and the West; and that the anxiety of the South to attract industry as rapidly as possible will both change its position as a "colony" of the North and make its industrial problems issues which call for federal action rather than for decisions separately made in each Southern state. The next age in American history is more likely than any previous period to dissipate the mythology of states' rights by a growing insistence upon equal and uniform treatment for things that are equal and uniform. It may then well emerge that the classic theory of federalism is obsolete in its historic American form; and there is no plane upon which its obsolescence is more likely to be demonstrated than in its expression in party organization. For an America that confronts relations of employer and employed which have been so long known in Europe may with some confidence be predicted to adjust those relations in terms which, whatever their names, repeat the experience of Europe. It is at least of the higher significance that this is what is happening in the Dominion of Canada.

Why a Labor Party?

Herbert Agar *

Many Americans have grown impatient with their illogical politics. They ask for political parties with clear principles and clear plans. They say the voter should know what he is getting, instead of having to choose between two vague and similar "platforms" which only become lucid when they discuss the vices of the other party. They say the Republicans and Democrats should reshuffle themselves into a progressive and a conservative party, each with a neat philosophy and an appropriate program.

Although this plea for logic and simplification sometimes comes from conservatives, it more often comes from radicals, in which case it usually leads to a demand for a Labor party. And in fact, if we were all to align ourselves ideologically, the emergence of a Labor party would seem inevitable.

In opposition to such a search for clarity and reason one may argue that parties based on ideas and principles may be suitable for a little country like England but would not be suitable here; that our strange form of politics grew up in response to a clear need and has served the country better than its critics admit; and that the substitution of the European type of party (and of political behavior) would alter our whole system of government.

The nature of that system can be suggested by reviewing how and why it came to pass. Then we can deal more cogently with the present.

The Fathers feared the rise of parties as the greatest of evils which might afflict the young Republic. Madison gave a clear picture of what he hoped would happen as an alternative. Because of the vast size of the country (and the variety of social habits and economic needs imposed by that size) certain pressure groups would form brief alliances when their interests were similar, but would then dissolve and look for new allies on new issues. This would force a healthy conservatism upon American politics, since no faction would be strong enough to govern alone, and when a group of factions came together in a temporary league each of them would have to water down its demands to win the help of the others. Conservatism, compromise, deference to class or regional bias: these would be required by the size and diversity of America. A local group might be as extreme as it liked in its own state or district; but when it joined with other groups to act nationally it would leave its radicalism at home.

Madison was very nearly right. American politics until 1825 can very nearly be made to square with his predictions. The Democratic party which he and Jefferson built was at first little more than a loose alliance of the

* Formerly special assistant to the American Ambassador in London. Author of *The People's Choice, A Time for Greatness, The Price of Union,* and several other books. The selection is from Herbert Agar, "Why Have A Labor Party?" *The Atlantic,* Vol. 186 (October, 1950), pp. 25–28. By permission of Herbert Agar and *The Atlantic.*

gentry who controlled the votes of their local factions: the Livingstons, the Clintons, and Aaron Burr in New York State; the two great Virginians; Charles Pinckney in South Carolina; and so on. Although this odd coalition of Southern landowners fiercely devoted to a cause and Northern bosses fiercely devoted to success did not dissolve, the opposing (Federalist) coalition did. From 1816 to 1825 there was in effect only one national party. This meant that there was in effect no national party, since each Democratic faction battled bitterly against the others.

An observer during the presidencies of Monroe and John Quincy Adams might well have thought Madison's predictions were coming true—but not with the benign results which Madison had expected. Every leader conspired for his own advancement with a stealth and bitterness which made the old party feuds seem friendly. Even within Monroe's Cabinet the Secretary of the Treasury found "ambitious and crafty and disappointed men on the watch for every mischief, and welcoming every disaster."

Instead of dividing the country, as the Fathers had feared, the political parties had canalized discontents and cupidities, discouraging the extremes of roguery or perfectionism so as to hold together as many groups as possible for the pursuit of power. Thus they gave a certain form and moderation to politics. And instead of uniting the country, the disappearance of the opposition led to a chaos which could only end in tyranny or in the rebirth of parties. When there is an orderly, respected alternative, a government will discipline itself and work as a team. But the members of Monroe's Cabinet had nothing to fear except one another, so they spent their time frustrating one another. Except in foreign affairs, the public business did not go forward.

All this was watched and judged by some of the ablest politicians America has bred. They saw the old Jeffersonian party, to which everyone was supposed to belong, unopposed and unhealthy, decaying in public and becoming a danger. They saw their chance to build (around the fame of Andrew Jackson) a disciplined opposition; and in the spring of 1825 they set to work. Because of the recent extension of the suffrage, the old-fashioned Jeffersonian alliance of a few gentry would no longer suffice. It was now necessary to reach the mass of the people.

Yet in basic character the new parties (for the Jackson men were soon opposed by a group as well organized as themselves) were like the old. They were a bundle of local pressure groups and local machines, concerned first of all with local interests and local victories but prepared to unite to win the prize of federal patronage: the jobs, the contracts, the personal favors which the national government could dispense.

It was no accident that the new parties had as little logical coherence as the old, that they stood for no clear idea except that victory is agreeable. The political form was imposed by the facts of a huge federal republic. Putting aside slavery for a moment, there were only three matters of primary concern to the central government: higher or lower tariffs; more or less road and canal building, river and harbor improving, at federal expense; faster or slower disposal of the national domain. Each question stirred fierce regional jealousies. No abstract philosophical principle connected the questions. They could not be divided on any system of Right and Left. They could not be "settled" once and for all. If the federal structure was not to be strained and the new experiment in government endangered, they could only be compromised, awkwardly, unsystematically, as the sectional and class pressures on either side waxed or waned.

In the 1820s, for example, when the new parties were beginning, South Carolina and Massachusetts were changing sides on the matter of tariffs. In the process they nearly plunged the country into secession, until the irrational party system produced an intellectually meaningless compromise which quieted the tariff war from 1833 until Fort Sumter.

II

Negro slavery was the one matter of "principle" before the country when our party system was developing. And the system, built to ensure compromise and to prevent regional groups from leaving the main party, tried of course to ignore the principle. Even this may not have been wholly bad, for man tends dangerously to treat all his opinions as principles, and ideological parties on the European model encourage the tendency. And even when the principle is genuine, even when the feeling on both sides is so strong as to preclude concession, there may be a case for the delay which nonideological parties ensure.

John Caldwell Calhoun, the philosopher in politics, early recognized that slavery was a question of principle. So he planned either Constitutional reform to protect slavery, or, if that failed, secession. He was right. No halfway measures would suffice. If slavery was to be saved, the North must give way or the South must secede. By the weight of his intellect and character Calhoun would probably have taken the South out of the Union in 1850, before the North had strength to resist; but he was defeated by a typical political compromiser: Henry Clay.

Clay had always laughed at Calhoun, whom he pictured as forever staring at an abstraction and muttering, "This is indeed a crisis!" Clay did not believe in crises. He thought "inevitable" issues could always be evaded, or postponed until they lost their interest. So when Calhoun was ready for secession Clay produced the famous "Compromise of 1850," which did not face the moral issue of slavery but which postponed the Civil War for ten years. By that time the North could win. By his cheerful, perhaps light-minded, feeling that if unpleasant issues were dodged "something would turn up," Clay saved the Union.

One cannot make a principle out of being unprincipled. One cannot defend as a virtue the refusal to face facts. Yet perhaps in the governing of men it is not always wise to push too fast, too furiously, toward the morally ideal. "Government is a very rough business," said Sir George Cornewall Lewis; "you must be content with very unsatisfactory results." Most Americans might agree today that even the Civil War was less "unsatisfactory" than a divided Union. Yet a little more logic and principle, applied a little sooner, would probably have assured disunion. . . .

Under the brave but inept Johnson, under the political baby, Grant, the Republican "radicals" imposed a policy of "thorough": no compromise, no concessions, nothing but the pure, logical idea. And as usual (since man is not good enough to be so sure of himself) the idea was quickly stained by hate and greed. The appeal to principles ended in the not infrequent combination of the Puritan and the blackleg. The Negro was betrayed in the hour of his deliverance and the white South was set against him for eighty years. The name Republican was made so odious throughout the late Confederacy that the region has been condemned to a one-party system. Yet in 1865 and 1866 there was a large ex-Whig, pro-Union group in the South. If Lincoln the compromiser had lived, the two-party system would have been re-established at once. . . .

III

This glance at history seems to show that in our huge federal society the political parties, to endure, must themselves be federations, with the maximum of home rule, which means the maximum of power (even within the party) to block, to delay, to insist on compromise. Thus we see today that the Democrats of the Northern industrial towns cannot impose their will on the Democrats of Mississippi, nor can the Republicans of Pennsylvania force conservatism upon the Republicans of Wisconsin. In the making of national party policy every region and every interest-group must have the right to interpose and to demand at least an abatement if it feels itself threatened.

This is what John Nance Garner had in mind when he said: "Each of the two parties is in a sense a coalition. Any party to serve the country must be a party of all sorts of views." But how can a party with hard-and-fast, logical principles be also a coalition with "all sorts of views"?

If we turn from the parties to the Congress, we find the same rules of federalism at work. When a bill is sent to committee the first job of the committee is to reach a compromise acceptable to all the major interests affected. Each member of the committee may be a statesman to his heart's content on other occasions; but when a bill affects the beliefs or the money of his constituents he must act as their agent, or look for another job. Who is to protect his district's interests if he does not? Will a representative from industrial Delaware understand (let alone stir himself to save) the business of a cattleman in parched Arizona or of an asparagus grower in the blazing, irrigated San Joaquin valley?

Even when a bill escapes from committee it may still be unacceptable to some region or some class. But under the system of federal concessions it can then be talked to death in the Senate. The filibuster has lately been called the last refuge of reaction. We should remember, however, that it has often been the last refuge of radicalism. Andrew Jackson's defender in the Senate, Thomas Hart Benton, said he would resort to "any possible extremity" to save unlimited debate. And the elder La Follette fought the moderate cloture rule demanded by Woodrow Wilson, saying that if the rule was accepted "you will have broken down one of the greatest weapons against wrong and oppression that the members of this body possess." And when Coolidge's Vice President, Charles G. Dawes, tried to speed the Senate procedure, a national convention of the American Federation of Labor unanimously condemned this "campaign to abolish free speech in . . . the only forum in the world where cloture does not exist and where members can prevent the passage of reactionary legislation."

The filibuster is an undemocratic veto in a chamber which is undemocratic by constitution. Nevertheless, like the amorphous party system, like the committee system in Congress, it has played a vital role in preserving our federal compromise.

All three of these put together comprise what Calhoun called "the rule of the concurrent majority." He wished to write it formally into the Constitution: that every major interest in the country, whether regional, economic, or religious, should have the right to veto any political decision which directly concerned it. Such an amendment would have left the government powerless to meet a crisis. Yet in normal times, when the nation does not feel itself in danger, Calhoun's plan is precisely how our federal system works. The question may be raised whether a very large federation can work in any other way. The proposal to introduce parties of logic and principle, and thus to weaken the power to obstruct, may lead to the more formidable proposal of remolding America into a centralized national state.

However, if we can preserve our present precarious balance, we may find ourselves with the best of both worlds—with as little government as possible in good times, and as much government as necessary in bad times. For side by side with our devices for obstruction we have invented (in the emergency powers of the President) a device for speed. When the people are roused to a sense of danger, the President can be given the strength of a Roman dictator. And when the sense of danger diminishes, the federal balance revives, and with it the power of a minority to block.

We have been living so long in economic or military emergencies that the federal power to act, rather than the federal power to deny, seems uppermost. This might be a reason for conserving our unique party structure. Neither the Congressional committee system nor the Senate filibuster could survive the rise of ideological politics. It seems fair to say that the parties, which the Fathers feared as the enemy of balanced powers, are today the chief bulwark of all their balances, the last defense of federal compromise.

If the Labor-party plan is to put all the progressives into one camp and all the unprogressives into another, and then to insist on strict majority rule (no matter if the majority lives in a corner of the country lying north of the Ohio and east of the Mississippi), the United States will cease to be a true federation or will cease to be united.

If the plan is to build a "third party" for labor, no one could object—except the leaders of labor, who have found they can do nicely by using the present system. Third parties have an honorable role in our history. They are not meant to come to power in Washington; they are meant to dramatize new ideas or neglected grievances. If they catch the public ear throughout the country, their projects will be taken over by *both* the major parties: witness the Populist party, in the case of neglected grievances, or the Prohibition party, in the case of a new idea.

But labor has won its fight for collective bargaining. It is winning the fight for large labor participation in the planning and in the conduct of business enterprise. It may even be winning the fight to persuade its own ranks that old-fashioned "feather-bedding" hurts labor as a producer and scalps labor as a consumer. Labor is of age—economically, politically, and socially. The cry for a Labor party comes chiefly from impatient intellectuals who think such a party would speed their favorite reforms. Less and less does the cry come from labor leaders, who have found that by using the traditional American party system they can win the traditional American benefits.

Finally, if the plan is to build a new party "of all sorts of views" and call it a Labor party, why bother? By the time the nation-wide coalition has been effected it will be found to resemble startlingly the two coalitions which are now called "Democratic" and "Republican." They are the product of pure professional effort. The fact that they are so much alike in policy is a credit to the profession. Every politician would delight in finding a new set of compromises which would not only win but which would leave his own party clearly distinguishable from the other. It cannot be done. By the time the Republicans have arranged to placate every large group among the hundred and fifty million Americans (except for Alabama and Mississippi) and the Democrats have done the same (except for Maine and Vermont) the chief issue must be the names they call each other.

We need more than one major party, or how could we turn the rascals out? We need fewer than three major parties, or most of us would be on a political payroll. That seems to leave a two-party system. If people choose to call one of the two parties "Labor," that can do no harm, so long as the party continues (by endless assuagements) to bring citizens of all sections, incomes, occupations, races, religions, and prejudices into an enjoyable combination for the pursuit of power. But in that case why change the name?

SECTION II
President and Congress

The system of separation of powers established by the Constitution was designed to give a large measure of independence to the three branches of our government in order to prevent concentration of power in one set of hands, which Montesquieu called the very definition of tyranny, and to safeguard the minority against the overbearing power of a majority. (See *The Federalist,* No. 47 and No. 51 in Topic 9.)

The office of the president is now the most powerful, responsible, and difficult in the democratic world. Yet, the author of a classic study of the American party system, after observing our convention method of nominating candidates for the presidency and the considerations which controlled its action, characterized the process as "a colossal travesty of popular institutions." The correctness of M. Ostrogorski's appraisal is clearly a matter of great importance. The issue is discussed by James Bryce, Harold Laski, and Pendleton Herring.

The members of Congress, selected from local districts and relatively independent of party discipline, are sensitive to the demands of pressure groups. As a result, it is charged by some, the legislative process in the United States is robbed of national purpose. The impact of interest groups upon law-making is evaluated by James M. Burns and Henry Bellows.

The gap between the Congress and the President has to some extent been bridged by political parties intent upon controlling all the branches of government. Nevertheless, as recent experience has shown, our system makes possible a President of one party and a Congress dominated by another. The result may be stalemate on important issues with responsibility difficult to establish. Furthermore, the rôle of presidential leadership in the legislative process, even when Congress is composed predominantly of members of his own party, is uncertain and varying.

Under these circumstances various measures to improve or even drastically alter legislative-executive relations have been advocated. Some critics of American government, like Henry Hazlitt, wish to create a system in America similar to British parliamentary government in order to concentrate power and responsibility, and minimize the possibility of stalemate. This view is challenged by Don K. Price, who emphasizes the great advantages of the American presidential system.

Topic 24
CHOOSING A PRESIDENT

Why Great Men Are Not Chosen President
James Bryce *

Europeans often ask, and Americans do not always explain, how it happens that this great office, the greatest in the world, unless we except the Papacy, to which any one can rise by his own merits, is not more frequently filled by great and striking men. In America, which is beyond all other countries the country of a "career open to talents," a country, moreover, in which political life is unusually keen and political ambition widely diffused, it might be expected that the highest place would always be won by a man of brilliant gifts. But from the time when the heroes of the Revolution died out with Jefferson and Adams and Madison, no person except General Grant, had, down till the end of last century, reached the chair whose name would have been remembered had he not been President, and no President except Abraham Lincoln had displayed rare or striking qualities in the chair. Who now knows or cares to know anything about the personality of James K. Polk or Franklin Pierce? The only thing remarkable about them is that being so commonplace they should have climbed so high.

Several reasons may be suggested for the fact, which Americans are themselves the first to admit. One is that the proportion of first-rate ability drawn into politics is smaller in America than in most European countries. This is a phenomenon whose causes must be elucidated later: in the meantime it is enough to say that in France, where the half-revolutionary conditions that lasted for some time after 1870 made public life exciting and accessible; in Germany, where an admirably-organized civil service cultivates and develops statecraft with unusual success; in England, where many persons of wealth and leisure seek to enter the political arena, while burning questions touch the interests of all classes and make men eager observers of the combatants, the total quantity of talent devoted to parliamentary or administrative work has been larger, relatively to the population, than in America, where much of the best ability, both for thought and for action, for planning and for executing, rushes into a field which is comparatively narrow in Europe, the business of developing the material resources of the country.

* British Ambassador to the United States, 1907–1913. Formerly President of the American Political Science Association. Author of *The Holy Roman Empire, Modern Democracies, The American Commonwealth,* etc. The selection is from James Bryce, "Why Great Men Are Not Chosen President," *The American Commonwealth* (New York, The Macmillan Co., 1922–23), Vol. 1, Ch. 8. By permission.

Another is that the methods and habits of Congress, and indeed of political life generally, give fewer opportunities for personal distinction, fewer modes in which a man may commend himself to his countrymen by eminent capacity in thought, in speech, or in administration, than is the case in the free countries of Europe. . . .

A third reason is that eminent men make more enemies, and give those enemies more assailable points, than obscure men do. They are therefore in so far less desirable candidates. It is true that the eminent man has also made more friends, that his name is more widely known, and may be greeted with louder cheers. Other things being equal, the famous man is preferable. But other things never are equal. The famous man has probably attacked some leaders in his own party, has supplanted others, has expressed his dislike to the crochet of some active section, has perhaps committed errors which are capable of being magnified into offences. No man stands long before the public and bears a part in great affairs without giving openings to censorious criticism. Fiercer far than the light which beats upon a throne is the light which beats upon a presidential candidate, searching out all the recesses of his past life. Hence, when the choice lies between a brilliant man and a safe man, the safe man is preferred. Party feeling, strong enough to carry in on its back a man without conspicuous positive merits, is not always strong enough to procure forgiveness for a man with positive faults.

A European finds that this phenomenon needs in its turn to be explained, for in the free countries of Europe brilliancy, be it eloquence in speech, or some striking achievement in war or administration, or the power through whatever means of somehow impressing the popular imagination, is what makes a leader triumphant. Why should it be otherwise in America? Because in America party loyalty and party organization have been hitherto so perfect that any one put forward by the party will get the full party vote if his character is good and his "record," as they call it, unstained. The safe candidate may not draw in quite so many votes from the moderate men of the other side as the brilliant one would, but he will not lose nearly so many from his own ranks. Even those who admit his mediocrity will vote straight when the moment for voting comes. Besides, the ordinary American voter does not object to mediocrity. He has a lower conception of the qualities requisite to make a statesman than those who direct public opinion in Europe have. He likes his candidate to be sensible, vigorous, and, above all, what he calls "magnetic," and does not value, because he sees no need for, originality or profundity, a fine culture or a wide knowledge. Candidates are selected to be run for nomination by knots of persons who, however expert as party tacticians, are usually commonplace men; and the choice between those selected for nomination is made by a very large body, an assembly of nearly a thousand delegates from the local party organizations over the country, who are certainly no better than ordinary citizens. . . .

It must also be remembered that the merits of a President are one thing and those of a candidate another thing. An eminent American is reported to have said to friends who wished to put him forward, "Gentlemen, let there be no mistake. I should make a good President, but a very bad candidate." Now to a party it is more important that its nominee should be a good candidate than that he should turn out a good President. A nearer danger is a greater danger. As Saladin says in *The Talisman,* "A wild cat in a chamber is more dangerous than a lion in a distant desert." It will be a misfortune to the party, as well as to the country, if the candidate elected should prove a bad President. But it is a greater misfortune to the party that it should be beaten in the impending election, for the evil of losing national patronage will have come four years sooner. "B" (so reason the leaders), "who is one of our possible candidates, may be an abler man than A, who is the other. But we have a better chance of winning with A than with B, while X, the candidate of our opponents, is anyhow no better than A. We must therefore run A." This reasoning is all the more forcible because the previous career of the possible candidates has generally made it easier to say who will succeed as a candidate than who will succeed as a President; and because the wirepullers with whom the choice rests are better judges of the former question than of the latter.

After all, too, a President need not be a man of brilliant intellectual gifts. His main duties are to be prompt and firm in securing the due execution of the laws and maintaining the public peace, careful and upright in the choice of the executive officials of the country. Eloquence, whose value is apt to be overrated in all free countries, imagination, profundity of thought or extent of knowledge, are all in so far a gain to him that they make him "a bigger man," and help him to gain over the nation an influence which, if he be a true patriot, he may use for its good. But they are not necessary for the due discharge in ordinary times of the duties of his post. Four-fifths of his work is the same in kind as that which devolves on the chairman of a commercial company or the manager of a railway, the work of choosing good subordinates, seeing that they attend to their business, and taking a sound practical view of such administrative questions as require his decision. Firmness, common sense, and most of all, honesty, an honesty above all suspicion of personal interest, are the qualities which the country chiefly needs in its first magistrate.

So far we have been considering personal merits. But in the selection of a candidate many considerations have to be regarded besides the personal merits, whether of a candidate, or of a possible President. The chief of these considerations is the amount of support which can be secured from different States or from different "sections" of the Union, a term by which the Americans denote groups of States with a broad community of interest. State feeling and sectional feeling are powerful factors in a presidential election. The Middle West and Northwest, including the States from Ohio to Montana, is now the most populous section of the Union, and therefore counts for most in an election. It naturally conceives that its interests will be best protected by one who knows them from birth and residence. Hence *prima facie* a man from that section makes the best candidate. A large State casts a heavier vote in the election; and every State is of course more likely to be carried by one of its own children than by a stranger, because his fellow-citizens, while they feel honoured by the choice, gain also a substantial advantage, having a better prospect of such favours as the administration can bestow. Hence, *cæteris paribus,* a man from a large State is preferable as a candidate. The problem is further complicated by the fact that some States are already safe for one or other party, while others are doubtful. The Northwestern and New England States have usually tended to go Republican; while nearly all of the Southern States have, since 1877, been pretty certain to go Democratic. *Cæteris paribus,* a candidate from a doubtful State, such as New York and Indiana have usually been, is to be preferred.

Other minor disqualifying circumstances require less explanation. A Roman Catholic, or an avowed disbeliever in Christianity, would be an undersirable candidate. For many years after the Civil War, any one who had fought, especially if he fought with distinction, in the Northern army, enjoyed great advantages, for the soldiers of that army rallied to his name. The two elections of General Grant, who knew nothing of politics, and the fact that his influence survived the faults of his administration, are evidence of the weight of this consideration. . . .

These secondary considerations do not always prevail. Intellectual ability and strength of character must influence the choice of a candidate. When a man has once impressed himself on the nation by force, courage, and rectitude, the influence of these qualities may be decisive. They naturally count for most when times are critical. Reformers declare that their weight will go on increasing as the disgust of good citizens with the methods of professional politicians increases. . . .

We may now answer the question from which we started. Great men have not often been chosen Presidents, first because great men are rare in politics; secondly, because the method of choice may not bring them to the top; thirdly, because they are not, in quiet times, absolutely needed. Let us close by observing that the Presidents, regarded historically, fall into three periods, the second inferior to the first, the third rather better than the second.

Down till the election of Andrew Jackson in 1828, all the Presidents had been statesmen in the European sense of the word, men of education, of administrative experience, of a certain largeness of view and dignity of character. All except the first two had served in the great office of secretary of state; all were known to the nation from the part they had played. In the second period, from Jackson till the outbreak of the Civil War in 1861, the Presidents were either mere politicians, such as Van Buren, Polk, or

Buchanan, or else successful soldiers, such as Harrison or Taylor, whom their party found useful as figureheads. They were intellectual pigmies beside the real leaders of that generation—Clay, Calhoun, and Webster. A new series begins with Lincoln in 1861. He and General Grant, his successor, who cover sixteen years between them, belong to the history of the world. Even the less distinguished Presidents of this period contrast favourably with the Polks and Pierces of the days before the war, if they are not, like the early Presidents, the first men of the country. If we compare the twenty Presidents who were elected to office between 1789 and 1900 with the twenty English prime ministers of the same period, there are but six of the latter, and at least eight of the former whom history calls personally insignificant, while only Washington, Jefferson, Lincoln, and Grant can claim to belong to a front rank represented in the English list by seven or possibly eight names. It would seem that the natural selection of the English parliamentary system, even as modified by the aristocratic habits of that country, had more tendency to bring the highest gifts to the highest place than the more artificial selection of America.

Crises Produce Great Presidents

Harold J. Laski *

The big problem that is raised by the American method of nominating presidential candidates is whether it puts a premium, as Lord Bryce argued, against the opportunity of first-rate men to receive consideration. I do not think his case is proved by making a list of first-rate men, Clay and Calhoun and Webster, for example, who missed nomination. The answer to that argument is, first, that many first-rate men have become president by reason of the system; and second, that the reasons which stopped others would have been powerful reasons against their elevation in any representative democracy. . . .

Granted, this is to say, the greatness of the prize, and the necessity of popular election, it is difficult to see what other method than the nominating convention is available; more, it is true to say that, on balance, it has worked well rather than badly. The criticisms that are brought against it are rather, in their real substance, criticisms of the place of the presidency in the American constitutional scheme than of the method whereby the president is chosen. It is regrettable that an inexperienced man may come to reside in the White House; the answer is that few of those who have reached it have been inexperienced men. If it be said that men like Harding and Coolidge were unfit for the great post they secured, the answer is that the first had considerable experience both in the Ohio legislature and in the Senate, while

* Late Professor of Political Science at London School of Economics. The selection is from Harold J. Laski, *The American Presidency* (New York, Harper & Bros., 1940), pp. 49–53. Copyright, 1940, by Harper & Bros.

the second had been a successful Massachusetts politician, twice occupying the governorship, for twenty years. If we take the presidents of the twentieth century, there is not one who had not been prepared for presidential office by a long experience of politics. . . .

It must be remembered that, in making the choice, there are two fundamental considerations in the background of which the meaning of "availability" must be set. The first is that the party choosing a candidate wants, if it can, to win; and second, it knows that if it does win, and its nominee becomes president, there is great likelihood of its having to adopt him a second time, since not to do so is to condemn an Administration for which it has to bear responsibility. While, therefore, it is quite true that a party convention provides an opportunity for the art of such a dubious wire-puller as Mr. Daugherty, it is also true that the managers of a great party are anxious to avoid, if they can, the consequences of success in that type of manipulation. . . .

All in all, I doubt whether the methods of the system are very different from those of other countries. They are, perhaps, more open and crude than in Great Britain. There is no generosity in the fight for power. There is a passionate determination on the part of organized interests to get the "safe" man who can be relied upon to live up to the commitments exacted from him. There is the fierce conflict of rival ambitions. There is the organization of every sort of cabal to win a victory for its man. Press and radio and platform are vigorously manipulated to this end. Immense promises are made, pretty ugly deals are effected. Yet I suggest that anyone who knows the life of a political party from within Great Britain will not feel inclined to cast a stone at the American system. It fits, well enough, the medium in which it has to work. It achieves the results that the needs of the people require.

For there is at least one test of the system that is, I think, decisive. There have been five considerable crises in American history. There was the need to start the new republic adequately in 1789; it gave the American people its natural leader in George Washington. The crisis of 1800 brought Jefferson to the presidency; that of 1861 brought Abraham Lincoln. The War of 1914 found Woodrow Wilson in office; the great depression resulted in the election of Franklin Roosevelt. So far, it is clear, the hour has brought forth the man. It is of course true, as Bagehot said, that "success in a lottery is no argument for lotteries." I agree that no nation can afford a succession of what Theodore Roosevelt termed "Buchanan Presidents"—men whose handling of the issues is uncertain and feeble. But the answer is that the nation has never had that succession; an epoch of Hardings and Coolidges produces, by the scale of the problems to which it gives rise, its own regeneration. The weak president, as I have argued, comes from the fact that a strong predecessor has set the feet of the nation on level ground. He is chosen because, after a diet of strong occasions, a nation, like an individual, turns naturally to the chance of a quiet time. "Normalcy" is always certain to be popular after crises. The issue is whether, when crisis comes, the system can discover the man to handle it. On the evidence, this has so far been very remarkably the case. To urge that it is chance is, I think, a superficial view. It is the outcome of the national recognition that energy and direction are required, and the man chosen is the party response to that recognition. . . . The more deeply we penetrate the working of the system the more clearly does it emerge that the result is inherent in its nature.

The Uses for National Conventions

Pendleton Herring *

The usefulness of our national nominating conventions has at times seemed obscure. Most of the criticism of party conventions grows out of the belief that they are held to discuss policy as well as to nominate candidates. Such a belief misinterprets the structure of our party system. . . . The behavior of any organization must be interpreted in the light of the elements that compose it if any understanding is to be achieved. To expect bands of local chieftains and their henchmen to come together and act as a deliberative national unit once every four years is to expect the impossible.

Our conventions could be orderly if they were the apex of a well-organized hierarchy. The most dignified, orderly, and impressive assembly for selecting an individual for a high office is the College of Cardinals. Even this august assembly is not without its political undercurrents, but it can function with its unexampled success because it is the final expression of a remarkably well-disciplined body. . . .

Our political parties are built not on the rock of faith but rather on the broad mud flats of popular desires and individual ambitions. The party convention is no better than the loose and undisciplined local and state organizations that send their delegates to bargain. If we cannot do much to change these underlying factors the question then is to consider anew what can be done with the materials at hand.

Judged as strictly rational and intellectual performances, these huge assemblies are flat failures; but are they to be measured by such standards?

Let us first hear some of the critics. No recent writer is more outspoken than Herbert Agar. He states that "the position of the average delegate at a national convention has neither dignity nor sense." "Never a wholly adequate device, the nomination convention," he says, "is now an anachro-

* Associate of the Carnegie Corporation, a research institution. Formerly Professor of Government, Harvard University, and Professor, Harvard Graduate School of Public Administration. Author of *Group Representation Before Congress, Public Administration and the Public Interest, Presidential Leadership,* and other works. The selection is from Pendleton Herring, *The Politics of Democracy: American Parties in Action* (New York, Rinehart & Co., Inc., 1940), Ch. 16. By permission of the publisher.

nism." He deplores the absence of serious discussion of public problems and the "atmosphere of lightminded carousal." This comes in for heartiest condemnation. "The delegates even showed signs of being ashamed of their own immoderate antics. They wondered whether the way to run a great political party is to get drunk and ride donkeys into hotel lobbies. . . . They knew they ought to be doing serious work. Yet there was no serious work to do, so they took refuge in idiocy." The author quotes Milton on the noises of Hell and concludes that conventions are worse. Agar's reaction is that of a cultured and sensitive man who evidently does not enjoy roughhousing. He would feel equally ill at ease at an American Legion convention or a conclave of the Elks.

Many of us would certainly prefer to see conventions less noisy, more thoughtful and "full of argument and heart-searching and high seriousness." My purpose here, however, is not to exhort delegates to be sober and meditative, but rather to raise the question as to whether a convention is primarily an intellectual activity. . . .

The attention of commentators has been focused most eloquently on sins of omission. The following views of Lord Bryce serve as a classic critique upon the shortcomings of the party convention:

> It goes without saying that such a meeting is capable neither of discussing political questions and settling a political programme, nor of deliberately weighing the merits of rival aspirants for the nomination. Its programme must be presented to it cut and dry, and this is the work of a small committee. In choosing a candidate, it must follow a few leaders. And what sort of leaders do conventions tend to produce? Two sorts—the intriguer and the declaimer. . . . For men of wisdom and knowledge, not seconded by a commanding voice and presence, there is no demand, and little chance of usefulness, in these tempestuous halls. . . . Large popular gatherings . . . are excitable in virtue of their size. . . . A national convention . . . is the hugest mass meeting the world knows of. . . . The struggle in a convention is over men, not over principles.

Such a sweeping denunciation hardly stands close scrutiny. The men influential in "these tempestuous halls" are the same men who serve as political leaders in Congress and the state governments. A huge mass meeting cannot be judged by its incapacity to perform tasks appropriate to a small committee. Unless we are to substitute for the convention a small executive council, we must accept the characteristics resulting from size. Moreover, its positive qualities are worthy of our respect. It is an indigenous institution and can be best evaluated with respect to our own peculiar needs.

What has our experience with national party conventions demonstrated their basic purpose to be? It is to find a man whom a majority of the voters will agree to support.

Farley has given us a perfect picture of the professional politician's attitude toward the selection of a candidate. On his way to the Elks' convention Farley called upon the national Committeeman of South Dakota, Bill Howe. Farley relates:

. . . We sat in a lunchroom at Aberdeen on a roasting-hot day. Bill was a canny politician who had been in the game for years; he knew it backward and forward. We sat there for some time, exchanging generalities, without disclosing what either of us really had in mind. Just before it was time to go, Bill plumped his fat fist on the table and growled in a deep voice, "Farley, I'm damn' tired of backing losers. In my opinion, Roosevelt can sweep the country, and I'm going to support him."

The desire to find a winner and thereby help the ticket back home is a force of no small importance. The primary task of the delegates is to find a winning candidate. The convention is designed to unite diverse sections and rival leaders behind a man, and to whip up the enthusiasm of party workers to fight for his election. This involves not questions of public policy but problems of party strategy. In view of the rivalries, the frank self-seeking, and the bitter jealousies arising in our party conventions, the ultimate adjustment almost invariably reached is a triumph of popular government.

The value of the convention lies in its permitting the rank and file of the party to participate physically and emotionally in a common enterprise. Here are the men who must carry the brunt of the campaign. Here they have their chance to meet, to shout together, to act together, to feel together. The excitement and the turmoil of the convention fulfill a useful purpose. The relationship of follower and leader is seldom an intellectual bond. A common bond of sympathy, a common symbol, is easily grasped and equally binding.

The party convention places a premium on party harmony. It reveals in a beating glare of publicity any thin spots and holes in the party fabric. Hence the impetus of the whole procedure is toward agreement. Prolonged dispute is greatly feared. As William G. McAdoo explained to the 1932 convention, when shifting the California delegation to Roosevelt: "Sometimes in major operations where skillful surgery is required, the life of the patient may be destroyed if there is unnecessary delay. We believe, therefore, that California should take a stand here tonight that will bring this contest to a swift and, we hope, satisfactory conclusion—a stand, we hope, which will be promotive of party harmony." A convention must try to unify a party not inherently unified. Its purpose is not to examine intellectual differences but to seek terms of agreement. When differences cannot be reconciled, the politicians seek unity in the face of disagreement. A party convention offers them the opportunity to negotiate and human materials with which to work.

As just noted, the basic function of the convention is to focus national attention upon the task of selection that is going forward, and then to align the regular party politicians behind a man who will lead them to victory. To do this the methods must be such as to attract and hold the attention of the great mass of citizens. Experience indicates that prizefights, football games, and similar sporting spectacles have characteristics that please the populace. Debating societies have a more limited following. The intellectually inclined may view this as an unfortunate situation. If a political spectacle is the way to arouse public attention, that is reason enough for the average politician.

The party convention may likewise be viewed as an excellent implement for compromise. Compromise in politics is not achieved simply through argumentation. The process entails bargaining and manipulation as well. There are various levels and types of compromise. To reach such peaceful adjustments of interest requires an area for movement and something with which to trade and barter. The party convention creates a human situation and provides scope under general rules of the game for elaborate interrelationships. Here concessions of many types can be made and victories in various terms are possible. The range of satisfactions is great, and disappointment on one count may be compensated for on another. There must be something wherewith to compromise. . . .

No one would think of planning an industrial development, an army campaign, or an educational program by devices similar to a party convention. No one can accurately regard our conventions as deliberative or planning agencies. Our conventions are a romantic and flamboyant attempt to get a high degree of popular participation in the high drama of democracy. It is not an institution to be dismissed contemptuously because of its noise and apparent confusion. It is characteristic of our free political system; the Nazis have pageantry of a different sort. Those who prefer order will find it at Nuremberg.

There is much that is not heroic in our system. The heroic mold has seemed ill suited to the peaceful routine of minding one's own business and working for a living. If we are approaching more dangerous times we will have less use for negative candidates selected because they came from the tactically important states with large electoral votes. Our easygoing, rough-and-tumble politics of compromise and barter may give way to a more efficient and effective control from the top. The demands made upon government may force our political parties to attempt a more authoritarian line. There would be no point in carefully devising a program unless the party leaders were determined to carry it through. This would entail sanctions to make such power effective. Our party conventions have sought not the strongest or wisest candidate but rather the man who would best serve to unite the party and attract the voters. This is one consequence of treating the presidency as a symbol as well as a job.

A party convention is a parley of state bosses accompanied by their henchmen carrying with them local jealousies and favoritisms. A convention might possibly become a meeting dominated by a clique of politicians in command of a national machine. Instead of selecting a compromise candidate, they might decide to put before the country their strong man who would—through all the arts of persuasion—be sold to the public as the leader.

The party convention is not an inappropriate device for serving our present purposes. In fact, it is admirably suited to testing the talents of our politicians. It demands organizational skill and manipulative genius—both of which qualities are exceedingly useful in democratic government. . . .

Much more can and should be done to give men of reason and knowledge a more strategic position within the party structure. Parties can aid in the political education of their own membership. Questions of public policy must now be thought of in national and even international terms. This means that the inadequacies of the local politician become more evident. Social and economic necessities push us forward in demanding more intelligence in the conduct of political affairs. Yet we would be shortsighted indeed if we placed our faith in the expert as the only man with the answer. The party convention is one institutional expression of human beings competing by their wits and emotions for some of the prizes available under popular government.

Topic 25

CONGRESS UNDER PRESSURE

The Pressure Politicians

James M. Burns *

We hear much of lobbyists and pressure groups, but a curious myth persists as to their role in American politics.

According to this myth, the member of Congress arrives in Washington eager to work for the national welfare, or at least for his constituents. He is ready to stand by the grand political principles that he expounded on the platform and as a result of which he received a majority of the votes. But trials and temptations beset him at the nation's capital. Greedy lobbyists for big business invite him to Bacchanalian feasts, where they seek to influence him with cash and chorus girls. Scores of labor lobbyists swarm through the corridors, buttonholing him and his colleagues and demanding legislative favors. He is mercilessly belabored and bedeviled by other pressure groups. If he is a good Congressman, he will reject all bribes and threats. If he is not, he will soon give in to cupidity and timidity.

This is a picture, in short, of unscrupulous lobbyists and of single-minded legislators. The trouble with the picture is that most lobbyists are discreet and honest men, while many Congressmen themselves are little more than lobbyists in disguise.

* Assistant Professor of Political Science at Williams College. Formerly Legislative Assistant, United States Congress. The selection is from James M. Burns, *Congress on Trial* (New York, Harper & Bros., 1949), pp. 18–31. Copyright, 1949, by Harper & Bros.

PRESSURE POLITICIANS AT WORK

The Congressman, as we have seen, represents not merely an amorphous collection of persons in a particular area. He is spokesman for the organized interests at home in their economic and political jousts with groups outside the district. Every member of Congress has a keen sense of the dominant economic enterprises in his district, whether he comes from a cotton-growing region in the South or a steel-producing city in the mid-West or a textile-making area of New England or a cattle-raising county of Montana.

The common term for organized special interests that exert influence on government is "pressure groups." Yet it would be to miscalculate the power and methods of organized minorities to say that the major groups in a district need bring "pressure" on a Congressman. Most Congressmen do not wait for pressure from home. They take the initiative, moving to protect the interest group before any pressure is in sight. They are ready with their arguments, their amendments, their parliamentary strategy the moment the interests back home seem to be endangered. As active propagandists, they convert their offices into temporary headquarters for a politically mobilized group. They are in fact lobbyists, but they work at the core of government rather than at the periphery. They are the makers of pressure, not merely the subjects of it. They are pressure politicians.

Some of the pressure politicians in Congress serve interest groups far more effectively than lobbyists could possibly hope to. Consider, for example, Representative Robert L. Doughton of North Carolina, who was for many years chairman of the House Committee on Ways and Means, and one of the chief policy-makers in tax matters and other national legislation. During consideration of the revenue bill of 1943—a measure of vital national importance—he made clear more than once that the tobacco grower in his district was "the man in whom I have my first interest." Doughton was able to scuttle an Administration move to increase taxes on cigarettes, cigars, chewing and smoking tobacco, and snuff. Watching this performance with admiration, a Republican legislator told representatives of tobacco interests: "While the tobacco farmers may not have a representative in this city, they have an excellent friend in the Chairman of this Committee, who is not only familiar with the problems of the farmers, but he watches out for their interests." There was no evidence that tobacco farmers put "pressure" on Doughton. They did not need to.

Some members of Congress are so zealous in protecting special interests that their nicknames carry the mark. Years ago Representative William D. Kelley of Pennsylvania was known as "Pig Iron" Kelley for his unceasing fight to gain tariff protection for a leading enterprise of his district. More recently we have had "Cotton Ed" Smith, who helped organize the Southern Cotton Association in 1905 and who never wavered in his fight for the cotton growers of his home state of South Carolina. The links between other members of Congress and dominant interests at home may be less obvious but they are no less important.

The great task of the pressure politician is to induce his colleagues to see things his way. Some of them, of course, already are won to the cause by virtue of the pressure groups in their own constituencies. Other Congressmen come from areas where those groups may be less powerful. With them the pressure politician may attempt the traditional bartering of legislative favors. This is known as log-rolling, or the process under which, as one Washington lobbyist puts it, "You scratch my back and I'll scratch yours."

The pressure politician also works closely with the lobbyists or "legislative agents" of the group supporting him. The alliance of lobbyist and pressure politician is an effective one. A publicity campaign is launched as the cause, however narrow, is elevated into a great moral or patriotic issue. An association headed by respectable leaders is set up. Citizens with local influence are brought to Washington to appeal personally to their representatives. A vast letter-writing and telegram-sending campaign is organized. The pressure politicians in Congress carry the campaign to the floors of the House and Senate and to the committee sessions with speeches and briefs. All media of publicity are exploited—radio, press, cinema, public forums, even schools and colleges.

Where aid from lobbyists is not available the pressure politician himself may actively recruit organized support. He may stir into action a slumbering interest group with dire warnings as to the effect of proposed laws. He may decide to take certain legislative action and then organize support at home for such action. Such activity is quite the reverse of the usual idea of "pressure politics."

Representatives of organized groups, whether members of Congress or not, follow two basic rules. One rule is to claim boundless support throughout the nation for a given policy, no matter how small a group would benefit from that policy. As Schattschneider says, "Never admit that it is only you who is talking." The other is to equate one's special interest with the national interest or the general welfare.

Spokesmen for sheep raisers argue that artificially supported wool prices will ensure a domestic supply of wool in the event of another war. Industry representatives assert that higher tariffs will benefit labor through increased wages, as well as help business. Organized labor pleads that extended social security programs will stabilize the economy along with safeguarding the less privileged. Whether true or not, such avowals would shift the argument from the area of crass group interest to the level of a higher morality and patriotism.

Witness a small incident taking place on the floor of the Senate on January 15, 1944. An important war-time tax bill is under consideration, and one clause provides for a tax on furs and fur coats. Senator John H. Overton of

Louisiana has just introduced an amendment to this clause exempting fur garments costing $150 or less from the new rate. He is doing this, he says again and again, for the sake of "poor struggling girls" who need to "protect themselves against the winter's blasts."

Other Senators object and tempers flare. Senator Champ Clark of Missouri, who has voted for the fur tax in committee, shouts that Overton "walked toward me and shook his fist at me and accused every member of the committee who voted for this provision . . . of being in league with a gang of manufacturers for the purpose of trying to render naked a lot of deserving girls who wanted to wear fur coats. . . . It almost breaks my heart to contemplate the pathetic picture drawn by the Senator from Louisiana of the poor, freezing girls in semi-tropical Louisiana being harassed and bedeviled because they are not able to wear these necessary fur garments for their protection from the cold."

What was behind this performance of Overton's? Perhaps he was genuinely concerned about working girls who lack fur coats. More likely he was thinking of the fact that over 20,000 trappers, fur buyers, and fur dealers in Louisiana specialized in cheap furs retailing for less than $150, and would be affected adversely by the proposed tax. Here was a special interest in camouflage.

Lobbyists always seem to be in public disfavor. Most of the states regulate their activities; the Georgia constitution outlaws lobbying altogether, and Alabama has made lobbying for or against a measure a misdemeanor. In the Legislative Reorganization Act of 1946, Congress provided for the registration of organized groups and their legislative agents, and for the filing of detailed accounts of their receipts and expenditures. This provision was designed to enable Congress and the public to judge the claims of lobbyists in terms of the pressure groups they represent.

Congress has done nothing, however, about those of its members who are in effect lobbyists in disguise, although former Representative Robert Ramspeck of Georgia took a step in that direction when he proposed a constitutional amendment forbidding Congressmen to deal with the executive branch except on legislative matters. Disguised lobbying is by far the more serious problem.

Few lobbyists try to conceal the fact that they speak for certain organizations. Testifying before a congressional committee a lobbyist will identify himself as national legislative representative of the Brotherhood of Railway Trainmen, or chairman of the Spinach Committee of the Baltimore Canned Foods Exchange, or vice-president of the Westinghouse Electric Corporation, or managing director of the Northeastern Poultry Producers' Council. There can be little doubt as to what and whom these spokesmen represent. Can one say the same of legislators who pretend to speak for the national interest, or at least for their constituents as a whole, and who in fact are acting for a pressure group?

THE PHYSIOLOGY OF PRESSURE

Pressure groups are powerful chiefly because they invade and envelop our regular political processes. This is the hard fact that we hate to accept. Any good democrat prefers to think that organized special interests gain their ends through trickery and dishonesty rather than through the democratic process. To be sure, the pressure groups sometimes stoop to questionable methods. But generally they are effective because they play the political game expertly and tirelessly.

Half a century ago the "interests" had a different basis of power. One spoke casually of the "oil" and "silver" and "railroad" senators who were the puppets of the industrial and financial giants of the day. These captive-congressmen owed their jobs to huge corporations that had little "ballot power" but enormous "dollar power." In politics, as in business, money talked. Whole legislatures were corrupted, officials were bought and sold by the job lot, governmental favors were purchased in vast financial transactions. From the Yazoo land frauds through *Crédit Mobilier* and the Harding oil scandals the men with cash to dispense have made their arrangements under cover of the patriotic outcries of the politicos.

Money is still a potent factor in politics, but today it is used mainly to sway elections rather than as a direct means of influencing politicians once the votes are counted. The strengthening of democratic machinery by such devices as the direct primary system of nomination, the direct election of Senators, and curbs on political activities of corporations, has forced the special interests to prove their power at the polls. Many members of Congress are still the creatures of pressure groups, but they owe their positions to the strength at home of an organized group as a whole, rather than to a few manipulators at the top. We still speak, for example, of "silver senators" but they are likely to represent the whole industry and not merely a handful of mine owners.

The Anti-Saloon League gave the classic demonstration a generation ago of how a superbly organized minority group could put over its program by cultivating its strength at the polls. The League carefully observed the three cardinal rules of effective minority politics: (1) Organize voting power in the members' constituencies; (2) maintain a legislative office to keep pressure on Congressmen with tendencies to waver; (3) never let the membership become divided over side issues. The League's great weapon was not bribery or propaganda as such, but its actual or vaunted power at the polls. "The surest way to secure needed temperance legislation," declared a League strategist, "is for the sovereign voters, through well planned organization, to elect men as their representatives . . . who will write the laws upon the statute books." This formula worked. It was reported that the average Congressman feared the League more than he feared the President of the United States. Considering how hard it is to amend the American Constitution, the adoption of the 18th Amendment was the ultimate tribute to the organized political strength of the Anti-Saloon League.

At the opposite pole from a high-powered group like the old League are the associations that have representatives in Washington but no strength throughout the states and districts. The "People's Lobby" is such a group. Benjamin Marsh, its director, regularly appears before congressional committees to testify in behalf of unorganized Americans. The committee members listen to him politely and duly incorporate his briefs in the committee's record. Some day historians may judge that Ben Marsh had the wisest suggestions of all the persons who appeared; certainly the low-income groups for which he speaks deserve representation before Congress. But it seems unlikely that the "People's Lobby" ever influenced an important decision in House or Senate. It would be hard to find a better example of the powerlessness of ideas in Congressional politics without organized power to back them up.

The strength of pressure groups lies only in part in the conscious mobilization and channeling of votes. Indeed, many organizations refuse to choose openly between candidates in order to protect their "nonpartisanship." Their influence may appear in more subtle ways. In most groups there are leaders and followers. The former are opinion-moulders, and they influence their followers in hundreds of casual face-to-face conversations.

These personal contacts often affect voting behavior to a greater extent than do even the press or radio, for the contacts are frequent, the "opinion leader" in the group is usually trusted, the argument can be tailored to suit the biases of the follower, and the follower is probably less "on his guard" against absorbing opinions than when encountering formal media of communication, such as the press or radio. As Lazarsfeld has pointed out, voting is essentially a group experience, and people vote with—and for—their group.

Even so, the voting power of pressure groups is often exaggerated. The rank-and-file of every organized minority is subject to a variety of sectional, occupational, religious, family, and other influences which cause the members to desert the group in the privacy of the ballot booth or to stay home on Election Day.

Unfortunately, the congressman himself is only too prone to do the exaggerating. But can one blame him? He has few ways of testing the group's voting power or the solidarity of its members. For the most part he deals with the group leaders, who naturally picture their followers as broadly and enthusiastically united. Trying to garner votes from an electorate that is erratic and nebulous and apathetic and often adrift, he naturally clutches for the support of groups and group leaders who are approachable and purposeful and who can swing at least a few votes in his direction.

The pressure groups, moreover, can speak with a loud voice. Many congressmen count their mail in an effort to see how the wind is blowing back home. Pressure can be turned on overnight. Price Administrator Chester Bowles once estimated that 5000 telegrams poured in on members of Congress in two days from automobile dealers seeking exemption from an OPA regulation. Many a congressman would like to resist "government by telegram," but he must be careful. Pressure groups have long memories. And they are articulate about legislative detail. The votes on amendments and the parliamentary maneuvers that might escape the attention of the average voter are spotted by the lobbyist sitting in the gallery.

The decisions of the important groups—the Cotton Textile Institute, the Legion, the CIO, the National Association of Home Builders, the NAM, the Grange, and so on—are front-page news, but the smaller, local organizations are important too. It is extraordinary how trifling an organized special interest may seem to be and still enjoy representation in government. The late Charles L. Gifford, who represented the Cape Cod area of Massachusetts in the House of Representatives, commented on this situation during debate over the price control bill in 1941.

"If a legislator is sent here from a 'bean' section," Mr. Gifford said, "he will—and seemingly must—protect beans. His constituents demand it to be his first interest. Difficult it is for most to sacrifice themselves and their 'bean' constituents. If one thinks politics easy, 'try sitting top of a high rail fence and keeping one ear close to the ground.' "

Mr. Gifford himself, however, had striven mightily to protect fish from the rigors of price control, for his 9th Massachusetts district had hundreds of miles of coastline. "I was very much interested in the gentleman's discussion of beans," declared Representative Merlin Hull of Wisconsin. "I wonder if the gentleman would not go a little further and take up the matter of fish."

"Yes, I will," replied Mr. Gifford. "I trust that I may have a little political sense. I asked that fish and fishermen be granted about the same consideration as the farmers. This was most cheerfully granted. However, no fishermen or fishermen's organization appealed to me. . . . But, of course, I should expect to watch over their interests when others are getting theirs."

One cannot blame Mr. Gifford for protecting his fishermen. Watching over their interests was part of his duty. If he had failed in that duty, he would ultimately have been replaced by someone who could defend the interests of the district. Even Abraham Lincoln won his election to the Illinois legislature partly as a result of demanding a canal from the Sangamon River to aid his constituents, according to his law partner. Nor can one pass judgment on the leaders of pressure groups. Inevitably those leaders will seek to bolster the group's economic position with political power, for they know that in a world of hotly contending groups, and in a society coming to be increasingly administered by government, their economic strength may ebb away if they have not the political vigor to back it up.

One can, however, pass judgment on a political system that lets pressure politics get out of hand. In a free society pressure groups are inevitable and desirable. But there must be limits. "If we do not eliminate selfish abuse of power by any one group," declared President Dwight D. Eisenhower in his inaugural address at Columbia, "we can be certain that equally selfish retaliation by other groups will ensue."

DEMOCRACY'S EXPOSED FLANK

Like an army probing for the enemy's weak point, pressure groups search out the sector of government that is least hostile to the attainment of their ends. In the United States that sector is held by the legislative branch. As between the chief authors of over-all national policy—Congress and President—it is the former that shows itself far more responsive to the drives of organized minorities. In times of sharp political conflict the Senate and the House, dominated by pressure politicians and their allies, over and again become deploying areas for mobilized pressure groups.

This is not to say that these groups operate only through Congress. Some administrative agencies have long been known for their close kinship with organized interests, which influence appointments, policy-making, policy execution. Nor is it to say that the President himself is oblivious to pressure groups. No political leader can be. But while the Chief Executive, dependent for support on a majority of the whole nation, can gauge the voting power behind the groups with a certain perspective, Congress tends to dissolve into a congeries of blocs and individual legislators who are unwilling and unable to withstand the organized minorities. Indeed, the responsiveness of many administrative agencies to minority pressures is partly a result of control by Congress over agency personnel and funds.

Striking evidence of congressional weakness in the face of organized minorities, and of presidential firmness, can be found in the story of veterans' bonus legislation. Presidents Warren G. Harding, Calvin Coolidge, Herbert Hoover, and Franklin D. Roosevelt each had the experience of vetoing bonus bills, only to have the House pass them over those vetoes. In none of the four cases did more than 90 Representatives out of 435 vote against the veterans' groups. The American Legion and the other veterans' organizations scored these signal successes because they were organized locally in states and districts. Although a minority, they made up for lack of numbers by working energetically for these special ends. They showed how to play the minority game.

Who represented the American people as a whole in these cases, President or Congress? There is no evidence that the pro-bonus Representatives suffered at the polls. But neither did the anti-bonus Presidents. The veterans' groups were never able to make the bonus an issue in the presidential campaign, but they succeeded in making it a factor in many congressional campaigns. This experience with bonus bills tells us little about the respective personal virtues of the Chief Executives and the Congressmen: the four Presidents felt that they would gain more by vetoing the bills than they would lose, and the Representatives believed that the safer course was to vote for them. This experience does illuminate our strange representative system, under which Congress responds to an entirely different set of forces than does the President.

How explain this contrast between President and Congress in their response to pressure groups? The key to it lies largely in the manner in which they are elected—that is, in the underpinnings of their political power. Organized minorities have a more significant role in congressional elections than in presidential. In the former contests the public issues are usually less well defined, national problems receive less emphasis, protection of local interests becomes a central question, and the organized voters exercise relatively greater weight. All these conditions strengthen the position of the pressure groups.

The presidential candidates, on the other hand, argue issues that often transcend the petty claims of the special interests. To be sure, they must handle with care the appeals of organized minorities, but at the same time they need not fear that any pressure group could make its demands a prime issue in the national campaign. For if any such attempt were made, the group would be swamped under by the far larger number of voters, organized or not, who would resent wholesale capitulation to special interests. In the case of the veterans' bonus bills, for example, not one of the subsequent rivals of the anti-bonus presidents made the veto an issue in the presidential campaign. To have done so would have won the support of some veterans only to have jeopardized the support of millions of non-veterans.

Viewing the situation from the Congressman's vantage point, one sees why it is not so easy for him to withstand the pressure groups. In the first place, his state or district may be so dominated by one or two interests—such as tobacco-growing, mining, or automobile-manufacturing—that he can aspire to no greater standing than that of the out-and-out pressure politician. But often he must submit even to the smaller pressure groups. For the disciplined rank and file of the organized special interest knows how to influence local sentiment and deliver the votes, while usually the mass of the voters can be counted on only for indifference or irresolution.

"The apathy of the many, in the face of the enormous complexity of our economic and political structure, is the common premise of all pressure groups," Max Lerner has said. "With it as a given, they are able through their condensed urgencies to translate their minority interest into a psychic majority."

But the translation is a false one, as Lerner points out. The minority wields power only because the majority has abdicated. Indeed, it is astonishing how much representation in Congress can be gained by a small but well distributed pressure group. John Gunther, noting this phenomenon while traveling through the states that maintain the sugar bloc in Congress, wrote: "Only 3 per cent of American farmers grow sugar beet and cane; the entire processing industry employs no more than twenty-five thousand people. But sugar is spread through many states—beets grow in seventeen, cane in two—which gives it thirty-eight senators out of ninety-six, and they can certainly make a noise." The President, elected by millions upon millions of voters, can assign the proper weight to the sugar growers and processors, and similar pressure groups.

Thus Congress occupies our government's exposed flank, against which the small but disciplined forces of the special interests take the offensive in order to invade the citadel of political power at the expense of the majority of the people. It is no accident that representatives of organized groups are called the "third house of Congress." Nor is it surprising that such measures as price control—the bulwark of consumers and other unorganized people—were continually under attack in Congress and finally dismantled there; that passage of the Taft-Hartley Act was the signal for labor to renew its efforts in congressional elections; that sectional minorities like the South, and occupational minorities like the farmers, receive their greatest political representation nationally in House and Senate. The pressure politicians and their allies hamstring action by the majority, and to the extent that popular government rests on majority rule, they are a threat to democracy.

In Defense of Lobbying

Henry A. Bellows *

No other trade in America to-day is subject to such widespread villification as that of the lobbyist. . . . The very term "lobbying" is in itself suggestive of sinister methods. It paints a grim picture of a furtive individual lurking in the byways of the Capitol, buttonholing a Senator here, a Congressman there, whispering secrets into quivering ears, a stealthy, malevolent perverter of truth. And in recent years this hideous figment of the imagination has grown to gigantic proportions. Not content with his pernicious activities beneath the dome of the Capitol, the lobbyist must needs reach out into every city and hamlet, and there stir up tornadoes of propaganda that writhe their way back to Washington in the form of myriads of letters and telegrams.

All very horrible, no doubt, but far from the whole story. Go to any

* Formerly Director of the Legislative Committee, National Association of Broadcasters, and Director of Public Relations, General Mills, Inc. The selection is from Henry A. Bellows, "In Defense of Lobbying," *Harper's Magazine,* Vol. 172 (December, 1935), pp. 96–107. Reprinted by permission of Mrs. Philip W. Pillsbury.

committee hearing on an important bill. Who is that man in the witness chair, answering innumerable questions, generally of a technical nature, and, as he finally withdraws, receiving the cordial thanks of the committee chairman? He, strange to say, is a lobbyist. He is paid to represent a group or an industry for the express purpose of affecting the course of legislation. It is quite possible that he will ultimately urge those whose interests he represents to communicate with their Senators and Congressmen regarding the pending bill. The members of the committee know all this, and yet it is clear that they look upon him, not as Public Enemy Number One, but as a serviceable and trustworthy ally.

The plain fact is that lobbying, properly conducted, is not only a perfectly legitimate exercise of a Constitutional right, but a direct benefit both to Congress and to the country at large. Most important bills involve the consideration of complex problems, which can be solved only on the basis of long practical experience and careful research. The lobbyist places at the disposal of Congress the collective experience of those whom he represents. That in so doing he is unbiased he would be the last to claim. Of course he is biased, but so are all the other witnesses, including, be it noted, such representatives of the government itself as may testify. The whole business of Federal law-making is, in this respect, remarkably like the functioning of the courts. An attorney is not expected to be nonpartisan, and the judge does not condemn him because he brings out the strongest points in favor of his client. Rather, the ends of justice are considered as best served when both sides are fully and ably represented, when all the evidence is clearly set forth, and when judge and jury have the benefit of whatever technical guidance the issues in the case may require.

The analysis and discussion of a proposed law, if it is to amount to anything more than superficial guesswork, normally requires weeks or months of intensive preparation. It cannot be done adequately by untrained persons, or even by experts who can devote to it only their spare time. Many a capable executive makes a lamentable witness before a Congressional committee because he neither speaks nor understands the special language of legislation; many an eloquent lawyer falls down when searching questions reveal his limited familiarity with practical details. The experienced lobbyist, on the other hand, intimately acquainted with his subject through long association with the people he represents, and fully cognizant of the special complexities of legislative procedure, including the peculiarly difficult technic of phraseology, frequently can and does render invaluable assistance in the shaping of proposed laws.

Proof of this is spread all over the pages of the published records of legislative hearings. Obviously there is nothing secretive or surreptitious about a type of lobbying that is thus publicly recorded, and yet lobbying within the ordinary definition of the term it certainly is. It is an effort to affect the course of pending legislation; it is openly conducted in the interests of some particular group, and not infrequently it costs a good deal of money. And yet the records show both its value to the public and the almost invariable cordiality with which it is welcomed by committee members. . . .

It will, of course, be argued that this is not the type of lobbying to which anyone seriously objects, that it is a far cry to the activities which warn Senators and Congressmen of dire consequences at the polls if they do not vote in such and such a way, that shake down avalanches of telegrams and letters on their defenseless heads, and, going one step farther, in the ominous vocabulary of practical politics "put pressure" on them.

After all, however, our entire system of government is based on the principle of representation, and each legislator must consider all questions of national scope as they may affect both the general welfare and that of the locality which has empowered him to represent it. A keen and constant interest in what people think "back home" is by no means, as is so often inferred, exclusively indicative of vote-counting spinelessness. It is distinctly and properly a part of the job, inherent in the provisions of the Constitution itself. The lobbyist in Washington, from the very nature of his residence and work, is commonly without immediate State affiliations; he must study pending legislation from the national rather than from the local point of view. Is he, therefore, to assume that Senators and Congressmen will disregard their direct accountability to those whose special interests they are required to safeguard?

The people "back home," however, normally have very limited access to detailed information about legislation. It is seldom that an issue is so sharply defined that the question is simply one of voting for or against a bill in its entirety. Even those whose interests are directly involved are, as a rule, far from clear in their own minds as to the precise things that they do or do not want. And yet, with complete propriety, every Senator and Congressman is eager to know what his constituents, and particularly the better-informed among them, really think about the matters on which his vote will be recorded.

At this point the lobby inevitably broadens its scope. Consider any extended group which may be directly affected, either favorably or the reverse, by some pending item of legislation. Its lobbyist has painstakingly analyzed the bill; he knows, as well as anyone can know, what effect it is likely to have on those whom he represents. He understands what amendments will increase the benefits or mitigate the hardships. From all over the country he receives urgent calls for information and advice, in order that the members of his group—and it does not matter whether they are producers or consumers, employers or labor, lenders or borrowers—may more intelligently transmit their own views to their Senators and Congressmen.

And so the lobbyist perforce launches a service of information. If he knows his business, his reports attempt no concealment of their frankly partisan nature. They do not try to hide their origin by masquerading as impartial news. They are careful never knowingly to misstate facts, and clearly distinguish between established facts and the inferences drawn therefrom. Above all, the wise lobbyist sees to it that his reports never contain a single line that cannot invite the widest publicity, and that is not actually, in substance at least, a matter of record. Provided such legislative service is honest within the requirements just set forth, it may be intensely partisan.

"Propaganda!" shout the hot-heads. Of course it is propaganda, and why not? How long since it has become a crime to disseminate legislative information? Is the political education of the American people to be left entirely to public agencies with an itch for self-perpetuation? The lobbyist's report is no whit more selfishly motivated than many a departmental press release or franked Congressional speech. Admit that it is not the whole truth; its openly proclaimed source is a virtual guarantee of that. Nobody is capable of telling the whole truth about any important legislative matter; otherwise there would be no debates in Congress. The legislative news service sent out by lobbyists, provided always it makes no concealment of its origin, is a definite and wholly legitimate contribution to public education, and to brand it as in any way improper is rank injustice.

Such information is sent out for the manifest and admitted purpose of influencing public opinion "back home." What are the recipients to do with it? File it, read or unread, in the wastebasket? By all means, if it does not coincide with their views. But if it provides satisfactory answers to the questions they have been asking themselves, and if they feel that they are in any way personally concerned in the matter, then it is not only their right, but actually their duty, to see that their chosen representatives are made acquainted with their opinions.

Occasionally some Congressional sleuth makes the amazing discovery that since many of the communications he receives are similar or identical in wording, they must have had a common origin. Certainly they had. How many good citizens and conscientious voters know enough about the details of any significant piece of pending legislation to frame a really helpful letter or telegram regarding it? Even the relatively well-informed and actively interested are commonly inarticulate when it comes to giving specific recommendations for action. And yet, as the numerous insertions in the Congressional Record demonstrate, Senators and Congressmen are keenly interested in such communications from their constituents as evince genuine understanding and provide logical reasons for the opinions set forth. It is, therefore, quite understandable that the lobbyist is constantly being asked to suggest the most effective wording for such letters and telegrams. . . .

Any form of legislative propaganda, however, undeniably opens the way for the sort of thing that has brought lobbying into such evil repute. Money can be and has been viciously used, and direct financial pressure of all sorts exerted, to color the views and actions of those who have influence either at home or with their Congressional friends. It may be impossible to buy a Senator or a Congressman, but it is sometimes quite feasible to purchase those to whom Senators and Congressmen must listen—the local political bosses who control the machinery of nomination and election. The most honest legislator who values his job—and the majority of them do—has his vulnerable spot, and if he owes his office to the support of crooks, money will talk to them and they to him. Many of the most outrageous political scandals have been of this type, with the elected representatives of the people, and still more, the appointed incumbents of high offices, mere pawns in the unscrupulous hands of local politicians who cynically offered themselves for sale to the highest bidder. . . . The seamy side of all attempts to influence legislation is, in truth, the ugly background of our entire politico-economic system of conventions, nominations, and elections, of the whole complex relationship between wealth and public service. With most of this the legislative lobbyist has little or nothing to do. . . .

In all this matter of seeking to influence public opinion, whether legitimately or otherwise, there is nothing of the traditional activity to which lobbying owes its repulsive name. The man who appears at public hearings, generally by express invitation, as the representative of some particular group, who assists, again commonly by invitation, in the drafting of legislation or of amendments thereto, and who sends out legislative information for the guidance of his clients or for distribution to the public, has so far done nothing which would require him ever to ask whether the Capitol has any architectural features denotable as lobbies. But the lobbyist is likewise accused of conversing privately with individual Senators and Congressmen. Well, why shouldn't he? Usually he calls on them, like any other visitor, in their offices, but there are times when he does have to earn his title by seeking them in the fusty purlieus of the Senate and House chambers. It is no indictable crime—though it may well prove an error of judgment—to talk with a Congressman even amid the blended aromas of the House restaurant, or to confer with a Senator on that scenic railway that careens underground between the north wing of the Capitol and the Senate Office Building.

This—this holding converse with legislators individually—is lobbying in all its pristine nakedness. It is excoriated as if it were a consorting of habitual criminals. And yet its hideous immorality is singularly hard to discover. Practically everyone who goes to see a Senator or Congressman "wants something"—a job, an introduction, a departmental favor, a card to the galleries. Why should it be perfectly proper to talk to him about anything else, but indecent to confer with him about his most important duties. . . .

Most lobbyists waste very little time in seeking to make possibly undesired calls, nor is there ordinarily much occasion for it. After all, legislation is made largely in committee, not on the floor. The members of the two committees, one in each House, to which any particular bill is referred, and frequently just the members of special sub-committees of these committees, are the persons whose opinions will be guiding, and probably determining. Even in debate on the floor, the lead in almost every instance is taken by not more than half a dozen members, most of whom have already had the advantage of studying the proposal in committee. These are the people whom the lobbyist makes a point of seeing personally, and he frequently does so by express invitation. . . .

The trouble with the personal conference, as distinct from most of the other phenomena of lobbying, is that since it is not a matter of record, it gives occasion for all sorts of sinister inferences. I remember once, in the Senate waiting-room, overhearing a conversation between two women, one evidently a Washingtonian, and the other a friend from afar who was being shown the sights.

"That's Senator So-and-so," said the Washington lady in the stage whisper with which one refers to marvels at the Zoo, "and that"—indicating the man with whom the Senator was in earnest conversation—"is Mr. Blank —you know—the lobbyist for the What's-its-name."

"O-o-oh," responded the visitor in awed tones. "Is he bribing him now?"

This state of mind is lamentably common. The lobbyist is supposed to go about bearing a brief-case stuffed with currency, or at the very least to do his nefarious work by the alternate application of financial threats and promises. Now, it would be absurd to claim that such things never have happened—there have been black sheep in Congress, as everywhere—but by and large there is amazingly little evidence of it. It must be remembered that every legislator who faces re-election, as most of them periodically do, lives in the most transparent of glass houses, with opponents goggle-eyed for any chance to "get the goods on him." Even for a legislator with an itching palm the risk is too great.

Of course, Senators and Congressmen are always being told that certain actions will win—or lose—untold numbers of votes, but it is hard to see what is inherently wrong in that. After all, we live in a democracy, and the only way in which a legislator can free himself from the tyranny of the ballot is by death or not choosing to run. "Pressure" of this sort is inevitable, but most of it comes, not from the lobbyist, but from the politically-minded friend from home. As for direct bribery, most of the talk about it is utter nonsense. I am told that somebody once prepared what purported to be a current market price list of Senators and Congressmen—a document which, if it ever really existed, which I doubt, would have made good reading. Washington is a hotbed of wild rumors on every subject, and anyone who has lived there awhile learns to discount them heavily. One would think, from the absurdities that periodically gain currency, that a Congressman could not so much as dine with an old friend without thereby selling his immortal soul. Nobody with a grain of intelligence imagines that one can buy a legislative vote with a dinner. If there is ever more direct bribery than this, the secret is unbelievably well kept, and that in an environment where secrecy is almost impossible. . . .

It is quite true that many of the lobbyists are on friendly terms with a considerable number of Senators and Congressmen, and that this personal relationship is sometimes assisted by a certain amount of entertaining. But, here again, why not? In every other sphere a reasonable amount of luncheon- or dinner-giving is regarded as entirely fitting, and an attorney may offer a cocktail to a judge without being in contempt of court. Accepting such an invitation occasionally does not put a legislator under the slightest obligation to vote as his host wants him to. Such entertaining as is done—and for obvious reasons it is seldom lavish or costly—is partly for the purpose of establishing friendlier personal contacts, but far more because the lunch or dinner hour is often the only time when Senators or Congressmen can get away from their tasks. . . .

Admittedly, however, the personal friendliness which exists in some cases between lobbyists and members of Congress, and which it is manifestly part of the lobbyist's business to maintain, opens the way to certain grave abuses. There are, unfortunately, plenty of people in Washington who seek to trade unscrupulously on alleged present or past "influential connections." Former Senators and Congressmen, lawyers or specialists who have been associated with administrative departments of the government, publicity agents, people of all kinds who claim to be somehow "on the inside," can be found among the ranks of those who undertake to render mysterious services for their prospective clients.

The trouble, of course, lies in the abuse rather than in the use of such contacts. It is exceedingly important, and indeed essential, for anyone who has dealings with any branch of the government to be fully posted as to procedure, to know whom to see and how to see him. The person who comes on business to Washington without a competent guide and adviser is likely to waste hours and days which could easily have been saved by a little timely counsel and a few entirely proper introductions. The moment, however, any person claims to have "influence" for sale then it is time for everyone concerned to look out. This is the most flourishing of all the Washington rackets, and, like all rackets everywhere, it fattens chiefly on the gullible. Nobody knows how much money is annually wasted in fees for this sort of "service," any more than we know how much is lost in any other form of confidence game. Here, indeed, are the frayed and tattered fringes of lobbying; here are the people who have done most to bring lobbying into disrepute.

Experience of governmental methods, a wide acquaintance among Washington's official population, long and special training in the analysis and interpretation of bills, laws, and regulations, and an established reputation, all these are parts of the wholly legitimate stock-in-trade of the attorney or other representative who does work in Washington on behalf of clients elsewhere. It is likewise legitimate that these qualifications should, in some instances, command exceedingly high prices. . . .

Enough has been said to indicate that the large fees sometimes paid to Washington attorneys and others for guidance and assistance in legislative matters—in simple language, for lobbying—do not necessarily imply the slightest impropriety. A man who, in an important civil suit, pays his attorney fifty or a hundred thousand dollars is not therefore assumed to be seeking to corrupt the judge or bribe the jury. Whether the attorney's services are actually worth that much is for the client, and for him alone, to decide. In exactly the same way, there are Washington representatives who, without having or claiming a particle of "influence," and without a single word or act that will flinch beneath the spotlight of publicity, are sufficiently experienced and capable so that they are fully entitled to charge high prices for their services.

Nobody would contend that all the money used for the purpose of affecting the course of legislation is wisely or honestly spent. Some part of it is at times diverted into wrong channels, above all when it gets into the hands of irresponsible underlings far removed from Washington itself. Expenses for general propaganda, whether legitimate or not, are always open to challenge, but the mere size of some of the amounts revealed whenever there is a lobby inquiry is not of itself enough to justify such an outcry. Any adequate legislative campaign costs money, even assuming, as is generally the case, that every cent of it is spent properly. A single item, such as the preparation and printing of a brief, may easily run into many thousands of dollars, and every lobby swells the receipts of the Post Office Department. The public ultimately pays the bill, of course, just as it pays the cost of the very active and efficient lobbies maintained by the various administrative departments of the government. In both cases the essential thing is full and accurate publicity as to how the money is spent; the fact that the amount involved may be large is no indication of improper use.

But what of the poor man in all this? The corporation may be able, with its customers' money, to hire expensive lobbying counsel, but how about the consumer, the man in the street, the housewife? The answer to that is that the strongest and most effective lobbies in Washington to-day are essentially "poor men's" lobbies. The American Legion compaign for the bonus bill, compared to which the efforts of the utility holding companies have been as the crackling of thorns under a pot, was certainly no plutocrats' party. To this day people recall the efficiency of the lobby which presided over the passage of the Adamson Bill. The lobby maintained by the American Federation of Labor, which is always on the job, has no support from millionaires. As for the farmers' lobby, it has been getting bills for the relief of agriculture passed in almost every session of Congress since the World War; if the farmers have not reaped the benefits thereof, it has certainly been from no lack of lobbying pertinacity. Anyone who thinks that lobbying unduly favors the rich has only to survey the laws enacted by Congress during the past five years—the period, we are told, of the lobbies' most insidious efforts.

Furthermore, the lobbies representing "the masses" have a tremendous head start. To begin with, they have the votes. When a labor representative tells a Congressman that his support of a certain bill will infallibly cost him the labor vote in his district, that Congressman pricks up his ears. When a consumers' organization advises a Senator that every woman in his state wants a certain thing done, that Senator is going to think twice before refusing to do it. There is, too, an enormous psychological advantage in championing what appears to be the cause of the people, even though the people may be in the end the chief sufferers. And nobody need imagine that the lobbies representing the consumers, labor, and the smaller producers are inefficiently staffed. True, they seldom go out and hire expensive counsel, but they more than make up for it by keeping their people on the job permanently. The intimate knowledge that some of them have of their business makes the highest-priced attorneys look like novices.

There are abuses in lobbying, of course. There are lobbying crooks who swindle their clients with fabulous tales of the wonders they can accomplish through mysterious channels. There are blunderers with distorted moral senses who fake telegrams and advocate whispering campaigns. There are subterranean workers who intimate that every legislator has his price. Above all, there are the people whose business is to squeeze money out of every phase of politics—the bosses who control elections and therewith the men they elect. Just so in every field; there are shyster lawyers, quack doctors, absconding bankers, labor racketeers, venal office-holders. But because these elements exist, in lobbying as elsewhere, it is grossly unjust to single out for public denunciation an occupation which not only exists by legal right but which—when properly conducted, as it commonly is—is a benefit and a necessity to the American people. It is largely through the instrumentality of lobbyists that legislation is adequately studied before enactment, and it is chiefly by way of the lobbyist that detailed information regarding such legislation reaches those who are most deeply concerned with it.

There can be no serious objection to having lobbyists registered as such, with full publicity as to their relations with their clients and with the public in all matters affecting legislation—provided there is a clear realization that the badge of the lobbyist is not a Scarlet Letter of crime. When a President of the United States referred publicly to the "lobbyists who, like a swarm of locusts, infest the halls of Congress," there was more than an intimation that the people had no longer the right of petition guaranteed by the Constitution, and that our laws ought to be enacted in Star

Chamber secrecy. Until that right is denied as contrary to the mechanism of dictatorship, the lobbyist has a legitimate, necessary, and honorable place in any system of government by the people.

Topic 26

CAN PRESIDENTIAL GOVERNMENT DO THE JOB?

THE SOLITARY PRESIDENT

Herman Finer *

The constitutional convention desired to secure an unmistakable focus of responsibility and avoid confusion; and to encourage vigor and despatch in judgment and decision. The weak colonial governors were in disfavor. Hence no plural or collective executive, like a cabinet or council of ministers, was established, though it must never be forgotten that a multiple executive was proposed only to be dropped for reasons not fully reported in the records of the convention.

All constitutional responsibility is focused on one man and one man alone. The constitution even provides for his impeachment. The consequences are interesting and dangerous.

No collective responsibility in a group of men equal in status, with perhaps some ascendency in a prime minister, was sought. None has developed. Something called the President's cabinet, always including the ten departmental heads and usually others, was evolved. Yet, in reality, no cabinet exists, in the sense of a constitutionally responsible multiheaded council for the exercise of the chief executive's power. The cabinet is a mere collection of Presidential minions, "clerks" as they have been called. The President's will is supreme, whatever they may advise, because his responsibility is sole and plenary. Indeed, it is rare that the cabinet is called together; rarer still that it discusses major issues; and practically never that it makes a corporate decision. The President makes up his own mind, whatever the votes—when, indeed, votes are taken.

The talk of a cabinet, then, is specious: it is a cabinet at a meeting to hold conversations, perhaps at times to deliberate, but hardly ever to create a collective will that shall govern all including the President. The President floats above it, and aloof. He is not merged in a team; he is detached.

Though business may be distributed, partly by the Presidential wish and

* Professor of Political Science, University of Chicago. Formerly Lecturer on Political Science, London School of Economics. Author of *British Civil Service, America's Destiny, Theory and Practice of Modern Government,* and many other works. The selection is from *The Theory and Practice of Modern Government,* Revised Edition, by Herman Finer. By permission of Henry Holt & Co., Inc. Copyright 1949.

his general executive power, and partly by statutes of Congress which vest various administrative powers in the several heads of departments, no real sharing of authority occurs. . . .

Every President is personally liable to be smitten in conscience, self-respect, and political reputation, by the boomerang of his own delegation of authority; responsibility—that is, punishability—is inescapable. He distributes business, or Congress does, but, whoever acts, he alone takes political responsibility. He therefore is careful not to devolve authority, which still attaches to him. It is always only a distribution of business. For whatever may be the actual demonstrable errors of his cabinet heads, political blame will come back to him. The President takes the greatest political risk in surrendering some of his authority into the keeping of others. If he is a conscientious man, this is a painful strain on him. He is torn between the impulse not to share power with others, though he has so crushing a burden himself, and the impulse to give it and then feel that unless he watches its use closely, Congress and public opinion will make him smart with blame. Congress may have given power and responsibility to a departmental chief, provided him with funds, instructed and encouraged him at its hearings, yet, since the President bears responsibility for executive competence, he cannot find relief from departmental concern, for he cannot cut the knot the constitution has tied.

It is an impossible burden. And, in fact, it cannot be borne in a governmental system so widely and deeply active as the American of the twentieth century is obliged to be. Too much responsibility paralyzes the will, for the imagined consequences are too fearful. An excessively concentrated accountability causes incomplete devolution of work to subordinate agencies, and a process of frantic intrusions and exits, by the chief executive, in the alternations between relief and accumulating anxiety. When the President is a weak man—which by the bargaining, contractual, almost casual, nature of the forces producing a nomination, he is liable at any moment to be—the pitiable man is reduced to a frightened whistling for courage, and policy to collapse.

The constitution and its conventional apparatus have provided him with no one he can fully trust; no one to lend him acceptable and dependable counsel; no one to encourage him with the sincerity that comes when a colleague's political fate is bound up with the results of the encouragement he gives. How much easier is the British cabinet minister's task, and how much lighter the prime minister's, even though the latter's power is not reduced and limited by any federal division of power, or checks and balances, or the exclusion of some matters from governmental jurisdiction altogether, as under the United States constitution.

It is not to be wondered that Presidents have been obliged to set up "kitchen cabinets" and "brain trusts" and "Assistant Presidents." . . . Instead of decision by cabinet, we have decision by tête-a-tête. Notice how on the death of one President, and the succession of the Vice-President of that same party, the former's departmental chiefs flee Washington, while the new chief executive brings in his own "gang." Frances Perkins's description of the Roosevelt cabinets fits the stories of previous Presidencies and corroborates that given verbally to the present author by other members of Roosevelt administrations.

> But as the years went on, Roosevelt's cabinet administration came to be like most previous ones—a direct relationship between a particular cabinet officer and the President in regard to his special field, with little or no participation or even information from other cabinet members. Certainly almost no "cabinet agreements" were reached. . . .

The effect of the last man in to see the President is most often decisive. The disputant who appears at the White House, as contrasted with the other man who stayed away, wins a superior influence. Cabinet members take deliberate care to safeguard their departmental concerns from cabinet discussion, with mutual understandings for suppression. One of those especially trusted by the President lunches with him weekly. Here is a fortuitous assemblage of regional, local, sectional, vocational, and "party" chieftains, each with his own fief; some, but few, with broad views of policy; some, but not all, loyal to the President's person and comprehending the import of his policy. They have come into politics for a time; they do not expect to stay; they will retire soon because they are sick or disagree with the President or are merely unwilling to shoulder an unprofitable burden or wish to repair their fortunes in their private business. Or they will cling to office, despite disagreement with the President, useful or not to the public welfare, and the President will not eject them as early as the public good demands because he may offend the chieftain's followers or clients, and so lose support in Congress or popular votes if he contemplates a second term.

Yet there is still a drawback: the President cannot wholly trust them. For they may involve him in trouble, and they are behind-the-scenes operators. In that case, what becomes of the Philadelphia Convention's desire to secure an indubitable locus of responsibility? The President is still "responsible," but it is a nominal responsibility. His backstairs mentors have not been tracked down and punished, or pilloried before an electorate which may make him or them or his party suffer for misgovernment at the next election. A cabinet on the British and even on the Continental model constitutes the principal part of the executive: there is little in the kitchen (I do not say "nothing"): there are enough advisers to render a "kitchen" unnecessary: the overt cabinet is the group, as a group, to be held to responsibility.

This element of solitary, and not plural, responsibility is the plague spot of the American constitution in the twentieth century. All remedial gadgets must break against its insidious obstinacy. For above all, it destroys from the beginning to the end the possibility of coordinating the work of policy making and administration that has been distributed, and the various work of the agencies and departments and commissions set up by statute. No one man can coordinate so much with so little. Nor can one man, with this unique responsibility, take advantage of the technical and personal devices which from time to time have been proposed and even established to assist him to coordinate the vast proliferation of executive bodies. For we revert always to *his* responsibility, his pride, and his conscience. . . .

When a President is swamped with responsibility he is, paradoxically, tempted to "off-the-cuff" decisions, for how can he genuinely let his duty invade him? The amount of business is beyond one man's capacity or conscience. One solitary man must, surely, look for short cuts. The President needs help, as the Committee on Administrative Management declared; but he needs the help of a dozen or fifteen men, good and true, who bear a direct responsibility *with* him (not *to* him) to the public and the party and the Congress. . . .

The Presidency needs to be put into commission. It needs distribution among fifteen equals, each of whom is fully the master and the servant of his own portion of responsibility and of all common policy which comes to them as a collective unity. You can coordinate if you have divided; you can divide if you can trust; you can trust if you alone are not saddled with all responsible decision. To apply a famous dictum of de Tocqueville's, used by him to describe the centralization of the *ancien régime* in France: when you centralize in a solitary President, you risk apoplexy at the center and anæmia at the extremities, or a red face and palsied hands. Nor is that all: if no full authority can be granted a departmental chief, how is one to induce men of stature to seek office and stay there?

All these proposed administrative gadgets may well help a little on lesser matters, and even that is to be much applauded. But every gadget calls for another gadget to stop up the still-existing leak, *ad infinitum*. Still, the reservoir of responsibility is so high and heavy that it will flood the channels made for it: what is needed is one collective reservoir and its sharing among a dozen or more interconnected basins, with free circulation among them all. The proposed reforms still leave the President high and dry, for they still leave him responsible for too much.

Nor is this all. The heads of departments are granted authority and are saddled with responsibility for their department by laws made in Congress. It has been found impossible to stop them from appealing to Congress for the funds and the legislation to implement their departmental policy, whether or not that conflicts with the President's. Close observers admit in desperation that independent staff work for the President (for example, especially through the Bureau of the Budget) may do much to enforce regulations and controls and prepare long-range plans, but *cannot* build up a unified program of policy and legislation.

Indeed, as one contemplates the collection of incongruous personalities in American cabinets from the beginning, but more especially since the end of the nineteenth century, it is ridiculous to mention the word "party." They are usually appointed because they have or are supposed to have some special interest or expertness in the field of that department—Henry Wallace in Agriculture, and then in Commerce; Jesse Jones in the Reconstruction Finance Corporation; Clinton Anderson in Agriculture; Henry Morgenthau, Jr., in the Treasury (because Mr. Roosevelt had a personal faith in him); Chester Bowles in price administration; Frances Perkins in labor welfare; or Wilson Wyatt as housing administrator, and so on. They are opinionated men; their natural pride is not moderated by party loyalty and solidarity with their chief executive. Their loyalties are divided between the President and their own department; they may sway between the President and Congress; they are torn between their own personal ideas and those of the President.

The memoirs of Sumner Welles, Raymond Moley, and Cordell Hull combined throw an authentic and tragic light on incoherence and mismanagement of foreign policy from 1933 to Pearl Harbor. The Pearl Harbor Report reveals a want of alert coherence between White House, the Secretaries of State, War, and Navy, and the Chiefs of Staff, with some proper blame on the first, or, more reasonably, on the system. Other studies throw light on the lack of solidarity at the center—fumbling in the formation of policy, and stumbling and staggering in its fulfillment.

Even with so potent and clever a President as Franklin Delano Roosevelt as compared with . . . Harry S. Truman, the President needs twelve or fifteen men of his own stature, of equal responsibility with him, equal in accepting party leadership and loyalty. And he and they need the ever-operative assistance of some sixty career men, heading the departments permanently, under the political secretaries—the cream of the crop of an "administrative group" of perhaps 10,000 or 12,000 at all ages on the scale from cadets to mature men and women, to be their advisers, their staff, their arms of administration. All need a Congress organized for, and alert regarding, its function of making collective and unified the policy of the scattered elements of the administration, by everyday, regular, organized, public criticism. Pearl Harbors, domestic as well as foreign, may be avoided where a collective fifteen are responsible, and where the Congressional five hundred badger them with relentless questions. . . .

The lack of a central *thinking,* focusing body of advisers at the top is acknowledged by observer after observer of the Washington apparatus of government, however reluctant in the beginning they may be to admit any deficiencies in the American constitution. . . .

In the British system of government, and even perhaps in the French, though it is weaker, the unintermittent merging of executive and legislature, the ever-continuing life in each other's physical presence, is some assurance of the unison of mind which leads to a unison of guesswork, and therefore to a sharing of responsibility for policy. It enables a measured trust in the executive that purges a peevish demand for "all the facts." The United States President is, on the other hand, compelled to face the task of correct inference from uncertain premises alone—this is a burden of all governments, everywhere, and at all times in human history. It is a dreadful burden for a solitary man, even if assisted by a few faithful friends, to bear alone. Accompanying it is a twin burden: that the knowledge of the facts and the consequent guesses must be carried forward in a state of tentativeness and uncertainty, in a condition merely of temporary probability and yet of possible final certainty, in face of a clamant people anxious to learn what sacrifices, what burdens, what happiness or unhappiness the future holds in store for them, and a people also, to whom the President owes an accounting. Particularly when the horror of war or the misery of depression is being faced is it difficult, as electorates now are, to release the secrets of fact and conjecture, when this may mean undeliberate, emotional behavior by popular groups, which would not occur later when time and events have ripened and made concrete the surmises which the statesman is obliged to nurse. The President is in a position where he can see much further than most people in the nation, even than the most enlightened publicists, but he is in a position where he must not talk as much as undutiful ones. He must bide his time, suffer the criticism until the day of reckoning, and hope that his prophetic thinking is sound enough to redeem his repute because it served his people.

Irresponsible Government

Henry Hazlitt *

Once we have recognized the vices of our form of government, we must act to remove them. This does not mean a generation hence, or in the next decade, or next year. We must begin *now*. . . . We cannot afford deliberately to handicap ourselves by adhering to a form of government that we recognize to be dangerously inefficient or unreliable in a crisis.

What is the central vice of our form of government? In a single word, it is *irresponsible*. All its chief defects come back to this. Either they are forms of irresponsibility, or they promote it. We arbitrarily separate the legislature and the executive. We choose each in such a way that there is no assurance that they will want the same policies—indeed, often in such a way that it is almost certain that they will want different policies. Congress can prevent the President from doing what he wishes, but cannot make

* Associate Editor of *Newsweek*. Formerly editorial writer for *The New York Times*. Author of *Thinking as a Science, Instead of Dictatorship, Economics in One Lesson*, etc. The selection is from Henry Hazlitt, *A New Constitution Now* (New York, Whittlesey House, 1942), Ch. XIV, pp. 277–286. Reprinted by permission of the publisher.

him do what it wishes. The President, through his veto power, can usually prevent Congress from doing as it wishes unless its desired policy is almost unanimous. He needs only the support of "a third plus one" in *one* House of the legislature to stop Congress from adopting a policy. Moreover, if he does not like a law that Congress adopts, he may enforce it either very feebly or in such a way as to make it seem obnoxious. If the President wishes any positive action from Congress, he must usually get his way, as Harold Laski has put it, "very largely by the use of patronage—about as undesirable a method of persuasion as the imagination can conceive." The Senate, again—indeed, a single Senate committee chairman unknown to the public—may through negative vote or mere inaction absolutely veto even the unanimous will of the House of Representatives.

The result is hopelessly to confuse the public regarding whom to hold responsible for a policy or for failure to adopt a policy. The public must wait perhaps through years of deadlock and paralysis to decide the question by its vote; and assuming even then that it knows *how* to decide, it may be powerless to decide. It cannot change whom it wishes when it wishes. It cannot change the government, or the government's policies, at any one election. At one election it can change the House of Representatives but not the President; so that even if it strongly disapproves of the President's policies it must nevertheless either endorse those policies or create a stalemate. At no election can it change more than one-third of the Senate. And if the voters of the whole country are almost unanimous in their opposition, say, to the influential foreign policies of the chairman of the Senate Foreign Relations Committee (who gets his position, not by the free choice of his colleagues, but by seniority), they are powerless to do anything about it. Only the voters of a single State—the State from which the Senator comes (at the present moment, Texas, representing less than 5 per cent of the total voting population), are ever consulted on that question, and then only once in six years.

All this makes for government irresponsibility of the most shocking kind. The only cure is the adoption of the principle of *concentration of responsibility*. This, as Ramsay Muir has pointed out, is the essential principle of the British Constitution, as contrasted with the *separation of powers* which is still the basic principle of the American Constitution.

Since the attack on Pearl Harbor the American public has been brought to recognize how disastrous can be the consequences of failure to fix and concentrate responsibility, even in the lower echelons of command. The Pearl Harbor disaster itself, in which the war was nearly lost in a day, was in large part owing, as the Roberts Commission report made clear, to the failure to concentrate responsibility for the defense of Pearl Harbor. Authority was divided between the Army and Navy commanders there; neither seemed to know exactly where his responsibility began or ended: neither was under obligation to consult with the other regarding the question; and so neither, apparently, condescended to consult the other. When the *Normandie,* the greatest shipping prize in the hands of the American Government, was burned at its pier through inexcusable carelessness, an investigation by Congress revealed no one whose authority had been so unmistakably fixed in advance that he could be held clearly responsible for the disaster. When Congress tried to find who was responsible for the Government's failure to build up a great stock pile of rubber and to begin effective steps to encourage synthetic production, it was confronted by more efforts to shift responsibility. At the time of writing there is no way to determine who was responsible for the failure to have sufficient air power at the Philippines or to protect that air power from almost instant destruction. Even the broadest facts necessary to form a judgment have been withheld from the public.

If these are the results of failure to fix and concentrate responsibility at lower levels, what must be said of our national failure to fix and concentrate responsibility at the very top? American officeholders are in the habit of using the word "responsibility" very loosely. They often declare roundly that they "take full responsibility" for this or that step; but they fail to recognize the implications of their statement. Responsibility implies, in public life, *accountability;* and real accountability implies *immediate removability*. There is no other political way in which responsibility can be made effective. We make a general in the field responsible in two ways: we give him the men, the equipment, the help and the full authority he asks for; we honor him for his success; and we remove him for his failure. So it should be with our political leaders. We should not place in power with them other men who conceive it to be their duty or function to obstruct them at every turn. We should clothe them with real authority for positive as well as negative action. But if they fail to carry out the wishes of the people, then the people, without long or disastrous delays, should be able to remove them.

Because America does not follow this policy, its public thought is hopelessly and chronically confused. We sink into endless argument over points that in England could not be the subject of argument at all. Who was responsible for American unpreparedness? This was a subject of dispute in the Presidential election of 1940 and has been since. We "analyze" the votes of Republicans and Democrats on a score or more of bills. In practically no case do we find a solid vote of Republicans opposed to a solid vote of Democrats; we decide in each case by comparing the percentage division of the vote within each party. (The Republicans alone, in fact, could not at any time have blocked a single "Administration" measure. Whenever the majority of Republicans was successful, it was through the aid of recalcitrant Democrats.) Who was responsible for the original Neutrality Bill? Was the President "forced" to sign this against his judgment? Who blocked the proposal for the fortification of Guam? What defense appropriations were the Republicans mainly responsible for blocking? What of the defense appropriations that the President never even asked for? What attitude *would* the Republicans have taken, or would "Congress" have taken, if these appropriations *had* been asked for?

Few questions of this sort could ever arise in England, or in any country with a sound cabinet government. The Prime Minister or a member of his Cabinet would state his preparedness policy and ask for his appropriation. If Parliament refused that appropriation, or attempted to cut it down, or tried to pass any neutrality bill in spite of "the Government's" wishes, the Prime Minister could announce that the vote was a vote of confidence and could resign or dissolve Parliament if it failed to meet his wishes. The public would never have the slightest doubt as to where responsibility lay. It might have the opportunity then and there, in fact, to decide between the Prime Minister and the parliamentary majority, if the two disagreed, and to make unmistakably known its own ideas of what the proper policy should be. *That* is responsible government.

It is a defect of the presidential system not merely that it scatters responsibility within the government itself among separate agencies insulated from each other, but that it has no organized opposition. This may seem a strange defect to complain of; nevertheless, it is a real and a serious one. "He who wrestles with us," wrote Burke, "strengthens our nerves, and sharpens our skill. Our antagonist is our helper." A good opposition forces a government to improve itself.

When there is no organized opposition, the criticism of the government's policies is the random and sporadic criticism of individuals as such. They are all saying different things; most of them are ill informed; they are only a babble of voices; they are likely to sound like mere carpers and scolders; and the public is confused. One criticism is often the opposite of another. The government seizes upon this fact, argues that the two criticisms cancel out, and that they prove it must be doing a good job. When individual Congressmen of the opposite party speak only for themselves, each says only those particular things that he thinks will help toward his own reelection in his own district. Criticism under presidential government is commonly aimless, moreover, because except at fixed intervals of four years no immediate result can follow from it.

But under a cabinet form of government the opposition is as organized as the government itself. It has a chosen leader. That leader is its spokesman. That leader must consult his colleagues, just as the premier must, and formulate a responsible program of criticism. The criticism is that of a party eager to prove that it is itself able to take over the government, if need be, at once. The leader of the opposition must therefore forego trivial and carping criticisms, which merely confuse the public, and concentrate on those issues that are centrally important. He must propose some constructive alternative to the course that he condemns. The criticism by an organized opposition, in brief, is not scattered and self-contradictory, but unified and consistent. The public is educated by this clarity. The opposition can itself help to frame issues. It can force the government to take a position on them. In Britain these vital functions are acknowledged. "His Majesty's Opposition" is recognized to be an integral part of the governmental system.

Responsibility, I have said, implies immediate removability. By that I mean immediate removability either of the chief executive himself, or of those in the legislature whose votes have effectively opposed him. It is not difficult to see why this must be so. If the executive's opponents in the legislature cannot be immediately removed by the people, they can continue to oppose his will and make it impossible for him fully to carry out his policies. In that case he cannot be held clearly responsible if the results are bad. If the chief executive himself, on the other hand, cannot be immediately removed when he is unable or unwilling to carry out the popular will, then the people in the interim before removal have a government that is not responsible to them because they cannot reach it. The absence of this immediate removability perverts public thought, for when the people know in advance that they cannot change their executive even when they are dissatisfied with him, they hesitate to hold him clearly responsible for his errors lest they discredit him at home and abroad and bring about a situation of mere chaos.

So difficult has it been under our system to fix responsibility, and so reluctant has the public been even to try to fix responsibility for disaster on men in high places whom it has no means of removing, that a strange doctrine has been preached in America. This doctrine tells us that we were "all of us responsible" for our general unpreparedness, for the loss of the Philippines, or for the disaster at Pearl Harbor. It is not necessary here to try to weigh elaborately the pros and cons of this remarkable contention. It is sufficient to notice that the notion of *universal* responsibility in such a context is a "non-operational" concept. That is to say, it is meaningless for practical action; nothing can be done with it.

The dictionary tells us that responsible means *answerable;* this implies answerable *to* someone. A whole people cannot be operationally answerable to themselves. They cannot replace themselves. They cannot resign, if only because they do not know what to resign *from*. The notion of universal responsibility, in short, is in this context operationally meaningless. It is a vague rhetorical mumble jumble in place of realistic analysis. The notion of the responsibility of specific officials, on the other hand, makes sense. It is an operational concept: one can act on it. If a specific official does well, he can be applauded, promoted or reelected; if he does badly, he can be removed and replaced by someone else who we hope will do better. That is what responsibility really means.

We Americans are usually acknowledged to be the most efficient people in the world as individuals. But we allow ourselves to be organized, or, rather, disorganized, at the top by one of the most miserably inefficient forms of government that it would be possible to conceive. This inefficiency is dangerous always; in time of war it may prove fatal. Our form of government will become increasingly dangerous to our national welfare and security until we reform it in accordance with the principle of Concentration of Responsibility.

Advantages of the Presidential System

Don K. Price *

To keep the administration of government under the control of the people, to invigorate it for effective action in their behalf, and to adjust national policy and its administration to the needs of various regions and institutions—these are urgent problems in this time of crisis.

While in Great Britain as well as in the United States new political and administrative institutions are being worked out to meet the needs of the hour, it is curious that much of the academic and journalistic criticism of government in America is based on a desire to imitate the classic parliamentary system of government. This is all the more curious since the British long ago abandoned the classic parliamentary system as definitely as they abandoned the classic theories of political economy.

Perhaps only a psychoanalyst could explain America's peculiar nostalgia for the obsolescent political institutions of the mother country, but the persistence of her obsession with the parliamentary system makes it not only an interesting theoretical problem but a practical political and administrative issue. . . .

In the British system the nice balance between the Cabinet and the Commons has long since been upset. A half-century ago it was not too unreasonable to argue that the power of the House to dismiss the Cabinet, balanced against the power of the Cabinet to dissolve the House, would always result in a perfect balance of democratic control and executive authority. Within limits, the system worked that way; the Cabinet could never outrage public opinion for fear of losing the support of the House, the members of which went home every week end to get the opinion of the county families if not of the people; the House would never yield to minority interests, for the Cabinet would have the House dissolved if defeated on a policy question, and the members, not wishing to risk their seats in a general election, would not vote against the Cabinet. The equation balanced until a new factor—

* Associate Director of Public Administration Clearing House. Co-author of *City Manager Government in the United States, The British Defense Program and Local Government*. The selection is from Don K. Price, "The Parliamentary and Presidential Systems," *The Public Administration Review,* Vol. III (Autumn, 1943), pp. 317–334. By permission of *The Public Administration Review*.

the electorate—became continuously instead of only potentially effective.

The British in effect did to the House of Commons what the Americans did much earlier to their Electoral College: they made it an automatic machine for registering the vote of the people, as organized into parties, for a Prime Minister. Once the Prime Minister is in office, with the Cabinet that he selects, the House remains in session to enact the bills proposed by the Cabinet, to vote the funds requested by the Cabinet, and to serve as the place where Cabinet ministers make speeches for the newspapers to report to the public but rarely remain to listen to the speeches of other members.

In theory, the House has the power to turn the Cabinet out of office or to refuse to enact the laws it proposes. But that constitutional power seems to be going the way of the King's power to appoint ministers and to veto legislation. Theoretically it exists, but politically it is rarely exercised. Since 1895 only two Cabinets have been refused a vote of confidence and turned out of office by the House, and neither of them had majority support to begin with. A political machine does not elect men to vote against its boss, and the Prime Minister is leader of the party and boss of the machine.

By invading and taking over the executive power the House of Commons destroyed its own independence. The very privilege of holding the Cabinet responsible makes it impossible for the House to think independently. No members of the House will accept office and serve in the Cabinet if the House will not support them. After taking office they will not accept defeat by the House without dissolving the House, calling for a new election, and appealing to the voters to return members who will support them. Because this is constitutionally possible, the members of the House who select and support a Cabinet put the desire to keep their men in office ahead of all minor considerations. The party machinery therefore controls the members fairly rigidly; if the Cabinet wants a measure passed, it will be passed, according to the schedule of debate which the Cabinet considers expedient. As soon as the House of Commons took away the power of the House of Lords by the Parliament Act of 1911 it had to surrender its independence to its leaders; in the cautious words of Sir William Anson, on that date "legislative sovereignty may be said to have passed to the Cabinet." . . .

This control by party machines over the political fortunes of members is a corollary of the similar control by the Cabinet over the legislative procedure. The Cabinet takes for its legislative program just as much of the time of the House as it needs, and during the 1920's and 1930's that was about seven-eighths of the total. The remainder went to consideration of measures proposed by private members (private members are all those except the seventy-odd members who are a part of the "Government" as ministers or assistants to ministers), who drew lots for the privilege of getting their bills considered by the House. No private member's bill could be passed if the Cabinet opposed it, and in practice private members who drew the right to introduce a bill would often ask the Cabinet (or its Whips) for a bill to introduce. . . .

The House of Commons has no committees, in the sense that Congress understands that term. At one stage a bill is referred to a committee—one of several large committees which do not deal with any specialized subject matter, which do not have any fixed membership, and which have no initiative or influence whatever of their own, being little more than devices to permit interested parties to testify. Funds are appropriated and statutes enacted without any independent review, and as the Cabinet requests.

The House votes the funds requested by the Cabinet; it does not have the constitutional power to vote more money for any purpose than the Cabinet asks for, and it has never during this century voted any less. In theory the private member may offer amendments to legislation proposed by the Cabinet, but in practice, as Mr. W. Ivor Jennings puts it, "Members appeal to the minister to accept amendments; they do not compel."

In short, through the party machinery the Cabinet controls the House of Commons on every question that is important enough to be called policy, and it *must* control the House as long as it is "responsible" to the House. The British short-cut the House of Commons to elect their executives as effectively as American voters short-cut the Electoral College. But between elections, since they have reduced their legislature to a voting machine under the control of the Cabinet, they have to rely on the executive to take complete charge of legislation, restrained and guided effectively only by public opinion as it is expressed through the press and through a multitude of private organizations as well as in the House. This is what Mr. Lloyd George meant when he told a Select Committee on Procedure on Public Business in 1931 that "Parliament has really no control over the Executive; it is a pure fiction." . . .

From one point of view, this system brings about an admirable coherence of policy; if a Cabinet is engaged in carrying out a certain program, it has a right to insist that its responsibility not be hampered by the enactment of measures that are inconsistent with it. But, from another point of view, the issue whether certain policies are consistent with each other is the most important issue to be decided, and the most important issue ought to be decided by the supreme authority. . . .

In practice, a legislature cannot exercise control or take an independent line unless it can set up committees to make investigations and recommendations. Under the parliamentary system, the Cabinet is the committee to end all committees; it can tolerate no rivals. It can let other committees conduct investigations and hearings or propose minor amendments, but on any question that a minister chooses to consider policy the House must fall into line. This lets the Cabinet define the scope of "policy," and it is not inclined to leave any controversial issue of importance outside the definition that it formulates. . . .

Thus the House cannot itself make decisions on the several major issues of policy that exist at any one time; constitutionally it can only choose which Cabinet to entrust those decisions to, and as a matter of practical politics it can only keep in office the men it is elected to keep in office.

What is true of policy is even more true of administration. The outlines of departmental organization are fixed by Cabinet action, without legislation, and so are the principal procedures of management, such as budgeting, planning, and personnel. The Cabinet itself now operates through a hierarchy of committees and subcommittees which have no hard-and-fast membership and no formalized existence; any decision on which agreement cannot be reached by common consent is passed on up the line to the War Cabinet, to be settled in the last analysis by the Prime Minister. The freedom of the Cabinet to handle administrative questions with this degree of independence undoubtedly makes for a high degree of coordination. . . .

Congress, since it has not taken over control of administration, has not had to feel responsible as an organization for getting the work of government accomplished. For that reason it has not had to organize itself into a tightly disciplined body, controlled by a single small committee that can act in a businesslike way. If it should do so, the individual members would have to surrender to their organization the individual freedom of action and decision that now enables them to criticize and restrain at their discretion even an administration that they generally propose to support.

During the Napoleonic war, according to Lord Mountararat in *Iolanthe,*

> The House of Lords throughout the war
> Did nothing in particular
> And did it very well.

The House of Commons, which was forced by the bombing of its own quarters to move into those of the House of Lords a couple of years ago, has succeeded to the role which Mr. W. S. Gilbert described with his usual precision of language. The House of Commons has influence, it does an important job, and it does it very well. But it does not control things "in particular." Its control has become so general, it is exercised through so rarefied a medium, that the Commons seem to be following the Lords into the status of one of the "theatrical elements" of the British constitution. . . .

But under the presidential system the public official is under no such restraint. The popular control of the executive is a double control: the people elect the President and the President holds his appointees responsible, retaining the power to discharge them at his discretion; and the people elect the Congress, which controls the executive by statutes, by appropriations, and by investigations. For failing to comply with congressional legislation, a public official is subject to legal penalties; for being so zealously opposed to administration policy that his administrative usefulness is ended, he is subject to removal by his administrative superiors. But since the advocacy of policy by the administrative official does not threaten the tenure of Congressmen, it does not need to be prohibited. Unlike the House of Commons, the Congress retains the power to regulate and control the executive in detail, without putting at stake on any issue the tenure of office of its own members or the President or (generally speaking) subordinate executives. For this reason, it largely divorces questions of policy from questions of party politics in its own proceedings, and executive officials are therefore free to participate in discussions of policy as much as they like—if they are willing to risk their jobs by making themselves no longer useful to the President or his successor. In public discussions of policy they are no more bound as a matter of democratic principle by the restrictions that apply to the British civil service than the President is bound by the restrictions that apply to the King—and for exactly the same reason. . . .

The presidential system, although it unifies responsibility for the execution of a program, does not unify responsibility for the preparation and enactment of a legislative program, as does the parliamentary system. Thus the voters are less able to hold a party clearly responsible for its administration of the program as a whole. On the other hand, the voters have a double check on their government—administratively through the President, their only national representative, and legislatively through the Congress. And they know that, however poorly the President and the Congress are carrying out their responsibilities, they are not kept from exercising their controls by a system of mutual deference that results from the fear of disturbing each other's tenure of office.

CONSTITUTIONAL FEDERALISM

It is easy to arrange complete harmony between executive and legislature by unifying them. But that only covers up the problem; any differences then appear within the legislature itself, and if they are serious enough the several factions, merely by refusing to cooperate, can simply bring government to a standstill. There is nothing automatic in the process by which various political groups combine in a two-party system. That process has to be impelled by a positive community of interest and a positive loyalty to a central symbol. If even a significant minority has different interests and no loyalty and wishes only to make the existing system of government impossible, there can be no orderly opposition, no gentlemanly alternation of "ins" and "outs."

During the nineteenth century there was little friction in the British parliamentary system because it reflected accurately the concentration of political influence. The two previous centuries had been different. . . . A federal constitutional republic needs a separation of powers to keep its federalism adjusted to the wishes of the people. If a single national representative body is omnipotent, it is likely to disregard subordinate loyalties in carrying out its program. Much of the friction that arises between the President and Congress grows out of the conflict between the national program as planned by the executive branch and the impulse of the legislators who modify it in the interests of their constituencies. Since the American executive is not a part of Congress, members of Congress have no institutional incentive to nationalize our system and to ignore the rights and interests of state and local governments. Their lack of individual responsibility for the administration of any federal program enables them to protect local interests and often to overemphasize them.

Senators and Representatives alike may be called to account more effectively by state and local interests than by their national party organizations. The existence of equal representation in the Senate, which the Constitution provides shall be permanent except by the consent of the states, would make it almost impossible to adopt a parliamentary system; it is difficult to imagine the more powerful of the two houses giving control over the executive to the lower house alone, and it is equally fantastic to imagine them acting jointly on every question.

Neither house of Congress has yet been willing to handle legislation by a committee system which is immediately responsible to the wishes of the house as a whole. If the isolationist Senator Reynolds heads the Military Affairs Committee during a world war, the Senate simply puts up with him. The advocates of "responsible" government will know they are making progress when either house decides to remove the chairman of any committee that differs with the house as a whole on a question of policy. And when both houses agree to hold each other's committees mutually responsible, and to discharge their chairmen whenever they disagree with each other, then we shall really be well along toward minimizing local differences and adopting the tightly knit system of parliamentary government.

But in the meantime, the flexibility of the presidential system has its advantages. We can make progress piecemeal, without waiting for a whole program to get approval in principle. The chief executive can get a majority from these groups on one issue, from those groups on another. The party discipline can be relatively loose; groups that oppose the administration on one issue for local or special reasons need not oppose it on the next. A parliamentary cabinet, by tending to command the same majority on all issues (since that majority wants to keep its administration in office) also tends to keep the opposition always against it. If that minority is concentrated in national or regional or social groups that appeal strongly enough to the loyalty of their members, such opposition is apt to become uncompromising and irreconcilable.

The kind of flexibility that the presidential system permits may be useful in dealing with various types of institutions, as well as with various regions or political groups in the state.

The neat logic of the parliamentary system requires the legislature to hold the executive responsible for a little issue in the same way as for a big one, for a technical detail or a subordinate's error in judgment in the same way as for a major policy decision. This was tolerable enough when government had very little to do with the daily lives of people. But now the dividing line between governmental and other institutions has become very shadowy, all sorts of hybrid agencies and corporations exist, and many private corporations and institutions carry on functions for governmental agencies. In such a situation, if a legislature is to keep the whole organism working in the public interest, it cannot depend mainly on a power to hire and fire the head of it, but it must approve one action and condemn another, encourage here and reprove there, expand this agency and restrict that one.

Under the parliamentary system the legislature must always hold a sword over the head of the executive and cannot stoop to slap his hand. To keep a discussion of the British Broadcasting Corporation from bringing up a vote along party lines on which the Cabinet might be ousted, the Cabinet had to set it up by a statute that makes it generally impossible for the House to control its detailed operations or even to ask questions about them. If an executive and a legislature have a degree of mutual independence, the legislature may review the budget of a government corporation and force it to change its policy without conflicting with the chief executive at all.

In their system of legislative control over the executive the British have let the Americans outdo them in refusing to conform to an abstract theory. The omnipotence of the House of Commons, the absolute responsibility of the ministers to Parliament—these ideas are so mystical that they can be explained only in terms of nostalgia for the nineteenth century. They are corollaries to other absolutes of the nineteenth century that we now see melting away—the idea of the absolute sovereignty of each nation, the idea of the complete freedom of private business from governmental interference. In the years that lie ahead, we shall probably work out a great many compromise adjustments between the world program and the interests of nations and their component parts; between governmental policy and the freedom of private corporations and institutions. If a legislative body is going to play an active role in such developments, it will need to be able to make up its collective mind coherently and responsibly, as the parliamentary system has been supposed to require it to do. But it will also need freedom to be inconsistent, to restrain the executive even when it wishes to support him, and to keep people and institutions from being fitted to the Procrustean bed of unified policy. Every step toward unification with the executive is a step toward the loss of that freedom. . . .

It is odd enough to find Americans who seek to increase legislative control over the executive arguing for the system that in Britain has given the executive control over the legislature, or Americans who seek to remove unpopular department heads arguing for a system that in Britain keeps the administrative heads from being known, much less responsible, to the people. But it is even more peculiar, at a time when people are thinking about the creation of international federal institutions, to find Americans proposing to discard the presidential system that has been associated with constitutional federalism, in favor of a system that has never proved its ability to accommodate the interests of diverse areas and populations in a federal republic.

America is a federation that is becoming a nation; the institutional system that has helped her do so will be of interest to the whole world as it moves toward greater unity. She gets her job of government done by popular control over two cooperating branches—an executive that provides unity and enterprise, a legislature that furnishes independent supervision and the restraining influence of local interests. Members of her public service are as varied in their origins and experience as the mixture of public and private institutions in her society itself; the leading members of that service come from private life and return to it freely, looking on the government as the people's agency open to their participation.

The assumptions that the legislature alone represents the people and that the administrative officials and departments are responsible to the people only through the legislature served the cause of democratic government well when the executive departments were under a hereditary monarch. They are the classical assumptions of the parliamentary system. Under the presidential system they can only set up an impossible relationship as the ideal to be attained and handicap the legislative and executive branches alike in their efforts to work together to meet the demands of a new age.

SECTION III

Government and the Economy

American government has continually expanded its functions; it now regulates wide areas of economic activity and is directly concerned with many aspects of the welfare of its citizens. More recently, there has been a demand for large-scale government planning to avoid depressions and ensure a more equitable distribution of wealth.

Most Americans would agree that an essential element of democratic politics is the ability of the community to control the government. If the tendency towards government planning of the economy continues, can our government remain democratic? Professor Hayek, in a widely read work, argues that planning leads down the "Road to Serfdom," but Professor Finer takes issue with him in a spirited rejoinder.

Topic 27

PLANNING AND DEMOCRACY

ROAD TO SERFDOM

Friedrich Hayek *

INDIVIDUALISM AND COLLECTIVISM

The common features of all collectivist systems may be described, in a phrase ever dear to socialists of all schools, as the deliberate organization of the labors of society for a definite social goal. That our present society lacks such "conscious" direction toward a single aim, that its activities are guided by the whims and fancies of irresponsible individuals, has always been one of the main complaints of its socialist critics.

In many ways this puts the basic issue very clearly. And it directs us at once to the point where the conflict arises between individual freedom and collectivism. The various kinds of collectivism, communism, fascism, etc.,

* Dean of the Faculty of Economics at the University of London. Author of *The Pure Theory of Capital, Individualism and Economic Order,* and numerous other works on political economy. The selection is from Friedrich Hayek, *The Road to Serfdom* (Chicago, University of Chicago Press, 1944), *passim*. Reprinted by permission of the University of Chicago Press.

differ among themselves in the nature of the goal toward which they want to direct the efforts of society. But they all differ from liberalism and individualism in wanting to organize the whole of society and all its resources for this unitary end and in refusing to recognize autonomous spheres in which the ends of the individuals are supreme. In short, they are totalitarian in the true sense of this new word which we have adopted to describe the unexpected but nevertheless inseparable manifestations of what in theory we call collectivism.

The "social goal," or "common purpose," for which society is to be organized is usually vaguely described as the "common good," the "general welfare," or the "general interest." It does not need much reflection to see that these terms have no sufficiently definite meaning to determine a particular course of action. The welfare and the happiness of millions cannot be measured on a single scale of less and more. The welfare of a people, like the happiness of a man, depends on a great many things that can be provided in an infinite variety of combinations. It cannot be adequately expressed as a single end, but only as a hierarchy of ends, a comprehensive scale of values in which every need of every person is given its place. To direct all our activities according to a single plan presupposes that every one of our needs is given its rank in an order of values which must be complete enough to make it possible to decide among all the different courses which the planner has to choose. It presupposes, in short, the existence of a complete ethical code in which all the different human values are allotted their due place. . . .

The dispute between the modern planners and their opponents is *not* a dispute on whether we ought to choose intelligently between the various possible organizations of society; it is not a dispute on whether we ought to employ foresight and systematic thinking in planning our common affairs. It is a dispute about what is the best way of so doing. The question is whether for this purpose it is better that the holder of coercive power should confine himself in general to creating conditions under which the knowledge and initiative of individuals are given the best scope so that *they* can plan most successfully; or whether a rational utilization of our resources requires *central* direction and organization of all our activities according to some consciously constructed "blueprint." The socialists of all parties have appropriated the term "planning" for planning of the latter type, and it is now generally accepted in this sense. But though this is meant to suggest that this is the only rational way of handling our affairs, it does not, of course, prove this. It remains the point on which the planners and the liberals disagree.

It is important not to confuse opposition against this kind of planning with a dogmatic laissez faire attitude. The liberal argument is in favor of making the best possible use of the forces of competition as a means of co-ordinating human efforts, not an argument for leaving things just as they are. It is based on the conviction that, where effective competition can be created, it is a better way of guiding individual efforts than any other. It does not deny, but even emphasizes, that, in order that competition should work beneficially, a carefully thought-out legal framework is required and that neither the existing nor the past legal rules are free from grave defects. Nor does it deny that, where it is impossible to create the conditions necessary to make competition effective, we must resort to other methods of guiding economic activity. Economic liberalism is opposed, however, to competition's being supplanted by inferior methods of co-ordinating individual efforts. And it regards competition as superior not only because it is in most circumstances the most efficient method known but even more because it is the only method by which our activities can be adjusted to each other without coercive or arbitrary intervention of authority. Indeed, one of the main arguments in favor of competition is that it dispenses with the need for "conscious social control" and that it gives the individuals a chance to decide whether the prospects of a particular occupation are sufficient to compensate for the disadvantages and risks connected with it.

SECURITY AND FREEDOM

There are two kinds of security, first, security against severe physical privation, the certainty of a given minimum of sustenance for all; and, second, the security of a given standard of life, or of the relative position which one person or group enjoys compared with others; or, as we may put it briefly, the security of a minimum income and the security of the particular income a person is thought to deserve. . . . There is no reason why in a society which has reached the general level of wealth which ours has attained the first kind of security should not be guaranteed to all without endangering general freedom. . . .

An incautious handling of these questions might well cause serious and perhaps even dangerous political problems; but there can be no doubt that some minimum of food, shelter, and clothing, sufficient to preserve health and the capacity to work, can be assured to everybody. Indeed, for a considerable part of the population of England this sort of security has long been achieved.

Nor is there any reason why the state should not assist the individuals in providing for those common hazards of life against which, because of their uncertainty, few individuals can make adequate provision. . . . There is no incompatibility in principle between the state's providing greater security in this way and the preservation of individual freedom.

There is, finally, the supremely important problem of combating general fluctuations of economic activity and the recurrent waves of large-scale unemployment which accompany them. This is, of course, one of the gravest and most pressing problems of our time. But, though its solution will require much planning in the good sense, it does not—or at least need not—require that special kind of planning which according to its advocates is to replace the market. . . .

PLANNING AND DEMOCRACY

It is not difficult to see what must be the consequences when democracy embarks upon a course of planning which in its execution requires more agreement than in fact exists. The people may have agreed on adopting a system of directed economy because they have been convinced that it will produce great prosperity. In the discussions leading to the decision, the goal of planning will have been described by some such term as "common welfare," which only conceals the absence of real agreement on the ends of planning. Agreement will in fact exist only on the mechanism to be used. But it is a mechanism which can be used only for a common end; and the question of the precise goal toward which all activity is to be directed will arise as soon as the executive power has to translate the demand for a single plan into a particular plan. Then it will appear that the agreement on the desirability of planning is not supported by agreement on the ends the plan is to serve. . . .

The difficulty is well known to socialists. It will soon be half a century since the Webbs began to complain of "the increased incapacity of the House of Commons to cope with its work." [1] More recently, Professor Laski has elaborated the argument:

> It is common ground that the present parliamentary machine is quite unsuited to pass rapidly a great body of complicated legislation. The National Government, indeed, has in substance admitted this by implementing its economy and tariff measures not by detailed debate in the House of Commons but by a wholesale system of delegated legislation. A Labour Government would, I presume, build upon the amplitude of this precedent. It would confine the House of Commons to the two functions it can properly perform: the ventilation of grievances and the discussion of general principles of its measures. Its Bills would take the form of general formulae conferring wide powers on the appropriate government departments; and those powers would be exercised by Order in Council which could, if desired, be attacked in the House by means of a vote of no confidence. . . .[2]

It is the essence of the economic problem that the making of an economic plan involves the choice between conflicting or competing ends—different needs of different people. But which ends do so conflict, which will have to be sacrificed if we want to achieve certain others, in short, which are the alternatives between which we must choose, can only be known to those who know all the facts; and only they, the experts, are in a position to decide which of the different ends are to be given preference. It is in-

[1] Sidney and Beatrice Webb, *Industrial Democracy* (1897), p. 800 n.

[2] H. J. Laski, "Labour and the Constitution," *New Statesman and Nation*, No. 81 (new ser.), September 10, 1932.

evitable that they should impose their scale of preferences on the community for which they plan. . . .

The argument by which the planners usually try to reconcile us with this development is that, so long as democracy retains ultimate control, the essentials of democracy are not affected. Thus Karl Mannheim writes:

> The only [*sic*] way in which a planned society differs from that of the nineteenth century is that more and more spheres of social life, and ultimately each and all of them, are subjected to state control. But if a few controls can be held in check by parliamentary sovereignty, so can many. . . . In a democratic state sovereignty can be boundlessly strengthened by plenary powers without renouncing democratic control.[1]

This belief overlooks a vital distinction. Parliament can, of course, control the execution of tasks where it can give definite directions, where it has first agreed on the aim and merely delegates the working-out of the detail. The situation is entirely different when the reason for the delegation is that there is no real agreement on the ends, when the body charged with the planning has to choose between ends of whose conflict parliament is not even aware, and when the most that can be done is to present to it a plan which has to be accepted or rejected as a whole. There may and probably will be criticism; but as no majority can agree on an alternative plan, and the parts objected to can almost always be represented as essential parts of the whole, it will remain quite ineffective. Parliamentary discussion may be retained as a useful safety valve and even more as a convenient medium through which the official answers to complaints are disseminated. It may even prevent some flagrant abuses and successfully insist on particular shortcomings being remedied. But it cannot direct. It will at best be reduced to choosing the persons who are to have practically absolute power. The whole system will tend toward that plebiscitarian dictatorship in which the head of the government is from time to time confirmed in his position by popular vote, but where he has all the powers at his command to make certain that the vote will go in the direction he desires.

It is the price of democracy that the possibilities of conscious control are restricted to the fields where true agreement exists and that in some fields things must be left to chance. But in a society which for its functioning depends on central planning this control cannot be made dependent on a majority's being able to agree; it will often be necessary that the will of a small minority be imposed upon the people, because this minority will be the largest group able to agree among themselves on the question at issue. Democratic government has worked successfully where, and so long as, the functions of government were, by a widely accepted creed, restricted to fields where agreement among a majority could be achieved by free discussion; and it is the great merit of the liberal creed that it reduced the range of subjects on which agreement was necessary to one on which it was

[1] *Man and Society in an Age of Reconstruction* (1940), p. 340.

likely to exist in a society of free men. It is now often said that democracy will not tolerate "capitalism." If "capitalism" means here a competitive system based on free disposal over private property, it is far more important to realize that only within this system is democracy possible. When it becomes dominated by a collectivist creed, democracy will inevitably destroy itself. . . .

If the law is to enable authorities to direct economic life, it must give them powers to make and enforce decisions in circumstances which cannot be foreseen and on principles which cannot be stated in generic form. The consequence is that, as planning extends, the delegation of legislative powers to divers boards and authorities becomes increasingly common. When before the last war, in a case to which the late Lord Hewart has recently drawn attention, Mr. Justice Darling said that "Parliament had enacted only last year that the Board of Agriculture in acting as they did should be no more impeachable than Parliament itself," this was still a rare thing. It has since become an almost daily occurrence. Constantly the broadest powers are conferred on new authorities which, without being bound by fixed rules, have almost unlimited discretion in regulating this or that activity of the people. . . .

ECONOMIC CONTROL AND TOTALITARIANISM

Most planners who have seriously considered the practical aspects of their task have little doubt that a directed economy must be run on more or less dictatorial lines. That the complex system of interrelated activities, if it is to be consciously directed at all, must be directed by a single staff of experts, and that ultimate responsibility and power must rest in the hands of a commander-in-chief whose actions must not be fettered by democratic procedure, is too obvious a consequence of underlying ideas of central planning not to command fairly general assent. The consolation our planners offer us is that this authoritarian direction will apply "only" to economic matters. One of the most prominent economic planners, Stuart Chase, assures us, for instance, that in a planned society "political democracy can remain if it confines itself to all but economic matter." Such assurances are usually accompanied by the suggestion that, by giving up freedom in what are, or ought to be, the less important aspects of our lives, we shall obtain greater freedom in the pursuit of higher values. On this ground people who abhor the idea of a political dictatorship often clamor for a dictator in the economic field.

The arguments used appeal to our best instincts and often attract the finest minds. If planning really did free us from the less important cares and so made it easier to render our existence one of plain living and high thinking, who would wish to belittle such an ideal? If our economic activities really concerned only the inferior or even more sordid sides of life, of course we ought to endeavor by all means to find a way to relieve ourselves from the excessive care for material ends and, leaving them to be cared for by some piece of utilitarian machinery, set our minds free for the higher things of life. Unfortunately, the assurance people derive from this belief that the power which is exercised over economic life is a power over matters of secondary importance only, and which makes them take lightly the threat to the freedom of our economic pursuits, is altogether unwarranted. . . .

The question raised by economic planning is not merely whether we shall be able to satisfy what we regard as our more or less important needs in the way we prefer. It is whether it shall be we who decide what is more, and what is less, important for us, or whether this is to be decided by the planner. Economic planning would not affect merely those of our marginal needs that we have in mind when we speak contemptuously about the merely economic. It would, in effect, mean that we as individuals should no longer be allowed to decide what we regard as marginal.

The authority directing all economic activity would control not merely the part of our lives which is concerned with inferior things; it would control the allocation of the limited means for all our ends. And whoever controls all economic activity controls the means for all our ends and must therefore decide which are to be satisfied and which not. This is really the crux of the matter. Economic control is not merely control of a sector of human life which can be separated from the rest; it is the control of the means for all our ends. And whoever has sole control of the means must also determine which ends are to be served, which values are to be rated higher and which lower—in short, what men should believe and strive for. Central planning means that the economic problem is to be solved by the community instead of by the individual; but this involves that it must also be the community, or rather its representatives, who must decide the relative importance of the different needs. . . . Since under modern conditions we are for almost everything dependent on means which our fellow-men provide, economic planning would involve direction of almost the whole of our life. . . .

Our freedom of choice in a competitive society rests on the fact that, if one person refuses to satisfy our wishes, we can turn to another. But if we face a monopolist we are at his mercy. And an authority directing the whole economic system would be the most powerful monopolist conceivable. While we need probably not be afraid that such an authority would exploit this power in the manner in which a private monopolist would do so, while its purpose would presumably not be the extortion of maximum financial gain, it would have complete power to decide what we are to be given and on what terms. It would not only decide what commodities and services were to be available and in what quantities; it would be able to direct their distribution between districts and groups and could, if it wished, discriminate between persons to any degree it liked. If we remember why planning is advocated by most people, can there be much doubt that this power would be used for the ends of which the authority approves and to prevent the pursuits of ends which it disapproves?

The power conferred by the control of production and prices is almost unlimited. In a competitive society the prices we have to pay for a thing, the rate at which we can get one thing for another, depend on the quantities of other things of which by taking one, we deprive the other members of society. This price is not determined by the conscious will of anybody. And if one way of achieving our ends proves too expensive for us, we are free to try other ways. The obstacles in our path are not due to someone's disapproving of our ends but to the fact that the same means are also wanted elsewhere. In a directed economy, where the authority watches over the ends pursued, it is certain that it would use its powers to assist some ends and to prevent the realization of others. Not our own view, but somebody else's, of what we ought to like or dislike would determine what we should get. And since the authority would have the power to thwart any efforts to elude its guidance, it would control what we consume almost as effectively as if it directly told us how to spend our income. . . .

That the ideal of justice of most socialists would be satisfied if merely private income from property were abolished and the differences between the earned incomes of different people remained what they are now is true. What these people forget is that, in transferring all property in the means of production to the state, they put the state in a position whereby its action must in effect decide all other incomes. The power thus given to the state and the demand that the state should use it to "plan" means nothing else than that it should use it in full awareness of all these effects.

To believe that the power which is thus conferred on the state is merely transferred to it from others is erroneous. It is a power which is newly created and which in a competitive society nobody possesses. So long as property is divided among many owners, none of them acting independently has exclusive power to determine the income and position of particular people—nobody is tied to any one property owner except by the fact that he may offer better terms than anybody else.

What our generation has forgotten is that the system of private property is the most important guaranty of freedom, not only for those who own property, but scarcely less for those who do not. It is only because the control of the means of production is divided among many people acting independently that nobody has complete power over us, that we as individuals can decide what to do with ourselves. If all the means of production were vested in a single hand, whether it be nominally that of "society" as a whole or that of a dictator, whoever exercises this control has complete power over us. . . .

It is pathetic, yet at the same time encouraging, to find as prominent an old communist as Max Eastman rediscovering this truth:

It seems obvious to me now—though I have been slow, I must say, in coming to the conclusion—that the institution of private property is one of the main things that have given man that limited amount of free and equalness that Marx hoped to render infinite by abolishing this institution. Strangely enough Marx was the first to see this. He is the one who informed us, looking backwards, that the evolution of private capitalism with its free market had been a precondition for the evolution of all our democratic freedoms. It never occurred to him, looking forward, that if this was so, these other freedoms might disappear with the abolition of the free market.[1] . . .

Once government has embarked upon planning for the sake of justice, it cannot refuse responsibility for anybody's fate or position. In a planned society we shall all know that we are better or worse off than others, not because of circumstances which nobody controls, and which it is impossible to foresee with certainty, but because some authority wills it. And all our efforts directed toward improving our position will have to aim, not at foreseeing and preparing as well as we can for the circumstances over which we have no control, but at influencing in our favor the authority which has all the power. The nightmare of English nineteenth-century political thinkers, the state in which "no avenue to wealth and honor would exist save through the government," would be realized in a completeness which they never imagined—though familiar enough in some countries which have since passed to totalitarianism.

As soon as the state takes upon itself the task of planning the whole economic life, the problem of the due station of the different individuals and groups must indeed inevitably become the central political problem. As the coercive power of the state will alone decide who is to have what, the only power worth having will be a share in the exercise of this directing power. There will be no economic or social questions that would not be political questions in the sense that their solution will depend exclusively on who wields the coercive power, on whose are the views that will prevail on all occasions. . . .

WHY THE WORST GET ON TOP

We must now examine a belief from which many who regard the advent of totalitarianism as inevitable derive consolation and which seriously weakens the resistance of many others who would oppose it with all their might if they fully apprehended its nature. It is the belief that the most repellent features of the totalitarian regimes are due to the historical accident that they were established by groups of blackguards and thugs. . . . There are strong reasons for believing that what to us appear the worst features of the existing totalitarian systems are not accidental by-products but phenomena which totalitarianism is certain sooner or later to produce.

[1] Max Eastman in the *Reader's Digest,* July, 1941, p. 39.

Just as the democratic statesman who sets out to plan economic life will soon be confronted with the alternative of either assuming dictatorial powers or abandoning his plans, so the totalitarian dictator would soon have to choose between disregard of ordinary morals and failure. It is for this reason that the unscrupulous and uninhibited are likely to be more successful in a society tending toward totalitarianism. Who does not see this has not yet grasped the full width of the gulf which separates totalitarianism from a liberal regime, the utter difference between the whole moral atmosphere under collectivism and the essentially individualist Western civilization. . . .

In order to achieve their end, collectivists must create power—power over men wielded by other men—of a magnitude never before known, and that their success will depend on the extent to which they achieve such power.

This remains true even though many liberal socialists are guided in their endeavors by the tragic illusion that by depriving private individuals of the power they possess in an individualist system, and by transferring this power to society, they can thereby extinguish power. What all those who argue in this manner overlook is that, by concentrating power so that it can be used in the service of a single plan, it is not merely transferred but infinitely heightened; that, by uniting in the hands of some single body power formerly exercised independently by many, an amount of power is created infinitely greater than any that existed before, so much more far-reaching as almost to be different in kind. It is entirely fallacious when it is sometimes argued that the great power exercised by a central planning board would be "no greater than the power collectively exercised by private boards of directors." [1] There is, in a competitive society, nobody who can exercise even a fraction of the power which a socialist planning board would possess, and if nobody can consciously use the power, it is just an abuse of words to assert that it rests with all the capitalists put together. It is merely a play upon words to speak of the "power collectively exercised by private boards of directors" so long as they do not combine to concerted action—which would, of course, mean the end of competition and the creation of a planned economy. To split or decentralize power is necessarily to reduce the absolute amount of power, and the competitive system is the only system designed to minimize by decentralization the power exercised by man over man.

We have seen before how the separation of economic and political aims is an essential guaranty of individual freedom and how it is consequently attacked by all collectivists. To this we must now add that the "substitution of political for economic power" now so often demanded means necessarily the substitution of power from which there is no escape for a power which

[1] B. E. Lippincott, in his Introduction to Oscar Lange and F. M. Taylor, *On the Economic Theory of Socialism* (Minneapolis, 1938), p. 35.

is always limited. What is called economic power, while it can be an instrument of coercion, is, in the hands of private individuals, never exclusive or complete power, never power over the whole life of a person. But centralized as an instrument of political power it creates a degree of dependence scarcely distinguishable from slavery. . . .

There is in the positions of [such] power little to attract those who hold moral beliefs of the kind which in the past have guided the European peoples, little which could compensate for the distastefulness of many of the particular tasks, and little opportunity to gratify any more idealistic desires, to recompense for the undeniable risk, the sacrifice of most of the pleasures of private life and of personal independence which the posts of great responsibility involve. The only tastes which are satisfied are the taste for power as such and the pleasure of being obeyed and of being part of a well-functioning and immensely powerful machine to which everything else must give way. . . . It is only too true when a distinguished American economist concludes from a similar brief enumeration of the duties of the authorities of a collectivist state that "they would have to do these things whether they wanted to or not: and the probability of the people in power being individuals who would dislike the possession and exercise of power is on a level with the probability that an extremely tender-hearted person would get the job of whipping-master in a slave plantation." [1]

We cannot, however, exhaust this subject here. The problem of the selection of the leaders is closely bound up with the wide problem of selection according to the opinions held, or rather according to the readiness with which a person conforms to an ever changing set of doctrines. And this leads us to one of the most characteristic moral features of totalitarianism: its relation to, and its effect on, all the virtues falling under the general heading of truthfulness. . . .

THE END OF TRUTH

The most effective way of making everybody serve the single system of ends toward which the social plan is directed is to make everybody believe in those ends. To make a totalitarian system function efficiently, it is not enough that everybody should be forced to work for the same ends. It is essential that the people should come to regard them as their own ends. Although the beliefs must be chosen for the people and imposed upon them, they must become their beliefs, a generally accepted creed which makes the individuals as far as possible act spontaneously in the way the planner wants. If the feeling of oppression in totalitarian countries is in general much less acute than most people in liberal countries imagine, this is because the totalitarian governments succeed to a high degree in making

[1] Professor Frank H. Knight in the *Journal of Political Economy,* December, 1938, p. 869.

people think as they want them to. This is, of course, brought about by the various forms of propaganda. . . .

It is not difficult to deprive the great majority of independent thought. But the minority who will retain an inclination to criticize must also be silenced. We have already seen why coercion cannot be confined to the acceptance of the ethical code underlying the plan according to which all social activity is directed. Since many parts of this code will never be explicitly stated, since many parts of the guiding scale of values will exist only implicitly in the plan, the plan itself in every detail, in fact every act of the government, must become sacrosanct and exempt from criticism. If the people are to support the common effort without hesitation, they must be convinced that not only the end aimed at but also the means chosen are the right ones. The official creed, to which adherence must be enforced, will therefore comprise all the views about facts on which the plan is based. Public criticism or even expressions of doubt must be suppressed because they tend to weaken public support. As the Webbs report of the position in every Russian enterprise: "Whilst the work is in progress, any public expression of doubt, or even fear that the plan will not be successful, is an act of disloyalty and even of treachery because of its possible effects on the will and on the efforts of the rest of the staff." [1] When the doubt or fear expressed concerns not the success of a particular enterprise but of the whole social plan, it must be treated even more as sabotage.

Road to Reaction

Herman Finer *

The most important historic consequence of the great depression was its grim, detailed, and unchallengeable demonstration of the chronic deficiencies of unbridled competition as the governor of the modern economic system. . . . Depression is a chronic disease of the competitive system. Twenty times, between 1854 and 1933, had the United States suffered such disasters, of varying severity; other countries had been equally afflicted. It can happen twenty times again. . . . The depression crisis and its pressure on the constitutional democracy of both the United States and Great Britain would have become unpredictably grave if World War II had not supervened. . . .

[From premises like these Finer assumes the desirability and necessity for "planning."]

[1] Sidney and Beatrice Webb, *Soviet Communism*, p. 1038.

* Professor of Political Science, University of Chicago. Formerly Lecturer on Political Science, London School of Economics. Author of *British Civil Service, America's Destiny, Theory and Practice of Modern Government,* and many other works. The selection is from Herman Finer, *Road to Reaction* (Boston, Little, Brown & Co., 1945), *passim*. Reprinted by permission of the author.

Planning, says Hayek, is dictatorship and totalitarianism, because it cannot be controlled by a democracy. If "conscious control" is sought by society in the name of one single goal over every end that man can imagine, then "conscious control" is not manageable by democracy. Then he proceeds with the argument as though the word *if* were not there.

The nature of a government, however, depends upon its purposes, upon who develops it, the terms in which its purpose is stated, the conditions attached to their fulfillment, and, above all, upon *where the authority rests.* Is the government one deputed to do a job by the authority of and with continuing responsibility to the people, or is it an alien body which has usurped power? This fundamental question is ignored by Hayek. He forgets that today, and for many a century past, all that is done by anybody in society is done by the sufferance of society. For society consists of more than a willing buyer and a willing seller. Hayek assumes a *single* purpose and "a complete ethical code in which all the different human values are allotted their due places." Thus, " 'the social goal,' or 'common purpose,' for which society is to be organized is usually vaguely described as the 'common good,' the 'general welfare,' or the 'general interest.' " Most would agree that the object of the economic system is the common good, or the general welfare, or, in Jeremy Bentham's phrase, "the greatest happiness of the greatest number."

"The common good," or something like it, is an extremely general phrase, and it was the starting point of Aristotle's *Politics.* Aristotle was sufficiently broad-minded and candid to see and say that there are many different kinds of government adapted to so large a goal. What is the *single* principle to which any planner has committed himself? I do not know of anyone who has made so sweeping a claim as to submerge all individual values or to direct everything. I hate Fascism, Nazism, and Communism, but none of them in fact came anywhere near this sweeping statement of Hayek's, and no planner in any democratic society would accept a totalitarian end. But if Hayek's supposition (*and it is nothing more*) were carried through, it still would not mean either dictatorship or the complete determination of all ethical ends and choices, as set out by him, *provided that its machinery were democratic*—that is to say, so long as its operators were appointed by, or at the behest of, a legislature freely and periodically elected, and changed, by the people. For in that elective process they would be judging the purposes of the plan, and the merits of the men and the measures to carry it out, and the question of repudiating them and choosing other ways and other legislators and executives.

He further maintains that planning will produce the defeat of morality. For, being total, it must require a complete ethical code defining what is right and wrong on everything. Where all the means to be used are the property of society, and are to be used in the name of society according to a unitary plan, "a 'social' view about what ought to be done must guide all decisions.

In such a world we should soon find that our moral code is full of gaps." Yet the code of the world of economic individualism, also, is fearfully full of gaps, and sinister ones; and those who wish to plan economic life better than it is planned today are not concerned with the control of everybody and everything—they are concerned with the serious gaps. . . . Why should he imagine that millions of individuals running a democracy should be more arbitrary than millions running the economic system on the principle of "individualism"? . . .

By insisting upon separating the ends from the means, Hayek can insinuate that *if there is the means*—that is, a central planning agency—it may then be used for the kind of purposes for which the Nazis built up their dictatorship! All his results are achieved by omitting from account the men who build and direct and manage the systems—whether of economic individualism, or planning. But what kind of economic guidance is it which leaves out the men? It is economics on a blackboard. . . .

Who says what "collectivism" is? No one, except Hayek, and he is hardly disinterested. Is it the "collectivism" of Robert Owen, or Karl Marx, or Saint-Simon, or Fourier, or Lenin, or Sidney and Beatrice Webb, or Eduard Bernstein, or Norman Thomas? He does not say. He is not interested in differences and distinctions, though he claims that freedom of choice is morality, and he disregards the teaching of Aristotle, the greatest political and ethical master of all times, who pointed out that the capacity for distinction differentiates the human being from the brutes. Is the species different according to different countries? J. S. Mill, full of good sense, urged the need of a special science to reveal the relationship between the character of different countries and their institutions, of which socialism would be one. Is the species different, and, if so, for what reasons, in Russia, Great Britain, and the United States? Of course it is. . . .

He cannot trust in the people, without limitation; nor in the authority of the majority; nor in the people as the source of power. Yet in Great Britain and in the United States democracy, with its ultimate reliance upon the will of the majority, is the product of at least three hundred years of severe mental labor, careful reflection, and piece by piece development. Most of its secrets have been discovered en route; and one of them, which is only one, and represents the spirit in which democracy has come to be worked, is that "liberty is secreted in the interstices of procedure." . . .

Democracy in reality consists of procedures, and they are such as to provide for steady reflection, to compel attention to argument, to proceed to legislation deliberately, to allow for amendment, to subject the executive to investigation. There are many others of the same nature. Why should it be assumed that this complex, delicately dovetailed but tensile piece of machinery does not exist? . . .

Hayek guys the parliamentary process; not that of the United States but Great Britain's, which, as all students of comparative institutions are aware, is more mature than that of the United States. The people, he asserts, will have adopted "a system of directed economy" on the plea that it will produce great prosperity. The goal will, in the discussion preceding the legislation, have been described by some such term as "common welfare." But in fact, as the discussions on postwar economic and social reconstruction down to the recent general election in Great Britain, the Wagner-Murray-Dingall social security and Kilgore full employment bills show, the party programs have been thoroughly elaborated in the greatest detail by intra-party discussion and amendment and reconciliation among the many interests that are domesticated in each political party, before they are put forward to the electorate in considerable particularity. Even in America the Presidential election of November 1944 showed a noticeable agreement on many such subjects of Republicans and Democrats, with the exception of certain "die-hards" who largely compose Hayek's school of thought.

Consider the list at the recent British general election. The Conservative Party submitted a platform on domestic affairs including the maintenance of a high and stable level of employment, with emphasis on free enterprise; a chance for the small man in industry; possible state co-ordination of the coal industry, certainly much control; assistance to all forms of transport; the reduction of taxation; much housing by both public and private enterprise; assistance to agriculture so that more food may be grown than formerly; the fulfillment of the promises of the government of a wide and important social security system based on the insurance principle; a state medical service for all; wide educational opportunity; stimulation of industrial research; regulation of monopolies. The Labour Party proposed to nationalize the coal mines, the iron and steel industry, fuel and power; to regulate banking heavily, to give full social security, full employment, a national health scheme, housing and education in greater measure than the other parties, and, when necessary, to take over monopolies otherwise unmanageable.

This discussion is not, as can be realized, merely about means but about ends. It would be ridiculous for any party to come forward with the demand for what a Conservative Prime Minister, Mr. Baldwin, once called "a doctor's mandate." This is worth noting, for the parties must reconcile all their own internal groups. . . .

Hayek cannot see how, in a planned state, groups can settle their differences over the course to be followed when the state is to undertake various business projects. He pretends that in this case it is necessary to leave it to "the discretion of the judge or authority in question" to decide what is "fair and reasonable." This again is hypothetical. The solution depends on how the law of the plan is constructed, and the ability and state of mind of the negotiators in parliament, in the courts, and in regulatory bodies such as the Tariff Commission, the Interstate Commerce Commission, the Federal Communications Commission, and the Securities and Exchange Commission, which are solving problems and building up important experience. But principally it depends on nationwide debate conducted over the course of years, assisted by the sifted results of scientific research and experience. The plan, such as it is, emerges from the majority; and only that emerges from the majority which the majority can thereafter operate. That is the answer to Hayekian obscurantism. . . .

What is troublesome about the idea of repealing a law or a set of laws which govern production and distribution of wealth? That there is wasted expenditure, and that people who have been living under the expectation of one kind of law now must live under another. But that is part of freedom and progress; and the effect of disturbance will be weighed against the possible advantages of change. Even the rule of *stare decisis* is not allowed by educated judges to hold up essential change forever.

The people will do what they can bear and afford to do. All this implies that there will still be in full operation periodical elections and freedom of speech. Of course it does. That is the condition which in democracies will govern the pace and the comprehensiveness of their planning. Whatever proves itself satisfactory to the people, they having the untrammeled right to say what is and what is not unsatisfactory with all the vehemence which they like to use, will remain—even though there are as now, in every form of government, people who remain unpersuaded by the opinion of the majority. They may still inveigh against the law and its administration, and try to persuade the majority to adopt their views. . . .

Why Hayek postulates a group of planners estranged from, but dominating, the nation he does not say. It is a perfect obsession with him: ". . . an authority directing the whole economic system would be the most powerful monopolist conceivable . . . it would have complete power to decide what we are to be given and on what terms." He doesn't say who would give "it" these monopolistic powers. . . . Hayek's assumption is that political power is neither limited in scope, restricted in authority, responsible in operation, nor co-operative and decentralized in execution. . . . There is much planning already in Great Britain and the United States, much more than Hayek likes—hence his book. The plans have worked and there has been no assumption of dictatorial powers. On the contrary, if we look into the operation of democracy we see more and more rather than fewer legislative, judicial, and popular controls over policy and its execution.

Hayek concludes, "It is for this reason [that the statesman would have to choose between disregard of ordinary morals and failure] that the unscrupulous and uninhibited are likely to be more successful in a society tending towards totalitarianism." He has fallen into this mischievous and almost irresponsible error because when he says totalitarianism he classes both the dictatorships we know and *any* planning in the same class, and so attributes to democratic planning the spirit, purposes, methods, and morals of dictatorship. From this it is but a step to foreseeing coercion, minority dictatorship, "regimentation" of all life, control over private lives as over men at work, propaganda, the teaching of a single view of life, and there is also thrown in "the communism of women"! Since the dictator is determined not to fail, he will, of course, bring in the scum at the top—the hangmen.

The reason that the worst got to the top in totalitarianism is simple: it is because there the worst *make* the top. They can get to the top only where they are allowed by society to make up the top. And one of the kinds of society in which the worst get to the top because the worst are allowed to make the top is, I suggest to Hayek (and he may consult Adam Smith about this also), a society of economic individualism. These are some of the more notorious names in the past economic history of the United States: Astor, Marshall Field, Rhinelander, Elkins, Hill, Gould, Stanford, Rockefeller, Vanderbilt, Morgan, Insull, Whitney. . . .

In our time the only system of government which will give Hayek what he wants—namely, the protection of economic individualism in the extreme form that he wants it—is dictatorship, which coerces whole peoples, and sneers at rule by persuasion.

The character of planning by government depends on which men plan; whether they plan totally; whether they plan swiftly, whether they intend to carry out their plan hurriedly; whether it is freely assented to by a public conscious of the issues involved; whether the public retains the right of dissent and reversal; whether there is a proper machinery of governmental responsibility, whether the schemes are decentralized; whether the public representatives are well-selected—in short, whether the whole process of planning is genuinely democratic. . . .

Is it not possible to decentralize the power of government—is it, indeed, not already what is achieved in the practice of government? Are there not many institutional devices to prevent the action of government from being oppressive and to keep it accountable? Why should more rationality and honor be attributed to millions struggling with each other economically, than to the millions democratically composing their own laws and controlling their responsible administration? If Montesquieu and the fathers of the American Constitution, facing this question, could answer it with the separation of powers within the government, why need Hayek answer it by excluding from the governmental field most of the activity ties of mankind that he regards as important? From Alexander Hamilton to the days of Hayek stretch one hundred and fifty years, and men have discovered and applied firm and fruitful devices, that Hayek knows not of; and even then, the devices depend on the continuing support and good sense of the men.

It is no accident that the system of economic competition leads steadily to centralization within the economic field itself; while in the state, centralization has been accompanied by the recognition of the need for decentralization and the practical establishment of it. . . .

It is from in and around the life of the parties and the contiguous and competing associations that the steady stimulus comes to state enterprise: to do or not to do; to make, supply, and deliver in such and such quantities the goods and services of various kinds. Not in all detail, for there are other well-known "market techniques" and "market research" developed by public administration no less than by private business, which can be the monitor of state-directed production and distribution. The idea that in a planned economy there would be no consumer's choice is one more of those suggestions which are refutable by the merest tyro in economic theory, and which Hayek could not have made inadvertently. . . .

The public in a planned state would demand goods and services of as many varieties as it does today. It would have just as much interest in abundance and change, and would express that interest to the managers of the state stores. Municipal planning of gas, water, and electricity supply was advocated in England by small and big business because government officials could be trusted better than their fellow businessmen to provide the services dependably, without discrimination between consumers, and at a lower cost of production. Secondly, there would be a focus of social demand in the legislatures and in the public services themselves, and they could be expected to continue to propose such vast enterprises as the Birmingham (England) gas department which operates the largest and most inventive artificial gas plant in the world, and such large projects as the Tennessee Valley Authority and other hydroelectric schemes, and the Maritime Commission, and the Reconstruction Finance Corporation. . . .

The two greatest inventions of the nineteenth century are representative and responsible democracy, and expert and impartial public administration. Public administration, besides the personnel, consists of three things to which attention is being given night and day by hundreds of anxious minds: the federal-state relationship, retaining the advantages of local thought and local application of measures; the written and personal liaison between the center and the extremities; and the securing of the responsibility of the official for the due fulfillment of the plan of democracy, as stated in the law. The checks internal to the administration are themselves almost a substitute for the old-fashioned separation of powers. . . .

CONCLUSION

There are two kinds of freedom. One is merely the absence of obstruction; it is essential; but it may be consistent with mere passivity. The second kind of freedom is strength or power, the ability to take action, or self-expression. It may be noted that there is in this second kind of freedom nothing which anyone would wish to restrict; on the contrary it is to the advantage of everyone to increase and use it.

Men have no freedom worth mentioning when they have no possibility of exercising their faculties and energy as they feel they must. Freedom in this dynamic sense cannot come to men, in all the abundance potential in our time, unless they collectively manage a large proportion of the social resources and economic equipment. The present economic waste by mismanagement is enormous; it is nothing but lost or unexploited strength; it constitutes a loss of freedom to many. . . .

There is certainly no need to be terrified by the bogey that social security provision will petrify society into a condition of "status." For the social security of today and tomorrow may change whenever the millions are convinced that change is desirable. . . .

Three mighty developments of the last century and a half offer men a high degree both of welfare and of freedom. They are the great technological advances, already immense, and about to be even mightier servants of man, administrative science, and the principles and practice of democracy. It is for the latter two to use the first for humanity's advantage. . . .

We have arrived at a technique and spirit of democratic government never equaled in human history, because there were never before such vast and dense agglomerations of human beings; never such a diffusion of knowledge and moral and practical wisdom; never such means of rapid communication among the people themselves and their myriad groupings. Immense areas have been reduced to the space-time-feeling dimensions of the single city of a hundred and fifty years ago.

Society as a whole, acting through its rationally constituted and deputed organs, is in a far better position than at any time in history to move forward to the collective management of many spheres of social life. When men attain to such a responsibility they certainly acquire freedom. This does not mean a government over all and everything. Society is now so able because what was before known only to individuals is now better known to social institutions, and can be even better known still through its own arrangements for the promotion and advancement of knowledge. Again, what was hitherto willed by individuals severally, and showed shortcomings in the consequent welfare for all, can be better willed and fulfilled by the social agents of all men freely choosing their purposes and deputies. The organs for fact-finding, analysis, interpretation, and the graduated and discriminating expression of popular approval and disapproval, were, in their contemporary quality, never before dreamed of. Finally, the organs of external control are sound and trustworthy. . . .

Justice is the great unknown quantity of political philosophy. Pascal said that man is ignorant of it. Yet man must act as though he were not. Justice is not a self-contained constant capsule, or a gift, or an instinct, with sure, objective, and unchanging contours. It is a relationship between men in society; and, revealed to individual minds in the passage of time, it is accepted in the shape and degree which are tolerable to all at the speed at which all can tolerate change. This process can surely never be better midwived than by popular sovereignty and the process of discovery by free debate. If it were not to risk the mixture of like and unlike, we could recommend Justice Holmes's opinion that the best test of truth (say, justice) "is the power of the thought to get itself accepted in the competition of the market. . . . It is an experiment, as all life is an experiment." Justice is recognized, revealed, stimulated by the play of competitors in the broad and open forum of politics. Justice in our time is above all likely to mean an appropriate degree of economic welfare and a settled insistence on the career open to the talents.

The regulator and producer of abundance and justice is public freedom, and this also creates those private felicities and security which constitute private freedom, in the sense of the capacity for continuous initiative. Public freedom unreservedly demands free association, election and recall of government, freedom of speech, writing, opinion, and opposition. It is within these that men learn their responsibility that marches with their endowment of authority, the common sense and tact of more than everyday affairs. The prospects of its free and advantageous use have been immensely improved by the remarkably able and at the same time magnanimous use of the power of democratic society in the successful conduct of World War II. Free government has truly come of age, and offers, to the millions upon millions whose minds and characters have never yet been given the opportunity to contribute to the common good, a broad avenue of advancement. Men have the right to comprehend and employ their confidence, and to make of their increasing abundance and power a yet more sensitive justice and more abundant freedom. With Walt Whitman, social democracy may respond, to the bare, poor, deprecating, and unsuccessful philosophy of "Snatch!" which is the spirit of economic individualism:—

> Come, I will make the continent indissoluble,
> I will make the most splendid race the sun ever shone upon.

Part IV

AMERICA IN WORLD AFFAIRS

East-West Conflict

What Policy for America?

SECTION I

East-West Conflict

Participation in two world wars in one generation suggests that the American system of government, and its very survival, are inextricably linked with developments abroad.

Most American political leaders believe that we are confronted with a pattern of Communist aggression similar to and perhaps more powerful than the Nazi aggression which led to World War II. On the other hand, the leaders of the Soviet Union contend that "the history of the Soviet state bears witness to its unswerving struggle for peace." Before considering alternative foreign policies available to us at this time, it is clear that we must examine the goal of Soviet policy. The question is discussed by James Burnham, Andrei Vishinsky, and George Kennan.

The exchange of British and Russian diplomatic notes which contains conflicting interpretations of recent international events is presented to provide some basis for judgment on this issue. (Though the discussion is in terms of Anglo-Soviet relations, the issues canvassed are also the basis of Soviet-American differences.)

Topic 28

THE GOAL OF SOVIET POLICY

STRUGGLE FOR THE WORLD

James Burnham *

We have already discovered, from several convergent directions, that the ultimate goal of communist, and therefore of Soviet, policy is the conquest of the world. This is not a surprising or a fresh discovery. It is a secret only to the ignorant or the deceived.

There has never been any mystery about this goal, except for those who have wanted it to be a mystery. From the very beginnings of communism,

* Professor of Philosophy at New York University. Former Editor of *The New International.* Author of *The Managerial Revolution, The Machiavellians,* etc. The selection is from James Burnham, *The Struggle for the World* (John Day Co., Inc., 1947), Ch. 7. Copyright by James Burnham. Reprinted by permission of author and publisher.

not only from the formation of the Bolshevik faction in 1903 but from the time of Marx' and Engels' *Manifesto,* this goal has been reiterated in theory and furthered in practice. Marx told his followers, "You have a world to win," just as Stalin proclaims in his chief textbook: "Here is the greatest difficulty of the Russian Revolution, its supreme historical problem—the need to solve international problems, the need to promote the world revolution." The Program of the International boasts in its introduction that it "is the only international force that has for its program the dictatorship of the proletariat and Communism, and that openly comes out as the *organizer of the international proletarian revolution.*" It announces with confidence and satisfaction "the inevitable doom of capitalism." Part III of the Program of the International has as its title: "The Ultimate Aim of the Communist International—World Communism." The official *History of the Communist Party,* required reading for all communists everywhere, declares: "Study of the history of the Communist Party strengthens the certainty of the final victory of the great task of the Lenin-Stalin Party: the victory of Communism in the whole world."

The fact that this is the communists' belief, that world conquest is, in their own minds, their goal, is not, by itself, particularly important. There have been, and still are, other groups and even individuals who have believed in this same goal of world conquest. . . .

When, however, we find that a belief in the goal of world conquest is combined with both sufficient means to give a chance of achieving it, and actions which in fact work toward it, then the purpose must be taken quite literally, at face value. This was the case with Nazism; and it seems also to have been true of at least one section of the Shintoist-militarist Japanese leadership. It is much more obviously true of communism. In communist doctrine, there is not the slightest ambiguity about the goal of world conquest. In action, communists work always and everywhere toward that goal. And at the present time the means at their disposal, in numbers, material resources, and psychological influence, are enough to give them a very substantial probability of reaching it.

However often this plain truth is repeated, very few of the leaders and citizens of the democratic nations really believe it. They do not believe it, I suppose, because they do not want to believe it. It is, we may grant, an uncomfortable belief, putting a pistol to the will, and demanding just Yes or No as an answer. Nevertheless, and in spite of however many exorcisms by Henry Wallace or the Dean of Canterbury, it is true, and will continue to be true, until the issue is decided.

II

The communist doctrine, hardened as it is into a fixed mental pattern by a century's tradition, is not the only force impelling communism toward the goal of World Empire, though it alone is sufficient to establish and maintain World Empire as the goal of communist activity. At least three other major pressures are operative:

1. We have already noticed, in some detail, the senses in which contemporary society is ripe for World Empire. This is evident to all observers, but seems particularly clear when analyzed from the Marxian point of view, in terms of which communists understand the world. The international division of labor, the development of rapid transport and communication, the complex inter-relationship of world industries, the unavoidable impact of each region of the world upon every other, the patent archaism of the present political divisions, the class stratifications ignoring national boundaries, all constitute what Marxists call the "material conditions" for a world state. A world state, Marxian reasoning concludes, must therefore necessarily come into being, since "political super-structure" is necessarily determined by "material conditions." . . .

The advent of atomic weapons makes the question of World Empire incomparably sharper and more immediate.

2. Another force driving the communists toward world expansion, of a type very familiar in historical experience, is the effect of economic and social failure within the Soviet Union, the primary base of communist power.

The stories about the mighty successes of socialist industry within the socialist fatherland, about the communist "solution of the economic problem," are, of course, mythical. The fact is that the great mass of the Russian people has lived, under the communists, at a material level well below that which it had under Tsarism, and that this level has declined during the Five Year Plans. Hunger, cold, and squalor, as well as terror and slavery, are the products of a quarter century of communist victories. Soviet industry is for the most part incompetent, inefficient, and qualitatively at a low level. The mass of the terrorized population, moreover, bitterly hates, as well as fears, the communist masters.*

Under these circumstances, the expansion of communist rule holds out several substantial promises.

First, according to the time-tested formula, it serves to divert attention from the internal difficulties. Victories elsewhere make up for defeats at home. A ready-made excuse is provided for the wretched living conditions. The discontent and anger of the people are deflected from the heads of the communist rulers.

Second, the looting of conquered territories means a temporary addition of desperately needed consumers' goods. From the start of the present stage of expansion in the Baltic nations, the communists have systematically stripped the stores, warehouses, barns and homes of the conquered territories. It should not be imagined that the individual soldiers who have done the initial looting have been permitted to keep commodities other than what they have put into their stomachs. After the first outbursts die down,

* See the note at the end of this article.

the soldiers are in turn looted by the state, and the goods distributed according to the plans of the rulers.

Third, the new territories yield the communists vast new reserves of manpower, upon which they rely to make up for industrial inferiority.

Fourth, the communists gain new capital goods—factories, mines, railroads, machines.

3. Finally, even if World Empire were not the positive goal of communism, it would, from the communist standpoint, be a necessary aim as a defensive measure. The communists believe, and have always believed, that there are only two alternatives for modern society: communism or capitalism. In spite of what people may "subjectively" think, they are all "objectively" lined up on one side or the other: there is no in-between. When, therefore, communism became a serious world force by conquering a large section of the earth and its inhabitants, an inescapable historical dilemma was presented. Either capitalism would destroy the new communist world, or communism would conquer the remainder of capitalism. (Somewhat paradoxically, the communists hold the latter result to be in the long run "inevitable.") The showdown might be drawn out or for a while postponed, but it cannot be avoided.

World capitalism (in which they include everything except themselves) is at present, they believe, in its death agony. It is driven by its internal contradictions to an ever more ruthless policy of world exploitation. Above all, it hopes to get renewed strength by opening up to exploitation the areas and peoples of the Soviet Union, now shielded by the proletarian dictatorship. This objective, the communists believe, has nothing to do with the personal opinions and wishes of the capitalists themselves, or their political leaders. It follows necessarily from the nature of capitalism in decline. It is inevitable, just as war under capitalism is inevitable; and just as it is inevitable that the "real meaning" of every war of the present time is an onslaught against the communist fortress of the Soviet Union.

Stalin, in his principal theoretical work, *Problems of Leninism,* has summed up the issue as follows:

> The basic fact . . . is that there no longer exists a worldwide capitalist system. Now that a Soviet country has come into existence . . . worldwide capitalism has ceased to exist. The world has been severed into two camps, the imperialist camp and the anti-imperialist camp. [Vol. I, p. 369.]
>
> We are living, not merely in one State, but in a system of States; and it is inconceivable that the Soviet Republic should continue to exist interminably side by side with imperialist States. Ultimately, one or another must conquer. Pending this development, a number of terrible clashes between the Soviet Republic and the bourgeois States must inevitably occur. [Vol. I, p. 56, quoting from Lenin, *Works,* Russian edition, Vol. XVI, p. 102.]

As if to make certain that the entire world should know that nothing of this doctrine had been abandoned as a result of the reformist demagogy of the Teheran Period, Stalin declared in his election speech of Feb. 10, 1946:

It would be incorrect to think that the war arose accidentally or as a result of the fault of some statesman. Although these faults did exist, the war arose in reality as the inevitable result of the development of the world economic and political forces on the basis of monopoly capitalism.

In terms of these beliefs, world conquest is for the communists the only means of self-defense. Any war which they conduct, no matter who fires the first shot or first invades—as, for example, the Finnish War of 1939—is by definition a defensive war.

The naive appeasers of the communists imagine that these beliefs of theirs can be altered if we show the communists that we are really their friends, if we talk softly to them, and grant everything they want. They overlook, to begin with, that what the communists want is the world. And they do not understand that, in the eyes of the communists, this friendliness from the class enemy must be either a hypocritical deception or a symptom of stupidity and weakness. Nothing is going to change these beliefs. Certainly no rational argument or evidence is going to change them, because, in the fundamental point that communism must either conquer the world or be itself destroyed, the communist belief happens to be true.

III

Within the framework of the ultimate goal of World Empire, the specific present communist objective is the preparation for the open phase of the Third World War. Preparation for the war is the basic communist "line." As always, this means that every communist activity, no matter how seemingly remote, is directly or indirectly subordinate to the "line." The Fourth Five Year Plan, the policy in the C.I.O., the new purges, Gromyko's behavior at the Security Council or the Atomic Commission, the seizure of Austrian industries, the coup in Iran, the formation of the World Federation of Trade Unions or the recognition of Perón, the fighting by the Chinese communists or the Anti-United States agitation throughout Latin America, the application by the British Communists to join the Labour Party or the campaign on the Franco question, the reorganization of the Red Army and Navy or the attempt to unify the United States seafaring and waterfront unions, the call for a monopolistic American Authors' Authority or the intransigence on Germany, the step-up in activities among the U.S. Negroes and the nursing of Moslem friendship: all these and all the rest are simply part of the preparation for the war. Soviet policies are mysterious only to those who persist in looking at them from the outside, separately and piecemeal, who refuse to use the key which the communists themselves supply to all who wish to use it. If we have a general understanding of the nature and goal of communism, all that we further need is a grasp of the main current line. Then everything fits into place, from slogans to assassinations, and the policy as a whole is revealed to be not in the least mysterious, but more direct and simple than any other in the world.

For convenience, the task of the preparation for the Third World War may be subdivided into the following:

1. The attempt to consolidate effective domination of the Eurasian continent.

2. The simultaneous attempt to weaken and undermine all governments and nations not under communist control.

In the present section, I shall confine myself to the first of these.

In August, 1939, the communists, in this respect heirs of the Russian Empire, held control of what geopoliticians call the "inner Heartland" of the "World Island." For the first time in world history, the inner Heartland (Central Eurasia) possessed a mass population, a high level of political organization, and a considerable industrialization.

In August, 1945, communist domination, though not yet fully consolidated, extended in the West to a line from Stettin south to the Dalmatian coast, and East to include all of the Balkans except Macedonia, Thrace, and the geopolitically unimportant Greek Peninsula. This line on the West, except for the omission of Macedonia and the Turkish territory north of the Dardanelles, corresponds exactly with what Mackinder defined a generation ago as the outer border of the Heartland.

In the East communist domination reached via the Kuriles to outflank the Americas on the North, and moved into northern Korea, Manchuria, and North China. Its two lines of egress from the Heartland into China (into Manchuria, and further south into Sinkiang) are also those previously defined by Mackinder.

In the West, the communist pressure pushes against the northern flank (Scandinavia), with the main force exerted against Germany, the key to the rest of Europe. This thrust is combined with an attempted envelopment from the rear (Spain) and what might be described as a temporary holding operation in France and the lesser European states.

In the Middle East, the pressure is felt throughout, in Afghanistan, Iran, Iraq, Turkey, down into Palestine and the lesser Arab states, and for that matter on into Egypt and North Africa generally. From the point of view of the thinking of traditionally naval powers, like Britain and the United States, this constitutes a "threat to the Empire lifeline," and is linked with the drive on Trieste and toward Italy. However, as understood from the point of view of land power and of fundamental geopolitical relationships, it is perhaps more fundamentally a drive across the land bridge to the southern adjunct of the Heartland, in Africa.

In the Far East, the pressure is directed toward all of China. In India, which is outside the Heartland and of secondary importance from a geopolitical point of view, the direct force from the Heartland is not yet being exerted. The pressure is felt from within, through the influence of the Indian Communists, the N.K.V.D. [now the M.V.D.] and military agents, and as an effect of the general pro-Moslem orientation.

We may picture the perspective through the geometrical analogy of a set of concentric rings around an inner circle.

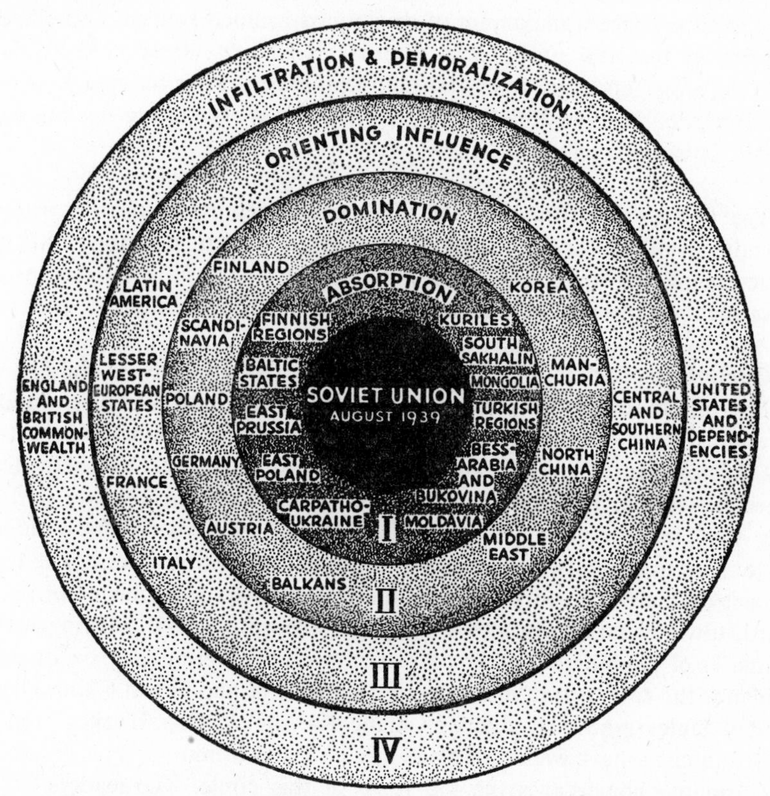

THE FIELD STRUCTURE OF THE COMMUNIST POWER

(This figure is not meant to be either complete or in every respect exact. Its purpose is to represent not a static state of affairs, but the general character of a dynamic historical process.)

The inner, magnetic core of the system is the established Soviet Union itself, within the boundaries temporarily crystallized, after the Civil War and until August, 1939. In preparation for the Second World War, this was the communist fortress. It now becomes, in preparation for the Third, the inner defensive ring of the greater Eurasian fortress.

The consolidation of the Eurasian fortress as a whole requires, for the inner core, a series of measures which are already well started. Economically, the new Five Year Plans are designed to expand at all costs the basic war industries, and to make a supreme effort to overtake the United States in the production of atomic weapons. New contingents of millions of slave laborers, drawn from the Russian people and from the conquered regions, provide a flexible mass labor force that can be concentrated at the will of the leadership on the economic tasks. The army, navy and air forces are being tightened and qualitatively developed, with the educational system revised to produce a maximum of disciplined, trained soldiers and officers. Politically, the new purges, the familiar N.K.V.D. terror methods, and suitable propaganda are re-establishing firm control over the people, which was somewhat loosened by the aftermath of the War, and are steeling them for the coming struggle.

The first ring, surrounding the inner circle, represents those territories already absorbed, or scheduled soon to be absorbed, directly within the structure of the Soviet Union proper. This step was prepared for, as we have seen, by the federalist revision of the Soviet Constitution.

Circle II represents those nations which the communists, in the first instance, aim to dominate (rather than absorb directly into the Soviet Union) through one or another type of puppet government. Poland, Yugoslavia, Czechoslovakia, Rumania, Hungary, Bulgaria, Albania, Northern Iran, Northern Korea, Eastern Germany, Eastern Austria, are already well inside this circle. To suppose that they will ever, voluntarily or by merely diplomatic maneuvers, be permitted to escape, is political idiocy. The communist design is, of course, exactly the opposite: to draw them further inward, toward and finally into Circle I of Absorption; and to bring within Circle II of Domination other nations now balancing uneasily on its edge. Finland, the rest of Iran and Austria, Manchuria and North China (if the United States graciously ditches Chiang Kai-shek), Iraq, Turkey, and all of Scandinavia have even today one foot over the brink.

Germany, however, is the top prize of this circle. The leaders of the democratic nations, who do not have an over-all political line, and who are always distracted by side issues, have yet to understand the meaning of the kind of concentrated Bolshevik *campaign* which is being directed toward the domination of Germany. Domination of Germany will in turn guarantee effective domination of the entire European continent, and will complete in the West the structure of Fortress Eurasia.

The importance assigned to Germany dates back to Lenin, and before him to Napoleonic days, when Prussian officers and divisions helped in the defeat of Napoleon. Lenin many times declared that German technology plus Russian manpower and resources would clinch the victory of the world revolution. From 1918 to 1924 the communists tried repeatedly to carry through a German communist revolution. Thereafter they continued intimate relations with Germany. They brought in German machines and technicians, and permitted German officers of the army outlawed by the Versailles Treaty to gain experience training the Red Army. The Stalin-Hitler Pact was by no means so unprecedented a reversal as the world found it.

Hitler's decision to launch the war against Russia did not end this more ancient perspective. As early as October, 1941, the communist veteran Walter Ulbricht was directing the formation of a communist-controlled league among the German war prisoners. In a speech delivered to the Moscow Soviet on November 6, 1942, Stalin assured all Germans: "It is not our aim to destroy Germany, for it is impossible to destroy Germany . . . It is not our aim to destroy all military force in Germany, for every literate person will understand that this is not only impossible in regard to Germany . . . but it is also inadvisable from the point of view of the future." On July 12–13, 1943, the Free Germany National Committee was formed in Moscow, under the nominal chairmanship of Junker General Walther von Seydlitz, captured at Stalingrad, and the real direction of Wilhelm Pieck, leading German communist and former Secretary of the Communist International. . . .

So alarming to England and the United States did the prospect of the Free Germany Committee become, that at Yalta they obtained Stalin's signature to a paragraph renouncing any plan to install the Committee as a new German government. As always, for the communists, such a renunciation was purely of form, not of substance.

The Free Germany Committee is the expression of the communist plan for Germany. Its program is a trap, baited for Germans with what seems to be the offer of a kind of junior partnership in the Soviet Eurasian, and future World, Empire. In reality, it aims at the incorporation of Germany under the monolithic communist control. This program stands unchanged by the Yalta Declaration, just as the Free Germany activities, under a variety of names, continue unabated.

The terms of the German capitulation gave eastern Germany to the communists. From eastern Germany as a base, they eye Germany as a whole. Already, by mid-1946, the progress in eastern Germany was sufficient to permit the preliminary moves toward the rest of Germany. The communists had swallowed the socialists by forcing them into the "Socialist Unity Party." The Free Germany Committee members, communist-trained abroad, were brought back from Mexico, New York, Latin America, London, Stockholm, Moscow. For the first time since the War, in Paris during June, 1946, Molotov came out against federalism and dismemberment, and for a "united Germany." By then he believed that the outcome was assured, that a united Germany would be a communist Germany.

The policy followed in the preliminary organization of eastern Germany is, in its fundamentals, the same as that throughout the area of "domination." There need not be any set formula under which the domination is to be achieved. Great flexibility, and many diverse forms of political movement, of social structure and of government, are possible. The one constant, as always, is the elimination of all power except communist power. Temporary concessions, favoritism, conversion, economic pressures, shuffling and re-shuffling of parties and governments, deception, and—essential and continuous prop to all the rest—the terror, threats, torture, killing, exile, forced labor, all of these, in mixed and varying dosages, gradually weed out all opposition, past, present, future, or imaginable. Coalitions, elections, treaties, mergers, these are shadows. The substance is the communist drive toward all power.

The boundary in the system of concentric rings between Circle II (Domination) and Circle III (Orienting Influence) is not always precise. Circle III represents those nations which the Soviet Union does not at the given moment feel in a position to absorb or reduce to outright puppet status, but within which it seeks enough influence to guarantee a pro-Soviet foreign policy, or at least to neutralize any tendency toward an anti-Soviet foreign policy. In Europe this includes the effort to hinder the formation of the so-called Western Bloc. In Latin America it means pressure to cut the nations loose from subordination to the United States.

The modes of influence in Circle III vary from direct pressure exerted by the Soviet state or the internal communist parties, to various forms of concession and conciliation. As examples of the latter, it may be noted that the Soviet government was the first to grant partial recognition to the De Gaulle Committee, and the first to grant full recognition to the Badoglio government in Italy and to Perón in Argentina. During 1946 it shipped grain to France. It offered, and in some cases put through, generous economic deals with various Latin American nations. Within all the nations of Circle III, the communist parties call for unity and collaboration in national fronts. They combine this call for unity with threats and strikes or other hostile actions to enforce abandonment of anti-communist or anti-Soviet tendencies. Within France and Italy and throughout most of Latin America, the communists have secured control of the greater part of the organized labor movement. There, and in China, they are ready to enter into coalition governments, where their veto power can be exercised in the cabinets.

In the nations of Circle III (including those, like the Scandinavian nations, which, though still in Circle III, are already drawn toward Circle II), the communists' policy is to strive for socio-political conditions that permit the communist movement to function effectively. That is why they advocate, for the present, a measure of democracy within them: communists abandon the forms of democracy when, but not until, communist domination is assured. That explains, also, their readiness to dissolve or merge national Communist Party organizations, and their acceptance of posts in multiparty cabinets. At the same time, they work to absorb or destroy any non-

or anti-communist revolutionary elements that tend to arise from the Left.

It is to be observed that the relations within this whole system of concentric rings are dynamic. As long as the Soviet Union retains the political initiative, the center acts as an attractive force, pulling the outer rings toward itself. As the first ring is absorbed into the body of the central circle, the second ring (Domination) tends to fuse, in part at least, with the first. Additional territories or nations tend to become candidates for outright absorption rather than for mere domination. We may rightly expect that, before so very long, applications for admission to the Union of Socialist Soviet Republics will be filed by some nations now within Circle II. Similarly, the third ring (Orienting Influence) tends, as the process develops, to fuse into the second; and the nations of the third ring thus tend toward the Domination group. The whole set of relations within the system of rings is summarily epitomized by the 1939–40 history of the Baltic states.

We have dealt, in this section, with the nature of Circles I, II, and III. The discussion, except for its inclusion of Latin America, has concerned the first part of the task of preparation for the Third World War: the attempt to consolidate effective domination of the Eurasian continent. Circle IV carries us altogether outside of Eurasia, and relates only to the second part of the general task: the simultaneous attempt to weaken and undermine all governments and nations not under communist control.

IV

The principal occupants of Circle IV are the United States, England, and the British Commonwealth. Though the ultimate communist goal with respect to these is identical with that for every other part of the earth, the specific policy for the present period of preparation for the Third World War is, in many respects, radically different from the Eurasian policies analyzed in the preceding section. Within this period, the communists do not expect to be able either to absorb or to dominate the nations of Circle IV. They do not believe that in the United States they can even attain a decisive orienting influence, though they may have a small reserve hope of swinging England into line.

Their policy toward the United States is, on the contrary, based upon the conviction that the United States is the only serious rival center of power to their own, and that the United States is their determining opponent in the developing Third World War. They believe that, in all probability, England and what is left of the Commonwealth and Empire will continue the *de facto* alliance with the United States on into the open stage of the War. The policy toward England is therefore subsidiary to the policy toward the United States, and I shall confine the following analysis to the United States.

The communist objectives in relation to the United States may be summed up as follows:

First, to try to prevent interference by the United States with the communist plans for the consolidation of Fortress Eurasia, and even to gain United States assistance in fulfilling those plans.

Second, to weaken, undermine and demoralize the United States to the maximum extent possible prior to the open war struggle.

Third, to become inbedded within the social fabric of United States life in order to be ready for direct action—espionage, sabotage, stimulation of riots and revolts, etc.—when the open war begins.

These objectives are furthered, of course, by communist activities and propaganda throughout the world. Within the United States and its dependencies they are promoted by a powerful and complex network. Many Americans, understanding nothing of totalitarian politics, dismiss the communists as "a negligible force in American life," because the Communist Party gets few votes in elections. For communists, elections—particularly the vote one gets in elections—are among the most minor of political exertions. It might be recalled that in 1917, at the beginning of the Russian Revolution, the Russian Bolshevik faction, which became the Communist Party, numbered only about 25,000 members. In general it is a law of politics that a small minority, tightly organized and disciplined, knowing in advance what it wants and planning consciously how to get it, has far greater weight than loose, amorphous majorities.

The communist apparatus in the United States, even quantitatively considered, is, as a matter of fact, very extensive. It is built out of a series of layers, which surround the inner steel, and merge at the outer edges into the general population. At the center, checking and supervising every activity, are thousands of N.K.V.D. agents. There are then thousands of other agents, of the military intelligence, and of the various special commissions, committees and bureaus of the Soviet State and the international party. All Soviet employees in this country, in whatever apparent capacity, are of course part of the machine. All foreign communist parties have their organized sections within all refugee and foreign-language groups in this country. Then there is the United States Party itself, with its own many layers; and the many communists who are instructed not to join any party. Then, in widening circles, there are the fellow-travelers, the sympathizers, the dupes, the simpletons; and the millions of honest citizens who, without knowing its source or its direction, drink up the propaganda because it seems to correspond with some sentiment of their own.

In order to carry out its triple objective, the communist network tries to infiltrate every level of American life. ("We must," Lenin commands in *What Is to Be Done?*, "go among all classes of the people as theoreticians, as propagandists, as agitators, and as organizers.") From the smallest sports clubs to the highest departments of government, from great trade unions to neighborhood debating societies, from the established political parties to minute farm cooperatives, from the army to organizations of pacifists, from *The Atlantic Monthly* to *The Protestant,* from Hollywood parties to strike riots, everywhere communist influence is actively penetrating. Where an organization is already established, they wedge from the outside; where there is none, they create it. As their grease for infiltration, they use everywhere the formula of the united front. . . .

The infiltration is in part opportunistic: that is, the communists seize any chance that may appear to entrench themselves in any kind of organization whatsoever. However, in accordance with their specific objectives, they have in the United States certain concentration areas to which they devote the greater part of their deliberate and planned efforts. The chief of these are the following:

[Here the author describes communist infiltration in the following fields:

1. *The public opinion industry*
2. *Maritime and Communications*
3. *Intelligence Services*
4. *Science, especially nuclear science and technology*]

From these and their other organizational vantage points the communists in the first place manipulate American public opinion in such a way as to permit the development of the communist Eurasian policy. Communism has by far the greatest propaganda machine that has ever existed, and its achievements in this country during recent years are notable. United States opinion was led, for example, to accept the turning over of Yugoslavia to the communist Tito; and of Poland to the communist-controlled Bierut government. Communists, with detailed advance preparation, acted as a catalyst for the "Bring the Boys Home" movement following V-J Day, which demoralized the armed forces, and weakened the world diplomatic position of the United States. Many Americans now believe, or half-believe, that totalitarianism is a new kind of higher democracy. They are persuaded that there should be "non-interference" in China: that is, that China should be turned over to the Soviet-supported and -supplied Chinese communists. They will soon be led to think that all American troops should be brought home from Eurasia. They believe, or many of them believe, that Americans abroad nurse fascists and counter-revolutionists. They are told horrifying stories about Greek monarchists and Turkish tyrants and Iranians and Iraqians subsidized by British and American big business. Whatever the immediate issue, the propaganda always finds a reason, a whole set of reasons, why the United States should do nothing to interfere with the communist organization of the concentric ring system, should, on the contrary, help in that organization with political friendship, food, supplies and industrial equipment.

And tirelessly the propaganda hammers in the Soviet myth, the fairy story of the happy, prosperous land of socialism, where forward-moving humanity marches ahead with one mind and one voice to new and braver worlds.

On another, related front, the communist propaganda and activities stimulate and provoke all latent conflicts between the United States and other non-communist states. In the Philippines, the Hukbalahaps, the guerilla force exploiting the discontent of poor peasants, directs its arms and agitation against the American-sponsored new government. In Puerto Rico, the communists join the separatist movement. Throughout Latin America, the communists and their allies denounce Yankee imperialism. Especially is every occasion seized upon to stir dislike and distrust of Great Britain.

Within the United States, the communists arouse and exploit every divisive possibility. Labor against capital, big business against little business, C.I.O. against A.F. of L., farmers against businessmen, Negroes against Whites, Christians against Jews, Protestants against Catholics, landlords against tenants, foreign born against native born, South against North, unemployed against employed: wherever there is a potential rift in the national life, the communist tactic is to deepen and tear that rift.

> To refuse . . . to maneuver, to utilize the conflict of interests (even though temporary) among one's enemies; to refuse to temporize and compromise with possible (even though transient, unstable, vacillating, and conditional) allies—is this not ridiculous in the extreme? . . . The old forms have burst. . . . We now have from the standpoint of the development of international communism such a lasting, strong and powerful content of work . . . that it can *and must* manifest itself in any form, both new and old; that it can *and must* regenerate, conquer, and subjugate all forms, not only the new but the old—not for the purpose of reconciling itself with the old, but to be able to convert all and sundry forms, new and old, into a weapon for the complete, final, decisive and inevitable victory of communism. [Lenin, quoted by Stalin in *Problems of Leninism.*]

It is of course true that many of these rifts, or potential rifts, exist, independently of communism, within the fabric of our society. There would be a Negro problem, a labor problem, a religious problem, a Jewish problem, if there were no communist movement. It is further true that many good citizens, non-communists and anti-communists, concern themselves with these problems. Their concern, however, is to try to solve them. What they do not grasp is that the concern of the communists—with whom they so often join their activities, frequently without themselves knowing of the united front into which they enter—is not to solve them but to make them insoluble. They do not understand that the communists do not want to mend the nation, but to smash it beyond repair. The good citizen is glad to find communist allies when he seeks, say, a fair trial for a Negro; he does not know that the communist will use him for the precise purpose, not of helping the Negro, but of embittering and poisoning race relationships.

The good citizen joins a committee to support, perhaps, the families of strikers; he does not know that the communists in the committee have as their objective not the well-being of labor but the hopeless exaggeration of class conflicts, and the undermining of the American economy. Or the good citizen, as a humanitarian, joins some committee "for Soviet-American friendship," equally unaware that the function of the committee is to protect and defend not the peoples of Russia and the United States, but the communist dictatorship today crushing the Russian people and tomorrow aiming for the people of America.

So, if all goes according to plan, the full war will open with the United States so isolated, and so internally weakened, divided, demoralized, that it will be unable even to make a good showing in the struggle. Meanwhile, in the war itself, with public communist activities limited or abolished, the infiltrated divisions will be in a position to take direct action to break down the industrial and military machine, and the morale of the nation.

The downfall of the United States will remove the last great obstacle. The Communist World Empire will begin.

AUTHOR'S NOTE

The evidence demonstrating the deterioration of the standard of living under the communist regime has been assembled and analyzed by a number of scholars. Among the relevant books that may be consulted in this connection, the following are representative: *Workers Before and After Lenin,* by Manya Gordon; *Soviet Labour and Industry,* by Leonard E. Hubbard; *Russia's Economic Front for War and Peace,* by A. Yugow; *The Real Soviet Russia,* by David J. Dallin. All of these books contain extensive bibliographies of first-hand sources.

Mass opposition among the Soviet people to the Soviet regime may be inferred from: (1) the size and scope of the internal secret police; (2) the periodic mass purges; (3) the prohibition of any travel beyond the Soviet border, except on official missions, by any Soviet citizen (a prohibition enforced by severe statutory penalties which apply not only to an individual who tries to leave the country but to members of his immediate family and to anyone who has knowledge of his intended act).

Let us ask: why are the secret police, the purges, and the prohibition of foreign travel considered necessary by the regime, and not merely admitted publicly in the controlled press, but constantly and spectacularly emphasized, especially in internal propaganda? The only possible explanation is that the regime recognizes the existence of profound mass discontent, however inarticulate and unorganized. [The above issues are dealt with in Topics 6 and 7.]

STRUGGLE FOR PEACE

Andrei Vishinsky *

Numerous facts and documents from the history of the Soviet State and its foreign policy bear witness to the unswerving struggle for peace, for the strengthening of international co-operation, which is determinedly carried out by the Soviet Government. These facts attest to the tremendous efforts and to the inexhaustible initiative which the Soviet Government has shown during its entire existence, since the first days of the Great October Revolution, in the course of the realization of its peace-loving aims and of the creation of conditions for the building of socialist society, of a socialist state of workers and peasants. The Soviet people, occupied with peaceful constructive labor, is far removed from any bellicose designs or plans for war. War is odious to it, and it is making gigantic efforts in order to avert the threat of a new war and to ensure peace and security, which are so necessary to our people for the successful solution of the great tasks of socialist construction. All the creative forces of the Soviet country and of our great people are focused on the fulfillment of peaceful aims. Science and technology have here been placed at the service of peace, of peaceful constructive labor. The development of all of Soviet industry, of the entire Soviet national economy, is going in the same direction. . . .

Nobody will succeed in covering his hostile schemes concerning the Soviet Union with hysterical cries that the Soviet Union allegedly considers the peaceful co-existence of countries of socialism and of capitalist countries to be impossible, that allegedly it, the Soviet Union, is not striving for co-operation and friendly relations with other countries, and in particular with countries of a different political and social system.

All these machinations, inimical to the Soviet Union, are confronted by numerous convincing facts, by all the history of the more than 30 years of the Soviet State, all the direction and content of peaceful Soviet foreign policy.

How then do matters stand in reality with the question, so often raised at international conferences and, in particular, in the United Nations Organization—the question of the possibility of peaceful co-existence and co-operation between the USSR—the country of socialism—and countries of the capitalist system? . . .

Here are these facts.

In 1927 in his conversation with the first American labor delegation, J. V. Stalin pointed out that the existence of two opposing systems—the capitalist

* Soviet Minister for Foreign Affairs. Author of *Law and the Soviet State* and other works on Soviet jurisprudence and politics. The selection is from speeches delivered by Andrei Vishinsky before the Political Committee of the General Assembly of the United Nations, October 23, 1950, and November 16, 1949.

system and the socialist system—does not exclude the possibility of agreements with the capitalist states in the sphere of industry, in the sphere of trade, in the sphere of diplomatic relations.

In this conversation, J. V. Stalin said:

> I think that such agreements are possible and expedient in conditions of peaceful development. Exports and imports are the most suitable ground for such agreements. We require equipment, raw material (raw cotton for example), semi-manufactures (metals etc.) while the capitalists require a market for these goods. This provides a basis for agreement. The capitalists require oil, timber, grain products, and we require a market for these goods. Here is another basis for agreement. We require credits, the capitalists require good interest for their credits. Here is still another basis for agreement in the field of credit. It is well known that the Soviet organs are most punctual in their payments.

Much time has passed since then; during this time our needs have changed. We have now no need, in many respects, of capitalist countries in the field of trade relations, but nevertheless the question of trade relations still has not lost its strength, has not lost its significance in the cause of the strengthening of international ties. I remind you of these words spoken by the head of the Soviet Government in 1927 to the American labor delegation, mostly in order to show how great are the possibilities, with good will and honest striving for real co-operation, of establishing and of strengthening international ties which in their turn will foster the strengthening of peace and the security of nations.

In that conversation, J. V. Stalin stressed that the Soviet Union is leading the policy of peace and is ready to sign pacts on mutual non-aggression with the bourgeois states, is ready to reach agreement regarding disarmament, etc. Having cited the agreements concluded at that time with other countries, J. V. Stalin in this same conversation with the American delegation stated that we would like these agreements to have a more or less prolonged character, but warned that: "That does not altogether depend upon us alone. It depends also upon the other parties."

The Soviet Union, being a partisan of peaceful co-operation with other countries, even though they be of another social, economic and political system, achieved improvement of relations with a number of countries and the conclusion of a number of treaties with them on trade, technical assistance, etc., despite the fact that certain countries, as, for example, the United States of America, at that time and from then on, during 16 years, did not recognize the Soviet Union and in every way opposed this recognition, resisted the demands of the American public and of progressive circles in other capitalist countries that it renounce this absurd policy of boycott of the young Soviet Republic.

But precisely at that time the Soviet Union, despite the boycott to which it was subjected on the part of certain capitalist countries, and such large ones as, for example, the United States of America, joined in the Kellogg

Pact, signed the protocols in connection with the Kellogg Pact with other countries, developed the active struggle for collective security. The Soviet Union then participated actively in a number of conferences which were held at that time, since the 20's, under the aegis of the League of Nations. The Soviet Government and no other in February of 1933 proposed the adoption of the definition of aggression and of aggressor. Despite the fact that this initiative was supported by many states and that the majority of the Security Committee, which consisted of the representatives of 17 states, approved this proposal in the main, it was nevertheless rejected by the conference, which acted under the leadership of representatives of the then English and French Governments.

But pacts defining an aggressor were nevertheless concluded by the Soviet Union with the majority of states neighboring it on the west and south, including Finland and Poland, and also with the countries of the so-called Little Entente. At that time pacts on non-aggression were concluded with these same neighboring countries, and also with France and Italy.

The majority of the League of Nations resisted this trend of foreign policy for which the Soviet Union was energetically struggling, and rejected the peaceful proposals of the Soviet Union. Nevertheless, the Soviet Union, overcoming all these obstacles, followed precisely this path of the consolidation of peace, concluding, on its own initiative and in support of the initiative of some other countries, agreements, treaties which certainly were not mere words but were practical deeds. And this is precisely the point which is insufficiently appreciated by certain delegates when they answer our proposals on peace, on measures to consolidate peace, always with the unchanging phrase: "Prove by deeds that these are not mere words, but that you are really ready to implement such measures in practice."

But are not these facts of which I just spoke a clear refutation of all kinds of attempts, by raising such questions, to avoid in reality the necessity of supporting the Soviet proposals, to disrupt somehow these Soviet proposals under the pretext, as I said, that these are mere words, and that you should show by deeds how these, your words and proposals, will be executed in living reality?

Here are the facts which I cited and which show how unchangingly Soviet words and proposals are executed into practical reality, into life itself, provided only that these proposals find at least a modicum of support on the part of other delegations, on the part of other states; provided only that these states display elementary efforts really to reach aggreement with the Soviet Union, with the Soviet Government, on some real issue.

Such was the peaceful Soviet foreign policy at that time.

The years immediately preceding the Second World War, as well as the postwar years, also give numerous examples of the establishment on the initiative and by the efforts of the Soviet Union, and not merely of proposals for the establishment, of friendly and business ties and relations with a number of states.

The leaders of the Soviet State have repeatedly pointed out that the Soviet Union proceeds in its foreign policy from its conviction of the inevitability and possibility of the co-existence of the socialist and capitalist systems for a long time, proceeds from the fact that peaceful co-operation of the USSR with all those states which are ready to reciprocate and are ready scrupulously to fulfill international obligations assumed by them, is fully realistic and possible.

When, in September, 1946, the Moscow correspondent of the [London] *Sunday Times,* A. Werth, asked the Chairman of the Council of Ministers of the USSR, J. V. Stalin, whether with the further progress of the Soviet Union toward communism, the possibilities of peaceful co-operation of the Soviet Union with the rest of the world would remain undiminished, the head of the Soviet Government, J. V. Stalin, then answered: "I do not doubt that the possibilities for peaceful co-operation, far from diminishing, may even grow."

In the same year of 1946, Elliott Roosevelt asked J. V. Stalin the question whether it is possible for the USA to live side by side in peace with such a communistic form of government as exists in the Soviet Union, with no attempt on the part of either to interfere with the internal political affairs of the other. J. V. Stalin answered at that time: "Yes, of course. This is not only possible. It is wise and entirely within bounds of realization. In the most strenuous times during the war the differences in government did not prevent our two nations from joining together and vanquishing our foes. Even more so is it possible to continue this relationship in time of peace."

In May, 1948, J. V. Stalin confirmed that the Government of the USSR believes that "in spite of the differences in the economic systems and ideologies, the co-existence of these systems and the peaceful settlement of differences between the USSR and the USA are not only possible but absolutely necessary in the interests of universal peace."

The historic answers of J. V. Stalin to the questions of the General European Director of the International News Service, Kingsbury Smith, are also known. In his answers the head of the Soviet Government stated the following: "Naturally the Government of the USSR could co-operate with the Government of the United States of America in taking measures designed to implement the pact of peace, and leading to gradual disarmament."

These words of the great leader of the Soviet Union define the entire direction of Soviet foreign policy, which unswervingly pursues purposes corresponding to the vital interests of the Soviet people and of all peace-loving peoples.

I believe these facts are quite sufficient to silence the slanderers at long last—all those who have adopted as their stock in trade dark insinuations against the Soviet Union, against its foreign policy, against its sincerity, against its real striving for co-operation in the interests of all peace-loving nations. . . .

Marxism-Leninism teaches that human society develops in conformity with the immanent laws of this society and is subject to their influence. Capitalist society has its laws of development. The concomitants of capitalism are war crisis, unemployment, crimes, prostitution. These phenomena follow from the laws of capitalist society. These are all scourges, concomitants, of the capitalist system, which is based on the exploitation of human labour, of some classes of society by others. . . .

The greatest service of Marxism-Leninism lies precisely in that it has found the key to the study of the laws of development of human society and thereby to understanding the laws of the history of this society. It has found this key, not in the minds of men, not in the views and ideas of society, but in the means of production, in the organisation of social relations and first of all of production relations in each historical period. But the subordination of the development of human society to certain laws does not signify that man is reduced to the role of blind subjugation to the action of these laws. Man is man. . . . Society is a society which is capable of organizing social relations. By his organizational activity, man can contribute to the development of the historical path. If this path accords with the laws of social development then it is of a progressive nature. If this path does not conform to the laws of development then it retards the development of society, it plays a reactionary role.

People, classes of society, therefore, play a tremendous role, and this means that the activity of people who are capable of regulating social relations plays a tremendous role. This task is effected by the internal and foreign policy of one or another State. . . .

[What are commonly misunderstood are] the elementary questions of Marxism-Leninism on the correlations between the laws determining the development of society and the measures which a conscious society undertakes in order to lessen the pernicious effect of negative laws and in order to create conditions—notwithstanding these laws—favouring the utmost alleviation of the crisis which periodically leads to the catastrophes that capitalist society is fraught with.

That is why we state also now that there is no contradiction whatever between the precept that war is an inevitable phenomenon in capitalist, imperialist society, which is taught by our teachers, which is taught by the entire history of humanity, and the striving to restrict, to curb the operation of this law. On the contrary, notwithstanding the fact that wars are inherent in capitalism, democratic forces are able to frustrate war, to prevent war by their solidarity, strength and the resolve to prevent war.

The stronger the unity of the masses in the struggle against war, the stronger the voice of protest of the nations resounds against war, the sooner will the danger of war be reduced to naught. The might of the solidarity of the peace-loving nations can paralyse the activity of such phenomena as war preparation and save the world from this horrible calamity. . . .

"If you consider that war is inherent in capitalist society then, consequently, you are for war," our opponents tell us. This is likewise absurd, because the task consists in overcoming this feature, law, if you wish, of capitalist society, in order by the conscious efforts of the nations to paralyse the effect of such features, the laws of capitalist society.

War Is Not Inevitable

George F. Kennan *

The air vibrates with controversy about America's proper course with respect to Russia. Much of it, it seems to me, is shallow or prejudiced or ill-conceived. It is hard to imagine that ever at any time in history has more error ever been poured out upon a single subject. And one enters with misgivings into this disorder. Where so much confusion lies about, what can we do in a few brief moments to disentangle the snarled skeins, to assemble and sort out and put together again the broken pieces of thought, to bring order out of the chaos—even assuming, which is not proven—that we might have some greater clarity in our own minds? How can we avoid adding to the bedlam, heaping confusion upon confusion?

The only hope I can see of avoiding these pitfalls lies in attempting to rethink our problem, but with a little greater depth in time than we are accustomed to give to it these days.

Thirty-three years ago—not two or three, mark you—*thirty-three*—there was a revolution in Russia. That revolution brought into power a political movement already committed, and long and deeply committed, to an attitude of hostility toward our own social and political system and to many other things elsewhere which we believe to be essential to world stability.

It is important to recognize that we did not create that attitude, nor was there really much we could do to prevent its rise or to alter it after it appeared. It arose out of ideology and preconception, out of things which were not our doing. To say that it stemmed only from the Allied intervention in 1919, or from the way we Westerners treated the Soviet regime generally in the early years of its power, reflects a very superficial view of the origins of the Bolshevik movement.

Lenin and his associates, I am sure, would not have been grateful for

* Member of the Policy Planning Staff, Department of State. American Minister-Counselor in Moscow, 1945. Author of several articles on world politics. The selection is from George F. Kennan, "Let Peace Not Die of Neglect," *New York Times Magazine*, February 25, 1951. Reprinted by permission of *The New York Times* and the author

the implication that their views about the capitalist world were so shallowly rooted that they could be basically altered by subjective reactions on their part to the actions of capitalist governments in the period immediately following the revolution. They would have rejected with resentment and contempt the implication that they could have been glad-handed into the abandonment of ideological principles to which they had devoted their lives.

This new political power, while not entirely a Russian phenomenon, did succeed in establishing itself in Russia and in bringing under a form of effective and stable control the energies of the peoples and the natural resources of that area. This fact—namely, that those energies and resources should have fallen under the control of a power hostile to Western civilization—was a serious and disturbing thing. It presented a major complication in the progress of the West. Those of us who were professionally occupied with Russian affairs in the Twenties and Thirties were very much aware of that fact. Perhaps that is why we are somewhat less than impressed when we are told today, by agitated and vociferous people, that this is the fact and that we ought to be much more excited about it than we are.

The Bolshevik leaders, in accordance with their ideology, did their best, in the years that ensued after the revolution, to achieve the breakdown of non-Communist power in Western Europe, in this country and elsewhere. They operated Communist fifth-column organizations in practically every area in the world. They unleashed civil wars and revolutions wherever they saw a chance. They sowed confusion and suspicion.

They peddled bitterness and bewilderment and despair. They earned a great deal of resentment in return, and no doubt a certain amount of subversive activity directed against themselves and their system, though nothing near what they claimed. They were a nuisance and a danger to everyone else. In these circumstances everyone else—inevitably and unavoidably—was a nuisance and a danger to them. Their relations with other countries faithfully reflected that fact.

Yet for over two decades nothing frightfully crucial happened in these relations. The Bolsheviks didn't succeed in destroying anybody; nobody succeeded in destroying them. Life was awkward—unnecessarily so—but not impossible. The impact of this Bolshevik hostility and dissatisfaction upon the mellow old democracies of the West led to many remarkable and usually unpleasant things; but it did not lead to war. It was not until another violent and neurotic political movement had raised its head in a neighboring country, Germany—a movement as hostile to Soviet Russia by preconception as Soviet Russia had been hostile to the capitalist West—that major war ensued.

But then, it was not a war between Russia and the Western democracies. The blow struck both Russia and the Western democracies together—like a bolt of lightning, like a reminder to them, from some disgusted deity, of the tragedy and unhappiness of their division.

The war that ensued had two main consequences which we ought to note here. First, by eliminating the armed power of Germany and Japan from certain very important areas of human habitation it opened up new and delicate sources of difference and controversy between the Soviet leaders and the West. These geographic areas, which had been placed by the outcome of hostilities in what might be called a power vacuum, included certain of the world's most sensitive spots, from the strategic and political standpoint. There was no reason to suppose that agreement about their future disposition, as between Russia and the West, would be easy to achieve. There was particularly no reason to assume this, because in a totalitarian regime like that of the U.S.S.R. defensive and offensive motives are always inextricably intertwined, and the anxieties of such a regime for the safety of its own internal power prevent it from reacting normally, or even from speaking frankly, in problems of this kind. All that was known long before the war.

So there these new problems were; and they proved, indeed, to be anything but easy; and because of them it even turned out to be impossible, in the immediate post-war years, to negotiate peace treaties at all. And meanwhile the disputed territories lay there, completely vulnerable in each case, as it happened, to the armed strength of the U.S.S.R., which wholly overshadowed that of the Western powers in the immediate vicinity. And there were many foreign ministers' meetings, many disputes, many disappointments, and much tension—but there was no major war.

The second consequence of World War II that I wish to mention is the establishment of the United Nations. We Americans took a leading part in this. The Russians reacted to proposals from us. You will recall that they were quite emphatic in their insistence on the veto power in the Security Council. This meant an insistence that the U.N. should not be used to settle security problems except where the great powers were in agreement. This applied particularly to precisely the problems we have just noted—the ones arising from the immediate dislocations of the recent war; and this was given indirect recognition in the Charter of the U.N. itself.

Now some of us liked these veto provisions and others didn't; but no one can say that the Soviet Government was not frank in stating its position at the time, or that we were not warned that there might be categories of problems which would be less susceptible than others of treatment in the U.N. forum.

Finally, we should note that when we established the U.N. we placed no barriers to the membership in it of Communist governments. We raised no objection to the Soviet Government's belonging to it, even though we knew it was a Communist government. We didn't ask how it had come by its power—whether by fair means or foul. We didn't ask it to disavow its ideology. We didn't even object to the admission of some of its satellites. It was clearly our view at that time that the U.N. was to consist of both Communist and non-Communist powers.

And we were plainly warned, I repeat, of what logic should have told us anyway: that there were distinct limitations on what such a universal organization, embracing both Communist and non-Communist governments, could be expected to achieve in this immediate post-hostilities period, and that among the things it could not be expected to do would be to serve as an invariably successful forum for the settlement of the problems arising out of the war, or for the resolution of the ideological differences between communism and all opposed to it.

Now we have on our hands today a situation the seriousness of which no one would deny. We find ourselves involved in a local military conflict, replete with the most grievous implications, over the problem of disposal of one of those disputed areas from which we required that the power of our recent adversaries be withdrawn. We are indignant over the refusal of Communist China, which is not a member of the U.N., to recognize the authority of that body in the dispute, and over its action in opposing that authority by force of arms. It is worth noting that, whereas we introduced our forces into the conflict, and I think properly and wisely so, the Soviet Government did not. It has preferred to operate, to date, with the forces of its puppets.

Meanwhile, we have come to the conclusion that the general world situation is one which requires a major effort of rearmament on our part and on the part of other Western nations. With this, again, I have no quarrel. I have long believed in the necessity for such rearmament. I think it should have come, to some extent, much earlier. But what I want to get at is not the fact of rearmament, it is the rationale of it.

We know many people in this country are coming to believe that war is not only unavoidable but imminent, and that the reasons for rearmament lie not even possibly in the long-term requirements of a relationship with Communist power short of major war, but in some new and recent developments, some new elements of menace in the Soviet attitude, which entitle us to despair altogether of avoiding major war for any considerable further period.

Now this is a very difficult thing to put forth: because anyone who tries to urge caution and sobriety in the judgment of these matters is apt to be accused of having said that war is definitely not coming, that we are not going to be attacked, that our fears are baseless, that we can relax and go home.

Let me make it plain! I am saying none of these things. Of course war is possible. Of course no one can say that we will not be attacked or that major war will not develop from the impetus and the cumulative complications of this situation. Who can say for sure what is in the minds of the Soviet leaders? Who can guarantee their behavior? Who can assure that they, peering out at the world through the muddied and myopic lenses of their bitter and fear-ridden ideology, have not come to the conclusion themselves that war is unavoidable? From such a conclusion anything could flow.

My purpose is not to make a plea for any certainty of a continued absence of major war. It is to make a plea against the assumption of any certainty that war cannot be avoided. It is to plead that before we assume that the world situation has turned basically and irrevocably against the chances of peace we make absolutely sure that we know what we're doing—that we test our views and retest them, putting aside all emotion and irritation and everything subjective—that we take care to see that we are not being carried away here by false assumptions or short memories or emotion.

Let us look carefully at these things which are often cited as the sources of despair.

It is true that the Kremlin is hostile and secretive, and a constant source of worry, danger and annoyance to us all; it has been that way for thirty-three years.

It is true that Western Europe is overshadowed by Soviet armed strength; it has been that way since 1945, and to some extent even earlier.

It is true that Russia has the atomic bomb. Did we then lack warning of this development? Does anybody suppose that we were in a position to assume, let us say three years ago, that they would not have it; that they would refrain from developing it out of some delicate regard for our feelings? I am not saying that these things are pleasant. I am asking whether they are new or unexpected.

It is true that the Kremlin unleashed its Korean puppets against the South Korean Republic. But there is nothing in this fact which is out of accord with the pattern of Soviet behavior we have known for three decades. At no time has there been any reason to suppose that they would not do this sort of thing, if circumstances seemed propitious. The assertion was made in a magazine article three years ago that the main concern of the Kremlin was "to make sure that it has filled every nook and cranny available to it in the basin of world power." There was no objective reason to assume that the Soviet leaders would leave the Korean nook unfilled if they thought they had a chance of filling it at relatively minor risk to themselves and saw time running out on them. I am not trying to justify their action. I am challenging our right to be surprised about it or to call it a manifestation of some "new aggressiveness" on the part of the Soviet Union.

Finally, it is true that Communist China has defied the United Nations. It is true that Communist China has committed acts in Korea which no one can condone and for which its leaders bear the gravest responsibility. If anyone needed proof that these Chinese Communist leaders are behaving hysterically and violently, with a distorted concept of the interests of their own people, and with no understanding at all for the nature and ideals of the non-Communist world, they have it, of course, in these events in Korea.

But the question at issue here is not, and has never been, whether the Chinese Communists were "nice people." The question lies in the amount of damage they are capable of doing, and are apt to do, to world stability. The question lies, for us, in the extent of the threat: in the measure of what we might call the intrinsic tolerances of the Far Eastern area against the effects of these tortured and neurotic attitudes we see in Peiping, and of what then remains to be done, and can only be done, by outside forces, and how much of that is within our capabilities.

Are we sure we have this so carefully figured out? Are we sure we have calculated correctly all the factors involved? China is a strange entity. She is called a world power, and doubtless deserves that designation from the standpoint of cultural and spiritual resources in her people. Actually she is the only country so considered which does not have the wherewithal to manufacture the sinews of her own military strength on a great-power scale. She has to get her major weapons from outside. I dare say that to date a considerable portion has come from us. Must that always be? It is true that China's resources as of today, while limited, are not negligible, and that they are in the hands of people who are foolish and excited and irresponsible. That is a dangerous and worrisome fact. But let us measure realistically the actual extent of this danger; let us be guided by that alone, and not by irritation over the fact that they are foolish and excited and irresponsible. They are not the first people that we have known that were that way, and they will not be the last; and we are not the keepers of their souls.

Now all of this might conceivably add up to the necessity for another world war; but before we decide that it does, let us be terribly, terribly sure we are right. In the old carpenter guilds there was a principle that you should measure seven times before you cut once. Are we sure we have measured here for the seventh time, or even for the third or the second? This is no time to make a false incision. The material will bear no more than one mistake.

A major American weekly recently devoted an article to combating the theory that co-existence with the present Soviet system may be possible. It attacked the Secretary of State for adhering to what it called "this pernicious fallacy." It called upon the President to drive from his councils at long last "all who have sold and fed him on the pap of 'co-existence' with Soviet Communism."

Now these are tricky words, and no one can ever be entirely sure what they mean. But if they mean what I take them to mean, I would range myself squarely and emphatically with the culprits: with the objects of these attacks and criticisms. What is the phenomenon of extremism and despair with which we are confronted?

Can this be realism, or is it a shrinking away from the first harsh implications of world leadership? Whoever said that world leadership would be easy or comfortable? "Co-existence" with Soviet Communism, as we have seen above, has been possible for thirty-three years. I do not know whether it will continue to be possible for a long time to come. But I would submit that these people who wrote this article do not know for sure that it won't; and in attempting to persuade the public that it won't they have taken upon their shoulders a grievous responsibility and one which I should never wish to have on mine.

They should not try to comfort themselves and their readers with the flimsy pretense that this counsel of despair does not mean war. It does; and if this is the view they are going to take, let them have the forthrightness with themselves and with others to come out and say that what they are talking about is war and tell us how and to what ends and with what resources they propose we conduct that war, and how we are to assure the agreement of the members of a great coalition to a course founded on preconceptions which they do not share, and how a better world is supposed to emerge from the other end of this entire process.

But better still, for them and for all of us, would be not to take this view at all; to admit that the dimness of our vision gives us the right neither to a total optimism nor to a total pessimism, and that our duty to ourselves and to the hopes of mankind lies in avoiding, like the soul of evil itself, that final bit of impatience which tells us to yield the last positions of hope before we have been pressed from them by unanswerable force.

As long as there is a one-thousandth chance that a major world conflict can be avoided—and I hold the chance far greater than that—let us guard that chance like the apple of our eye—let us remain considerate of the hopeful possibilities as well as the discouraging ones—let it not be said of us that we allowed any hope for the avoidance of war to die, like an unwanted and unappreciated child, by abandonment and neglect.

I know that this is the view which has been held by my former associates in the Department of State, and that they will continue, despite all discouragements and opposition, to act on this. If these efforts succeed, the world will have been spared a great catastrophe. If they fail, there will always be time for the other things, the unhappy things, later.

Topic 29

THE ISSUES: DIPLOMATIC EXCHANGE BETWEEN GREAT BRITAIN AND THE SOVIET UNION

The British Note *

At the end of the war there existed in the United Kingdom a vast fund of goodwill toward the peoples of the Soviet Union who had fought so gallantly as Allies of the peoples of the West in defending their country against

* Reprinted in *The New York Times,* February 18, 1951.

Hitlerite aggression and in contributing to the overthrow of the Nazi regime.

The British people and His Majesty's Government eagerly desired that this war-time collaboration should continue. They believed, and still believe, that the peoples of the Soviet Union had the same wish. In response to this common desire, His Majesty's Government earnestly sought, in the words of Article 5 of the Anglo-Soviet Treaty of 1942, "to work together in close and friendly collaboration, after the re-establishment of peace, for the organization of security and economic prosperity in Europe."

Soviet Violations Detailed. His Majesty's Government has always based their policy and actions on strict adherence to the two principles mentioned in Article 5 of the treaty, of "not seeking territorial aggrandizement for themselves and on non-interference in the internal affairs of other countries."

After the conclusion of hostilities they drastically reduced their armed forces in order that the energies and resources of the country might be devoted, in collaboration with their Allies, to restoring the ravages of war both at home and abroad and to advancing the social and economic well-being of their people.

The Soviet Government, on the other hand, soon showed by its actions that it had no real intention of permitting the Soviet people to take part in this work of peaceful collaboration in the spirit of the Anglo-Soviet Treaty or of itself basing its policies on the principles enshrined in that treaty.

Despite the agreement reached at Yalta in 1945 providing for three-power consultation to uphold the democratic rights of the liberated peoples of Europe, the Soviet Government has unilaterally assisted Communist minorities to seize power in all the Eastern European countries.

When, later, the Communist regimes thus established in Bulgaria, Hungary and Rumania constantly flouted the human rights provisions of the peace treaties concluded with those countries in 1947, the Soviet Government obstructed all attempts to invoke the enforcement procedure laid down in the treaties.

From 1945 onward it aided and directed attempts by Greek rebels to overthrow the legally elected Government of Greece. In February, 1948, a Communist coup d'état took place in Czechoslovakia and the Soviet representative vetoed the attempt of the Security Council of the United Nations to investigate this event as a threat to peace.

Since June, 1948, an increasingly violent campaign of vilification and subversion has been waged against Yugoslavia for refusing to subordinate her national interests and independence unreservedly to Soviet dictates.

Obstruction in Germany. In Germany steps were taken by the Soviet authorities at an early stage after the war to seal off the Soviet zone from the West, in violation of the agreement at Potsdam to treat Germany as a single economic unit, and attempts were made to prevent the recovery of the Western zones.

After constant obstruction by the Soviet Government of all efforts to reach a German settlement at successive meetings of the Council of Foreign Ministers, the Soviet Government withdrew its representatives from the Allied Control Council and, by imposing a blockade on the Western sectors of Berlin, sought by force to compel the three Western powers to abandon their legal right to be in the city.

These actions in the political sphere have been accompanied by constant efforts on the part of the Soviet Government to delay economic recovery and to prevent the establishment of tranquillity in Western Europe.

Thus, when in June, 1947, the United States Secretary of State made his proposals for American aid for the economic recovery of Europe, which were closely in harmony with the provisions of Article 5 of the Anglo-Soviet Treaty relating to the organization of European economic prosperity, the Soviet Government not only refused to cooperate itself but influenced other Governments, with which it was in close relations, equally to refuse to participate in the plan.

In September, 1947, on the open initiative of the Soviet Government, the Cominform was set up and in its first manifesto made clear its purpose of organizing and directing every possible form of agitation and action designed to defeat the recovery of Europe.

To this purpose the Soviet Government, in a statement by its official spokesman at the inaugural session of the Cominform, pledged its full support.

The Soviet Government, itself, in the United Nations and elsewhere, increased its propaganda against the Western Governments and sought, through various agencies, to encourage strikes and social unrest aimed at preventing the economic and social consolidation of those countries.

The Soviet Government, moreover, has refused to participate in the activities of those international bodies which have been set up with the express purpose of restoring prosperity, strengthening the social order and furthering international cooperation.

Thus, the Soviet Government has refused to cooperate in the activities of the Food and Agriculture Organization, the United Nations Educational, Scientific and Cultural Organization, the International Monetary Fund, the International Bank, the International Civil Aviation Organization, the International Refugee Organization and the International Labor Organization, and it has withdrawn from the World Health Organization.

Accusation on U.N. Activity. In the United Nations it has repeatedly abused its right of veto, in cases where vital Soviet interests could not be said to be involved, to block the settlement of disputes or the admission of new members, and it has refused to accept plans regarded as reasonable by the vast majority of members for the control of atomic energy and the reduction of armaments.

Its unilateral policies have likewise been a major cause of the total lack of progress in the work of the Military Staff Committee which had been designed to provide a system of collective security based on cooperation of the permanent members of the Security Council.

The general attitude of the Soviet Government in the United Nations has been one of complete and rigid lack of cooperation and compromise, an attitude which strikes at the very roots of that organization. This culminated in the total withdrawal of Soviet representatives from the Security Council and all other organs of the United Nations for a period extending from January to August, 1950.

Furthermore, during the whole of the post-war period the Soviet Government endeavored so far as possible to ensure that the peoples of the Soviet Union and its allies were isolated from the outside world, kept in ignorance of the true facts and inspired with hatred of the Western nations.

Slowly and unwillingly His Majesty's Government were forced to the conclusion, not only that the Soviet Government had no intention of fulfilling its treaty obligations to collaborate with them, but also that it was the aim of the Soviet Union to undermine the independence of the free nations of Western Europe.

Pressure with Propaganda. The policies and actions of the Soviet Government in the fields of politics and propaganda were backed by the huge forces which the Soviet Union maintained under arms. No doubt the Soviet Government demobilized a number of men from the war-time peak but their forces remained far superior in numbers to those of all the Western powers put together.

At the same time they were busily engaged in rebuilding the forces of their allies, some of whom had formerly been the allies of the Nazis, in Eastern Europe, and maintained in Germany and Austria garrisons far in excess of those retained by the Western powers.

In the face of the aggressive and subversive policies of the Soviet Government, backed by the threat of overwhelming force, the Western nations were constrained to take the first steps to organize their self-defense. The North Atlantic Treaty of April, 1949, was the direct consequence of Soviet policy and actions and, as was pointed out in His Majesty's Government's note of 5th January, was strictly and solely defensive in its intentions. The Soviet Government, while persisting in its own threatening policies, nevertheless sought to represent the North Atlantic Treaty as an instrument of aggression and to mislead world opinion as to the true causes of world tension by a campaign of so-called "peace" propaganda.

Since the autumn of 1949 the Soviet Government has used various expedients to prevent the conclusion of a treaty with Austria which would lead to the evacuation of Allied troops and the restoration of normal relations with that country, in accordance with the declaration of Moscow of Nov. 1, 1943, whereby the Soviet Government, together with His Majesty's Government, the United States and French Governments, affirmed their wish to see Austria re-established as a free and independent state.

In the Eastern zone of Germany the Soviet authorities began to build up a force known as the Bereitschaften, which is trained on military lines, with artillery and tanks. The creation of this force is a violation both of the Anglo-Soviet Treaty and of the Potsdam Agreement.

Aggression Aid in Korea. In the Far East the Soviet Government has applauded the action of Communist rebels in Malaya and elsewhere, and in Indo-China has openly supported them by recognizing them as a government. Finally, after the unprovoked aggression of the North Korean forces against the Republic of Korea and the subsequent intervention of the Central People's Government of China, it supported the aggressors in the United Nations and opposed all attempts to restrain them.

These acts of unprovoked aggression proved to the peoples of the free world that Communist imperialism will not stop at agitation, threats and subversion, but is ready to use force to obtain its ends by conquest. These developments have made it plain to the British people that the Soviet Government, ignoring the provisions of the Anglo-Soviet Treaty, is intent on building up a coalition directed against the United Kingdom and other peace and freedom loving countries, and aimed at undermining their social order and independence.

It is in the light of all these circumstances that His Majesty's Government, like the other governments of the West, have been obliged in pure self-defense to set about strengthening their defenses and considering the participation of German units in the defense of Western Europe.

To attempt to disguise these facts by accusing the democratic and peace-loving countries of the West of aggressive policies will deceive no one. The Soviet Government itself is fully aware that the governments of the Western powers seek only to improve the social and economic conditions of their peoples; it knows that the free democracies of the West have neither the desire nor the means to enter upon a war of aggression.

Assurances Are Repeated. Nevertheless, His Majesty's Government repeat their often stated assurances. The measures of collective security in which they are at present participating as the result of Communist policy and actions since the war are purely defensive. His Majesty's Government have no aggressive intentions toward the Soviet Union or its allies. They have no intention of reviving aggressive German militarism and they will not allow their zone of occupation in Germany to be used as a base for aggression.

They reaffirm their readiness to seek, in discussion with the Soviet Government and in the spirit of Article 5 of the Anglo-Soviet Treaty, the settlement of the principal problems whose solution will make possible a real and lasting improvement in their relations.

The Soviet Note *

The facts prove that the Government of Great Britain is guilty of pursuing . . . not a policy of preserving peace but a policy of aggression, a policy of unleashing war. . . .

Suffice it to cite such examples of unilateral actions of the Government of Great Britain with regard to Germany as the fusion, by way of separate action, in 1946 of the British and American occupation zones in Germany, to which subsequently the French zone was also joined, as a result of which Germany was split into two parts; the introduction in Western Germany of a special currency which finally disrupted the economic unity of Germany and resulted in the liquidation of the Control Council of representatives of the four powers; the formation by way of separate action, of the Bonn Government for Western Germany, which created obstacles to restoring the unity of the German state; the separatist refusal to prepare a peace treaty with Germany and the institution of the occupation statute imposed on the Western zones of Germany with the object of maintaining the occupation for an indefinitely long time.

All these measures were carried out by way of separate action, without coordinating them with the U.S.S.R. and without its participation. Thus not the U.S.S.R. but Britain repudiated the policy of cooperation on the German question. The Yalta and Potsdam conferences on the German question oblige the participants in the conferences strictly to pursue a policy of the demilitarization and democratization of Germany.

Yet contrary to this, the British Government started to carry out not the democratization of Germany but the reinstatement of Fascist leaders, the gradual fascization of Western Germany; when Krupp was released from prison it returned Krupp and his imperialist friends to power in the Ruhr, and released from prison and returned to power well-known Fascist generals of the Hitlerite camp, suppressed and continues suppressing democratic and peace-loving elements in Western Germany.

Simultaneously with this the British Government, instead of demilitarizing Germany, started the restoration of German war industry, having turned the Ruhr into a base of the war industry, started the re-creation of a regular German army headed by Fascist generals, started turning Western Germany into a bridgehead for new aggressive war. . . .

Thus Britain definitely violated its obligations to prevent the revival of militarism in Germany, to democratize and demilitarize Germany, thereby undermining the foundations of the Anglo-Soviet Treaty and the Yalta-Potsdam agreements.

The Government of Great Britain, together with the Government of

* Reprinted in *The New York Times,* February 26, 1951.

France, was the initiator in setting up the so-called "Western Union," which from the very outset has not concealed its hostility toward the U.S.S.R. Following this, Great Britain and the United States of America set up the North Atlantic grouping of powers; of the great powers comprising the anti-Hitlerite coalition only the Soviet Union was excluded from being a party to the North Atlantic Treaty. . . .

At present the aggressive nature of the Western Union and the North Atlantic grouping has been completely exposed. All the statements about the defensive aims of these groupings, headed by the Anglo-American bloc of powers, lost their meaning after the efforts had been initiated to draw into these groupings Western Germany with its revanchist [seeking to regain lost territory] Bonn Government and West German army headed by Hitlerite generals.

In its note of Feb. 17 the Government of Great Britain resorts to crude slander against the Soviet Union as well as Bulgaria, Hungary and Rumania where democratic regimes were established which once and for all did away with the vestiges of fascism in these countries. The Government of Great Britain would evidently prefer to see in these states governments which would follow in the wake of the aggressive policy of Great Britain.

It is time, however, the Government of Great Britain understood that the peoples of Bulgaria, Hungary and Rumania have the same right as the people of any other state to arrange their domestic affairs, proceeding from their national interests and not from whether the democratic regime established in these countries is liked or disliked by the government of one foreign state or another.

It is well known that the Government of Great Britain, seeking to restore by forcible means the power of the Fascists and other aggressive elements in the peace-loving democratic states of Eastern Europe, encourages in these states the hostile activity of Fascist groupings which set themselves the object of organizing conspiracies to overthrow the People's democratic regimes. . . .

The Government of Great Britain resorts to similarly slanderous assertions also regarding the changes in the composition of the Government in Czechoslovakia that occurred in February, 1948, which the Government of Great Britain tries to present as some kind of coup allegedly threatening peace. It is known, however, that these changes were caused by the fact that a coup d'état was being prepared in Czechoslovakia under the guidance of American and other foreign agents, including also official diplomatic representatives of the United States, with the object of depriving the Czechoslovak people of their national independence and subordinating Czechoslovakia to the Anglo-American diktat. . . .

The Soviet Government, further, considers as an oddity the attempt of the British Government to assume the pose of defender of the national interests of Yugoslavia. The Soviet people stigmatize and will continue stigmatizing the present Yugoslav rulers because they established in their country a fascist regime resembling the regime of Franco in Spain and deprived the peoples of Yugoslavia of elementary democratic rights. The Soviet people stigmatize and will continue stigmatizing the Yugoslav rulers because they organized a conspiracy against the Hungarian People's Democratic Government and thereby became the sworn enemies of the countries of people's democracy. . . .

The Government of Great Britain, just like the Governments of the United States and France, will not succeed in evading responsibility for delays in concluding a treaty with Austria, and will not succeed in shifting responsibility for this on the U.S.S.R. It is time to end the protracted examination of unagreed articles of the treaty, and, what is most important, it is necessary that Great Britain and the United States abandon plans for turning Austria into their new military base in the very heart of Europe, as they have done in Trieste, trampling upon the peace treaty with Italy signed by them.

In the note of Feb. 17 the Government of Great Britain made crude attacks on the Korean people and the Chinese People's Republic, advancing against them the slanderous accusations of aggression. Yet it is evident to all that the Korean people are waging a liberation struggle for their national unification and do not interfere in the affairs of any other states. It is likewise evident to all that the Chinese People's Republic defends lawful national interests, upholding its right to the Chinese island of Taiwan [Formosa] and to the defense of its frontiers from the Anglo-American troops which broke into Korea and threaten the frontiers of China.

It is not China and Korea, defending their national interests, their national territory, which are the aggressors. The aggressors are the United States of America and Great Britain, which have sent their troops several thousand kilometers from their frontiers to the territory of Korea, where these troops have already for several months been destroying Korean towns and villages, robbing the Koreans, violating Korean women and killing Korean children and the aged.

The Soviet Government regards likewise as not serious and ridiculous references in the British note to the liberation movement in Malaya, Indo-China and other countries, containing the accusation that the Soviet Government, expressing sympathy for the liberation struggle of the oppressed peoples, thereby allegedly violates the Anglo-Soviet treaty.

Similarly, not serious and ridiculous is the mention the British note makes, borrowed evidently from the lexicon of Hitler and Mussolini, of some kind of Communist imperialism. . . .

It is necessary to explain that as long as imperialist oppression exists in the world, there will exist also the liberation movement of the oppressed peoples, irrespective of the will and sympathies of some rulers or others. To accuse the Soviet Government of the existence in different countries of liberation movements caused by the oppression of imperialism is just as absurd as it would be absurd to accuse it of the occurrence in the world of earthquakes or tides.

The note of the Government of Great Britain asserts that the Soviet Government by voicing disapproval of the Marshall Plan thereby allegedly hampers the economic restoration of the European countries. This is absolutely wrong. The Soviet Government opposes the Marshall Plan not because it promises financial aid to some countries, but chiefly because it makes financial aid conditional on renunciation by these countries of their economic and political independence, renunciation of their sovereignty.

Great Britain has fallen under the subjugation of the United States of America, she is more and more losing her independence and being turned into a military base of the American armed forces because without this she could not obtain so-called Marshall Plan aid. The same should be said of France, Belgium, Turkey and the other so-called Marshallized countries.

Nor is it possible to ignore the fact that the Government of the United States used the Marshall Plan and attendant financial hand-outs to certain states in order to undermine by all kinds of unlawful means normal international trade and to impose a regime of discrimination against such states as the U.S.S.R. and the People's Democracies which firmly and resolutely defended their lawful economic interests and rejected all attempts at interference in their internal affairs.

The British note takes upon itself even such an affair as defense of the prestige of the United Nations, reproaching the Soviet Government for unwillingness to follow in everything the lead of those who unceremoniously are ruling supreme in this international organization upon which the peoples placed certain hopes not so long ago. However, as is clear to all, in any case it is not the Soviet Union which bears responsibility for the unsatisfactory situation that has arisen in the United Nations.

Obviously absurd are the attempts of the Government of Great Britain to shift on to the Soviet Union responsibility for "strikes and social disorders" or to ascribe all this to no one else than the Cominform. . . . It is well known in Britain that "strikes and social disorders" occurred not only long before our days and before the establishment of the Bureau of Communist and Workers Parties but also long before our generation.

The note of the British Government [says] that the Soviet Government demobilized only a certain number of servicemen from among the maximum call-up during the war. This assertion of the British note is a slander against the Soviet Union. In reality the Soviet Government effected a fundamental and extensive demobilization of its troops, having demobilized thirty-three age classes. No one needed an extensive demobilization of the Soviet troops as much as the Soviet Union, since without the returning of millions of demobilized men to the fields and factories the Soviet Union, far from being able to organize an economic advance after the war, would not have been able even to rehabilitate the areas, towns, railways, industry and agriculture destroyed by the German occupationists. Only people who have the intention of vilifying the Soviet Union can deny these facts.

The British note further asserts that at present the armed forces of the Soviet Union numerically exceed the armed forces of all the Western countries taken together. This assertion contained in the note is likewise a slander against the Soviet Union. At present the numerical strength of the armed forces of the Soviet Union, counting land forces, air forces and navy, is equal to the numerical strength of the armed forces of the U.S.S.R. before the outbreak of the second World War in 1939.

Yet three members alone of the North Atlantic aggressive pact—the United States of America, Britain and France—have at present in their armed forces, counting land troops and air forces as well as navy, more than five million men, with the numerical strength of these three powers continuing to grow rapidly while the industry of these countries has already been mobilized for a further increase in the production of armaments. We speak of the armies of these powers as one military force first and foremost because the armed forces of these three countries are now not three independent armies but one army combined by the American military men and put under the command of the American General Eisenhower.

It should be noted that this numerical strength of the armed forces of France, Britain and the United States is several times greater than that of their armed forces prior to the second World War in 1939 and is more than twice as great as the numerical strength of the armed forces of the U.S.S.R., at present. . . .

But from this it follows that, having attained a twofold superiority of its armed forces compared with the U.S.S.R. and seeking to expand them further, Great Britain, the United States and France prepare not for defense but for aggression, for unleashing a new world war. . . .*

As distinct from the Government of Great Britain, which has given up concern for the consolidation of peace among nations and now links its destiny with the untrammeled armaments drive and with reckless propaganda for a new war, the Soviet Union continues firmly to adhere to its peace-loving stand. The Government of the U.S.S.R., together with the entire Soviet public, day in and day out educates the Soviet people in the spirit of the consolidation of friendship among all nations, in the spirit of upholding the cause of peace and preventing a new war, exposing the intrigues and machinations of the warmongers.

* [Editors' Note] A French spokesman said on February 27, 1951, that the Russians have "four to five classes of 1.2 million men each" under arms, and challenged the Soviet Union to permit outside inspection of the size of its army. The U.S. Senate Armed Services Committee estimated, the same week, that the Soviet Union has 4 millions under arms, its satellites exclusive of China another million, the Atlantic Pact nations (including the United States) 4.5 millions. (See *The New York Times* for February 28, 1951.)

It is for this reason that the Soviet Government attaches such great importance to honest observance of the Anglo-Soviet Treaty as well as to strict observance of the Yalta and Potsdam agreements on the German question; especially at a time when violations of these agreements seriously harm the cause of the preservation of peace.

SECTION II
What Policy for America?

The foreign policy of this government since the promulgation of the Truman Doctrine of 1947 has been based primarily on the assumption that the Soviet Union is exerting constant pressure on all non-communist countries, and that the United States must take the lead in resisting such pressure. The necessity for "containing" the Soviet Union was argued in an influential article which appeared in *Foreign Affairs,* written by a Mr. "X," later identified as George Kennan, a high State Department official. Although supported generally by both major parties, the Administration's policy, highlighted by aid to Greece and Turkey, the Marshall Plan, the North Atlantic Pact, and armed support of the United Nations in Korea, has been subjected to much criticism. Observers like Walter Lippmann and Herbert Hoover have repeatedly warned that some of our policies may lead to the dissipation of our strength, leaving us too weak to provide for our own defense. What foreign policy will enable America to avoid war and yet safeguard her legitimate interests?

The victory of the Communists in China has not abated controversy over America's future rôle in the Far East. The nature of Chinese communism, the ties between China and the Soviet Union, and the best course of action for the United States are discussed by two well-known authorities on the Far East—Stanley Hornbeck and John Fairbank.

And, finally, is there any possibility of finding a solution to the recurring problem of war by building a world federation? This may perhaps be the question upon which world peace will ultimately be found to depend.

Topic 30
THE GREAT DEBATE

THE POLICY OF CONTAINMENT
"X" *

The maintenance of [the] pattern of Soviet power, namely, the pursuit of unlimited authority domestically, accompanied by the cultivation of the

* The selection is from "The Sources of Soviet Conduct," by "X," *Foreign Affairs* (July, 1947), pp. 571–582. Reprinted by permission of *Foreign Affairs.*

semi-myth of implacable foreign hostility, has gone far to shape the actual machinery of Soviet power as we know it today. Internal organs of administration which did not serve this purpose withered on the vine. Organs which did serve this purpose became vastly swollen. The security of Soviet power came to rest on the iron discipline of the Party, on the severity and ubiquity of the secret police, and on the uncompromising economic monopolism of the state. The "organs of suppression," in which the Soviet leaders had sought security from rival forces, became in large measure the masters of those whom they were designed to serve. Today the major part of the structure of Soviet power is committed to the perfection of the dictatorship and to the maintenance of the concept of Russia as in a state of siege, with the enemy lowering beyond the walls. And the millions of human beings who form that part of the structure of power must defend at all costs this concept of Russia's position, for without it they are themselves superfluous.

As things stand today, the rulers can no longer dream of parting with these organs of suppression. The quest for absolute power, pursued now for nearly three decades with a ruthlessness unparalleled (in scope at least) in modern times, has again produced internally, as it did externally, its own reaction. The excesses of the police apparatus have fanned the potential opposition to the régime into something far greater and more dangerous than it could have been before those excesses began.

But least of all can the rulers dispense with the fiction by which the maintenance of dictatorial power has been defended. For this fiction has been canonized in Soviet philosophy by the excesses already committed in its name; and it is now anchored in the Soviet structure of thought by bonds far greater than those of mere ideology. . . .

It is clear that the main element of any United States policy toward the Soviet Union must be that of a long-term, patient but firm and vigilant containment of Russian expansive tendencies. It is important to note, however, that such a policy has nothing to do with outward histrionics: with threats or blustering or superfluous gestures of outward "toughness." While the Kremlin is basically flexible in its reaction to political realities, it is by no means unamenable to considerations of prestige. Like almost any other government, it can be placed by tactless and threatening gestures in a position where it cannot afford to yield even though this might be dictated by its sense of realism. The Russian leaders are keen judges of human psychology, and as such they are highly conscious that loss of temper and of self-control is never a source of strength in political affairs. They are quick to exploit such evidences of weakness. For these reasons, it is a *sine qua non* of successful dealing with Russia that the foreign government in question should remain at all times cool and collected and that its demands on Russian policy should be put forward in such a manner as to leave the way open for a compliance not too detrimental to Russian prestige.

In the light of the above, it will be clearly seen that the Soviet pressure against the free institutions of the western world is something that can be contained by the adroit and vigilant application of counter-force at a series of constantly shifting geographical and political points, corresponding to the shifts and manœuvres of Soviet policy, but which cannot be charmed or talked out of existence. The Russians look forward to a duel of infinite duration, and they see that already they have scored great successes. It must be borne in mind that there was a time when the Communist Party represented far more of a minority in the sphere of Russian national life than Soviet power today represents in the world community.

But if ideology convinces the rulers of Russia that truth is on their side and that they can therefore afford to wait, those of us on whom that ideology has no claim are free to examine objectively the validity of that premise. The Soviet thesis not only implies complete lack of control by the west over its own economic destiny, it likewise assumes Russian unity, discipline and patience over an infinite period. Let us bring this apocalyptic vision down to earth, and suppose that the western world finds the strength and resourcefulness to contain Soviet power over a period of ten to fifteen years. What does that spell for Russia itself?

The Soviet leaders, taking advantage of the contributions of modern technique to the arts of despotism, have solved the question of obedience within the confines of their power. Few challenge their authority; and even those who do are unable to make that challenge valid as against the organs of suppression of the state.

The Kremlin has also proved able to accomplish its purpose of building up in Russia, regardless of the interests of the inhabitants, an industrial foundation of heavy metallurgy, which is, to be sure, not yet complete but which is nevertheless continuing to grow and is approaching those of the other major industrial countries. All of this, however, both the maintenance of internal political security and the building of heavy industry, has been carried out at a terrible cost in human life and in human hopes and energies. It has necessitated the use of forced labor on a scale unprecedented in modern times under conditions of peace. It has involved the neglect or abuse of other phases of Soviet economic life, particularly agriculture, consumers' goods production, housing and transportation.

To all that, the war has added its tremendous toll of destruction, death and human exhaustion. In consequence of this, we have in Russia today a population which is physically and spiritually tired. The mass of the people are disillusioned, skeptical and no longer as accessible as they once were to the magical attraction which Soviet power still radiates to its followers abroad. The avidity with which people seized upon the slight respite accorded to the Church for tactical reasons during the war was eloquent testimony to the fact that their capacity for faith and devotion found little expression in the purposes of the régime.

In these circumstances, there are limits to the physical and nervous strength of people themselves. These limits are absolute ones, and are binding even for the cruelest dictatorship, because beyond them people cannot be driven. The forced labor camps and the other agencies of constraint provide temporary means of compelling people to work longer hours than their own volition or mere economic pressure would dictate; but if people survive them at all they become old before their time and must be considered as human casualties to the demands of dictatorship. In either case their best powers are no longer available to society and can no longer be enlisted in the service of the state.

Here only the younger generation can help. The younger generation, despite all vicissitudes and sufferings, is numerous and vigorous; and the Russians are a talented people. But it still remains to be seen what will be the effects on mature performance of the abnormal emotional strains of childhood which Soviet dictatorship created and which were enormously increased by the war. Such things as normal security and placidity of home environment have practically ceased to exist in the Soviet Union outside of the most remote farms and villages. And observers are not yet sure whether that is not going to leave its mark on the over-all capacity of the generation now coming into maturity.

In addition to this, we have the fact that Soviet economic development, while it can list certain formidable achievements, has been precariously spotty and uneven. Russian Communists who speak of the "uneven development of capitalism" should blush at the contemplation of their own national economy. Here certain branches of economic life, such as the metallurgical and machine industries, have been pushed out of all proportion to other sectors of economy. Here is a nation striving to become in a short period one of the great industrial nations of the world while it still has no highway network worthy of the name and only a relatively primitive network of railways. Much has been done to increase efficiency of labor and to teach primitive peasants something about the operation of machines. But maintenance is still a crying deficiency of all Soviet economy. Construction is hasty and poor in quality. Depreciation must be enormous. And in vast sectors of economic life it has not yet been possible to instill into labor anything like that general culture of production and technical self-respect which characterizes the skilled worker of the west.

It is difficult to see how these deficiencies can be corrected at an early date by a tired and dispirited population working largely under the shadow of fear and compulsion. And as long as they are not overcome, Russia will remain economically a vulnerable, and in a certain sense an impotent, nation, capable of exporting its enthusiasms and of radiating the strange charm of its primitive political vitality but unable to back up those articles of export by the real evidences of material power and prosperity.

Meanwhile, a great uncertainty hangs over the political life of the Soviet

Union. That is the uncertainty involved in the transfer of power from one individual or group of individuals to others.

This is, of course, outstandingly the problem of the personal position of Stalin. We must remember that his succession to Lenin's pinnacle of preeminence in the Communist movement was the only such transfer of individual authority which the Soviet Union has experienced. That transfer took 12 years to consolidate. It cost the lives of millions of people and shook the state to its foundations. The attendant tremors were felt all through the international revolutionary movement, to the disadvantage of the Kremlin itself.

It is always possible that another transfer of preëminent power may take place quietly and inconspicuously, with no repercussions anywhere. But again, it is possible that the questions involved may unleash, to use some of Lenin's words, one of those "incredibly swift transitions" from "delicate deceit" to "wild violence" which characterize Russian history, and may shake Soviet power to its foundations.

But this is not only a question of Stalin himself. There has been, since 1938, a dangerous congealment of political life in the higher circles of Soviet power. The All-Union Party Congress, in theory the supreme body of the Party, is supposed to meet not less often than once in three years. It will soon be eight full years since its last meeting. During this period membership in the Party has numerically doubled. Party mortality during the war was enormous; and today well over half of the Party members are persons who have entered since the last Party congress was held. Meanwhile, the same small group of men has carried on at the top through an amazing series of national vicissitudes. Surely there is some reason why the experiences of the war brought basic political changes to every one of the great governments of the west. Surely the causes of that phenomenon are basic enough to be present somewhere in the obscurity of Soviet political life, as well. And yet no recognition has been given to these causes in Russia.

It must be surmised from this that even within so highly disciplined an organization as the Communist Party there must be a growing divergence in age, outlook and interest between the great mass of Party members, only so recently recruited into the movement, and the little self-perpetuating clique of men at the top, whom most of these Party members have never met, with whom they have never conversed, and with whom they can have no political intimacy.

Who can say whether, in these circumstances, the eventual rejuvenation of the higher spheres of authority (which can only be a matter of time) can take place smoothly and peacefully, or whether rivals in the quest for higher power will not eventually reach down into these politically immature and inexperienced masses in order to find support for their respective claims? If this were ever to happen, strange consequences could flow for the Communist Party: for the membership at large has been exercised only in the practices of iron discipline and obedience and not in the arts of compromise and accommodation. And if disunity were ever to seize and paralyze the Party, the chaos and weakness of Russian society would be revealed in forms beyond description. For we have seen that Soviet power is only a crust concealing an amorphous mass of human beings among whom no independent organizational structure is tolerated. In Russia there is not even such a thing as local government. The present generation of Russians have never known spontaneity of collective action. If, consequently, anything were ever to occur to disrupt the unity and efficacy of the Party as a political instrument, Soviet Russia might be changed overnight from one of the strongest to one of the weakest and most pitiable of national societies.

Thus the future of Soviet power may not be by any means as secure as Russian capacity for self-delusion would make it appear to the men in the Kremlin. That they can keep power themselves, they have demonstrated. That they can quietly and easily turn it over to others remains to be proved. Meanwhile, the hardships of their rule and the vicissitudes of international life have taken a heavy toll of the strength and hopes of the great people on whom their power rests. It is curious to note that the ideological power of Soviet authority is strongest today in areas beyond the frontiers of Russia, beyond the reach of its police power. This phenomenon brings to mind a comparison used by Thomas Mann in his great novel "Buddenbrooks." Observing that human institutions often show the greatest outward brilliance at a moment when inner decay is in reality farthest advanced, he compared the Buddenbrook family, in the days of its greatest glamour, to one of those stars whose light shines most brightly on this world when in reality it has long since ceased to exist. And who can say with assurance that the strong light still cast by the Kremlin on the dissatisfied peoples of the western world is not the powerful afterglow of a constellation which is in actuality on the wane? This cannot be proved. And it cannot be disproved. But the possibility remains (and in the opinion of this writer it is a strong one) that Soviet power, like the capitalist world of its conception, bears within it the seeds of its own decay, and that the sprouting of these seeds is well advanced.

It is clear that the United States cannot expect in the foreseeable future to enjoy political intimacy with the Soviet régime. It must continue to regard the Soviet Union as a rival, not a partner, in the political arena. It must continue to expect that Soviet policies will reflect no abstract love of peace and stability, no real faith in the possibility of a permanent happy coexistence of the Socialist and capitalist worlds, but rather a cautious, persistent pressure toward the disruption and weakening of all rival influence and rival power.

Balanced against this are the facts that Russia, as opposed to the western world in general, is still by far the weaker party, that Soviet policy is highly flexible, and that Soviet society may well contain deficiencies which will eventually weaken its own total potential. This would of itself warrant the United States entering with reasonable confidence upon a policy of firm containment, designed to confront the Russians with unalterable counter-force at every point where they show signs of encroaching upon the interests of a peaceful and stable world.

But in actuality the possibilities for American policy are by no means limited to holding the line and hoping for the best. It is entirely possible for the United States to influence by its actions the internal developments, both within Russia and throughout the international Communist movement, by which Russian policy is largely determined. This is not only a question of the modest measure of informational activity which this government can conduct in the Soviet Union and elsewhere, although that, too, is important. It is rather a question of the degree to which the United States can create among the peoples of the world generally the impression of a country which knows what it wants, which is coping successfully with the problems of its internal life and with the responsibilities of a World Power, and which has a spiritual vitality capable of holding its own among the major ideological currents of the time. To the extent that such an impression can be created and maintained, the aims of Russian Communism must appear sterile and quixotic, the hopes and enthusiasm of Moscow's supporters must wane, and added strain must be imposed on the Kremlin's foreign policies. For the palsied decrepitude of the capitalist world is the keystone of Communist philosophy. Even the failure of the United States to experience the early economic depression which the ravens of the Red Square have been predicting with such complacent confidence since hostilities ceased would have deep and important repercussions throughout the Communist world.

By the same token, exhibitions of indecision, disunity and internal disintegration within this country have an exhilarating effect on the whole Communist movement. At each evidence of these tendencies, a thrill of hope and excitement goes through the Communist world; a new jauntiness can be noted in the Moscow tread; new groups of foreign supporters climb on to what they can only view as the band wagon of international politics; and Russian pressure increases all along the line of international affairs.

It would be an exaggeration to say that American behavior unassisted and alone could exercise a power of life and death over the Communist movement and bring about the early fall of Soviet power in Russia. But the United States has it in its power to increase enormously the strains under which Soviet policy must operate, to force upon the Kremlin a far greater degree of moderation and circumspection than it has had to observe in recent years, and in this way to promote tendencies which must eventually find their outlet in either the break-up or the gradual mellowing of Soviet power. For no mystical, Messianic movement—and particularly not that of the Kremlin—can face frustration indefinitely without eventually adjusting itself in one way or another to the logic of that state of affairs.

Thus the decision will really fall in large measure in this country itself. The issue of Soviet-American relations is in essence a test of the over-all worth of the United States as a nation among nations. To avoid destruction the United States need only measure up to its own best traditions and prove itself worthy of preservation as a great nation.

Surely, there was never a fairer test of national quality than this. In the light of these circumstances, the thoughtful observer of Russian-American relations will find no cause for complaint in the Kremlin's challenge to American society. He will rather experience a certain gratitude to a Providence which, by providing the American people with this implacable challenge, has made their entire security as a nation dependent on their pulling themselves together and accepting the responsibilities of moral and political leadership that history plainly intended them to bear.

Strategy of the Cold War

Walter Lippmann *

An anonymous article on "The Sources of Soviet Conduct" † appeared in the quarterly journal *Foreign Affairs* for July 1947 and shortly afterwards it was republished in *Life* magazine. By its quality alone it would have commanded wide attention. For it was manifestly the work of a man who had observed the Soviet regime closely with a trained eye and an educated mind, and had arrived at a theory as to why the conduct of the Soviet government reflects "no abstract love of peace and stability, no real faith in the possibility of a permanent happy co-existence of the socialist and capitalist worlds, but rather a continuous, persistent pressure towards the disruption and weakening of all rival influence and rival power." . . .

We must begin with the disturbing fact, which anyone who will reread the article can verify for himself, that Mr. X's conclusions depend upon the optimistic prediction that the "Soviet power . . . bears within itself the seeds of its own decay, and that the sprouting of these seeds is well advanced"; that if "anything were ever to occur to disrupt the unity and the efficacy of the Party as a political instrument, Soviet Russia might be changed overnight (*sic*) from one of the strongest to one of the weakest and most pitiable of national societies"; and "that Soviet society may well (*sic*) contain deficiencies which will eventually weaken its own total potential."

Of this optimistic prediction Mr. X himself says that it "cannot be

* Newspaper columnist. Formerly newspaper editor. Author of *Public Opinion, A Preface to Politics, A Preface to Morals, The Good Society, U.S. Foreign Policy,* and numerous other books. The selection is from Walter Lippmann, *The Cold War* (New York, Harper & Bros., 1947), *passim*. Copyright, 1947, by Walter Lippmann. Reprinted by permission of Harper & Bros.

† See foregoing selection, retitled "The Policy of Containment."

proved. And it cannot be disproved." Nevertheless, he concludes that the United States should construct its policy on the assumption that the Soviet power is inherently weak and impermanent, and that this unproved assumption warrants our entering "with reasonable confidence upon a policy of firm containment, designed to confront the Russians with unalterable counterforce at every point where they show signs of encroaching upon the interests of a peaceful and a stable world."

I do not find much ground for reasonable confidence in a policy which can be successful only if the most optimistic prediction should prove to be true. Surely a sound policy must be addressed to the worst and hardest that may be judged to be probable, and not to the best and easiest that may be possible. . . .

In Mr. X's estimates there are no reserves for a rainy day. There is no margin of safety for bad luck, bad management, error and the unforeseen. He asks us to assume that the Soviet power is already decaying. He exhorts us to believe that our own highest hopes for ourselves will soon have been realized. Yet the policy he recommends is designed to deal effectively with the Soviet Union "as a rival, not a partner, in the political arena." Do we dare to assume, as we enter the arena and get set to run the race, that the Soviet Union will break its leg while the United States grows a pair of wings to speed it on its way? . . .

Surely it is by no means proved that the way to lead mankind is to spend the next ten or fifteen years, as Mr. X proposes we should, in reacting at "a series of constantly shifting geographical and political points, corresponding to the shifts and maneuvers of Soviet policy." For if history has indeed intended us to bear the responsibility of leadership, then it is not leadership to adapt ourselves to the shifts and maneuvers of Soviet policy at a series of constantly shifting geographical and political points. For that would mean for ten or fifteen years Moscow, not Washington, would define the issues, would make the challenges, would select the ground where the conflict was to be waged, and would choose the weapons. And the best that Mr. X can say for his own proposal is that if for a long period of time we can prevent the Soviet power from winning, the Soviet power will eventually perish or "mellow" because it has been "frustrated." . . .

Now the strength of the western world is great, and we may assume that its resourcefulness is considerable. Nevertheless, there are weighty reasons for thinking that the kind of strength we have and the kind of resourcefulness we are capable of showing are peculiarly unsuited to operating a policy of containment.

How, for example, under the Constitution of the United States is Mr. X going to work out an arrangement by which the Department of State has the money and the military power always available in sufficient amounts to apply "counterforce" at constantly shifting points all over the world? Is he going to ask Congress for a blank check on the Treasury and for a blank authorization to use the armed forces? Not if the American constitutional system is to be maintained. Or is he going to ask for an appropriation and for authority each time the Russians "show signs of encroaching upon the interests of a peaceful and stable world"? If that is his plan for dealing with the maneuvers of a dictatorship, he is going to arrive at the points of encroachment with too little and he is going to arrive too late. The Russians, if they intend to encroach, will have encroached while Congress is getting ready to hold hearings.

A policy of shifts and maneuvers may be suited to the Soviet system of government, which, as Mr. X tells us, is animated by patient persistence. It is not suited to the American system of government.

It is even more unsuited to the American economy which is unregimented and uncontrolled, and therefore cannot be administered according to a plan. Yet a policy of containment cannot be operated unless the Department of State can plan and direct exports and imports. For the policy demands that American goods be delivered or withheld at "constantly shifting geographical and political points corresponding to the shifts and maneuvers of Soviet policy."

I find it hard to understand how Mr. X could have recommended such a strategic monstrosity. For he tells us, no doubt truly, that the Soviet power "cannot be easily defeated or discouraged by a single victory on the part of its opponents," and that "the patient persistence by which it is animated" means that it cannot be "effectively countered" by "sporadic acts." Yet his own policy calls for a series of sporadic acts: the United States is to apply "counterforce" where the Russians encroach and when they encroach. . . .

There is, however, no rational ground for confidence that the United States could muster "unalterable counterforce" at all the individual sectors. The Eurasian continent is a big place, and the military power of the United States, though it is very great, has certain limitations which must be borne in mind if it is to be used effectively. We live on an island continent. We are separated from the theaters of conflict by the great oceans. We have a relatively small population, of which the greater proportion must in time of war be employed in producing, transporting and servicing the complex weapons and engines which constitute our military power. The United States has, as compared with the Russians, no adequate reserves of infantry. Our navy commands the oceans and we possess the major offensive weapons of war. But on the ground in the interior of the Eurasian continent, as we are learning in the Greek mountains, there may be many "individual sectors" where only infantry can be used as the "counterforce." . . .

Yet the genius of American military power does not lie in holding positions indefinitely. That requires a massive patience by great hordes of docile people. American military power is distinguished by its mobility, its speed, its range and its offensive striking force. It is, therefore, not an efficient instrument for a diplomatic policy of containment. It can only be the instrument of a policy which has as its objective a decision and a settlement. It can and should be used to redress the balance of power which has been upset by the war. But it is not designed for, or adapted to, a strategy of containing, waiting, countering, blocking, with no more specific objective than the eventual "frustration" of the opponent.

The Americans would themselves probably be frustrated by Mr. X's policy long before the Russians were.

The policy of containment, which Mr. X recommends, demands the employment of American economic, political, and in the last analysis, American military power at "sectors" in the interior of Europe and Asia. This requires, as I have pointed out, ground forces, that is to say reserves of infantry, which we do not possess.

The United States cannot by its own military power contain the expansive pressure of the Russians "at every point where they show signs of encroaching." The United States cannot have ready "unalterable counterforce" consisting of American troops. Therefore, the counterforces which Mr. X requires have to be composed of Chinese, Afghans, Iranians, Turks, Kurds, Arabs, Greeks, Italians, Austrians, of anti-Soviet Poles, Czechoslovaks, Bulgars, Yugoslavs, Albanians, Hungarians, Finns and Germans.

The policy can be implemented only by recruiting, subsidizing and supporting a heterogeneous array of satellites, clients, dependents and puppets. The instrument of the policy of containment is therefore a coalition of disorganized, disunited, feeble or disorderly nations, tribes and factions around the perimeter of the Soviet Union. . . .

In the complicated contest over this great heterogeneous array of unstable states, the odds are heavily in favor of the Soviets. For if we are to succeed, we must organize our satellites as unified, orderly and reasonably contented nations. The Russians can defeat us by disorganizing states that are already disorganized, by disuniting peoples that are torn with civil strife, and by inciting their discontent which is already very great. . . .

There is still greater disadvantage in a policy which seeks to "contain" the Soviet Union by attempting to make "unassailable barriers" out of the surrounding border states. They are admittedly weak. Now a weak ally is not an asset. It is a liability. It requires the diversion of power, money, and prestige to support it and to maintain it. These weak states are vulnerable. Yet the effort to defend them brings us no nearer to a decision or to a settlement of the main conflict. Worst of all, the effort to develop such an unnatural alliance of backward states must alienate the natural allies of the United States.

The natural allies of the United States are the nations of the Atlantic community: that is to say, the nations of western Europe and of the Americas. The Atlantic Ocean and the Mediterranean Sea, which is an arm of the Atlantic Ocean, unite them in a common strategic, economic and cultural system. The chief components of the Atlantic community are the British Commonwealth of nations, the Latin states on both sides of the Atlantic, the Low Countries and Switzerland, Scandinavia and the United States. . . .

Now the policy of containment, as described by Mr. X, is an attempt to organize an anti-Soviet alliance composed in the first instance of peoples that are either on the shadowy extremity of the Atlantic community, or are altogether outside it. The active proponents of the policy have been concerned immediately with the anti-Soviet parties and factions of eastern Europe, with the Greeks, the Turks, the Iranians, the Arabs and Afghans, and with the Chinese Nationalists.

Instead of concentrating their attention and their efforts upon our old allies of the Atlantic community, the makers and the shapers of the policy of containment have for more than a year been reaching out for new allies on the perimeter of the Soviet Union. This new coalition, as we can see only too clearly in Greece, in Iran, in the Arab states and in China, cannot in fact be made to coalesce. Instead of becoming an unassailable barrier against the Soviet power, this borderland is a seething stew of civil strife. . . .

The nations of the Atlantic community are not occupied by the Red Army. They cannot be occupied by the Red Army unless the Kremlin is prepared to face a full scale world war, atomic bombs and all the rest. Though impoverished and weakened, the nations of the Atlantic community are incomparably stronger, richer, more united and politically more democratic and mature than any of the nations of the Russian perimeter.

If the Soviet Union is, nevertheless, able to paralyze and disorganize them, then surely it can much more readily paralyze and disorganize the nations of the perimeter. They are already paralyzed and disorganized. They have never, in fact, been organized and effective modern states. Yet we are asked to believe that we can organize the perimeter of Russia, though the Russians are so strong and so cunning that we cannot consolidate the Atlantic community.

By concentrating our efforts on a diplomatic war in the borderlands of the Soviet Union, we have neglected—because we do not have unlimited power, resources, influence, and diplomatic brain power—the vital interests of our natural allies in western Europe, notably in reconstructing their economic life and in promoting a German settlement on which they can agree.

The failure of our diplomatic campaign in the borderlands, on which we have staked much too much, has conjured up the specter of a Third World War. The threat of a Russian-American war, arising out of the conflict in the borderlands, is dissolving the natural alliance of the Atlantic community. For the British, the French, and all the other Europeans see that they are placed between the hammer and the anvil. They realize, even if we do not realize it, that the policy of containment, in the hope that the Soviet power will collapse by frustration, cannot be enforced and cannot be administered successfully, and that it must fail. Either Russia will burst through the barriers which are supposed to contain her, and all of Europe will be at her mercy, or, at some point and at some time, the diplomatic war will become a full scale shooting war. In either event Europe is lost. Either Europe falls under the domination of Russia, or Europe becomes the battlefield of a Russian-American war. . . .

It will be evident, I am sure, to the reader who has followed the argument to this point that my criticism of the policy of containment, or the so-called Truman Doctrine, does not spring from any hope or belief that the Soviet pressure to expand can be "charmed or talked out of existence." I agree entirely with Mr. X that we must make up our minds that the Soviet power is not amenable to our arguments, but only "to contrary force" that "is felt to be too strong, and thus more rational in the logic and rhetoric of power."

My objection, then, to the policy of containment is not that it seeks to confront the Soviet power with American power, but that the policy is misconceived, and must result in a misuse of American power. . . .

The policy concedes to the Kremlin the strategical initiative as to when, where and under what local circumstances the issue is to be joined. It compels the United States to meet the Soviet pressure at these shifting geographical and political points by using satellite states, puppet governments and agents which have been subsidized and supported, though their effectiveness is meager and their reliability uncertain. By forcing us to expand our energies and our substance upon these dubious and unnatural allies on the perimeter of the Soviet Union, the effect of the policy is to neglect our natural allies in the Atlantic community, and to alienate them. . . .

I am contending that the American diplomatic effort should be concentrated on the problem created by the armistice—which is on how the continent of Europe can be evacuated by the three non-European armies which are now inside Europe. This is the problem which will have to be solved if the independence of the European nations is to be restored. Without that there is no possibility of a tolerable peace. But if these armies withdraw, there will be a very different balance of power in the world than there is today, and one which cannot easily be upset. For the nations of Europe, separately and in groups, perhaps even in unity, will then, and then only, cease to be the stakes and the pawns of the Russian-American conflict.

I do not think there is any doubt, therefore, that the evacuation of Europe by the Red Army would alter the situation decisively. There would then be in the internal affairs of the European countries no alien and irresistible military force actually deciding or threatening to decide the internal issues of power and authority. . . .

The next question is whether the objective of obtaining the withdrawal of the Red Army is attainable. A certain answer to this question is, of course, impossible. We can only calculate the probabilities, and we can say that the objective I am contending for is concrete, substantial, intelligible to everyone, and a normal and universally accepted objective at the conclusion and settlement of a war.

We may begin, moreover, by noting that in all our disagreements with the Soviet government the Kremlin has always agreed that the purpose of these tedious negotiations is in the end to conclude treaties of peace with all the enemy states. . . .

In making the withdrawal of the armies the objective of our policy, we are seeking to accomplish a result which the Soviet government by the very act of negotiating peace treaties has agreed to in principle.

If the Kremlin really means to dominate Europe, it will not withdraw its armies which are halfway across Europe. Standing on the Elbe line in the middle of Europe and Austria, and on the vulnerable frontier of Italy, the Kremlin is in a far better position to advance farther west than it can be if it withdraws and stands on its own frontiers. The withdrawal of the army is, therefore, the acid test of Soviet conduct and purpose, incomparably clearer, more definite, more practical than whether or not they observe the Yalta Declaration in countries liberated from the Nazis but still occupied by the Red Army. Verbal agreements like the Yalta Declaration and the Atlantic Charter can be made the subject of endless tactical maneuvering. For agreements of this kind do not change the balance of power. But the evacuation of a continent would change the balance of power.

The Kremlin will understand this, and we must expect it to exact the highest price it can obtain for what would be a deep reduction of its present power and influence in Europe, or, if it means to conquer Europe, to obstruct any settlement which meant that the Russian armies must evacuate Europe. . . .

If, nevertheless, the Soviet government will not negotiate an agreement, if the price of a settlement is impossibly high, if the ransom is deliberately set in terms which mean that Russia does not intend to evacuate Europe, the situation will be no more dangerous than it is today. But our energies will be concentrated, not dispersed all over the globe, and the real issues will be much clearer.

We must turn then to the problem of Germany, and how that problem is defined if we adhere to the Truman Doctrine and how defined if we adopt the alternative policy for which I have been contending. . . .

The underlying assumption, which is implicit though unavowed, has been that since Germany has lost the eastern provinces to the Russians and to a Russian satellite, Poland, German national feeling will naturally be directed against the Soviet Union. Historical experience and the logic of the situation indicate, I believe, that this is a profound miscalculation. For we are encouraging the Germans to want something—namely, national unity—which we cannot give them except by going to war with Russia. Germany cannot have unity, as all Germans must understand unity, except by recovering the lost provinces of eastern Germany. We would have to conquer Russia and Poland in order to restore the eastern provinces to Germany.

But Russia can return them to Germany whenever she decides that an alliance with Germany is a vital Russian interest. This can be done by performing another partition of Poland, an act which the men who signed the Molotov-Ribbentrop pact of 1939 could carry out if they deemed it expedient and necessary. Or if they deemed it inexpedient to partition Poland again, but necessary to enlarge the truncated Reich, they can offer the German nationalists compensation in western Europe and elsewhere for the lost provinces in the east. Just as they gave the Poles the German provinces as compensation for the territory east of the Curzon line, so they could offer Austria to the Germans, perhaps Alsace-Lorraine, perhaps Denmark, perhaps the Netherlands and the mouth of the Rhine.

We do not need to know exactly what the Soviet Union would offer the Germans for an alliance. It is enough to know that in an auction for the support of the Germans the Russians could offer them great prizes, and that we can offer the Germans absolutely nothing—except some help in rising from squalor and misery and prostration to the position of a fifth-rate power living a prosaic and stunted national existence. The idea that we can foster the sentiment of German unity, and make a truncated Germany economically strong, can keep her disarmed, and can use her in the anti-Soviet coalition is like trying to square the circle. Applied to Germany, the policy of containment is a booby trap, constructed by men who do not understand the politics of power. . . .

At the root of Mr. X's philosophy about Russian-American relations and underlying all the ideas of the Truman Doctrine there is a disbelief in the possibility of a settlement of the issues raised by this war. Having observed, I believe quite correctly, that we cannot expect "to enjoy political intimacy with the Soviet regime," and that we must "regard the Soviet Union as a rival, not a partner in the political arena," and that "there can be no appeal to common purposes," Mr. X has reached the conclusion that all we can do is to "contain" Russia until Russia changes, ceases to be our rival, and becomes our partner.

The conclusion is, it seems to me, quite unwarranted. The history of diplomacy is the history of relations among rival powers, which did not enjoy political intimacy, and did not respond to appeals to common purposes. Nevertheless, there have been settlements. Some of them did not last very long. Some of them did. For a diplomat to think that rival and unfriendly powers cannot be brought to a settlement is to forget what diplomacy is about. There would be little for diplomats to do if the world consisted of partners, enjoying political intimacy, and responding to common appeals.

AMERICA: GIBRALTAR OF THE WEST

Herbert Hoover *

The Kremlin-directed horde has under arms and in reserves probably 300 combat divisions, with 30,000 tanks. I am now told they have over 20,000 mostly tactical planes and they have with their satellites fifty million men available for cannon fodder. In World War II, when Russia was without the satellites, the Germans failed with 240 well-equipped divisions to overcome her. With her allies of General Manpower, General Space, General Winter and General Scorched Earth, she had stopped the Germans even before Lend-Lease had reached her. The nations of Europe in the Atlantic Pact have at the present moment less than twenty equipped and trained combat divisions available for European action.

There is here a stark reality upon which our foreign policies must be based. With any seeable land forces from non-Communist nations, even including the United States, a land offensive against the Communist could bring no military victory, no political conclusion. But that does not mean that there are no other methods of stopping the Kremlin's ambitions.

The second stark realism upon which our foreign policies must be based is the defense of the Western Hemisphere. Its defense is not only in our interests but in the interests of free men everywhere.

I may say at once that with proper economic action this hemisphere can be made self-contained in critical raw materials. From a long professional career and from years as Secretary of Commerce dealing with such questions, I might qualify in this field. Further, unless we so dissipate our strength as to become a beaten and crushed people, we will be able to keep sea lanes open. Moreover, this hemisphere can be defended from Communist armies, come what will. It is still surrounded with a great moat. To transport such invading armies either 3,000 miles across the Atlantic or 6,000 miles across the Pacific would require transport ships and naval protection which the Russians do not possess and could not build or seize, no matter what further countries they occupy.

If we have a proper naval and air strength, we could sink them in mid-ocean. With somewhat more attention paid to our defense, this would apply to invasion via the Bering Straits. Hitler could not even cross the English Channel. Atomic bombs do not transport troops over the ocean. Communist armies can no more get to Washington than any allied armies can get to Moscow. No responsible military man denies these two conclusions.

The American people should not be frightened into rash action by fear

* President of the United States, 1929–1933. Author of *The Challenge of Liberty* and other works. The selection is from a radio broadcast by Herbert Hoover, February 9, 1951. Printed in *The New York Times*, February 10, 1951.

that we cannot survive. I am not advocating isolationism. But if other nations should fail, we may be isolated by force of circumstance and against our will. We might go into a period hard to endure, but this nation can stick it out.

AMERICA'S COMMITMENT TO EUROPE

Harry S. Truman *

Our own national security is deeply involved with that of the other free nations. While they need our support, we equally need theirs. Our national security would be gravely prejudiced if the Soviet Union were to succeed in harnessing to its war machine the resources and the manpower of the free nations on the borders of its empire.

If Western Europe were to fall to Soviet Russia, it would double the Soviet supply of coal and triple the Soviet supply of steel. If the free countries of Asia and Africa should fall to Soviet Russia, we would lose the sources of many of our most vital raw materials, including uranium, which is the basis of our atomic power. And Soviet command of the manpower of the free nations of Europe and Asia would confront us with military forces which we could never hope to equal.

In such a situation the Soviet Union could impose its demands on the world without resort to conflict, simply through the preponderance of its economic and military power. The Soviet Union does not have to attack the United States to secure domination of the world. It can achieve its ends by isolating us and swallowing up all our allies. Therefore, even if we were craven—and I do not believe that we could be—I say, even if we are craven enough to abandon our ideals, it would be disastrous for us to withdraw from the community of free nations.

Topic 31

THE UNITED STATES IN THE FAR EAST

COMMUNIST IMPERIALISM IS THE ENEMY

Stanley K. Hornbeck †

The most portentous and most tragic fact about our policies in relations with and regarding China of the years under reference is that most of the

* President of the United States since 1945. The selection is from the text of President Truman's State of the Union message delivered in person before a joint session of the Eighty-second Congress. Printed in *The New York Times*, January 8, 1951.

† Former member of faculty of the University of Wisconsin and of Harvard University; former Chief of the Division of Far Eastern Affairs, U.S. Department of

persons whose views have prevailed in the formulating and implementing of those policies have, until very recently, believed about China, and about China's National Government, and about China's Communists, and about the part played or not played and playable or not playable by Russia in and regarding China, a great many things which simply haven't been so. They've believed that the United States should do things which it shouldn't, that China could do things which it couldn't, that China's Communists both were what they weren't and weren't what they were *and are.* The same regarding their view of the Soviet Union. Wishing the *people* of China well, and perturbed over ways in the political and social life of China that they considered dark, they failed—until recently—to take adequate account of a fact in international political life much more warrantably of concern both to the United States and to the Chinese—namely, the fact that "Communism," no matter where or of what brand, is being used by the Government of the Soviet Union as an instrument of imperialism and is committed to objectives which call for subjugation of all mankind.

World War II began when, in 1931, Japanese imperialists staged an assault on China, *in Manchuria;* and the League of Nations and the United States *in effect acquiesced.* Before that War was ended, Russian imperialists began a new assault on China, *via Manchuria,*—and for five long years, until seven weeks ago, the United Nations and the United States *in effect acquiesced.*

Now, eight years plus after Pearl Harbor and five years after VJ Day, we are living in *a world politically divided—divided three ways;* a world of *free peoples;* a world of *enslaved peoples;* and a world of those *peoples* who, *neither free nor enslaved,* are seeking freedom and are in danger of becoming enslaved. The *United States* is outstanding in the first, the *Soviet Union* outstanding in the second, and *China* outstanding in the third of these worlds.

We, the United States, are today confronted with probably the greatest test of our capacities that has ever been imposed upon us. Wanting peace, yet having since 1914 been drawn into *two World Wars,* we have become a party to and are a leading figure in an *even greater conflict: the Kremlin and Communism versus Democracy.* . . .

President Truman sensed danger some three years ago. He declared it his belief that it must be the policy of the United States "To support free peoples who are resisting attempted subjugation by armed minorities or by outside pressures," and that "If we falter in our leadership, we may endanger the peace of the world—and we shall surely endanger the welfare of our

---

State; former United States Ambassador to the Netherlands. Author of *Contemporary Politics in the Far East (1916)*, other books, and many articles on international relations. The selection re-presents, with the permission of the author, major portions of an address delivered at The American University, Washington, D.C., on August 16, 1950, entitled, *The United States and China—in a World Three Ways Divided.*

own Nation." The policy makers formulated, and the Congress approved, a plan which committed us to the principle but whittled down the scope of that utterance. Toward resistance to the Communist assault, we undertook to give *some* support to *some* countries, but *some* only, menaced by that assault. The principle of combatting the spread of Communism by giving support to resistance to it has since loomed large in our foreign policy as a whole, but with some glaring inconsistencies.

In two countries, Greece and China, the Communist assault was pressed simultaneously in terms of "hot" war. In the case of Greece, we, the United States, gave moral support and economic and military aid to a government which, under armed Communist attack, made armed resistance, a resistance which but for our support would soon have proved hopeless. In the case of the other, China, we ostentatiously withdrew our moral support and discontinued our material aid; and the resistance there of a government which was likewise under armed Communist attack became ineffectual but did not cease.

Strategically, China was and is of extreme importance in relation to the conflict between Democracy and the Kremlin because China lies in a buffer position, both geographically and politically, between the free peoples of the Pacific area—including ourselves—and the main base (Moscow) from which Communist operations are conducted. An anti-Communist China would be at least a barrier—to the advantage of the free peoples. A Communist China, if and as, will be a highway by which and a base from which Soviet influence will move and Communist armed forces be able to strike southward and eastward, i.e. toward Australia and toward the United States. Manchuria is so serving today.

Politically, China was and is of importance because she has vast potentialities and she has a permanent seat on the Security Council of the United Nations. An anti-Communist China votes there on our side. A Communist China, if and when, would vote—and veto—there on the Soviet side.

Yet, with that country, China, the largest, the most populous, the most richly endowed country in Asia, the enduring "Middle Kingdom," a neighbor across the Pacific, long our friend, lately an ally, under armed attack and in process of being subjugated by militant Communism, and with Korea, Japan, the Philippines and other Far Eastern countries, in fact most of Asia, almost sure to go as she goes,—our policy makers caused this country, the United States, to refrain, from August 1946 to June 27, 1950, from giving any real support to those who there are resisting Communist aggression. They said, successively and cumulatively, that we should not, we could not and we would not "intervene" in what they declared to be a "civil conflict."

That was just what the Kremlin and Communism wanted and worked for. William Z. Foster said some four years ago: "The war in China is the key to all problems of the international front . . . the key task . . . is to stop American intervention in China . . . the question of China is our key concentration."

President Roosevelt and Prime Minister Churchill made to Generalissimo Chiang in 1943, at Cairo, certain commitments. Most important: it was the agreed "purpose" of the three that Manchuria and Formosa (and the Pescadores) "shall be restored to China," and that "in due course Korea shall become free and independent."

Later, President Roosevelt—who did not understand the Russians, who thought he had persuaded Stalin, who was told by his military advisers that without Russian participation in the war against Japan the American casualty list in achieving Japan's defeat might be enormous,—President Roosevelt made, with Prime Minister Churchill, to Marshal Stalin, in 1945, at Yalta, concessions, at China's expense, inconsistent with earlier international agreements and with the commitments made at Cairo. (Incidentally, Stalin had already promised Russian participation.)

In the same transaction it was agreed that President Roosevelt would, upon signal from Marshal Stalin, take measures to obtain the concurrence of Generalissimo Chiang Kai-shek. The United States thus, with a view to saving American lives, paid Russia, in advance, with a draft drawn on China, guaranteed to Russia by Mr. Roosevelt and Mr. Churchill, kept secret from China for many months, and honored later by China on American official advice. . . .

True, we could not have prevented the Russian aggression which ensued; but, by giving, in advance, our assent to a predatory trespassing on Russia's part, we did in Russia's favor in relations with China a thing which we had for many years refused to do in Japan's favor; and in the giving we disregarded principles and pledges of our own and we authorized a violation by Russia of pledges which both she and we had given. No matter how much or how well our part at Yalta may be explained, defended and justified, we there bargained in and with China's rights and interests, for expected advantages to ourselves. We bought, with Chinese coin, unneeded Russian action and worthless Russian pledges. We later caused the Chinese to buy, with their confirmation, a made-in-Moscow Trojan horse. And—all too few of our people, including some in high places, seem subsequently to have taken any account of the extraordinary moral obligation which we thus incurred.

The Yalta and early post-Yalta developments had weakened the position of China's National Government and strengthened that of the Communists. Many of the things done and things said by the American Government and by some parts of the American public since then have had similar two-fold harmful effects.

There has been much loose, prejudiced and prejudicial talk about the amount of "aid" which we have given China. The facts do not bear out the impressions created by various statistical exhibits and official interpretations thereof. Much of what appears in various accountings is in no way warrantably describable as post-war aid to the National Government or as contribution to the military effort of that Government in its battle against the Communists. Our economic assistance was sent both into Nationalist held and into Communist held areas. It is more than questionable whether on balance the aid which we have given the National Government since VJ Day has not been more than offset by the encouragement which our other courses, in words and in deeds, have given to its Communist opposition, whether we have not in effect given the National Government more of hindrance than of help.

Surely, for instance, the embargo in 1946 on export to China of munitions, official statements in 1947 after the Marshall mission, testimony officially given in 1948 in public hearings, the "White Book" in 1949, the announcement in January, 1950, that we would not provide military aid or advice to Chinese forces on Formosa,—surely such and various other of our contributions have been the opposite of helpful to the Nationalists and highly encouraging to the Communists. The withdrawal of our moral support, with substitution of official criticism and abuse, probably did the Nationalists more damage than our munitions (while, and as given) had ever done them good. . . .

As of 1946, the Communists, after twenty-five years of effort, had no substantial following outside of the ranks of their own armed forces. In that year we began our withholding of material aid to the Nationalists and the Russians began their giving of material aid to the Communists; in the next year the Communists began to win armed victories; and thereafter, where the Communists appeared in force the Chinese people accepted them on a basis of hope and of fear, not, with the exception of a few intellectuals, on a basis of enthusiastic choice.

The Communist conquest of the mainland was not a victory of, by or for the Communist ideology. The Communists won by skillful use of armed forces, an abundance of munitions and a marvellous propaganda of big lies and bigger promises. They were the "outs" capitalizing on conditions of distress, which, after the Japanese, they themselves had helped create and which the "ins" were unable—as the Communists now are unable—to alleviate. They broadcast to the Chinese people and to the world that these conditions were all the fault of the Nationalists; they, the Communists, would liquidate those rascals, set up a government of and by and for the people, and make everything all right. And many of the Chinese people and many of the Nationalist soldiers—impoverished and frustrated by two decades of warfare, yearning for peace, discouraged and demoralized by the discontinuance of American moral and material support of the National Government, and noting the successes of the Communist armies—were easily taken in by that "line."—Many Americans, with no such preconditioning, also. . . .

The "yoke" in China will not be a "foreign" yoke: it will or would be a local copy of the totalitarian system which, effective in the Soviet Union and countries satellite thereto, is giving at this moment in Czechoslovakia and elsewhere new demonstrations of its methods. Communist totalitarian regimes are ruthlessly effective in anticipatory elimination of would be—or even might be—"revolters."

There is the wishful thought that Mao Tse-tung may become a Chinese Tito and a Communist China under him become an Asiatic Yugoslavia. But how can any statesman or any thoughtful layman seeking to combat the spread of Communism and to make the world safe for peoples that are free or hoping to become free,—how can any such person find comfort or cause for cheer in a hope for such a consummation? Tito is a proponent of world revolution. Tito's Yugoslavia is a totalitarian state. Mao Tse-tung has declared that Chinese Communism is a part of World Communism, and Mao's China will be a totalitarian state. Can it be imagined that a Communist China will ever become more antipathetic to Moscow dictation than Chiang Kai-shek's Nationalist China has been?

There is no warrant for an assumption that a "Communist" regime in China could or would be friendly or helpful to the United States. Communism is by nature intolerant of democracy. The Chinese Communists are avowedly committed no less than are the Russian to the objective of overthrowing all "capitalistic" or "bourgeois" or "imperialist" governments and making the victories of Communism universal. The Chinese Communist leaders have—openly, emphatically and repeatedly—declared that Chiang Kai-shek is their enemy Number One and the United States their enemy Number Two. They've copied the Russian pattern; they use the Russian methods; they follow the "Moscow line." Wherever they gain control they conduct themselves just as their counterparts or prototypes in other countries have done and are doing. They have told us over and over, and they show us day by day, to whom they consider themselves indebted, where their allegiance lies, what they envisage, and how they intend to operate. . . .

More serious, however, than any of these matters: If the Communists gain unchallenged control in China, the natural sequel, China then having passed completely into the Kremlin and Cominform orbit, will be intensification of Communist pressures in areas to the South, to the West, and to the East of China; the influence of the democracies (Western Europe and North America) will be diminished; Russian influence will be expanded; the interests, investments and commitments in general of the United States throughout the Far East—especially in Japan and in the Philippines—will be gravely endangered; the chance of our being involved in a "shooting" war with Russia will be increased; and the likelihood of our having any allies in Eastern Asia will be reduced to approximately zero.

The authors and factors of the Marshall Plan portrayed the foreign aid program as an "investment" in security—to be implemented on a basis of "calculated risk." They envisaged economic aid—to certain countries. They figured that this would require expenditures up to a certain amount. They said that we could afford that amount but no more; that we therefore could not include—could not find funds to include—China. But, less than a year later they saw and they declared that economic aid to Western Europe must be supplemented by military aid. They then decided that we could afford that supplement. Next, they perceived that Europe could not make a full economic recovery unless access be regained to the resources and trade of Eastern Asia. But the Communist advance in China was creating obstacles to that restoration. So, they thought and said, the Communist advance must be stopped—at China's borders. Hence the idea of economic aid to countries peripheral to China—with particular thought for Korea and the Philippines, and general thought, under a "Point Four" program, for several other areas. Next, they realized that in Asia as well as in Europe economic aid must be supplemented by military assistance. So, plans for such aid. . . . All the while, however, a studied insistence that China, including Formosa, not be included.

Was it not and is it not patent that the more the Communists gain in China, the stronger would be Russia's over-all strategic position and the greater the "risk" feature of the investment, under the Marshall Plan, in aid to and for Western Europe? Could it not be seen, be foreseen, that if Communism gained undisputed control in and of China, the initiative, in the struggle in the Far East between Communism and Democracy, would thereafter be overwhelmingly at the disposal of the Soviet Union and any likelihood of firm resistance by indigenous governments or populations to Communist pressures against or within the areas peripheral to China be greatly diminished?

Could it not be foreseen that with a Communist domination of China we would stand to lose all that we have with a century of effort gained—not only in China but at other, or at all, points in the Far East; that the relief which we had gained at a great price from the threat to our security which had all along been implicit in Japan's policy of expansion by force would be gone; more, that our losses might easily become the Kremlin's gains and the whole of our investment in the Far East, before and in World War II, be turned against us?

The Kremlin-planned and Russian-supported invasion of South Korea is a sample of the fruit to be expected from a policy of first letting a middle and key area go by default and then hoping that a modicum of aid to weak peoples in scattered peripheral areas will serve as a quarantine.

The whole question of what the United States could afford was and is a question of relative evaluations. We must, of course, at all times consider our national economy. But in war we spend freely in order that we may save. Now the simple fact is we've been at war with Communist totalitarianism. We've talked of "cold" war. But our policy makers have shown little awareness of the fact that war, whether "cold" or "hot," is nevertheless *war* and calls for planning and action accordingly. Compared with the expenditures that our people are now demanding be made, and which no one now says we can't afford, in response to a top level decision to support resistance to Communist aggression in Korea, the cost of an aid to Nationalist China such as we gave to Greece would have been a small amount indeed. We couldn't afford it because the people who said we *couldn't* were the same people who said we *shouldn't*. They were at outs with China's Nationalists because the Nationalists had declined or been unable to adopt and implement a program for China which *they* had prescribed. They believed that, as Stalin had said, China's Communists were "not real Communists." They believed that Democracy and Communism could exist, and be at peace, side by side. They refused to believe that a Communist domination of China could have serious—to say nothing of tragic—implications in regard to our policies and our position in the "cold" war which they expected to win by giving much economic and some military assistance to a few countries in Western Europe and in Western Asia. They insisted that the issue between Communism and Democracy was one of ideologies. They reasoned that we could check and roll back the tide of Communism by showing *some* peoples and telling *all* peoples that our Democratic way of life produces a better standard of living than does the Russian Soviet way.—They simply did not understand the Communist, the World-Communist, movement. They did not and would not see that Soviet Russia is, as was Tzarist Russia, expansionist minded, bent on conquest, and ruthless. We must not, they said, support a "corrupt" government in China. We must not intervene—though we already had intervened—in a "civil conflict" in China. If China's Communists won in that conflict, we could, they affirmed, thenceforth give them economic and cultural assistance, enroll them on the side of democracy, and see them become a thorn in the side to Soviet Russia.

One year ago, in August 1949, the Department of State, in the *White Book,* declared China's National Government bankrupt. It said that the Communists had won and that nothing that the United States had done or had not done could have changed that result. At the same time it declared itself at last awake to the fact of Soviet Russian imperialism, and it admonished China's Communists that an attempt on their part to engage in aggression against China's neighbors would be an affront to the United Nations.

At that time China's Nationalists still had a government, they still had armies, they still had a treasury, they still had bases, they long had been and they still were resisting the armed advance of militant Communism, and they still were hoping for American assistance. Moreover, what remained of the Nationalist organization was the hard core of the Kuomingtang and its armed forces. What they most lacked were the very things which but for the United States the Greeks also would have lacked, the things but for which Greece would have been overrun by the Communists.—Yet our government all but crossed them off, and perhaps worse, told them and the world that we were doing so.—Today, a year after that cross-off, those Nationalists still carry on. They have more and better political and military assets than they had then.

When China's Communist leaders created a government in Peking and proclaimed that government the government of China, the Kremlin and all of its satellites promptly accorded that government recognition. Our policy makers, along with those of Great Britain and several other non-Communist countries, gave favorable consideration to a plan which, had it been fully implemented, would have brought about recognition of that government by the United States shortly after that accorded by the United Kingdom, India and others. Popular opposition in this country, aroused by observation of the treatment accorded American interests in China by the Communist regime, spared us the making of that mistake. . . .

In the course of the past two years our Government, impelled partly by dictates of a "Europe first" strategy, party by a belated realization that economic assistance without military assistance is not only a "risk" but a "risk" which invites aggression, and partly by a feeling of alarm born of Communism's gains in Asia,—our Government has entered into arrangements for mutual defense between and among the free peoples of Western Europe and ourselves. We are giving to the North Atlantic Pact countries economic assistance and moral support and weapons and military collaboration. All to the good—in principle—but it does not go far enough.

The North Atlantic Pact and the Military Aid Program . . . may have strengthened us in *one* theatre, but they could not and can not give us security, all theatres considered. Strength and vulnerabilities have to be considered together. In today's world, security is, as is peace, indivisible, a condition for all or a reality for none. There can be no real security in the North Atlantic area, none in Europe, none in Asia, none in fact in America—no real security anywhere—so long as it is left possible for "Communism" or any other "ism" or system to impose itself or be imposed anywhere by force. . . .

There persist a number of serious questions to which, answered indifferently during recent years, renewed attention must now be given:

Can we afford to abandon a friendly Government, to the fashioning of whose predicament we have contributed, while that Government still lives and still is resisting a common enemy?

Can we afford to add, by such an act, to the doubts regarding our standards and our reliability which already exist in the minds of various governments and peoples whom we exhort to stand with us in a common effort to combat Communism and produce conditions of national and international security?

Can we afford to accept—by facilitating the completion of the Communist conquest of China and consolidation by the Communists of their position in the pivotal and crucial area—the increase which will inevitably result therefrom of Communist pressures upon and against other areas in the Far East in which we have interests and involvements, especially Japan and the Philippines?

Can we afford to accept by default the loss of the advantage which it might be to us to have remain alive in China at least a nucleus of organized resistance, some element allied with us in the common cause of resistance by free men and peoples to the armed advance of Communism?

Communist propaganda long has declared the conflict in China to be strictly a "civil conflict." The American Government has taken and has expressed the same view of it. But now, a similar conflict having developed in Korea, and the Communists (witness Mr. Malik) declaring *this* conflict strictly a "civil conflict," the American Government and the United Nations say: "No. This is a case of Communist aggression, Russian inspired and Russian supported. It must be stopped." (Witness the recent discussions and the Resolutions adopted at Lake Success.) "Even if it were merely a civil conflict, where there is a danger to world peace it is a right and may be a duty of the United Nations to intervene" (witness Sir Gladwin Jebb, on August 11, 1950).

No matter what may have been before 1946 the character of the conflict between China's Communists and China's National Government, that conflict has been since that year a conflict the fundamental characteristics of which have been and are Communist aggression, Russian inspiration and Russian support. What has been going on *in* China since 1946 differs little from what has been going on *in* Korea since June 24, 1950. In both cases Communism, engaging in armed aggression, has been on the march. In China, Chinese Communist armed forces have overrun the country; in Korea, Korean Communist armed forces have overrun the country. The American Government and the United Nations are right in declaring the developments in Korea a case of Communist aggression and in giving support to South Korean resistance thereto. They would have been right had they so done in regard to the conflict in China. They would be right were they now to do so. President Truman was right when in March 1947 he said: "I believe it must be the policy of the United States to support free peoples who are resisting attempted subjugation by armed minorities or by outside pressures." He is right now in coupling with United States action toward resisting Communist aggression by armed Koreans United States' action toward resisting Communist aggression by armed Chinese. The conflict in Korea is not a "civil conflict." The conflict between China's Communists and China's Nationalists is not a "civil conflict." The attacking forces in both cases bear a made-from-by-and-for-Moscow stamp.

A policy of resisting aggression by giving support to resistance to aggression calls for action not only toward repelling aggression but toward preventing aggression. Our operations toward repelling a Communist aggression in Korea would be jeopardized if concurrently therewith there occurred a Communist attack on Formosa. Success for our side in Korea would be a hollow victory if at the same time Communism made gains in Formosa or in the Philippines or in Indo-China. President Truman doubtless took all these considerations into account in the making of the decisions which he announced collectively and in combination on June 27. He gave us, for the region involved, a co-ordinated program toward comprehensive resistance to an enemy which, unfortunately, is in position to strike at any one or several of many points.

In a leading role, as we are, in this third world conflict; involved as we are in an armed resistance to Communist aggression in one region; and perceiving as most of us now do that Communism may attack and we be compelled, along with other peoples, to make armed resistance elsewhere (even to the point of there eventuating a third World War)—it behooves us to do, now and in particular, two things: (a) to "tie tight the cords of our helmet," gird on our armor, toward preventing an all out war if possible and, if war is forced upon us, defeating the aggressor; and (b) to make friends wherever possible, toward the same ends.

The question of making friends brings us back again to the question of relations with China. There has been in this country and elsewhere an advocacy of an idea of making friends with China's Communist regime: "Be nice to them, recognize them, give them the seat on the Executive Council of the United Nations which is now that of China's National Government; they are only superficially and temporarily allied to the Kremlin; they would, of their own volition and in gratitude for favors received from and expected of us, turn against the Russians, become friends with us, and be on our side in the world conflict."

Of that idea let me say only, in this context, that in my opinion the most stultifying action that the United States could take now would be to give any form of political encouragement or support to the Communist regime in China or to any advocacy, no matter by whom, of such a course. That regime cannot be won over to, nor will it come over to our side. Mao Tse-tung may, as Tito has done, quarrel with Stalin; but neither is Communist China nor is Communist Yugoslavia likely to side with us and Democracy against Communist imperialism. And, in my opinion, the most stultifying thing that the United Nations could now do would be to take from China's National Government and give to China's Communist Government China's seats in the Executive Council and elsewhere. The Soviet authorities could be appeased only by a total surrender, and the Chinese Communist authorities are almost as hostile to the Democracies as is the Kremlin. In the practical politics of international relations, the eyes, the ears, the voices and the acts of nations are, at any given moment or period, those of their own governing authorities. This is especially true where peoples are ringed 'round by "iron curtains." We cannot under present conditions reach and make friends of the people in Russia or the people in Communist China.

On the other hand, China's Nationalists have been our friends, still wish to be our friends, and are committed even more firmly to resistance to Communism than are we. We can influence them and, through them, China. Both the United States and the United Nations should take full stock of those facts and make the most of them.

No country in Europe, no nation in Asia has been won over to Communism by Communism's ideology. None has been saved from Communism by Democracy's ideology. But a dozen countries have been subjugated by Russian manipulation of the forces and resources, including manpower and arms and propaganda, which Communism has put at the Kremlin's disposal. Others are in jeopardy—and we are in danger. As Sir Gladwyn Jebb said on Friday last at Lake Success (August 11, 1950) "Whatever their (Europe and Asia's) relations in the past, they are likely both to be lost unless they both realize the danger and concert to meet it. For this purpose, what has happened in Korea must not be allowed to occur again."

For our own good, toward defense and survival of our country, our democracy, our own and other peoples rights to freedom and security, we need to prepare *now,* to the maximum of our ability, to discourage aggressors, to prevent attacks, to support those who resist attacks and, if we are attacked, to defend our own soil and from it, with help from others, whom we may have helped, put an end to aggression. The Communist attack is global. We cannot all by ourselves meet it on every front. But it must be met. We need friends and our friends need friends. We should think of China in that setting and of Nationalist China and Communist China in terms of relative potentialities. In a world three ways divided, the free peoples and those who seek freedom must stand together or, failing that, be one by one destroyed.

Competition with Communism, Not Containment

John K. Fairbank *

Current recrimination as to whether we gave Chiang Kai-shek too little military aid, or wasted what we did give him, obscures the lesson of his collapse. Not only our China policy but our whole Asian policy should profit by this lesson before it is too late.

* Director of the Regional Program on China at Harvard University. Author of *The United States and China.* The selection is from John K. Fairbank, "Competition with Communism, Not Containment," *Foreign Policy Reports,* Vol. 25 (March 15, 1949), pp. 6–9. Reprinted by permission of author and publisher.

WHY U.S. FAILED

Our policy failure in China has been due to our inadequate understanding, and even naïvete, concerning the complex revolutionary process there. As a country with a dominant middle class, devoted to political freedom, we have failed to grasp the dynamics of revolution in a peasant society where food and civil order are more highly esteemed by the masses than political self-expression. China's low economic standard of living has gone hand in hand with a low political standard of freedom, yet China's masses have become increasingly susceptible to organization through economic, political, social, and ideological appeals and devices. This has made it possible for the Chinese Communists to establish themselves as the leaders and organizers of the Chinese revolution, even though the Communists' "democracy" is phony according to our American standards. To say that the resulting turmoil in China is not a genuine social revolution, in the proper sense of the term, is a refusal to face facts. The revolution may be unpalatable to us and ominous for China, but let us not deny its real vigor. To do so betrays the same wishful thinking as the argument, never yet advanced with solid evidence, that the Chinese Communists have defeated the demoralized Nationalist forces only because of superior armament. If this is so, let us have the proof. If there is no proof, let us not base a policy on a pleasurable supposition.

Our greatest danger lies in our underestimating the strength of Chinese communism and assuming that because we would not tolerate communism in our country, therefore the peasant masses of China, in their far different and less happy circumstances, cannot regard it as a "liberation."

It is quite true that the United States and Russia are unhappily locked in a power struggle, the evil features of which may be mitigated but cannot be side-stepped. This great power conflict, however, goes on in many local areas in which the American and Russian state systems find themselves ineluctably in competition. We should have learned by now that the one sure path to American defeat is to judge the local regime in each area not on its merits, but solely by its attitude toward us and the Russians. Mere anti-communism, in short, will not save us. This is especially true in Asia, where the most anti-Communist elements are likely to be most closely linked to a *status quo* which has long been undermined.

Support of social change. It follows that our only hope of maintaining a position in China more extensive than the range of our own artillery lies in allying ourselves with the forces of social change and working with, not against, the long-term process of revolution. Such an effort to compete with communism for the leadership of revolution in Asia is not foreign to our heritage. The destruction of the old social structure of China was begun by Western missionaries, their concern for the individual soul, their education of girls as well as boys, their leadership in Westernization. Political revolutionists all over Asia have for decades drawn inspiration from the American revolutionary tradition. Only in this latest phase, with world power suddenly thrust upon us, do we find the United States cast in the role of defender of the *status quo*.

SOURCES OF COMMUNIST STRENGTH

The need to re-examine our policy makes it essential and urgent that we accurately assay the sources of Communist strength in China. What are the elements of the revolutionary process which Chinese communism thus far has used in its rise to power?

These forces can be grouped under four heads. The first is *nationalism* which brought Chiang Kai-shek to power. During the war, however, the Chinese Communists in North China assumed the leadership of a patriotic resistance to Japan. Since the war, they have further developed their claim to patriotic leadership by denouncing American "imperialism" and aid to Chiang as a continuing phase of foreign capitalist aggression. Whatever the merits of this interpretation, it is noteworthy that the Chinese Communist rank and file seem to be motivated by a genuine and ardent love of country.

Peasant rebellion is a second element which gives much of its substance to the Communist movement. The Communists, however, have improved upon the ancient tradition whereby the disaffected peasantry, slaughtering landlords and redistributing the land, paved the way for a new dynasty on the old pattern. Chinese communism has changed the pattern of oriental despotism by creating a method for the political activation of the formerly inert peasant masses. This activation, making the common farmer a political animal rather than a passive spectator of the course of government, has been accomplished by means both good and bad. Terrorism and intimidation, the gruesome killing of the rich to commit whole villages to the new order, have gone hand in hand with the idealistic evangelism of the cadres of young party workers and the promise of order and prosperity. The fact remains that by their hopes and their fears Chinese villagers in Communist areas have been led as never before to participate in public bodies, join movements, and take part in meetings and elections.

Chinese Communist success in the political organization of the peasantry as the basis for military power—providing troops and the food to feed them—has by no means used political methods alone. The third and most important secret of the Communists' rise to power has been their use of certain forces of *social change*. Bringing the peasant into the process of government, even at the level of controlled elections, has created new political energy. Giving the peasant literacy, that ancient prerogative of the scholar-official class, has ended the old bifurcation between the literate who governed and the illiterate who toiled. Communist literacy campaigns must be counted a forward step, even though they pave the way in the first instance for intensified indoctrination and thought control through the printed word. The organization of youth movements and the recruitment of young people for party work or for the newly respectable armed forces provide outlets from the family system. Like women's associations and co-operative movements, they offer alternatives to the old dependence upon family. The Chinese kinship system, like the old class structure, is split apart, and this process generates tremendous social energy, not unlike the splitting of the atom. The Communists, in fact, advertise it as a "liberation" or "emancipation." It is this ideal of the liberation of the common people which has fired the enthusiasm of young Chinese. The peasant masses, or *lao-pai-hsing,* are indeed the object of a cult in which party workers and intellectuals sacrifice and outdo themselves "for the people."

The fourth and by no means the least ingredient of the Chinese Communist revolution is its Marxist-Leninist-Stalinist *ideology.* As set forth in orthodox terms by Mao Tse-tung, Chinese communism is fighting to liberate the Chinese masses from the shackles of feudalism, reinforced as it is by imperialism from the West. Since the two chief enemies on whom the wrath of the Chinese countryside can be focused have been the rapacious absentee landlord and the foreign invader, this explanation of China's ills as due to feudalism (landlords) and imperialism (foreign invaders) gains easy credence. It is all the easier when American-made planes strafe the villages.

BASIC U.S. ERROR

The error of the United States in dealing with the Chinese revolution has been to focus upon its Communist ideology and anti-American aspect to the exclusion of the three other elements described above. In taking an anti-Communist position in China we have paid too little attention to the local circumstances, and particularly to the forces which communism is using there. This led us to back the National government and Chiang Kai-shek. But while Chiang has been anti-Communist, he has also lost the allegiance of the great bulk of Chinese patriots, set himself to oppose peasant rebellion, and in large measure failed to use the forces of social change. As a result, after twenty years' competition with Communist leader Mao Tse-tung to see who could solidify peasant support on a nation-wide basis, Chiang has lost. For years he has contended that the reforms which were generally acknowledged to be necessary in the countryside must wait until unity and peace had been achieved. Unfortunately, the Communists have disproved this doctrine that one cannot reform while fighting, by devising a system for reforming and fighting both at once.

The meaning of the Chinese revolution lies in its totality as a process of change on the political and economic, social and ideological levels. It cannot be dealt with by military means alone, either by Chiang or his successors, or by 600 American officers and $800 million a year as proposed by William C. Bullitt. The lesson of our failure in China is that we cannot deal fruitfully with Asia's revolutions by putting military means at the forefront of our policy. Force in reserve must be part of any policy in a power struggle, but the local circumstances in Asia demand that it occupy the background, not the foreground. There is no indication that increased military aid to anti-communism in Asia, either in China or Indo-China or Indonesia, will solve our problem.

The view that American military aid to Chiang could have saved him if only it had been greater is not only wishful thinking. It is a positive menace to the American future in Asia. If we continue to put our faith in material goods, economic and military, we continue to disregard the many complex forces from which Chinese communism has drawn its strength.

This dangerous wishful thinking is most evident among those who quote statistics to show that our aid to Chiang, although it cost us $1.5 billion during the war and $2 billion afterward, has actually amounted to a good deal less in real terms. It is quite true that shipments were withheld for a period in 1946–47, that they were delayed by various causes including Chinese inefficiency in making their requests, and that Nationalist government armies were not thoroughly equipped. We may also assume, although concrete evidence is almost entirely lacking, that the Russians have been giving some military advice and assistance to the Chinese Communists. We have long heard of the Japanese arms captured by the Communists in Manchuria, with Russian connivance. But when all the debated statistics are added up, it is not possible to show that the Chinese Communists have had superior matériel on an over-all basis.

On the contrary, we know that Central government forces received extensive American equipment and training both during and after the war. The National government has had both an effective air force and a small navy. Its record of defeat is due to demoralization, not lack of matériel—caused partly by unsound strategy, against which both General Marshall and General Wedemeyer were vigorous in their advice. The factor of demoralization—350,000 unarmed Nationalist troops helplessly surrounded south of Hsüchow by 300,000 Communists, as Chiang's chief of staff admitted—is a clear indication of the psychological and social factors mentioned above. It is not primarily a case of American military aid being too little or too late.

The attack on then Secretary of State Marshall by members of the Eightieth Congress, evidently in an effort to find a scapegoat for their own ill-advised military aid policy which Marshall opposed, is one of the regrettable manifestations of current politics. General Marshall's alternatives when he was mediating in China were either to get the opposing factions into a political agreement and a coalition government, or to let civil war develop. In a coalition government we know from the example of Czechoslovakia that the Chinese Communist minority would no doubt have tried eventually to seize power. But there was also the possibility that the still dominant National government, by effective reforms with extensive American economic aid, could have competed successfully against this Communist threat. The chance was worth taking. The alternative was civil war. Civil war came and we now see the result.

COMPETITION, NOT CONTAINMENT

Our new policy toward the revolution in China, as in the rest of Asia, must aim to ally ourselves with the long-term forces of social change. It is not fruitful for us to aim merely to *contain* the forces of revolution in Asia, particularly when the great part of them has not yet been organized under Communist control. We must approach Asia more positively and constructively and on a broader scale in order to *compete* against the Communist attempt to capture revolutionary leadership.

This calls for a *local approach* to each area according to the local realities. There is no use in our settling down to back the *status quo,* whether it be Chiang Kai-shek, or French and Dutch patriots who wish to reimpose their colonial rule. We have nothing to gain by opposing social change—literacy or freedom of marriage, for example, or the emancipation of women. Although Chinese Communists use them, these things were not made in Moscow. Actually, most of the movements for "liberation" and "emancipation" were begun in Asia by American missionaries and educators.

In practical terms this means that we must treat local regimes in China and elsewhere strictly on their merits and according to their deeds. In non-Communist areas of China and in Southeast Asia, where we may have relatively free access, we should offer our technical aid as proposed by President Truman to governmental and private groups whose aims we genuinely approve. Our aid should be given on the basis of principle, not of expediency; because it will be constructive, not because it will be anti-Communist. This is our only way to compete for the allegiance of the genuine revolutionary forces in non-Communist Asia.

Thus our new program for Asia must be greatly expanded in its scope, using not only technology but also education and educational exchange, information services, public health and hygiene, and all the ways of applying technology to the soil. Shipments of goods and programs of military aid should occupy a smaller proportion of such a total program than has been the case in China. This should keep its cost within our means while actually expanding its impact.

The application of this broadened program to Communist areas of China or to a Communist-dominated coalition government must be on a basis of hard bargaining. We know that any regime which attempts reconstruction in China will feel the need of outside aid in equipment as well as technology.

We know also that the Soviet Union is in no position to provide these things on a lavish scale. It would be in keeping both with Chinese temperament and with Mao Tse-tung's pronouncements to bargain from the Chinese side. On our part we should realize by this time that Communist regimes are controlled by minorities who fear the contact of our world. North China today in its leading cities has thousands of modern Chinese who have been educated very much in the American tradition and who hope to see us play a part in China's future. We should not consign the non-Communist Chinese of Communist areas to the other side of an Iron Curtain if we can avoid it. Therefore the first object of our hard bargaining in Communist areas should be to maintain American contact with the local scene. Most of the American missionary community is remaining in North China. Our consulates are being left there, and so are many business representatives. We should see to it that this American representation in China continues to be actively desired by the articulate groups which form Chinese public opinion. For some time to come the Chinese Communist party must govern its regions of China with the co-operation of non-Communists, administrators and technicians who have independent views. To these people it is essential that the United States stand forth as a champion of freedom and constructive progress, not as a source of continued warfare or as the supporter of regimes that have been discredited with the Chinese people.

The lesson of our defeat therefore is that we must avoid relying on a military-aid approach to the Chinese people. We must make a much broader and more energetic nonmilitary approach to any non-Communist areas of China and to the rest of Asia, and maintain contact as best we can with China's Communist areas. This is not as easy as shipping more arms, but will be much more successful in our long-term competition with Russia.

Topic 32
WORLD GOVERNMENT

We Are Not Ready for a World State

Edward R. Lewis *

Since the atomic bomb was loosed on Japan, stunning the Japanese people, and the minds of all of us, the demand for the formation of a world state has taken on new vigor and insistence. The majority of the persons attending the Dublin, New Hampshire, Conference last October, declared

* Lawyer. Author of *A History of Political Thought in America, 1860–1914* and contributor to legal periodicals. The selection is from Edward R. Lewis, "Are We Ready for a World State?" *The Yale Review,* Vol. 35 (Spring, 1946), pp. 491–501. Reprinted from *The Yale Review,* copyright Yale University Press. By permission.

that "The implications of the atomic bomb are appalling," and that only a world government, with a world parliament, and a world executive responsible to the world parliament can save us. Albert Einstein, likewise, has demanded world government, chiefly in order to control the atomic bomb; and to that end he recommends that exclusive military and naval power be vested in a world government. Norman Cousins, in his eloquent and moving book, "Modern Man Is Obsolete," adds his voice to the same demand. It is the old cry of "Unite or Perish." The time is short, tragically short, we are told. The atomic bomb will not be a secret long. We must act at once before it is too late.

The intense idealism and sincerity of the demand are unquestionable. But despite these earnest appeals, the time cannot be so short that we have not time to consider what a world state implies, what the difference is between a world state and the present United Nations, so far as effective control of the atomic bomb may be concerned, whether a world state gives promise of successful operation today, and above all, whether it is likely to furnish us with a protection from the atomic bomb.

We have been told, of course, that the world state should have a parliament and an executive. Naturally, it would have a supreme court to decide cases appealed from the highest courts of its member nations which involved questions under its constitution. Likewise, probably, a world state would have its own courts in which a citizen of one nation could sue a citizen of another nation.

Many believe that the chief purpose of a world state would be to have an army, a navy, and an air force, and to have a monopoly of military, naval, and air power. If a constituent nation could have a separate army, navy, or air force, there would be no purpose in a world state.

If the problem of the control of war power were answered, the problem of the constitution of the parliament of a world state would come next.

Russia has 192,000,000 people; China about 450,000,000; India 388,000,000; the countries of South America about 88,000,000. I think it is not unfair to say that the people of China, India, Russia, Germany, Spain, Italy, Thailand, Poland, the Arab nations, the Malay States, Burma, Iran, Afghanistan, and the countries of South and Central America have as yet shown no long-term capacity for representative government; nor have they developed the ingrained habits requisite for it. Their combined population is about 1,650,000,000.

On the other hand, it can be said that the only countries which have shown sustained capacity for self-government, with an effective desire to govern themselves, are Great Britain, the United States, France, Norway, Sweden, Denmark, the Netherlands, Switzerland, and the British Dominions—Canada, Australia, and New Zealand. It might be added that the Union of South Africa, the Irish Free State, and Czechoslovakia in its brief but promising career cut short by the ruthless Nazis, have shown evidence of capacity for this type of sustained political achievement. The combined population of all these countries is about 275,000,000.

Thus the countries without fairly long records of substantial success in self-government would on a per-capita basis outnumber those with such records by more than five to one.

The Dublin Conference suggested that representation in a world state be based not merely on population but on industrial and natural resources as well. Yet it is difficult to see how, on any basis that can be imagined, the countries that lack the political habits and achievement of representative self-government would not overwhelmingly outvote the countries that have them.

Even if a world parliament were bi-cameral, and in the upper house each nation were allowed but one vote, the politically experienced nations would still be badly outvoted in the upper house by the politically inexperienced nations, and in the lower house, if it were based on population, the balance would be overwhelmingly against the politically experienced nations.

Obviously, it is no answer to say that this argument is based on political conceit, and that it may be merely the misfortune and not the fault of the politically backward countries that they have not yet shown political ability in self-government. One cannot avoid replying that the people of many of these countries have had long periods, some of them centuries, in which to assert and develop their ability, more time in a number of cases than the people of the politically more competent countries have had, and that many of them have shown not only no aptitude for self-government but no sustained interest in it. Certainly this is true of the people of Germany and Italy. But the point need not be argued. Let us assume that the people of all these countries have the innate capacity for self-government. The fact remains that they have not yet shown this capacity, and that a world state is being demanded immediately. We may well ask that it should not be the task of a world state to educate backward member nations in self-government.

But composition of a world parliament is only the first of the problems involved in grievous discrepancies between the nations of the proposed world state which would create clashes at every turn.

It is difficult to see how a world state could deny free movement of people from any nation to any other nation in such a state. Indeed, there are those who insist now, under the United Nations Charter, that one of the fundamental freedoms should be the right of people to move freely from any part to any other part of the world. . . . The problem of free migration suggests the real reason why the nations of the United Nations organization are not yet ready for entrance into a world state. They have vastly different political experiences and backgrounds. Their political traditions are different. Their systems of law are different. Their cultural roots and habits are different. Their languages are different.

Surely, it takes a naive optimism to imagine that a closely integrated world state with a world parliament, a world law, perhaps a world bill of rights, could be formed of so heterogeneous and unevenly developed a concourse of constituent nations.

Yet we are told confidently that this is the attitude of querulous Bourbonism. Not only, it is said, does necessity today call for a world state but the formation of our own country points the way. The assertion has been made repeatedly that the United States of America was formed of thirteen separate, sovereign States, with great diversity in population and with jealous and antagonistic views. If the United States could be formed in 1787 out of the weak league of the Articles of Confederation, it is but political intransigence, many argue, to doubt that a world state can be formed now by the nations of the United Nations.

Our school and college courses in argumentation and logic teach that the argument from historical analogy is the most unreliable and the least convincing of all arguments. But the advocates of a world state, like the advocates of "Union Now," are indifferent to, or perhaps unconscious of, such doubts.

I think, however, that the only similarity of the United States of America to the proposed United States of the World lies in the word "united." The comparison is completely at variance with the facts. It is amazing that such a distortion of our history should have attained such a vogue. It has run through the arguments of "Union Now" and the eloquent advocates of a world state. The comparison has been repeated so often that by many it is now accepted as an established fact that our country was formed by the union of thirteen separate States, separate in the sense that the nations of the United Nations are now separate.

Such a distortion of our history is puzzling. Perhaps it may be due to the fact that in the forty years before 1924 we received such masses of immigration from countries of vastly different backgrounds that our sense of continuity with our past has become blurred. This theory goes far beyond the extreme States Rights theory of Calhoun, for even Calhoun did not claim that the thirteen colonies, which he stubbornly and erroneously called "sovereign," had ever been independent nations.

Those who argue that the formation of the United States is analogous to the proposed formation of a world state would probably be surprised to learn that Rufus King of New York declared in the Constitutional Convention of 1787: "None of the States are now sovereign or independent. . . . This is a union of the men of those States." James Wilson, one of the great constitutional lawyers, if not the greatest, of the Convention, asserted: "The States under the confed. are not sovereign States—they can do no act but such as are of a subordinate nature." He declared that the States "are now subordinate corporations or Societies and not Sovereigns." He asked whether we were forming a government for "men, or for the imaginary beings called States." Elbridge Gerry of Massachusetts, "urged that we never were independent States, were not such now, & never could be even on the principles of the Confederation. The States & the advocates for them were intoxicated with the idea of their *sovereignty*." Madison said, "Some contend that states are sovereign, when in fact they are only political societies. . . . The states never possessed the essential rights of sovereignty." In the summer of 1861, Lincoln admirably summarized his theory of the States Rights question in his Special Message to Congress, in which he said that none of the original thirteen States had ever been States "either in substance or in name outside of the Union," that none of them had ever been independent or sovereign, but "passed into the Union even before they cast off their British colonial dependence."

Advocates of a world state who cite the example of the formation of our Union are ignoring a great deal of our history. The truth is that our Union was formed in 1776 of thirteen colonies all of which were colonies of Great Britain. New York, New Jersey, and Delaware had for brief periods been under either Dutch or Swedish rule, but after 1673, all the colonies were colonies of Great Britain, and ten of them had been from the beginning. None of our colonies or States had ever sent an ambassador to a foreign country, or received one; none had ever made war against or signed a treaty with a foreign nation. None had ever been an independent nation.

Moreover, the thirteen colonies had powerful historical forces making for union when they declared independence. The colonies were all under the English common law. They all had legislatures modelled on the English system. Save for a few Swedes in Delaware, some Dutch in New York, New Jersey and Delaware, some Germans in Virginia and a considerable number in Pennsylvania, all spoke the English language. The United States Census Bureau Report, "A Century of Population Growth," estimated that in 1790 more than 90% of our population had originated in Great Britain and North Ireland. The National Origins figures, presented to Congress in 1928 and accepted as a basis for immigration quotas, estimated the percentage as 80%.

It is mistaken, therefore, to say that our population was notably diverse and heterogeneous in 1790. Certainly it was remarkably homogeneous compared with the populations of the United Nations today.

Advocates of a world state who are fond of emphasizing our diversity in 1790 like also to emphasize our present diversity. Always, they stress diversity instead of our essential unity. So, likewise, there are people who invariably stress the minority elements of any problem instead of the major factors. They seem to think that there is some magic in diversity. But while a reasonable amount of diversity may add variety and interest to a body politic, an undue amount with too great extremes is a definite danger to it.

Diversity, indeed, never of itself makes for union. Our Union in 1787 was not made because of diversity but in spite of it. Benjamin Franklin, for example, testified to the weakening effect of the racial diversity in Pennsylvania. This held Pennsylvania back while the homogeneous States of Virginia and Massachusetts led the way in the Revolution and in the creation of the Union. Our Union was formed in 1787 despite the diversity which then existed but which was not great enough to overcome the forces for union; we were brought by integrating common aims and traditions into essential unity.

The people of the thirteen colonies had also had vital experiences which had welded them together. Many had fought side by side in three French and Indian wars. They had so fought in the Revolutionary War. They had come after a century and a half of pioneer life on this continent to think of themselves as one nation, as Americans, so that Patrick Henry could say in 1774, "I am not a Virginian, I am an American."

Moreover, the people of the thirteen colonies had reached, generally speaking, the same stage of political development. The United States, then, was made from a deep feeling of unity. When that feeling became dominant, but not until then, the Union came.

The contrast between the thirteen colonies in 1776, or the thirteen States in 1787, on the one hand, and the nations of the United Nations today, on the other hand, could hardly be more crucial. The differences of these nations in political capacity and achievement, in traditions and background, in race and language, are, as all know, immense. To make any comparison hold, it would be necessary to show that in 1787 each of our thirteen States had been an independent nation, with a centuries-old political tradition, a law and a proud history of its own. In short the analogy of the formation of our Union with the formation of a world state now is lame and faulty.

Throughout the course of the Second World War, we have seen many examples of what may be called the "blue-print state of mind," which likes to make elaborate charts of world organization, to make detailed statements of plans, based upon the hope or the assumption that political constitutions can be evolved in the study or conference room.

It is, of course, natural that the emotions generated by war have tended to produce grandiose and doctrinaire proposals. Emotionally stirred, many of us like to imagine that democracy can be produced by a few courses in the schools, and that without a common basis a world state can be brought about by a mere agreement. But reason should remind us that states are not made that way. During the French Revolution, Edmund Burke warned that "The science of constructing a commonwealth, or renovating it, or reforming it, is, like every other experimental science, not to be taught a priori." He exerted all his power and energy in eloquent argument against the theory that a constitution could be made to order by the members of the Constituent Assembly. He declared that state constitutions are the result of growth, that they depend on long-evolved political habits and institutions.

William James once said that "the civic genius of our people," the "mystery, at once the secret and the glory of our English-speaking race, consists in nothing but two common habits, two inveterate habits carried into public life, habits so homely that they lend themselves to no rhetorical expression, yet habits more precious, perhaps, than any that the human race has gained." These two habits, he went on to say, are, first, "the habit of trained and disciplined good temper towards the opposite party when it fairly wins its innings" and, second, the habit of "fierce and merciless resentment towards every man or set of men who break the public peace."

It may safely be said that no world state can survive if these two habits are not ingrained in the peoples which make it up. And, surely, no one can say that these two habits are now recognized or followed by the great majority of the people in the nations of the present United Nations.

The advocates of a world state are in too much of a hurry to realize a lofty ideal. There is some reason to believe, as I have already said, that the crashing blows we have all had during the past six years, the carking anxiety, the grievous losses, the death and desolation, have warped us so that we no longer think in terms of gradual and fruitful change necessary where great new goals are concerned. Rather we think in terms of abrupt and even cataclysmic revolution. We are often impatient when anyone even counsels delay. Yet only last summer, in San Francisco, we found that the U.S.S.R. could not be induced to enter the United Nations Organization, unless each of the five big powers were granted the veto power. The Charter was accepted, weak as it was, on the statesmanlike ground that it was the best that could be obtained at the time, and in the hope that it could be broadened and strengthened. It seems incongruous, to say the least, that within six months after it was found impracticable to make the Charter of the United Nations stronger, through such a first step towards abatement of national sovereignty, it should be proposed to jump over all intervening steps and form a world state at once.

What, then, of the argument that the alternative to a world state is now destruction? In these days when black predictions of catastrophe are common, it may seem foolhardy to venture an opinion that our choice is not so compelling. Yet it may be ventured. If, owing to the atom bomb or other destructive weapons, it is certain that we are doomed if the people of the United Nations cannot be convinced in a year or so of the necessity of a world state, then perforce we are doomed, because men's minds in a score of countries cannot possibly be convinced or action achieved so fast. But I agree with the famous statement of Justice Holmes, that he had "no belief in panaceas and almost none in sudden ruin." Even in the present circumstances, his words may still well be heeded.

What reason is there to believe that a world state is a panacea against the atomic bomb, or if that question seems unfair, what reason is there to think that a world state could control the atomic bomb more effectively than could the United Nations?

The people of the world state would still be scattered as people are now over the entire globe. No world-state army or navy or air force could be big enough to police every corner of the globe. If scientists can produce atomic bombs in some nation of the United Nations, it is difficult to see why they could not produce them in some corner of a world state. What reason have we for believing that a world state could prevent their use any more effectively than could the United Nations? There have often been civil wars in single states as there have been wars between nations.

A world state offers no more protection against the atomic bomb than can the present United Nations. On the other hand, a world state would face all the obstacles we have considered—a Babel of tongues, a Babel of diverse laws and customs, peoples at different stages of development, with no common backgrounds, the majority of them with no sustained political habits, no tried traditions of self-government. A nation, wrote Renan, is a soul, a spiritual principle. It is, he said, both of the present and the past. It is formed of a rich legacy of memories, and the desire to live together, to maintain the heritage from the past. A nation, he went on, cannot be improvised. Nor can a world state.

The advocates of a world state would try overnight to manufacture a world state to order. It cannot be manufactured. It must grow and develop naturally, out of ever closer association of nation with nation in a common effort, if it is to come at all. Nature, an old Latin proverb says, does not make jumps. All political experience would seem to warn us to go forward in the path on which we have started, persistently step by step, instead of attempting an uncertain leap into the unknown.

One World or None

Norman Cousins *

The beginning of the Atomic Age has brought less hope than fear. . . . Where man can find no answer, he will find fear. While the dust was still settling over Hiroshima, he was asking himself questions and finding no answers. The biggest question of these concerns himself. Is war inevitable because it is in the nature of man? If so, how much time has he left—five, ten, twenty years—before he employs the means now available to him for the ultimate in self-destruction—extinction? If not, then how is he to in-

* Editor of *Saturday Review of Literature*. Author of *The Good Inheritance, The Democratic Chance*. Editor of *A Treasury of Democracy*. The selection is from *Modern Man Is Obsolete* by Norman Cousins. The book is an expanded version of an editorial in *The Saturday Review of Literature*.

terpret his own experience, which tells him that in all recorded history there have been only three hundred years in the aggregate during which he was free of war? . . .

It should not be necessary to prove that on August 6, 1945, a new age was born. When on that day a parachute containing a small object floated to earth over Japan, it marked the violent death of one stage in man's history and the beginning of another. . . . At present he [man] is a world warrior; it is time for him to grow up and to become a world citizen. This is not vaporous idealism, but sheer driving necessity. It bears directly on the prospects of his own survival. He will have to recognize the flat truth that the greatest obsolescence of all in the Atomic Age is national sovereignty. Even back in the old-fashioned Rocket Age before August 6, 1945, strict national sovereignty was an anomalous hold-over from the tribal instinct in nations. If it was anomalous then, it is preposterous now.

It is preposterous because we have invested it with non-existent powers. We assume that national sovereignty is still the same as it always was, that it still offers security and freedom of national decision. We assume it still means national independence, the right to get into war or stay out of it. We even debate the question of "surrendering" some of our sovereignty—as though there is still something to surrender. There is nothing left to surrender. There is only something to gain. A common world sovereignty. . . .

Can it be that we do not realize that in an age of atomic energy and rocket planes the foundations of the old sovereignties have been shattered? That no longer is security to be found in armies and navies, however large and mighty? That no longer is there security based on size and size alone? That any nation, however small, with atomic energy, is potentially as powerful as any other nation, however large? That in an Atomic Age all nations are now directly accessible to each other—for better or worse? That in the erasure of man-made barriers and boundaries all the peoples of the world stand virtually unarmed in the presence of one another? That they are at the mercy of one another, and shall have to devise a common security or suffer a common cataclysm? That the only really effective influence between peoples is such influence as they are able to exert morally, politically, ideologically upon each other? That the use of disproportionate wealth and abundance of resources by any nation, when applied for bargaining purposes, do not constitute influence but the type of coercion against which severe reaction is inevitable?

All these questions have been in the making for centuries, but the triumph over the invisible and mighty atom has given them an exactness and an immediacy about which there can be no mistake. The need for world government was clear long before August 6, 1945, but Hiroshima and Nagasaki raised that need to such dimensions that it can no longer be ignored. And in the glare brighter than sunlight produced by the assault on the atom, we have all the light we need with which to examine this new world that has come into being with such clicking abruptness. Thus examined, the old sovereignties are seen for what they are—vestigial obstructions in the circulatory system of the world.

Much of the attachment to old concepts of sovereignty, as well as the reluctance to face squarely its severe limitations in the modern world, grows out of apprehension over the control a world authority might have over the internal affairs of the individual state. There is the fear, for example, that the individual Constitutions would be subject to central control. There is the fear that institutions built up over centuries would exist only at the pleasure and discretion of a super-state.

Natural and understandable though these concerns may be, they have their source in confusion over a distinction that should be made between world *sovereignty* and state *jurisdiction*. A common world sovereignty would mean that no state could act unilaterally in its foreign affairs. It would mean that no state could have the instruments of power to aggress against other states. It would mean that no state could withdraw from the central authority as a method of achieving its aims. But it would *not* mean that the individual state would lose its *jurisdiction* over its internal affairs. It would *not* mean the arbitrary establishment of a uniform ideology all over the world. It would *not* mean the forcible imposition of non-democratic systems on democratic states, anymore than it would mean the forcible imposition of democratic systems on non-democratic states.

Though the idea of bestowing democracy on all other peoples throughout the world seems both magnanimous and attractive, the fact remains that democracy is not to be had just for the giving or the taking. It cannot be donated or imposed from without. It is an intricate and highly advanced mechanism capable of existing, like man himself, under certain conditions. It depends not only on the love of freedom, but on the ability to carry the responsibilities of freedom. It requires enduring respect for numberless principles, not all of them incorporated into formal law. It requires adherence to the principle of majority rule with preservation of minority rights. It is as much a way of living and a philosophy of life as it is a form of political organization.

This does not mean, however, that peoples not now democratic must be restrained from moving toward democracy. Nor does it mean that the conditions under which democracy can come into being cannot be nurtured and developed. So far as a central authority is concerned, one way to help in that development can be by providing a greater external harmony that will permit a greater internal harmony.

In creating this higher sovereignty, we naturally wonder whether history has any advice to offer. History tells of two experiences worth our examination. The first happened in Greece more than two thousand years ago; the second happened in America a century and a half ago. Neither experience can properly be termed a parallel or a precise guide to the present. Strictly speaking, no precise guide to the present is to be found anywhere. Never before has the world known such profound and sudden shocks; never before has there been so little in the way of previous experience to build upon. But while we should not overstretch historical analogy, neither should we fail to take into account the operation of certain historical principles whose validity might seem to apply to our own time. . . .

The causes and the effects of the Greek failure, said *The Federalist,* "cannot be too highly colored, or too often exhibited. Every man who loves peace, every man who loves his country, every man who loves liberty, ought to have it ever before his eyes. . . ." Readers were told that if the Greeks had been "as wise as they were courageous," they would have transformed their loose and competing leagues into a real union. *The Federalist* believed that had such a union been formed after the war against Persia, when both Athens and Sparta were, for once, united in defense of Greece, there might never have been a Peloponnesian War culminating in the ruin of both states and in the decay of Greece itself. America, said *The Federalist,* should be the "broad and solid foundation of other edifices, not less magnificent, which will be equally permanent monuments of their errors."

There is a disposition to deny the value of America's success at international organization one hundred and sixty years ago because the states were supposedly so compact, so homogeneous, so closely knit in their cultural and political and economic patterns.

Let us see.

There were thirteen American nations in the Revolution against England. They came out of that Revolution as former allies rather than as partners in a continuing enterprise. There were varying and frequently conflicting systems of political, economic, monetary, and social organization. Sovereignty, separation, sectarianism—these fixed the thinking of the day. A man who went from one state to another found that his currency would shrink ten per cent just in the act of crossing a state line. At one point, Vermont, New Hampshire, and New York were on the brink of war. In the absence of an outside threat after the Revolution, the colonies began to fall apart. . . .

In all the discussion over the making of America, a fact frequently overlooked is that the American Revolution did not create the United States. The United States were created largely through their differences, differences so intense that only a common sovereignty could prevent international anarchy within the American group.

John Fiske, in his *Critical Period of American History,* writes that each little city or district regarded itself as an island. "Local prejudices were intense. It was not simply free Massachusetts and slave-holding South Carolina, or English Connecticut and Dutch New York, that misunderstood and ridiculed each other, but even between such neighboring states as Connecticut and Massachusetts, both of them thoroughly English and Puritan, and in all their social conditions almost exactly alike, it used often to be said that there was no love lost. These unspeakably stupid and contemptible local antipathies are inherited by civilized men from that far-off time when the clan system prevailed over the face of the earth and the hand of every clan was raised against its neighbor. They are pale and evanescent survivals from the universal primitive warfare, and the sooner they die out from human society, the better for every one."

Or listen to Thomas Paine on the "homogeneous" quality of the Colonial peoples at the time the international organization that is the United States was founded:

"If there is a country in the world where concord, according to common calculation, would be least expected, it is America. Made up, as it is, of people from different nations, accustomed to different forms and habits of government, speaking different languages, and more different in their modes of worship, it would appear that the union of such a people was impracticable. But by the simple operation of constructing government on the principles of society and the rights of man, every difficulty retires, and the parts are brought into cordial unison."

Paine's footnote to this paragraph indicates that the melting-pot was not peculiar to a later period in American history. "That part of America," he said, "which is generally called New England, including New Hampshire, Massachusetts, Rhode Island, and Connecticut, is peopled chiefly by English descendants. In the state of New York, about half are Dutch, the rest English, Scotch and Irish. In New Jersey, a mixture of English and Dutch, with some Scotch and Irish. In Pennsylvania, about one-third are English, another third German, and the remainder Scotch and Irish, with some Swedes. The states to the southward have a greater proportion of English than the middle states, but in all of them there is a mixture; and besides those enumerated, there are a considerable number of French, and some few of all the European nations, lying on the Coast."

Paine went on to point out that the American experience proved that diverse peoples did not have to be subjugated to be brought together, but that they could achieve common government through common consent. Government, he said, was not a "thing made up of mysteries," but a "national association acting on the principles of society."

In examining, therefore, the Greek and American experiences, we find one central point worth considering in relation to the problem before us today: States within a related group must live as one or suffer as many. A corollary is that the differences among peoples are not a deterrent in meeting the need for over-all government, but actually both a pre-condition and a basic reason behind the need.

What validity does this have for the world today? First, do the nations of the world belong to a related group? If so, how and to what extent?

The world has at last become a geographic unit, if we measure geographic units not according to absolute size, but according to access and proximity. All peoples are members of this related group, just as the thirteen American colonies belonged to a related group, and just as the city-states of Greece belonged to a related group. The extent of this relationship need only be measured by the direct access nations have to each other for purposes of war. And the consequences of disunion are as applicable to the world group today as they were to individual groupings of states in the past. The unorganized geographic units of the past have given way to the unorganized unit of the present. It is a unit without unity, an order without any order.

In a world where it takes less time to get from New York to Chungking than it took to get from New York to Philadelphia in 1787, the nature and extent of this geographic entity becomes apparent. All natural distances and barriers vanish. Never before in history has the phrase, the human family, had such a precise meaning. This much all of us—American, European, African, Asiatic, Australian—have in common: Whether we like it or not, we have been brought together or thrust together as members of a world unit, albeit an unorganized world unit. Within that unit, to be sure, are divisions and subdivisions, but they are all heavily interdependent. There is little point in musing or speculating whether this unit is desirable or whether it deserves our support. The fact is that it exists.

Here we must meet the argument that even though the world may be a geographical unit, it is too large, too unwieldly, for the creation and operation of a governmental unit. But size alone does not limit the area in which government can function. Unwieldiness is entirely relative to the instruments of control. For harmony among states depends upon relationships; and relationships among states depend upon law and respect for law. . . .

Radio is only one of the instruments available for drawing the peoples of the world together under a common sovereignty. The revolution in transportation can give them a mutuality such as even the people of any one nation a hundred or more years ago never knew among themselves.

This mutuality—a mutuality built on present and future needs—is more important than physical dimensions. A common ground of destiny is not too large a site for the founding of any community.

But reject all other arguments for world government—reject the geographic, economic, the ideological, the sociological, the humanitarian arguments, valid though they may be. Consider only the towering job of policing the atom—the job of keeping the smallest particle of matter from destroying all matter. This means control. But control is no natural phenomenon. It does not operate of and by itself. Control is impossible without power—the power of investigation, the power of injunction, the power of arrest, the power of punishment.

But power, like control, cannot be isolated, nor is it desirable except under carefully defined circumstances. Power must be subordinate to law, unless it is to take the form of brute, irresponsible force. Here, too, we are involved in an important interrelationship, because law can be derived only through government. Law is a product of moral, judicial, executive, legislative, and administrative sanction—all of which adds up to government. And government means what it says: the process of governing. It is not decentralization, it is not informal organization, it is not the right of veto or the right of secession by any state or states. It is a central body none of whose members has the right or the means of aggression or withdrawal. It is the source of legitimate action and legitimate redress.

Approach the problem in reverse. We are all agreed that war must be "outlawed." If that is what we really mean, then we shall have to apply law. Law based on what? On general agreement? With or without sanctions? With or without protective as well as punitive power? With or without a judiciary? To the extent that the answers to these questions are subtractive, we shall fail in our agreed purpose. Outlawry of war is a noble phrase but its translation into tangible effectiveness requires, by its very nature, the existence of the basis and the instruments of legality, by which we mean government.

We are left, then, with three basic principles necessarily related to an effective system of international control:

No control without power.

No power without law.

No law without government. . . .

It is claimed that warfare has now become so horrible that no nation will dare to unleash it. The argument is not new; it was heard when the bow and arrow were used in Egypt more than five thousand years ago. It was heard when the phalanx was developed to supposedly invincible strength in Macedonia more than two thousand years ago. It was heard when gunpowder was introduced more than five hundred years ago. It was heard less than thirty years ago after a World War in which dynamite took to the sky. But each time, though the horror of war increased, though the size of the battlefield grew larger and larger until the world itself became the arena of combat, new wars continued to break out.

So fallacious is the war-is-now-too-horrible theory that actually the reverse is true. The possibility of war increases in direct proportion to the effectiveness of the instruments of war. Far from banishing war, the atomic bomb may in itself constitute a cause of war. In the absence of world control, it may create universal fear and suspicion. Each nation may live nervously from one moment to the next, not knowing whether the designs or ambitions of other nations might prompt them to attempt a lightning blow of obliteration. The ordinary, the inevitable differences among nations which might in themselves be susceptible of solution might now become the signals for direct action, lest other nations get in the first and decisive blow.

Since the science of warfare will no longer be dependent upon armies but will be waged by pushbuttons, releasing armadas of radio-controlled rocket planes carrying atomic explosives, the slightest suspicion may start all the pushbuttons going.

It will be argued that each nation will realize this; that is, that the first button might lead to universal catastrophe as all the other nations rush to the switchboards of annihilation. This presupposes the existence of reason—but reason is hardly something likely to flourish in a world of international anarchy, by which we mean the absence of central government. Moreover, there may always be the feeling that one nation can escape though all the others may go down. What a temptation for the blitzkriegers!

More popular than any of these suggestions for controlling the atom is the plea, advanced in Parliament and in Congress, that England and America keep the secret of the atomic bomb to themselves. Conspicuously absent among those urging such action are the scientists—not because they do not believe it may be desirable to retain exclusive possession of the bomb, but because they do not believe it is in our power to do so. They know of Germany's advanced experiments with atomic energy; they know of Japan's development of plutonium; they know that the very demonstration of the successful fission of the atom is crucially valuable knowledge for other nations in rounding out their experiments; they know that in the very act of attempting to keep the mechanism of the atomic bomb a secret we stimulate other nations to undertake whatever additional research is necessary over their present experimentation to yield the desired results. They know, too, that in all history there is not a single instance of a new weapon being kept exclusively by any power or powers; sooner or later either the basic principles become generally known or parallel devices are invented. Before long, the atomic bomb will follow the jet plane, the rocket bomb, radar, and the flame thrower into general circulation. We were not the only horse in the atomic derby. We just happened to finish first; the others will be along in due time.

Still another suggestion is that the nations of the world agree to a system of voluntary inspection. Behind this is the knowledge that it is difficult and almost impossible to hide the large laboratory and production facilities required to produce atomic bombs. It would be possible, according to this suggestion, to train a force of "atomic detectives" who would have freedom of examination anywhere in the world.

Even granting the infallibility of the inspectors to ferret out atomic bomb plants wherever they may be in the world, two weaknesses clamor for attention. The first is that any system of investigation is only as strong as the agency behind it. The agency in this case is nothing but a gentleman's agreement lacking executive and police power. The second weakness is that any nation at any time can revoke its part in the agreement and refuse admission to the inspection force.

So far, it will be observed that all the methods proposed have one thing in common. They all rest on naked chance. The chance that a counter-weapon may be developed. The chance that war will be self-liquidating because it has become so horrible. The chance that no other nation is smart enough to develop its own atomic weapons without our help. The chance that an inspection system can work with nothing behind it. At a time of dimensionless peril, we are asked to build on random chance.

In looking beyond random chance for a firmer footing on which to build for tomorrow, we naturally turn to the United Nations Charter. There can be little question that when the delegates from forty-four nations concluded their Conference at San Francisco in June 1945, they had made a promising start in the direction of international security. Whatever its imperfections, the Charter was a signal contribution to world peace. In the statement of its principles and objectives, in the provision of machinery for making it stronger and more effective, in the very fact that men from many lands had come together, reflecting the desire of peoples of every continent to plan for world peace as they had planned for victory in the war—in all these respects, the Charter was of historic importance. Moreover, so far as the United States was concerned, it kept the door of isolation from slamming abruptly in the faces of the American people.

It is no reflection on the Charter, or on the men who joined in its making, to say that it has become a feeble and antiquated instrument for dealing with the problems of an Atomic Age. It is no reflection, because even the calendar is hopelessly out of date. A thousand years of the world's history were compressed in that brief fraction of a second during which Hiroshima was leveled. The world which the San Francisco Conference met to consider no longer exists, even though the same nations and same people represented at the Conference belong to both the old and new worlds.

After the Charter was drafted, even its warmest advocates did not claim that it was equipped to cope with war or the threat of war. But it was felt that time might work to the advantage of the United Nations—time in which to build up the habit of peace, time in which to strengthen and implement the Charter so that within fifteen or twenty years it might take the form of a real and durable world structure.

But the time factor has been reversed. Time no longer works for peace. Time today works against peace. The longer we wait the more difficult it becomes to achieve world government. There is a desperate though quiet scramble in almost every nation of the world to duplicate the success of America, Canada, and Great Britain in prying open the atom. This race is not only based on distrust but generates distrust. The feeling grows everywhere that it must be every nation for itself. Are these the foundations of a common security? Are these the building blocks of lasting peace?

Do we realize that time is running out? Do we realize that victory has given us no real "respite," as has been claimed, but has created instead an emergency not less intense than the world knew at Dunkirk or Stalingrad or Pearl Harbor? Do we realize that victory imposed obligations from which we cannot shrink? These obligations are directly related to the responsibility we have to assume for the invention and use of the most hideously successful and indiscriminate killer in history. This is not so much a matter of justifying our use of the atomic bomb as it is a matter of following up the unprecedented use of raw power with real moral leadership. In short, it is the obligation and opportunity to equate the atomic bomb with an atomic solvent, to equate force with reason, stating to the peoples of the world the full implications as we understand them of atomic energy, and filling the vacuum created by the atomic bomb by calling upon them to join in the building of a real world structure for the greater welfare and safety of all.

This atomic solvent operates not through a chemical compound or a gadget but through an active world public opinion in bringing peoples together. Once the nature and imminency of the peril are clearly understood by the peoples of the world, their differences will not be a bar but an incentive to common government, as was demonstrated earlier in the case of the American colonies. For it is not in spite of these differences but because of them that the world is now in need of a general amalgam. The very purpose of government is to regulate differences. If these differences did not exist, if man's actions were uniform and uniformly predictable, then man would be as free of war as the vegetable kingdom. The differences point up the problem, not the problem the differences. The primary consideration is not how great an obstacle the differences may be to the setting up of a closely knit world structure, but whether men will be in a better position to reconcile those differences within world government than without it.

Moreover, there are few differences that confront nations in their dealings with each other that they do not have to meet within themselves. Man himself is a magnificent summing-up of differences, of which the larger differences on the international scale are only a reflection. Macneile Dixon, in *The Human Situation,* reminds us that "many are the races and many the temperaments. There are vehement and hot-headed men, selfless and conciliatory men. They display, varying as they do in appearance, talents, behavior, every type of unpredictable reaction to their surroundings. There are sybarites and ascetics, dreamers and bustling men of affairs, clever and stupid, worldly and religious, mockers and mystics, pugnacious, loyal, cunning, treacherous, cheerful and melancholy men. There are eagles among them, tigers, doves, and serpents. 'He was a comedian on the stage,' said the wife of a celebrated funny man, 'but a tragedian in the home.' "

World government will not and cannot dissolve these differences. All it can do is operate on a level which can keep those differences, when raised to international dimensions, from dissolving the globe itself.

This is the propitious moment, the grand moment, with the tremendous psychological advantages it offers at the end of a great war, to take the moral leadership in bringing the atomic solvent into play. But that propitious moment is slipping. The world is slipping, too—back into old systems of power politics and spheres of influence—the ovaries of war.

By itself and of itself, the United Nations Charter cannot arrest this trend. Nor would any amount of implementation do the job so long as nations can act unilaterally and so long as nations can withdraw from the over-all organization at their own discretion. Nor can we sit back comfortably and wait several generations for the world to evolve naturally and progressively into a single governmental unit which would erase those dangerous privileges. Whatever is done must be done with an immediacy which is in keeping with the urgency. Not another Conference but a Constitutional Convention of the United Nations is needed—not only to undertake a general inventory of the revolutionary changes in the world since the San Francisco meeting in the long-ago spring of 1945, but to design the form and fabric of real government.

The difficulties confronting such a Convention would be far and away the most comprehensive and complicated that any group of men anywhere, at any time, have had to face. But of one thing the Convention can be certain, and that is a knowledge of what failure will mean. The Convention has some advantage, too, in knowing that if world government sounds as though it poses methods or solutions above the reach of mortal man, some answer is to be found in the fact that the reach of mortal man was long enough apparently to push science and invention ahead by perhaps a thousand years during a few years of experimentation with atomic energy. His ability to do this not only indicates that he can extend or overextend himself when pressed, but emphasizes the need to do the same with government.

There is no need to discuss the historical reasons pointing to and arguing for world government. There is no need to talk of the difficulties in the way of world government. There is need only to ask whether we can afford to do without it. All other considerations become either secondary or inconsequential.

There comes to mind a scene from one of the old "silent" films. An outcast, lost somewhere in a mountainous forest, stands on the edge of a canyon. Behind him rages a forest fire, drawing ever closer. In front of him is a sheer drop of several hundred feet. But the gap across this canyon to the other side is only ten feet wide. Ten feet! He has never jumped ten feet before. He has no way of knowing that he can jump it now. He has no choice but to try.

The precise outcome of this episode we are unable to tell, for it was one of those Saturday afternoon adventure serials which was discontinued at just the crucial second. But we never entertained any doubts that at least the jump was attempted.

Mankind today is involved in a somewhat similar predicament. It would be comforting to believe that we could leisurely build a footbridge across the gap. It would be comforting to believe that time is working in our favor, or that the fire has changed its direction. But it happens that there is no time to build a footbridge. It happens that we cannot take just a step forward but must jump. It happens that the longer we delay the less space we shall have for a running leap. It happens that if we wait too long we shall have the disadvantage of jumping from a stationary position. Perhaps we have never jumped ten feet before. But under the circumstances that is the poorest of all reasons not to try.

And even if we make the jump successfully, we still have not disposed of all our problems. For though world government provides a better method and a better chance of preserving world peace than man has ever possessed, it cannot provide a guarantee of world peace. It provides man with time—time to think, time to change, time to keep decisions in his own hands, but it cannot make the right decisions for him. It provides only the minimum and not the maximum requirements of a common security. It provides the broad and solid ground in which to sink the foundations of a genuine sovereignty, and on which to build a floor under tomorrow; but it does not provide a finished structure. It provides the form but not the substance. That finished structure and that substance can be provided only by the vision and the day-by-day wisdom of man himself.

Peace under world government is only half the job. Peace is a big word; there are all kinds of peace. Peace can be slavery or it can be freedom; subjugation or liberation. It can be static or dynamic, stagnant or vibrant. Alfred North Whitehead once described peace without purpose as "anesthesia." The real peace is more than non-war. It is a vital peace, a restlessness to get on with the work of the world, an anxiety to meet the future. The real peace means progress. That is the other half of the job.

Directly related to the danger of a purposeless peace is the danger represented by a perverted use of power. World government requires the manipulation of power on a larger scale than man has ever known, but unless this power is carefully defined, unless it is surrounded with workable checks and balances, unless it is *representative* rather than *dictatorial,* unless it is subject to changes in its officers and in its laws in response to changing needs and the freely expressed will of the peoples of the states—it can lead to a world tyranny against which insurrection will be difficult if not impossible. The instruments of control will have been necessarily concentrated and centralized in order to guard against the use of unlimited destructive power in the hands of lawless forces, but those same weapons can become the instruments by which a tyranny might attempt to entrench itself and enforce its decisions.

The prospect is frightening, but it is a problem man has had to face in the creation or operation of government on any level. Power inevitably constitutes an invitation to tyranny, whether on a community or a national or an international scale. The crucial question is whether the need for power exists, and, if so, what type of power will be used, how, and by whom? In starting World War II, Germany recognized that the world had become a geographic unit; and it was her intention to organize and rule the world order. The power in that case would have been exercised even more arbitrarily outside Germany than it had been inside Germany. But in defeating the Axis, we did not automatically destroy the need for power on a world scale any more than we destroyed the geographic world unit itself. We succeeded only in creating the opportunity to refine and channel that power through properly constituted and representative government. If we refuse to meet or fail to meet this opportunity, we automatically create a vacuum which will be filled by a single nation or bloc of nations, or which will result in crude international anarchy. . . .

So that we return full circle to man himself, to the animal that must operate the world government. Is he wise enough to use greater power for greater good? Is he wise enough to create a common sovereignty and yet keep the ultimate power in his own hands?

This is the multiple nature of the challenge to modern man—to bring about world government and to keep it pure; to keep his social, economic, and political institutions apace with his scientific achievements; to make whatever adjustments are needed in his own make-up, conditioning, and outlook on life in order to exist in an Atomic Age.

This is a large order, perhaps the largest order man has had to fill in his fifty thousand-odd years on earth, but he himself has set up the conditions which have made the order necessary. We can put on blinders; we can laugh it all off as just a false alarm; we can claim that talk of an Atomic Age is sheer fancy; we can protest that the threat of the destructive use of atomic energy is exaggeration, overstatement, hysteria, panic.

But all the manufactured calm and scorn in the world cannot alter the precise fact that the atomic bomb plus another war equals global disaster. Nor that the crisis is fast approaching and may be upon us within a few years unless we act now to avert it. Nor that this crisis is created not only by the explosive atom but by inadequate means of controlling international lawlessness. Nor that control is inoperative without power, that power is dangerous without law, and that law is impossible without government.

And if we reject the multiple challenge before us? And if we decide that we are not yet ready for world government? What then? Then there is yet another way, an alternative to world government, an alternative to change in man. This way is the second course. Absurd as this second course may seem, we describe it in all seriousness, for it is possible that through it man may find a way to stay alive—which is the central problem before us.

This second course is fairly simple. It requires that man eliminate the source of the trouble. Let him dissociate himself, carefully and completely, from civilization and all its works. Let him systematically abolish science and the tools of science. Let him destroy all machines and the knowledge which can build or operate those machines. Let him raze his cities, smash his laboratories, dismantle his factories, tear down his universities and schools, burn his libraries, rip apart his art. Let him murder his scientists, his lawmakers, his statesmen, his doctors, his teachers, his mechanics, his merchants, and anyone who has anything to do with the machinery of knowledge or progress. Let him punish literacy by death. Let him eradicate nations and set up the tribe as sovereign. Let him, in short, revert to his condition in society in 10,000 B.C. Thus emancipated from science, from progress, from government, from knowledge, from thought, he can be reasonably certain of prolonging his existence on this planet.

This can be a way out—if "modern" man is looking for a way out from the modern world.

(10)